"A magnificent achievement to the oral-history sources available on the American West. This collection of Ricker's interviews provides a rich resource on the Old West for the scholar and those interested in an accurate analysis of the lives of Indians, soldiers and settlers. . . . The strength of the volumes is in the stories told by the interviewees, with their perspectives on key historical events from the Old West, which is equally suited to the student and the academic scholar."—*American Studies*

"The interviews are a gold mine of information, and researchers will be rewarded for digging through them. . . . Ricker left Nebraska and the West an important source of information, and Jensen has made this more user-friendly by his organization and commentary."—*Great Plains Quarterly*

"Ricker proved himself a patient and meticulous oral interviewer, giving voice to people mostly ignored by historians of his day. His subjects document the Ghost Dance as a genuine religious movement, not as a 'craze' as described in white accounts. . . . Editor Richard Jensen provides a true service, for having translated Ricker's arcane handwritten notes into readable form and for his endnotes filled with biographical information."—*Kansas History*

"Priceless sources of information that offer more balanced perspectives on events than were accepted at the time. . . . There is no doubt that the voices and stories captured here in both books will be of significant value."—*Lincoln Journal Star*

"Anyone wishing to know more about Wounded Knee, the Little Bighorn, the history of the western frontier in general, and many other topics will certainly want to refer to Jensen's work."—*North Dakota History*

Eli S. Ricker worked for the Office of Indian Affairs in Washington DC when this portrait was taken in 1916. RG1227.PH:1–4

Voices of the American West
Volume 2

The Settler and Soldier Interviews of Eli S. Ricker, 1903-1919

Edited by
Richard E. Jensen

UNIVERSITY OF NEBRASKA PRESS
LINCOLN AND LONDON

All illustrations are courtesy of the Nebraska State Historical Society.

Set in Bulmer by Tseng Information Systems, Inc.
Designed by R. W. Boeche.

Library of Congress Cataloging-in-Publication Data
Ricker, Eli Seavey, 1843–1926.
Voices of the American West, volume 1: the Indian interviews of Eli S. Ricker, 1903–1919/
Eli S. Ricker; edited and with an introduction by Richard E. Jensen.
p. cm.
Includes bibliographical references and index.
ISBN-13: 978-0-8032-3949-4 (hardcover: alk. paper)
ISBN-10: 0-8032-3949-1 (hardcover: alk. paper)
ISBN-13: 978-0-8032-3996-8 (paper: alk. paper)
1. Indians of North America—Historiography. 2. Indians of North America—Interviews.
3. Pioneers—United States—Interviews. 4. European Americans—Interviews. 5. Indians of North
America—History. 6. Frontier and pioneer life—United States—History. 7. Ricker, Eli Seavey,
1843–1926—Relations with Indians. I. Jensen, Richard E. II. Title.
E76.8.R53 2005
970.004'97—dc22   2005012016

ISBN-13: 978-0-8032-3967-8 [vol. 2, hardcover]
ISBN-10: 0-8032-3967-x [vol. 2, hardcover]
ISBN-13: 978-0-8032-3997-5 [vol. 2, paper]

Contents

Chapter Five: Lightning Creek Incident 165

Chapter Six: Biographical Sketches 174

Chapter Seven: The Old West 190

Illustrations
following page 210

Figures

Introduction

Eli S. Ricker was forty-two years old when he settled in Chadron, Nebraska, in 1885. His wife and family joined him a year later. For the next two decades he practiced law, acquired a sizeable ranch, and then in January 1903 he and a partner began publishing the weekly *Chadron Times*. Ricker owned the paper for just over two years. It was during this time that he began interviewing people who could give him eyewitness accounts of historical events on the Plains. This was to be the basis of a book on Plains history, which he never wrote.

Voices of the American West, Volume 2

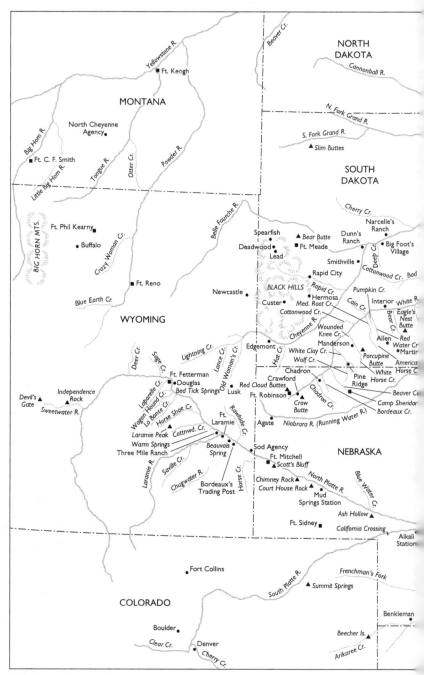

The West of Eli S. Ricker

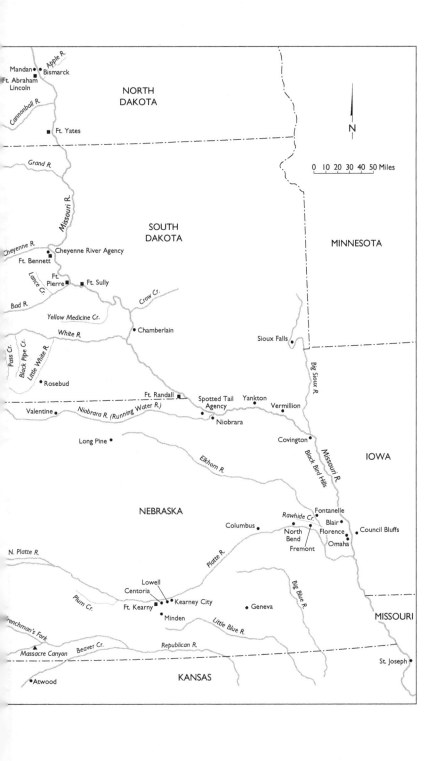

1. Wounded Knee

[Peter McFarland's Interview]

[Tablet 31]

Personal Sketch of Peter McFarland who is (April 20, 1905) 35 years old and was 21 at W. Knee battle.[1] He was teamster for the Indian scouts under Capt. Taylor. Was at W.K. fight and all through it and in the center of it. He came back from W.K. & was ambulance driver for Col. Biddle.[2] In January, 1896, he began service in the Pack Train at Camp Carlin, near Cheyenne, Wyo. and in 1898 went with pack train to Alaska where he was three months and then shipped from Dyea, Alaska, to Tampa, Florida, via Seattle and St. Louis, and reached Cuba June 22, 1898, and was there four years, barring one trip back to the states which lasted three months. Was in the pack train service from the time he went in January, 1896.

Was first employed by the gov't. as ambulance driver in 1888.

Shipped from Cuba in 1902 and arrived at Fort Riley, Kansas, May 6, 1902, and came to Fort Robinson in August, 1904.

April 18, 1905. Wounded Knee

Peter McFarland, Packmaster at Fort Robinson, of Pack Train No. 3, says: He was a gov't. employee driving team for the Quartermaster Colonel Humphreys who was in charge of all the teams at Pine Ridge. (He is General Humphreys now.) Humphreys was the Quartermaster at P. Ridge then. McFarland was assigned to Capt. Chas. W. Taylor, Chief of Scouts, and served under him and Lieut. Guy Preston.[3]

McFarland went out from the Agency after Christmas (probably the 27th) with a four-line team which was in charge of Capt. Taylor, hauling grain, ammunition tents, etc; went with 7th Cavalry. Camped that night at Wounded Knee where the battle came off. Baptiste Garnier with some of the Indian scouts went out on the morning of the 28th and captured 2 or 3 of Big Foot's scouts who were watching the troops.[4] He brought them in and they were kept in McFarland's tent. Baptiste saw on the night of arrival at W.K. some of Big Foot's scouts hovering around. Next morning he went out and got behind these scouts and captured them. He discovered the location of Big Foot's camp on the Porcupine and on his return he conducted the 7th Cavalry out to the camp and Big Foot's band was brought in, arriving about, as it seems to him, as late as 2 or 3 in the afternoon. Tents had been put up by a detachment which had been left behind in the camp of the 7th at W.K., for the Indians to occupy, but on their arrival they would not occupy them for they seemed to want to camp near the dry gulch. They pitched their tepees in an irregular half moon. About 10 or 12 Indians sat up all night manifesting no desire to lie down; they stayed over by McFarland's tent where Big Foot was lying therein on Mc's buffalo overcoat which I have seen at Fort Robinson. Big Foot was very sick with pneumonia and had a white cloth tied around his head as though he was in pain. Little Bat [Baptiste Garnier] was at Mc's tent also and he sat up all night talking with the Indians in a low tone; they seemed to be discussing and talking over affairs. Bat told Mc that as Mc was lying in the tent asleep & was 20 yrs. old, that he himself stayed up all night to watch, saying that if the Indians had broke out that they would have killed Mc, & Bat was keeping them engaged in conversation to keep them quiet. Big Foot and Mc slept together in same tent. Big Foot was a man of large stature. A close chain guard was placed around the Indians and it encompassed the scouts. That is, the tent occupied by the scouts and Bat and Mc was in the enclosure.

Following is a description of McFarland's map of the W.K. field:[5]

[Figure 1]

1. House on Hill. There was a small shack on this hill and some hay was stacked there. Mc and Lt. Preston went up there and got some hay for their horses. Here were planted the Hotchkiss cannon. He thinks there might have been 3 or 4 of these. Cannot tell the number.[6]

2. Is where the hospital was. The wounded were brought and laid around this wagon. It was not a tent. They were laid on 2 stretchers and on blankets & anything else at hand. This is what he calls the Red Cross Ambulance, but it was handled by the military. It has a white flag with a red cross.

(There were some pack mules on the field with the wagon train.)

3. Troops and Transportation. The Transportation was parked in rear of the troops and close to the hospital wagon. The dots just above the words "Troops

and Transportation" mark the "Kitchen wagons." The dots between the troop quarters and the "Officers" tents are the First Sergeants' tents.

4. Officers Tents.

5. Close Chain Guard. On the east side of the ground enclosed by the chain guard are tents put up by the troops for the Indians to occupy when they came in, but which they would not use. He says it was understood that there were 319 Indians of all kinds in Big Foot's band brought in; this is what Bat told him.

About 8 o'clock in the morning four dismounted troops were formed in a circle within the enclosure formerly made by the chain guard which had now been taken up. This circle is marked 5 and was an oblong & not a circle.

The night or day before, word was dispatched to the Agency stating that Big Foot's band was captured and more troops were wanted to help disarm them. Four troops came out in the night accompanied by Col. Forsythe. Before his arrival Capt. Whiteside had been in command of the 4 troops and transportation of the 7th.[7] These four troops which came in the night were camped behind the hill at the north and out of sight of the Indians. About the time the battle started Mc saw these 4 mounted troops dispersed to the southwest of the camp up on the high land evidently to prevent the Indians, if they should break away, from gaining the hills in that direction.

The Indian warriors were ordered to come into the oblong "circle" and to bring their arms and turn them over. They showed reluctance, looked downcast—mad—but finally 60 or 70 or more out of 129 warriors came straggling in. They were asked to give up their guns, but none had any. Then they returned to their tepees. They all had on ghost shirts, which were covered up by their blankets.[8] All had on the war paint; ~~their faces painted green striped with yellow~~ many had on their war feathers; some of the ponies were decorated with feathers in their tails and striped with the paint of battle. After awhile they began to come back; this time they sat down on the ground. Now 2 or 3 were taken at a time from the main body to the west end of the oblong "circle," the guns were received there by a soldier who carried them out through the guard and piled them on the ground 30 or 40 feet away and beside the wagon to which the team was attached ready to haul them at once to the Agency. Lieut. Preston was sitting down on the pile of guns when the fight began. The search produced only 8 or 10 old firelocks [flintlocks].

When the warriors collected the second time Big Foot, assisted by another, came out into the "circle" and in the center kneeled down and remained there and in that position until he was killed. Shortly after the search began the medicine man began to chant his war (?) song. The Indians had their arms concealed under their blankets. When the search began to bring out the good weapons the medicine man still singing facing the rising sun, his back to the Indians, waving his arms, he stooped down and with both hands grasped some soil and threw both arms outwardly scattering the dust. Instantly came an Indian volley. The fight was on with deadly effect. It was at close quarters and hand to hand. The Indians used guns, knives and war clubs. The women fired from the Indian tents. Philip Wells was wounded early in the action. Capt. Wallace was also killed near the east end of the "circle."[9] Lieut. Preston, at the beginning of the action, mounted his horse and within an hour was at the Agency with word of what had happened. (It was safer than staying there.)

(The scouts were Indians and Little Bat was the chief. There were 24 or about that number. Excepting 4 or 5 of these scouts they all disappeared the first night that the 7th arrived at W.K. Nothing more was seen of them until two or three weeks afterwards they returned to the Agency.)

The center of the fight was at the "circle." One of the Indian scouts was High Back Bone who was thought to be half crazy. Early in the action he was seen by a soldier to flourish his revolver and whether it was excitement or a bad heart which was his incitement is not known, but his actions being seen, his running around was interpreted to mean that he had turned against the whites, and when he got down by the officers' tents a soldier shot him down.[10]

Where the center of the fight was were 50 or more Indians killed.

After the fight had continued awhile and the smoke rose so the field could be seen and the soldiers had been formed in line at 6, and some soldiers were formed in line on the top of the hill by the artillery, the Hotchkiss guns on the hill fired into an Indian wagon standing at 7. Several Indians were firing on the soldiers from behind this wagon. The shell sent into it knocked it into pieces and killed a number of warriors.

During the progress of the fighting an Indian slipped into the tent belonging to the scouts and occupied by Bat and McFarland, and he got Bat's gun and shot 2 soldiers. McFarland saw the smoke from Bat's rifle coming out of the scouts' tent at 8. Mc was standing behind his wagon at 9 which had been overturned; one of his mules was shot and the others, when the mule fell, cramped around and tipped the wagon over. When Mc saw what this Indian was doing (he saw two men fall when the shots were heard from the tent) he ran forward and notified some soldiers in the line at 6, and as they could not fire from that position without striking the tents of troops nor without hitting some of the horses, they ran back to the first tent in the officers' row at 10 and from here they fired 2 or 3 volleys into the scouts' tent. An officer with the men who were firing on this tent told a trooper to go up to the tent and fire it; he said he would fix it, and he ran up and cut it open whereupon the Indian on the inside shot him in the breast and killed him instantly. This firing party continued to shoot into the tent while Mc ran up to the top of the hill where the cannons were and told the officer in command of the artillery that a Hotchkiss gun was wanted down on the bottom to shell the tent. One cannon was brought down and planted at 10 and a few shells were thrown into the tent. Then a soldier ran up and set the tent on fire and it was quickly burned down, and his [the Indian's] clothing took fire and he was burned and bloated up 2 feet high. He was found to have a bullet hole through his body and it is not known whether he had been killed by a rifle shot before the cannon was brought into requisition. Bat's gun which he had been using was burned "a little" on the stock. It was his best gun, the Hotchkiss rifle.

Dr. Seward Webb of N.Y. who used to come out on hunting trips gave Batteesse a fine breech-loading arm which Bat called his Hotchkiss rifle.

All the foregoing occurred in about three-quarters of an hour.

The Indians were pushed back into the gulch; some crossed it, others went up the gulch. Those who crossed fell back one by one going up the rising ground to the southwest where they made a stand at 11; the mounted cavalry above their position had before this time ~~disappeared and he does not know where they went~~ moved around to the west to get out of line of fire and here they found something to do in pursuing Indians who had escaped by running out of the gulch at the upper end or head. A lot of Indians were killed by these mounted men who had one of their number shot through the body. The fight of the Indians at 11 was kept up till the last one was killed. A Hotchkiss gun was run out on the flat in front of the Indian tepes and towards the gulch. From here a searching fire was kept up on the Indians who were lying low in the gulch; whenever and wherever one was seen to move, as they often did in shooting at the troops, a shell would be dropped where he was which either killed him or hunted and chased him out; he would spring right up and march toward the soldiers singing the death song, and was quickly killed by the watchful soldiers.

A straggling fire was kept up till the middle of the afternoon. This was due to the fact that the gulch was occupied by Indians who did not show themselves, but when a soldier got exposed a concealed Indian would pick him off.

5

So it was not only extremely hazardous but was almost certain death to advance towards or along the gulch, and this Hotchkiss gun was kept in action to drive them out whenever the position of an Indian was discovered or from any sign suspected. The gun was moved from position to position as was found necessary. A lieutenant with this Hotchkiss was wounded while the gun was doing its work against the Indians in this protected part of the field.[11]

Mc says he saw one Indian who was scalped. He was lying in the gulch on his back.

McFarland went around by the road and got up where the Indians had all been killed at 11, and there he found a little girl about three years old, had light hair, she was standing and holding on to her dead mother's hair. He took the child and carried it to the Red Cross ambulance and it was received by an attendant. What became of the child afterwards is not known.

Wounded Indians got down to the creek in some manner (supposed to have crawled down the gulch) and many were found there afterwards both dead and wounded, some of them frozen.

A rumor got in circulation that a large force of Indians was coming from among the hostiles at the Agency.[12] This was late in the afternoon. Troops began making breastworks out of the bags of oats in the supply wagons, by carrying them up and putting them down on the hill north of the flat. This work had not gone far when there came an order to load up and start for the Agency. The dead and wounded soldiers and the wounded Indian women and children and the train and troops moved in and arrived at the Agency about one o'clock next morning. The Agency was all excitement, nobody being in bed.

Peter McFarland's Pine Ridge story continued: He says:

About Sept. 1889, Capt. Gilfoyle took an escort from Fort Robinson (McFarland was with him) and met General Miles at Rushville and took him to Pine Ridge Agency where Miles remained 2 or 3 days and was having some kind of a conference with the dissatisfied Indians.[13] The party brought back four Indian chiefs who went with General Miles to Washington.

He further says:

That after he came back from W. Knee to the Agency on the night of Dec. 29, arriving about 1 o'clock on the morning of the 30th.

Early on the morning of the 30th the 9th Cavalry came into the Agency, having left their wagon train abt. 5 miles north of Agency in charge of D troop under command of Capt. Loud. When the wagon train or transportation was within about 2½ miles of Agency just at break of day, they had an advance guard out, a party of 2 Indians advanced toward the advance guard & were mistaken for friendly Indians because ~~they were wearing~~ one wore U.S. Soldier overcoats with yellow cape lining, & when close to the ad. guard he shot one of the guard dead. The other advance guard then broke for the Agency and the other two Indians tried to head him off but he escaped from them and gave the alarm at the Agency. The wagon train then parked for protection till reinforcements could be brought out. The 9th came right out and dispersed the Indians and the train came in.[14]

The smoke down in the valley of the White Clay [Creek] from fires made by the hostiles the day before was rising lazily, and there was rumor that the Indians were going to attack the Mission, so the 7th Cavalry was sent out. (They were setting fires on the 30th.) The troops got into the bottom on the creek just north of the Mission, and at one time it looked as though the Indians had them in a pocket; the 9th was sent out to their assistance and they were extricated. Several were wounded and killed.[15] The troops returned to Agency in the evening abt. 4 or 5 o'clock. The Indians went on down the valley. The night the troops came in from W.K. and the night of the 30th there was a chain guard around the Agency and teamsters and all able bodied persons were up all night and doing duty apprehensive of attack by the Indians.

On January 1, Gen. Brooke with an escort of 9th Cav. and 2nd Infy. went west & a little north 18 miles to the White River and camped that night. Leaving these troops there the next morning he went down the River visiting all the camps till he arrived at the mouth of W.K. where there was the 6th Cav. under Col. Carr. Between these two camps were, beginning next to Henry's camp and following the river was first, as you recollect, Ofleys, Wells and Sanford's camps but he does not know their order. ~~and says there may have been more~~. From Carr's camp the general and escort returned up the river. There was a simultaneous movement now of all these camps converging toward the Agency.[16]

It should have been said before that when the general was going down the river they saw where two troops of the 6th Cav. had had a brush with the Indians, there being a little breastwork thrown up.

Henry's camp and Carr's were on the south side of White river, and the intervening ones on the north side. Carr's was in the angle of W. River and W. Knee creek.

Carr moved his camp up the river toward White Clay and the intermediate camps took up the march for the same point on the White Clay above the mouth and just below (or north) of the Mission and all, comprising it was at the time said, 39 troops and companies, and all went into camp together at that place.

As Genl. Brooke went down the river he left his escort as he successively reached one camp after another, and took a fresh escort & went on.

He stayed in each camp a day while Little Bat went out over the hills and looked and watched to see if any Indians were around. One of these camps was called the Leavenworth camp because it was the camp of M [Troop] of the 5th Cav. and C Troop of [the] 9th Cav. which had come up from [Fort] Leavenworth. This is the camp where Lieut. Casey who had charge of the Crow scouts, was killed. (Thinks these scouts had come from up abt. Standing Rock.)[17]

Casey went out from Leavenworth camp against Bat's warning not to go out too far in that direction and up the valley. The hostiles were between Leavenworth camp and the Agency and Casey went out from this camp going south or nearly so and went up the valley, while Bat made a detour to the west through and over the hills west of White Clay creek. Casey went out with 2 Crow scouts of his command. As he went up over a hill an Indian scout (a hostile scout) shot him. His own scouts returned to Leavenworth camp and a detachment was sent out and his body recovered. He was a man large of stature, raw boned, etc.

McFarland says that the 8th Cav. was out there somewhere but does not know how they got there unless they were the ones that Big Foot's band got away from when they started from Standing Rock [Cheyenne River Reservation].

When the troops had all concentrated in the single camp north of the Mission and east of White Clay they were out of rations, and a wagon train of 25 or 30 wagons was sent in to the Agency for supplies with an infantry escort & McFarland was in the lead. They followed the road from the Mission to the Agency and on the way passed the hostile Indian camp which was surrounded by a chain guard & was flying a red flag (ticklish movement). The train had no trouble. The hostiles remained in their camp a few days and then they moved over south of the Agency, passing it on the west, moving up White Clay past Red Cloud's house going in single file with their ponies and teams on their right flank and the women and children in rear drawing out like a thread uncoiling from a spool, and they camped on White Clay just above American Horse's camp of friendlies.[18]

The troops then came right in behind them and were then put into camps around the Agency. In three weeks more by departures of a few at a time the tepees had all disappeared—the Indians had gone. There were 600 Brulé Sioux Indians there at [the] Agency—he says the meanest of all the hostiles.

On the first ridge north of the Agency and left of the road to the Mission stood four Sibley tents serving a secret purpose in the concealment of four Rodman cannon which were placed there under cover of darkness and trained on the hostile camp, so that if a break had been made by the Indians these guns would have opened as a surprise on the enemy.[19]

Two Strikes was a leader of the hostiles. Also Jack Red Cloud.[20]

Returning to Wounded Knee. Both McFarland and [W. F.] Clark say:

That a man named Campbell got his lower jaw shot off and afterwards was furnished with a silver jaw. He was loquacious to a degree but it is not said whether this change in his anatomical mechanism ever effected a cure of his habit of much speaking.

The wounded soldiers when brought in from W.K. in army wagons over frozen ground suffered terribly from the jolting and their groans were ~~terrible and~~ heartrending.

A light haired recruit for [the] 7th Cav. went up to W.K. with McFarland to join his command; he got a bullet through his head just below the ears. He was brought in with the wounded and dead and it was thought he was dead and was left out all night in the wagon in the cold night. Next morning when they were removing the bodies it was noticed that this young man moved. He was taken into the hospital, his wound was bandaged, in two days he was strolling about the Agency and he finally recovered (see Book 4, page 17, 62 recruits for 7th Cavalry).[21]

Capt. Mills of the 2d Infantry was sent out with his company north of the Agency to occupy the ridge with his company. He and his Co. had come up from Omaha with Gen. Brooke. He was well along in years. He marched his company to the foot of the ridge by the little creek & left them there till he went up on the hill himself to see if there were Indians before exposing his men. Nothing was done and he was at length recalled. This was on the afternoon of the 29th after the Indians had been firing and burning. He occupied his tent that night and in the morning was found sitting in his chair dead.[22]

Jack Red Cloud was a bad Indian during these disturbances. After the trouble had subsided he was seen in the post-office by [W. F.] Clark and McFarland with streakings of ghost painting and with ghost raiment adorning his muscular frame.

Red Cloud was out in the hostile camp some time and on his return he stated that the hostiles obliged him to go, but it was believed that he went of his own accord.[23] The only reasonable supposition is that Red Cloud's native sympathies were with the hostiles — they could not well and naturally be placed elsewhere; but from his visits to the eastern section of the United States he had acquired visual knowledge of the strength of the white people, and he was too ~~shrewd~~ wise not to know that the power of the government was irresistable. On a former occasion he had expatiated to his people upon the grandeur of the white men's possessions and the vast number of their population, and because he was yielding to a sensible discretion there is good reason to say that his influence had to some extent declined among the younger and rasher members of his tribe.

When a Big Foot squaw was dying in the hospital she told another person that there was a plan for the Indians to carry secret arms on their persons and to simulate friendship for the whites, and at a concerted moment to begin a massacre of the white soldiers and people when they did not suspect danger. A lady school teacher on the Reservation who understood the Sioux language overheard this and reported it (Miss Emma ? Steckel; write her).[24] An order was issued by Gen. Brooke requiring all persons to carry arms all the time as stated in [W. F.] Clark's foregoing statement.

The first troops at the Agency were the 2d Infy. from Omaha and Co. C. of the 8th Infy. and 4 troops of 9th Cavalry. These troops all disembarked from trains at Rushville.

[Tablet 41]

Scalping of Indians

Indians were scalped at Wounded Knee. Peter McFarland told me of one lying in the draw scalped. He also said that he scalped one. Somebody was trying to get a scalp from an Indian without success, not knowing how to do it; and he volunteered to take it off, which he did with a jerk after he had made the circular incision.

[Charles W. Allen's Interview]

Charles Wesley Allen came west in 1871, and worked at Fort Laramie, Pine Ridge, and at Valentine, Nebraska, where he first learned the newspaper business. In 1885 he and two partners moved to Cha-

dron and published the Chadron Democrat. *Allen left the paper
in 1891 to take up ranching south of Martin, South Dakota. In
the 1930s he prepared a manuscript about this period of his life.
Nearly one-third of it was devoted to his eyewitness description of
the Wounded Knee massacre and events surrounding it.*[25]

[Tablet C]

Wounded Knee Statement of Charles W. Allen

Chas. W. Allen of Merriman Neb. Dec. 23, 1903, says: He reported from Pine
Ridge Agency for the New York Herald during the Indian troubles 1890. There
were three New York Herald correspondents on the ground at Pine Ridge
Agency during the war, viz; Chas. W. Allen, Alf. Berkholder and J. W. Jones.
The latter remained only abt. 2 weeks & left. Allen remained until within
2 weeks of the time of the departure of the soldiers and Berkholder stayed till
last minute.[26]

A man named Miller who had a paper down at Blair or Mo. Valley was there
only 3 or 4 days in the early part of the matter & did not show Berkholder who
was the reporter in charge, that he had any authority from James Gordon Ben-
net who signed all the telegrams authorizing reporters to act for the Herald.[27]
He finally left without writing anything for Bennett. Jones was there 2 wks. &
left day before W. Knee Massacre. Write K. Managury [?] Editor New York
Herald & ask for copy of all the correspondence from the War Correspondents
at Pine Ridge Agency & W. Knee including Red Cloud's speech to the hostiles. Red Cloud had influence with the hostiles.

Charley Allen was the only N.Y. Herald reporter who was at W. Knee; Berkholder did not go out that trip.

The only papers represented on the ground of W. Knee were the Herald,
Omaha Bee and Lincoln State Journal. Cressy represented the Bee & Kelly the
State Journal. Journal's account was a fair general one; but the Bee & the Herald were the only ones that were full & perfect in detail. The Bee correspondent was a sensational writer & the bulk of stuff he sent in was exaggerated;
but his a/c of the W. Knee fight is good, as he and Charley worked together
in preparing their dispatches. He and Charley paid a messenger $75 to carry
their dispatches & letters to their papers to Gordon P.O.[28]

Reinhart, the Photographer in Omaha has all the pictures ever taken &
a fine collection. He made a national reputation.[29] Charley Allen says that at
W. Knee the soldiers' tents were at the foot of the hill on which the monument

stands.[30] That south of these was the council which was surrounded by the soldiers. He thinks the cordon of soldiers was open one side—probably on one side—the side next the tents of soldiers south of the council where the pole stood was a row of Indian tents. Officers were searching these tents for arms and Charley Allen was with them when the firing began. It was from here that Charley ambled off on hands & knees, going west and finally up the hills to save himself. He says several times soldiers essayed to shoot him & he heard officers say to them that he was a white-man, and soldiers afterwards told him that they came near shooting him.

The soldiers that surrounded the council were between the army tents on the north at the foot of the hill and the Indian tents on the south. Charley Allen says about 20 of the Indians had been disarmed and their guns were stacked at one side with a guard over them (I should think from the way he pointed in his description that these were stacked on the west of the council circle; at any rate he pointed and said "they were stacked off to one side"). He says the Indians had guns concealed under their blankets and cartridge boxes shoved down their trowsers. He is the best authority for the reason that he was there with the business mission for the Herald to know the facts & was actually present witnessing the search for the purpose of reporting the facts. Besides, he is a calm man not inclined to fiction, fancy or sensation but his characteristic methods are careful, accurate and truthful. It is manifestly true that only a part of the Indians were disarmed, and the smaller part at that. It was thus possible for the Indians to have the chance to kill as many soldiers as were killed. This can be the only reasonable solution. Charley says he heard a shot and then as he expresses it "it went like pop corn."

I asked him the question how it started, and his answer indicated that he did not know definitely, but said what I have stated, and spoke as though it is the common agreement that a "crazy" or excited ghost-dancing young Indian discharged his piece at the guard over the guns, and then the shooting began in deadly earnest and became general.[31]

Here is where coolness and discipline should have been displayed to avert the tragedy. If these had been present no doubt a more humane result could have been recorded. Instead of allowing the act of this one Indian to become a pretext for starting the fire which led to loss of many lives on both sides, the transgressor should have been seized and put under guard till all the Indians had been disarmed. Charley Allen & Berkholder went out with the first detachment of 7th Cavalry which went to intercept Big Foot's band, and after they had been met matters dragged along without any occurrences & these two men were out there with only a camping outfit and tent; so they returned to the Agency. When the rest of the 7th was sent up to W. Knee Charley went along but Berkholder stayed behind, and so Charley was the only authorized reporter who witnessed the W. Knee fight. But when he and Burkholder got together at the agency they prepared the report in conjunction.[32]

[Tablet 11]

Following is Charley Allen's Map of Wounded Knee [Figure 2]

Ask Allen how long the battle lasted.

" Abt. cannon

"   " commands of officers

"   " calls to Inds. to sit up

Wounded Knee (Continued)

Allen, S.D. Wednesday, Aug. 21, '07.

Charles W. Allen says: He was at the battle of W.K. and was on the field during the fighting.

He was present at the council. He saw Big Foot brought out of his tent and placed close to the circle. The Indians were stubborn and opposed to surrendering their arms. Big Foot talked to them feebly but without much influence. The medicine man harangued them. He was a fine orator, if there ever was one. (As Mr. Allen could not understand what he said, and has given me what he was told that he said, I will not put it down.) He says that the medicine man gathered up some dust and swirled it [in] the air to illustrate as he was told. Getting tired of the council which to him resembled a ward caucus, he went over to where the soldiers were disarming the Indians. Little Bat was here and John Shangrau. The soldiers had got about two thirds the way around. In front of one tent a woman was lying on the ground. A soldier engaged in the search said: Roll that woman over; maybe there is a gun under her. Another turned her over exposing a gun handsomely concealed. In another place a girl was found covering up some kind of firearms in like manner. The soldiers were searching the bags of knives and forks and taking all the murderous weapons. The wagons that the squaws had partly or wholly loaded were unloaded and examined for arms.

He saw the little children in numbers playing about the tents like little children around a country schoolhouse. Two hours afterwards he saw the same children lying dead or wounded where they had been cavorting in mirth just a little while before.

While this search was going on he heard a shot. In a moment came the popping of soldiers' guns, and men, women and children began to fall. The Indians broke to get away. He says the officers could have had no expectation of battle, or the dispositions of the soldiery would have been different.

Big Foot was killed in this manner: Some of the Indians feigned that they were dead; Big Foot did so as one of that number, or he laid down because he was unable to sit up; at any rate, he was lying on his back. He raised up. ~~(Was it when the call was made to the Indians, as Paddy Starr says, to raise up and be saved? Others have said that calls were made to the Indians.)~~[33] Big Foot raised up; as he did so a soldier who was standing among other soldiers and one officer, leveled his gun at the chief and shot him in the back and he fell back dead. Big Foot's daughter was standing by the Big Foot tent; she saw this dastardly deed and ran towards her father; as she did so, a lieutenant snatched a gun from the hands of a soldier and shot her in the back. She fell dead on the spot and her spirit kept company with that of her sire. This officer was Lieutenant Reynolds. My informant stood with this group of officers and soldiers and saw these things done. These facts are absolute and certain. (In writing, the name of the officer is to be suppressed. My pledge was given never to let it be known who it was that gave me the name of this officer. It was on this condition that he gave it. There is no mistake as to who it was. My informant rode by his side to the Agency after the butchery and heard him addressed by name many times. My informant is an acquaintance of 22 years and thoroughly trustworthy. Lieutenant Reynolds was the man.)[34]

Lieutenant Garlington was on Cemetery Hill with a troop. He was wounded in the elbow.[35]

He [Allen] says the bright sun was shining in Big Foot's face and he thinks he rose up on that account.

He says the council was not assembled until 8 or 9 o'clock A.M. The fighting began about 11 A.M. The main fighting was done in half or three-quarters of an hour, but the excitement lasted two hours. The troops and train did not leave the field for the Agency until about 3 o'clock P.M. It was after one o'clock at night when they arrived at the Agency.

Says no cannon was fired into the tent where the Indian was shooting from; but a soldier went up and cut a slit in the tent and the Indian shot him in the breast. Then the cry came to burn the tent. It was set on fire. The Indian was scorched brown and the stock of Little Bat's gun was burned.

Lieut. Garlington had his troop on Cemetery hill. He was wounded in the elbow. He was left there with a guard and his troop was sent west along the road and up the hill to head off and beat up the Indians. The troop of gray horses was the farthest west and on the road up the ridge to the west; this was commanded by Capt. Jackson, and was stationed out there to ward off Indian reinforcements & to pick up straggling Indians.

The military took all the wounded, red and white into the Agency when they went in; but when the party went out a few days later—the party Dr. Eastman and George E. Bartlett were with—this party found a few, as stated by Dr. Eastman—a few who had been missed.[36]

Charley Allen says the squawmen taught the first lessons of civilization to their wives—taught them to make tables and get their meals off the ground—taught them to make garden and raise vegetables, taught them to dress like white women.

Squawmen filled an honorable place—did a necessary service—they learned the Indian languages and were indispensable to the military, to the civil power—to the government in every way—as interpreters, guides, trusted assistants and helpers.

(Read the letter of Reno in the back part of Tonda. Charley Allen says what he affirms of squawmen is untrue.)[37]

Charley Allen says it was not possible for white men of any character to be with the Indians against Reno. White men cannot live among the Indians in time of war with the whites, though they be squawmen. If white men at such time fight on the side of the Indians against the whites and attract attention by their bravery and prowess, they arouse the jealousy and enmity of the Indians, of those especially who are ambitious for honors. Again, their lives would be unsafe from other cause. The squaws mourning for their dead, killed by white men, would in obedience to the law of their race which is the law of Israel—"an eye for an eye, and a tooth for a tooth"—would have killed them. A squaw seeing a white man, for instance lying asleep, having lost a relative at the hands of a white man would bury an axe or a war club in the sleeper's head. This would appease the spirits which were calling out from the ground for her dead to be avenged with the blood of a white man.

Appleton, chief clerk and acting agent at Red Cloud furnished atonement with his life for a white man who killed an Indian.[38] This was the law of Indian society and government. When any person says that white men were fighting in the ranks of the Indians against the whites it is pure fabrication.

At Wounded Knee C. W. Allen heard no commands of officers at the opening of the fight. He thinks the affair was an accident of war, very deplorable, yet an accident. The officers were free from the influence of liquor in the morning. During the night before, there had been some conviviality. Allen was with Major Whiteside, Captain Wallace and other officers that night; they were not intoxicated, but felt well.

Allen says there were soldiers drawn up as Philip Wells avers; but there were also a cordon of soldiers thrown around the council, and it was impossible for these soldiers to shoot without killing one another.

Suppose (I say) that it was an accident. Why should the soldiers have fired when no shots had been poured into them? Was there no authority and no discipline among officers and soldiers? Could they not wait till the recalcitrant Indian or Indians who forcibly refused to deliver their guns were overcome and restrained? It is said Indians in the council arose when the first shot occurred. Was it not natural that they should do so without intention to fight? The action of the troops was overhasty, premature, and more like a mob than trained soldiery.

[Meded Swigert's Interview]

Meded Swigert was an eyewitness to the Wounded Knee massacre. Charles Allen met him and said he was a "hotel man" from Gordon, who came to Pine Ridge simply to satisfy his curiosity.[39]

[Box 19]

M. Swigert who lives 15 miles southeast of Gordon and has a son in business in G. [Gordon, Nebraska] was on the battle ground at the outbreak and is the man who on foot outran Jim Asay to a log house for protection. Asay was in a light wagon with a barrel of whiskey.[40] See Swigert. He has a telephone.

[Tablet 14]

M. Swigert's Map March 31, 1905 [41]

M. Swigert of Gordon says: _____ Miller was correspondent of the Neb. State Journal.[42]

He says: That the 7th Cav. went up from the Agency before the battle on Monday, and he followed them up.

He says the only troops in the battle were the 7th Cav. & no Infy.

After breakfast the Cav. got ready and went up over Cemetery hill and headed down toward the trader's house and came around up to the east of the tepees. (See map.) The two leading companies were dismounted and four horses were held by one trooper. Col. Forsythe ordered the Indians to come to council, and Little Bat interpreted to the haranguer who cried "Come to Council! Come to Council!"

The Indians came out of the tepees bringing the little boys with them and they sat down on the ground. Col. F. ordered a chain guard thrown around, in an oblong hollow square abt. 60 x 100 feet, the soldiers standing 4 to 6 ft. apart. Col. Forsythe observing that Indian boys were in the council asked why they were there. And Chief Big Foot said those boys had proved themselves brave and they had a right there by that reason. That when an Indian boy had proved his bravery he was recognized of right as a warrior. Forsythe then said if they want them in the Council let them stay. The Colonel then told them that the Great Father had sent him there to take their arms and ammunition and that the G.F. would pay them what they were worth; that they should go back to their homes at Standing Rock; that he would send a wagon train with them to help them back and a company of soldiers to guard them and see them safe home; that the Indians at Pine Ridge were excited and that there were some bad Indians among them, and that if these were to go there it would make trouble. The Indians cried out in one acclaim "Lille Washta, lille washta" (Very good; very good!).

Then Col. F. said to let ten (Indians) go from this end of the council & ten from the other end go to their tepees and get their guns & ammunition. At first they hesitated, then went strolling off leisurely or slowly as though they were disinclined to do as told. They were gone to the tepees abt. ½ an hour and seemed to be moving around uneasily. ~~When they returned (the first 20)~~ When some had returned more went out, and abt. an hour was consumed before all had come back, and it was declared by them that they had brought all they had. They turned over a lot of old, worthless guns numbering about 60; these were piled in 2 piles, one pile in front of Big Foot's tepee at the east end of the council or square, and the other pile near the west end, as parties had been sent out from each end and they returned where they had respectively gone out. These piles were under guard of soldiers. Col. Forsythe now said to them, "When you passed under examination as prisoners yesterday you had 160 good guns, and you have brought only 60 old, worthless guns that were not counted." The Indians, it must be remembered, were now standing up; they did not sit down on their return as is usual in council. He then said, "You must go and get those guns & fetch them in, for we know they are here inside our guard line, and we must have them. And I will have the men search the tents and the grounds till we find them." The Indians stood there talking and declaring that these were all, Little Bat interpreting what was said, the Indians remaining in their places, showing no disposition to go as directed or to give up their arms.

Six soldiers were now sent to search the tepees. They returned in abt. ½ an hour bringing two guns and stated that these were all they could find & that they found 2 Indians with the guns. While they were talking one of the guards called out, "This Indian right here has a Winchester; the wind blew his blanket up against it & I saw it;" another guard said this Indian [had] a six shooter and a belt of cartridges on him; then another guard cried out, "They are all armed!" "Search them!" said the Colonel, directing the searching party to search the Indians. Then 2 or 3 seized the Indian with the Winchester and took it from him; then the medicine man threw off his blanket and revealed that he was painted blue, being naked except leggings, and breech clout & a head dress, and covered with yellow spots [the] size of ½ dollar (silver). He began to jump and dance backward and forward before the Indians and sing a war chant; he stooped down to the ground and took up a handful of dirt and made two signal motions—opened 2 fingers and threw up a part of the dirt, then made 2 steps sideways and threw up the balance over the heads of the Indians.[43] Little Bat the chief interpreter cried out in a loud voice, "Look out, they are going to shoot!" Just then the whole band of Indians threw their blankets in the air and opened fire. The troops were taken by surprise. The men holding the horses turned them loose. The civilians (11 in number) fled to shelter. Teamsters sought protection behind their wagons and any other objects. The horses tied on either side of camp [by] ropes instinctively lowered their heads and held them down crowding close together; the women and the little girls poured over the bank into the gulch where they had dug a ditch the night before abt. 18 inches wide & deep and abt. 80 or 100 ft. long, in which they laid down for protection.

(After the chain guard had been placed these men were ordered to load their pieces which they did.) Everything was in instant panic on the field. The chain guard returned the fire. Opposite lines poured relentless shots into comrades as well as into Indians. The soldiers, as well as Indians were under double fire. Many fell by the hands of their own men.

Mr. Swigert ran down to the trading house distant 175 paces and took shelter and remained about an hour.[44] A soldier also came (also Asay and 2 or 3 others with him) behind this house. The bugle sounded the order to fall back into line. Then followed several volleys of small arms. The Hotchkiss guns were fired at this time. (There were 3 or 4 of these, but one became disabled at the outset.) When the firing had about ceased all behind the house went back to the field. When the soldiers fell back under orders & formed the line of battle the troops came into view of the trench on the north side and at the bottom of the gulch under the bank, and the killing and wounding of the women & girls here now took place. As soon as the fire was directed on these they began to move about and it was discovered that they were women and the firing on them was stopped. The Indians fled in all directions, mostly to the south and west, and were pursued and shot down. Some were killed half a mile from the central field. The dead lay thickest on the council ground, soldiers and Indians together, in places 3 deep. Big Foot who was sick and during the council was sitting in front of his tent was killed there. An Indian sprang into the scouts' tent, where there were a lot of guns and ammunition and from this place he shot several of the soldiers; when the firing from this place was noticed a return fire was directed to this spot. A Hotchkiss threw a shell into the tent, which set the tent and the ammunition on fire, and the Indian was killed and burned. After the firing had ceased on the field two Indians were in a little depression up the gulch abt. 300 yards from the field, and they were concealed by big grass and from here they kept up a fire on any soldiers in sight. A soldier was detailed to go up the gulch to tell these to stop firing and to come in as prisoners, and that they would be protected. They refused to surrender saying that their friends were all dead and that they were ready to die too. A cannon was then trained on them. One shell was all that was needed to stop shots from there. At this moment a team appeared in sight hurrying as fast as they could going up out of the gulch. The officer asked the gunner what they were. He looked through a glass and said they were Indians, and the officer said, "Can't you stop them?" The gun was trained on the wagon; there were five in the party — 2 men being on the ground whipping and urging the horses; the shell exploded with terrible effect, tearing horses, wagon and Indians in pieces. An eye witness says the sight was as if a pile of rags had been thrown into the air. All were killed except a small baby which General and Mrs. Colby afterwards adopted. This child was in this wagon. Mr. Swigert says ask the mother of Frank Goings at the agency whether this is the baby that the Colbys took.[45]

He says that the soldiers did not bury the Indian dead. A party of citizens went out from the Agency and buried these.

He says he saw a woman running west with a pappoose on her back. A shot killed her. The child was old enough to sit up but could not walk. He told one of the Indian scouts to go and get this child and take it to the squaws near the hospital. The scout tore open the mother's dress and pressed the infant down to the mother's breast, when it went to nursing.

An Indian man & woman mounted on horseback were escaping along the road toward the Agency. These were torn into fragments by a shell. There must have been 30 or 40 Indians who got away and saved their lives. An Indian boy and girl in the early part of the action, caught two of the horses which were turned loose by the soldiers who were holding them when the firing began, and rode to the hostile camp and told the hostiles to turn back, as those at the creek had been disarmed and killed. There were a number of women who were uninjured and these with the wounded women were taken to the Agency. The wounded women and men were taken to the Episcopal Church at the Agency.

Mr. Swigert thinks that under the orders that Col. Forsythe had there was no escape from the fight as the Indians would not give up their arms. Forsythe was obliged by orders to disarm the Indians and the Indians would not be disarmed. It was like an irresistible force meeting an immovable object.

Afterwards, within a few weeks, a convoy of wagons and soldiers took the surviving Indians back to Standing Rock.

He says that in the old and unused building in N.E. cor. are piled the old arms and remnants which were gathered up after the battle.

About the 3d or 4th of Jan., 1891, word was bro't to the Agency that the Indians had burned the large log school house at the Mission and several houses belonging to friendly Indians. The report was that the people at the Mission were standing the Indians off. The 7th Cav. was sent out to the Mission. The Comdg. officer sent back for reinforcements. The 9th was then sent out. These were colored soldiers. The Indians drew off down the White Clay.[46]

This affair on the W.K. was hushed up; there was anxiety to keep a part of the truth from the public; this was evident from the uneasiness manifested by some in authority; officers had at least one conference with the civilians asking what they knew and warning them not to say too much. This was probably to shield Forsythe who had been put under arrest.[47]

Mr. Swigert says there were eleven civilians at the battle namely; James F. Asay, Charles Cressy, _____ Miller, Charley Allen, Dick Stirk, J. H.

[Thomas H.] Tibbles, Jack Newman, M. Swigert, Joe Brown Jr., Father Craft the priest who was afterwards wounded, and Philip Wells.

(April 23, 1908. Mrs. Keith told me about Tibbles' coming out to W.K. but I think he had gone back to the Agency when the fighting occurred. I think Mr. Swigert was mistaken as to him.)[48]

Write to J. H. Tibbles and ask for anything he can furnish abt. W.K.

The Indians relied on the medicine man's incantations and pretensions. When the fight began and they saw their friends falling around them they were cruelly disenchanted and fled for escape. They were truculent in disappointment. This was shown by the maddened hatred of the wounded Indian who asked to be moved and placed by the side of the misleader, and who when this was done viciously plunged his knife into his dead body three or four times.

(Apr. 23, 1908. This incident is partly confirmed by some other person whom I do not recall.) It turns out to be Guy Vaughn.[49]

[Guy Vaughn's Interview]

[Tablet 14]

Guy Vaughn of Chadron says: That he was present at the battle of Wounded Knee as a courier with Capt. Wallace when his command left the Agency to go to W.K. The 7th Cavalry all went out from the Agency at the same time and were most of two days in reaching W.K. They went into camp that night, the 28th as near as he can recollect, and next morning 29th, after breakfast the command formed in line and moved forward from the camp which was on the opposite side of W.K. creek from where the fight took place, and advanced to the creek facing the Indian camp and crossed the creek and formed in the shape of a letter V.

The Medicine man threw dirt in the air and yelled and the braves threw off their blankets and began firing. The soldiers threw themselves on the ground. Thinks no order was given by any officer to fire. The firing at once became general. The positions of the soldiers were changed several times.

As Guy recollects Capt. Wallace was wounded in the left shoulder and pretty high up. Does not think the wound would have killed him, at any rate not immediately, and so he thinks he was first struck with the war club. When he saw him the Captain was lying on his face. Saw Big Foot first after he was killed; he was lying flat on his back, his arms spread out, and a bullet hole through the middle of his body. Several dead bodies were lying close by him.

Guy saw a wounded squaw crawl on her hands and knees some ten yards with a butcher knife in her teeth and plunge the knife into his [a soldier's] breast. She was found after the battle was over clutching the knife in her hand, lying beside the dead soldier with a bullet hole through her head, showing that someone had given her this as a recompense for the vengeance she had wreaked on the dying soldier who had tried to evade her blow.

(Guy belonged to the Nebraska National Guard and left W.K. with a dispatch from Capt. Taylor, chief of scouts. Delivered the message at Rushville, remained 12 hours at R. and then went by rail to Long Pine and went to drumming up the company to which he belonged which rendezvoused at Long Pine.)

[Francis M. J. Craft's Letter]

Father Francis M. J. Craft, S.J., a longtime missionary to the Lakotas, accompanied Forsyth's command to Wounded Knee on the evening of December 28. He said he went there "to see if I could be of any service . . . by going among the Indians and reassuring them." During the mêlée he received a serious stab wound that pierced his right lung.[50]

[Box 2]
St. Matthew's Rectory
East Stroudsburg, Pa.
Jan. 16th 1907
Dear Mr. Ricker,

Your kind favor of Dec. 22d received. I regret very much that I have not the time to write up for you the matters you mention, as they should be carefully prepared, if mentioned at all. I can only say that any reports as to soldiers or officers being in any way to blame for the battle of Wounded Knee Creek, or that they hunted down & killed Indian women & children are entirely false. The women & children were killed—most of them at the beginning of the battle—by the fire of the Indians themselves, when they fired, without provocation, upon the troops, beyond whom the women & children were standing. All the women & children who were saved, were saved by soldiers, at the risk, & in many cases, at the cost of their own lives.

The enclosed copy of a sketch [not found] is not quite correct. I have seen it before, & learn that it was sketched from a description, (& not by an eyewitness) & probably refers to the death of either Private Kelly, or Private McCue of the 7th Cavalry. [Here appears a long paragraph on the derivation of his name.] I regret very much that I have not the time to aid you as you request, but it would take more time than I can possibly spare.

With kindest wishes, I am, very sincerely yours,

Francis Craft.

[John W. Butler's Interview]

[Tablet 16]

John W. Butler of Agate says he was at W. Knee as a packer in charge of the pack train. He says that the Indians were got into a circle, as others state, to be disarmed. Col. Forsythe came to him the night before & told him to be ready next morning at 6 a. m. with the pack train to start for the Agency, and he got ready as ordered. Butler was not a soldier then but had been employed by the Q.M. at Fort Robinson as a civilian packer.

The Indians were ordered to come & turn in their guns but as only one or 2 were bro't Forsythe ordered Capt. Wallace by saying, "Capt. Wallace, select a detail and go and search those tepees, & see whether they have any firearms and steel pointed arrows and if they have any take them; if they haven't any we will proceed on into the Agency." (Wallace was the ranking Captain on the ground.) Wallace told Butler to come with him, remarking to him that he did not want to take any of those white soldiers as they would fool with the squaws etc. Wallace was accompanied by Lieut. Smith of D Troop to which Capt. Wallace belonged, and Lieut. Preston of 9th Cav. who was in charge of the scouts.[51] These 4 went to a tent & searched it & found a lot of new guns & passed them out to soldiers & then went to next tent. It was at the first tent that Butler passed out a new war club to Wallace who said he would keep it & hang it in his office. He put it under his arm. Butler & Smith went into the tent and found guns & handed them out. They were carrying them out to number them & put them into a pile. They were each numbering them & laying the guns down between these 2 officers. Wallace got Butler's knife to mark a gun for Butler. He told Butler he could have [?] it. He handed the knife back & stooped down to lay the gun on the ground, and while in the act an Indian in the circle jerked the war club from under Capt. Wallace's arm & struck him in the head & he fell dead. Lieut. Smith instantly shot the Indian who fell by Wallace; their feet lay between the legs of each other.

[Shorthand next six pages]

[James R. Walker's Interview]

Dr. Walker received his medical degree at Northwestern University in 1873. He practiced medicine at Leech Lake, Colville, and the Carlisle Indian School before coming to Pine Ridge in 1896. In 1902 anthropologist Clark Wissler visited the reservation and encouraged Walker to carry out investigations into Lakota culture. Even the most conservative Lakotas came to trust Walker, which enabled him to gather a massive amount of data on native religion and beliefs. Walker retired in 1914.[52]

[Tablet 17]

Interview with Dr. J. R. Walker, Agency Physician, Pine Ridge, November 21, 1906.

Dr. Walker has been at this Agency in official capacity eleven years.

He it was who wrote the article on Wounded Knee published in Appleton's Book-Lovers Magazine in ———— 1906, and which was sold through Rex Beach. This was the statement of Dewey Horn Cloud (now Beard) in his own words as near as could be.[53]

Upon the subject of Wounded Knee the doctor states:

That Beard told him that Big Foot's mission was peaceable; he was coming to the Agency for a peaceable object; that he encountered the soldiers drawn up in battle array, but he approached them in careless order as he had been moving across the country, without hostile attitude on his part, and showed all possible intention to be friendly. The commanding officer took Big Foot into a conveyance and moved off with him, followed by the troops, and these were followed by the Indians themselves. Thus they all came to Wounded Knee; the soldiers went into camp; Big Foot was put into a tent; and the Indians went into their own camp untrammeled by orders from the military.

The critical question is on the beginning of the action—the spark from which the flame arose. The father of the Horn Clouds was a doubting Thomas in the matter of the new Messiah worship. When affairs were drawing to a head in the search for arms, Horn Cloud tauntingly told the medicine man that now was the time to test and prove the efficacy of his new gospel.

The medicine man has been accused by the whites of throwing up dirt into the air and waving a blanket or some emblem as a signal for action. This was only the ordinary procedure through which he went in the ghost dance. It happened at this moment that the searching party came to two certain young men who had Winchester rifles for which they had paid good prices, and they were not willing to give them up, though their disposition was peaceable and they would have surrendered their ammunition without resistance.

An officer ordered a noncommissioned officer and a private to disarm the two young men. They advanced toward these, and one of them dropped his piece nearly to the position of guard against infantry, when the two soldiers retreated as though they anticipated that he would shoot if farther pressed. The Indian laughed at their evident fear. Just then Beard heard a shot and he looked around. A moment later he heard two shots and saw the two Indians fall. This was the beginning of bloodshed, and from now on it flowed continuously till the madness for blood and murder had ~~nothing more to feed on~~ left nothing but dead and dying.

It should be said that the conviviality among the officers the night before was well known by enough responsible persons to leave no doubt on this point.

(Mr. R. C. Stirk has told me that this pleasure was carried to a pretty high pitch, and that the line officers were going from tent to tent congratulating Col. Forsythe on his capture of the Indians.)

Dr. Walker is of the opinion that intoxicants had undue effect in producing the result of the disarmament.

Black Fox and Yellow Turtle were the two young men who opened the battle of W.K. See Dr. Walker's article published in Appleton's under the name of Rex Beach.

In 1897 the authorities began getting the Indians to take the names of their fathers.

My Map of Field of Wounded Knee [54]

(This is not Dr. Walker's narrative. One of the Indian police told it to me. The policemen are paid $20 a month. They are distributed over the Reservation. They come into the Agency from their homes on detail, as it were, and stay at the Agency on duty about three weeks and then return home and continue on duty there. They keep eight here at the Agency on duty.)

Dr. J. R. Walker says that Chas. W. Allen told him that Big Foot came out of his tent and sat down in front of it. When the firing began Big Foot's daughter ran towards him and he was shot just before she reached him; she gave an outcry and stooped over him. An officer seized a gun in the hands of a soldier and shot her and she fell over on her father.

Dr. Walker speaks of the cannon being trained on a wagonful of Indians escaping in a southeast direction and fired into them and all and everything were killed and demolished.

A woman and two children escaped down the ravine and got into W.K. Creek and were followed by soldiers and shot in the creek. Dr. Walker says he has heard from other sources of this incident of the killing of these in this manner. Antoine Herman, an intelligent half-breed who helped bury the dead, told Dr. W. that these bodies were found in the creek. Antoine Herman lives in Kyle.

Dr. Walker says that Red Cloud was not a chief but a head warrior. Mr. Samuel Deon has told me the same thing. Dr. Walker adds that Red Cloud was cruel. Once he and some other Indians held up a train or engine on the U.P. R.R. and fed the fireman into the fire box.

Another story of this character is, that the Doctor mentions, that at another time Red Cloud and some of his friends tied a railroad employee to a telegraph pole and shot his body full of arrows. These acts are not unlike what American Horse related to me about his shooting stealthily some Indians that he crept up on.[55]

Dr. Walker's management of Ghost Dancing at Leech Lake where he was Agent in 1890.

When the Messiah delusion gained some progress at Leech Lake some of the Doctor's Indians brought the matter to his knowledge, and he invited them into his office and talked the subject over with them in a deliberative manner. They told him that the Messiah was to come and destroy the white people and to restore the earth to the Indians as it once was with all its benefits; that their dead would be restored to them, and a new era of the ancient happiness which blessed their fathers would descend upon them. They particularly stated that their Messiah taught them to do no wrong.

Their confidence was very strong that they were to see a period of great rejoicing long delayed. Dr. Walker told them that if what they had told him was true, the Great Spirit was behind it all, and if he was planning this good for them it would come to pass and be right; but if they were mistaken in these pleasing anticipations—if these truly good things had not been planned for them by the Great Spirit, they would fail to realize them and all their dancing and rejoicing would come to naught, and they would know whether they were in error. They made known to him their purpose to do no harm nor wrong and that their Messiah had taught them these principles.

He admonished them that they must cleave to this determin[ation] if they would obey the Messiah whose interposition they desired, and so long as they did this their dancing and worship would be all right and not be opposed, and he advised them to continue it. In less than a year it had died out and some of the Indians spoke of it in jest.

Agent McLaughlin did nothing against the dancing till the government called his attention to the subject, then directed [blank].

[Tablet 25]

Dr. J. R. Walker says: That on the 4th July, 1903, Red Cloud formally abdicated his Chieftancy in favor of his son Jack at a celebration of the Indians. Dr. Walker took down the speech, and he has read it to me. It is a fine piece of eloquence. The doctor will publish it and then I may get it.

[George E. Bartlett's Interview]

As far as is known, Ricker's first interview was with George Bartlett on November 30, 1903. It is the only time Ricker wrote all of his questions and the answers he received. A week later Bartlett gave Ricker a biographical sketch.

[Tablet 45]

Sketch of Capt. George E. Bartlett. Was born Aug. 25, 1858, at New Haven, Conn., and came with his parents to Sioux City, Iowa; and a year later he went up to the Yankton Agency and were employed in a trading store continuously from that time up to 1876.

A party of 14 outfitted at Yankton for the Black Hills, among them were Milloy, an old California miner and Charley Green, who afterwards [was] killed on Centennial prairie (near Whitewood) by the Indians when he was hunting some hobbled horses, and Alex. Sands, Frank Munson, and Irving Smith & several French Canadians whose names the Captain cannot recall. Capt. Bartlett joined this party and went into the Black Hills in the month of August & went into Two-Bit Gulch and located claims and in November the Captain came out of the Hills & returned to Yankton & remained there that winter. The whites were driven out by the government because this was before the treaty.[56] On Feb. 24, 1877, with another party he left Yankton driving one of Charlie Marshall's teams to take the party to the Hills, and they arrived in March. The trip was for awhile very pleasant and when they reached the Cheyenne river a terrible blizzard was encountered & they were snowed in there several days.

They arrived at Rapid City & weather was fine. There were a blockhouse just west of where the flouring mill now is, 2 or 3 cabins, and John R. Brennan had a little log house there and he afterward kept the American House. Noah Newbanks had a log store. "Red-headed" Johnson had a log livery stable. Frenchy had a stone shack for a saloon. The blockhouse was in the middle of the street & had a well inside of it. In a few days the captain went up to Spring Valley ranch where he worked for Garvey & Adler a year in making the ranch improvements. This place was 14 miles above Rapid City. Here some complications arose between the two partners over a woman who was cooking at the ranch; Garvey became infatuated with the woman and tried to drive Adler off the place and Adler killed him. Garvey ran toward Adler with a hammer and the latter ran into the house and took a Sharp's rifle and shot Garvey. Adler was tried and acquitted.

When the pony express was established from Fort Pierre to Rapid City he was employed by the mail contractor Harvey Horton to carry the mail, and he carried it from Cheyenne river to Deadman creek between Rapid City & Fort Pierre. He rode all winter a distance of 30 miles, leaving Cheyenne river at sundown and returning and arriving at sunrise next morning, making a night ride of 60 miles. He got off the road one night in a blizzard and got into the head of Bull creek and crawled into a hollow Cottonwood stump and remained there three days and 2 nights. He had one jack rabbit to eat while lost. His horse browsed around. He found his way out the evening of the third day. Following this service he was in 1879 appointed deputy U.S. Marshal for Dakota by John B. Marshal, U.S. Marshal for Dakota Territory. He held the office ~~continuous~~ under different marshals 14 years. Captain Bartlett traveled anywhere as deputy U.S. Marshal, for in those times a marshal went anywhere and did not pass over his papers to other marshals as is now done. He had his house at Pine Ridge and Deadwood. He went on to Pine Ridge Reservation along on White river — went down from the Hills to prospect. He went with a party, but found nothing.

In 1883 (?) he started a trader's store at Wounded Knee where he established a post-office in an Indian camp, for W.K. was nothing but an Indian camp then. While at W.K. he established a Nebraska horse ranch in the northern part of Cherry Co. close to the reservation line. He held them for quite a while on the reservation till the govt. officers began to make a fuss abt. it, then he moved them over the line & hired a man to take charge of them.

He was a trader at W.K. nine years and until 1892.[57]

In 1893 he took a band of Indians to the World's Fair for exhibition purposes for another party. While there he made an engagement with ~~Adam Forepaugh~~ Howe & Cushing's Circus to travel with the circus with the Indians in a Wild West taking some Pine Ridge Indians, & doing fancy shooting. He formed like arrangements with others afterwards in the following order: Adam Forepaugh's Circus which had also a Wild West attachment, and used an old Deadwood stage coach; Robert Hunting, commonly known as Bob Hunting. With these he toured the south, making all the southern states where the Indians attracted a great deal of attention, especially among the negroes, and where his shooting of walnuts and pennies and loaf sugar thrown into the air also attracted great interest from the old mountaineers who themselves had been raised from children to the use of the rifle, some of whom were surprisingly incredulous as to his practice being genuine & the walnuts being broken by a bullet, and would not believe that he had not used shot cartridges until he had allowed them to throw up pieces of silver money in the air and sent a rifle ball through them.

~~The author I saw him shoot.~~

The author has witnessed shooting by him even more marvelous. He saw Capt. Bartlett, using a Marlin 30–30 rifle loaded with a 30–30 cartridge with a soft point bullet, manufactured by the Peters Cartridge Co. of Cincinnati, Ohio. At the time I saw this he was in the employ of the Peters Cartridge Co. and gave an exhibition for the purpose of demonstrating the superior quality of all kinds of ammunition made by that company, including the cleanliness and introduction of King's semi-smokeless powder, a patented article. I saw him repeatedly pierce with a bullet a piece of boiler plate steel two and a half inches square and one quarter of an inch thick, thrown into the air. I also saw him shoot small washers the size of quarters and half dollars. I saw him place a common oyster can on the ground and shoot under it throwing it into the air and then shooting and hitting it five times before it descended to the ground. I saw him throw such cans into the air and shoot each six times in their descent. I saw him shoot, holding his gun in various positions and with his back to the mark, and holding the gun upside down and also at arm's length, with the aid of reflection from a small round mirror about the size of a silver dollar, and hitting the mark at each trial.

The Captain will send ~~cuts of some of his cuts~~ me photos of some of his attitudes in these shooting exploits, for cuts to accompany his sketch. Notify him when they are wanted.

Continuing the show engagements, the Captain was next engaged to Davis

& Keogh in a western melo-drama called the "Great Train Robbery," showing the perils and excitements of railway travel on the southwestern frontier, the scene being laid on the Chicago & Rock Island R.R. in the Indian Territory. The scenery in this melo-drama was very grand, the scenic effects being very powerful, exhibiting the train on the prairie, the robbers holding it up and overpowering the express messenger and blowing ~~open the safe~~ up the car and robbing the safe. The specialties were particularly interesting and exciting. Capt. B. was with this three seasons and did the fancy shooting in the specialties. There were ten long haired Sioux Indians from the Pine Ridge Indians with this show and which the Captain himself furnished.[58]

Capt. B. quit the show business and in 1898 went to work for the Marlin Firearms Co. of New Haven, Conn., shooting their new repeating shot gun at gun clubs and shooting tournaments advertising their guns. In the spring of 1901 he made an engagement with the Peters Cartridge Co. of Cincinnati, Ohio, & has been with it since to date (Dec. 8, 1903). Since he has been in their employ his travels have covered the entire western country, a part of old Mexico and a part of Canada.

The foregoing was written Dec. 8, 1903, and taken down from Capt. Bartlett himself. His address: Capt. George E. Bartlett, Peters Cartridge Co. Cincinnati, Ohio.

[Box 19]

Capt. Geo. E. Bartlett in a fight with thieves in Montana got a wound in his knee & the Indians called him "Wounded Knee" & he is known by them by that name; but the creek went by that name before he was an Indian trader at Wounded Knee. He was there 9 yrs.; went there in 1883. He was Deputy U.S. Marshal 14 yrs. in Dakota Territory — first appointed in 1879. He held office of Post Master, was special agt. for the Department of Justice, & was Inspector for the Black Hills Live Stock Assn.

Capt. Bartlett was appointed Capt. of Indian Police by Gen. Brooke, & this is how he got his title. He was not app. by Gen. Miles as stated in my notes elsewhere. He was the man who brought word to Gen. Brooke of the massacre at Wounded Knee. Brooke would not believe his story, & said it is Impossible! impossible!

Rough map of Wounded Knee by Capt. Geo. E. Bartlett. [Figure 3]

Capt. George E. Bartlett represents the Peters Cartridge Co. of Cincinnati and travels with W. H. Kleinke who travels for Hibbard, Spencer, Bartlett & Co. of Chicago.

Statement of Capt. Geo. E. Bartlett made Nov. 30, 1903, in the office of The Chadron Times. Lee Card, Stenographic Reporter. [Ricker edited the type-script.]

Q. You may state when you came here?

A. Well, I was down there the first after the war, the fall of 77, along the White River down to the forks. It was in the spring of 78 when they went up and located at Pine Ridge

Q. Were you there continuously from that time?

A. No, I was in Deadwood a good deal of the time and travelled back and forth there many years, but spent about half of my time at the agency head quar-ters which were really at Deadwood but I was appointed for the [Pine Ridge] Indian Reservation, but used to do lots of work north on the hills[,] in Mon-tana and over into Wyoming and all around the country.

Q. Well, when did you come to the reservation to stay continuously?

A. I think it was in 1883, I went over there to Wounded Knee from White and Gillingham. They bought out the Tom Cogle's store.[59]

Q. Was he a ranch man?

A. He did have a ranch down here on Beaver. Had a store at Pine Ridge and a branch store at Wounded Knee.[60]

Q. How long were you there?

A. Nine years.

Q. Now, I wish you would make a statement about the Indians that were there at Wounded Knee. Where was Big Foot's Band?

A. Well, as I understand was at Standing Rock Agency. The Indians of Stand-ing Rock Agency on hearing of the dance down here at Pine Ridge are sup-posed to have started down here for the purpose of joining it, whether they had any intention of joining in or not, there cannot anybody tell and as soon as the soldiers intercepted them at the Bell Fourche River or Bear Butte Creek and made them prisoners, that is, in a way, and they skipped out at night and come on down through the bad lands and the Indian Police first noticed them coming up Porcupine Creek. They crossed the bad lands and come over to the White River and started up Porcupine Creek. Porcupine Creek from Wounded Knee is 8 miles off the road. When they came across, parties of soldiers were sent to intercept them and bring them in and they had trouble there. I think they were under Captain Wallace. He was the captain killed there. He was with them when they went down to intercept them. They intercepted them down on the Porcupine Creek. They come up from Porcupine Creek and then crossed over to Wounded Knee and went into camp the 28th day of December 1890. Well then they were getting ready to move the next morning about 8 o'clock and the shooting commenced after having disarmed them right there. I think they took their guns away from them the night they got in there.

Q. Well, I always heard they had them about surrounded there and got them out into line and some of them did not bring their guns.

A. They had everything that you could think of—old muzzle loaders with [blank] lock and everything else, and Wallace was killed there as he was going around among the tents.

Q. I did not think that was so, I thought Wallace was killed after the shooting commenced, that is what I always heard. That is different from anything I ever heard. I understood they delivered up all arms they had.

A. They might not have delivered up all the arms but nearly all. They might have held out a few guns. There [are] always a few in every kind of a crowd, you know, of either whites or Indians that would kind of naturally hold out a few revolvers. They did not have very many guns. Most of their guns were given to the police and they promised to deliver up their guns when they got to the agency and the Indians were going into what they called a friendly camp. A great many Indians camped up there which was on White Clay Creek.

Q. Did you see the guns?

A. Now [No?], I had been down in camp. The hills where I was (when the massacre was going on) are well off Wounded Knee Creek in the direction of the Agency.

Q. Just tell him anything about it you saw and know. The fight coming off. Can you give the positions of the guns?

A. This Hotchkiss gun stood on the hill north of the camp—right in that locality (showing) right out here on this flat is where the camp was, then there is a succession of hills; that cannon stood up there on one of those hills some-wheres. This is the hill where the body was found. I was told that one was planted way up there. It might have been this gun that was trained on that woman and child and killed them. (The woman and child that Marrivall told about.) This road (pointing) runs toward the agency. The hills are very low and slope on the east side and when that gunner wrecked that squaw and wagon, that was right in front of the store. Right (pointing) up here is a dry creek that is down in a deep gulch and there was a deep bank of snow there and quite a number of Indians that were shot would run and fall into this snow bank and die. There were several places where the Indians dropped off this bank right into this snow and there were a big pile of Indians lying dead in one bunch here and in some places there were five and six squaws in a pile and in one pile of squaws was that Indian baby alive — right in the bunch of squaws that were frozen stiff and cold.

Q. You saw that wagon load of squaws that moved away from the camp towards your store and that that Hotchkiss gun was discharged at the wagon.

A. It hit the wagon or ground under the wagon and burned the wagon half up.

Q. Do you know of any other incidents like that?

A. Only those two boys, and the old man that I spoke of that was followed way up the creek and he and his two boys killed trying to get away. (They were found killed by gunshots three miles up Wounded Knee creek from the battle ground.)

Q. You said something about a couple of women?

A. Five of them run from this camp up across the flat and where this deep gulch is and up in here (pointing) I guess in the clear space and got up on those hills and two soldiers followed them and as soon as they saw they were being followed by the soldiers they sat down on the hill and faced them and the soldiers killed all five of them. When they saw they were going to be slain they covered their faces with their blankets and awaited death.

Q. You saw that?

A. Yes. Two little boys were killed also. One soldier shot him through the eyes. The article says he was dead. Both his eyes were shot out. They were both probably in the neighborhood of 12 years of age. One was a half breed boy and was shot through the hip. He was found dead, so the article says, but he was found alive. (Capt. Bartlett speaks of the article meaning that published in the "Great Falls Leader." He says that both these boys were alive but the one shot in the eyes died in a few days. Doesn't know what became of the one shot in hip.)

Q. Did you see that?

A. No, the half breed boy told me that.

Q. Well, you know of any other incidents like that?

A. Only those two boys — Indians — found on the creek five miles east of

Wounded Knee several days after that. It is presumed the soldiers found them waiting around over there. It was learned afterwards that it was a woman and a girl. I can't remember all those things, there was so much happened about that time.

Q. Now, tell as to how the Indians came to kill the soldiers as far as you know.

A. When the shooting commenced the soldiers being in a semicircle around the Indians that probably killed each other and I suppose several of the Indians got hold of soldier's guns and ammunition and done the best they could with it. Every Indian I saw was laying on the ground with his inwards all out. You have to put this and that together—where he was killed, how he was found lying, etc., but it was pretty conclusive that they was right.

Q. Did you state that that Hotchkiss gun was trained on that Sibley tent.

A. Well, the Indian looking out of the tent was hit with the Hotchkiss ball enough to tear him all to pieces. There were chunks taken out of his body as though they were pulled out. He certainly had the gun pointed that way and if it was an accident, it hit the Indian all right.

Q. How many machine guns did they have?

A. I don't know.

Q. The Indians tried to escape?

A. Oh, they run in every direction and the soldiers followed them and killed them while they run and some of them sat down on the ground and did not try to do anything.

Q. Did you see anybody trying to stop their firing on the Indians?

A. I was not close enough for that.

Q. How close were you?

A. In the neighborhood of three quarters of a mile. I just happened to be coming out from the agency riding along the hill tops. This little girl Mrs. Colby has [Lost Bird] we found here on the first day of January—three days after the so called fight. You will get the account of that in the clipping there. I think the name of the Indian that got her was Feather on the Head and I never heard of her until Mrs. Colby wrote me about taking land in severalty. The girl is 13 or 14 years old now.

Q. You don't know who the commanding officer was?

A. I think the Captain's name was Forescythe. [In the margin Ricker noted, "It was Col. Forsythe."] There were so many of those officers that I did not know and that I did not try to keep any track of them.

Q. You did not know who the army officer was that was in command at the agency?

A. Well, Brooke was in command, the man whom I reported the fight to and he said that he did not believe it and acted very strange about it and said it was "Impossible! impossible!"[61]

Q. At that time you were captain of the Indian Police.

A. Afterwards, I was appointed by General Miles.

Q. Anything else you are willing to communicate? I wish you would state how many there were that were killed.

A. I always understood that there were 400 Indians and about forty soldiers.[62]

Q. Did any Indians get away that escaped alive?

A. Possibly there was [a] few that got out that they did not overtake. All that were left were supposed to have been left dead but we heard at the agency on the last day of December that would be on the 31st of December, the day before New Years that there were a few Indians left—that they were alive and I was instructed to go out there and find what there was alive and bring them in and that was the time we found the little girl.

Q. Did you have anything to do with the bringing in of the dead soldiers?

A. No, the soldiers brought them in. They were brought in right at the time, that day.

Q. Don't know anything about the wounded?

A. No, I did not pay attention at the time.

Copy of Bartlett's map. His route of Big Foot's march is not correct according to the Horn Clouds. This makes him cross the White River above the Stronghold, when there is no dispute that he descended the Wall in the neighborhood of Interior.[63]

[Tablet 44]

Capt. Bartlett says: He took the Indian child which Mrs. Colby has out of a pile of dead squaws (abt. 7 or 8) all squaws, all dead, & it looked as though they had been piled together by the Indians, & it was evident the Indians had been there between Dec 29 and Jan. 1 for numbers of the wounded had been covered with blankets. The child was heard to cry. The Indians being superstitious were loath to approach the pile of dead bodies. Those on top were frozen. Capt. Bartlett helped get the child out from underneath the bodies and he gave the child to Long Woman (Wiyan Hanska) who was the wife of Feather on Head & she took charge of the baby, and next he heard of it he learned that Mrs. Colby had it.

Mrs. Colby's address is: Mrs. Clara B. Colby, Care of Woman's Tribune, Washington, D.C.

Capt. Bartlett says that he was in command of the Indian Police and moved his men down to the bluff north from the town toward the White Clay Creek at the time the Indians fired into the agency and set fire to the log cabins north of the town and the creek. He moved his men from the west side of the long government buildings and from a point just north of the agent's office, in a northwesterly direction to the house of Fred Ammon the engineer. He was fired on here, a bullet striking the ground about twelve feet in front of him. He took shelter behind the house. Gen. Brook shoved his head out from behind the government house and told the Captain to tell the Indian Police not to fire. He had been telling his men to fire. His Seargent asked him what the General said. The Captain answered that he ordered the men to fire.

See Capt. B.'s map made Dec. 7, 1903. Capt. B. disputes Col. Corliss in some of his statements; but most of those disputed are immaterial ones.[64] Where Col. Corliss says "Ten minutes afterwards all of the hills to the northwest of the agency were alive with Indians firing at the Second Infantry," Capt. Bartlett says the Indians were not on the hills but down on the White Clay bottom.

Capt. B. agrees that Capt. Wallace was killed with a war club.[65]

Where Col. Corliss says that he visited the church where the Indian wounded were and they made no sound of complaint or of pain, etc. Capt. B. contradicts him and says he was in same place and that there was a good deal of moaning and groaning, and that the women particularly moaned because they realized their condition and what the end must be.

Capt. Bartlett read Col. Corliss' statement published in the Denver Post, and made his contradictions knowing what Col. Corliss had said. Capt. Bartlett says a great many of the wounded were removed from Wounded Knee & died in other places. This would make it seem that more lost their lives on account of the action at W.K. than the Indians state, and it helps to support the Captain's statement that about 400 lost their lives. He says he did not count the dead but the talk around Wounded Knee by all was that the loss was about 400. It is said by Capt. B. that about all the Indians were killed, and the fragmentary statements seem to confirm this. If it be true, then Col. Corliss' statement is a strong corroboration, in which he says Capt. Varnum had in searching for guns "passed something like 200 Indians in his search and was half through his task."[66] According to this there were about 400 Indians.

[Box 18, Tablet 209]
Copy[67]
From Cincinnati Times-Star
An Awful Vengeance
The Battle of Wounded Knee

George Bartlett tells a Sensational Story, Which Reflects on the Old Seventh Cavalry. Soldier Boys Wantonly Massacred Defenseless Indians. It Was, He Claims, to Even up for the Custer Massacre.

A remarkable version of the battle of Wounded Knee was given to the Times-Star recently by Capt. George E. Bartlett, who was an eye witness to the whole affair, who is now playing with "The Great Train Robbery" at Heuck's Opera House. In December, 1890, Bartlett was acting as scout for Gen. Brooke, commanding the forces at the Pine Ridge agency. Bartlett had been prior to that time a U. S. Marshal, Indian trailer and scout, and had a little store in a valley near the agency. Bartlett who had been wounded in a fight with horse thieves ten years before, was known among the Indians as Hu-Stse, which means in English, "Wounded Knee," and this name, painted on a sign above the entrance to his store, gave to the battlefield its designation. Big Foot's Sioux had left camp and headed for the Pine Ridge agency for the purpose of joining the ghost dance. They were headed off by U. S. troops and taken to the Black Hills, but escaped, and again made for Pine Ridge. Here a good part of the army had been assembled under command of Gen. Brooke to suppress the dance, and, the band having been detected by the agency scouts, Capt. Wallace of the Seventh cavalry was detailed by Gen. Brooke to go out and bring in Big Foot and his band. It was significant in the light of after events, that the Seventh had been known as Custer's old command, and that memories of the famous massacre still lingered in the minds of many of the troopers.

"Big Foot's band," says the captain, was surrounded in the valley near my store. They surrendered without a struggle, and pitched their tents near to one side of the soldiers' camp. During the night the officers thought it would be safer to disarm the Indians, who were generally armed with excellent repeating rifles, and upon the promise that their rifles should be restored to them as soon as the ghost dance had been suppressed, they were induced to give up everything save a few pistols and muskets. After disarming the Indians the soldiers took up a position in the shape of a horseshoe on three sides of the valley, and a Hotchkiss gun throwing an explosive shell was so placed as to command the only outlet.

From a dispute of some kind arose between the Indians and soldiers, and one of the former thru a handful of earth into the air. It was afterwards claimed that this was a signal to the Indians to begin fighting, but I was on horseback on top of the hill at the time, and I think the idea preposterous. A single shot was fired, and then came a volley from the soldiers which killed men, women and children indiscriminately. The Hotchkiss gun, too was soon in operation, and the fight did not last long, for it was too one-sided. One Indian secreted himself in the soldiers' tents, and as soon as he was detected there a shell from this gun blew the tent, the Indian and his gun into fragments. Another shell struck an Indian camp wagon, destroying its contents and setting the wagon on fire. The troops fired recklessly and it was in this way that Capt. Wallace met his death, although in the official report he is said to have been killed with a tomahawk. Women and children who tried to escape were pursued by the cavalrymen, and finding their attempt futile, stopped of one accord and covered their heads with blankets. They were killed as soon as the cavalrymen reached them. Four hundred Indians were killed and in all forty-three soldiers in this so-called battle.

When I described the affair to Gen. Brooke he could not at first believe me, but was soon convinced as the troops came in with their dead and wounded.

About the investigation which followed? Naturally my feelings were with the Seventh, and this is the first time I have ever told the story of what I saw. Many soldiers were afterwards heard to remark that the accounts with the Sioux for the Custer massacre were partly squared.

[George A. Stannard's Interview]

[Box 19]
Stannard and Kocer's Accounts. Wounded Knee

George A. Stannard of Gordon, Neb., says: I was in the employ of the government as farrier at the time of the Wounded Knee Massacre, and was, in relation to the ground at the time, one mile southwest of the field. Could see but little of the battle. The main fighting lasted about ten minutes and being upon elevated ground, I could see the general operations and the dispersing and escaping Indians, and give it as my opinion that no Indians got away; at any rate I never knew of any escaping. I saw a team and wagon containing nine bucks going leisurely away towards the southeast at a distance of about a mile and a half at least from the Hotchkiss cannon which was fired into it. I saw a lieutenant draw the gun up on to a little sand knoll and train and sight the piece at this wagon. A shell was thrown into it. The horses were killed, the wagon destroyed and the 9 bucks mangled. (The fellow who went with Stannard to view the scene remarked that you about get enough out of what remains to make a funeral.) A large hole was made in the ground about 10 or 12 feet in diameter. I went over and saw the results of this shot within an hour after it was done.

I was told by Swigert and another man, that they did not think the Indians fired more than one volley before they broke and ran east toward the creek above the trading house.

Over 300 Indians were killed. There were in the neighborhood of 500 soldiers.[68]

I saw a boy and a girl, probably 8 or 10 yrs. old, running from the field in a southeast direction towards the creek, and I saw two soldiers drop down each on one knee, and taking a knee and elbow rest of their pieces, kill these little children who, when hit, carried by the momentum of running, went rolling over.

When the fight began there was one person with me, a blacksmith from Omaha whose whereabouts are unknown to me now; and we started towards the field and by the time the main action was over he and I had come up within 200 or 300 yards of the center of the ground.

I came here to Gordon from Independence, Iowa, in 1889 and ran a blacksmith shop in Gordon 6 or 7 years and have since been on my farm 1½ miles east of Gordon.

Before the fight at Wounded Knee the Sioux Indians were camped on the ridge north of the Agency, north of (Wolf?) creek. The time that Capt. Bartlett went out with the police under Gen. Brook's orders, the Indians fired into the agency & 2 soldiers were wounded down at the sawmill on the creek. Thinks the Indians would have come in at that time had it not been for the police.

The Cheyennes were camped south of town.

The Sioux north of town at a later time suddenly struck camp and withdrew, and on leaving, stopped back on the hills and shot about half an hour into the agency, and then retreated to the bad lands and joined the band under Young Man Afraid of his Horses and Two Sticks.

[Joseph Kocer's Interview]

Kocer came to Pine Ridge in 1880, and was employed as an "industrial teacher" at a school on Wounded Knee Creek eighteen miles northeast of the agency. Charles Allen knew him and wrote he "made a record for honor and integrity in his long life as farmer, merchant and stockman."[69]

[Box 19]

See Jo Kocer at Gordon who was at Wounded Knee. He has a store at Kyle and a ranch 18 miles north of Gordon & close to W. Knee. His family lives in Gordon.

Wounded Knee, Dec. 11, 1904.

Joseph Kocer of Gordon and Kyle says: He was on the battleground next day after the fight.

The battle was on Monday. Tuesday there was some fighting on the White Clay near the [Holy Rosary] mission between the Sioux and the troops. Wednesday a blizzard came and he thinks it cooled off the ardor of the Indians and led to a cessation of hostilities. The Indians said they would wait till spring when they could throw away their blankets and fight without such encumbrance and could fight better. White men told them that the soldiers would not have to wear buffalo overcoats and could also fight better.

Tuesday, next day after the battle, Mr. Kocer who was a scout and was patroling along the line with other scouts, viz., Walter Scott, Bill Truax, W. M. Coffield, Ed Noble and Louis Eddy. These men were private citizens who were employed by militia officers and received their pay from the state. They were scouting along the line between Nebraska and the Reservation to watch for Indians and give information of their movements.

He was getting breakfast when one of his comrades spied the 6th Cavalry approaching from Fort Niobrara and mistook them for Indians.[70] When Mr. Kocer saw the army wagons he replied that they could not be Indians and must be troops. These came up and he and Ed Noble and Bill Truax were put in the lead to show the way to W. Knee. He knew of the battle the night before; he and Wm. M. Coffield went down that (Monday) night within three miles of the field and could see nothing, but could hear the relations and friends of the slain, who were in scattered bands over the hills, moaning and crying.

He says that some of the Indians got away from W.K. alive. Four at Kyle now, were in the fight, viz., Dewey Beard, Daniel Whitelance, Frank Horncloud and

Joe Horncloud. These four are all brothers. When the two latter went to mission school they were given the name of their parents which was Horncloud. The two older ones, Beard and Whitelance, never went to school and so they were not constrained to bear the parents' name, but kept those which were given by the parents. Indian children are named by the parents according to some trait or peculiarity they possess and never take the name of the parents. These four brothers lost both parents and a brother at W.K. Does not know of any others who escaped out of Big Foot's band. He says many others escaped.

The moaning and crying referred to was the lament of natural grief for their dead, and was particularly the sorrow expressed by relatives of the dead.

The custom among the Indians now is that relatives who are bereft of close kin put a white sheet on, cut their hair off and mourn; and formerly they were in the habit of cutting their bodies and limbs, but this has now been abandoned, except in rare cases when it is kept up by some of the old ones.

The 6th Cavalry went to the ground and after traveling over the field these scouts returned. The cavalry camped there and Wednesday buried the dead on the hill where the monument is. Mr. Kocer saw Big Foot and six others lying in a row, Big Foot in the middle—laid out—done by somebody, probably friends, and a white sheet was spread over Big Foot.[71] The other Indians were lying promiscuously on the field as they fell. Women and children were lying dead among the slain and in great numbers. In one place three women, the inference being that they were a mother and two daughters, were lying, the mother on her back, and the daughters across her chest. In another place was an old gray haired mother who evidently died in great agony, her hands clutching the grass, lying upon her back, and her daughter with her own child in her arms lying across her chest—all dead.

A needless slaughter. They were all getting ready to move. It was decided to search and disarm the Indians, and instead of taking out a few at a time and examining them they got them all up together.

Says he heard the account of the battle from both whites and Indians and they all agree that the Indians fired first. When camp was broken and abt. ready to move, Capt. Wallace who was in command of the camp under Col. Forsythe, ordered a double guard to be placed in the regimental formation of a V, the apex being near the canyon on the west. Some Indian, supposed to be lunatic, fired a shot and the Indians began shooting. Capt. Wallace was the first one killed & was struck in the head with a war club. Mr. K. says this is the way Wallace was killed, and he is very positive on this point, contradicting all other versions, say[s] that he has received it from the Indians. Wallace was searching tents; he was shot by the crazy man and fell in front of a tent, and he raised upon his knees and was then struck by an Indian in the head with a war club. This started the battle.

About 187 were buried. Thinks a good many bodies were carried away.

The two Hotchkiss cannon stood on the knoll where the monument is.[72]

Owing to the regimental V formation the soldiers killed their own men.

In the ravine south of the plateau where the Indians were camped & the massacre took place women and children & men went over the bank & fell dead as they went over, being shot at the bank as they came to it in their flight. The dead laid in three directions — or in three great rows, so to speak, as they went in their flight for safety. The three lines of dead all lay in westerly directions — one northwest, one west and one southwest. There were some, a more scattering number, lying dead along the Wounded Knee creek.

Two girls were fleeing up the ravine shown in the Stannard picture to the right.[73] Two cavalry horses which had lost their riders were following them; finally the girls came to the end of the ravine where the bank was perpendicular and here they caught the horses, and mounting them, got away and made their escape to the Standing Rock Agency after a ride of 250 miles.

Two old women (abt. 60 yrs. old) both wounded, went down to the Porcupine creek and lived in a cave in a bank three weeks and maintained themselves on rose buds. When found they were taken to the Agency and placed in the hospital, and next day after coming to the fire they both died.

A mule and pony hitched to a wagon were right down in the bottom of the ravine just south of where the fighting was. The horse was killed in harness and the mule had a leg broken. He stood there braying.

Another team, farther up the ravine, where the road winds around and crosses, was standing. One horse lying dead in harness, the other standing with a broken leg.

Thinks it was figured that close to 80 soldiers were killed.[74]

See Coffield and Mr. Cleveland abt. these things.[75]

One tent which was occupied by scouts who had gone out to see the operations in the camp when the Indians were being disarmed and had left their guns in the tent was taken possession of by a single Indian when the trouble began, and he used these loaded guns to shoot the soldiers. He killed a good many, and at length the soldiers turned rifles on the tent he was in and riddled him with bullets, one in each cheek, one in the forehead and some in his body.

Mr. K. says it is not true that a Hotchkiss was turned on the tent for there were no evidences of this as he saw the man & tent after the battle. Tent was partly burned. The Indian's hair was nearly all burned off. Fire had been set to the tent after he was dead and before the battle was over.

Saw a girl abt. 16 yrs. old lying dead about 20 paces from the main camp. By her side lay her school case in which she carried her pencils and pens & penholders. Mr. K. brought it away and subsequently gave it to Wm. Margrave, of Reserve, Kansas. Chas. Margrave, a brother, lives in Gordon.

Mr. K. has a Hotchkiss shell which he picked up on the hill where the Hotchkiss cannon stood.

[W. F. Clark's Interview]

[Tablet 31]

(April 21, 1905)

W. F. Clark, saddler and trainmaster at Fort Robinson, says:

He was at the time of the Wounded Knee fight a driver for Co. C, 8th Infantry and was on duty when Lieutenant Preston and a soldier of the 7th Cavalry arrived from W.K. at the Agency at about 11 o'clock a. m. on the 29th day of December 1890. (See Fred [Peter] McFarland's statement abt. Lieut. Preston's starting from W.K. when the action began.) These two brought to the Agency the first news of the fighting on W.K. creek.

When these swift messengers with the bad news of what was going on out there had been heard stating that Big Foot's band had been "massacred," (would not "destroyed" be the word here) an educated Indian standing near, who was either a doctor or a preacher (he says some one of the wounded women died at Agency and he himself hauled the body and this man preached the sermon, and he had seen him taking the children up to the church, and thinks he was an Episcopal minister; was it Dr. Chas. A. Eastman?)[76] spoke up and said he would not be surprised if all the Indians on the Reservation would now go out, meaning that they would take to the warpath. (Capt. — now General — Humphrey was quartermaster at the Agency at the time.) Lieutenant Preston hurried with an ambulance to the scouts' camp a mile and a half south of the Agency and at American Horse's camp where there were a lot of unpacked guns which he loaded up and brought in and placed in the hands of men who were without weapons, asking of each at the same time if he was familiar with the use of firearms, designing to distribute the pieces only to those who would be most likely to do effective work with the ~~guns~~ them. There were but few

troops at the Agency at this moment and feeling was intense and fully justified because the danger could not be measured, everything depending on the
self-restraint of the Indians themselves which just then was looked upon as
a slender thread. There was at this instant skirmishing between the hostiles
and the Indian police. Lieut. Preston had not been at the Agency to exceed
an hour when the firing between the hostiles and the police began. What has
been called "firing into the Agency" has been misleading by making it appear
that the object of aim was the Agency itself, whereas the police had been under
Capt. Barlett (the mention of Bartlett is my own statement) rushed down to
the vicinity of the creek north of the Agency and the hostiles shot at them, and
the Agency being in the line of fire the bullets fell there. Thinks two soldiers
of the 2d Infantry were slightly wounded in the feet by this fire.

(I will anticipate here by saying that after conditions had become quiet at
the Agency an order was issued requiring all formations to sleep upon their
arms, and Clark says that the cavalry when going to water, carried their carbines and revolvers, and he himself when taking his mules to drink slung his
gun over his shoulder.)

(The police was the Agent's own force and under his orders.)

As soon as the hostiles got word of the fighting at W.K. they began their
warlike demonstrations—firing on the police and burning the three or four
shacks down on the little stream (some on each side of it) and what hay was
stacked there.

Mr. Clark remembers the remains of the fort on White River at the junction
of Beaver Creek. He thinks it was called Halleck; says the ruins were there in
1877. This is the one Leslie mentions.[77]

[E. C. Swigert's Interview]

[Tablet 14]
March 31, 1905.

E. C. Swigert of Gordon says: Chas. Cressy was correspondent at the
Agency and was at Wounded Knee during the battle and took refuge behind
the creek bank when the firing began. He was correspondent for Omaha Bee.
Mr. Swigert was not at the battle, but he was there after the dead had been
gathered up. Stakes had been driven to mark the spot where each Indian fell.[78]

He speaks of Short Bull leading a band up later to take part in the fight.[79]

He tells of the disorder and how the firing was carried on, and how Col. Forsythe was rattled and was put under arrest and court martialed at the Agency

for allowing the 3 Hotchkiss guns which were on cemetery hill, to fire down on the flat at the Indians, shells from which, exploding, killed a lot of soldiers.

(Get the report of the court-martial of Col. F.)

He does not believe that there was a Gatling gun at that fight.

He does not believe that Capt. Bartlett was there.

He speaks of and describes the council had with the Indians. See him further on this point.

He says one or more of the Hotchkiss guns was moved from Cemetery Hill to another part of the field.[80]

He tells how 2 or 3 Indians went up the dry run and concealed themselves in some weeds and picked off soldiers. These were hunted out and killed. By the side of one of these was found 30 or 40 empty shells, and this fighter was engaged in reloading them when he was killed.

E. C. Swigert of Gordon, traveling man who has been on the road for nine years but will be at home in his store on the corner north of Wilhite's [?] this year, is full of W.K. Cites me to Philip Wells who had his nose cut off by a squaw in the battle.[81] The nose hung by the skin on each side at the base and the surgeons replaced it, sewed it on, and he recovered. Wells was official interpreter and is a man of fine education. He can tell me all about W.K. as no other man can. Swigert says that some of the Pine Ridge Indians were acting as scouts for Big Foot's band, but he does not remember who they were.

[W. A. Birdsall's Interview]

[Tablet 3]
Dec. 22, 1906.

W. A. Birdsall who was an employee in the service & sent out to count the Indian dead when the burial party went & recd. $10 a day for self and horse (while Frank Gruard got $10.50 for self) says that there were 182 dead Indians, women and children. Joe Horn Cloud's list of the slain at Wounded Knee foots up 185. William Peano's count of the number buried in the single grave on Cemetery Hill is 146.

[Tablet 25]
Chadron, May 6, '07

W. A. Birdsall says: Speaking of the troubles of 1890 when he was a guide on the Reservation for the military from about the latter part of December,

1890. He began when he was employed to pilot the California soldiers, infantry, from Chadron to the Agency.[82] He served about 5 weeks.

Says that Carl Smith, correspondent of the World-Herald, and some New York paper he thinks, was the only correspondent who was truthful, honest & reliable. Smith was with General E. A. Carr. He was so good & careful in gathering his facts, & this was so contrary to the methods of all the others that he was given the cold shoulder & crowded out. He had to leave the Agency and the W-H got another correspondent.[83] The way war news was manufactured was this: It was in the back room of ~~H. A. Dawson's~~ Asay Brothers store (J. A. Asay and Ed. Asay) at Pine Ridge, which is now the Catholic Church on the corner north of Dawson's.

Doc Middleton, John Y. Nelson, Nick Janis, Ott Means, et al. (John Y. Nelson was the author of "Nelson's Forty Lies.")[84] Tom Crimmins whose real name was Tim Crimmins was messenger for the war correspondents & carried their messages to the R.R. He was the camp scavenger who gathered the grape vine material and retailed it in the back room to these men, and they worked it up into stories for the correspondents who sent it off by Crimmins for their papers. This gave employment and pay to all concerned. By this means the country was excited and fired and criminally misled.

Al Dorrington and Jim Dahlman and John Maher were sending out exciting and lurid accounts from Chadron.[85] This is the way war turmoil was stirred up. A man named Frank McMahan, a half-breed, educated in Colorado, was & now is living on the Reservation. It was currently reported that he read this incendiary war stuff to the Indians with the effect that the Indians were scared and driven to confusion, fear and disorder.

Birdsall says that the Indian in the W.K. pictures who has a scarf tied on his head is Big Foot. He got to the field and saw Big Foot before any of the others. He knows this is Big Foot. Big Foot wore a dark gray overcoat, such as were issued to the Indians. Birdsall took a whetstone out of one of the pockets; he also got his knife etc. The Indian in that collection of pictures, who has an exposure of his privates was the crazy medicine man who was using the incendiary talk when the disarming was going on.

Birdsall says that he went over to the battleground the day of the burial, under orders to count the dead, & was in company with Lieutenant Cloman or Kloman.[86] Birdsall counted the dead on the field on the south and west of the ravine, and the Lieutenant counted on the other side. He says they counted in aggregate 184 dead. The snow fell next night after the fight. This count took place before the burial by the military. Says they went up the ravines and up to the top of the hills west. It was the day before this that Clem Davis had his "experience."[87]

The burying of the Indians was on Jan. 2, 1891.

Clem Davis had come out from the Agency as it was reported there were some crippled Indians out on W.K. He drove down with his team of mules in the vicinity of the Keith buildings & left his team on the west side of the creek. He found a wounded Indian lying across the creek & he attempted to bring him over. He laid a slab across and got him over. At this point some Indians had appeared off on some hills & some half breeds came along and reported it. Every body stampeded. Clem saw them running, friendly Indians and all, and he took the panic too. He claimed that the Indian on his back got scared and clung to him. Clem tried to throw him off before he tried to climb the creek bank, but could not, and finally he climbed the bank carrying the Indian up. Clem could not then disengage himself, so Charley Usher jerked the Indian off & into the wagon. The fleeing crowd had struck for the Agency, going by the lower road. Clem knew of a cut-off through the hills which joins the main road, between W.K. Creek & Wolf Creek. By taking the shorter route Clem got into the Agency before any of the others. When he struck the main road, he supposed he had fallen in behind the other escapees or refugees. Here he cut his good mule loose from the wagon and flew to the Agency. Arriving there he found none of the others had arrived; and so he reported that they were all massacred. Troops were dispatched toward W.K. and met the escapees coming in. They also found the wounded Indian whom Clem left in the wagon, trying to mount the mule Clem had left attached to the wagon. This mule was a lame one. The building that this Indian was found in was on the east or north of the creek & Clem brought him over.

W. A. Birdsall says that Frank [Mc]Mahan taught the Indians that the ghost shirts were impervious to bullets, and got to believing it himself, so much so that he went off with the hostiles after the W.K. fight.

When the W.K. battle took place and the hostiles were going, they dashed into the Friendly Indian camp which was on the flat between the present Boarding School & Red Cloud's house & they swirled through the camp & took with them all there were in the camp, mainly women, children, old men and a few able bodied Indians, and they drove them off with them as they would drive a lot of cattle. It was several days before these abducted Indians all got back: a few strung in every morning, escaping at night and returning to the

Agency as they could do so. Before the hostiles executed this scoop, an Indian, Birdsall does not remember whether it was Big Road or He Dog, dashed into the Agency & circled up around Dawson's, swinging his gun and defying the military, & rode away presenting a lively scene.

[Cornelius A. Craven's Interview]

[Tablet 3]
Cornelius A. Craven of Interior S.D. Interviewed Oct. 13, 1906.

He says: He came west in 1868 to Kansas City.

He had charge of the beef herd at Red Cloud Agency in 1875 when the conference was held on Chadron Creek for the purchase of the Black Hills.[88] He says it was in 1875; that very great credit is due Young Man Afraid of His Horses for preventing bloodshed there at that time. Says that at that time Red Cloud's spokesman and right hand man was Two Dog (?)or an Indian of an other name. He says John Farnham can give correct name.[89]

Red Cloud has been and still is the King Bee among the Indians. His influence has been for peace ever since he made peace. The three leading chiefs among the Og-la-las were Red Cloud, Little Wound and Old Man Afraid (until the latter retired in favor of Young Man Afraid) (date not recollected).[90] Old Man Afraid was father of Young Man Afraid. Whatever any of the above-mentioned chiefs said was just about the law. American Horse is sharp and shrewd for American Horse. He is for American Horse first, last and all the time, and he has done a good deal for himself but mighty little for his people. Red Cloud and Little Wound are the really meritorious chieftains who were true to the interests of their people. During Mr. Craven's time the chiefs named above and also Big Road were the important leaders. Jack Red Cloud never amounted to anything. He was a peaceable Indian during the difficulties.

One night in the night during the troubles of 1890–1 Gen. Miles sent for Nick Janis who was then living at the Agency, as everybody had been ordered into the Agency for protection, immediately after the W.K. battle, and Nick came to Miles Hd. Qrs. Red Cloud was at this time in the hostile camp. The hostiles had told him that there was no use of talking, he must go with them; if they were going to be killed they would all die together; he was not kidnapped.

Miles told Nick Janis that if he had any influence with the Indians he wanted him to use it now; that if there was going to be bloodshed he did not want, and he had orders to that effect, and the gov't. did not want Red Cloud there, meaning in the hostile camp, and he wanted him to get him away. Nick sent for Jack Red Cloud who came & then went over to the hostiles that night and brought him home.

Nick used to go up to Gen. Miles' headquarters every night after things had quieted down and give him all the news he had heard during the day—gave every circumstance.

General Carr commanded the Sixth Cavalry, all of which had been concentrated from various posts, at Rapid City. Mr. Craven was one of Gen. Carr's scouts.

A week before Gen. Carr marched with his regiment out from Rapid City, he had dispatched two troops under command of Major Kramer to Cheyenne River, nine miles north of the Indian stronghold which could be seen with a fieldglass. This stronghold is the Table or mesa described by P. F. Wells as the place near Sheep Mountain which is near the eastern extremity of the mesa.[91]

The object was to be north of them to prevent their escaping. This stronghold where the Indians had assembled was at the head of Corral, Quinn and Battle River draws which ran thence north to the Cheyenne, and 32½ miles southeast from Hermosa. Major Kramer with this battalion scouted in this neighborhood several days to protect the ranches, to prevent their going north, and in case of their attempting anything else to watch and report their movements. General Carr marched down Rapid Creek and camped at the mouth, on Cheyenne River. Major Kramer was then ordered to move down Cheyenne River and join General Carr. About the same time Major Adams with four troops was directed to move south and scout on White River.[92] The remainder of the regiment did scouting duty at this point, and a few days later Major Kramer received orders to move with his battalion to Heart Springs which was a drawing closer to the Indian stronghold. The duty at this place was the same as that at Cheyenne River had been, and he was camped here again several days. Christmas eve Major Kramer received orders from General Carr stating that Big Foot had escaped, and to move with his command in a northeasterly direction and intercept the regiment. Major Kramer marched as directed and instead of intercepting the regiment, struck its trail twelve miles in its rear and followed and overtook it at 2 o'clock in the morning finding it "cached" in the Bad Lands watching for and expecting Big Foot. General Carr seemed both surprised and pleased at this union of the regiment; and now he sent off his scout Craven through Sage Creek pass to find Major Adams' battalion on White River. He started about 2:30 A.M. and found him at daylight. Adams had been scouting up and down White River, and had he not been disconcerted by the orders received he would have intercepted Big Foot that day; but the orders commanded him to move up White River and intercept Big Foot. He had no alternative, and hence he obeyed strictly, and Big Foot crossed White River below him a few hours later. He had come over The Wall, the upper strata of the Miocene formation, which is 50 miles long and varying in height from 100 feet to 300 feet, through which there were at that time 3 well known passes and through which Big Foot now constructed another near the center, which bears his name. By this piece of strategy he eluded his pursuers.

Gen. Carr's headquarters had not been moved from the mouth of Rapid Creek. He now returned with the six troops he had with him and after a short delay crossed the Cheyenne and advanced to White River and camped at the mouth of Wounded Knee. In the meantime Adams had moved up White River and established three different camps, the last at Iron Springs on the night of the 29th of Dec. Major Adams had orders to join Carr next morning. As the camp was about to settle down to sleep an Indian by the name of Capt. John Long Dog, one of General (continued in No. _____, Scratch Book)[93]

[James White's Statement]

This account discusses Colonel Sumner's search for Big Foot. It was written on four loose sheets. Although the sheets were numbered one through four, the statement does not seem to start at the beginning. The handwriting does not appear to be Ricker's.

[Box 19]

Commanding officer went on up the trail about 2 miles after all the excitement was over he stopped them, as the Indians were going on all right, and called a council. The Indians agreed to go on back to the main camp of Big Foot on Belle Fouche, Sumners camp was about 6 miles farther on from B. F.'s camp.[94] They agreed to come and have a council the next day at noon at Sumner's camp. The Indians did not come but, started all the women and children on toward the Bad Lands south toward Big White river. Then the warriors (Back) laid for the soldiers in a ravine where it was heavy timbered waiting for the soldiers to come back to force them to go. They laid there till evening but the soldiers did not come, so they pulled on after the main force of Indians. In the meantime when the Indians did not come, Gen. S. [Colonel Sumner] had his scouts out. The scout reported to Sumner that the Indians had broken camp and gone to Big White River. After they were gone about 2 days he detailed 3 companies of cavalry to follow but they never overtook them.[95] He let them get clear out of the country and then broke camp himself and went to Ft. Mead. The soldiers were not satisfied at his cowardly movements so every chance the soldiers would josh him about it. One Sunday he was inspecting his company's quarters, he had got through inspecting and started to go out the door, one of the mischievous called "Big Foot," it enraged the old commander [?] so that he came back and had the Captain march them all out on the parade ground in front of the quarters, line them up and tried for 2 hrs. to find out who it was called out "Big Foot," but failed. It would have been a sad day for the offender if he had found him out. Courtmartialed and imprisoned.

In the meantime Sumner had dispatched a courier to Gen. Brooks, commander of head quarters at Pine Ridge that he had Big Foot and what should he do with him. Brooks dispatched a courier back at once to Gen. S. to hold Big Foot and band for further [illegible]. Big Foot was well on his way toward Pine Ridge to join the hostiles and was captured at Porcupine Butte.

The author of this story was James White, a private in the command.

[John H. Dixon's Statement]

The handwriting in this account suggests that it was written by two different people. It is apparent from the handwriting, and especially the poor spelling, that Ricker did not write either section.

[Box 19]

Generl Miles comander of Dpartmt ordered Generl Sumner then comander of Fort Meed So Dak 89–90 to take his comman and go over on Belfush River and intercept Big foot that had left his camp on Cheyene agency. When he got to mouth of Belfuche Big foot had past that point and went down Big White about 40 miles from mouth of belfush that runs in Big White River. He had in all his Band about 400 in all wimon children. They was killing cattle and runing settelers from home and other Depredations. Thoes indines were on warpath and on their way to join the Ogalala Sux of Pine Ridge [illegible] Generl Sumner followed [?] down Belfush to mouth then down Big White River to in 10 miles of where Big foot Band was suposed to be in camp. Somner camp his comand at a mexican ranch by the name of Goussia [?] then he detailed captan with fiftey solders with severl empty 4 horse wagons to go to where the Indians was suposed to be in camp. His instructions was to get Big foot to break camp and to come up to where Somner's command was in camp and he Somner wold give them a fieast and Somner had in mean time kild 2 Beefs. The indians were scatered all over bad lands and when capton got to where the indians was suposed Be in camp they was now indians in sight but in little while they begin to come in from all directions and the old men got in to wagon and went with soldiers to main camp. He gave them theair fieast and held cunsel and the indians agreed to go to generl Hed Quarters on Belfush but after the counsell was over and the indians returned to theair tepees heavey gards was thrown a round the indians camp unbeno [unbeknown] to the counslers this Decption on part of General Sumner incensed [the Indians. It was an] unnessasry pecausion when they agread to go with him. next morning just as the solders was just about [to] brake camp about 100 of young warrers broke through its gard and run to theair horses about 3 hundred yds on hill where these horses was picked (picketed) out in full war paint. Got theair horses and were hoping [whooping] a round the solder camp [Begins different handwriting] Sumner got scared so badly that he took his escort and rode on toward his camp, told the man that was in command to not get into trouble with the Indians but to let them have their own way. The Indians broke camp in all directions till they came to a narrow place where they threw out their camp outfit and blocked the road so the soldiers could not follow. The soldiers cleared the road and followed, rounded the Indians up about a mile from camp, fetched them back on the road they wanted them to go. There, instead of going with the other Indians who were in the wagons, 100 rode off to the left with their guns ready for action. Just then if an accident had occurred or a gun gone off a massacre would have been the result. The soldiers and Indians were ribbed up for a fight and anxious to fight.

Statement by John H. Dixon of Gordon

[T. L. Williams's Interview]

[Tablet 48]

Major Williams of the First Nebraska National Guard made this sketch of W.K.[96]

T. L. Williams of Geneva, Neb. who was major of the 1st Neb. in the troubles of 1890–1 says: That Col. Forsyth told him at the time he was under arrest in the following words:

He was ordered to disarm Big Foot's band; not to let any of them get away; and that none of them got away; and when he said this he broke down and cried. He said he had been put under arrest because he had done what he was ordered to do.

The charge against him was that he had made a bad disposition of his troops. The order was from Gen. Miles.

[W. A. Ballou's Letter]

[Box 2]
Hemet, Calif. Sept. 24, 1905 [97]
Mr. E. S. Ricker
Dear Sir
I received your letter some time ago but have been away for nearly a month and expect you began to think I never would ans. Now as to the pictures I would like the one where the troops are on review in line of march in colume by companies. One of the troops a long line extending across the Plain from their camp all mounted over at the agency on review by Gen. Miles. One of the battery trained on the hostiles under Capt. Corliss, Making three pictures in all. Please send them to me and I will send money for same as soon as I get them. Now as to the account of the march our division took I will tell you to the best of my ability but of course as to dates have forgot some of them also the name of the Capt. of Co. E 1st Reg. NNG which was with us on the march. Co. F 1st Reg. Nebraska National Guards was raised and stationed at Juniata, Adams Co. Nebraska, one of the oldest companies in the Reg. and state having seen service for a good many years before the Sioux out-break of the winter of 90 & 91. The writer of this piece enlisted as a private at 14 years of age. Promoted to musician of the co., served in Reg. drum corps about 8 years, promoted to 2 lieut., served one term, promoted to 1st lieut. and was in that capasity at the time of the Sioux out-break, and ranking 1st lieut. of brigade. The company was commanded by my brother Capt L. A. Ballou at the time we was called out. Co. E was from Fremont Neb. and belonged to my Reg. and was with us on the march. Do not remember their capt. name you can get it from the Adgt. Gen. at Lincoln. Our company was called out the 2 of January and proceeded to Crawford. Their was halted and waited orders where we was joined by several co. of our brigade. In the evening we received orders to go to Chadron arriving their about midnight where one of the Co. F men received their first accident in handling cartridges in the night. A box of 1000 Rounds fell crushing his finger. We was then conducted to the new court house and Co. E to the skateing rink to await further orders. Major Woolcott of the 1st Reg. was in command of that division. Capt. L. A. Ballou being senior officer of the other companies E of Fremont 1st Reg., E of Chadron 2nd Reg., F of Juniata, 1st Reg. and one other co. which I have

forgot the letter & reg. We remained quartered in Chadron 2 days and most of 2 nights when we received orders to secure 10 scouts and 3 teams and be ready to march to the front in the morning. Having secured the scouts and having them propley armed and equipped, Ed Cameron a tried and well known scout was placed in command of the scouts with full instructions to keep in touch with the hostiles and report when he deemed it nesisary. When the troops arose in the morning for the march they was confronted with a blizzard which did not add very much comfort to situation. By noon all was in readiness to move and the troops drawn up in line in the street suffering with cold.

The line of march was formed with the 10 scouts in front and Co. F 1st Reg. then Co. E 1st Reg. This band of troops marched all afternoon until dark facing a snowstorm. When they arrived at a deserted house and order was given to camp for the night. Part of the troops prefered to camp in the house while the balance put up tents having to shovle away about 4 inches snow to lie down on the frozen ground. At dark it set in to storm harder than ever sleet & snow together. The soldiers quartered in the house suffered several frost bites and hardships than those did in the tents but either was bad enough and the guards took the blunt of it all. I can hear them yet as they paced back & forth on there lonley beat out in the storm far away from there homes. The morning dawned clear and cold. Thermomiter ranging below the zero mark. After breakfast camp was broken Capt. L. A. Ballou taking Co. E 1st Reg. proceeded north about 3 or 4 miles to White River where they received orders to go into camp and dig rifle pitts and protect themselves as best they could and watch for any stray bands of Indians which might break through the regular line of U.S. troops. Co. F, 1st Reg. under command of 1st Lieut. W. A. Ballou broke camp and moved about one half mile to the mouth of Big Bordoux Creek and went into camp and dug rifle pits for protection the same as Co. E. Do not remember the name of the man who owned the farm where we camped. Their was a farmer near by whoe had not left yet with his family and after the arival of the troops stayed and this is the place the wounded soldier from Co. E 1st Reg. was taken care of by men from both co. Then proceeded the rotene of camp life, the scouts reporting each day. It was the pleasure of the writer to have a chance of accompaning Ed Cameron on one of his scouting trips and seeing the country and to have the misfortune to nearly run into a band of nearly 200 Indians but through the knolledge of Indian warefare he eluded them and arrived at camp at midnight having riden about 40 miles. The weather the ballance of time while their was clear & cold. Do not know the exact time we were

there but stayed untill the war was over. When we received orders to return home being held at Chadron by Gen. Miles awhile for fear the Indians would make another brake. The gen. health of the troops was good but after our return several was laid up from exposure including the writer whoe was sick for 4 long years, finally recovering. The headquarters of brigade was at Rushville Neb. This may not be of benefit to you but if you can get any help or I can help you latter will do so and please let me know when your book is printed as I would like a copy and their is 3 or 4 of the boys here whoe would like one. Hoping to hear from you again I remain yours very respectfully
1st Leut. of Co. F 1st Reg. N. N. G.
W. A. Ballou

[Ricker added the following.]
It was on G. W. Lowry's ranch where these militiamen were stationed. Lowry has so told me. He says they were about on the line between his ranch and M. M. Wild's, the latter being north of his. He says the militia was out there about a week.

[Elbert Mead's Interview]

[Tablet 24]
Statement of Elbert Mead.

On the 8th and 9th of August, 1906, E. Mead of Chadron removed the bodies of the soldiers who fell at Wounded Knee and were buried in the cemetery at Pine Ridge Agency. This was done under contract with the Chief Quartermaster at Omaha. Thirty bodies were exhumed; 29 belonged to the 7th cavalry and these were transferred from Rushville to Fort Riley, Kansas, where they were re-interred. The thirtieth belonged to the 9th Cavalry and was removed to Fort Robinson for re-interment.

(Write to Sergeant Peterson, Fort Robinson, who was present during the disinterment for the names of the dead.)[98]

[Eli S. Ricker's Statements]

Ricker's Tablet 44 was written in the latter part of 1903. It is a diary containing his thoughts on Wounded Knee and comments about people he had or would meet in his search for interviewees. He also wrote about the crops, the weather, and reminders that an

individual had purchased a subscription to Ricker's newspaper.
He wrote other discourses on Wounded Knee in Tablets 3 and 22.
Only the Wounded Knee items are included here.

Ricker went to Wounded Knee Creek on at least two occasions
in 1903 in conjunction with a series of articles he was writing on
reservation schools.[99] *It was during one of these trips that he copied*
the inscription on the Wounded Knee monument.

[Tablet 44]

Wounded Knee unfortunate, unnecessary, blundering and revengeful slaughter of both sides, butchery.

Arnold Short Bull was agitator of the ghost dance. He loaded guns for Ind. with powder & without shot & had Ind. shoot at him, to show them that the ghost shirt was a protection.

Chas. Marrivall licensed Indian trader under $10,000 bonds. Served 2 yrs. in regular army in 2d Infy.[100]

On May 30, Memorial day 1903, the survivors of the Indians who were sacrificed & slaughtered at W. Knee, from Cheyenne River Agency & Standing Rock Agency & Brulé of Rosebud Agency, & Lower Brule Agency & neighboring Indians of Pine Ridge Reservation assembled at W. Knee and the monument in the enclosure securely locked was put up by W. R. Kimball of Lincoln, Neb. Monument was procured by subscription made by the Indians & cost abt. $400. Chief Firelightning who is an aged man & chief of the Indians in W. Knee neighborhood & lives in the old commissary, he has charge of the burying ground & keeps the key & admitted us to the grounds. Some 146 Indians were killed & buried there. 74 white soldiers killed.[101]

Memorial Day the Indians decorated the graves with flowers after the white man's custom & will observe the ceremony hereafter & have a feast, and prayers in the cemetery. This is a Protestant settlement with a Presbyterian church and Episcopal church, both abt. 80 rods apart. The two churches unite in the Memorial ceremonies. The Presbyterian in charge of the church is a Santee half breed Indian not ordained. The Indian in charge of the Episcopal church is a full blood & is not in orders, but is what they call a catechist. Both are married, both hold services every Sunday. There is a Y.M.C.A. here with a membership of between 30 & 40. The Indians are about as good Christians as the whites. The women have serving societies, each church has one.

The Episcopal leader is named Paul Hawk; the Presby. is Sam Roulard.

In the last summer abt. last of July when the Indian races came off at Porcupine it was reported from the Agency that Red Cloud was dead, a contribution was taken at the races and over $100 was collected to bury Red Cloud, not that the old chief did not have property enough to bear his funeral expenses, but this was done out of respect for him.

This money is now on deposit held by a treasurer whom the donors appointed, & the money is in his hands to be used for his burial when he dies. Red Cloud has abt. 60 or 70 head of horses & as many cattle; these are kept down at the mouth of White Clay for him by his 2 sons-in-law. Red Cloud is 80. His wife is said to be between 60 & 70 & looks abt. that.

Send Times to Charles Jordon, Rosebud Agency, S. D. Jordon is an Ind. trader there, a white man who is an admirer of Red Cloud & always upheld.[102]

At W. Knee is an Omaha Dancing House where they dance Friday nights.[103] The Indians used to dance whenever they felt like it, but the Agent stopped this and they were allowed to dance as stated.

Joseph Horn Cloud at Kyle, has the names of all the Indians killed at W. Knee.[104]

Inscription on monument "This monument is erected by surviving relatives and other Ogallala and Cheyenne River Sioux Indians in memory of the Chief Big Foot Massacre Dec. 29, 1890, Col. Forsythe in command of U.S. Troops.[105]

"Big Foot was a great chief of the Sioux Indians. He often said, 'I will stand in peace till my last day comes.' He did many good and brave deeds for the white man and the red man. Many innocent women and children who knew no wrong died here.

"The erecting of this monument is largely due to the financial assistance of Joseph Horn Cloud whose father was killed here.

1	Chief Big Foot	12	Wounded Hand
2	Mr. High Hawk	13	Red Eagle
3	Mr. Standing Bear	14	Pretty Hawk
4	Long Bull	15	Wm Horn Cloud
5	White American	16	Sherman Horn Cloud
6	Black Coyote	17	Scatters Them
7	Ghost Horse	18	Red Fish
8	Living Bear	19	Swift Bird
9	Afraid of Bear	20	He Crow
10	Young Afraid of Bear	21	Little Water
11	Yellow Robe	22	Strong Fox

23	Spotted Thunder	34	Charge at Them
24	Shoots The Bear	35	Weasel Bear
25	Picked Horses	36	Bird Shakes
26	Bear Cuts Body	37	Big Skirt
27	Chase in Winter	38	Brown Turtle
28	Tooth Its Hole	39	Blue American
29	Red Horn	40	Pass Water in Horn
30	He Eagle	41	Scabbard Knife
31	No Ears	42	Small Side Bear
32	Wolf Skin Necklace	43	Kills Seneca
33	Lodge Skin Knapkin		

(On north side is as follows)

"Horn Cloud the peacemaker died here innocent. Courage Bear. Crazy Bear."

Harry K. Cloud told me that Fred Badge of Porcupine can also give me a list of the Indian killed at Wounded Knee.[106]

Capt. Wm. A. Roe who was Act.A.A. Gen. on the staff of whatever troops were on duty at the Pine Ridge Agency at the time.[107] He claims to have given the order to fire on the Indians at Wounded Knee.

Capt. Casey is the N.C. officer who was killed.

At Wounded Knee 146 Indians were slain and 74 regular soldiers gave their lives.

April 4, 1907. There [were] 147 put into the grave, but more were slain — 182 (?) says W. A. Birdsall

Mary Thomas is the little girl sent to the Holy Rosary Mission on Pine Ridge Res. and was 8 days old.

The mission was started July 23, 1889.

Rev. Father Schmidt is at the head of the mission. The Father Superior.

Mother Lucia the Mother Superior.

98 girls here & 85 boys.

Among the reasons why the W. Knee battle was needlessly begun are: The whites began it without provocation. If they feared that the Indians would fight it was only rational for them to wait till an overt act had been committed, for they had all the advantages — they had 2 machine guns and besides other cannon, all skilfully posted and surrounding the Indian camp.[108] They had disarmed the Indians of their guns (to some extent), which gave them a numerical advantage. In the Indian camp was confusion of both sexes and of all ages from infants of a few days to men and women of extreme age. These Indians were the wards of the nation, and therefore concurrent caution and justice were due from the government.

The seventh cavalry which fought the Indians was Custer's old regiment, and the men felt they had a debt to pay. We talked with some of these men only a few days before the fateful action and we discovered that the spirit was deeply fixed to balance the account for the action on the Big Horn. The Indians were completely in the power of the whites. Intoxicating drink was not sufficiently restrained to avoid rashness and excess. There was a feeling all too prevalent (rife) that a solution of the Indian problem would be assisted by reduction of the number of the red skins. If it should appear brutal to say this, what is to be thought of the spirit which makes the statement a fact?

The disposition to wipe out the band can hardly be questioned. The cannon which stood at the north west angle was discharged at an Indian woman escaping with her child over the ridge to the S.E. (am not sure of these directions) and she was killed. This was simply murder.

Capt. Geo. E. Bartlett tells me of Philip Wells an Indian interpreter ⅞ white & ½ Indian. Lived after W. Knee fight, over in that neighborhood. Can give good a/c of the battle. Charley Allen tells me that Wells P.O. is Sterns, S.D. in N.E. Cor. of Reservation.

Father Kraft, Catholic priest, was stabbed in the back in the W. Knee fight. Did not kill him. Made trouble—advised Indians not to go to school—and tried to prevent them from going to Carlisle.

Meded Swigert of Gordon, a German, was at the fight but when firing began ran & concealed himself behind Read [Red] Bear's house which was in front of Bartlett's store. Swigert can tell me about the whiskey at Agency & at Wounded Knee. Charley Allen got Swigert to go out from Pine Ridge to W. Knee. He had come over from Gordon. He was at the fight & ran down by the buildings. Alex. La Buff worked for Bartlett in the store. Is a half breed. He is truthful & honest & I can depend on him. He helped gather & bury the dead & [at] W.K. & knows all abt. it.

Charley Allen says Le Buff lives at Allen S.D.

Paddy Star was there & helped bury the Indians. Has one eye. Can't depend so much on him. Liable to tell anything.

Capt. Bartlett was at W. Knee till 1892.

Charles Allen says Paddy Star's P.O. is Allen S.D.

Charley says Le Buff is the one who has the single eye and not Starr.

[Tablet 3]

My opinion is that Col. Forsythe was a brave and careful officer but blundered in making his dispositions. Evidently was surprised by the sudden and disastrous turn which affairs took; had not the slightest suspicion that there would be any fighting; thought that his gravest care was to obtain the Indians' arms. Having them closely surrounded he believed was a means to prevent outbreak, as the situation would impress the Indians that odds were much against them and thus overawe them and restrain any impulse of resistance. The positions of his troops were well taken for the night. It is strong evidence that he did not expect fighting to result from his the attempt to disarm by his failure to station his forces in new positions with ampler spaces before the disarming began, so in the event of an engagement his men would not fire into one another, as they unquestionably did, and no time would be wasted in changing positions, and if the Indians instead of leading an attack upon him should try to escape and put up a defensive fight endeavoring to keep the soldiers from overtaking and surrounding them. The contingency of a battle was not in his mind else he would not have been so fatally unfortunately surprised and would not have gone into the action at disadvantages producing so high a percentage of fatalities. The surprise was universal to both sides; the firing began nearly simultaneously. The Indians, having a peaceable purpose and being in a friendly mood, were aggravated (?) and excited by the stern measure to take their guns from them, and moreover they were suffering from alarm because they reasoned among themselves that they were to be killed afterwards, some of their number having insisted that that was the object of the disarmament. On the side of the soldiers a different incentive was in their minds. This was the Seventh Cavalry. It had once suffered terrible sacrifices on the Little Big horn—at the hands of the red men—no doubt some of whom were now within the narrow circle of Colonel Forsythe's guns. These men had no feeling of terror or cowardice; but there was a tension of nervous sensibility—hard to describe but sometimes felt. With slightest touch upon this delicate string and there was an instant volley, flames of angry aim streamed out from leveled guns and yawning muzzles; in the roar of musketry the voice of war rose up never to be stilled until the last red skinned warrior had met the final conqueror. In

the sudden breaking down of patience and restraint the soldiers showed defi-
ciency in discipline; the commanding officer had issued no orders to fire; but
the action commenced and went on in the spirit of total destruction—soldiers
beyond all command eagerly and irregularly pursuing women and children
upon the hills and shooting them to death without remorse or mercy.

The scene was terrible; there is no use of denying it. To say the affair was
badly managed would be giving it too much dignity of description. It was not
managed at all, more particularly in the beginning, and after it was under way
the men had too much freedom, for they did not seem capable of the Christian
impulse to spare life in cases where it ought not to be taken. Like a magazine
touched off by secret means, there was an explosion; then the disaster ran its
wild course to the end with nothing to direct it but ungovernable rage. If men
would speak upon the sodden field concerning the cause and certain of the actions, they were hushed up and silence enjoined. That utterance in relation to
some of the features that might excite inquisition was hedged about by pru-
dential limits is not to be wondered at, for it is apparent that there was no want
of necessity for caution.

[Tablet 22]

The affair at W.K. was a drunken slaughter—of white soldiers and innocent Indians—for which white men were responsible—solely responsible. A
little reason and patience & forebearance and patience would have avoided the
murderous clash. Any man of ordinary competency knows that with a considerable body of armed people there is present at all times a certain degree
of danger. In this case it might have been known that there was more than the
natural degree, owing to the unsettled and excited conditions and inflamed
conditions prevailing throughout the Indian country—owing to the ease with
which misconceptions were engendered among both the authorities and the
Indians—owing to the ignorance of most of the men on whom devolved the
duty of dealing with the Indians, and of their domineering authority, and their
supercilious assumption of superiority which forbade their taking counsel of
rough men who, though without knowledge of books, were as familiar with
Indian character and needs as they were with their own life-long personal history. Fools and bigots and vain men are always at the front. Sometimes good
men make mistakes that they would not if they were sober; and these are often
made as well under the best of conditions.

The order to Forsyth to disarm the Indians was as unfortunate and unnecessary as it was unwise and fatal. The orders of Forsyth to the sergeant in command of a troop, which it must be presumed was given to all the troop commanders as they volleyed simultaneously to fire at the first report of a gun, was unmilitary under the circumstances, and destitute of all intelligence. He might have delivered to his subordinates a string of orders before they left the Agency and then remained behind in cozy quarters. He was present with his command to use it according to circumstances as they should severally develop. Otherwise, he instead of being a benefit he was an encumbrance. Such an order exceeds in magnitude most examples of foolishness recorded of reasonable commanders. An accidental discharge of a piece by a soldier, a scout, or a teamster was bound to precipitate wholesale destruction of life on both sides. It happened that an Indian gave the deadly signal which fitted into Forsyth's injudicious order, by firing into the air. It cannot be said what was his object, whether there was an object, or whether it was simply an accident. That there was not the slightest necessity for that awful answering volley is as plain as the unclouded sun at midday. Insult honest judgement as much as some may, it can never be denied that the superior race first opened living veins of blood and made corpses for unmerited graves. At that moment what need was there of killing? No one had been hurt or shot at. A report and an Indian's bullet speeds higher than the morning sun. A volley! What for? Malice or cowardice? One or the other; perchance both. Could there not have been a minutes waiting for time's solvent to show what was best to do? Every principle of sound action was thrown away. It was not battle. Nay. It was butchery, it was a crime. I have tried to find out if the officers were not drunk that morning hoping there might be as poor an excuse as intoxication for the sins of omission and commission; but beyond the conviviality of the night before preceding the battle nothing could be established.

2. Agents and Agencies

[Mr. and Mrs. E. M. Keith's Interview]

[Tablet 29]

Interview with E. M. Keith, Day School Teacher at Wounded Knee, No. 7, Nov. 17, 1906.

He says that the employees on the Reservation were ordered in to the Agency about the middle of November, 1890.

He says there were some Indians encamped between the Agency and the slaughter house east of the Agency. There were some encamped on the Ridge north of the Agency and Wolf Creek, and about noon these latter came down like a single tent. He states a circumstance about the stage coach showing that it was noon. He says an officer arrived early in the day—by 10 o'clock A.M. bringing news of the action. I suppose this was Lieut. Preston.

The hostiles, a part of them, moved north of the hills to the vicinity of W.K., but a lot of hostiles remained near the Agency and shot into the Agency and at a few infantrymen who were camped in front of Mr. Cleveland's house. There was great uneasiness at the Agency during the day of the action at W.K. until the troops came back that night for there were [enough] Indians at the Agency to have destroyed it.

The Indians on Wounded Knee were all friendly and alarmed and at the prospect of trouble, and were offended when the Keiths went into the Agency without their knowledge, so they could not go in with them. The Keiths were told to go in without making their object known. These Indians all went in and camped south of the Agency in the friendly camp. The Keiths returned to their home about the middle of February, 1891; but would not do so till the Wounded Knee Indians would all go back with them.

It was Eagle Bull who lived on Cemetery Hill. He had two houses—one in which he lived, and the other in which his mother-in-law lived. Eagle Bull is now dead.

The Keiths left nearly everything moveable in their house and some valuable presents and other property which were stolen and destroyed and their house torn up inside. Mr. Keith honestly estimated his losses at what he believed actual value and was cut down by the government one-half; while some that lost little or nothing got a good deal of money.

Mr. Keith tells of a wagonful of Indians starting up southeast from the crossing of the ravine and were fired into by a shell and conveyance and people were wrecked and killed except a baby.

He says the Indians almost invariably reckon themselves one year too old. He has noticed this particularly and seen no end of trouble of this tendency in his neighborhood among them. He accounts for it this way: That they figure that they are a year old when they are born.

He has noticed one particular Indian trait, as a teacher; this, that they are very deliberate, cannot be hurried, slow in coming to a conclusion or decision. They have never had to be in any hurry, and now it is hard to get them to acquire speedy action. He says they are in sufficient hurry when they want anything.

He says they seem indifferent, and this is one of the most discouraging things a teacher has to encounter. He and Mrs. Keith consider that they are stubborn and refuse to become enthusiastic and to answer questions because they think you want them to do so—the whites want them to do so—and they are downright contrary and stubborn. He thinks that the old Indians tell the younger ones not to talk.

Mrs. Keith says that Indian girls who have been off to school and have come back do not talk English, but they talk to Mrs. Keith in Indian, and she has asked them why they did not speak English, they replied that when they got home back from school they heard nothing but Dakota and had forgotten so many English words that they were afraid they would make mistakes and be laughed at.

Mrs. E. M. Keith says: That she read of a case of an Indian mother whose only child was torn from her—no matter for the rest; get the Oglala Light for September-October for article entitled "A Cry for Reservation Schools," taken from "The Philistine."[1]

Mr. and Mrs. Keith say that Capt. Pierce was the acting agent at Pine Ridge after Royer's departure and while the military were there.[2]

Mrs. Keith says she would rather live among the Indians on W.K. than in the white settlement south of the Reservation. ~~They are more kind, just, peaceable, less selfish, covetous, and grasping than the whites.~~

Indians never quarrel among themselves (as a rule). They are far more kind and unselfish than the whites. No matter how bad an Indian may be, other Indians will not let him suffer from hunger. They never have trouble in the division of property. I have seen four families kill and divide a young beef (not older than a yearling) and the pieces were thrown out in several piles without weighing to the satisfaction of all. They do not complain that somebody has had more than his share and they less than theirs.

The Indians, like white people, have their classes. They will associate with some while not with others. This is along lines of respectability.

Mr. Keith says that it seems that everything the Indian scholars learn has to be pounded into them. In most cases patient and laborious effort is required to make them learn.

Docility of the Indian children is a remarkable trait, it is a quality of child nature of the highest importance. Love of parents for children is much stronger among Indian fathers and mothers than among the white race. Indian children are better than white children; their obedience to and reverence for their parents are phenomenal; they are not quarrelsome and they are very obliging and playful and happy; and above all are not given to gasconade and smartness as the children of white parents are.

Mrs. Keith says Cleveland's Episcopal Church was turned into a hospital for Indian wounded after the action at W.K.[3] The church was filled with the suffering. She did not count the number. A good many died of their wounds. Infants from a few months to tender years of age were shot in all parts of their bodies and presented a pitiable spectacle. The battle had begun early in the day and these children were received at the Agency about 10 o'clock P.M. A lady (Mrs. Keith) (and her husband) who worked among these poor little things all that night feeding them and ministering to their extreme thirst tells me that their cries, faint from weakness and long suffering, were something never to be effaced from memory. These little objects of humanity could not be satisfied by eating and drinking; it appeared that their long fast had created in them excessive thirst and hunger that could not be appeased. Mrs. K. says one of these children was under a year of age, because it was wrapped up after the Indian custom. This was badly wounded in the lower bowels. She does not know whether it lived. The mother was in the hospital. Mrs. K. does not know whether she recovered, but thinks she did. Mrs. K. says she is sure there was not a man in the hospital. This shows how effectually the soldiers killed all the men who could not escape. They did not spare age or sex.

Mrs. Keith says that Julia Blackfox and her mother saw the soldiers hunting and killing women, and this so frenzied them with fear that they fled up the western hills until they had no strength and breath to fly farther, then they laid down beside a log as snugly as they could expecting to be overtaken and slain. But they were not seen; so their lives were spared and they are living today on Pine Ridge Reservation.

Mr. Keith says that before the battle he was passing some soldiers of the Seventh Cavalry at the Agency and he heard one of them remark that if they could just get to the Indians "they would give them hell." These Indians (Big Foot's) I have been told by another, were in the Custer massacre, and these soldiers were desirous for an opportunity to square accounts with them.

I myself talked with infantry soldiers marching to the Agency from Chadron who expressed to me the sentiment that all they desired was to get to the Indians and they would do them up.

Mrs. Keith tells me that she and they were well acquainted with Dr. Charles A. Eastman and Miss Elaine Goodale, and that they were all good friends. That Miss Goodale never saw Dr. Eastman until after the battle of W.K.; that Dr. Eastman treated the patients in the hospital at the Agency and Miss Goodale assisted some in the hospital and that there they met, and soon afterwards Miss Goodale told her that she and the doctor were going to be married.[4] They were married in a church in New York. They live now at her home in Amherst, Mass. Mrs. K. says that Miss Goodale taught first for three years in a Day School on the Lower Brulé Agency; then she was supervisor for the district that Mr. Davis now has. She was a teacher at Hampton before she came out to the Lower Brulé school.[5] She has three sisters. All of these have written poems of some merit.

Mrs. Keith says the Eastmans were sent away from this Reservation because they wrote a good deal of complaint to the Commissioner of Indian affairs about faults that they thought should be corrected.

Dr. Eastman was liked on Pine Ridge Reservation; when an Indian was sick he jumped on his horse and went out immediately and attended to him.

Mrs. Keith says that the Day School teachers are required to furnish the measures of their school children and are particularly instructed to be careful in taking measures; but when the goods come they have not been made according to measure nor according to any form of a human being of which there is any model from human or divine hand except in Puck or Judge or other humorous publication. A suit for a six-year-old boy would squeeze a three-year-old infant out of recognition by its mother.

Mrs. K. tells of a deaf and dumb girl that was among the wounded in the hospital at the Agency after the battle of W.K. The nurses tried hard at first to attract her notice by speaking loud to her, while she continued to moan and groan piteously without giving recognition to their efforts. At last an old woman told them of her condition.

Mrs. Keith says that the word squaw is a vile and uncomplimentary word to apply in the Indian language to an Indian woman; that it imports what, if applied to a white woman, is the worst that can be said of her. She adds that if white people only knew what the word means in Indian, they would not use it.

[Tablet 15]

Jan. 4, 1907

Mrs. Keith says Julia Black Fox is the daughter who escaped at W.K. with her mother by lying behind a log. They are living near Thos. J. Jackson's school on White Clay below Clarence Three Stars.

Mrs. Keith tells me that Geo. E. Bartlett was greatly liked by the Indians on the Reservation; that he ought to know much about them for he was with them a great deal and had a perfect knowledge of their language.

[Robert O. Pugh's Interview]

Pugh was a native of England. He had prospected in the Black Hills before starting a ranch twelve miles south of the Pine Ridge agency about 1878. He held a variety of jobs at the agency, including hauling freight and superintending the Pine Ridge school. His career ended in 1900 when he was the chief clerk at the agency.[6]

Ricker planned to meet with Pugh as early as 1904 because he "will give me the inside of the Indian affairs."[7]

[Tablet 11]

Wounded Knee

Allen, S.D., Aug. 21, 1907.

Robt. O. Pugh says: He was issue clerk at Pine Ridge Agency before and during the troubles of 1890. He was in service under Col. Gallagher.[8] Says Gallagher was one of the best Indian agents ever in the service. Was honest, did not steal a thing during his incumbency. When Gallagher went out [of] office the wood, of which there were about three hundred cords; and the hay, of which there were about 150 tons; and the grain (corn and oats) of which there were some 600,000 pounds, were all in store at the Agency. After Royer came with his chief clerk, Bishop J. Gleason, (the present Farmer at Manderson) they received six thousand head of cattle at 1,200 pounds per head when they actually weighed less than 1,000 pounds. There were about 250 pounds on each head to be divided among the contractor, agent, chief clerk and possibly others, making the aggregate 1,500,000, which at two and three-fourths cents a pound, gave these grafters the snug sum of $40,000 (exactly $41,250). A good profit for a single dishonest transaction. But this was not all of the stealing. The wood, hay and grain were stolen remorselessly — stolen clean. The wood went with such dispatch that the Boarding School had to burn tree tops and such inferior fuel. The school children did not leave the Boarding School; they were kept, this is positive.

Agent Royer and Chief Clerk Gleason were broken down small politicians of South Dakota. Senator Pettigrew was their patron.[9] They were overwhelmingly in debt. They came to this reservation as political adventurers in search of fortunes, of which they were much in need. From the day of their arrival to the day of Royer's departure stealing went on at a galloping rate. Rations (sugar, coffee, etc.) went as though they were blessed with animated life and were on a stampede. The only thing that escaped the cyclone of robbery was the annuities which could not be disposed of without leaving tracks of easy detection. Assistant wise heads who were beneficiaries of the transactions counseled the bringing of the army. The army is a mammoth consumer — a safe destroyer. The "wise" ones borrowed these supplies from the Agent. The "wise" ones then sold the borrowings to the military. Vouchers which were signed by an Indian, whose mark was witnessed by the clerk, were forged. The "wise" ones said if the troops came there would be large demand for forage fuel and other supplies, and that the opportunity for a harvest was at hand. The agent was advised that the need for troops was wholly wanting; but he insisted that he had private advices which settled the question in his mind. He went away and came back with the troops. He had previously disposed of Pugh by telling him that he must have a man in his place whom he could depend on. So Pugh was put out to look after the beef herd.

Gleason did not depart the Reservation when Royer left but having, with his chief, demonstrated his incompetency, he was given the position of Farmer.

The ghost delusion was a religious craze, similar in many respects to religious excitements which have penetrated communities of the white race, notably the _ _ _ _ (see the history of the Jerks and other like affairs in some Cyclopedia). Pugh saw ghost dancing. These dancers would exert themselves till they fell in a trance. The medicine man went to one and received from the entranced his statement in a low tone. The medicine man cried out in a loud voice what he heard from the prostrate dancer. He had seen the Black Eagle; he had seen the Christ; he had been told that the white men would disappear; that the Indian would again come into his own; the buffaloes and other kinds of game would come back; the Indians would be filled and happy. These visions were assisted by empty stomachs—the gnawings of protracted hunger working upon the superstitious, untutored intellect. The dancer, coming out of his trance would bite into the turf. He would lie quivering, as with an ague.

Pugh had, after he took charge of the Agency, Indians out in the camps in blankets acting as emissaries, who reported the condition of sentiment among them, showing that there was no contemplation of war.

Commissioner Morgan was a Baptist preacher filled with more religious zeal than sound judgment.[10] He did not realize the importance of creature comforts as a foundation for religious conversion. Instead of meat he gave tracts. Told that the Indians were hungry, he inquired what kind of religious reading would be best for them. He acted as though a diminishing ration would create a spiritual appetite. He was zealous for God, expecting the Indian to take care of his own stomach before the time of his enthrallment. The difficulties were serious for all concerned. Ignorance and dishonesty were holding carnival. The people would make good the expense. The Indians would be blamed for the trouble. And they would be butchered too. The whole thing was bad from the start. It wound up in the worst disgrace that has signalized our fighting for a hundred years. It seemed as though the devil had come in capricious mood to do all the wickedness he could invent. At any rate it was done. This is beyond controversy. Let the historic page blush with crimson color, for it is written in the blood of murder.

Bob Pugh and Charley Allen say that the burden of the ghost song was, "Father, my Father has said my Saviour will come." This was a sort of chorus or refrain.[11] See the clipping from the Cowboy, entitled "Holy woman of Wounded Knee." Bob Pugh has the same clipping & showed it to me.
[Tablet 12]
Allen S.D., Friday Oct. 26, 1906. Short Interview with R. O. Pugh.

He says: That he was issue clerk and chief of police when Col. Gallagher went out as agent at Pine Ridge and Dr. Royer came in. Royer had a political pull with Senator Pettigrew and got the appointment. Royer was a man of no ability and no knowledge of business, weak and timid to an immoderate degree. He came to the Agency in October, 1890.

Mr. R. O. Pugh is a native Englishman, and has a half-blood Indian wife. At the time of the disturbances he had two small children.

The Chief Clerk at the time Royer was in the office was a person of no capability and lacking in force.

One day Mr. Pugh went in to his dinner. When the one o'clock bell rang he came out as usual to go to work. He saw the front office crowded with Indians and Indian police, and Dr. Royer was at the back door beckoning to him. The Agent was in great fright and could scarcely speak above a whisper. Pugh asked him what was the matter. "Don't you know?" asked the terrified man. When the clerk told him he did not, the Agent replied "We have almost been massacred," and much more of the same tenor betraying his agitation. He declared further that he was going to leave at once and take his family. Mr. Pugh advised him not to do so; that such a course would bring his official career as Agent to an end speedily; and tried to calm his excitement with the assurance that there was no danger and that no trouble would ensue. But the Agent was prostrated and could not regain his composure.

There had been a sharp scene between the Indians and the Indian police, but it was only a war of words.

Mr. Pugh went among the Indians, most of whom he personally knew. Two of them were Sitting Bull's followers; these he was well acquainted with, and stepping up to one of them, he took him by the collar and led him away, to the issue office, talking to him in a comprehensible way. After loading him with eatables he turned to the crowd which had followed and threw out some boxes of crackers and other provisions and told them to go home, as they were making it unpleasant at the Agency and when hungry to come back and get more. They went away satisfied and perfect quiet reigned. By this time the affrighted Agent had his team ready and his family in the buggy to leave. He told Pugh to act as Agent. Pugh suggested that he appoint the Chief Clerk, but he said that as Pugh had successfully quelled the disturbance that he would devolve the conduct of affairs on him. Pugh could not help saying to the agent as he was departing that he could not be deceived as to Royer's intention to make a demand for troops on his arrival at Rushville, and he warned him against doing so, as there was not the slightest need of the military. But the agent, victim of panic, was no longer susceptible to reason, and putting whip to his horses hurried to Rushville. From here the fatal message went over the wires. Had there been in this man's place another of cool judgement, the painful story which follows could not be written.

Three days afterwards Mr. Pugh heard the clear notes of a bugle, and going out a little way, he espied the winding column of three troops of cavalry approaching with the redoubtable agent Royer driving safely in the center.[12]

To go back a little, this account would not be complete if it was not stated that after the Agent had quit the Agency the resident Presbyterian minister, Rev. Mr. Sterling attempted to visit the Boarding school and work up a high feeling among the teachers over the situation, but he was promptly stopped by Mr. Pugh who could not check his desperate intention until he threatened, as the acting Agent, to place him in the guardhouse if he did not desist. The minister also went that night with his family to Rushville.[13]

The disturbance in the Agent's office was occasioned by the attempt of the police to put a man by the name of Little, a member of No Water's band, in the guardhouse. It was insisted by some of the Indians that Little's arrest was improper under the circumstances, and these were resisting the police.[14]

Mr. Pugh, speaking of the higher qualities of the Indians, says that they are deep reasoners; sound and profound readers of human character; they excel he thinks any other race of people in their insight into motives, and they are capable of right conclusions. He says he came among them 36 years ago with the usual impression of the white man that the Indians are more like wild beasts than human beings; but he has changed his mind—has reversed his opinion, and affirms that they should be treated as men—dealt with as men—entitled to as fair and honorable treatment as any other class; that the government has never done right, its policy has always been wrong; that it has driven them from place to place contrary to all justice; then it has herded and corralled them and regarded them as childish criminals to be put into reformatories (This last idea is my own, but his talk led me into the thought); the Indians should be put under law and be answerable thereto the same as the white man. He should have been treated in all respects as a man. He is a man the same as any other.

What Mr. Pugh relates: Mr. Pugh disclaims any spiritual or psychological knowledge or any opinions on those subjects; but he says that he has often observed that the Indians have some mysterious and to him incomprehensible mode of receiving impressions; that some have explained it by saying that it is their flash light system a theory which he scouts; and he relates the following incident to illustrate what he means. He thinks it is like Hindu telepathy.

Mr. Pugh was taking the census on Pine Ridge. He says the rule was to have it completed in June. Young Man Afraid (His name was always abbreviated for convenience to this) lived with his band ten miles north of the Agency. He was going one year to the Crow Agency on a visit, and was waiting until the census should be taken; when Mr. Pugh enrolled him he said that he was going to start next day. (I can find the date of his death at the Agency. Can also find it in the clipping giving account of the conference on Chadron Creek in 1875.) When Young Man Afraid reached Newcastle, Wyoming, he fell dead in the street about noon. About two o'clock P.M. of the same day he [Pugh] saw an Indian, a member of Young Man Afraid's band, coming down the hill north of the Agency as hard as his horse could run. He dashed into the Agency and gave out the information that Young Man Afraid was dead. He had evidently ridden in from the camp ten miles north of there. At four o'clock the same afternoon a telegram was received from Newcastle announcing to the Agent that this Chief was dead, and inquiring what disposition should be made of his body.[15]

The Indian could have had no communication by the ordinary means.

Mr. Pugh and William Garnett, speaking in relation to the date when the Red Cloud Agency was moved over from the Platte 28 miles below Fort Laramie to White River say it was in the fall of 1873. George Stover agrees with these two, and he says he helped to build the Agency. These men contradict John Farnham as to the date, he having stated that it was in 1872. But they confirm him in this, that the removal was made in the fall, but not finished till the next spring.[16]

Mr. Pugh says that Capt. Wessels was a little man — a Dutchman; and that Lieut. Robinson was a large and jovial man.[17]

Mr. Pugh says that the flagstaff raising affair was in the fall of 1873. He says there were about a dozen in the squad which came down from the Fort to protect the Agency, under the command of Lieutenant (afterwards Capt.) Crawford. George Stover says it was Crawford and no mistake. Farnham is wrong when he says it was Lieut. Ray.[18]

Mr. Pugh and George Stover say that the American Horse killed at Slim Buttes was a Minniconjou Indian who belonged over on the Cheyenne River.[19] Stover says he knew him.

[Tablet 26]

Mr. R. O. Pugh says that it was in 1878 that the Price & Jenks ranch was started on Chadron Creek at the old Half Diamond E.

Mr. Pugh says that the Brulé or Spotted Tail Agency was located on the

White River just below Crawford in the big bend of the river, on the flat where the three buttes are, and that it was moved to the Beaver Creek when Red Cloud Agency was moved over from the Platte in 1873.

Mr. Pugh says he was at the conference when the first attempt was made to obtain the Black Hills, and that instead of its being held on Chadron Creek it was on White River at the mouth of the first creek east of Crawford, and at the big and lone tree about a hundred yards from the mouth of the creek.[20]

Why Residents on the Reservation Keep Their Mouths Closed

Because of the stringency of the regulations. The Agent is as absolute as the Czar of Russia. His orders are supported by the Indian office in Washington. He may make whatever representations he chooses and supplement these with an expression of his wishes, and these will produce action corresponding thereto. If his peculations are the source of an abundant stream of wealth into his money chest, and any man living on the reservation over which his charge extends, dares to make any noise about it, or raise a protest, no matter what the spirit, or whether mild or vociferous, the offending Agent can formulate the assertion that he is a nuisance stirring up strife—making trouble on the reservation—and ask that he be expelled and the Comr. will promptly approve an order to such effect. There will be no hearing to determine the right or the wrong in the premises; the ax of authority descends, and the just man suffers punishment while the public servant arrogantly plunders funds which are not his own.

The aggrieved man can have costly redress, if redress at all. If he returns to the reservation he becomes liable to heavy fine. Few men can afford such luxury as a suit in a federal court. Between himself and the government there is a great difference in the chances for success. In nowise is it difficult for the agent to obtain testimony; he can have willing witnesses whose expenses of travel to the distant court will be paid; whose board will be free, so far as the obligation to pay will affect him, at a good hotel; the favor of the Agent has strong tendency to create favorable testimony for him; and the government has its regular counsel to prosecute its case. The poor citizen has no means to bear heavy expenses. If he can get anybody on the reservation to testify for him, generally it must be an Indian—this man, the moment he gives testimony unfavorable to the agent is in disfavor and is marked for persecution. The forms of persecution are as numerous as the devices of Satan. He has no security from charges being preferred against him at any time; and whether they be true or false, (and they can just as well be false as true) it is immaterial, for there will be nobody to investigate the matter but the interested Agent, and any order which he sees fit to make has the force of law — it is the only law. There is therefore no real redress for the man wronged by arbitrary and selfish power. The system is anomalous and un-American, and, if it was ever necessary, it is now no longer so in view of the present improvement of the Indians, and is a scandalous delegation of authority which cannot be too speedily abolished. Its retention can have no object except to aid in frauds and wrongs which have effect both ways, that is, against the people collectively and against them as individuals. (The above from page 32 [to this point] was principally outlined to me by Mr. Pugh.)

Mr. R. O. Pugh says that Crazy Horse was singular in some ways. He never painted like other Indians.

[H. A. Mossman's Interview]

[Tablet 25] Dr. H. A. Mossman of Chadron, on Dec. 4, 1906, stated to me that he and his wife, Mrs. Nellie Mossman, were Day School employees on Pine Ridge Reservation eight years, first located at No. 12 (mouth of Wounded Knee Creek) and next at No. 9 (Manderson).

He was under Brown and Penny and Clapp and Brennan.[21] Capt. Brown gave the first impetus to the Day Schools, and was always in the saddle riding among his aboriginal wards and seeking every item of interest connected with his charge, and studying the needs of the people under him, who were, according to civilized requirements scarcely above the comprehension and ability of children.[22] He was an officer of rare merit, for the reason that he did not regard his position as a sinecure, and understood that he occupied it for the good of the natives and the honor and benefit of the American people. It was not a station in which dishonest third persons had a paramount interest. He did not forget that he was the agent of the government and the servant of the law in all its integrity.

Capt. Penny did not conceal his dislike for the Day Schools, and among the teachers he could not count any friends who would experience delight in offering a charitable word for him when lowering clouds hung above his head. He got into difficulties, and there are those who say that he trusted too much to those about him, and that this negligence rather than obliquitous design brought him to grief. Be this as it may, inspectors began to examine into the affairs of the Reservation, and the Agent soon resigned. Subordinates who had had long experience in this kind of governmental service, and so far as mental qualifications figured were worthy of instant recognition, also fell from the good places which were destined to know them no more. (Did Pugh and [clerk

George] Comer drop out now? Pugh told me that he was issue clerk as late as when Royer was in office as Agent.)

[A. F. Johnson's Interview]

Rev. and Mrs. A. F. Johnson, Presbyterian missionaries, arrived at Pine Ridge in 1892.

[Tablet 13]

Rev. A. F. Johnson of Pine Ridge, March 13, 1907, says:

Active work of the Presbyterian church of the U.S.A. began on the Pine Ridge Reservation in 1886 by the Rev. C. G. Sterling, Ph.D. a graduate of McCormick Seminary, Chicago. He had missionary buildings erected at the Agency and at different points on the reservation.

Miss Jennie B. Dickson came with Miss McCreight. The latter was a helper to Miss Dickson who was the missionary. The Misses Dickson [and] McCreight established a Presbyterian mission at the Upper Porcupine Station.

At [the] same time different out-stations were established by Mr. Sterling. These ladies, though acting in conjunction with Mr. Sterling, were independent of him. This work was first under the Foreign Missionary Society of the Church, but in 1893 was transferred to the Home Missionary Society.

These ladies began by teaching the Indians in their own language, and preaching to them and imparting religious instruction on the Sabbath.

Miss Dickson was a woman of very positive and striking personality possessing great force of character. Mr. Sterling's wife's health failed and he was obliged to retire from the work in 1890.

The next white missionary was the Rev. John P. Williamson D.D. of Yankton Reservation, and on account of a throat trouble had to return to Greenwood after a year and a half at Pine Ridge. He is general missionary of all the Presbyterian work among the Dakotas.[23]

Mr. Johnson followed him here in 1892 & is still here.

There are nine churches of the Presbyterians on the Reservation at this date (1907) & there are others in process of erection.

An important feature of their work is the adjunct of the Y.M.C.A. with work laid out and adapted to the Indians' varying needs. Good work is done; it draws the young men to places where they hear elevating discourses and are under uplifting influences instead of attending the Indian dances and listening to harangues against the whites and scornful deprecations of civilization.

(When I come to write on this topic I am to write Mr. Johnson and ask him to tell in addition to other things what the "Presbyterial Native Missionary Society" is doing, etc. etc. Also ask how the gov't. has dealt with the churches in allotting lands for the church edifices.

May also write to the Missionary at Sisseton where lands have been allotted for a long time, & ask him.)

The congregations are growing.

[Tablet 15]

Rev. A. F. Johnson of Pine Ridge in an interview March 13, 1907, speaking of the moral and spiritual influences which are being absorbed by the Sioux Indians as a result of the patient and ceaseless labors of the missionaries among them, said there was much improvement and reason for encouragement, and comparing these to the Winnebagoes and Omahas, stated that the latter are in a very deplorable state owing to their demoralizing laxity of discipline and manhood.

[William J. Cleveland's Interview]

Rev. William J. Cleveland began his Episcopal missionary work with the Lower Brulés in the fall of 1872. A year later he married Hannah Stiteler, a member of the small mission community. In 1875 the Clevelands moved to the Spotted Tail Agency and then to Rosebud. During this time Reverend Cleveland began publishing the Anpao, *a Lakota-language newspaper. In 1887 he returned to his family home in New Jersey. A year later he was back in South Dakota, serving the white community at Madison. Reverend Cleveland continued to edit the* Anpao *and maintained close ties with his Lakota friends. After serving briefly in Pennsylvania, he returned to missionary work at Pine Ridge in 1900. In 1908 he moved to California, where he died two years later.*[24]

[Tablet 29]

Interview with Rev. W. J. Cleveland Nov. 20, 1906.

Zit-ka-la nuni

Zitkala nuni-Little lost bird.

The first mission of the Episcopal Church among the Sioux Inds. was established by Rev. S. D. Hinman among Santee Sioux at or in the neighborhood of Red Lake, Minn. The mission to the Yanktons was begun on the Yankton Agency S.D. by Rev. Joseph Cook in 1870. The Santee Sioux were sometime held up at Crow Creek where the Epis. mission was begun by Rev. H. Burt in Oct. 1872; the mission work among Lower Brulés was begun by Rev. W. J. Cleveland in Oct. 1872, & the mission work on Cheyenne River Reserve was begun by Rev. Henry Swift in Oct. 1872 — these 3 all went up together at the same time.[25]

The Santees were sent down from Crow Cr. into Nebraska before this time.[26]

Get from Bishop Hare date of the beginning of Epis. mission at Standing Rock &c.[27]

The work among the Upper Brulés and the Oglalas was begun at the old Spotted Tail and Red Cloud Agencies in Neb. by Rev. W. J. Cleveland in 1875. The Upper Brulé was at Spotted Tail Agency on Beaver Creek.

The Lower Brulés are on the opposite side of Missouri River from Chamberlain and from the Crow Creek Reserve.

The Upper Brulés are now on the Rosebud.

Rev. Wm. H. Hare was elected first missionary Bishop to the Sioux Indians in 1873; his missionary District was called "Niobrara." Afterwards was given the State of South Dakota, including now whites as well as Indians.

Previous to this the Indian work was under Bishop Clarkson of Nebraska, but the church did not have a bishop for the special Indian work till 1873.[28] The work has grown rapidly till now there are upwards of ninety native congregations among the Sioux and two boarding schools — one, St. Elizabeth's at Standing Rock, the other St. Mary's at Rosebud. The two that were abandoned were the St. John's at Cheyenne River and St. Paul's at Yankton Agency. The Hope school at Springfield S.D. (right across from Santee Agency) was sold to the government.

The government made at one time a singular ruling that if an Indian child attended a mission school he should be deprived of his rations and clothing to which he was entitled under treaty or law; but if he attended a government school these benefits were not cut off. This was the reason why the above two schools had to be abandoned and & the bishop had to sell the buildings for almost nothing. The injustice of this ruling was finally recognized by the government after protracted representations by Bishop Hare and others, and it was revoked.

Mr. Cleveland was not at Pine Ridge Agency at the time of the W.K. battle but came right after. He was sent during the summer before by the Indian Rights Ass'n. over all these agencies — Standing Rock, Cheyenne River, Crow Creek, Lower Brulé, Rosebud, Pine Ridge, &c, to find out all about the ghost dance and to report upon it.[29] He says it is his belief that the ghost-dancing Indians had one purpose only, namely, to withdraw from these Reserves and go to some wild region of the country where they could lead their old life of hunting. [Tablet 25]

Rev. Mr. Cleveland says, as Phillip Wells did, that squaw and papoose are not Indian words, and he supposes that Indians use them because they think these are our words. He does not know where they originated, but supposes they came through the Canadian French. Nepo is a word the Indians use meaning "dead," but he is at a loss for its origin.

[Edmund Thickstun's Interview]

On April 24, 1907 Ricker was at Day School number 3, fifteen miles west of Pine Ridge Agency, where he noted, "I came over from Chadron Neb., a distance of 25 miles, yesterday, with Mr. Thickstun." Thickstun had recently delivered a lecture at the Chadron Y.M.C.A. "in opposition to the views of Scout E. H. Allison who had addressed an assemblage at the same place on the night of April 9th (1907)."

While visiting Thickstun, Ricker reviewed his host's library of various government publications relating to Indian schools. He then interviewed Thickstun on April 29.

[Tablet 16]

Rev. Edmund Thickstun, Teacher at Day School No. 3, Pine Ridge Reservation, S.D., says, April 29, 1907.

That many of the traits of Indians are the products of conditions. I have not the least doubt of this; for it is well established in inquisitorial literature that physical causes in the cosmos create the modes of life of a people, and these are seen to vary in habits, customs, methods and peculiarities according to the differing features of climate, landscape, productions and other controlling material facts. This is not peculiar to the red race; all peoples and communities of peoples are subject to these influences. Out of these is evolved the education, such as it may be, of gens, phratries, tribes, class, and even families who have in a more or less marked degree a local or individual system of living which may be distinguished in some points from the modes of all others. While the general instruction is practically the same, these minor distinctions become fixed and exert a widening influence till they have made a subordinate conquest and have a recognized dominion. A traveler passing from one region to another is struck by differences in speech, in forms of labor, in traits of hospitality, in ways of pleasure, in acts of worship, in singularities of belief, in surprises of superstition (for I question whether there is a people wholly free from this hurt) and other observable differences from most other localities. There will be seen, besides, similarities and likenesses, which will remind the itinerant of a relationship between two or more sections, showing that in reasonable probability one has been ancestor to another. Science has been fortunate in tracing linguistic affinities, and therefrom establishing racial or national descent.

Mr. Thickstun has coined, as explanatory of much that is abhorrent in Indian conduct, the term, "Religion of Revenge." This, it will be easily seen instead of being a reproach to the Indian character, may be taken as a considerable extenuation of horrors and barbarities which mark the history of the aborigines. Reflection is convincing that beliefs and convictions and practices are the outgrowth of instruction; and if this has been misleading and erroneous — nay, criminal or barbaric, the lives of the learners, it may be justly apprehended, will measureably conform thereto. As the ancestors have eaten grapes, so have the children's teeth been set on edge. All Christian humanity, at least, have imbibed this lesson from long centuries of direct observation; they have witnessed the defective models of prevailing thought and the universality of selfish instinct, both culminating in acts of daily life; and it has been the almost immemorial endeavor of the students of true principles — of pure models of life — to elevate and ennoble by imparting good instruction and supplying harmonious environment to all the race as indispensable to oppose the natural effect of the moral gravitation of the finite nature of mankind. The effort that has been made by Christian peoples, both by associated and individual energy, covering centuries of time, to uplift the aboriginals, is an enduring evidence of the spiritual discontent of the divine or godly impulse to supplant the false with the true. It is illogical and reprehensible to marshal against this ages-long, godly movement of men who have endured sufferings of rankest kind and spent themselves completely in this unselfish service, the vicious and criminal deeds of members of our own race when in contact and intercourse with the native inhabitants of this continent and their descendants. Fruitage of the Christian propaganda does not yet comprise entire subjugation of the brutal instincts and evil propensities of the human intellect; and despite all endeavors to purge society of wrong-doing there continues to be a lamentable amount of wickedness existing and propagating everywhere. This is not with the sanction, but in opposition to the appeal, the example and the sacrifice of Christian precept and combination. It is a grossly unrighteous charge against humanitarian desire and principle to accuse the fairly disposed citizens of our country of sympathy with the lawlessness and debauchery and crime which have signalized the intercourse of the white with the red race on the remote frontiers and far beyond them. Many of these white men had forfeited the respect and protection of civilized association; many found flight to the deep recesses of the expansive wilderness a welcome escape from the pains and penalties where law and order were enforceable and dominant; others were allured by the fascinations of unlimited freedom; some were enticed by love of hunting, while numerous congeners were attracted by the profits of fur-trapping and sallied forth either as employees of the large and powerful companies or as independent laborers. These adventurers were not conspicuous for lofty spiritual virtues, though they are justly canonized in song and story for courage, endurance and hospitality. Not all of these were in any sense really bad men; the historian often derives delight in contemplating the best known of these useful characters when he recognizes that they were truly high-minded and honorable, regardful of the rights of others, scrupulous in performing their obligations, and industrious and thrifty in their occupations. If some carried the seeds of vice and the poison of bad example among the red children of the forest and the plains, it should be borne in mind that these men were far from the elevating restraints and influences of the settled communities, and that even in these communities themselves remained a powerful element which, had it also disappeared beyond civilization, would have been hastily absorbed into the new conditions without change to them or shock to itself.

Mr. Thickstun speaks of the communal system prevailing among the Indians, and tells me that boys attend his school wearing several pairs of trowsers, while girls also have on several dresses. His inquiries disclosed that this practice was caused by the fear that if the extra garments were left at home they would be appropriated by older members of the family if not by persons outside of the family. Mrs. Cora Fisher told me that an Indian woman had come to her house wearing eight dresses. But her explanation of this freak was that the woman put a clean dress on over a dirty one till she had on this number— that she acted on the principle of overlaying instead of exchanging; whereas it seems reasonable from Mr. Thickstun's statement that this woman did not dare to lay off her dresses because she felt that the extra ones would be appropriated by other persons. It should be observed that Mr. Thickstun avoids as much as he can a direct question to his pupils; for if they can discover from his question what answer will be pleasing to him, they are pretty certain to make such answer.

[John R. Brennan's Interview]

John R. Brennan came to the Black Hills in 1876 and was one of the founders of Rapid City, South Dakota. He was appointed agent for the Pine Ridge Reservation on November 1, 1900, and served until July 1, 1917. Brennan returned to Rapid City to look after his many business interests. He died there in 1919.[30]

[Tablet 17]

Major John R. Brennan says: That the $1 tax on excess live stock was laid during the second year of his incumbency (1902) for the specific object of shutting out the cattle belonging to outsiders who made a sham sale to Indians so they could be got on and kept on the Reservation. The individual brand of the reputed Indian owner was put on the cattle so they could be identified. But it was required also that the Reservation brand of F o F should be put on the same stock; this was too dangerous for foreign owners to allow this latter brand to be used and outside stock was cut out. This is the Major's idea why there are not more cattle on the Reservation; he thinks the Indians have as many as formerly. He says the tax did not affect but two or three Indians, and he once asked one of these why he did not divide his stock among his family so that no one would hold more than 100 head.

Major John R. Brennan, Agent at Pine Ridge, Nov. 23, 1906, says: It is his understanding that the Indian Court here was the first experiment made in this line.

It was organized here in 1892 with three judges; this number was increased in 1903 on this Agent's recommendation to six judges, one from each district.

Each term begins on the 25th of each month and terminates on the 5th of the next month. Each judge during the time that this court is adjourned, acts in conjunction with the Farmer in his district in hearing petty cases, civil and criminal. If there is a case that justifies holding the accused, he is sent to the Agency and confined till the court meets to dispose of it at the next term. The jurisdiction is both civil and criminal in a small way — civil as to disputes over possession of personal property, questions of tresspas, etc; criminal extends to misdemeanors. These judges hold at the pleasure of the Agent or Department and receive $10 a month. (Apply to the Indian Office for information — for Rules for Government of Court of Indian Offense.

"Regulations of the Indian Office for the Guidance of Indian Agents;" this is about the title. Get it from Washington.)

The Reservation Police serve at the Agency 15 days every month, the detail being made at the Agency, and the policemen alternating regularly. They receive $20 a month now and the officers $25. This is a new law raising the salary from $10 to $20 & officers from $15 to $25, & was started to be agitated by Major Brennan and was passed in the session of Congress 1905–06. There are 50 policemen on the Pine Ridge Reservation now. Pine Ridge Reservation is 100 miles from east to west and 60 miles from north to south.

There is killed on this Reservation 2,000,000 lbs. of beef each year, or abt. 2,000 head of cattle. The hides are sold for the benefit of the Indians, and the grazing tax, or $1.00 a head for all over 100 head, a tax fixed by the Comr.'s office, together with the interest on the Indian fund is distributed yearly to the Indians, making about $4 apiece.

[George Stover's Interview]

[Tablet 26]
Allen, S.D., October 27, 1906.

Mr. George Stover says: He says that the first battalion of the 13th Infantry to which regiment he was transferred when he was veteranized remained the 13th regiment; and that the second battalion was made the nucleus of the 22d Infantry, and the 3d battalion was made the nucleus of the 31st Infantry.

In 1866 he went with his regiment to old Fort Rice at the mouth of Knife River which flows into the Missouri from the north and there left three companies. The following spring they went up the river to Fort Stephenson [Stevenson] and there dropped four companies of the command, and thence the remainder went to Fort Buford. Fort Rice was treated as the headquarters of the regiment.

In 1867 four companies of the 22d Infantry came up the river to Fort Stephenson and marched to Devil's Lake and built Fort Totten. The remainder of this regiment was stationed farther down the Missouri; a part at Fort Sully and the rest lower down at Fort Randall, above Yankton. (Wagoner [Wagner, S.D.] is now just below Fort Randall.) Fort Sully was then the headquarters of the 22d.

Fort Stephenson was built in the summer of 1867.

Fort Buford was built in 1867 and finished in 1868. This fort was built on part of the ground where the graveyard of old Fort William was; this Fort

William was torn down and old Fort Union was built out of the materials. Mr. Stover says that the government bought Fort Union and tore it down and used the materials in the erection of Fort Buford. He says further that there were adobes in Fort Union which the interpreter told the men had been made, as his mother told him, at Fort William before he was born, and at this time he was 38 years old. These adobes were moved back to the site of Fort William and rebuilt into the sutler's store.

Mr. Stover says that Muggins Taylor was sent by the government to Salt Lake to study secretly and write the history, theory and doctrines of the Mormons, and that he worked on it five years, and finally died near Junction City, this side of Billings, Montana. He was always traveling and writing and had a large amount of manuscript, but Mr. S. does not know what became of it.

Mr. Stover, speaking of Frank Gruard, says that Gruard told him that he was a cousin to the mother of Frank Goings, who was a colored woman. He came from the Missouri River, up near Apple river just below Bismark, N.D. when he went to the Indians. Mr. S. heard that Gruard killed a man up there when he was 13 years old, and he ran away and went to the Indians. Frank told S. that he had had trouble there. Gruard told S. that he ran off with Caddy [Cadet] from the Chouteau family and went to the Indians. Mr. S. thinks he was the first white man at Fort Robinson who made his acquaintance when he came down from the north with the Indians. He was painted like an Indian and his hair was braided.[31]

Gruard began his career as a scout at Fort Robinson.

Mr. Stover let Col. Mackenzie know of him and his qualifications and his knowledge of the Powder River country and his acquaintance with the Indians of that region, and the Colonel gave him employment.[32]

S. says that Congress passed a special act making him a captain, but that he at length got to dissipating and became such a wreck that he was courtmartialed and cashiered. (?)

Mr. S. says that he has heard the stories from officers and others that he [Frank Grouard] was a Kanacke and that he was with an emigrant party when the Indians killed all but him and took him prisoner.[33] Mr. S. thinks Gruard told these stories to cover his identity. Gruard spoke of knowing Caddy, and Mr. S. says Caddy was never west of the Missouri that he ever knew of. S. also says that the fact that Gruard had such good English is a point in favor of his having come from near the Chouteau family where his early life was spent.

Mr. Stover, speaking of political conditions says that Maj. John R. Brennan kept hotel in Rapid City, at which the stockmen made headquarters. He feasted and entertained these men till he was broken up. The stockmen selected him as the man they wanted for agent. The influence of the association was thrown in favor of a legislature that would support Kittridge for U.S. Senator. Kittridge was their man as well as a railroad tool. Martin of Deadwood and Burk of Pierre were the choice of the Assn. for Congress. They were elected. So Major Brennan got the appointment and he is here for the interest of the stock association.

A man named Bland published a paper in Washington titled "The Council Fire." He had criticized the Indian Bureau. Afterwards he came out here to Pine Ridge and the Commissioner of Indian Affairs was informed of his presence on the Reservation and he ordered him removed and he was removed. This was about the year_____.[34] In 1879 a Catholic priest was put off.

In President Grant's time he caused the Agencies to be apportioned among the sectarians. Standing Rock was given to the _____ Cheyenne River Reservation went to the _____ and Pine Ridge became the field of the Catholics and Episcopalians.

Mr. George Stover, Allen, [South Dakota] says there was a measure passed by Congress at the last session which provides for more liberal treatment of the Indians in relation to citizenship, and also in relation to allotments, so that the provisions of the Crook treaty of 1889 are extended to include any Indians and give them right to land, no matter where they were born or were residing at the date of the treaty. He will try to get me a copy.

Stover says that the cry has been going up from the Indians for several years for allotment, but that the entire official place-holders have reported that they did not want it. The object has been to stave off citizenship so as to keep the Indians under subjection, and from the department to have something to pick. Allen, South Dakota, Sunday October 28, 1906.

Interview with George Stover.

Reasons Stated Why the Indians Have No Stock.

Captain Brown of the [Eleventh Infantry] who became agent in 1891, succeeding Royer and held the office [two] years, inaugurated the plan of encouraging the Indians to raise and accumulate live stock. They were allowed to sell no steers under three years of age except old cows that were not liable to pass the next winter; the object was to husband the breeders so that the increase would be as rapid as possible. The Indians were getting a good ration which was due them from the government, and consequently they were in a position to make the most of their stock both by increase and sales. Captain Brown was a live and active agent who, like Joe Hooker as a correspondent said of him in the war, had his headquarters in the saddle. He delighted in horse back exercise and was a great deal out among the Indians under his charge, looking minutely after their concerns, directing them in the matter of building and improving their homes, making gardens, planting small fields, and taking care of and adding to their holdings of horses and cattle, and the grading up of their animals. It was through his recommendation to the department that a supply of thoroughbred bulls was sent to these Indians, though they were not delivered till his successor, Captain Penny, had taken his place as agent. Captain Brown's orders forbade outsiders coming on the reservation to round up cattle, but on one occasion during his horseback excursions in the interest of the Indians he discovered some outsiders rounding up over on White River. He put them off the Reservation summarily without taking any cattle with them, and discharged his boss herder who was privy to what was going on and had failed to inform his chief.

Captain Penny continued Captain Brown's policy with fair success. He remained true to the prohibition of sales of live stock as above stated, and prevented buyers from coming on the Reservation; and also stood in the way of promiscuous buying, selling and trading among the Indians themselves and would not allow white men on the same ground who were legal residents by reason of the marriage relation, to bargain for Indian stock, thus protecting the Indians from being overreached by the shrewder ones. By the end of his term of service the Indians were prospering; their herds had grown into large numbers, many of them having as high as 150 to 300 head; and they were doing well otherwise, the majority living in houses on their own places, and keeping hogs and poultry, and were raising garden vegetables and field crops so that there was a reasonable degree of comfort and happiness among them. Large shipments were not uncommon, and many a carload and special trainload went into the South Omaha market from the Reservation. With the departure of Penny and the advent of his successor, Captain Clapp, this provident system which was giving the Indians a remarkable uplift, began to decline; buyers were permitted to come on to the reservation; traders living on the reservation were allowed to purchase; the restrictions as to ages and classes of stock sold were removed, so that the young stock and the females went upon the market as well as the other kinds, and the detrimental effect was soon noticeable. Clapp was persistent in his efforts to keep outside cattle off the Reservation, and at one time he took up a large lot of them and held them for damages; but after a long fight over the matter an order from the department directed him to turn the stock over to the owners and remit his claim. Clapp ran affairs loosely; he trusted too implicitly to employees who brought him to grief; and he went out under a cloud of enforced resignation. He made a specialty of promoting school instruction, and along this line there seems to be no scar on his record, except the regular "rakeoff" which came from the extensive building of school structures and appurtenances. One case may be mentioned as an illustration of the manner in which certain of his favorites profited by his friendship (some of these favorites being George Comer ex-chief clerk, R. O. Pugh, issue clerk, and H. A. Dawson post trader at the Agency). During his term the commissary building about 18x60 and the slaughter house about 16x30, both mere shells, were moved two miles into Allen, the work being accomplished in a week, and the Indian fund suffered a depletion of $1,800 for the job. Comer was now out as clerk, but he and his brother-in-law, H. A. Dawson were in partnership in the contract. Comer resigned while Penny was in office for the reason that it was thought that a crisis had come; but Pugh took hold after Comer was gone and pulled Penny through. Stover says that Pugh told him that he got his rake off on the removal of these buildings and that Comer told him that they got $1,800 for moving them.

Clapp brought a man named Lang as his chief clerk. This fellow, when he had got Clapp into impending trouble, resigned. Then "Bob" Pugh took up the fight for Clapp and stayed by him to the end. This was the act which marked him for doom—it was the beginning of the end for Pugh.

Mr. Stover says that a delegate (R. O. Pugh) was sent by the Indians (and mixed bloods) to Washington about 1902 (about the time Jenkins went and Brennan came in) to confer with the Commissioner of Indian Affairs in regard to the tax of $1.00 a head on stock in excess of 100, to see if he could not get the rule revoked. He had a conference with the commissioner who asked him how long he had been in the service on Pine Ridge Reservation and he answered, "Eighteen years." "Did you go out when Agent Clapp retired?" "Yes." Then said the Commissioner: "If you want to stay on Pine Ridge you better go back and keep still."

When Captain Clapp resigned Special Agent Jenkins filled the interregnum which lasted about two months, when John R. Brennan of Rapid City S.D. received the appointment of agent. This special agent was the one who established the rule requiring the payment of $1.00 a head on all stock in excess of 100.

At this date (Oct., 1906) the stock interests have so dwindled in magnitude that the Indians have few cattle and horses remaining. These people have to live. They have been so dealt with that their own cattle are gone. Before they will starve they will steal. The result is that they kill live stock belonging to others in order to live. This makes the evil conditions on the Reservation increasingly worse. People who but for this last added burden would do well, are willing and eager to quit and go somewhere else, because they see in the near future no bettering of gainful chances.

There are two leading features on this reservation; one is the practical business part of leading the natives in the way of agriculture, stock-raising and business principles and practices, and raising them up in the scale of material welfare; the other is the school system which deals with the mental status; but the former is so managed as almost to defeat the genuine hopes of the friends of the school. The former impoverishes the Indians and tempts them to crime, while the teachers and the preachers are doing what they can to head off the devil in these forms. It is the way the government generally works; it employs one force against the other, and the result is a standstill.

The Special Agent Jenkins who established the $1.00 a head rule had been tarrying in the Hills before he came to take charge of the Agency affairs. He put this rule in force and asked the department to sustain him in what he had done. It is remarkable that a man who was taking so important a position for a few weeks should show so strong a desire to make so radical a change in the administration and create such a burden of taxation unless he derived a direct personal benefit from his own act. The influence of the South Dakota Stock Association has been recognized as the power which caused this thing to be done.

George Stover says he was on the road close to Clark the mail carrier when he was killed. Denny Regan was with the bull train starting for Laramie. Stover was along and his wife and a lot of men he names. The train went back to the Fort that day after the killing. Stover saw Clark fall.[35]

[Tablet 12]

Stover was with Farnham at Farnham's Suttlers' Saloon between Fort Robinson and Red Cloud Agency at the crossing of the River, and confirms Farnham in his account of the killing of California Joe by "Red Dog" Tom Newcomb.[36]

[John B. Sanborn's Letter]

[Tablet 36]

The Sanborn Letter (copy)

Law Offices of John B. and E. P. Sanborn, Rooms 66 to 69, National German American Bank Building, Cor. Fourth and Robert Sts.

Gen. John B. Sanborn. Edward P. Sanborn. St. Paul, Minn., February 25th, 1896. Dictated.

Little Wound,

Chief of Ogallala Sioux.

Dear Sir:

In answer to your question where was the south line of the Sioux Reservation located by the Commissioners of 1867 and 8, I will say that there are two ways of answering it; 1st; By the language used in the Treaty, which as matter of law is controlling; and by that language the southern line of the Sioux Reservation, was the northern line of the state of Nebraska, or 43rd parallel of latitude, from the Northwest corner of Nebraska to its crossing of the Keya Paha, thence down that river to the Niobrara River, thence down the Niobrara River to the Missouri River.

2nd; Relative to the understanding of the parties to the treaty, as to where that line would be on the surface of the earth, I recollect distinctly that there was a great deal of conversation and controversy as to this point: The Commissioners knew as little concerning this as the Indians, and from what you now state as to the actual location of this line on the earth's surface, it is certain that the Northwestern corner of Nebraska, it is twenty five or thirty miles farther north than either the commissioners or Indians, parties to the treaty, supposed it would be. I know the Indians contended strongly for the Niobrara as their southern line, but the Commissioners were unable to concede this, as their instructions from the Department at Washington, limited them in setting off reservations, as I recollect it, to lands in the territories, and Nebraska was at that time a state. There was an understanding between the Commissioners and the Chiefs, that certain lands containing the springs and rivulets, at the head of White River, should be retained for the use of the Indians as far and as long as possible, and I believe this understanding was carried into effect by the Commissioner of Indian Affairs.

All matters connected with that treaty sink into insignificance when compared with the open palpable violation of its provisions by the United States, in failing to preserve the integrity of the territory of the reservation and the exclusive control of it by the Indians, subject only to such officers and agents of the United States as were necessary to carry into effect its provisions, and protect the Indians in the enjoyment of their rights under it. Like all error and wrong this led to the greatest disaster to the Sioux Indians in habitating the territory, and was not unattended with loss and disaster to the people of the United States.

I hope your visit to Washington, will be successful, and that the United States will be ready to make reparation as far as possible for the losses and sufferings that have resulted from the wanton violation of the stipulations of the treaty of 1868.

I am glad to be able to furnish you with the same map possessed by the commission of 1868, and on which it acted in making the treaties of that and the preceding year.

Very respectfully yours,

John B. Sanborn

Indian Peace Commissioner 1867–8.[37]

The above letter I copied verbatim et literatim at the log cabin home of George Little Wound, son of Chief Little Wound, deceased, Feb. 28, 1907. I copied it exactly, capitals, punctuation, misspellings, errors and all. E. S. Ricker

[Oluffine Nelson's Interview]

Oluffine Johanson and Peter B. Nelson were married in Chicago, Illinois, in June 1874. In 1877 she and her two daughters, a two-year-old and a baby of three months, joined Mr. Nelson at the Yellow Medicine Creek Agency for the Oglalas on the Missouri River in central South Dakota. In 1884 the Nelsons moved to Bordeaux, a small community east of modern Chadron, Nebraska. There they opened a store and Peter became the postmaster. In 1887 they moved to Chadron and built the Nelson Opera House.[38]

[Box 19]

Statement of Mrs. Oluffine Nelson, taken at Chadron, Neb. in May, 1905. Lee Card stenographer.[39]

At the age of 19 I left my home in Norway, Oluffine Johanson and came to Chicago, Illinois, and was there 6 weeks. I knew Mr. P. B. Nelson in Bergen, Norway, and after I was in Chicago six weeks I married Nelson and then lived in Chicago two years and a half, perhaps not quite. Had been corresponding with Nelson for more than two years before he asked me to come to America. Nelson left Chicago and went to Yankton about the year 1876. I left Chicago by rail and with two children, both very young came by rail to Yankton and Nelson was then above Yankton on the Missouri and 45 miles below Pierre. I took a boat up the Missouri River. I had always lived in a large city and Bergen was quite a large city and therefore I had no knowledge of country life and especially American Frontier life—had never seen an Indian and had no knowledge of the race except what little I had read from books. I had read some about the Indians when a little girl but did not know any such people as Indians. Mr. Nelson told me nothing about them nor frontier life and when I came out he did not want to discourage me and I came out there with no knowledge whatever of what I was to encounter any more than expecting to find things as in a great city. A girl came from Chicago with me but did not like it there and went over to the Fort [Hale] just a mile from there, after I got there.

When I came to Yankton from Chicago I staid over night in a hotel there and it was [a] pretty rough place in that hotel and I had not had any experience in the hotel that perhaps is not worth telling. I had two little children and the first thing I knew after I woke up in the night, I heard some shooting—two fellows were shooting right in the hall next to my room. I never told Nelson about that as he did not appear to care to listen. I heard some one hollowing that somebody had got killed and the land lady came to my door and knocked at my door and I could not talk because I could not talk English very good. She told me to get up and dress as there was a man out there dying. I did dress and took the children and as I was coming out I stumbled over a dead man—you know the feeling of one when—then come several policemen—they went after those fellows—I was pretty scared—it was my first experience. Coming down in the hotel the next morning there was a drunken fellow coming and hollowing and said he had to have some whiskey and I did not know what to do. I hollowed and went into the next room but did not know where I was going. He came into my room and wanted something to drink about five o'clock in the morning. I forgot to lock my door. Then I had another scare. The next morning I got away from there and took the boat and some lady helped me with the children when I got into this boat. I got along on the boat nicely and was 8 days going until I got to the Yellow Medicine Agency. The girl I brought from Chicago with me. Her name was Hanna and could talk English pretty well. When I got there, it was night and the bell commenced to ring and I asked what that was and thought it must be some stopping place. The boat stopped then and the first thing I knew some people came down to the boat and we got off. It was a little ways up hill that we had to walk and then we were on a flat. Mr. Nelson and Hank Simmons came down to meet me. One took one baby and the other took the other one. When they came down to the boat he—Nelson—was all dressed up. I never see him dressed this way. He had his great big boots on and his pants down in his boots and a great big wide hat and six shooter on a belt and knife. I kind of looked at him and did not know whether it was him or not. Took me kind of surprise way he was fixed up. Hank Simmons was dressed the same way. Then we walked up this big hill from the landing and then we got up onto the flat and I was saying to Nelson—to him—is not this a lovely city—Hank Simmons I noticed kind of laughed when I called it a big city. It was a lovely night and when I came up there I thought it was a big city. I could see tents and tepees and I thought it was new houses—it was the top part of the buildings, you know. Instead of that it was the tents and tepees. Then, when we got up to a little log house, I thought it was his barn, because he told me by writing that he had bought a couple of government horses. He opened this little place—this little house with one little window, and I saw a table set. It was a long table—he(Nelson)used to run the hotel. Then there was just a dirt floor. You had to step about two feet over the door sill and then a long way down to reach the dirt floor. He did not want to coax and humor me and I had to make the best of it. So, as I got there, I see in his little room there was a table—his table and benches. I asked him if he had a chair to sit on—two little babies, one only three months old and one two years old. He said, now you got to get used to this. I asked him where he slept, and he pointed over to the corner and said that is where we all sleep. There was some old clothes and old sacks there; and _____ Then I say we have to have some supper. The table was all set— some biscuits several inches high—nice biscuits—platter of bacon, a basin of dried apples. Oil cloth on the table. I think it was dried apples.

Do you set the table in the barn? I asked. No, he said, this is my house. This is our home. Then I sat down to my supper with the children. One child looked at him and one looked at me. They were afraid. There was another fellow there called Broncho Bill. He had long curly hair. Looked scared at me. He had a big six shooter on him too. I asked who that fellow was. I asked Nelson in Norwegian so that he could not understand as I was afraid of him. Then after we was through supper he showed me his bed. Then I thought of the big holes and ridges in the floor. He said I could throw the coffee grounds in the holes and make the floor level. It was very uneven. The bed was just made of logs, some old sacks, a blanket and an old slicker under his head. When we went to bed, I and he sleeping on top it was rough and I could feel the logs with my feet and body. He said I got to get used to it. Everything I told him, he said I got to get used to it. I took everything—and considered. I had goods on the road. For three weeks I slept that way. Did not have very much with me because it was so expensive and not very much money for anything. Sold everything I could you know when I left Chicago. I asked where Hanna was going to sleep, and he says the girl sleep in the little room off to one side, with some bedding on the floor. I made a bed for her I think of some deer skins and some wolf skins—and I didn't know where she would sleep and I had gone and fixed up this place, and, she says, I never would stay here; and she was mad at me. I felt bad and commenced to cry. I said I had to put up with it—we both had to put up with it. I was only 22 years old and she 36 and had more experience than I had. He told me he had a nice house there, and I took the girl out with me. She went away the next day. Next night it rained and poured down and the rain came through and I did not have any place to stand, so we got under this long table for a place because there was an oil cloth over the table. This was the second night. I was glad the girl was off my hands—she was ugly at me. It rained so not a place to stand or sit, and I was so down hearted. Oh, he says, the sun will come out and every thing be all right. He says, you put the children in the bed. Then it got cleared up but it rained more in the house than out doors, through the dirt you see. It was dirt roof and moss on it. Next day he says, here is a pair of boots & he told me to take off my dress. I was dressed up in a traveling dress, you know, and didn't have my trunk yet. He just said "put your dress off and go to work; here is a pair of boots." I just looked at him—I says I can't do it. He says, "you do this way," and I did and I went to work and done it. I was so upset and done it. My poor little baby, one nursing, here I had them setting there crying and left them two in the bed, and so I had to work and help— doing this work—cleaning out; and here came this doctor Irwin himself.[40] His wife sent him up there—knew it had rained. He knew it was an awful place for me; she sent for me to come down there and stay in their frame building. Irwin told me to stay there, and I went down with the children. Nelson did not like it very well. Everything then dried out and so he fixed the house up the best he could. Then Dr. Irwin let us take a tent. He was the agent. And then he put up the tent for us and I slept there in the tent. I was scared to death with the Indians. I asked him who they was and one came creeping and looking in the window and said "How." I didn't know whether they were animals or what. Oh, he says they are Indians and I says, "What! Indians here!" and I was all scared up. And he says "There is lots of them; and he says "I have been here all the time and why should you be afraid of them?" One squaw came in and says "How." She was black and painted up red and yellow; and she hollered and laughed and made fun. That was the first I saw of the Indians.

[Peter B. Nelson's Interview]

Peter B. Nelson was born on March 6, 1853, in Bergen, Norway. After a career as a seaman he set out for the Black Hills in 1876. When he arrived at Yankton he accepted a job as a cook at the new Yellow Medicine Agency.[41]

[Box 19]

Peter B. Nelson's Statement

The lumber of which the agent's house was built was shipped from Yankton. The house of mine was of old cotton wood logs, I think somewheres about thirty or forty feet long. It was an old trading store that had been built at the Brule Agency over thirty miles below there. I paid for hauling the logs up there $75.00. We built up on a high knoll just about a half dozen rods from the agency and we built on the finest location. I don't recollect how much we paid for the building. We put it up after we had hauled it up there, and chincked it and fixed it up and then put poles on top of the ridge poles, and on top of that of course there was straw and hay and such things of that kind, and on top of them there was dirt and when it quit raining on the outside then it began to rain on the inside.

The Indians used to come around and visit me. My first trouble that I had — Mrs. Nelson came there in the spring and month of March, I think of 1877. American Horse, chief of his band of the Sioux, was a good friend of mine; and finally when she came there and had been there for a short time, he came and informed me that he was very much infatuated with my wife, and he wanted to know if she could not be purchased, and what the price would be as he would like to have her for his wife. I took it in a kind of jocular way and told him that the question would be whether he would be able to purchase her at the price that would be demanded for her. Well, he said, he did not have very much money but he said he had lots of horses. I finally asked him what he thought he could afford to pay. Well he said he could buy the best of the Sioux maidens from two to ten or 15 horses, and of course maybe a calico dress and a few little trinkets and notions for the old folks put in to make them feel happy. I then told him that I was afraid his price was too low; that he would not be able to purchase a white woman at that price and especially the one that he was talking about or offering to buy. Well he kept raising; he said he liked very much to get himself a wife and that he was very much taken and that he would make the price forty head of horses, and I told him that he was far below the value and that he could see for himself that forty head of horses would be nothing in price in this deal if it would go through; so he raised the bid to sixty five. At the time, as we was talking about the transaction, I began to fear that I might be going too far in this business, as I saw American Horse seemed to be in great earnest about it; but it was getting so [blank] at the time that some of the other Indians came up and our conversation ceased. I went off on some other excuse, but I told him as I left, that we perhaps might make a deal. (Mrs. Nelson interrupts: "He used to come often and dressed and slicked up in war paint with feathers in his hair, and was a very clean Indian.") So, one morning—after this transaction—American Horse came very often and always with this thing on his mind and wanted to talk about this matter. Well, I kept it up in a jocular way all the time, but finally one day in the morning he rode up on a fine sorrel horse—rode up and had a beaded blanket and another horse along with him as he informed me for Mrs. Nelson. That his band of horses, sixty five head was right there and waiting for the deal to take effect immediately, and, in looking over where he pointed, here was the whole band of horses. I saw then, of course, and was rather taken back, seeing that he was in such deep earnestness about the matter, I felt not a little confused, but I told him to come over to the house where we sat down. I then told him that our talk about this matter was jocular on my part, and that our way of doing that sort of business was not the Indian's way and that we never buy or sell any women or wives, or any of our daughters, but that there was only certain ways to go about it. That it did not cost us anything for so doing, and that we go through matrimony according to a certain rite. I told him then that I was very sorry that matters had gone so far and that he had been fooled; that I was not well informed of the Indian ways of getting wives and never thought for one moment when he spoke to me about the deal that his intention was serious. (Mrs. Nelson interrupts—I came out and he showed me his horse. Nelson could talk to him in the Sioux language.) But Mrs. Nelson could not understand anything he said, but knew what his motions meant. American Horse was very much put out and went away with a sad heart—he seemed to think I had played a great trick on him. He went off not only in great disappointment, but he felt very grudgingly towards me for leading him on and making him believe that he could get her. A week or ten days elapsed before I saw him again. After that time he seemed to return to his own self and came around very frequently. (Mrs. Nelson interposing: — later they told me that he might steal me, and so I was always afraid.) Quite awhile afterwards he would refer to the matter laughingly and talk to me about the deal for my wife. I always thought a great deal of American Horse. He was a good Indian and he was a man that you could rely on what he said.

Now, the trader at the Rosebud Agency, Charley Jordan then chief clerk at the Yellow Medicine Agency came to me and informed me that several Indians had come and spoken to him and the agent that they would like to do a little trading with me in changing their supplies for some of mine, and I told them that such could be done provided the same was satisfactory with Dr. Irwin the agent. My answer was carried to the agent who informed me that it would be a good thing for the Indians if I would trade with them that way, because they did not know how to use the same, etc. I did to a certain extent give them supplies for flour especially, and at one time several hundred Indians came and got quite a lot of supplies from me in payment for which I received about 3,000 pounds of flour and had it put in my house. I had an addition there in which I stored it. The Indians all seemed friendly and were willing, more or less, to do most anything I wanted them to. A great many of them seemed friendly; still more were a very sorry looking crowd and when I had to shut down on this trade and I had a lot of stuff then to lock up. Their method of surrounding the house with their blankets drawn all about them and nothing visible but their eyes and staring in at all the windows or doors or any cracks where there was any chance to get a view. They would stand there for hours and hours and just look like statues and at first it was the greatest wonder to me how they could hold their composure and stare so long at one time. A great many of them seemed to be under the spell or impression that anything they could lay their hands on, whether it was theirs or not, they would keep it and it made no difference. They would take everything under their blankets and then leave for the tepees. In the fore part at the first appearance of them at the agency, I would call them in and give them something to eat. I would set them down to the table and furnish them with the best I had in the house, but to my sorrow I found out it was a very unwise thing to do. One morning four Indians appeared at the door with a note from the Doctor asking me if I could do something for them in the line of eatables, as they did not have anything at the commisary at that time.

I was running a mess-house (Hotel) at the agency at that time. I then told the Indians to come in, and as breakfast was then just about over but the table was set, I told them to sit down and get their breakfast. My supplies was quite large as I had just received a shipment by the Steamer "Black Hills" from Yankton, South Dakota, then Dakota, but after supplying the Indians awhile in feasting them up during this breakfast episode, I thought that my supplies would not last very long if they happened to be my boarders for any time. I thought they never would fill up. It seemed their stomachs would extend and protrude so that they looked as round as good sized barrels. They were having a feast and they were bound to take advantage of it. But I got exhausted in placing eatables on the table and gave up furnishing them any more. Before they arose from the table my eye discovered that they had left nothing on the table—not even a sugar bowl. There was nothing left but the bare table. That was my first surprise in taking Indians for boarders. The Indians would still come around before day light in the morning. They would be there continually during the day and long into the night; standing around all the time on all corners of the building. It got so after while it was no novelty to me; to my sorrow I found it was a great annoyance, as they were the greatest beggars that I ever seen. A few days after, one or two officers, I think it was a lieutenant of the 3rd Cavalry from the post, was invited and entertained at dinner. After the dinner was over and we had sat and talked and the officers had departed for the post on their horses, and it was supper time some Indians appeared and wanted me to furnish them with some bread and other supplies. I told them it was impossible for me to do so as I was getting rather short of supplies and did not want to take any chance of taking any of their stuff as I had more than I was able to carry and pay for in flour, etc. They were rather disappointed. I told them to come back in a day or two, and when the steamer arrived I might be able to give them something. The next day about noon Herman Bosler of Philadelphia, who had the contract to furnish the agency with beef, having then brought the herd to the agency for issue, was going to issue beeves the next day to the Indians. Mr. Charley Woolworth had charge, being interested with Bosler in the contract and he stopped at my place. Mr. Woolworth and one of his men and I sat down to dinner and all were through when two large Sioux Indians came in through the door into the room and stood up along the wall. They were two large Indians, over six feet high, and I should judge were between 35 and 40 years old. They had been there before; I partly knew who they were. They asked and begged as usual for something to eat. Before dinner was over, as was said, both stood against the wall and they commenced to fart. We were sitting at the table. I turned around to them and pointed to the door and told them in the Sioux language to go out. They paid no attention but stood there immovable. I put my chair back, raised up from the table, went over, grabbed one of them by the blanket and shoulder, took him to the door and gave him a kick out and then proceeded with the next one in the same manner. They were too hot to be hostile. They were in just about as bad humor as could be and went away. I could not understand or hear what they said. I was satisfied that I was threatened with vengeance. About four o'clock in the afternoon, Mr. Leon Pallady, then the interpreter for the Agency, rushed up to the hotel, came in and called me by name and said "Mr. Nelson, you had better leave the agency at once, as I would not give one cent for your life."[42] I said, "Mr. Pallady what is the matter? What has struck you?" "Why," he says, "I mean just what I say. If I was you, I would not stay here for one hour; I would get out before sun set." "Well," I says, "Mr. Pallady, if you will be kind enough to inform me what is the matter and what you refer to, I will be thankful to you; but, as it is, I do not know what you are driving at." "Why," he says, "you went to work and kicked those Indians and they have sworn vengeance that they will take your life and they will do it. I know those Indians." I said, "If that is all, I will stay just where I am. If those Indians want anything of me, they know where to find me." I then told Mr. Pallady to sit down while we talked the matter over; that I thought he was too much exercised about so small a thing. He said he had been among the Indians all his life. The way he had come to find this trouble out was that he had been to the tepee where these Indians were holding out and that he had overheard their talk and plans to do him up in the regular dog fashion. I told him to let the matter drop, as far as I was concerned, and not to waste any sleep over it that if they got me, it couldn't be helped; but that I should not leave the agency on account of these threats. "Just as you like but you will find out that what I tell you will be so," he said. "I just give you warning as a friend that they will lie for their prey until they get their satisfaction." I then told him that when it came to a final point if he could inform me of anything serious going to happen, I would be greatly obliged to him, and so the matter for the present ended. In those days I was generally in the habit of going over to the post during the early evenings and passing an hour or so at the post trader's store among the officers or merchants or up to the post quarters, and going over and returning I had to cross a flat about a mile wide covered with the Indians' tepees and then I had to go through a piece of woods down towards the Yellow Medicine Creek over which we built the bridge there in the early part of the seasons, and after crossing the bridge, I then had to go through a small piece of woods before getting to the rise of ground on which stood the sutler's store, and from there on up the further rise towards the post. In passing some of my evenings over there I had gone across many times alone and unarmed but since the trouble with those Indians I had gone across to the post armed. I kept a good lookout going and coming. I used to stay over there rather late and at times it would be close onto midnight before returning. I have spent many enjoyable evenings there. After the trouble with those Indians I went armed; and it was just about a week afterwards that I was coming back from the post to my home and was walking as usual along the road and had got as far as the bridge, it being unusually dark so that nothing could be discerned; while crossing the stream and walking in the middle of the bridge, I became instinctively aware of something dark coming up before me, and recognized in the darkness the gleam of steel and heard the swish, before it struck me between the arm and the side where I found on investigation after getting home quite a cut in the side of my coat. It was my habit on returning after night to carry my gun in my hand. The instant I was aware of this danger I raised my gun and began to fire and discharged several shots but I don't know whether I hurt anybody or not. I then started on a run, but the road was rough through the woods, some of the stumps were knee high and unable to choose my stepping places, at last I fell headlong to the ground. Springing to my feet again, I continued my flight until I got out of the woods and into the prairie and in sight of the tepees where the lights were and the Omaha Dances were going and other sounds of revelry were rising. In taking an inventory of myself I found I was pretty whole with the exception of my hat which was left behind. I finally got down to a walk for home and arrived there in pretty good shape. After getting home I thought over the matter and came to the conclusion that the Indians were very cute after all, as they had fire arms and it was clear that they did not want to use them as such use might lead to apprehension; but had laid their plans to stab me, and having failed in the attempt desisted from further attack. My body would have been thrown into the Yellow Medicine Creek and the affair obscured in mystery. The stream was muddy and the banks bad and nobody would have been the wiser if they had got me over the bridge into it. Next day Mr. Palladay was at the house, I confessed to him that he was a very good guesser and asked him to take me to those Indians whom I had not seen since the date of our trouble when I expelled them from my house. But all my persuasion could not induce

Mr. Pallady to connect himself with this difficulty and he did not want me to have anything to do with those Indians, and he claimed that if he had anything to do with the trouble that he would get the enmity both of those Indians and all their relations. Consequently I could do nothing but inform the agent of the matter and get his advice which was to be careful how I proceeded. It was then but a few days after this occurrence that I made the acquaintance of Little Bad [Big] Man.[43] He came into my house and we had a talk. He seemed to take quite an interest in me and I also liked his appearance as an Indian. I told him what had occurred. He told me that provided I could get the name of those parties that he would set things right even if he had to fight for me to do so.

During the day Mr. Antoine Janis came to the hotel and he being a good friend of mine, I also informed him of what befell me. He also advised me to be very careful of those Indians as they were as treacherous as could be, and that I had better quit going over there in the darkness. At that time General Hammond, then the inspector and overseer of all the agencies on the Missouri River was coming up to make us a visit. The General was one of my best friends in that part of the country in that day, I was very glad to hear that he was coming. He arrived with his ambulance from Ft. Sulley on the Missouri and came right to me and I had the pleasure of being the first man he shook hands with at the agency. After talking with me half an hour he went to the agency to make his visit to Dr. Irwin, and after staying there awhile proceeded to the fort across the river, staying there over night. I had another interview with him the next morning before he left for Ft. Thompson. The General's first remark to me was to ask how I was getting along and his inquiry always was, "Nelson, have you got a loaf of bread to give me?" I always had the bread to give him, when I knew he was coming, because he claimed that he got the best bread at my house of any place on the whole road, and sometimes he would have a dozen or more rolls of bread that he would bring from the army posts or from any agency bakery where he used to stop. These he would exchange with me, sometimes almost a dozen for one.

In my talk with the General I informed him of the agent's request to changing supplies of mine for the Indian's goods, to give flour especially, and beans or any other stuff that they might be willing to exchange for equal in value to their goods. He stated that if I was willing to do so it would be a benefit to the Indians and would be all right. While at the agency and when it was taken charge of by Dr. Irwin as the agent of the Sioux Indians he brought with him men under his charge whose names, if I recollect right were, Jim Oldham, Clerk of the Commissary, _____ Jacobs, boss farmer, Ben Tibbits butcher, Hank Simmons seems working on agency as herder.

[Mabel M. Dawson's Interview]

On February 12, 1906, Ricker wrote in Tablet 10, "Antoine Herman, Kyle, S.D. says Mrs Mabel M. Dawson, Kyle, S.D. (formerly Miss Mabel M. Gould) who has a great collection of Indian curios known as the Gould collection. From Her catalogue 'The Smith and Gould Collection.' A collection of rare Indian work." Ricker's interview with Mabel Dawson includes copies of her letters from the Indian Boarding School at Fort Sill, Indian Territory.

[Tablet 32]

Kyle, S.D., Feb. 27, 1907.

Mrs. Mabel M. Dawson says:

She began at Fort Sill, Okla., & taught there about six months; from there she was transferred by Hon. J. S. Sherman to Santa Fé where she remained about the same length of time, and held the highest salaried Kindergarten position in the service, and on her resigning at this place the salary was reduced to $600 per annum. She was Kindergartner at these two places. She resigned on account of sickness. Believes she and others were poisoned. She was next appointed as teacher and sent to Cherokee, N.C., & was there about six or seven months. She resigned at Charlotte.

She was next Kindergartner for two years at Flandreau, S.D. She left here on a telegram that her mother was dying.

Her next place was at the Pine Ridge Boarding School from June till October, 1901. This was but temporary. She was married to J. L. Dawson in 1902.[44] From Pine Ridge she went to the Pima Indians 5 months.

[Tablet 10]

Mrs. Mabel M. Dawson tells me that the story told by Gen. Miles in "Recollections" about his campaign in the Comanche country, citing an instance of a person's experience with a rattlesnake and of getting rid of him by spitting tobacco juice in his eyes, refers to Capt. Baldwin who was the soldier who had the experience.[45]

Mrs. Mabel M. Dawson (nee Gould) says that she was well acquainted with Geronimo at Fort Sill and the Kiowa Agency.[46] He told her that if there was any hope he would go on the warpath and stay as long as one of the Apaches lived, but it was no use, as there were too many whites. (See her catalogue for more of him.) He was a scout at Fort Sill, & it was after the soldiers had left there for the Spanish war that his conspiracy to break out by killing the inmates of the Boarding School first, was discovered.

In that sandy country in Arizona the Apaches used to lie down and cover themselves in the sand so that an enemy or travelers would unsuspectingly come immediately upon them and not know of the presence of a hostile foe till the later had risen up and "thrown down" on them so that the surprised party was not able to move without fear of instant death or wounds. Geronimo on such occasions would do all manner of childish and silly things such as making faces at his captives, and doing immoral and indecent acts before them, compelling them to see his performances. These preceded his reserved choice pleasure of killing the victims. He told these things himself to Miss Gould through an interpreter.

The Indians learned to scrutinize these little sand mounds with suspicion; if they had no sage or mesquite growing upon or around them they were suspected of concealing Apaches, but if there was this growth they gave no rise to fear.

[Tablet 32]

Copies of Letters written by Miss Mabel M. Gould to her mother, Mrs. Helen R. Gould. At the age of sixteen Miss Gould took examination for admission as teacher into the Indian school service and received her appointment when a little under seventeen. (They are not allowed by law to take examination under the age of twenty-one.) Her first appointment was to the Indian Boarding School at Fort Sill, Okla. I begin with her correspondence with her mother from this place with the following letter written soon after her arrival at Fort Sill.

Fort Sill, Kiowa Agency, O.T., Nov. 27th, 1897.

My Own Dearest Mamma:

At last I have a little time I may call my own. I am so busy during the day, and the duties so break up the day that I hardly have time to do anything for myself.[47]

We are pleasantly located on a prominence three miles from the Post. Our buildings are located around a large circle, in the middle of which is a very large bell. This bell is the signal for almost all of our duties. We have three large buildings and many small ones. The largest are the Boys' building, the Girls' building, and the School house. The dining halls are in the Girls', and my room in the Boys'. The sick room and most of the employees' rooms are also in the Girls'. The three crosses indicate the storehouse, meat house and sawmill. Farther back, and between the Girls' building and the first cross, are the laundry, windmills, stables and other buildings. [Rough sketch.]

Now you know where I am. I put an arrow in the direction of the Post from us.[48] We can see it, the country is so level. We have had several prairie fires, and the coyotes snarl about the buildings almost nightly, but as one of the boys here says, "they are much heap 'fraid"; so that is nothing to fear.

Anadarko is 35 miles away; and Rush Springs, the nearest railway station, is 30 miles off.

The first bell rings at 5:45 for the children to get up and dress; at 6:15 another bell tells them to come down stairs. At about seven they hear again a summons to go over to the dining rooms to breakfast. At 7:25 a small bell calls the employees to breakfast. At 7:45 the work bell rings & a detail of children are sent to the different school rooms to build fire, sweep and otherwise make the rooms bright and clean under the teachers' supervision. We can't do one thing ourselves, but have to stand and teach those boys how to do it. At 8:30 another bell tells them to prepare for school, and at 9:00 school bell rings. At 10:45 recess comes until 11:00, and at 11:30 school closes and the bell to prepare for dinner rings. Dinner is at twelve and the teachers dine at 12:25. The bell rings at 12:45 for boys to attend to rooms again, and at 1:30 school bell rings. Recess at 2:45, and school (for me) closes at 3:30. At 4:30 the bell rings to prepare for supper, and at 5 the children all file in to supper. We have ours at 5:25. At 6:30 we prepare for collection, to me the pleasantest part of all. The children dress in their best and march to the large school room up stairs (which we also use for chapel) and say some psalms and sing hymns and other songs for nearly an hour. Twice each week some one addresses them. It is my turn to-morrow night, but I am going to tell them a Thanksgiving story instead.

There are a few mountains about ten or more miles from us. Otherwise the country is rolling prairie. Most of the children who come here are Comanche, although there may be a few Kiowas.

Have I told you that Anadarko is named after a tribe of Indians and they are all dead but one. He lives over at the seat. One could weave a story about him and name it "The Last of the Anadarkos."

The Doctor and his wife are very refined people. Also both Matrons. X X X X X

The children seem to think a great deal of me. They are quite bright children. It seems to me the sun never shone so bright & the sky was never so blue as out on these western plains. I may have written much that is not interesting, but I thought I'd put it all in and you would know how I am situated. We are a little more than two hours behind you. One of the teachers here is a little Indian girl, 19 years old, from Wisconsin. She & the Superintendent keep guard over the children at breakfast & teach them to eat properly, my room-mate and the S's wife at dinner, and then he & I do duty at night. X X X

From your loving Mab.

Monday A.M.

My Own Dearest Mamma:

It is very cold this morning. We had a sand blizzard last night. This country is subject to them. Yesterday afternoon it was so warm that we were out in light clothes, and without any outside wraps. In less than five minutes after we saw the cloud it was so cold that we were nearly frozen. Saturday it was issue day. Once a month—every fourth Saturday—the Government issues beef to the Indians from different points on the reservation. That is the visiting day at the school here. The grounds were covered with Indians. They came laden with everything you could imagine for the children—doll trunks, sachels, candy, nuts, fruit, crackers, & jewelry of all kinds. There were lots of little babies strapped in their cradles to the squaws backs. The cradles are beautifully beaded all over, and some are plain buckskin. Different tribes have different kinds. The Comanche people and some other tribes have them like this. I am going to send one to Esther for Christmas if I can find a pretty one. The Apache cradles are more like this, [Figure 4] and the baby lies on the lacing, covered with buckskin or blanket. Of course this is not Apache country, but there are some Apache prisoners of war near by; Geronimo the chief is down in history as the most cruel chief that ever lived. I met him yesterday and talked to him through an interpreter. When asked how many white men he had killed, his eyes lighted up with a cruel fire and he waved his hands above his head, meaning "As many as the leaves on the trees." He couldn't count them. I have his picture. Some day I'll let you take it to see. I think much of it, because he gave it to me himself. There is a Comanche chief near by—Quana Parker. I have two of his children in my kindergarten—Honey and Johnnie. They were given names upon their entrance to the School. I don't know their Indian names. Quana has had nine wives and twenty-eight children. He has cast off two wives. Some of his children are in Carlisle school. I ought to have my bicycle here; there are lots of them here. I could buy a fine pony for ten dollars & the keep would be little. I don't have much time though, only on holidays.

I went to a beautiful dinner party at the Superintendent's home Thanksgiving day. They are very kind to me. They take me driving a great deal. Twice we have been pecan hunting and once persimmons gathering. Then they take me to the Fort and Sub-Agency a great deal. I like it very much here. We went down two evenings to the camps near by. When issue day approaches the Indians begin to bring their tents and tepees & camp about here. Thursday we took the girls to one camp, and Friday we took the boys to another. Friday was the best. The camp was composed of about thirty tents & tepees. Each had a windbreak. These wind-breaks are made of wild sunflower stalks, something like this:[49] Just a sort of brush fence around the tepee. Their doors are nothing more than a curtain over the little opening. It is spread over the outside. We went to the tepees and pushed back the curtain & walked right in! Imagine our feelings if they should do it to our homes!! Opposite the entrance blankets are spread against the tent on the ground. This is the guest seat. On the left of entrance is the host's seat & on the right is where the old women & children sit. Between the latter & the guest seat is where the young couples, if there are any, sit. That is the general rule. The little hot fire in the center, the bright blankets spread around the inner edge of the tents, the old, grizzled, witch-like women and the tiny babies in the cradles, the younger people in their bright garments, with long flowing hair, and their arms and hands covered with silver bracelets, rings and other ornaments, the buckskin moccasins with their beautiful beadwork and silver buttons, and last but not least, the tall dome-like tepee smoked black inside, with the firelight playing upon the whole, cast a weird, romantic spell over us all. We looked at our boys and we saw just what they would go back to someday. Some never will. But others love it all. Little Nellie would much prefer and appreciate a string of beads, no matter how cheap. She would see no significance in a card. She is a sweet little thing — one of the prettiest Indian babies I have seen — only three or four years old. X X X X X

Miss Casey has been real nice to me, although we are not very congenial. She is rather uncouth, and an ex-Catholic. She has had lots of trouble and has left the Catholic Church. I am not much with her. I spent last evening with Dr. Shoemaker & his wife. You would love them if you knew them. He is a Washingtonian. I have written a long letter and will close now, as it is almost school time. X X X X X

With dearest love,

Yours always, Mab

Fort Sill, O.T., Dec. 14, 1897.

My own dearest Mamma:

For a wonder I will be able to write you a whole letter without the thought that I must hustle for my life.

We have been quite gay here for over a week—had company. First Capt. Baldwin came with the Commission (a Congressman from Wisconsin).[50] Then an Indian Minister named M. Wright, and Sunday the Cheyenne boys (pronounced Shy ánn). Last night we had a fine time. Everybody, children and employees, went to the Assembly room, and two young men, merchants at the Sub-Agency, brought their graphophone and the Cheyenne boys played, and I recited "Raggedy Man" and "A Little Man Bought Him a Big Bass Drum." That was a hit on the Cheyenne Band, and it brought the house down. The building isn't a very staunch one anyway. The hard winds have undermined it some; so between chuckles and giggles and roars on Mr. Cox's part, he finally had to tell them to stop cheering, for fear we'd all go down. Mrs. Cox made 69 big popcorn balls, and after the littlest ones went to bed, Willie, the Indian Captain of the boys, passed them around. After everything was over, there was a reception or something over at the reception room, but I didn't go. I was too tired. They had music & candy and two young men.

We will have a ~~Christmas~~ Xmas tree next week, either Friday or Saturday night. X X X Mrs. Shoemaker, the Dr.'s wife, has gone to Rainy Mountain for a month. I don't know what I'll do without her. She is the only one I have much to do with, except Mr. & Mrs. Cox.

Friday, Jan. 28, 1898, Fort Sill, O.T.

My Own dearest Mamma:

I have a few minutes and so will write to you again. I am in school, and havn't anything but Kindergarten material to use over here. I received a nice long letter from Peg yesterday. Is she going to be married, and if so, when? She said you enjoyed the Indian things. I am glad someone appreciates their work. You know I have never told you how I get along in the Kindergarten. It is the most fascinating work I ever did. It is exhausting, yet I hardly notice how the days go by. They just fly. They are some of the brightest children I ever saw, too. They are all building towers just now, and their funny little talk is most entertaining. "Look at de mine, Pahbee!"————"Sho nuff, indeed, mine beat him; Look, my brother!"———— "Dis boy he make him bery good, ain't it?"————"My dear brother, look at de Emos!"————"Miss Goulda, I want 'scuse'." This last has just been addressed to me.

Does Peg really want an Indian dress? Or is it just an odd fancy? If she sends me two large pieces of chamois skin, long enough to reach from her foot to half way between her knee and hips, I'll send her a complete Indian outfit; not a buckskin one, but what the majority of the camp Indians wear. One Indian woman promised me long ago to make me an Indian dress. If there is nothing in it, why, I won't have her make it until she gets ready, but if there is an occasion for Peg to wear it, I can tell her to make it right away. The chamois skin is for the moccasins. The moccasins that the Indian women wear are beautiful. They come almost to their hips, are tied above the knee to keep them up, and the upper part falls over in beautiful fringed skin. That is one of the things that love nor money cannot make the Indians make for a paleface. But Jennie is my "dear friend," and so her mother will do anything for me. I say "Nah-mah-kah-mah-ki-tee-nah," and she will do anything for me; that is, "My sister, I love you." I must close now.

With Dearest love,

Mab.

Fort Sill O.T., Feb. 3, 1898.

My Dearest Ma:

X X X X X The young man in our pictures is (or was) a trader here. Now he has gone to Kansas City to study law. A trader, originally, was a man who bartered with the Indians for skins, etc., and gave in exchange anything they needed. At the present, a trader is best described as an Indian skinflint. They are storekeepers, and it is shameful how much they charge the Indians for everything. A blanket they would sell to white people here for $10.00 they ask 15 or 20 dollars for from an Indian; and just so with everything they sell. Miss Casey and I are partially outwitting them though, and the others are following suit. We take the children's money and buy for them, and get about three times as much as the children. One of the traders goes with Miss Casey. He has red hair and a red mustache, but is withal good looking. He is very tall. The Indians call him "Mr. Acca poppy," or that is what it sounds like although not the proper spelling. It means Mr. Redhead.

I was going to tell you about the friendship of friends among the Indians. I don't know how they first come to be friends, but they are the truest friends I ever saw. Willie and Clarence are friends, and I asked them one day how they first came to love each other so very much, and they told me it was "just somehow." And when I asked Willie again he said: "Me don't know; me always just love him for my friend." If Willie tells anything to Clarence which he doesn't want told, Clarence would kill himself before telling it. They will lie, steal, murder, anything, if their friend not only says to, but wishes it done. They are together always, and always with their arms around each other just like two girls. They call each other "Brother" and "Friend," and that word is the talisman by which one does everything for the other. If you go out in camp and say, "Brother give me that," they will give it to you. Of course that is where the whites have deceived and taken advantage of the Indians, for they just used the word and didn't care to keep faith with the Indians, so that now they are more wary. One or two girls call me "My sister." I could do anything with them, for they have adopted me when they call me that, and love me like [their] own sisters. Four or five of them want me to take them "up in my home" next summer. There is a Seminole Indian here, the baker. He has such a peculiar way of expressing himself. When he is sitting around the fire, he "sits with men where the smoke go up in the air," and instead of saying last night, he says the "evening (or night) of last." You have Willie's and Clarence's pictures. When Willie gets a wife, she will be as much Clarence's as his, and vice versa. And when one friend goes away into another camp or country for a time, the other is instructed to take care of the first one's wife, and she is brought over to the second friend's tepee, and his own wife cast aside until his friend returns.

Major Baldwin is in Washington undergoing examination and investigation. He of course works for the Indians' interest, and necessarily against the traders? He encourages them to build houses instead of roaming all over the prairies, and the money they use for this would go to the traders otherwise. So they are always trying to get something against him. X X X X X

With dearest love from your own Mab.

Fort Sill, O.T. Feb. 9, 1898.

My Dearest Mamma:

I have been making everyone here envious over all the bundles which have come in lately. The shoes are just fine, and a perfect fit. The red cloth has been admired by everyone. I made a curtain, and there was enough left to cover my old pillow. It is so hard I never can use it, so I just put the cover on it and laid it on top of my bed for effect. It has brightened up the room so much. You don't know what a bare old room we have. We have up all our photographs and books, but the red stuff made it so much brighter. I am wild to know how you liked your skirt. When Mrs. Shoemaker saw it, she sent right off for one too, to wear with her fancy waists.

We have had some changes here. Our nurse and seamstress has been transferred, and because she didn't like where she was going, she resigned. The woman at Fort Totten, N. Dak., is here in her place. Our dear old Mrs. Cannon, boys' matron, was transferred to Rainy Mountain, and Miss Freeman, an old employee here, has come and taken her place. Miss Casey cried like a baby, because Miss Cannon was like a mother to us.

Thank you very much for Peg's dress. It will be just right to teach in, for they say it is so hot here in the summer that you cannot wear a heavy skirt and shirt waists.

The minister at the Sub-Agency took me to an Indian burial the other day. The coffin was a box covered with black calico, and a cross of brass headed nails on top. It was lowered into the grave and we sang, "What A Friend We Have In Jesus." Preston interpreted what the minister had to say. Mr. Forrester (the minister) then asked them if they had anything they wanted to bury with the Indian woman, for it is the custom to bury all she has had on or around her when sick. The husband then spread what calico was left from covering the box, on top. Then they brought a large quilt or comforter, and then friends threw in such offerings as their love for the dead woman suggested. One poor white girl who was raised with the woman dropped in a bead necklace from her neck. Then the preacher read the service and the grave was filled up. While the man was digging the grave all the men and woman sat around the little burial place and smoked. That is the loneliest little burial plot I ever saw. One man who was murdered is buried there, and a big medicine man who died last November is buried there too. Hu wa yah prayed after the things were put in the grave, and then the Indians began to mourn. They yelled and cried out loud until he told them to stop, then they listened to the service. After it was over they mourned again. There are about 12 graves over there and only [one] is a white man. They bury money, jewelry, blankets and everything in the graves, and no one would rob a grave any more than he'd kill himself. The little burial plot is about 60 feet square, on the open prairie, with not a tree in sight. When the big medicine man died his squaw filled in the grave with handfuls of earth, and it was so frozen she could hardly break it apart. The medicine men are supposed by the Indians to be imbued with some divine power, and everything they say or do is considered holy. I am going to enclose one or two little letters the girls have written me—the ones who are my "sisters." The boys are very fond of me too. Yesterday, Preston heard me wishing I had a few spring beauties, and he ran away over on the prairie to hunt these two or three little things, and sent them wrapped up in the little note. X X X X X

How I wish you were here. It is all such beautiful sunshine, and singing birds and blooming flowers. Two or three weeks, and the prairie will be a veri-table flower garden, to remain so until next November. The air is full of the sweet scents and feathered warblers of spring. Flocks of bobolinks, sometimes many thousands of them, fly all about us. Their songs are the first sounds I hear in the morning. X X X X X

From your loving Mab.

P. S. When the girls talk Indian in school some pleasure is taken away from them. Last Tuesday they all talked Indian, so they cannot talk with any of the employees for a week, & we do not go into their playroom for a week. That is what the girls mean.

Following are copies of two of the letters referred to in the forgoing:

Fort Sill, O.Ty., February 7, 1898.

Miss Gould:

My Dear Sister:

I thought I would write to you this morning. I am so sorry that you can told to us my heart was so sorry because I love you so deary your sister write to you and Miss Hosinger put it in the stove. We are both very sorry because we never told to you. This is just a short letter this time. We won't again at you. We love you better than any of ladies because you so kind to us. I hope you are well I am getting along very well some time I will write to you again This is all I can said to you Well my sister I have no more to said to you This morning from you sister Leora good morning good by with much love and good kiss

Fort Sill, O.Ty. February 7, 1898.

Miss Gould

My dearest loving sister I am just going to answer your letter I was very sorry that you can't talk to us this week. My dearest sister I will not get angry with you. I will be very glad to talk with you next week. You are my best loving sis-ter and I love you very much because you are my best and sweet sister. I am in great hurry because it is most bell time. I will sent this letter by Leora. I think you are the best lady I ever saw you must remember me again I love you very dearly I will not close without a kiss for you I saw you going to walk with you children. My friend Leora is getting along well. This is all I can say.

From your sister Jennie.

The other is a brief note enclosing a few flowers.

Thursday.

My Dearest Mamma:

I have just a minute & not much to write. There is a terrific sand storm raging & I can't get to the house. Half an hour ago the sun shone & it was warm & balmy, but it is freezing. It came up in about five minutes. Preston meant Mrs. Cannon by "Mother" the first time. She was the boys' matron but was transferred to Rainy Mt. They call their kind friends "Mother." Half the little boys here have called me "Mother." This morning the children made some shields to wear on Washington's birthday. Little Otis Wah wah sent his to Aunt Helen, and would like to have you wear it the same day that we wear ours. We are going to put a piece of white baby ribbon through the hole & wear it over our hearts. Some of our work has gone to the I. K. U. Convention in Philadelphia this week. It was beautiful work too. You can see they are painstaking, and they work very rapidly too. Mrs. Gregory the city or State (I don't know which), instructor at Utica, asked Miss Smith to have me send some. So I did. It was not much of a variety, but beautifully done. Their drawing is something marvellous. X X X I wish you could see the sand fly. It's awful.

Your own loving Mab.

Eugene is Preston's "dear friend."

Fort Sill, O.Ty. March 10, 1898.

My own dearest Mamma: X X X X X X

It is raining here to-day. It seems so odd to have it rain, because the sun is almost always shining. But the rain has freshened all the earth up so nicely. We have very heavy dews here. They, in part, take the place of the rain. Last evening Mr. Holland and Mr. Cox and a lot of little boys went out with burning torches and set fire to the prairie all around the buildings, so as to burn the old grass off for the new to come up fresh and green. X X X It is beautiful to sit out on the piazza evenings now. It is so nice and warm that Miss Casey and I just take our chairs right out and sit there. We can't hardly walk unless we step on flowers, the prairies are so covered. X X X X X

Did I tell you about one girl's grandmother making me some leggings like the Indian women wear? X X X X X X

We cannot leave the school grounds without permission from the Superintendent. Up till now we didn't care, because it wasn't warm out after we were through with our work, but now we rather be out than in for just an hour or so after all the day's work is over, and we can't leave without permission! X X X X X X

Miss Casey is going to send a few little flowers to you. The children bring in such heaps of them from the prairies.

With dearest love from Mab.

The following letter was not dated, but it was written at Fort Sill and mailed April 11, 1908 [1898].[51]

My own dearest ma:

I have no need of Easter rigging out here. Altho the employees dress to kill; even the Indian employees have their silks and satins. I will need either a big sun hat or sunbonnet. It is already terribly hot here. The sun is dreadful, and I am out so much. X X X X X

The flowers are all out again—a hundred different kinds—violets, spring beauties, daisies, blue & white heart's ease, and a lot of little, tiny purple ones looking like forget-me-nots. Then we have a little flower that grows all over, that grows & looks like our little northern snow drops, but they smell like English violets. The grass looks yellow—with several varieties of yellow flowers—mustard and little bell-like flowers that smell like some tall yellow flowers of the north.

I went down to church twice yesterday. In the morning Miss Casey and I took the little girls' and big boys and Honey Parker, a little girl 7 years old, was taken sick and couldn't walk & I had to carry her almost a mile home. In the evening I was taken sick and one of the older boys brought me home. He is studying to be a minister under Mr. Forrester, but expects to be called to [Camp] Chickamauga in a few days. He was telling us yesterday about their rations on the march and in camp. They are given a small box of pills or tablets, and one pill is a day's rations. Then they have little sacks of pea flour, weighing a few ounces, and that is a day's rations. Then they have hard tack and ten ounces of bacon, and that is another day's rations. We were very much interested in it all. X X X X X X

If we didn't have a good room I don't know what Miss Casey & I would do, for we don't have anything fit to eat except when we send to the Post privately and get some bread from the bakery and meat from the meat market. And they made us pay our board in advance too, or nearly the whole of it. Poor Miss Casey didn't have a cent left on account of her brother's death & the expense of going home. She always tells me to give you her love, but I generally forget. Poor Preston has gone home to Mt. Scott. The Doctor went out for two days & then came back. He wasn't here a day when Preston came galloping in to the school on his pony, saying his mother was worse. So now they think it is only a matter of a few hours of life with her. Poor little Georgie & Preston have cried and cried. Preston is coming back to school though.

There is one boy, Walter Komah, who has fallen in love with Peg's picture, and he calls her his "sweetheart." He says he is going to write to her. He is only a little fellow of 14 years, but has a very sweet disposition, and they seem to think that if any one only belongs to "Chah-tee-nipe," it is good enough recommendation X X X X X

Your own loving Mab.

Fort Sill, O.Ty., April 15, 1898.

My own dearest Ma:

X X X X X X Among those letters I sent you was one from Henry. I have often told you Miss C. and I are uncongenial. You can get some idea of her innate delicacy and good breeding by a sentence in Henry's letter. He asked her to write something pretty in that letter because it was to his best girl. So she thought it was to one of the girls, and she wrote that sentence: "I can kick your hat off your ear." Isn't that refined and pretty for a teacher to write in her boy's letter to a girl? Well, the letter happened to be to me, and of course I read it to her, and I wish you could have seen her face when she saw I had found out!!! X X X X X X

The girls are all making me cradles again. Posseweah is making Miss Casey a fine large one. Inetassy made me a pretty one, and half beaded it, but she got tired and one day the girls stole all the beads from it, and so I have only the buckskin cradle left. But lots of the real cradles have no beads, so I don't mind. When they don't have beads they are painted yellow (the skin part). X X X X X X

I have a beautiful Navajo blanket for you. It will last a lifetime, either as a floor rug or a bed rug. It is made by hand, of pure wool, on a loom that resembles a rag carpet loom just a little. They dye the wool themselves, and they can be washed forever.

Cherokee, N.C., Nov. 17, 1898.

My own dearest Mamma:

I have arove. It is lovely here. Among other things of lesser importance I have made good friends with the Superintendent and his wife.[52] They are lovely, and through Miss Sylcott they embraced me almost as soon as I mentioned her name. They are lovely people; but as usual the employees are all on the verge of a wrangle.

The mountains are just lovely. We are in a tiny valley, hemmed in by the beautiful mountains, with a lovely river flowing right past the door. It makes me think of Mt. Vernon. The employees quarters are on a hillock sloping down to the river, and we have pretty buildings. I room with the Kindergarten teacher. I need never have been afraid of what I didn't know. She took a course and then a post graduate course in Chicago, and the Superintendent is wondering how soon he can get her away from here. She don't know beans. The rest don't know very much. Think of a class of children four years in school and can't read or write yet! This is some of the wildest scenery in the U.S. It is grand. The holly and mistletoe grow wild here. These mountains are a spur off the Smoky mountains & they are well named as they almost always look blue and hazy. X X X X X

With much love from your loving Mab.

Geronimo's Conspiracy at Fort Sill. She says:

This conspiracy was discovered abt. 10 P.M. and Mr. Holland, an employe of the school, ran to the Fort, 3 miles distant (it was 2 miles beyond the sub-Agency and the sub-Agency was one mile beyond the school). Geronimo and the rest of the Apache prisoners occupied a row of houses on the ridge back of the Fort. It was said he had knives, bows and arrows and arms—knives of every kind made from hoops of tubs & pails, which he had been collecting for a long time. He & the other prisoners had been confined in Florida; some agreement had been made between him and the government to send their children to Carlisle, & these were allowed to come west as far as Fort Sill, but not allowed to go farther west. There was quite a large number of prisoners.

Mr. Holland ran to the Fort. It was reported or rumored that an Apache Indian employe at the school named Francis, they wanted him to go about and show the sleeping rooms to the Apaches. These rooms were filled with Comanche children, & these the Apaches hated; they hated all others but their own tribe which they greatly loved. Francis shrank from this dastardly deed & thus got knowledge of the conspiracy. "They" said that Ramona Chihuahua (not certain abt. the spelling but it is pronounced Che wa wa, the Mexican name of the mountains & a province). She was the daughter of an Apache sub-chief, was engaged to show the sleeping rooms when they could not get Francis. It was rumored around the school that when Francis failed them, that Ramona was secured. She was a great favorite of Cox, the Supt. & he would believe nothing against her. This affair was hushed up & kept from the world so not to alarm the people in that part of the country. The soldiers had started to march to the R.R., going to some place of rendezvous in Spanish-Am. war. They had gone a day's march when they were overtaken by a messenger and they returned as rapidly as possible. No one had been left behind but the chaplain and the officers' families, it is said. When they (the soldiers) got back everything was quiet & settled & hushed up, and after 2 or 3 days the soldiers again took their departure. Geronimo was put into the guardhouse for a night or so. The Indians all said the story was a lie. It was declared there was no danger. But his weapons were found just the same.

Geronimo was said to be a scout of the Gov't.(?) He used to come to the school in his scout's uniform & make addresses to the children & tell them to be good. He was religious (in his villainous way); there was a little church at the sub-Agency where he always attended. He was several times converted, she says, though nothing was said about it in the papers. His conversion was a rotatory affair.

[Tablet 18]

An Agent at a Southern Indian Agency, who was an army officer at W.K., remarked to a teacher in the Indian School at Fort Sill (as, &c., see Major Baldwin's remark, next page).

He said that soldiers stripped the dead, women as well as men. This was Major Frank D. Baldwin. Major Baldwin showed Miss Gould that the soldiers were posted so as to fire into one another.

Notes

Mrs. Mabel M. Dawson (nee Gould) says that Major Baldwin who was a lieutenant at Wounded Knee, told her, speaking of the tragedy [torn] that that was one thing [in his] life he wished he [could] blot from his memory.

3. Little Bighorn

[A. F. Ward's Interview]

A. F. Ward was a soldier in Col. John Gibbon's column that marched out of Fort Ellis in 1876 to intercept the so-called hostile tribes.

[Box 19]

Interview with A. F. Ward of Chadron, Neb.[1]

Chadron, Nebr., June 28th, 1904.

In the early spring of 1876 the order came to Ft. Ellis where four companies of the 2nd Cavalry and four companies of the 7th Infantry were stationed that a vigorous campaign was to be inaugurated that summer for to round up Sitting Bull with his Sioux Warriors that was threatening the northwestern [blank] at that time there was considerable pillaging going on and the neighboring ranches were being burned and stock was being run off and they saw that the time had come when this kind of campaign was necessary—that something had to be done to curb the ravages of the savages in that part of the country and orders came to Ft. Ellis about May 15th, 1876, to get ready to act in conjunction with the Army of the Department of the Platte and also of the Missouri in conjunction with the Department of Montana and instructions was given from the War Department for us [and?] to Montana troops to move towards the Yellowstone proceed down the Yellowstone towards the mouth of big Powder River and until further orders patrol the north side of the Yellowstone as Sitting Bull's Warriors [were] known to be between the Big Missouri River and the Yellowstone on a tributary of the Yellowstone River and to keep, if possible, the Sioux's from crossing toward the north as they had already got wind of the movement of the troops both from Ft. Lincoln and the department of the Platte which were coming against them.

We arrived at the mouth of the Big Powder River about June first and then proceeded up the Yellowstone again as far as the Big Horn River then turned and proceeded again to about 20 miles below the mouth of the Big Powder River turning up said river again to the mouth of the Rose Bud where the Montana Troops were in camp and receiving a courrier from Gen. Custer who was then on his way from Ft. Lincoln and also was accompanied by the Far West, a steam boat that had been pressed into service by the government to convey supplies up the river for the command, with Gen. Terry on board.[2] At this time Sitting Bull was camped on the Rose Bud about five miles from the mouth. When our scouts crossed the Yellowstone they discovered this to be the fact and that the main body of the Sioux was camped about five miles up the Rose Bud. Orders were given the Montana Troops to cross the Yellowstone with a command and try and to drive Sitting Bull from his position but owing to the June Raise which is characteristic of all Montana streams the river was very swollen and we found it impossible for [us] to ford the river. Abandoning that scheme and having the Indians under surveillance and knowing where their main camp were we accordingly threw up entrenchments at the mouth of the Rose Bud on the north side of the Yellowstone and awaited for the arrival of Custer's command which we knew was cooped up on the south side of the Yellowstone. About June 18th, Custer's command came up, also the steam boat, Far West, Captain Grant Marshall being commander of the Far West and a man who understood navigation of steamers of that kind and who was considered a very valuable man for the guide [of] the movement of vessels in a campaign of this kind.[3] Now scouts from the Indian Camp had been — that is the hostile camp — observing the slow approach of Custer's large command coming up the south side of the River — of the Yellowstone — and had taken advantage of the slow movement of the large command which Custer had and had moved across Tongue River and went into camp on the Little Horn and when this fact became known through Custer's scouts that Sitting Bull had changed his position, instructions were given, as it was understood at that time, that Custer should follow the hostile camp hold them, if possible in the position that they then occupied and wait for the concentration of the forces both from the north side of the river — Yellowstone and also of the command from the department of the Platte, Gen. Crook being in command of the troops from the Platte.[4] Then orders was issued to the Montana troops that the 2nd Cavalry and the 7th Infantry to move up the Yellowstone and take position at the mouth of the Big Horn which is commonly known as old Ft. Pease.[5] Then at the time when Crook got in the vicinity of the Big Horn River the Montana troops was to move up the Big Horn from the junction with the troops from the department of the Platte and also with Custer's command and attack the hostile Sioux in force. The Montana troops had been in camp at old Ft. Pease two days when a courier arrived from Custer's command which we found to be "Curly" a Sioux Scout which we had loaned to Gen. Custer for the simple reason that Curly was very familiar with the topography of the country being the old hunting ground for the Sioux Indians for centuries past and for that simple reason Curly was considered a valuable scout.[6] Myself being on the vidett that day noticed a commotion down on the river bank in the shape of an Indian waiving his blanket. When I called for the sargeant of the guard who was ordered out with a relief and by the aid of a field glass we discovered that it was Curly our old and familiar Sioux scout. That was June 26th. Then we proceeded to camp, got a Yaul [yawl] boat from the Far West and brought the messenger into camp when he gave us the first news of the Custer fight telling us that the "pony soldiers" were all killed and that he was the only one that had escaped from the battle field alive. Orders were at once issued by General Terry who was in command at this time to proceed at once to cross the command over onto the other side, the south side of the Yellowstone River which was completed about three o'clock in the morning. Then we immediately proceeded in lead marching order with the pack train on our way towards the battle field which was about 35 miles distant arriving there about 8 o'clock in the evening where we found that part of Custer's command which was given to Colonel Reno for to attack the lower part of the camp.[7] We found them entrenched on a little hill with a good many of their men killed and wounded. The Indians had at this time all left the battle field and had started towards the Rose Bud. In reconnoitering the battle field we found that Custer and his men had all been killed where they lay in the order that they charged from the upper end of the camp. We found that Custer in making the attack had divided his command, sending Reno down the river to attack the lower part of the camp while he with two hundred and sixty two men had charged the upper end of the camp and by this time the Indians were out in force and from the upper end of the camp where he had attacked and making his detour towards the lower or middle part of the camp had begun to string his men and horses as was evident from where their boys fell which we found to our horror had been horribly mutilated—being stripped of all their garments and clothing and lay naked in the blazing sun. As the thermometer in those days will stand about 100° in the shade and the stench of the battle field could be scented for five miles and the mutilation was something horrible to behold. Tongue cannot describe or pen tell of the horrible cruelties and barbarism that was perpetrated upon these poor soldiers who doubtless were horribly butchered and scarred with knives and axes previous to their death. Now, in the mean time the Far West had proceeded up the Big Horn to the mouth of the Little Horn River where it was tied to the bank and on the arrival of this vessel orders were at once given to bury the dead and also to remove from the battle field the wounded to the Far West. The wounded which was 61 in number belonging to Reno's command, and one of the noted survivors of this memorable fight was Custer's old war horse that stood in the middle of the field with three gaping wounds but the old war horse stood as a living monument to savage butchery and treachery, receiving one wound through the lower jaw, one through the shoulders and one through the thigh and this old warrior was placed upon the Far West with the wounded men and we can assure you he was handled as careful and as tenderly as any living human being could have been handled. A blacksmith led the old warrior to the boat and in crossing over the gang plank while the tears rolled down his cheeks he said this is all that is left of Custer.[8] Then the Far West proceeded with its load of wounded men for Ft. Lincoln where they could receive hospital attention. And it is a fact that Capt. Grant Marshall has got the honor of making the fastest time for that number of miles which lay between the little Big Horn and Ft. Lincoln that was ever made on the upper river where he arrived safe with his boat load of human freight.

The wounded was first attended to and then an order was given to bury the dead which was indeed a solemn task and after this was done, that is, as well as the inconveniences and scarcity of tolls [tools] would allow, the command proceeded to return to the Yellowstone. Owing to the condition of the ground the graves were made very shallow for the ground was baked very hard under the summer sun. When the order was given to proceed to the camp at the mouth of the Big Horn where we proceeded to get our supplies and the wagon train crossed the river, where as soon as possible, we got our command in marching order and proceeded up the Big Horn and, across the battle field where we found that the coyotes and wolves had not even then allowed the poor fellows to sleep undisturbed but had burroughed into the shallow graves in which they were buried and strewn promiscuously about. Taking up the trail at this time the trail led directly to the upper waters of the Rose Bud where we met General Crook that is the troops from the Department of the Platte and here was a funny incident which we thought at first was not going to be so funny after all as we expected Sitting Bull coming to take another dig at us and when coming up

over a little ridge we saw a great dust in the distance and our Sioux scouts being
out in advance came back and reported that Sitting Bull was coming back and
we began to think there was going to be something doing and now the funny
part comes in when it happens to be Gen. Crook's command coming in from
the department of the Platte and they had their scouts out ahead of them returned to their command and reported that Sitting Bull was coming to them
which give them somewhat of a scare but we accordingly drew up in line of
battle. This happened about 3 o'clock in the afternoon and a more desirable
place could not have been built to throw out troops into position to repel an attack for just on our left was a little round hill which gave us a good commanding
position for our artillery which was directly drawn up and planted which consisted of two nine pound Rodney [Rodman] guns and two 24 pound napoleon
guns, four gatling guns and seven mountain howitzers.[9] The remenant of the
7th Cavalry which consisted of Reno's command or that part of Custer's command which was given over to Reno drew up and deployed [as] scirmishers
and with 2nd Cavalry drew up in relief while the infantry drew up on our right
which made a formidable line of battle and without doubt, if Sitting Bull part
of it had materialized and was indeed coming to give us battle, [we] would have
given them a warm reception. Myself being orderly of the day was in a position
to hear and see just what was going on and when General Terry's Staff drew
up in a commanding position to take observation of the oncoming savages as
we expected they were, a white man was seen to merge from the undergrowth
and come out into plain view. Then it was discovered that it was William Cody
better known as "Buffalo Bill" and a shout of relief from the strained position
we were holding broke out as the officer who held the glass cried out that it
was Buffalo Bill and then there was a season of great rejoicing. Hats went into
the air and strong men wept with joy as it was a well known fact now that the
long looked for command from the department of the Platt had been successful in forming a junction with our command for vague fears of apprehension
had been present with us that Sitting Bull had started to cut off the advance
and attack that little company of troops that we knew could not possibly expect to withstand the onslaught of the savage host and as we went into camp
that night on the upper waters of the Rose Bud there was many of [a] prayer
of thanksgiving went up for the deliverance of that little band which we knew
was coming from the department of the Platte but now when forming a junction with our troops composed a band of about 2,500 fighting men and several
pieces of artilery added.[10] Then a council of war was held and it was decided

that the command should take up the trail and proceed towards Tongue River
and farther, if necessary, in order to overtake the fleeing savages. Now commenced a long weary march over a desert plain. Forty miles without any water
in sight for man or beast, so accordingly canteens were filled and water kegs
and every receptacle that could be found that would hold water was filled and
we proceeded on the march. Every thing went well until about noon the second day when the dearth of water commenced to tell both on man and beast
and a good many men and horses fell by the way. Those who fell were picked
up by the ambulances and brought along but with parched lips and tongues
and fever stricken frames and toward the close of the second day we sighted
Powder River and it was a welcome sight for to see living water once more as
the whole command was about fagged out. We had followed the trail closely
from the battle ground which trail when leaving the battle ground was about
a mile wide trod hard as if a buffalo herd had been over the ground. Indians
could be seen every day on the mountain tops and along the high ridges flash-
ing looking glasses in our faces and seeming to mock us as we were on our
journey. Here is where Indian strategy had been handled to perfection. Little
bands had broken away from the main band or body of Indians scattering off
into the mountains as they proceeded toward the Big Powder River and that
was the last sight of any Sioux Indian. After striking Powder River and going
into camp next morning about 8 o'clock we proceeded to strike camp and proceeded down the river to what was then known as Powder River cantonment
or depot of supplies which had been established by General Terry.

In the winter of 1875 word was brought by a courier to Ft. Ellis that a party
of hunters and trappers was surrounded in a stockade at old Ft. Pease and that
several men had been killed in their endeavor to get away. Finally two men on
a dark stormy night made their escape from the stockade without being seen
and brought the news to Gen. Brisbane who was in command at Ft. Ellis at
this time and that immediate relief must be sent them or they would all perish
at the hands of the Sioux. On receiving this intelligence the wires was made
hot between Ft. Ellis and the War Department [from] which General Brisbane
received orders to immediately proceed with his command which were four
companies of cavalry to the relief of the besieged hunters. Starting from Ft.
Ellis about January 1st, in the dead of a northern winter, there was considerable suffering added to this movement but the boys in blue were used to this
kind of hardship and weather longing for revenge for the other depredations
which had been perpetrated upon a few of our outlying posts were things for

revenge and consequently with high spirits launched out into the cold winter on what proved to be a severe journey. Arriving at Ft. Pease none too soon for the hunters were about starved out and several had been killed before the troops had arrived.[11]

Arriving at Ft. Pease the little frost bitten command went into camp about 4 o'clock in the afternoon. Scarcely had the tents been pitched when stock foraging expeditions had already been started out and one Ingram who was noted for his detective qualities had somehow or other found his way into the cellar of the stockade and had discovered a barrel of "red Liquor" and had returned to the tent taking a couple of camp kettles with him—one in each hand proceeded to relieve the barrel of its contents or a part of it at least and it was not long before the boys in camp Custer had proceeded to use the antidote for frost bites and when a lively time ensued in camp but it was soon discovered by our officers that the men were becoming somewhat hilarious and an investigation was started and it was discovered that the men had found their way into the wine cellar of the post trader and had already relieved one barrel of its contents and not wishing to have the rank and file use quite all of this antidote they proceeded to store it away in a more secure place as the boys said "for their own use" but, of course you will see later in my narrative it is a hard matter to beat the boys who are our fighting strength for Uncle Sam. After a rest for three days order was given to strike camp and start for Ft. Ellis again taking along with us the besieged hunters. Being myself a fair teamster I was given one of the teams to drive and in this wagon the liquor was stored—that which remained—but the boys with a liking toward that thing which makes a man feel good were equal to the emergency and it was not long before they had one of these barrels drained by an ingenious device. After cutting an elder from the bank which is hollow and driving a little peg into the end of it taking a bit and brace cutting the bottom of the wagon bed and finding the direct location of the barrel and bored a hole up from the wagon bed into the barrel and then driving the reed into the hole in the barrel the problem was then solved as to how to get the liquor and where to get it. The officers soon discovered that the men were becoming hilarious in camp again and an investigation was started to find out where they got it and when the ingenious plan was discovered to get or procure this much longed for stuff and especially in the rigors of a northern winter, they found to their horror and shame that but one small keg was left when they proceeded to remove this from the wagon and put it as they thought in a more secure place, that is, placing it in their tent at the head of their bed but it could not, of course, remain in this secure place very long as the boys had discovered its whereabouts by the dent of the keg on the surface of the tent when all was asleep in the silent watches of the night they proceeded to mutilate the tent by cutting a hole through it and rolling the keg out and after the contents had been dispoiled the keg was rolled back into its place and the officers slumbered on but in the morning what was to their horror and surprise when they discovered that their morning nip before breakfast that is if they had any would have to suffice by simply a smell from an empty keg.

Of course, several of the boys were compelled to walk and lead their horses for the rest of the journey, yet, as they had outwitted their superiors and was only looking for another chance which did not come until after they had served their time in the guard house and got leave to go to town.

Alfred H. Terry Chief of Command

This general was over Crook, General Custer and Major Reno. General Gibbons commanded Montana troops. The orders to Custer were overheard by several at headquarters so that the soldiers knew what Custer's orders were that he was to go to locate the Sioux Camp and hold them in check until he formed junction with Montana troops and the troops of the Platte and then attack the force. When Custer came up on the south side of the Yellowstone, his scouts had been or seemed unfamiliar with that part of the country so one scout by the name of Mitz Boyer and Curly this scout was turned over to General Custer because it was a known fact that these two scouts knew the country. These scouts were given over to Gen. Custer from Gen. Gibbon's command because they were familiar with that part of the country and Mitz Boyer and Curly went in with Custer's part of the troops and Mitz Boyer was killed and Curly was the only one that had escaped alive from Custer's part of the detachment and he explained to us how he made his escape.[12] He pulled the blanket over his head and run toward the river and run through the Sioux camp down to the river and plunged into the river and swam down the little horn to the mouth of the Big Horn, then got onto the bank and made his way back to the mouth of the Big Horn and that is what I saw and when I saw him when I was on vidette that he wanted some one to come over for he had something to tell and he is the only live mortal to tell of Custer's last fight, as the monument shows on one side an excellent picture of the Sioux Scout leaning upon his gun the sole survivor of Custer's detachment.

Q. How far was Reno away when Custer's men fell.

A. It must have been one half mile or more perhaps. When the detachment was separated and Custer took his part and went to the upper part of the camp and Reno took his part and went to the lower part of the camp but when Reno attacked the lower end he found such odds that it was impossible for him to come against them. Taking into view this fact that he was going against such a force and he saw it was madness to try to break the savage line, he with a true generalship drew his men to a commanding position around the little knoll and while surrounded by the savages he entrenched himself as best as he could and proceeded to hold his position when it was an evident fact from taking a good observation from the camp as it was that if Reno left his position on that hill he would have left all his men there would not have been one left to tell the tale and all who have been there and looked over the ground say that it would have been madness for him to ever have left his position. In speaking of the battle and in talking with the Indians after the fight — years afterwards — when they become more familiar they said that at the time the battle begun that they did not need guns to have killed Custer's men that those big corn fed horses run back with the troops and that it was all they could do to handle them. They could have knocked them off their horses with their war clubs. A great many of Custer's soldiers were recruits from New York and never had been astride of a horse and the Indians called them pony soldiers and in my estimation Custer was to Blame. I believe that if he had obeyed orders we could have cleaned them out.

[Charles Clifford's Interview]

[Tablet 10]
Deer Springs, S.D., Feb. 4, '07. P.O. Kyle, S.D.

Charles Clifford, son of Henry Clay Clifford, deceased, says that ten years ago about a dozen Indians had a sweat at Kyle and he and his wife were present and heard a discussion among these Indians, a majority of whom were men who had participated in the Reno and Custer battles.[13] All of them but two sneered at the soldiers of the army as fighters. They were bragging of their exploits, and while the talk started out jocosely, in the end it grew to be very earnest and biting. They divided with the two on one side and all the others on the other side. The majority spoke of the two as women, as they said they had never fought anybody but soldiers, and it was a small matter to fight them. Yellow Horse was the one who did the talking for the two and defended himself and his fellow from the slurs of the braggarts, one of whom had said that Custer killed but one Indian, an old man. Yellow Horse said that five of them had stood off at one time the whole of the Crow nation when they occupied an advantageous position behind rocks. He cited this feat as proving they were not women. Then he went on to describe the fighting done by Custer and his men. This discussion was hot and fierce, and this is why Clifford believes Yellow Horse gave a truthful account. He hurled his statements straight into their teeth and they did not once dispute him. He gave an account of the Reno fight also, and said that if Reno had fought with the desperation that Custer did the Indians would have been whipped. Probably this was an excited [statement] and should be so considered. He said Reno began the action about sunrise. Reno, he said, did not offer much of a fight. He acted as though his aim was to get into a safe place. When his men went down over the bank in crossing the Little Big Horn a lot of them were lost. When Reno had got to the hills the Indians quit him on hearing by messengers whom he called "runners" that there was another attack. He described the appearance of the country—the hills and the valley of the River—as covered by swallows darting in every direction. He said you know that Indians do not go in any order—every man goes on his own account—in his own way; and the country was alive with them going in all directions like myriads of swallows, yet the great body all the time moving down on Custer.

(Yellow Horse was a Christianized Indian who did some preaching among his people, and was an intelligent man, and proved too much for his opponents.)

Yellow Horse's conclusion of the whole matter was that if Reno and Custer had attacked the village simultaneously from above and below according to the original plan, that the Indians would have been routed. His idea was that being in doubt as to the numbers of the troops and thrown into sudden confusion and assailed from opposite directions, that the Indians would have retreated from the valley. In the excitement of his argument he said that they would have been captured. There was everything in the situation, I will say, to assure and enspirit the Indians. They had met Reno and driven him back disastrously. They had put him across the river in disorder and with much loss. This was high encouragement to fight Custer determinedly. Reno's retreat was the beginning of disaster. He had not suffered materially before he ran away from the woods out into the open river bottom where he was fully exposed and passing a long distance with backs to the foe. The initial fault of the whole affair was Reno's failure to give the Indians a death struggle while his command was in the woods. If that had been done many of the Indians would have been obliged to confront Reno while Custer was gaining position and delivering his attack lower down. The resistance to him would not have been overwhelming. Benteen and the pack train would then have gone to Custer instead of being absorbed contrary to orders by Reno.[14] It was a miscarriage through Reno's cowardice. Reno could have gone to Custer if he had had any disposition to do so.

Yellow Horse said that the Indians lost eighty-three killed in the fight with Custer himself, and that Indians were dying from wounds for three weeks afterwards.

Reno got the Indians all awakened. Custer fought hard. The battle began by sunrise. The fight lasted till into the afternoon. Yellow Horse said he himself fought till he almost fell for want of water. The Indians suffered for want of water; some of them gave out because of thirst. The day was very hot. Mr. Clifford asked Yellow Horse at another time at Clifford's own house in regard to mutilation of the dead, and he said they were not mutilated, that is, the Custer men were not, except one man who had not been killed, and opened his eyes to get a little view, and a squaw was standing over him and noticing this crushed his skull with a club. The Indians had no time to mutilate Custer's men, for they went right away; but they took all their clothing and arms. They call Terry's column the "Big Outfit." They knew of the approach of this all the time, but Custer's column surprised them, and the old men and women began at once to flee. The Indians, as Yellow Horse told them, did not go at Custer in bodies, but they went into the fight, every man on his own hook, but they surrounded him at last. Yellow Horse said Custer fought and Reno did not; Custer went in to die, and his fighting was superb; he never saw a man fight as Custer did; he was conspicuous in the battle waving his sword and directing the men,[15] and making charge after charge, charging after he was surrounded, first with one body of his troopers in one direction, and then taking another body charging the Indians in an opposite direction; and so on in every direction he hurled troop after troop against the encircling enemy. When one body charged and turned to come back the horses of some of the returning troopers could not be stopped, but they ran in spite of their riders right into the Indians in the opposite direction to what the charge had been made, and then these riders were killed, while some Indians grabbed the horses by their bridles other Indians would either shoot the riders or club them to death, while others were pulled off their horses and killed on the ground. I never before had the true idea about the soldiers' horses running into the Indians and the riders being knocked off. Custer was making charges, and in returning the horses got momentum and ran right on into the Indians.

Some officer's voice could be heard a long time above the din; he was everywhere, waving his sword, charging like a giant; but after a time his voice was less heard; it grew shrill and less powerful under strain as the conflict raged on and on, and finally Yellow Horse heard it no more. Yellow Horse told those who were defaming soldiers that Custer could have done as Reno did, entrenched, made breastworks of his horses and saved himself; that he could have cut his way through the Indians in spite of them and, he said, "you know it;" the Indians would not stand and face the soldiers; of course, he said, Custer would have lost some men doing this, "but you know he could have led his command through the Indian line anywhere; that his charges were terrific and the Indians would not stand before him; but he was there to fight," and he fought as never Yellow Horse saw a man fight before.

Yellow Horse told these Indians that he was arguing against that there are no men they dread as they do the soldiers, because these will march right up into the heaviest fire and stop at nothing.

Yellow Bear said that the Indians quit the Custer field and went back to Reno; but at this time nobody was left in the Indian camp—they had all fled —old men, women and children—all the warriors did not remain investing Reno's position until the last—until evening of the next day; but they began early next day to withdraw in small parties, until evening of the next day not many warriors remained. These finally left. Some chief told them early that it was no use to fight Reno; that he was in an impregnable position, and that the "Big Outfit" would soon be up there. The Indians cleared out. No attack was made on Terry. (As some one has told me, I think Respects Nothing, some boys rode down to Terry's camp in the evening and did some foolish firing, and this has been called an attack).[16]

Yellow Horse emphasized this; that Custer did fighting; that Reno did none.

Yellow Horse told them that Custer kept his ground clear to the last; it is popularly believed that the Indians mingled among the soldiers and fought them hand to hand; but this is not so; Yellow Horse said that the Indians kept their distance; that Custer held them back; the soldiers kept them at bay, standing until all had been shot down but a handful when the Indians closed in. Even at the last one man—the last one—pushed through the Indian line and nearly escaped.

Yellow Horse said that when any soldier got out of his own troop he seemed to be unnerved; and when any were borne by their horses into the midst of the Indians they lost all courage and energy and were nerveless.

Yellow Horse further said that Custer could have rushed through the Indian line if he had so chosen and taken to an eminence as Reno did and saved himself. "We would have given way for him," said Yellow Horse "and you know it." He told them that Custer could have opened his way through them, taken to an eminence and fortified, and "all we would have done would have been to skirmish around him as we did around Reno; we would not have run up on him, and you know it."

Mr. Clifford says that it is in such ways as this—the Yellow Horse discussion—that we can get the truth from the Indians. They will not, as a rule, tell the story correctly; they keep back, conceal what is against them. All information goes to show that they are boastful of their prowess, and reserved and reticent as to things unpleasant to them.

[Edward H. Allison's Statements]

[Box 2]
State of South Dakota
Miner County

Edward H. Allison[17] being first duly sworn deposes and says: That in the year 1881 he was employed by the United States Government as Chief of Scouts for the Military Department of Dakota, then commanded by Brigadier General Alfred H. Terry with Head Quarters at St. Paul, Minnesota;[18] That he was ordered to report to General Terry in St. Paul, which he did on the 9th day of June of said year; That he was at that time and for some months previously had been engaged in negotiating and securing the return of the Sitting Bull Indians from Canada to their own country, and afterwards completed the transfer of said Indians. That he was summoned by General Terry to confer with him as to the disposition to be made of the Indians already surrendered and who were then under military guard at Fort Yates, Dakota. That he, the said Edward H. Allison having served many years under General Terry during which time he had been entrusted with many important duties which, together with those upon which he was then engaged, were always brought to a successful termination, by reason of which he found General Terry in a very complaisant and approachable mood. That he therefore took the liberty of saying to him that as there was dispute regarding General Custer's action at the Little Big Horn, some saying that he disobeyed orders, would like to ask for information on this subject, and for the truth of the matter, for his own personal satisfaction. That the General was sitting at his desk, and some papers were lying before him. Without any apparent design he placed his hand on these papers, spread them round with a nervous motion and then turning to him said: "I told General Custer that if he found the Indians too strong to warrant an attack, to simply hold them in view until reinforcements could reach him." He further says that General Terry added something about Custer's judgement in the matter, but that he does not remember his exact words.

Edward H. Allison

Subscribed and sworn to before me this 30 day of April 1907, J.[?]D. Bell Notary Public

Nat.' Mil.' Home, Kan. 1, 25, '06

My dear comrade:

Yours came this evening. I wish you could hear me tell the story of "Custer's Last Rally." You would then catch some of the fires of indignation which burn within me when I recall the story as told me by the Indians. How a brilliant victory was turned into a crushing defeat by the miserable, cowardly cur, Reno.

I could tell you more in two hours, and tell it better, than I can write in two weeks. I make no claim to ability as a writer, yet I have, in my eagerness to get the truth before the people in a way that would convince and satisfy, so that men would no longer ask "How in the world did it happen?" contemplated writing the story for publication. But now that you have begun the work, I will leave it to you, hoping that at last the mystery which has hung like a pall for 30 years over the valley of the Little Big Horn will be cleared away and the truth, however distasteful to some, told.

At the time of Custer's last battle in 1876 I was interpreter and chief of scouts under Gen. Wm. P. Carlin who was in command of the military Post at the Standing Rock Agency, 55 miles below Fort Lincoln, the Post commanded at that time by Gen. Custer.[19]

Fred Girard was Ree Indian interpreter at Fort Lincoln and accompanied the expedition.[20] I think he is still living. His address is Mandan, N. Dak. Word of the battle came to me at Standing Rock 7 hours before it reached Fort Lincoln through official channels via Yellowstone and Mo. rivers. It was this way: Early one morning a few days after the battle—after so many years I am not sure of dates—Chief Bear Face of the Hunkpapa band came into my office and sat down. I asked him if he had heard news from the field. His reply was evasive. He said that he had heard something, but what it was he could not fully understand. He said that a bird flew over a lodge in the night uttering cries of awful import. But not being a bird himself he could not of course understand the bird language. Of course I laughed at his ingenious evasion and tried to persuade him to tell me just what he had heard and how he had heard it, but he persisted in his statement, so I changed the subject and talked for a while on matters of local interest. At half past 7 I told him that I had an appointment with Gen. Carlin and if it would be agreeable he might go with me and shake hands with the General. An honor greatly coveted by the petty chiefs. He accepted the invitation with eagerness and we were soon in the presence of the commanding officer. Briefly as possible I told the General what the chief had told me about the mysterious messenger of portentious news and then told the Indian to repeat his story to the great white chief. He did as requested, whereupon the General flew into a violent rage, assumed of course, declared that the chief had deliberately insulted his intelligence by reciting such a silly story and demanded of him the truth, the whole truth and nothing but the truth, and that to be told then and there, instantly, or the consequences to the Indian would be something terrible. The ruse was successful. The Indian told all that he knew, how seven young warriors from S. Bull's camp on the Little Big Horn came into his camp in the night bringing a report of the battle, and after inviting all the fighting men of the nation to join them took their departure before daylight in the morning.

In 1879, 3 years after the battle I was transferred to Fort Custer, Montana, a post established soon after the battle and situated in the forks of the Big Horn river, 15 miles, if I remember rightly, from the battle ground.[21] Here I had an opportunity to study the battle ground thoroughly. I went over the ground with scouts, guides, Indians and soldiers who were there or near there at the time when the battle was fought and assisted in the burial of the dead after the battle. I was thus well prepared to intelligently receive the story as it was told me a year later by the very warriors who defended their village on the Little Big Horn in '76, and some of the most interesting incidents of the battle were told me by the women and children, hundreds of whom are still living and will retain a clear and vivid recollection of that awful day as long as they live. Their story should be heard and embodied in your work. It would be incomplete without it.

If you get a copy of "Surrender of Sitting Bull," that will tell you how it happened that I began the diplomatic service which ended in the surrender of Sitting Bull and his band of hostile Sioux in 1880–81.[22] It was while I was engaged in this work and much of the time domiciled with the Indians, that I heard the story over and over again a hundred times. That story I will endeavor to tell you as soon as I can find a suitable place to write. We will not get our pension here until about the 20 of Feb. so that I cannot promise any copy before that time. I receive a pension of only $10.00 per mo. The most of that goes to my halfbreed daughter who is widowed with a little son 4 yrs. old. She is teaching a district school this winter in Chas. Mix Co. S.D. but her salary is only $30.00 per mo. insufficient for support thro the summer months when she will have nothing to do.

As an inmate of the Home I could get half rates to Chadron, and I really believe you would find it well worth the cost to have me make the trip. We could visit the reservation, or I could bring Indians, men and women, with whom I am personally acquainted, to you in the city, so that you could have the story at first hand. And I can assure you there is not now living, and there never did live a man, White, half-breed or Red who can or could do as much with an Indian as I can. I have the honor to enclose copies of letters, one from Gen. P. H. Sheridan and one from Dr. W. J. McGee, which I will ask you to return.

I will submit a proposition for your consideration and such action as you may deem advisable. It is this: If you will pay my expenses and pay me $1.00 a day for my services for 30 days or less, I am ready to answer your summons. If you should find it necessary to keep me longer than 30 days in your service, you may then reduce my pay to 65 cents per day. I am willing to work thus cheaply because I am eager to have the work done.

Hoping that I may live to see the work issue from the press. I remain yours In F. C. & L.

E. H. Allison

Co. A.

Nat. Mil. Home, Kansas, Jan. 31, 1906.

Judge E. S. Ricker
Chadron Neb.,
My dear comrade:

Yours of the 28 inst. is at hand. Referring to the "proposition" in my last letter I will explain. I meant to say that I would visit you in Chadron and devote all of my time to your service for as long a period as you may find it proffitable, you paying my necessary expenses and a salary of $1.00 per day for 30 days or less. Further, if you found it desireable to retain me longer than 30 days in your service I will then accept the nominal salary of 65¢ a day and expenses. In further explanation of that letter I will say that the Indians brought back from Canada and surrendered by me to Maj. David H. Brotherton, Commanding Fort Buford, were subsequently brought down the river to Fort Yates, from which point they were distributed among the several Sioux Agencies west of the river, including Red Cloud and Spotted Tail, according to their tribal relationship.[23] Thus I meant that you should understand that I could bring Indians to you in Chadron from whom you could hear the story at first hand, or I could take you to their homes on either the Pine Ridge or Rosebud or any of the Sioux reservations. I could bring you face to face with the man who, with his own hand, slew Lieut. Harrington something like 2 miles down the stream below where Custer fell, for whose body a fruitless search was made at the time all the others were discovered, and whose young wife, it was said, was frantic with fear that the savages had taken him alive and were holding him for torture. His bones were found and identified by the gold filling in his teeth in 1884 in a deep ravine, where they had lain for 8 years since that awful day in June 1876. The story of Lt. Harrington's fate is a most pathetic one and filled with unusual interest from beginning to end.[24] As I have stated before, in 1876 I was serving as interpreter and chief of scouts under Gen. Wm. P. Carlin at Fort Yates, near the Standing Rock Agency. Soon after the Custer battle I purchased $100.00 worth of goods and trinkets, such as Indians prize and sent them by two trustworthy Indians to Sitting Bull's camp to be exchanged for plunder taken by the Indians. After an absence of several weeks the Indians returned and delivered to me 3 watches, a Hospital Steward's morning report book and $12.00 in money, a $10.00 and a $2.00 bill. All of these I turned over immediately to Gen. Carlin. One of the watches, a cheap silver case, was not identified at the time and I don't know that it ever was. Two were valuable gold watches both immediately identified by officers who were present. One had been the property of Captain Keough and was said to be worth $325.00.[25] This was uninjured. Of the other only the heavy, double gold cases remained. The works had been entirely removed. On the inside of the case was the inscription: "From Wm. Harrington, Philadelphia Pa. To his Son" &ct. So we knew then that Lt. Harrington was dead.

I suppose the watches were restored to the friends of the officers who had owned them. But I have never received as much as a penny, not even a thank you sir, to reimburse me for the cost of recovering the property. After mature reflection I suppose my name was not even mentioned in connection with the affair.

It was not until 4 years ago, in Oct. 1901 that I listened to the story of the killing of Lt. Harrington from the lips of the warrior himself who struck the fatal blow. The fact that the bones were found 2 miles distant and down the river from where the battle was fought and every incident of his fatal encounter as vividly described by the Indian forced upon me conclusions so pitifull, so pathetic, and with all so tinged with a suspicious dishonor that for the sake of possible living friends who loved him and honor his memory I have refrained from giving the facts to the public.

The name of the Indian who killed Harrington is White Bull. He lives on the Pine Ridge reservation. His story freely translated is substantially as follows: "After all the soldiers were killed I joined a number of warriors in making a thorough search of the surrounding country for possible fugitives, though none had been seen to escape. I rode swiftly down the river carefully scrutinizing the ravines and river bottoms and every probable hiding place until I came to a long stretch of table land, at the lower end of which I discovered a single mounted soldier. He was standing still when I first saw him with his face towards me. I kept under cover a little while and watched him. He seemed to be listening. Presently he moved forward a little way, halted again and again advanced as if undecided what to do. Thus he continued slowly to advance until he came within about 300 steps of the place where I was concealed when I suddenly rode out into his view. He was plainly startled but stood still facing me. He carried a rifle which rested across his saddle bow in front of him. He called to me, but what he said I didn't understand, and he lifted up his hands. I don't know what that was for. Did he offer me his blessing? Did he lift his hands to bless me? He had witheld it too long. I was not in a mood to receive anything at his hands. I was about to move forward and close with him when a warrior a little to my right and rear, who had that moment sighted the lone horseman, fired at him. He missed his mark but it put the soldier to flight. Turning his horse's head down stream he fled as fast as his jaded horse could carry him. My horse was comparitively fresh and I followed, gaining upon him rapidly. I was soon close upon him. I could easily have shot him as he fled before me, and at first that was my intention. But now I determined to club him to death. He kept looking back and talking all the time but of course I didn't understand what he said. I think he was trying to tell me that I was his elder brother. But he had chosen a bad day to make the relationship known.

"Suddenly he drew his revolver, emptied it into the ground and flung it away. Then while we were still moving as swiftly as our animals could go, he siezed his rifle by the centre of the barrel and proffered it to me. I was already upon him. I had clubbed my rifle which I held high in the air. Leaning forward I struck with all my strength. The blow fell upon the soldier's head and he plunged forwards to the ground. He was dead. His horse, his guns, his equipments, everything that he had was mine. I left him there, food for the hungry wolves."

This is the story as told by the Indian himself.

Now, what does this story reveal?

Simply this. Harrington run. There is no other possible explanation. It was his first baptism of fire and he was not equal to the ordeal. Your experiance in the civil war enables you to understand the conditions. And he ran upon the very first contact with the enemy at the riverside, before the Indians had crossed to the east side and before Custer had been forced back to the higher and open ground, else his flight would have been seen by the Indians. But protected by the bushes which grew along the bank of the river he escaped unseen. Beside himself with fear of a savage foe, a fear inherited, over which he had absolutely no control, a fear that has blanched the face and curdled the blood of many a veteran who, in a score of hard fought battles of our civil war had boldly stormed the works of a civilized enemy, he flew. Away, away, anywhere to hide himself from that awful hell of which he had had but one glance. A hell indeed, filled with painted fiends perfect in hediousness, while the air resounded with the demonical war whoop. He found himself at last a long distance away, down the river. He realized that he was alone, that he was not followed, that he was safe. Safe?! Safe?!! No! Poor boy! Though he live a hundred years he will never find safty. His conduct has placed him in peril more dreadful than death at the hand of a painted savage. He has come to himself. He reflects. "What can I say to General Custer?" "How can I explain?" "Oh! if only they have not missed me." "I must hurry back and rejoin my company." "It is better after all to die at the hand of an Indian than to live in disgrace." So for a little way he hurries back toward the scene of battle. In his mad flight he noted no land marks and made no rational estimate of distance, so that though he is still more than two miles away, he thinks he is near the place where he left his command. But he hears no sound of battle. (Custer lies cold in death.) He halts and listens, moves forward slowly and halts again. From here on White Bull has told the story as far as he knew. But there was a sad sequel. An awful ending is the story that White Bull never knew, which we find by resorting to the method employed by the hero of Sir Conan Doyle's detective stories. The Indian struck Lt. Harrington down near the lower end of the stretch of table land mentioned in his story. He says he left him there dead, food for the hungry wolves. The officer was not dead. Only stunned. After the Indian had stripped him and carried away the plunder he revived and undoubtedly, in a measure at least, regained consciousness. Instinctively he sought safty. Nearby was a deep ravine filled with a dense growth of shrubbery. Into this he crawled. But here we must draw a curtain over the scene. Imagination stands paralized in the presence of such awful suffering. What an atonement! What a penalty to pay for his boyish panic!

In conclusion I will say that I will, as soon as possible give you all the facts that I have learned relating to the battle of the Little Big Horn, and I am sure you will find them O.K.

I referred to Fred Girard of Mandan N.Dak. I never had any use for Frank Gruard, the Kanaker, a man utterly without principle, ready at any time to betray his best friend for a farthing.

I will have no money before the 20 of Feb. — to-day is the 1st, and I am out of smoking tobacco, stamps, stationary &ct, but not yet having furnished you anything of value I suppose I should not ask anything in advance. But there is no harm in telling you how I am fixed.

Yours in F. C. & L.

Co. A

E. H. Allison,

Feb. 2nd

P. S. A journalist of this city who writes for the N. Y. Herald and Harper's Publications whom I permitted, under the seal of confidence, to see this letter, urges me to withold it until he can communicate with his employers. He claims that the story is valuable. I disregard his advice, feeling myself in a measure pledged to you.

E.H.A.[26]

Nat. Mil. Home, Kan. March 7th 1906.

E. S. Ricker Esq., Chadron, Neb.

I am glad you got the pamphlet.[27] In reading it you will see that I had exceptional opportunities for accumalating facts. On the occasion of my first visit to S. Bull's camp in Canada I accepted an invitation to eat in Chief Gall's teepy. While eating I engaged the Chief in conversation which, after a while, turned upon the Battle of the L.B. Horn. The story about Rain in the Face had been published and by this time, 4 years after the battle, was fully established as part of the history of Custer's last battle. So I asked Chief Gall if it was true. He hesitated as if recalling the events of that awful day. Then turning to his wife as if for confirmation, he answered, "Why — no." "Was not he one?" this to his wife. "Yes, He was one of 17 young men whom I sent south to watch the movement of soldiers reported coming from that direction." (Crook's Command.) "They left camp the day before the battle and did not rejoin us until 5 days after the battle when we were moving north along the base of the Big Horn Mountains. No, he took no part in the battle." His, (Gall's) wife confirmed what he said. Later the Chief's statement was confirmed by many, among whom were Black Bull, Low Dog, Four Horns, Black Moon and Patriarch Crow, all leading warriors of the Tribe. Rain in the Face, upon his surrender, found himself famous. He gave confirmation to the fiction because it was a source of revenue. The same kind of people who carry flowers to condemned murderers in their cells were eager to shower quarters, halves and dollars on the man who (they supposed) killed Gen. Custer. So much for that story.[28]

Patriarch Crow or Kan-gi Ya-ta-pi, improperly interpreted Crow King, was a name of influence in the Tribe second only to Chief Gall, and absolutely fearless. For these reasons I cultivated his friendship and support. I often visited him in his lodge where I heard from him, his wife and his children and other men, women and children who were visiting there, the story of the attack at the upper end of the camp. I will repeat; as near as I can recall them, the exact words as I heard them. I asked if they were forewarned. If they knew the soldiers were coming. They answered: "We had heard that soldiers were approaching from the South, but they were reported so far away that we had no fear of them. We had no knowledge whatever of the approach of the soldiers who attacked us that morning. The very first intimation we had of the presense of an enemy was when we heard the report of fire arms and the whistle of bullets and the shriek of a woman who was wounded in the shoulder while standing near our teepy. Our horses were grazing away in the bluffs west of the camp. We didn't know how many soldiers were upon us" and of course the wildest confusion seized the entire village. The women seized their little ones and fled, screaming with terror toward the hills west of the camp. Those who had no children seized such valuables as they could carry and fled with them. One woman was so badly panic stricken that she seized a bundle of fagots brought to the lodge for fuel and fled with that on her back. So beside herself with fright that she imagined she was carrying away something of value. Sitting Bull's own wife had twin babies 3 weeks old, both boys.[29] She was so frightened that she forgot that she had twins. Seized only one and fled with it for the hills. She was almost to the hills when an acquaintance asked who had the other twin. She then realized what she had done. Passing the child she carried to her neighbor and ran back to her teepy and brought away the other twin. The one she carried away first was named Yu-ha Nan-pa-pi. The one left in the lodge was named Ih-pe-ya Nanpa-pi. The word Yu-ha means to have, to hold, to possess. The word Ih-pe-ya means to cast away, to abandon, to loose, Nan-pa-pi—They Fled. So there you have the names of the twins, Fled With and Fled and Abandoned, One [twin] Fled With, is still living and still bears the name given him on acc't. of that event. An unimpeachable wittness to the fact that the Indians were taken by surprise and that they fled in fear before the attack of Reno's command. Had Reno possessed half the courage of even a Chinaman he would have charged down thro the camp as Custer ordered, and he would have met with no opposition, for warriors, women and children all fled together to the hills where their ponies were grazing. Benteen would have swept down the valley on Reno's left flank and if need arose could have joined him in the central attack. Custer on the right flank would have struck the enemy lower down and the victory would have [been] complete. But what's the use of telling it all over again. We all know how Reno entered the timber and how he run. Run before he had lost a man. The Indians were running for their lives to the hills West of the camp when they discovered Benteen's advance. "There they come too!" they cried. Others looking back saw Custer's men moving down thro the bluffs on the East side of the river. "Yes and look yonder! the country is full of soldiers!" All this intensified their terror and accelerated their flight, so that if Reno had even held his place in the timber just a little while longer, and there was no reason why he shouldn't, the Indians would have continued their flight indeffinatily and Custer would have taken possession of their camp and being left with nothing but what they carried on their backs they would have been compelled to sue for peace.

The warriors looking back while they ran saw Reno in his reckless ride to the rear (For the first time in his life he led his command). The Indians wondered, and said to each other "See! The soldiers are running away. What can they be running from? Surely invisible allies have come down from the skyes and are fighting for us." And then they said to each other "What are we running for?" "Surely there is nobody fighting us," and they halted in their crazy flight, and turned on Reno, many had by this time reached their horses and came back mounted. The trouble's all over when you once get a man on the run. The Indians had a picnic sending Reno, who was joined by Benteen, to the East side of the river. Then realizing that they had nothing to fear from him they left perhaps 200 of their old men and boys with sawed off shot guns, muzzle loaders and flint locks to keep Reno scared to death while the entire fighting force, no longer panic stricken, but flushed with an easy victory rushed to the lower end of the camp which they saw was threatened by Custer.[30]

Comrade: I havn't time to write more to-night. I am sleepy and tired, will try and send you the story tho in fragments, badly broken at that.

Yours Fratly.

E. A. Allison

[No date]

Dear Comrade:

Louie Bordeaux has promised to come in and give me the story of Crazy Horse's death. I will write it down as he gives it.[31]

I think it is what you want. It corresponds with the impression I had received from other sources.

My stomach is not quite right yet. However, I am growing better.

I trust the enclosed [?] is what you want.

Yours in F:

E. H. Allison

Greenwood, S. Dak. May 7, 1906

Dear Comrade:

The number of men on my company roster ranged from 237 to 343. I had but one helper, a Seargent. You can imagine the work I had to do. Requisitions for all kinds of clothing for from 5 to 20 men every day but Sunday, besides requisitions for Co. property. Passes and applications for furloughs, passes and transfers, complaints and petty grievances to listen to, morning report to make out every day, and every Sunday I had to inspect some other Captain's Co. Oh! it's tiresome just to talk about it. And for all this I re'd. the munificent sum of $15.00 per month. My first month's salary I accepted and spent in riotous living without any concientious scruples; but after due consideration I refused longer to be a party to what appears to be a deliberate attempt by the distinguished managers of the National Homes to bankrupt the U.S. government and have it placed in the hands of a receiver. $15.00 per month! How long will it take to swamp the Treasury and force the government to fall back on the "gold reserve?"

I resigned and took a furlough for 90 days to be extended at my pleasure, and I am back here on the Yankton Sioux reservation.

I am glad enough to be back here too. I found my daughter and little grandson well and glad to see me again.

Let me hear from you. Comrade, I will get my wits together perhaps after a while, when I will be able to write you something worth reading.

Yours in F. C. & L

E. H. Allison

[Ricker's note on a single loose page. Box 24.]

Killed from 4 to 6 antelopes at a time for the fat, and with this fed his fires.

Scout Allison when on one of his lonesome journeys, traveling all alone through an extensive wilderness flanking the Missouri river on the north, a distance of three hundred miles, for seven successive days was drenched by the copious rains which spoiled his matches, found his ingenuity taxed to the utmost to make fires when necessity compelled him to have them. Tearing a piece from his wet handkerchief, he would put it under his arm till it was dry then holding it close to the muzzle, discharge his revolver and thus set it on fire. By blowing a blaze was produced, and a little careful management finally led to a cheerful fire.

[Edward S. Godfrey's Letter]

Edward S. Godfrey joined the army in 1861, and two years later entered the military academy. Lieutenant Godfrey was assigned to the Seventh Cavalry where he remained for thirty-three years. Godfrey won a Medal of Honor in 1877 in the battle at Bear Paw Mountain. He retired with the rank of brigadier general. General Godfrey died in 1932.

In 1896 Godfrey wrote the following letter in response to questions posed by artist Edgar S. Paxson. Paxson was gathering information for his painting titled Custer's Last Stand. *This and other Paxson paintings were displayed in the Montana state capitol.*[32] *Ricker misspelled his name as Papson.*

Ricker visited the Little Bighorn Battlefield in August 1906. While there he copied Godfrey's letter and interviewed Walter Tucker and F. E. Server.
[Tablet 7]
Extracts from the letter of Col. E. S. Godfrey to Mr. E. S. Papson of Butte, Montana, who painted a picture of the Custer battlefield for the Montana Capitol:
San Carlos, Arizona, January 16, /96
Mr. E. S. Papson,
Butte, Montana
Dear Sir:

Yours of Sept. 4 was forwarded to me and would have been answered long ago, but our recent move and the fact I have not had my property unpacked so that I could have access to my notes etc. It gives me pleasure to attend to your requests. When you refer to my article, I suppose you refer to the one published in the Century Jan. 1892, and later quoted by President Andrews in Scribner's Monthly, June, 1895.[33] I have consulted some of my comrades, of whom a few are left in the regiment, that took part in the engagement, as to details asked for. I would suggest that you correspond with Major H. J. Nowlan, 7th Cavalry, Fort Sheridan, Ills. for further details, especially as to the lay of the bodies, for he gave that matter particular attention and made a sketch showing the location at the time of the burial, and the following year superintended the removal of the remains.[34]

Your questions are answered in the order made.

1st Gen. Custer rode "Vic" into the fight (F. E. Server says "Vic" was a sorrel horse; the letter at this point is mouse-eaten; Server says the horse was found in Indian camp in British Possessions) X X X X four white feet and legs and a blaze face. (Godfrey says he has heard "Vic" was found in possession of an Indian in British Possessions.) The dogs were left with wagon train X X (mice-work).

2nd Gen'l. Custer carried a Remington sporting rifle, octagon barrel, two Bull Dog self-cocking English white handled pistols with a ring in the butt for a lanyard, a hunting knife in a beaded fringed scabbard; and a canvas cartridge belt. He wore a whitish gray hat with broad brim and rather low crown, very similar to the cowboy hat, buckskin suit with fringed welt in outer seams of trowsers and arms of blouse; the blouse was double breasted, military buttons, lappels generally open, turn down collar and fringe on bottom of skirt.

3rd Captain Tom Custer was dressed about the same as the General.[35] He was found near the top of the hill. North and a few yards from the General, lying on his face; his features were so pressed out of shape as to be almost beyond recognition (eaten by mice) X X X X not mutilated at all (eaten by mice) X X X on the ground the hands folded or spread over the body about over the stomach; his position was natural and one that we had seen hundreds of times while taking cat naps during halts on the march. One shot was in the front of the left temple, and one in the left breast at or near the heart. Boston, the youngest brother, was dressed similar to the younger [older] brothers;[36] his body was found about two hundred yards from "Custer Hill," between that and the Little Big Horn, at the foot of the ridge that runs up from the river, and as it were, forms the lower boundary of the battlefield. The body was stripped except his white cotton socks, and they had the name cut off.

4th. Yates, Cook, Smith and Reilly lay on Custer Hill and in the vicinity of the General but nearer the (mouse eaten)[37] X X X depression just north (?)

below Crittenden Hill and on the slope of the ridge that formed the defensive line furthest from the river; the body was stript, except the socks and these had the name cut off; in life he wore a Catholic medal suspended from his neck, it was not removed. All the officers wore the dark blue shirt with rather wide falling collar, which when the blouse was worn, was over the blouse collar; most of them had cross-saber and 7, like the old cap ornament; worked in white or yellow silk on the points of the collar. Yates, Cook, Smith, Porter and Calhoun, and some times Keogh, wore buckskin blouses, but I don't think any of them wore other than blue trowsers;[38] Harrington wore the blue blouse and white canvas trowsers, with fringe on the outer seams. The day was very warm and few had on any kind of blouse. (mouse eaten) X X X Sergeant Robert Hughes, Troop K, who carried the General's battle flag, was killed near the General on the hill.[39] Nearly all the men wore the blue, but many, perhaps most, of them had their blouses [trousers?] re-enforced with white canvas on the seat and on the legs from the knees half way up. Nearly everyone wore the short top boot (that was then uniform) not high like these now worn, although a few of the officers wore the Wellington boot and some had white canvas leggings.

5th. The command was armed with the Springfield carbine and the Colt revolver, every officer carried the revolver. No one carried the saber (nearly every illustration I have seen of that fight or campaign have officers and men armed with the saber. Adams painting of Custer's[40] (mouse eaten) X X X X Trumpeters rode grays X X X as a rule the officers were then X X X which they belonged X X X there were none X X X the dead horses and X X X field, but thickest on and X X X tufts of redish brown grass X X X soil depicts a scene of X X X bows down the heart in sorrow. I re X X sight. The early morning was bright as X X X X of the highest point whence the whole field X X X view with the sun in our backs. What X X X several as they looked at what appeared X X X X had a small canvas sack about 20 inches long in which was carried 12 pounds of oats, strapped on the cantel; there was no hood on the stirrups used by the men.

6th. There were no "Good Indians" left on the field at the time we saw it; they were all removed; our dead were alone! There were not so very many dead ponies found on the field, nor many dead horses, indeed surprisingly few, and most of them, were on or near Custer's Hill; it would seem that they were turned loose that the men might better defend themselves, or were wounded and broke away. The scene on the left (N. & E. of Crittenden Hill or near the point on the map marked "Spring") where the Indians stampeded the "led horses" of Troop I & L, must have been a (End of all of the letter I saw.)

[F. E. Server's Interview]

Ricker was on a trip to the Little Bighorn Battlefield when he talked to Server. The notes on this interview are scattered throughout the tablet. A more logical arrangement has been attempted here.

[Tablet 7]

Mr. F. E. Server was 18 years in the army—3 years in volunteer service during Civil war, and 15 yrs. in regular service. In the Volunteer service he was a member of the 7th Pennsylvania Cavalry but was on detached service all the time being an orderly first for General Franklin in the army of the Potomac and when General Sheridan succeeded to the command of the Cavalry he continued as his orderly to the end of the war.[41] It was on the advice of Sheridan and [George A.] Forsyth that he continued in the army.

He says it was "Sandy" Forsyth who commanded at Wounded Knee, and he was a brother to "Tony" Forsyth who fought at Beecher Island. Does not know how these men got their sobriquets. Knew "Tony" as he knew any officer of the staff; for "Tony" was on Sheridan's staff and he himself was Sheridan's orderly.[42]

Mr. F. E. Server was made First Sergeant of Troop G, 2d U.S. Cavalry, under peculiar circumstances [not explained], when he joined the command.

He says that after the war the riff raff of the Federal and Confederate armies went into our regular army and it became a desperately tough organization.

He approves what Scout Allison has written about his conversation with Gall concerning Rain-in-the-Face being in Custer fight.

He says that the Indians don't know who killed Custer—has heard Gall and Two Moons say so. When men are fighting with great desperation they do not know what is going on around them six feet away. It is impossible. They see only that closely in front. It is not like a stage play in a theater—it is no opera bouffe. Each man sees just what he is doing himself—little else; if he knows what everybody else is doing he is merely an on-looker, a do-nothing.

Mr. F. E. Server, Crow Agency, says that 310 dead Indians were left buried by the Indians. There were several buried on platforms, and three lodges were filled with dead and sewed up. Gen. Terry's Report shows this. Capt. Ball of Troop H, 2d Cavalry followed the Indians up the river a day and a half to track the natives and when he found that they had scattered in all directions he turned back.[43] He found over 100 dead Indians in this pursuit. His report showed this, Capt. Edward Ball, 2d Cavalry.

Lodge, Tepee and Wickiup Distinguished

In those days a lodge was accounted by the Indians to be a large teepe usually made by 24 skins. A teepe was a smaller habitation and made with about 18 skins. A Wickiup was the smallest and was a nondescript owing to its indefinite and uncertain size.

Says Terry's Report shows that Sergt. Becker or Decker of the Signal Corps with Terry followed Terry all through the campaign and with a two-wheel cart with an odometer attached, and drawn by a mule, he measured the extent of the Indian village which was 5 miles and a fraction long, and it covered the whole width of the River bottom which is a mile. Says it was the largest Indian camp ever on this continent in our day.

He is convinced that there were 7,000 at the very lowest fighting men and boys on the Ind. side. Thinks there might have been 10,000. He saw the whole camp of Indians after Terry's arrival. Terry opened with one Hotchkiss (rapid firing) gun and a Gatling on the Ind. camp on arriving and these guns scared the Inds. who fled precipitately leaving their camp which Terry destroyed. Thus Mr. S. knows the size of camp and can intelligently estimate their strength. Terry had four big guns, he says.

Mr. Server says that none of the men in Custer's party were mutilated, but those under Reno who were killed were shamefully mutilated—arms and legs cut off—heads cut off—in one case two heads tied together with thongs were thrown up over tent poles. There were no marks on any of the Custer party except such as were caused by the elements. He adds these reasons why the squaws did nothing to these men viz. the scorching sun of the 25th had beat down on the bodies all day; the night following a tempest of rain came, the night was black as ink (the hardest rain he ever saw) and the 26th was also a scorching rain; the bodies were bloated and offensive; the squaws were prevented by the conditions from mutilating the dead. The river was swollen too, which made crossing of it difficult and dangerous, and the Indians were on opposite side.

He says Gall has told him and others have, that he was at the lower end of the camp when the fighting by Reno began; that he did not want fighting and was trying to avoid it; but when he went up to where his tepee was and found his wife and child killed his heart turned to stone.

Gall and Two Moons and others have told Server how the fight with Custer began.[44] They told him ten years afterwards, when there was an anniversary gathering of the officers of the 7th Regiment on the battlefield, and they had got Gall and Two Moons and other prominent Indians to attend. Mr. Server is a good interpreter. He was also a sergeant in his command. Custer was moving down the river to cross. He had not yet tried to cross. Instead of going on down past where the buildings now are and following where the road leads down the canyon towards the Crow Agency on to the flat and reaching the river by that route, he turned down from the ridge at Custer Hill where the Monument is and followed the deep ravine thence to the River, supposing that he could make a crossing there. When he reached the outlet of the ravine he found that it was several feet to the water and his horses could not get down. At this instant Gall with his followers coming down the river from the south, after having withdrawn from Reno, finding that he had taken final position on the hills, came up, and Two Moons with a strong party came up the river from the north at the same time, an unfortunate conjuncture for Custer. Here 12 of Custer's men were suddenly killed, not having had time to fire a shot themselves, and these were the only soldiers with the general who did not have any empty shells to show that they had attempted to do execution. There were headstones put up here but the erosion by the water has cut them away and all have disappeared. Custer fell back up the ravine.

Mr. F. E. Server says that the reason that Two Moons came up the river and met Gall and Custer at the discharge of the big coulie was that the Indians were coming up in a grand sweep around and in rear of Custer Hill.

He thinks the line between the Crittenden-Calhoun Hill and Custer Hill must have faced north or northeasterly, possibly faced both ways, that is, some men shooting southwesterly toward the summit of the ridge while others fired toward where is now the line of cemetery fence, running approximately northwest and southeast. These might and probably did direct their line of fire obliquely to the left at first to strike the advancing foe squarely in the face as he came up from the north on the northwest and north flanks of Custer Hill. The topography of the region and the marble monuments disclose as distinctly as any grim and silent evidence can that the heroic little command was surrounded and overwhelmed by tremendously disproportionate numbers.

(He says that by actual count there were from 12 or 14 to 68 empty shells left by the troopers. The lowest found was either 12 or 14—he is not sure which—

and the highest 68.) The Indians themselves say that Custer's ammunition gave out; then they were merely helpless victims of fury and fate, there not being a sabre in the command.

Frank Grouard

Mr. F. E. Server says that he was thoroughly well acquainted with Frank Grouard; that Frank could not write his name; that he was not to blame for DeBarthe's lies; that DeBarthe told lies in the Grouard book to give it savor; that he heard DeBarthe admit this fact in a little quarrel that Grouard had with his historian when Grouard complained because of the story of his visit to the Custer battlefield, and DeBarthe said he had put that in fictitiously. Grouard accused him of other falsehoods. Server says DeBarthe lied when he stated that he had almost superhuman difficulty to induce Grouard to submit to be written up.

He says that Grouard died a practical pauper and was buried the same as in the potter's field.

Custer Again

Custer's horses were held after the men were dismounted in the (almost) north and south coulie (give dimensions) at a right angle to Keogh's eastern flank (not knowing which way he faced it is not competent to say on which — right or left — flank). The horses were huddled together in this safety-spot, the only one on the now circumscribed field. They must have been packed in like livestock on shipboard, for this retreat was _____ yards long, _____ yards wide, with very steep sides, the rims _____ feet above the bottom.

Mr. Server says the battle began about nine in the morning. He is sure it was fought in the forepart of the day.

(To write the history of the Custer disaster with strict regard to truth is a perplexing difficulty. It is enough to know that no amount of industry and no degree of conscientiousness conjoined can ever produce a complete and accurate account of that affair.)

F. E. Server says:

That in the fight with Lame Deer and Iron Star, Gen. Miles was not present till the fighting was all over, though it was Miles' command which overcame the Indians. Miles was behind with the infantry. His A.A.G. was with the cavalry which was F, G, H, & L troops of the 2d Cav. Lame Deer and Iron Star had surrendered and were disarmed. Miles on coming up engaged in the hand shaking described by David L. Brainerd on page 335, Brady's book. Mr. Server was present and saw the whole affair. He says Brainard's statement that Lame Deer shot at Miles is a mistake; that an Indian behind Lame Deer drew up his gun and shot at him. He says that Brainard was a corporal under him (Server). Now Brainard is Colonel in Commissary Dept.[45]

Mr. F. E Server says of the changing of the Crow Agencies: The treaty of 1866 or 67 or 68 (the Laramie treaty) fixed the middle of the Yellowstone river as the northern and western boundary of the Crow Reservation; the line between the present Wyoming and Montana, and the eastern line ran to the Wolf mountains in Montana.[46] The first gold & silver discovered within the Crow Reservation was at (principally) Cook City, Emigrant Gulch and Bear Gulch; these names were given to the places after the miners came and made discoveries. At that time the Agency was at a place called Mission Creek, abt. 12 miles east of where Livingston now is.

As soon as these metals were found white greed raised a howl for the country, and a commission came to treat with the Indians for the land. A pow wow was held and the poor Crows sold this mineral land for agricultural land at $1.25 per acre, the western boundary now becoming Bridger Creek, they giving up the lands between Bridger Creek and the Yellowstone; the Crows had before this sale a piece of the Yellowstone Park. The Agency was then moved down to the junction of the Stillwater River and Rosebud River (both are only creeks).

The next event was discovery of coal in the Clark's Fork country and the whites then wanted that and got it by treaty for $1.25 per acre; then the agency was moved to the present place on the Little Big Horn.

The Little Big Horn was not known by any name but Little Horn until it came out in Boots and Saddles as Little Big Horn.[47] It was called by the Indians Little Horn from a deer's and antelope's horn which is small. The Big Horn was named for the Elk's Horn which is a large horn. The Yellowstone river is named for the gold rock found in it by the Indians.

The Mandans are practically gone, but quite a number are scattered around, some being now on the Crow Reservation.

Blackfoot was chief of the Crows when Mr. Server came to this country in 1869 (July 4), came from Camp Douglas at Salt Lake City where he soldiered 6 months. Blackfoot was then abt. 50 yrs old.[48] The Crows split under him. Old Two Belly arose and wanted to be chief instead of Blackfoot, but he was not smart enough, so he took what followers he had, abt. a third of the tribe and moved north to the Missouri river near the British possessions, to the Cow Island country (this name lost its identity long ago); they were migratory, not remaining anywhere absolutely; there was but one Agency; Two Belly's Indians had to come to the Blackfoot Agency.

These Crows at the Crow Agency have now lost the Crow designation and are known as Black Lodges. After Two Belly went off these were called River Crows.

Blackfoot stood 6 feet 4 in. in his moccasins, & he was built proportionally from the ground up, straight as an arrow, splendid specimen of humanity physically and mentally, a grand orator, the greatest the Crows ever had, a wonderful orator his gestures surpassed in grace any Frenchman or Spaniard. He died abt. spring of 1875. In 1872 the first delegation of Crows went to Washington direct, thence to Baltimore, Philadelphia, New York, Boston, Buffalo, to Pittsburg, Harrisburg, again to Washington, thence to Cincinnati, Chicago, Omaha and home. Mr. Server was sent as a soldier with them. The trip was a tour to impress the Indians. The bear episode was at Walnut Street theater.

The president, U. S. Grant gave an audience to the Indians in the Blue room. Blackfoot made a speech, also Iron Bull, Two Belly, Old Crow. Blackfoot made an address that caused the audience to open their eyes; a good many public officials were present; the room was full of people. He was a man of strong character which was written all over his face.

Moran (the artist) painted a picture of Blackfoot.

Jim Bridger

Died at the mouth of Bridger Canyon on his ranch abt. 5 miles N.E. of Bozeman. He was buried by the U.S. troops at Fort Ellis, 2d Cavalry, under command of Col. Eugene M. Baker, a great Indian fighter who wiped out the Piegans. Bridger lived on the north side of the Gallatin River and Bozeman lived on the south side. The two men were great friends.[49]

Mr. S. thinks Bridger first died. Bozeman was also buried by troops of the 2d Cav.

Mr. Server says the name of the sergeant who was posted on the left west of Calhoun Hill was Shaughnessy. He thinks it was this: See the name in the list on monument.[50]

Crow Census

Mr. F. E. Server says he helped take the first census of the Crows in 1869 and there were then over 4,700. His part of the work was to tabulate returns of enumerators. The census is now taken yearly. In 1906 the census shows 1,830 Crow Indians.

Dog Soldiers

Were the same as the police of a city, and the Chief of the Dog Soldiers was the same as the Chief of police. The Dog Soldiers had charge of the camp; they said when the camp should be moved and when and where pitched, and attended to the tribal discipline and kept order and enforced the laws. The Chief of the Dog Soldiers was generally the War Chief of the tribe. Each tribe had its own Dog Soldiers.

In 1877 the Custer battlefield was surveyed. Uncle Dave Mears assisted in the work. The bones of the dead were collected and deposited in an excavation on the top of Custer Peak (Mr. W. H. H. Garritt tells me that Custer Peak is the official designation) immediately S.W. of where the monument stands. They were covered and a monument of wood piled in pieces was raised over the sepulcher. In 1879 the present monument of granite was erected. A new crypt was made N.E. of and as close to the old one as it could be digged; this was floored and walled with stone and cement; a stone collar was placed around the top, drawn in so as to diminish the size of the opening at the top; inside of this was placed in a box or coffin the remains of the soldier "Kid" Holcomb of 11th Inf. who was shot when painting the tablet marking the spot where one of the officers fell, and the bones of the dead were transferred and the base of the monument was laid over, all in cement, completely closing the aperture, and above this the monument was reared. The monument is abt. 12 feet high from the ground & is a heavy, durable structure. Accursed vandals so chipped and defaced it that it had to be re-dressed and the names upon it re-chiseled.

"Kid" Holcomb was shot in 1879. His remains, in a coffin, were put into the crypt with the bones of all.

Mrs. Server tells me that she was on the field in 1877 when the bones were gathered together, that they were lying either on top of the ground or partly in sight and pieces of clothing, accouterments, cans which constituted part of the soldiers' outfit were scattered over the field so that it looked like an unclean backyard.

Mr. Server says that Crook's camp on Goose Creek was about at Beckton, some 15 miles south of Sheridan, Wyo.

[Walter Q. Tucker's Interview]

[Tablet 7]

Dr. Walter Q. Tucker says that the creek which Godfrey calls Reno Creek is rightly called Medicine Tail and the one which he marks as Benteen Cr. they call up at Crow Agency Reno's Creek.[51]

He says that H. M. Mechling who got a medal for going down to get water, piloted Dr. Tucker, Col. Grover, Mr. Burgess, the missionary at the Agency to the field 2 yrs. ago, and pointed out where Custer camped before he came on to the Little Big Horn, & where Custer made his disposition of troops.[52] Up about 7 miles from the mouth of Reno Creek Benteen broke off to the left; somewhat nearer down Custer broke off & went over by the neighborhood of Custer Butte, & he says Mechling told them that Custer and his scouts might have gone up on Custer's Lookout. He said Custer was in the habit of pitching camp and then taking his scouts and riding around over the country and taking observations.

[Archie Smith's Letter]

[Tablet 48]

Extract from a letter written by Archie Smith to his "Folks" at home after his visit to the Custer Battlefield.

A quarter of a mile to the southeast of the custodian's residence is the monument, at the extreme north end of the ridge which divides the field. Right in the shadow of the monument on the west slope is where Custer made his last stand; and from there down toward the Little Horn are scattered the marble slabs which indicate the line of march as the leader struggled to get back on to the high ground, upon meeting the horde of redskins who unexpectedly rose up before him from out of the gulches below.

To the south of this line of march, the west slope is sparsely dotted here and there with stones, singly and in pairs. It is supposed these mark the spots where fell the horseholders. After starting down the west slope part of the band dismounted, one man out of every four remaining in the rear to hold the horses. The Indians encircled the advance, cutting off the unmounted steeds from the main body, and with their demonical war-whoop frightened and scattered them to the south, the few widely separated slabs telling the sad story of the troopers' unsuccessful efforts to check the frantic animals.

It seems that when Custer started down the hill he sent a detachment southward along the east slope, out of view of the Indians, which was to swing around and assail them from their rear. But the Indians drove them back over the crest of the ridge, and huddled together in the southeastern section of the field about the cross which shows where Captain Keogh fell I counted 28 of the marble slabs.[53] Beyond a gully forty rods to the east stands one lonely stone far from all the others, the one to which the pamphlet refers as being that of the trooper who tried to escape; he was almost over a little ridge out of sight of the savages. From the spot where Keogh died, angularly up the slope, in a northwesterly direction, is a promiscuous dotting of the marble stones, mostly in pairs, fewer and fewer as they approach the site of the monument, indicating the heroic effort to reach the ill-fated leader. The nearest is that of Kellogg, the New York Herald correspondent,[54] who almost reached Custer; a little farther away I noticed a cluster of six pairs, and, altogether, strewn along that eastern slope I counted some ninety stones. X X X X X X

Of course there is a certain amount of mystery surrounding this event, and, as the Indians told many conflicting stories part of what I have written is the "interpretation of insensible records." I gleaned it from conversation with the custodian, a very sociable old veteran whom we pumped both before and after going upon the field. X X X
Archie Smith.

4. Beecher Island

[Allison J. Pliley's Letter]

*Allison J. Pliley was seventeen years old when he came to Kansas
in 1861. He worked for a company hauling freight across northern
Kansas to Denver. During the Civil War he enlisted in the Fifteenth
Kansas Cavalry.[1] Pliley's experience made him a prime candidate
for Maj. George A. Forsyth's civilian scouts. Their objective was to
harass the Indians in western Kansas to prevent them from raiding white settlers.*

*Pliley and John J. "Jack" Donovan left Beecher Island to find
help for the besieged scouts.*

Ricker made the following notes at the end of Pliley's letter.

[Tablet 6]

[Pliley's letter was] copied October 29, 1905, from the original document
which was lent me by John Donovan son of Jack Downing [Donovan]. The
original is the property of the Beecher Island Memorial Association.[2]

The "Annual" of the association was prepared by Robert Lyman of Wray,
Colorado, or Beverly or Salina, Kansas, who is one of the Beecher Island de-
fenders. Others of the same heroic band are J. J. Peate, lumber merchant, Kansas City; _ _ _ S. Schlessinger [Sigmund Shlesinger], cigar dealer, Cleveland,
Ohio.[3]

Miss Alice Donovan, daughter of Jack Donovan, is a clerk in the drug department in the Denver Dry Goods Store. She and her mother now live at 573
Evans St., Denver. _ _ _ Donovan is a clerk in the Burlington Freight office at
1900 16th St., Denver. Miss Alice unveiled the monument at Beecher Island,
September 17, 1905, on the 36th anniversary.

Statement by A. J. Pliley one of the Forsythe Scouts at Beecher Island

To the Beecher Island Battle Memorial Association, Wray: In view of the approaching unveiling of the monument to the memory of the dead and surviving members of the Forsythe scouts who stood between the defenseless settlers of our frontier and the bloodthirsty and relentless savages.[4] It may not be amiss for me to relate some of my recollections of that bloody struggle, since named the battle of Beecher Island, skipping the many marches and incidents that finally on the evening of the 16th of September, 1868, found the little band of scouts in camp near the fateful island.[5] I will pass over the thrilling scenes of the next day, at the dawn of which commenced one of the most bitter and stubbornly contested fights, considering the numbers engaged, it was ever my fortune to witness; (and up to that time I had participated in many a forlorn hope) and relate to you the experiences of myself and my brave, patient and big-hearted comrade, Jack Donovan: and wherever he may be, dead or alive, my heart goes out to him in love.

As you remember, Donovan and I, in response to a call from Forsyth for two volunteers to go to Fort Wallace for re-inforcements, on the 3rd night after the fight commenced, after changing our boots for a pair of moccasins apiece, which we took off of two dead Indians, in order to make as light a trail as possible; and after filling our pockets with tainted horsemeat, we bid a silent "so long" to our comrades and started to crawl down along the north side of the island, stopping frequently to let a party of the Indians, who had the island surrounded, pass by.

After getting outside of their lines we straightened up and, taking our course by the north star, started on our long and weary walk; and we soon found we had made a mistake in putting on moccasins. In crawling away from the island they got wet and the cactus thorns which was very plentiful went through them into our feet like pins in a cushion.

That night's walk took us not quite across the divide, and we hid away in a buffalo wallow, laying there all day in the hot sun without water, eating that rotten horse meat in order to keep up strength to make the trip. About 3 o'clock P.M. our attention was drawn to a party of 25 Indians coming towards us from the south—coming straight towards us as you could point your finger—10 minutes more and they would be upon us. We got our cartridges where we could get at them, and prepared for the closing acts of our lives. When they got within a ¼ of a mile of us they halted, and after a short consultation they bore off to the northwest and past us without seeing us. Jack who was always light-hearted in danger, commenced singing: "Oh for a thousand tongues to sing!" After dark we again took up our weary walk—footsore and almost famished for water. About 12 o'clock that night we struck the south fork of the Republican. After spending an hour drinking, and bathing our sore and swollen feet, we hurried on our mission. It appeared that every hour added more thorns in our feet and more pain from those that were already in them, until it seemed impossible to go on; but the thoughts of our comrades who depended upon us spurred us on. When we started from the island we laid our course to hit the Smoky Hill stage route at Cheyenne Wells, and on the 4th night out at 3 o'clock we struck the road at a ranch about 3 miles east of the wells. Our feet were a sight to look at—swollen to twice their normal size, festered with thorns pro-truding out of the numerous festering pimples on them—tired out, sick from eating the putrid horse meat, and drinking warm water, we were indeed hard lookers when we aroused the ranchmen and explained to them where we were from, and what we wanted, which consisted of a little whisky, something to eat, and a chance to lay down and sleep with their promise to wake us when the stage to Wallace came along: all of which they cheerfully complied with, waking us about 6 o'clock, and we had no trouble arranging terms with the driver for our passage in to Wallace. And within less than one hour after we reported to the commanding officer every available man at the post was gallop-ing to Forsyth's assistance.[6]

Donovan went with them as guide. That night I was sent with a message to Gen. Bradly at the mouth of the Frenchman's fork of the Republican river. I struck his command at 8 o'clock the next morning, and in a few moments his command was hurrying to Forsyth's assistance. I then returned to Wallace. And I will here say that Donovan and I beat Stillwell and Trudell (Trudeau) (this name not plain) who left the island two nights before we did, on the same mission, into Ft. Wallace by about one hour.[7]

Hoping to be with you next September on Beecher Island, I remain your comrade,

A. J. Pliley

Late Forsyth Scouts.

[John J. Donovan's Letter]

[Tablet 6]

Letter from J. J. Donovan of Los Angeles, California, brother of Jack Donovan. Transcribed from a copy of the same which was lent to me by John Donovan and his sister Alice Donovan, son and daughter of Jack Donovan, but in October, 1905, in Denver.

(Copy)

936 Ramona Ave.

Los Angeles, Cal., June 25, 1905.

My Dear Nephew:

You wrote Ella in regard to your father's trip from Beecher's Island to Ft. Wallace for reinforcements. I have heard him say that the third night of the fight Colonel Forsyth called for volunteers to carry a dispatch out through the Indian lines, as he feared Stilwell and his partner had failed. So John and A. J. Phyley (Pliley) were chosen out of the men that offered their services. John was known to have a very strong constitution and knew the country and would not have to follow creeks and trails and could take a short cut. Plyley (Pliley) was brave and was the man that was considered to be the best shot on the plains, but was not quite so strong as John. John said that the first night that they had a hard time trying to steal through the picket line, but they soon made up their minds that they could not steal out, so they concluded to fight their way out or die in the attempt. They were up near the head of a little draw and a big Indian was walking and his beat was directly in front of them. They concluded to shoot and then instead of running out over him they would just run back down the draw and go through the line a little way from there, as the Indians would run to their comrade's assistance and would naturally look for their enemy to go out over his beat. John and Plyley got out by that trick and made about fifteen miles before daylight, on foot. They had no horses and had to travel by night and hide all day. They had nothing to eat either. The next night they made better time, but the next day were close to a band of Indians nearly all day and were in fear of the dogs finding them and leading the Indians to them. Plyley said he wished the Indians would find them, as he never expected to go through with his sore feet, and as he told John he would rather die fighting, and he said to John: "You know I could not miss them." But John would never say die and told Plyley they would go through all right and bring back the reinforcements to their comrades on the Island. Plyley and John separated the fourth night,

John going to the stage road and caught the stage in to Ft. Wallace and told the news. Stilwell had got to the Fort that Bankhead was at and Bankhead had sent a dispatch to Colonel Carpenter to go to the battleground, but Carpenter had no guide and John knew he had a poor chance to find Forsythe and he feared they would all be dead before help found them, so he determined to go back and guide him to the Island.[8] There was nothing in camp but work mules and John mounted one of them and with a sack of hard tack started to trail Carpenter. He soon seen Carpenter was going wrong and rode night and day to catch him and turn him toward the Island, which he did, and Carpenter moved as lively as he could, but John was always ahead on his old work mule which proved to be a good one. Carpenter would ask him to go slow, as the ambulance mules with supplies and medicine could not keep up. Carpenter doubted John's ability to guide him right but followed, and John told him they would find a dead Indian right over the next ridge and they then [knew] that John was right. John rode on ahead and as he came in sight over the ridge the guns of the scouts on the island were trained on him in an instant, as they first thought him an Indian, but he rode down to them, and he said he would never forget the sight. The men came dragging along up to him to shake hands. They were more dead than alive but they said they knew Jack would come back.

Now to my mind John's brave and unselfish nature shone out at its best when he saddled that work mule and started back into the heart of an Indian country on a work mule so as to take no chance on not getting reinforcements to his starving comrades in battle. Most men and even brave men would not have started back in John's condition on a poor mount especially. I heard John say that he had nothing to eat except a little piece of bacon the size of his two fingers, that he had used to grease his gun with. He was seven days without food.

I hope you will come out and see us sometime. You know that you, or any of John's children, would be most welcome. We are all well here and I hope this will find you all the same.

Your Uncle, J. J. Donovan

Letter from D. Donovan of Los Angeles, Cal. to his nephew John Donovan of Denver. John Donovan was the son of Jack Donovan, the hero. D. Donovan was a brother of Jack Donovan. This letter is in the original handwriting of D. Donovan, and it was lent to me by John Donovan in Denver in October, 1905.

(Copy)

Los Angeles, Cal. 7-4-05

John Donovan

Denver, Colo.

Dear Nephew

I read with pleasure your letter of June 6th to Ella and in reply to your request write what I know of your father's trip from Beecher Island & return to the rescue of Forsyth. The battle began on the morning of the 16th (17th) of Sept. and your father stayed and fought until the night of the 18th (19th), then with a comrade whose name I think was Sam (A. J.) Plyley (Pliley) he started out for reinforcements. The Indians were very thick round close to the Island and it took them several hours to get past the first lines of pickets and when they had reached a point about two miles from they (the) Island they ran up against another and closer line of pickets and a large camp of warriors. They skirmished round for sometime to find a weak place in the picket line but failed to do so and finally concluded they would have to break through that line or die. Plylie was one of the best shots on the plains at that time. He had plenty of courage and experience, and your father gave him the credit for the plan that carried them through the line. The camp was on a table land near the brow of the table land overlooking the valley and the Island, and your father and Plylie chose a point near the camp to break through the picket line. The plan was to crawl as close to the picket as possible, and in case of alarm to be sure and kill the picket so he could not keep them in sight. The picket line was along the edge of the table land, and this a sharp raise with gullies running up and down its surface. They chose a point about one hundred yards from the camp and stole as close as they could to the picket; he saw them and gave a sharp cry of alarm. Your father was within twelve feet of him and shot him with a 52 caliber Spencer carbine. He fell like a log. Then your father, and Plylie dropped just below the brow of the cliff and ran a short distance toward the camp and hid in a gully, while the Indians from the camp ran past them going to the place of alarm. Then as soon as the bunch of Indians had gone by, your father and Plylie ran through the camp and passed the Indian line where by daylight they had secured a hiding place for the day. Here they separated, your father going to Fort Wallace, while Plylie went to Fort Hayes. Two scouts Stilwell and Truesdell had gone out from the Island on the night of the 16th (must be 17th, if on the first night), and your father and Plylie went out on the night [of the] 18th. Stilwell and Truesdell reached Fort Wallace at 10 P.M. on the 22nd, and your father reached there two hours later. On Stilwell's arrival at Fort Wallace Col. Bankhead had ordered out all the cavalry, and started out immediately with Stilwell as guide to go to the Island. He had also sent scouts to find Captain Carpenter who was out with two companies of cavalry, with orders to go to the rescue of Forsythe. So when your father arrived at the Fort it was abandoned as far as available men or horses were concerned. Now I hope you will impress the balance of this letter on the reporter, as all the reports I have seen either overlooked or misrepresented this part of the performance and it shows better than any fight could, the real character of your father. He had three days of hard fighting and four days and nights of tramping with scarcely anything to eat. He wore moccasins, and as he walked in the river the first night and they got wet, they were worn out, and his feet were in pitiable condition. Under these conditions I believe any other man would have stayed at the Fort, but he would not stop until he knew these men were rescued. He learned from the Post Adjutant where Carpenter's Command was supposed to be scouting. He secured a mule from a government train and two hours after his arrival at the Fort found him riding on his return to the Island; and although he made a detour of about thirty miles off of a straight line, he made the return trip to the Island in 34 hours from Fort Wallace, reaching there nearly a day ahead of Col. Bankhead, after having found Col. Carpenter. I believe his trip on this occasion should show that he had as many points of a real hero as any man of whom history shows any authentic record.

Hoping this will find you well, I remain

Yours truly,

D. Donovan

[Beecher Island Veterans' Interviews]

Ricker attended a reunion of Beecher Island veterans and their families and friends in 1908. It offered the opportunity to interview some of the scouts.

[Tablet 42]

Reunion at Beecher Island 1908. Interviews with 6 of the Scouts, Pliley, [Thomas] Ranahan, [Elijah A.] Gilbert, [George] Green, [Howard] Morton and [James J.] Peate.

Beecher Island, Yuma Co. Col., Sept 17, 1908.

Elijah A. Gilbert, one of the scouts who fought on this ground 40 years ago to-day being interviewed by me while traversing the locality and pointing out the important locations, says:

The river as at present has filled in on the north side west of the present bridge forming a new bottom 3 or 4 rods wide & about 10 rods long, so that this branch of the river was then some six rods wide, whereas now it is not more than three. The north bank was about five feet high.

Louis Farley & [G. B.] Clark & [Frank] Harrington who were on the north bank took their horses to the Island & then returned to the north side & took places in little ravines in the bank which for shelter & remained there all the first day. These ravines have disappeared. Farley had position about a rod west of his companions, and the three were due north of the monument.

John Wilson was the guard at the northwest corner of the camp on the north side of the river; his post was north & a little west of the monument; he was the guard that gave the warning that Indians were coming at daylight & the one that Forsyth says he was with. He stood not more than 100 feet from the camp, & when he fired his piece to give warning, the Inds. were so close that they [were] almost in the camp.

Morton & Pliley fix the location of the camp farther east than Gilbert does.

Gilbert says the morning surprise party of Inds. came right over the little ridge just west of the camp & swept past the camp close to the north side of it yelling & rattling their rawhides. The horses were picketed in among the scouts; Gilbert's picket pin was right where he slept and he was close to the second bank & his horse could go down over the bank & graze on the lower bottom where grass was ranker.

The charging Inds. passed the camp. The scouts poured shots into them; they swung a little to the north but went right on down and up on to the hill N.E. of the camp & just east of the ravine where Pliley & Morton say that the daylight charging party came down & swept up stream instead of down stream as Gilbert avers.

George Green, one of the Beecher Island Scouts of Sedrowoolley, Washington, being interviewed by me this 18th September, 1908, Mr. Green being seated on the monument at Beecher Island says:

That when the Indians first charged on the morning of 17th Sept. to stampede the horses, they came down from the ridge north of the camp, in one of the little ravines northeast of the camp. Mr. Green thinks the camp was abt. where the wagon road now is after it crosses the river to the north in its course over the ridge to Wray. Morton and Pliley say these Indians charged down from the canyon on N.E. of the camp. These men have the camp farther east by about 4 rods. Gilbert has it farther west than Green has it—due north of the monument Gilbert has it. Green and Pliley and Morton all say the Inds. charged up stream, and after passing the camp veered N.W. over the ridge. They could tell the course taken only from the sounds of the horses' hoofs, it being yet dark in the morning, so that the Inds. looked like mere shadows.

Hutch Farley and [Eli] Ziegler went up to the west ridge and about to the top when they saw the Inds. coming towards the camp, & the scouts ran back with all haste. This party of Inds. was the first ones who came to attack — came after the stampeding Inds. had charged.

J. J. Peate says that he has met 14 of the scouts on this ground within the last ten years, and 13 of them, including Forsyth, all these agree on the point on the place where Roman Nose fell; where the 3 scouts lay on the north side of the river, namely Louis Farley, Frank Harington (Peate says Harrington spelled his name with one r) and G. B. Clark, and the direction from which the attack was first made, and they also all agreed as to where the Inds. came from who tried to stampede the horses.[9] He says Gilbert is the only one who differs in statement from these. Their statement is as follows:

That the 3 scouts north of the river laid about north of the monument, as stated by Gilbert; that the stampeding Inds. came from the northeast direction and dashed westward past the camp trying to stampede the horses westwardly toward the Indian camp up the river.

George Green says the first charge of the Inds. came from the west or N.N.W. from the ridge; some scouts say they came from the west while others say they came down more from the southwest. Gilbert says after the stampeding party of Inds. had charged that he asked Col. Forsyth if he should not go up on the ridge & see & find out what he could & the Col. told him to go. He went up, showed me & took me over the ground where he went to the top of the big ridge west; he says that he saw no Indians in the ravine west of the ridge, but on looking up the valley of the Arikaree he saw the valley filled with Inds. coming; on the east side of the section of the river which runs from south to north across the valley a distance of half a mile, were some of the Inds., and these were coming on the run. He went back & told the Colonel — went on the run to avoid getting cut off — that the country to the west, up the river, was full of Indians and all coming.

Green and Peate and Gilbert and all say there was no wagon on the expedition. Two mules were taken by the stampeding Inds.; these were pack mules.

J. J. Peate says my account on page 19 of Annual for 1908, beginning in 5th line with, "Ahead of this reconnoitering party, &c" is not correct in this:[10] The body of the dead man was not on a pile of brush in the white tepee, but it was on a scaffold six feet high, standing in the white tepee; he was wrapped in blankets and robes and lashed on the scaffold with rawhide thongs. This was not

Roman Nose, but was a medicine-man. Hanging to the scaffold was an Indian tom-tom drum and a war-bonnet. Peate and 8 or 10 others, in advance of Bankhead's command, on the return from the Arikaree to Fort Wallace found the white tepee in which this medicine [man] was. These men kicked down the scaffold & the body of the dead Indian came to the ground and rolled down the steep hill some 75 feet to the bottom of the canyon. Then the men cut out pieces of the tepee for leggings. This tepee was made of tanned buffalo hide, hair off. This tepee was not seen on the trip of the relief party to Beecher Island, but on the first day of the return from the Island to Wallace. Peate tells me that one of his articles was published in two Annuals, and advises me to follow these; it is in First and Second Annual, or Second and Third. This tepee was on a branch canyon of the Republican river.

Roman Nose was buried on a scaffold seven feet high, half a mile south of the South Fork of the Republican river and about south from Beecher Island.

Peate says his article aforesaid gives the full history of the relief & to follow that. He adds that the name of the chief of the Wallace scouts nine in number was Victor Clark. Peate was in command of the Forsyth scouts of this party of relief.

Pliley says that my account in the Annual for 1908, of his and Donovan's trip from Beecher Island to Wallace is all right. He calls attention to my omission of what is stated in his letter as to his journey with a dispatch from Wallace to Brisbin.[11] He made the journey.

A. J. Pliley says that he did not go into Wallace with Donovan; that he was so prostrated and so sick from eating vile horsemeat and drinking warm water that he had to leave the stage at the first stage station west of Wallace ten or twelve miles distant, namely, Goose Creek and rested there three hours, when he rode in on a mule team, arriving at 1 o'clock p. m. Donovan had got in about 10 o'clock, and was gone with the four men that Lieut. Johnson had hired to proceed to Beecher Island. He had been at Wallace till about 4 P.M. Then he was sent by the Quartermaster at Wallace from whom he received his orders & instructions to the mouth of the Frenchman's Fork where Colonel Brisbin was supposed to be, and next morning about 8 o'clock he overtook Brisbin half a mile below the mouth, his command being then in motion, but Pliley does not know where he was going. Pliley bore a message from Sheridan ordering him to go to Forsyth's relief. Brisbin started immediately for the Island with great celerity. Brisbin sent a dispatch back by Pliley who returned without delay & traveled half a day till he came to a stream and considering it unsafe to go farther by daylight, he tarried there till after dark and then rode all night, arriving at the Fort after daylight. The distance between Wallace and mouth of Frenchman's Fork was 75 miles.

E. A. Gilbert on this 19th day of September, 1908, went over the ground with me and showed where Roman Nose died, as nearly as can be determined. He obtained his information from an Indian, afterwards. This Indian and he could not talk except by the sign language. The Indian mapped the landscape on the Arikaree with sand, and Gilbert says he made a good profile of the ground; he had the river, the Island, etc., and he laid off the grassy draw 375 yards southeast of where the monument stands. This draw was not deep, but furnished perfect shelter, & is now covered on sides & in bottom with grass. The draw is in this form:[12]

This draw is where the Indian said that the squaws tended and watched and waited with Roman Nose through the day till he expired when the sun was about an hour and a half high the same day he was wounded.

After relief came to the men some of them, says Gilbert, & he thinks Stillwell was one, came over to this ravine, and they said that all up and down it was marked by blood spots on the ground and bloody rags scattered around.

In the diagram the main draw is only about 20 rods long; it debouches into the river bottom probably 20 rods or more from the river. The two prongs at the head of the ravine or draw are six or seven rods long.

I stepped the ground between the draw and the monument at 375 paces.

Gilbert and Morton tell me that northwest of the Island, in one of the little ravines coming down from the big ridge north of the river, probably 200 or 300 yards N.W. of the Island was a place where the Indians collected their wounded, and this the Scouts called the Indian hospital. At this point, and on the big ridge and beyond it, and also on the river bottom above the Island, at safe distance, say about the mouth of the ravine; and also at the bloody draw southeast where Roman Nose died, the wailings of the women were heard.

James Curry is one of the Scouts omitted from the monument and all the lists. I should add his name. Pliley, Ranahan, Green, Morton and Gilbert, all say that Curry was a scout in the battle. Pliley says Curry was immediately by his right side in the fight. All agree that he was a desperate fighter; a dead shot, and a killer. He killed numbers of persons. Was a locomotive engineer. Everybody dreaded him, for no one could be sure that Curry would not kill him in an hour. The Scouts say he was the most desperate fellow they ever saw. After killing seven persons at one time in the Redlight house in Ellsworth he escaped in the tank of a brother engineer who assisted him, and went to Kansas City. Ranahan says that afterwards he and a companion met him in Memphis. He was running an engine to Fort Scott. He was running an engine when he did the killing at Ellsworth, and his own engine was searched at several different points on his route or run. Ranahan says Curry was killed in a mining camp in New Mexico. Fate of a desperado, which he was.

Ranahan says Wild Bill told him that Jim Curry was the only man he dreaded. Curry was fearless.[13] He could not read or write.

Morton says that Ziegler and Hutch Farley and Tucker all went up west of the camp after the stampeding Indians had charged. Gilbert says he also went up.

Charley Reech, this 19th Sept. 1908, at his home 3 miles southwest of the Monument, tells me:

That he and his brother Frank came here from near Denver in 1878, and they have been here since; for 4 or 5 years they were more or less disturbed by the Indians, and in 1879 the Inds. burned them out.

He says that in 1879 [1878] when the Cheyennes broke out in Indian Territory & came north, 40 white people were killed at Atwood, 60 miles S.E. of Beecher Island; at Benkleman, Nebraska, the Inds. took a corralful of cattle.

Speaking of the Inds. killed at Beecher Island, he says that 6 were buried in a small canyon about 3 miles N.E. of the Island; 2 were buried north of the big ridge north of the river, on its northern slope towards the Black Wolf Creek; in Jack's Gorge, 4½ miles west of the Island, a good many Indians were buried in tree tops, and judging from the scaffolds he saw in trees he thinks there were 50 or 60 Indians buried; he did not see graves of any others.[14]

Morton and Gilbert have both told me that that the main fighting was done on the first day. Gilbert says that as late as the 20th it was not safe for a scout to show his head above the trenches. He further says that Indians were all around in the vicinity till the relief came. This is fully corroborated by others.

The monuments to the several scouts who died, are placed where it is believed they each had pits and fought. When they buried the dead the latter were placed together, as Gilbert says, about where Beecher's position was.

I heard some of the boys tell that when the wounded were gathered into the hospital pit this was covered over with brush to protect them from the sun's rays. No earth was put on this brush.

Pliley thinks the Island is higher than when the battle was fought. Gilbert says the Island is higher but it [is] because the channel has deepened. He cites

Charley Reech who says that the first bottom on the north side of the river, which Gilbert thinks is a "fill," was on a level with the bottom of the river when he, Reech, came here in 1878.

Length of Island as pointed out by Pliley is 275 paces and the width at widest place 70 paces. Gilbert says the Island was blunt at upper end, rounding, and was not more than 150 yards long. He had his pit at this end and killed an Indian there. He had best position to see and know. Pliley was nearer on south side and Morton nearer on north side of Island.

Gilbert and Pliley say that the trees now on the Island and others were there in 1868. There are 5 now immediately around the monument.

Below this point and about at the lower end of the old Island are 6 other large trees. There was shrubbery at different places along the banks. On the south side of the river on the bank, and opposite where Gilbert was posted, were little bunches of plum bushes, around the roots and stalks of which the sand had blown up into mounds; these formed a line about 60 feet long; behind these the Indians in considerable number took position, and poured a galling fire into the scouts. Gilbert insists that it was from here that Louis Farley was wounded; he says these Indians could see the three men on the north side of the river.[15]

Pliley told me this 20th of Sept. on the grounds, that the stories about Donovan and himself running into an Indian camp when they were starting for Wallace, and their killing an Indian, etc., is false; that they had only two incidents, the first was when they were leaving the Island, they had to stop several times and keep still while patrolling parties of Indians were passing round to guard against escape of scouts. The same night when about 5 miles on the way, going round a sharp point of a hill they came on to some ponies within a few feet; they could not see them but could tell by the noise that they were within a few feet of the ponies which snorted and stampeded. The two scouts changed course instantly farther east, and hurried their pace, not knowing but fearing that there might be herders with the ponies who might be aroused by the noise of the ponies.

These were the only incidents except the additional one given in his letter, of which I have a copy, when a party of Indians were seen coming toward them and they prepared to sell their lives as dearly as possible; but the Inds. after a consultation turned and went off in a new direction.

All the Scouts agree that Roman Nose was shot about south, possibly a little east of south of the monument; that he fell forward on the neck of his horse to which he clung with his arms around his neck, and that he rode on east about ten rods and then dropped to the ground. From here he was borne by his friends to the draw where he died abt. an hour and a half before sunset. He was shot abt. 10 o'clock a. m. This charge came from the west. Gilbert had been wounded in his left lung where the bullet has ever since remained, just before Roman Nose's charge, and was in an unconscious, or semi-conscious state, so that he did not see this charge. He had heard that Roman Nose charged up-stream, and had always had that impression. But, I may say, all the scouts' that I have seen except Gilbert, agree that the charge was from the west, and on the south side of the river.

Roman Nose was buried on the South Fork of the Republican.

Gilbert thinks that if Roman Nose could have had his way in controlling the attack the Scouts would have been destroyed. He says there was no concord of opinion how it should be made; that Roman Nose wanted to rush or ride the Scouts down, which would have been successful, but other views prevailed; the Sioux and other warriors would not give up to the Cheyenne suggestion.

Gilbert says he and Stilwell rode as right flankers to the column, and some two days before the battle they had seen the heads of Indians above the ridges looking over at them.

Pliley says that he and Donovan, on starting out for Wallace took down along the north side of the island, and when they reached the lower end they angled across to the southeast.

Scouts Present at Beecher Island Reunion, September, 1908

Elijah A. Gilbert, A. J. Pliley, George Green, Howard Morton, Thos. Rana-han, James J. Peate.

Charley Reech who lives nearly three miles southwest of Beecher Island, and who has freighted a good deal between his place and Fort Wallace, says that the distance is 100 miles.

As my own observation I will say that Red Cloud, Crazy Horse, Roman Nose and all the great chiefs, saw the white frontier steadily pressing their people back like a rapidly encroaching sea.

H. H. Tucker Sr. was wounded in battle at Beecher Island. He held pub-lic office in Ottawa County, Kansas. His son, H. H. Tucker, Jr., is Secy. and Treasurer of the Uncle Sam Oil Co., and lives in Kansas City, Kansas. H. H. Tucker Sr., died in 1908.

The location of the gravestones with reference to the monument at Beecher Island is as follows: Farley's is northwest of the monument; Mooer's is due north; Beecher's is west (about four feet north of a straight line due east and west through the monument; Culver's and Wilson's is southwest and within eight feet of the corner of the iron fence. It is rather more E.S.E. I have these locations stated wrong in the Annual of 1908.

Arthur Chapman of Denver Republican, call on him in afternoon at Republican office, will sell me copies of pictures taken at Beecher Island Sept 17, '08. He has pictures of Custer field, & others & a good deal of stuff he has published in magazines.

M. R. Shahan, Bird City, Kansas, at 1908 Reunion took photo of the six scouts present at the reunion, and other views. These scouts were standing at the Monument. Price 35¢.

The Song Arikee. Composed on the grounds on the morning of Sept. 17, the 40th anniversary of the first day's battle, by Dr. _____ and was sung for the first time, that morning at the monument with the surviving scouts present, sitting upon the pedestal, myself being there then. Again, after dinner this song was sung in the auditorium in presence of the people, and at the close the applause given was the Chataqua yell which consisted of the waving of handkerchiefs.

5. Lightning Creek Incident

Eli S. Ricker's Newspaper Articles

In the early winter of 1903 a group of about twenty-five Indians from the Pine Ridge Reservation were in eastern Wyoming hunting small game. They were accused of violating the state's hunting laws, as well as slaughtering settlers' cattle. When a sheriff's posse was sent to arrest them a gunfight erupted, resulting in several deaths.

Ricker published four articles about the incident in the Chadron Times. *Two were general summaries taken from other papers and two, reproduced here, were written by Ricker. Years later Ricker's son Leslie recalled that "Pa made a trip to the scene of trouble and got the inside facts and aspoused the Indian cause. This act of justice on his part endeared him to the Indians and ever after that he was widely known by the Indians over [at] the Agency."[1]*

A Fight With Indians

[*Chadron Times,* Nov. 5, 1903]

Last Saturday [Oct. 31] a battle occurred on Lightning creek near its confluence with the Cheyenne river, about forty miles south of Newcastle and forty five miles north of Lusk, between twenty-five Indians, said to be Sioux from Pine Ridge reservation, and a posse led by sheriff W. H. Miller of Weston county, Wyoming. The Indians were hunting game and had established a camp on Beaver creek north of the Cheyenne and in the direction of Newcastle, where they had been staying the last two weeks. When this camp was reached by the posse it was found to contain some squaws and children and a few old men who were skinning game and preparing the meat for winter. Lieut. Hilton took these in charge and proceeded with them to Newcastle while Sheriff Miller with the posse went in search of the band who were hunting in violation of the Wyoming game laws, and crossing the Cheyenne came upon them awaiting in ambush.

Deputy Sheriff Faulkenberg fell mortally wounded at the first fire. The Sheriff himself received a fatal wound and died in three hours. Only four others were left, but they kept up the unequal contest for an hour when the Indians began to slip away in small numbers, and finally all withdrew carrying their wounded with them. Several of the Indians were reported killed.

A strong posse went out from Douglas, and the settlers began to gather to aid in their capture. Our last report from the scene of operations was received Wednesday night and it was stated that twenty of the Indians had been taken.

The settlers complain that this band had been slaughtering their live stock as well as hunting the wild game.

Between the Wind River reservation in central Wyoming, the Crow reservation in southern Montana and the Pine Ridge reservation in South Dakota the Crows, Sioux, Arapahoes and Shoshones have traveled for a long time, and eastern Wyoming has been hunted over by them every year, especially in the fall when game is plentiful, and this has caused much dissatisfaction among the people. Wyoming has enacted stringent laws for the protection of the game, but the redskins have succeeded in evading them or standing off those who attempted to enforce the law, and by these means escaped punishment.

The Paleface Outbreak in Wyoming

[*Chadron Times*, Nov. 19, 1903]
The trouble with the Indians in Wyoming is over and the net result in bloodshed is two white men and four red men killed and a buck and a squaw wounded.

On the 30th of October two small parties of Indians belonging to the Pine Ridge reservation and bearing passes from Major Brennan, Indian Agent, returning from an expedition into Wyoming, as a result of ordinary good fortune came together on Little Thunder creek and formed a single party and were quietly and peaceably pursuing their homeward journey when sheriff Miller with a small posse from Newcastle intercepted them for the purpose of making a wholesale arrest and marching the whole body to the Wyoming town.

The two original bands were headed respectively by Wm. Brown who had three with him, and Charlie Smith who had a much larger number; and when united the travelers and their train consisted of sixteen men, some women and children, and fifteen wagons. These people had been abroad to gather roots and herbs, and the Indians say that they had killed rabbits, sage hens and prairie dogs, but no large game, and moreover state that they had traded with the whites who came into their camps giving moccasins and bead work for sheep and venison, and Last Bear, a member of the Brown party, says that these had no beef at all except the offals of a carcass for which they traded a blanket at Hot Springs on their outward passage. The claim was made on the part of Wyoming settlers that they were hunting the larger game in violation of the state law, and also that they were killing cattle. We would not greatly doubt that they had shot large game, but it is not so probable that they molested cattle on the range. The excited imagination of men who think Indians have no right to live would have little difficulty in mixing a few cows in with antelope in the indictment against them.

After the two parties had united Charlie Smith was, on account of his superior attainments and ability to speak English, practically the head man. He was fairly educated at the Carlisle school, had been assistant farmer on the White Clay, and during the present year had been one of the Agent's foreman and in charge of 40 or 50 laborers on the national work on the reservation, and was a peaceable and useful man. There was therefore united to his own Indian cunning some of the white man's knowledge and experience. But for this knowledge and experience there would probably have been no blood shed.

The sheriff wanted the Indians to go with him, but Smith refused to do so, saying that they had done no wrong, and were attending to their own business going to the reservation, and that he knew if they were to go with the sheriff they would be stripped of their ponies and wagons and everything else they had; for this had been their experience in a former like case. Brown advised Smith that he was willing to go with the sheriff, and it is under stood that there would have been no objection by the other members of the party. The sheriff and his men took dinner in Brown's tent. He told Smith as they were leaving that he was going away to get reinforcements and that he would return and take the Indians back. They all moved away together from the dinner encampment at the same time but had gone only a short distance when they reached the forks in the road, one going to Newcastle which the sheriff took, and the other bearing toward the reservation which Smith who was in the lead followed, at the same time beckoning to the Indians to come with him. Not being able to understand English they supposed that some agreement had taken place between Smith and the sheriff and that it was the proper thing for them to go with the latter.

They traveled until 11 o'clock that night before pitching camp and at sunrise next morning took to the trail again. At noon they went into camp for dinner. About 5 P.M. they came to Lightning creek. They had now covered upwards of 70 miles since they separated from the sheriff. At this point a girl went to open a gate to let them down to the stream. She returned with the information that a body of white men were down there and were going to shoot at the Indians. The Indians were moving along without a word. Their guns were put away in the wagons and only two or three on horseback had guns in their hands when the shooting began. The Indians deny that the conflict was begun by them, and it is said by some familiar with the evidence on both sides that when the truth is fully known it will be seen that the white men were the aggressors. Sheriff W. H. Miller was killed and Deputy Faulkenberg mortally wounded. Of the Indians, Smith and three others were killed and Smith's wife and Last Bear were wounded. The Indians scattered and fled leaving ponies, wagons, and nearly everything they had. One Indian who had a wagon and a buggy left the wagon and escaped with the buggy. Last Bear who was wounded was put into a conveyance and taken away with his family. Black Feather and Chief Eagle with their wives got away with Brown. Several of the Indians were captured by the posse and taken to Newcastle. Those that got away made all possible haste to reach the reservation. They traveled all that night and the next day, intending to camp the next night on Hat creek where there was a settlement, but here three shots were fired at them by somebody and they kept on till they reached Horse Head in the vicinity of Oelrichs where they went into camp. It is said that this party, traveling in every possible way, was in a pitiable condition. Indian Agent Brennan dispatched some officers from the Agency, who, taking Chief Eagle with them, went to gather up the abandoned property and to bring back some families that were behind. The Agent also urged the department to take active measures to investigate and to protect the Indians in their rights and see that they had proper defense.

Last Saturday [Nov. 14] the Indians in custody had their examination at Douglas. When the State rested the United States District Attorney moved for a discharge of the prisoners on the ground that no case had been made against them, and the magistrate sustained the motion. There were nine of these who came down Monday night on the train and went to Rushville on their return to the reservation.

[Hugh Houghton's Interview]

[Box 19]

Lightning Creek, March 31, 1906.

Hugh Houghton, speaking of the tragedy on Lightning Creek says: The whites reported that the Indians had been killing range cattle, which was not true. They had killed some antelope and rabbits and other small game. Hypocritical complaint was made that they were violating the game laws of Wyoming. This the white complainants themselves did at pleasure. The trouble originated in the selfish hatred of the lawless element in and around Newcastle against the red race.

The sheriff went out after the Indians, but failing to bring them in with him, the "element" jeered him, and smarting under their taunts and jests he returned with a bitter purpose in his heart to take them dead or alive.

Indians on the Pine Ridge reservation had been trading with the Crows for ponies. These got away and were returning to their former owners. At New Castle they were taken up by citizens and Major Brennan was notified that they could be recovered upon payment of the charges claimed against them. He sent Louis Martin, a half breed, after them. Martin took along his wife and three children. He had no suspicion that his life would be in danger and drove up to a livery barn in the town without concern. There was a public gathering there that day. Threats against the Indian were instant and violent. Martin was advised to get out of the town with his family as quickly as possible upon a train, and was promised that his team and wagon should be delivered to him at a place named where he should be in waiting the next day. He escaped from the place, and his horses being returned according to pledge. The family, fearing pursuit, lashed the animals in terror to gain the reservation.

When they had driven fifty miles and their horses were too much used up to go any farther, Martin was permitted by a ranchman who showed him every kindness, to pitch his tepee close to his house, and being assured that no harm should be done to him or his family by any one, he rested there two days and recuperated his ponies, when they made their way without molestation to their home.

Before this affair, whenever the Indians had gone over into Wyoming they had been arrested and fined and all the good ponies they had were taken from them to pay these fiendish fines; and it was the memory of this kind of confiscation of their property that made them resolute in refusing to go with the sheriff when he first overhauled them, being persuaded by their past experience that to go with him to Newcastle would be but to suffer a repetition of the malicious dispossession of what they had.

When Martin arrived at Newcastle he was confronted with exorbitant bills in the nature of costs which were designed to leave few if any of the ponies to be returned to the owners. Some of us who have lived in new communities in the West a few decades and seen justice dispensed from the throne of the blind goddess have little difficulty in understanding how swift and overwhelming is the fiat against an unfortunate Indian when court, jury, witnesses, prosecutor and the community, having little noticeable regard for the law themselves, believe that no one of that race is good until he is dead.

[Roy Lemons's Interview]

[Tablet 31]

April 22, 1905.

Roy Lemons of Crawford says: That he recd. on the evening immediately after the trouble on Lightning Creek (He was then in Edgemont) a telegram to have 20 saddle horses ready when the midnight passenger train should arrive from Newcastle. He and his partner Mike Carroll, who were in livery stable business. Eight men came down on train, and the sender of the telegram was one of them. They bro't. saddles. A wagon was taken and a part of the party went in this & the rest on the horses. They went out to LO (L. O. bar) ranch; got there at 3 A.M. They got up out there & got breakfast, & by daylight they had fresh saddle horses for all the party. Directly after daylight these men started out to look for the trail of the Indians who it was said had gone past the evening before towards the Agency. When they got out on the divide 3 miles east of C. A. Lampson's of the LO ranch, with aid of glasses they could see Indians in the distance about 7 miles away (3 or 4 miles west of Hat Creek, while these men were 3 miles east of Hat Creek) coming towards them with pack ponies, having left their wagons, & driving the ponies ahead, and themselves going behind for better concealment of their persons, the dust rising as though it was a moving herd. Only a little bedding was on the ponies. They had left their wagons where the fight was on Lightning Creek.

(To go there, go to Lusk and drive out abt. 60 miles N.W.)

These men watched them through their glasses abt. an hour and finally could see what they were—could see the red blankets, & when a pony turned out to one side to graze they could see the Indians go out to put him back into line. Next could hear them singing what was supposed to be war songs. Next the Indians came down on Hat Creek, & 2 young bucks came up on white ponies—came up within ¾ mile of these men & stopped. These men had an interpreter with them & they told him to go down & tell the Indians to come up and give up their guns. He demanded a white horse before he would go and was given one. He went down and talked to the 2 young men. The Interpreter was an Indian. They said they did not want to give up their guns, but wanted to go to the Agency. These men sent the interpreter back with another message for the Indians to come & give up their guns and go with them to Edgemont. They sent back word that they did not want to give up their guns, but that they would go with him. He was sent back again to tell them that the white men did not want to hurt them—would not molest them—but that they must give up their guns and go to Edgemont. That time they came back with the interpreter carrying their guns butt foremost to hand them over. They gave up their guns & rode back with the white party to where the rest of the Indians were on the creek. These Indians all shook hands with the whites and all gave up their guns. The whites asked them how they were—whether they had had anything to eat & they replied they were very hungry. They were taken down to Lampson's ranch and gave them a quarter of beef, some flour, & they built fires & in 30 minutes they warmed it up in water & had it nearly eaten up. They didn't wait for the meat to cook. Their ponies were played out; as soon as they stopped they would lie down with their packs on. When the Indians had eaten the whites selected out of their ponies such as seemed able to make the trip back; they got a wagon from Lampson and after mounting Indians on the selected ponies and filling the Lampson wagon and their own conveyance, they all started for Edgemont, moving very slow on account of the weakness of the Indians' ponies. There were 23 Indians besides some children. None of these were wounded. Arrived at Edgemont abt. 6:30 P.M. and they fed the Indians at a restaurant after which the Indians were put into an empty building and provided with bedding for the night. They were kept two days, when the bucks were taken to Douglas on the train via Crawford. Some Indian police came over to Edgemont from the Agency and took the squaws and children and ponies and all home.

Roy Lemons was hired as a liveryman and had no other connection with the affair here related.

He stated to me the first time I talked with him that Sheriff Miller belonged to Weston County, Wyo., and that he went out of his county into Converse county to do the killing.[2]

[Isaac Robbins's Interview]

[Box 19]

[August 24, 1904]

Isaac Robbins says I may use his name in my account.

He says that a young Indian helped him a whole afternoon to herd and bunch his sheep. R.'s dog had got poisoned and R. needed some help with the sheep. When the boy left R. gave him some mutton. The Indian party to which the Indian boy belonged was camped a week or so there & R. could hear them shooting jack rabbits and sage hens. They did not get big game. A number of people had live stock in the neighborhood, but R. who was acquainted with them & saw them never heard any of them make complaint of anything against the Indians. The Indians were doing no harm.

The Indian boy could talk English and told R. that there were no Ind. police with his party.

This statement was made to E. S. Ricker by Isaac Robbins Monday, August 25, 1904, in the courthouse at Chadron, Neb.

Statement of Isaac Robbins Showing his Meeting and Interview with Sheriff Miller who was killed in the Fight on Lightning Creek, Wyoming. 1903.

Fight on Lightning Creek, Wyo. [Figure 5]

4 men came along on above road. One left the party and came to Isaac Robbins who was herding sheep on the divide between Horse Creek & Spring Cr. and he inquired of Mr. R. if he had seen any Indians. R. said he had but they had gone over toward Antelope 4 days before. R. told him that he (Robbins) heard some shooting over there the night before, but he told this sheriff that he did not know who was doing it, it might be herders, for there were some over there tending sheep and it afterwards so turned out.

Ques. by Sheriff: How many were there of them.

Ans. I don't know only what a young buck told me; he said there were a dozen in all—squaws men and children.

Then R. asked the sheriff if they were Indians from the Reservation.

Ans. "Yes."

Ques. Did they have any police among them?

Ans. "I'll make them think if I find them that they ought to have police with them. If they don't go along with me without any pow-wowing I will leave them where I find them."

Robbins could see the three men who were with the sheriff off some distance and that they were armed.

The sheriff had a new rifle and a new six shooter, a belt around him filled with cartridges.

6. Biographical Sketches

[Tablet 2]

Wind Creek, Pine Ridge Res., S.D. Jan. 23, 1907.

W. R. Jones being interviewed says: That he was a member of the 1st Nevada Cavalry & enlisted in 1864 & was mustered out in 1866. He served under Gen. Connor in Utah; was stationed at Fort Douglas.[1]

He tells of the Battle of Bear River, Utah, fought in January 1863, he thinks. Connor fought the Piutes in a canyon; his scouts found them; and he surrounded them; he entered the canyon with cannon, and there were willows between him and the Indians who were backed up in a cul de sac & could not get away.

They would not surrender and Connor slaughtered the entire band, men, women and children, something like 400 in all. Connor's loss was 38 men.[2]

Mr. Jones says Connor's practice was not to report the full number of Indians he killed; he reported a small number only; so he would not be recalled.

Says Joseph Bissonette (not the old man) was a good interpreter, and was employed at Fort Robinson.[3] Leon Palladay was not related to Alfred Palladay who was killed on the Running Water [Niobrara River] with John Richard Sr. He was a fine interpreter. But according to Garnett was untrustworthy. Garnett says these two Palladays were from St. Charles, Mo. & were related.

Says Little Big Man was a small man & would not weigh more than 130 pounds. He was [a] snaky, sneaking Indian; a man of bitter disposition. Mr. Jones lived near neighbor to him on White Clay Creek on Pine Ridge Reservation 4 or 5 years and L. Big Man was at his house as often as twice each week & he knew him well. He killed a man once over on the Laramie when riding along by his side, a man who was on his way to Montana with a drove of stock

& was wintering there. The man was repeatedly cautioned to beware of the Indians, but he thought they were safe and he went a long way off from camp one day, 5 or 6 miles & was killed.

This Indian's strong hold was to make trouble.

Mr. Jones says that Crook did outrageously in his treaty of 1889. He came and feasted the Indians on beef for two days till he had them full, & then he told them what he wanted. He received anybody as a signer — any way to get signers. He got 11,000,000 acres on the north, for which the Indians were to have $1.25 each year for a short number of years; then 75¢ an acre the next few years on all that remained; then 50¢ on all that was left after that. The Indians got only 50¢, for none of the lands were taken at first.[4]

After the battle of W.K. a man named Miller who was the cook for the agency herders started to go in to the Agency. An Indian met him and told him the Indians were bad and not to pass among them; other persons also warned him; but he knew many of the Indians & thought they would not harm him; but on his way up from White River where the herd was being kept & was going up White Clay Cr. the Indians killed & mutilated him. They did not interfere with the beef herd.[5]

John Y. Sechler was not a swearing man. "By thunder" was about the extent of his imprecations. Mr. Jones was with him a great deal. Saw him "set afoot" a good many times by the Indians. It was nothing in those days to be set afoot. When you turned your team out at night you had no assurance that you would have one next morning. Indians would steal the animals. It was their business. Mr. Jones has been "set afoot" a good many times. It was never long after "Arkansaw John" was set afoot till he would have another outfit. He was an industrious, energetic man; had ability to get along. The last time he saw "Arkansaw John" was in Chadron. He and Ben Tibbitts were on a stout spree. "Arkansaw John" died up on the Northern Pacific R'y. and his body was brought to Gordon and buried in the cemetery at that place where a good monument has been erected.[6]

Mr. Jones says outbreaks, killings, etc., were so common that people thought nothing of such occurrences. There was something of that kind going on all the time.

Frank Salaway was a finely built man, powerful almost beyond belief; and a foot racer who had no equal and could run like an antelope. An honest and truthful man, nothing tricky about him; harmless old man.

Broke himself down drinking and carousing. Has been a very hard worker all his life; never idle—worked hard for the lazy gang around him who kept him down.

Rations used to be drawn at the Agency, and then people living on the Reservation always met often; but after the issuing was given over to the Farmers nobody went to the Agency except for special business, and since telephones have been put in such business as this gives less occasion to go there.

Little Bat's father was killed by the Indians, Mr. Jones thinks. Says he Bouyer (father of Mitch Bouyer and of Little Bat, both had the same father) was out hunting or trapping on the Laramie River (he thinks) with a man who had been a member of the 11th Ohio Cavalry. The latter had been out from camp; on his return he found Bouyer killed. The Indians fired on him; he ran till nearly exhausted and got into a thicket of bushes where the Indians would not follow and escaped. This run affected his wind so that he never got over it, but he was a saving man and became well off and lived in later days at Cheyenne.[7]

Little Bat was the most wonderful hunter ever in the Rocky Mountains. Could run down and around game as no other could. He could see a deer pointing for some place and he would run for an hour to get ahead of or around him, and after a long race his aim would be as quick, steady and sure as though he had not run at all. One time Mr. Jones was with him going out for some ordinary game (in the fall) and they came on a she bear and her two cubs. Bat threw up and fired—crack, crack, crack sounded his rifle—a shot for each and each was dead. Jones says he does not see how he could fire so quick and take any aim at all. He was quick as lightning.

Beauvais he did not know much about—had not much acquaintance with him.[8] He says Beauvais was a man of herculean frame. He left Wyoming and went to the Black Hills, and it was there that Mr. Jones last saw him. He was once well off, but they broke him; that is, he endorsed for people.

Another thing to be noted. Not one man among the traders out here in early days but what "went broke"—not one that Mr. Jones has ever been able to think of. Blanchard who ran for the legislature in Nebraska was a heavy trader, but he went to pieces and settled on a little place in the south. Dr. McGillicuddy's wife died in Rapid City. Blanchard had twin daughters. One of these used to be around with McGillicuddy when he was agent. After the death of Mrs. McGillicuddy the doctor married one of these twins.[9]

McGillicuddy was in some respects a good agent. In others not so good. He had a bitterly revengeful and unrelenting nature. Once he got down on a man he could scarcely let up; after this poison in him was once stirred against a person, any kindness from the latter was no anti-dote. He was overbearing and tyrannous toward Red Cloud, haughty, domineering and mean. Used Red Cloud very ill. A man of large ability, great courage, but in those affairs where tact and kindness were great and sometimes the greater factors in gaining ends, McGillicuddy was without knowledge or means for action. His only argument and resource was force. He was always on the firing line. He was of the kind known as "rantankerous!" The chip was never off his shoulder. He was eternally embroiled. Mr. Jones once heard him say that if he had it to do over again as Indian agent he would do differently. McGillicuddy could not do too much for any person he took a fancy to. I read this ¶ to Mr. Jones and he says it is about right.

Garnett heard him say same thing.

Mr. Jones says there is a gloomy outlook for the Indians on the reservation. People cannot buy from the Indians, but the traders buy, not only the old stock but all kinds and ages. It did not use to be so. The Indians are becoming destitute. They had a great amount of stock ten and fifteen years ago. The present policy is breeding crime instead of lessening it among the Indians. When these people were taken in hand by the government they needed instruction that would improve their respect for the rights of person and property, but the system in vogue is breeding crime; the reducing of the Indians to poverty by allowing them to sell off their stock to the traders for much below its value, has been a breeding of crime—when an Indian is hungry he will eat—will kill somebody's cow to eat; and the Indians are now slaughtering stock on the range to live. The object should have been to encourage the breeding of cattle and the strengthening of the moral fiber, the respect for law and private right.

The Indians have been allowed to sell their horses with more freedom by getting permits.

Then there is the store business resembling the "company store" of the mining and other employing companies.

The Mitchell Flats, called Fort Mitchell where there was a one-company post.

It was here where John Hunter, step-father of Billy Garnett, lived, and where Mr. Jones first got acquainted with Billy Garnett who was then 12 years old.[10] Billy used to come around the hay camp on the flats where Mr. Jones was at work. Billy was a very talkative boy. John Hunter was killed up on his own ranch on Baptiste's Fork (a little spring branch) about six miles above Fort

Laramie, just outside the Reservation. He was a trader—kept a little store. He was killed by Bud Thomas. Hunter had sold whisky to the government teamsters in the corral and told that Bud Thomas was the one who did it; so Bud settled it by killing Hunter. Thomas was a tough follow and in his time killed several persons. Bud Thomas was himself killed on the Platte. Mr. Jones says that after this Bud Thomas and _____ Bulger stole a four-horse team from Portuguese Phillips. The owner recovered his team. The soldiers went down the Platte River and arrested Thomas. On the way up to Laramie the soldiers under a Lieutenant told Thomas to get out of the wagon. He knew they were going to kill him. He was nervy and called them all kinds of cowards. Portuguese Phillips was along. Thomas proposed to him that if he had anything against him that they should take guns and have it out. But Phillips declined. Then the soldiers shot Bud Thomas. Bulger was a natural born thief.

Portuguese Thomas [Phillips] was the man who carried the dispatch from Fort Phil Kearny to Laramie after the Fetterman massacre, for which service he was paid $1,000.[11]

~~Mr. Jones says there were good and honest men in this country who kept out of trouble. These did not drink whisky and carouse. They attended to their own affairs with assiduity and gave no offense to anybody. Some of these men who, it would appear, were desperadoes, were fine men to be with—to do business with, gentlemanly in deportment. But they could not be crossed in some matters with safety. Bud Thomas was such a man.~~

Mr. Tibbitts killed a little lame man named Palladay—not related to the other Palladays. Two of Antoine Janis' sons and some others sent this Palladay up to Laramie for whisky. These men had a drinking carouse and the two Janis' were killed. They were laid out in Nick Janis' house. Palladay came to look at the corpses and Nick's daughter Emily shot him.

In relation to what Mr. Jones said of Red Cloud and McGillicudy Garnett says that Red Cloud was a good deal to blame. The first year and a half of McGillicuddy's incumbency of the office of Indian Agent the two rode together a great deal. Red Cloud's people were continually bringing complaints to him; as soon as one was disposed of another would arise; the Indians have a faculty for consuming the time of a man who will incline his ear to listen; and this fault finding harassed the Agent till the opposition of one to the other got to be acute. After McGillicudy was removed and the Indians were starving under Gallagher, Mr. Garnett heard Red Cloud say that he wished they had McGillicuddy back in his old place.

[Tablet 11]

L. B. Lessert (who is called Ben Claymore by all the Sioux Indians and white people in this region. His father's name was Claymore Lessert).[12]

Mr. Lessert came from Kansas City, Mo. in 1853 to the vicinity of Fort Laramie. In 1858 he took up residence in Colorado & lived there 20 yrs. He was at Denver, Collins, Cache L' Poudre &c. In 1858 he made the first trail from Denver to the road called the California road. He intercepted this road at the junction of the North and South Plattes. He established this road by throwing up a few sods at proper points or sticking up a willow, or anything which answered the purpose of a landmark. People coming from the east to Denver in this way reached the main road to California. A well defined road was soon worn into use.

Knows that the Indians came close to Fort Casper; that the soldiers went after them & Lieutenant Casper [Collins] with whom he was well acquainted and for whom the fort was named got too close to the redskins & was killed. He was killed about the beginning of the Civil War.[13]

For some years Mr. L. used to come over from his home in Col. to the California trail and have dealings with the emigrants to the west—buy lame cattle from them & take them back to his home & winter them.

He knew Jim and John Baker well; he and Jim were neighbors for a time. Thinks these Bakers came to Denver from Fort Bridger in Utah in 1859. He first settled on Clear Creek on the north and south road from Denver to Laramie. This was adjoining Mr. Lessert. Lived there a few years. Mr. L. was there only two years after Baker located there. When Baker went away he returned to Utah and remained till his death.[14]

Baker had taken the hard knocks as other frontiersmen did. Had to live as the Indians did on the wild meat that they could kill. To get flour was out of the question because of scarcity and high price. Mr. L. says he bought flour from the emigrants and sold it out in the winter at a dollar a pound. Could not get much to sell. Canned roast turkey, roast chicken and oysters pound and a half cans sold for $2.50 a can; poor calico sold for 50 cts. a yard; coffee and brown sugar sold for 50 cts. a tin cupful, and the cup was filled by taking the sugar up with the fingers and dropping it into the cup, and without waiting to pack or fill the cup, it was quickly emptied before the sugar could settle in the cup.

Jim Baker was a typical western man, hospitable, generous, anybody could come into his house and have anything he had and be welcome. Nothing could be said of him but good. Nothing scared him; brave, fearless & had had many adventures and terrific struggle. He had the side of his face mangled, and his under jaw broken by explosion of a Spencer Rifle magazine. A new one was presented to him by a friend. Jim used to go out on big bear and buffalo hunts with big men from England and the east. This gun was a present from some big man. Thinks Baker had been in the west 25 or 30 years when he came; his oldest and only boy was old as Mr. L. Baker was at least 50 yrs. old when he got acq. with him. His children were this son and two daughters, the latter married when Mr. L. came there to know them. Jim Baker had two Indian women who were sisters, for wives at the same time, the oldest was named, according to the sound, Morook. These were Snake or Shoshone Indian women.[15]

Mr. L. says the Mormons were in the habit of confiscating the property of the Gentiles, taking them prisoners and confining them; some of these, at least one or two, never came back to their old neighborhood. But the Mormons always let Jim alone, supposedly because he had a plurality of wives, though Mr. L. says he was not a Mormon, but he was wise and knew enough to keep his mouth shut.

Baker was a trapper and hunter & made his trips spring and fall. He was well fixed, at one time had a lot of cattle; thinks Baker's son William got most of his property; William was a good son who stayed at home and saved his father's effects. Wm. remained in Utah and looked after the property while the old man was over in this country (Colorado).

William also had an Indian wife—a Shoshone, married her in 1855, just before Mr. L. left that country.

Mr. Lessert also knew Jim Bridger and his partner Vasquez. The latter was a French Canadian. (Vasquez came up from the south & could not have been of Canadian origin. He had as much Spanish as French blood. Was very dark.) These were in partnership at Fort Bridger. Bridger was always employed by the government when it needed a guide and scout. He knew the country by heart—needed no map or compass; it was all clearly outlined in his brain. He was the best in his line in the west. He saw Bridger when he made his last trip either in 1866 or 1867.[16] He was on his way from Fort Laramie to his home at Westport Missouri. He said to Mr. L. "Well, my friend, I'll bid you goodbye; this is my last trip; I am getting too old and am going to my home." He was at this time past 80. He went to Denver & was taken sick & sent word back to Antoine Janis & old John B. Provost and Mr. L. and all the old friends to come and see him; that he thought he had his last sickness and would not get any farther. Antoine Janis and another one or two went to see him, but he recovered and lived a few years longer.

Mr. L. says that the Mormons hated Bridger, for he got to talking against them, and all who did that got the worst of it and they robbed him of his cattle at Fort Bridger, though he saved a lot of his horses.[17] In the early 50's the Mormons cleaned him out at Fort Bridger, and he came down to Westport, Mo., and made his home for the first time there and built a large house and he made this his home till he died there. He always came out from there to serve as guide and scout for the Govt. & for emigrants.

Mr. Lessert (Ben Claymore) says he himself left La Porte, Colorado, in July, 1878, upon the written request (a letter) from Dr. Irwin, Indian Agent at Yellow Medicine on the Missouri, who asked him to get together 100 Indians and 400 ponies & to draw 100 wagons to begin to haul provisions and stores for the Indians who were on the road from the River to Pine Ridge. Mr. L. got the Indians and the ponies and with these went to the Yellow Medicine, & there he procured the wagons & loaded & began his hauling to Pine Ridge, starting with his first train of supplies the 27th day of October. The doctor Irwin had also written in some letter to him to gather up 100 citizens who had teams and wagons and bring them also to help haul. These latter started out from Yellow Medicine a few days behind the others. A trip was made once a month and 600,000 pounds of freight was hauled each trip, and during the fall and winter he made 3 trips, hauling 18,000,000 pounds aggregate. Then the agent was changed, McGillicuddy succeeded Dr. Irwin. McGillicuddy said he was ordered not to employ any of the employees who had served under Irwin (a falsehood, of course).

Mr. L. says that the ponies were raw and the Indians were raw and that first trip was a Picnic with a big P. They were green and awkward and ignorant. They often failed to control & manage their loads & the wagons would plunge over the ridges and hills & go down pitches and break out a wagon tongue, and the contents of the load would be dumped in a heap. Then here would come an Indian flying back on a pony & tell Mr. L. that he had broken the "handle" out of his wagon. L. would tell him to get his wagon out to one side so the others could pass & when L. came up they would take a tent pole or anything else that could be had (for timber was scarce there) and would bind up the broken tongue. He says there must have been at least 25 tongues broken.

Dr. Irwin was a fine man and agent. He had been Agent of the Shoshones before. When he was down here the Indians up there had another they did not like & wanted Irwin back. He resigned here & was immediately appointed Agent again for the Snakes. Not too much can be said in praise of Dr. Irwin.

McGillicuddy, speaking of him as an Indian Agent, he was all right. After Mr. L. lost his job as freighter, he got employment at the Agency of T. G. Cogill, Indian trader, & worked for him 3½ years. Cogill and McGillicuddy got mixed up in trouble & Cogill got up a petition to have the affairs of the Agency investigated, and Mr. L. signed it. Cogill then had his license revoked & Mr. L. lost his place in the trader's store.

Returning to the old frontiersmen and Mountaineers, he says Jim Beckworth, with whom he was well acq. was a trapper & hunter and went out spring and fall hunting & trapping. Beckwourth was a mulatto & spoke good French. He was a man of great physical strength, no extra flesh, was tall, a six-footer, somewhat slim, but all bone and sinew, a powerful man; was a truthful man; it was a mistake to call him a liar; he was truthful and was so recognized. He was a peaceable man; Mr. L. has seen him in all conditions & knows he was a peaceable, truthful man, and particularly a peacemaker, always endeavored to make peace. Says Beckwourth never denied having colored blood in his veins, showed it plainly, hair was curly etc., must have been ½ or ¼ blood. He was honest and kind. Mr. L. has been at Beckwourth's ranch about a mile from Denver, up on Cherry Creek many times when B. lived there. A colored man got too intimate with B.'s wife at this ranch, and he killed the fellow. This wife was an octoroon, or a woman of colored blood. Beckwourth left the woman there. Nothing was done with him by the authorities, but he left, having parted with about all his possessions, and taking a couple pack horses and his gun he went north. Mr. L. was at this time living on the Cache L' Poudre when Beckwourth came along, and B. stayed with him over night. Beckwourth said to Mr. L. that he was going to his people (meaning the Crow Indians) and live with them till he died; that he would leave his bones with them before he would go anywhere else. He went to the Crows and Mr. L. studied it out and says B. died about 1865 or 1866, as nearly as he can calculate. Beckwourth's one fault was his drinking habit. He was a thoroughly good man.[18]

Mr. L. was an Indian trader on his own account at Pine Ridge Agency 8 years.

[Alexander Baxter's Interview]

[Tablet 18]

Kyle, S.D. Feb. 28, '07.

Alexander Baxter, Henry McKenny, Do Good For All (colored): This the name, he says, his father gave him. He says:

That he was a servant around Grant's & Sherman's Hd. Qrs. in the war down on the Mississippi.

Four or five years before the Civil War he went out west, was taken prisoner by Inds. at 7 yrs. of age with 6 or 7 white boys who were afterwards recovered by the traders. He was a prisoner when he first saw Pike's Peak. The Indian chiefs sent him and the white boys back to their parents in the south. He was captured by the Navajos and Bannocks.

After the Civil War the U. S. troops came from St. Louis to Fort Leavenworth; thence to Fort Riley & Harker, & at Fort Larned and Fort Zero [Zarah] in Kansas they divided, some going north, some northwest, & others southwest. He went with the latter, as he had previously been in that country. Gen. Miles & Gen. Grover [Maj. Cuvier] went in the latter direction in command.

He says Little Wound, chief of the Cutoffs who were the Southern Sioux, was the recognized friend of the white people. This colored man went up from the south with troops to make a treaty by Gen. Harney with the Blackfeet and Modocks. It was hard in those days to get the Indians in, because they had been fired on so much they were suspicious. The scouts, guides & interpreters had the hard work to do.

Alexander Baxter says: That the following were some of the early scouts who guided the troops on the frontier:

Bill Rowland, right after the Civil War, was among the southern Indians — Indian Territory, New Mexico, Arizona; wherever Uncle Sam's troops went, down there he went. Rowland went up north with the Cheyennes. He had a Cheyenne wife. He was a versatile interpreter, speaking Spanish, Arapaho, Cheyenne and Lakota, besides the English, and being an expert in sign-talking.

Cherokee Bill was in the Indian nation and was guide and interpreter. A mixed blood, half colored and half Indian.

Kiowa Charley, a full blood Indian, lived among the Kiowas; was a guide and interpreter for his own people.

Navajo Jim was a full blood Navajo and lived in Arizona, and was a guide and interpreter for the troops.

California Joe was guide, scout and interpreter.

Joe Marivaill was a Mexican and was a scout, guide and interpreter, and worked all over, in the south and north.

The Janises were interpreters.

Leon Palladay was an interpreter.

Hank Clifford worked for the government but was not much of an interpreter. He was at Sidney, Laramie and Robinson.

He mentions the following Forts:

Time when he was in service.

Fort Union, New Mexico

   "   Craig where Gen. Grover commanded   "   "

   "   Beard [Bayard]   "   "

Fort Santa Fé (1865) New Mexico

    Troops were in it before the War.

Fort D. A. Russell, near Cheyenne,   Wyo.

   "   Laramie   "

   "   Steele, above Laramie on Platte River,   "

   "   Washakie, on Wind River,   "

He speaks of the following U.S. Indian Agents:

Major Wahlen, on the Platte

Dr. Daniels   " "   "   He moved the Agency from the Platte to the White river.

Dr. J. J. Seville followed him

Major Hastings next.

Lt. Johnson temporary military supply.

Dr. Irwin from Wind River, Washakie.

  "   McGillicudy

    Col. Gallagher; Dr. Royer, Capt. Brown next; Capt. Chas. G. Penny followed; then an Inspector came and took charge a little while and sent Penny to his command, but the Captain was sent back.

He gives names of old chiefs as follows:

Arapahos: Friday, Black Coal (so-called by whites, but Black Powder by Indians) Six Feathers, Sharp Nose, Shakespeare, Eagle Dress.

Cheyennes: Turkey Legs, Black Crow, Wild Hog, Dull Knife.

Shoshones: Washakie.

Utes: Colorow.

Oglalas: Little Wound, Red Cloud, Blue Horse, Conquering Bear (who was injured by a street car and died on Corn Creek); Red Dog, who is dead and young Big Road a northern Indian has his place; American Horse &c. White Bird who was a northern Indian but is dead; Rocky Bear and Fast Thunder, both living on Wounded Knee Creek; Face, who is dead, his descendants live on W.K.; he was an uncle to Billy Garnett; he was a northern chief; Charging Shield, a northern chief, is dead; Yellow Bear was a northern chief and is dead.

The Dakota dialect is that spoken by the Santees; the Lacota is that spoken by the Oglalas. The former sound the d, while the latter articulate in the same place the l.

[Tablet 32]

Alexander Baxter says: That at the council at Laramie when the treaty of 1868 was made, Spotted Tail who was a Brulé Sioux stirred up quite a commotion by speaking in favor of having Indian farmers and teachers and preachers to instruct the other Indians. He was opposed in this by a young brave who arose in the council and ridiculed his proposition and judgement, and sharply reminded him that the chiefs were not the repositories of all authority; that they had no power—no right—to bind the Nation by their exclusive action, but should submit all vital questions to the Nation at large for decision. This was the spirit of democracy. It will be, perhaps, a pardonable digression to note in this connection, that the American Indians have furnished the best example of democracy in government of any subdivision of the human race in modern times; and if the fathers of the United States Government were too proud to acknowledge it, they nevertheless modeled their incomparable system after the pattern devised and tested by the Five Nations in their great and successful Confederacy.[19]

Spotted Tail was further reminded by his bold antagonist that to insist that instructors in the various arts of civilization should come from the identical people who were deficient in knowledge savored of foolishness; that these were to be found at that time only among the white race from whom they must come for several generations; and his advocacy was so pointed and irritating that the more Spotted Tail reflected on what had been replied to him the more his anger swelled, till the dinner hour when on his way to the hotel he opened a fusillade with his revolver on the brave who had wounded his pride. The controversies natural to the occasion engendered more or less excitement. Finally, Man Afraid of His Horses, who was powerful in influence, settled this disturbance in a strong speech in which he pronounced it wholly impracticable to attempt the instruction of the Indians by the Indians at that early period in the new career then dawning.

Red Cloud ran away from this council and would not take part in it. Baxter, of course, has no good word for this old Chief, as he was adopted, as he claims, into the Cut Off band and into the Little Wound family. He says Red Cloud was a knavish disturber of peaceable relations. He gives Chief Little Wound a distinguished place, because he cultivated amicable intercourse with the white men, and carefully promoted the interests of his people. He says Little Wound organized a large body of several hundred Indian "militia," as he denominates it, for use by the government. There may be some truth in this, but it must be probed and verified. It is certain that he was a scout; for I have seen four of his discharges, one of which mentioned him as a sergeant.

Baxter says that the leading and far-seeing Indians wanted to get away from the Platte, and did remove at last to the White river; because over on the Platte they were on the great highway of travel to Oregon and California and were thrown into too intimate contact with the tide of emigrants which poured in a continuous stream westwardly, and afflicted them with all manner of vices, especially the habit of intoxicating drinks, the paramount curse of mankind.

Baxter says, but I think he is in error, that the sentiment among the prominent Indians was in favor of banishing the white men who had intermarried, and the mixed bloods; for it was through these, he says, that so much whisky was introduced among the Indians; and these also dealt in it, besides consuming it inordinately, making themselves the responsible instruments in producing drunken quarrels, conflicts and murders.

Baxter states that Little Wound and his people, Cutoffs, lived in the south of the Sioux country from about Fort Harker on the Smoky river north to the Republican and the Platte and were called the Southern Sioux; while Red Cloud, and his people lived up on the White river and around the Black Hills.

Baxter states (verify it) that American Horse carried rations to the Northern Indians in 1876, and that Sioux Jim told this on him and when American Horse found him cached he killed him. He says that the Gov't. withdrew its confidence in American Horse because of his giving aid as aforesaid to the hostile Indians. (Needs corroboration.)[20]

Baxter says, and in this I have reasons to believe him, that Spotted Tail had become arrogant and refused to respect the domestic rights of other men; that he had acquired the habit of appropriating the wives of others, or stealing them, as it is called among the Indians, at his pleasure. An Indian husband against whom the old Chief had offended in this manner came one day to Crow Dog and related his wrongs. Crow Dog said he would not steal any more wives, and taking his gun, he shot Spotted Tail as he was passing in a buggy. Crow Dog was tried and acquitted (verify).[21]

[Harry Dean's Interview]

[Box 19]

Wild Bill

Dec. 26, 1906. Interview with Harry Dean.

He came up to Red Cloud which was down below where Crawford stands, in October, 1874, but the danger from Indians was so threatening that he and those who came with him remained only three days and went back to Cheyenne whence they had come to get work chopping.

He was in Deadwood in 1876; worked in the Homestake mine six years. He knew Wild Bill. Says the pictures I have of him are good, though they make him look a little fleshy in the face, but he admits that he probably was so when he was a younger man in Kansas, when it is most likely these pictures were taken. Says Bill was a tall, square-shouldered man, a bundle of bones and muscles, fine looking in the face, made in the noblest mold—after nature's choicest pattern—big hearted, lion hearted, free from all disposition to quarrel, patient under abuse and long suffering, but inspired fear in other men who knew the might of his wrath when he was provoked to anger and action. Dean relates that in a house in Deadwood where the business place was upstairs, Bill with others was up there one day when a fellow came in and stepped up to Bill asked him if he was Wild Bill, Bill replied that that was what they called him. His interrogator said, "I've got you now; I've been looking for you for three years," at the same instant drawing his revolver; but before he could raise his arm Bill had seized his hand and wrenched his gun from it, and then taking him by the back of his collar and the seat of his trowsers pitched him down stairs. Then putting the gun into his pocket he sat down as though nothing had happened. Another time some men were together in a rough house quarreling. Bill always carried a cane. He happened this time to come around while the disorder was going on, and stepping into the doorway leaned up against the jamb and was looking on. As soon as he was noticed the disturbance ceased; such was the awe his presence inspired.

In his later years he was dissipated; liquor, the women of the town, and the hard life he had led combined to impair his noble physique. Dean never saw him till he was greatly broken, and yet he speaks of him with admiration.

[John W. Brafford's Interview]

[Tablet 22]
At the late homestead of the late Henry C. Clifford, Deer Springs, Pine Ridge Reservation, S.D., Jan. 23, 1907.

John W. Brafford says that in June, 1905, he met William F. Drannan, at Perry, Oklahoma, and had several conversations with him. Says his picture in his book is perfect. Says Drannan was selling his book for a living and Drannan said he was doing well. He was dressed in buckskin & he wore a large slouch white hat. Brafford lived 11 miles north of Kit Carson at the Big Springs 18 years and knows many places that Drannan described to him minutely — one place where Carson and Drannan and others made breastworks and resisted the Indians. Brafford says Drannan marked out the works and fully described the ground with all familiarity. Drannan said he neglected to give an account of this in his book. Brafford has full faith in Drannan's book. Drannan told Brannan [Brafford?] that Carson had never dictated his life. He Drannan said he could give a pretty complete history of Carson.[22]

Brafford advises me to find Newt Vorhis who lives about 15 southeast of Denver & was with Carson much of his life and can give Carson's history. Vorhis' own history is exciting.

Brafford tells of Cheyenne Wells where Wild Bill gave a gang of outlaws and killed them all and was himself badly wounded. Brafford says the stable where Bill did the fighting still stands and has been fenced in for preservation. Cheyenne Wells is in S.E. Colorado.

[Marion Spencer's Interview]

[Tablet 20]
Mrs. Marion Spencer nee Vasquez, being interviewed at the house of her daughter Mrs. Rosella Brengman, in Grand Junction, Colo., January 28, 1908, says:

She was born at Fort Bridger, Wyoming, in 1849. Her father was Louis Vasquez, at that time a partner with Jim Bridger.[23]

In 1851 her parents moved back to St. Louis and her father lived ever after in Missouri and died in Westport in 1868. It was near Westport where Bridger had his farm.

Mrs. Spencer remembers Jim Bridger from the time she was eight years old. She saw him a great deal in Missouri; he was at Vasquez's much of the time.

In 1851 the Vasquezes moved back to St. Louis. Bridger had been back down the Mo. River [a] good many times. Vasquez lived at St. Louis 2 years & moved to Westport. Bridger came down and bo't a farm near the place & about four miles from Vasquez. Westport has been absorbed by Kansas City. It was once a separate town with a post-office.

Before Bridger bought his land near Westport he was at St. Joseph very much where he had two children, a son and daughter in school. Bridger went from there with his family to Westport and bought his land, leaving the two children at St. Joe. He had at this time six children & took four to Westport. Afterwards, these two in school died at St. Joe.[24]

Mrs. Spencer says the last time she saw Bridger was about 1878. Bridger had a Flathead squaw for a wife. She died at Westport before the war, probably abt. 1858 or 1859.[25] When she died Vasquez was at Denver and Bridger was out west.

Mrs. Spencer says Bridger died at his farm at Westport, & his body was moved to Kansas City where the monument was erected.[26]

Bridger's squaw could talk a little English before she left Fort Bridger; after she removed to Missouri she learned to speak the language with ease. She was an expert maker of fancy needlework.

7. The Old West

[Tablet 28]

~~Interview with Mr. Magloire Alexis Mousseau. Buzzard Basin, Pine Ridge
Reservation, S.D. October 30, 1906.~~

I was born in Canada Nov. 22, 1830. My parents were French Canadians.

At the age of 17 he went alone to join an older brother, Zephrin, near West
Stockbridge, Mass. He had while there a lingering illness lasting more than a
year. When he was fully recovered he and his brother went to St. Louis in the
fall of 1848, they going by way of the lakes and the Illinois River. The second
fall following, the brothers separated, Zephrin going down the river to New
Orleans and taking passage to California, and Magloire in the spring of 1850
(the next spring after the departure of his brother) he joined a party which was
collected by Pierre Choteau, or rather the American Fur Company of which
Choteau was the principal one, though he did nothing himself, Mr. Sarpy doing
the work in the company's office in St. Louis. (Sarpy shot himself for the reason that he lost $40,000 on one expedition; but he did not die; however he
could not do any more business.)

Mr. Mousseau went up the river on the company's boat which carried 285
men who were employees and a cargo of goods for the Indian trade. Mr. Mousseau stopped at Fort Pierre (where the city of [Fort] Pierre now stands) but the
boat ascended the river to Fort Union at the mouth of the Yellowstone.

The Fur Company had a still at Fort Union and made corn whisky which
was traded to the Indians for robes. Buffalo robes were shipped by the company to Europe where they fetched a good price.

The same year that Mr. Mousseau went up from St. Louis, the government
sent an expedition up to Fort Union. The object of this expedition was a mystery to the people who saw it pass up the river on a steamboat. There were

two head men and 50 men. This was not a military expedition. The object was to ascertain whether the Fur Company was manufacturing illicit whisky. This expedition was supplied with interpreters and guides from the Rees, the Grovans, the Mandans, Crows, and Assinniboines. This body of men he calls detectives, they were not military men; it must have been that they were employed by the government and sent out on special service. They found the company distilling and they closed the still. He says that Henry Pichot, the member of the company who attended to the business at all of the trading posts, "fixed" the chiefs of this expedition so that a report was made to the government that the company was not making whisky. Pichot did not make any more liquor.[1]

During this summer of 1850 Mr. Mousseau was engaged in chopping and hauling wood into the fort for use the next winter. He also worked at burning charcoal in the summer and getting out the wood to be used in this way. Great quantities of this coal were required for blacksmithing at the posts.

Only a part of the employees were set at this kind of work; the rest of the men were mostly going down the river to St. Louis during the summer with Mackinaw boats loaded with robes. These boats were loaded in the spring and kept moored & waiting for the rise in the river which comes in May, when the boats are set adrift with their cargoes. The buffalo robes were folded in uniform size in a press, then a heavy weight pressed them down and they were tied with ropes by two men who worked at the press. These robes were tanned when purchased. Ten made a pack. A Mackinaw boat carried 300 packs. Sometimes there were loaded on one of these boats, in addition to the robes, 40 or 50 sacks of buffalo tongues, salted and dried. These brought in the market $1.00 apiece.

In the spring of the year it was a part of the usual labor to make what was called green hide boats. The manner of constructing these which were called "bull skin canoes" was to make frames and cover them with green buffalo hides with the hair on the inside, and to sew the several parts together, and then cover the seams with buffalo tallow. These "bull skin canoes" would hold 40 or 50 packs. These little cargoes were brought down the tributary rivers like the White, the Cheyenne and the Cannonball to Fort Pierre where they were unloaded and stored. I should have said that these Mackinaw boats were manned by five persons; four were oarsmen and the fifth was steersman.

The trading season began about September when the men went out in twos to open bargainings with the natives. Two men started off alone into the interior to some camp, there being five or six horses and one mule in charge of each man, the whole going in single file, the mule leading and the man walking behind. Each man had his particular mule for this service. The camping places were always the same. The wise mule invariably knew the camping place at night. He would stop when he had arrived at the right spot, and the driver made his camp. There was no stopping from morning till night. On the going out trips the animals' burdens were goods for traffic with the Indians. These consisted most often of beads and vermillion, which were in high demand, blankets, shirts, calicoes, muslins, hatchets, axes, knives, firearms, gunpowder, lead molded into bullets, traps, and a great variety of goods suitable for their use.

As soon as one of the two men who had gone out could be loaded he started back to the trading post; then the other would pack his burden-bearers and start in, and the two generally met midway; and thus they passed and repassed the entire season if trade was regular and there were no untoward circumstances.

He says this was a very hard life.

In the late summer after the low stage of water had come of 1851 Mr. Magloire A. Mousseau came down from Fort Union (he had in the meantime from his arrival at Fort Pierre gone up there) to Fort Pierre, and after a stop at that place came on down to Fort George about 40 miles below Pierre.

This Fort George was an island in the Missouri which the government reserved for the occupation and use of the white people who chose to resort there, and it was tilled and some dairy cows were kept there. There was also a like island called Farmer's Island in the River at Pierre, which was also cultivated and tended and made a resort for people passing up and down the river.

After Mr. Mousseau reached Fort George he started down to St. Jo with two sick men—George Cronyn and Francis Babby—both of whom had the dry scurvy. Both these men were cured when they got to St. Jo. They bought a skiff, that is Cronyn bought it, at Fort George, and they pulled up to the shore every night and camped. Mr. M. rubbed the men all over with Missouri River mud and water at night and made them good beds on some brush and on arrival at St. Jo they were well men. They subsisted on fish from the River which they caught with hooks and lines. There were no provisions at the fort when they started. Mr. M. was well rewarded for his services to these men in restoring them to health. The distance down was 1,200 miles as he remembers, though he is not certain.

George Cronyn was the chief clerk of the Fur Company. He became very wealthy and died in Provo, Utah. He was Irish. He invited Mr. M. to come and bring his family and visit him a number of times, but he did not do so.

Mr. Mousseau stayed in St. Joe all winter shaking with fever and ague, and in the spring of 1852 he came up to Independence Rock in the Sweetwater country and there he went to clerking for Hubert Papin & Charley Perat who were in partnership in a trading post, and they also had a toll bridge across the Sweetwater. Emigration was at this date very heavy and these partners were doing a large business. He continued at this until his employers were in 1858 ordered away from there—to go either to Green River Utah or Fort Laramie. This company now had a fine place on the Sweetwater; their building[s] numbering fourteen were laid up square-hewed logs with well-laid floors, and windows, and covered with boards and dirt, and these structures were built on three sides of a square. He explains that Independence Rock is seven miles below Devil's Gate; that the post was above Devil's Gate about a mile. The bridge crossing was at the Rock; then the road ran up on the opposite side of the river between the bank and the ridge. When within about a mile of the post the road passed Devil's Gate which is formed by the river bank on one side and high bluffs on the other, the passage being only about 200 yards. Springs lined all these rocky ridges, flowing down from the top. Devil's Gate was so called because the Indians took position among the rocks of this cliff and killed many a white man.

Mr. M.'s employer moved when ordered by Gen. Harney, and went to Fort Laramie. This order was because of the Sioux war in which the general fought the battle of Ash Hollow.[2] So Mr. M. may not be right as to the date of 1858, and he so states; but the removal of his company was in the year of the Battle of Ash Hollow. He states that the first troops were sent to Fort Laramie by the government two years before his company went there (look this up). He says this war lasted ten years.

Life at Devil's Gate was most always exciting; hardly a month passed without a visit from a war party composed of Sioux, Cheyenne and Arapahoe Indians who stole and carried off the horses belonging to the post. Good horses were kept here, and the Indians were good judges (as they are now) of horses and they had a great liking for them. These parties had a special motive for raiding this post because they were all at enmity with the Shoshones; and the men owning and working about the post including the proprietors and Charles Lajeunesse, August Archambeaut and his two brothers, Moses Perat and a brother of him and Charley, some Canadians and others, and Mr. Mousseau, all of whom were from the Green River country which belonged to the Shoshones, except Mr. M., and the raiders regarded them as Shoshones, which Indians always had good horses; so this post was an attractive point to them for horse stealing. The Shoshones used to come down to Wind River to winter. It was a great country for game, and the government has set off here the National Park to furnish a retreat, among other objects, for wild animals, to preserve them from destruction and extinction.

Here at Devil's Gate the post people had fights with their successful enemies "too numerous to mention," as Mr. M. expresses it. The Indians always got away with the best horses, but none of the men at the post were killed.

Mr. M. says that eight or ten years afterwards he was living at Casper, Wyoming, and had 200 cattle and 120 horses and mules. The Sioux Indians raided him and carried off 27 of the best horses and mules that he had and killed the three men he had herding them. He had another man out hauling wood.

He says that the soldiers were too slow to cope with the Indians. They spent too much time counting—1, 2, 3, 4, 1, 2, 3, 4; says he used to laugh at them; says the Indians would make a sudden dash, fire a volley, and be out of sight and hearing, and the whole incident occupied but a minute or two.

Mr. Mousseau had a ranch across the Platte opposite where Fort Casper stood twelve years before the fort was built. There was peace then, and he had no trouble except the occasional loss of a horse when stolen by Indians.

Fort Casper was built in 1865. Troops were camped there before that in tents. Casper was named after Lieutenant Casper Collins who was killed close to the fort. His father was Colonel Collins who commanded the District and had headquarters at Fort Laramie.[3] There were troops stationed along the road —100 to 200 in a place—from Fort Kearny to Fort Laramie, thence to Fort Casper, thence to the foot of Rocky Ridge some hundred miles west of Devil's Gate. At Rocky Ridge is where Mr. M. discovered the first gold in the Sweetwater region. Lawyer Blair from St. Louis came along with his train when Mr. Mousseau was picking in the hill, and Blair asked what he was doing. M. showed him a piece of gold he had taken from a crevice which Blair declared was worth five dollars. Blair crossed the ridge and went to prospecting and stayed there that winter. He sent for miners and this was the beginning of the Sweetwater gold mining.

These troops were posted along the trail to protect the emigrants. No train was allowed to go with less than 50 soldiers as an escort.

Fort Casper was occupied about nine years. The garrison had a great deal of fighting. First Lieutenant Collins' company was at the Sweetwater bridge, Independence Rock and he had been ordered from Fort Laramie to join his company by General Connor who had just taken command. He had ridden

from Laramie to Fort Casper. He started out from the fort to continue his journey, but before he was out of sight of the garrison he was attacked by Indians
who knocked his brains out with their clubs. Mr. M. says this sad event took
place about a week before the following occurrence, which he avers was in
1868 [1865]. A wagon train had been out to the Sweetwater delivering stores
for the troops along the line of travel and was returning and expected in a day
or two. There was some discussion whether a scout should not be sent out to
meet the train a few miles beyond and have the drivers leave the wagons and
by a circuitous route attempt to get into Fort Casper without encountering the
Indians, as the country was swarming with thousands of them and they were
dangerously active and warlike. A council of the officers decided to let the train
with its escort, numbering 55 men, take its own chances of getting in the best it
could. When within four miles of the fort it was attacked by 200 Indians wearing the army uniform and carrying the Stars and Stripes, which enabled them
to approach very close before the deception was discovered and gain the advantages of a surprise at short range. The best defense was made that could
be, but the overpowering force of Indians, after a considerable loss (he says
40) succeeded in killing every man except one who, after some hair-breadth
escapes, reached the fort. The Indians burned the wagons.

Colonel Plumb was in command of Fort Casper at this time.

When Mr. Magloire A. Mousseau went to Fort Laramie his employer discharged him and he went to work for the government. Right away General
Harney arrived with a large force of troops and after a short stay at that place
he marched his men to Fort Pierre to see what he could do against the Indians
who were very hostile and threatening. He had 5,000 soldiers — cavalry, infantry, artillery and two companies of engineers.[4] At Laramie the General found
some good whisky in the sutler's store and he ordered the sutler to sell to the
soldiers without reservation or limit; and Mr. M. says that there was a devil of
a time but no trouble, the troops drinking like fish but making no disorder.
When he got to Pierre with the army (he and three others went carrying express) they found fine residences already for occupancy by the officers. The
government had been sending buildings in the "knock down" shape up the
Missouri and putting them up at all government posts in large numbers. The
General had taken over with him from Laramie all the old timers he could get
together as scouts, namely Jim and John Baker, Hubert Papin, Suise Lewis and
Joe Merrivall two Mexicans, the latter father of Alexander Charles Marrivall,
Sam Deon, Louie Morrisett, _____ Provost, John Colombe. These are all

Mr. M. can name, though he can recall many others who were from Missouri but who belonged on the frontier. This expedition was in 1866 (I must verify all his dates; I doubt their correctness).

Mr. M. had his home at Fort Casper, but owing to the hostilities everybody came or went away from there at this time. A party with 40 wagons would not return to Laramie; they said they would starve there; but they went to Oregon, they said they could get plenty of game if they went that way. These were people who lived at Casper and were hardy and fearless men and could fight their way through. They got out there and found the natives on the warpath, but they built blockhouses and were successful in defense.

After General Harney got to Pierre he called some of his old scouts around to consult about getting supplies of meat, and when he was told of a large herd of buffaloes not far away on the east side of the Missouri (Pierre is on the west side) he sent out hunting parties from among his scouts who of course were all old and good hunters, and these marksmen sent across boatload after boatload of buffaloes to the commissary. He also had cattle driven over from Laramie.

Harney remained at Pierre with his forces all winter. In the spring he received orders from Washington to make peace whether or no. He felt a little chopfallen at this, for he would much rather have made war. But the effect of this formidable array of soldiers had produced a change of attitude of the Indians.

Kelly, Laramie [Larimer] and Wakefield

Mr. M. knows well of the Kelly-Laramie[5] party, with Wakefield, which was attacked on the Box Elder Creek. He says there were two emigrant roads along there. One was down by the Platte river. The other was half way between the river and the foot of the Casper mountains. He says the Wakefield party were on this upper road. At the time of this fight he was going to Laramie with the 6th Michigan regiment which was going to Laramie to be mustered out of service. He saw a girl belonging to this party, who was up on a hill, tied by the Indians for a decoy to get the soldiers into ambuscade; they called to her and asked how many Indians there were and she said she did not know but there were a good many. They passed. Mr. Mousseau told them that she would be hacked to pieces. When he came back from Laramie some of the officers of the 6th had to return to Fort Casper on some business and they found this girl's body in the road hacked as he had said it would be.[6]

He was at Deer Creek when Mrs. Laramie came in. He saw a figure on a hill across the river early in the morning. He called the attention of Captain

Rinehart to it. They could not distinctly make out at first what it was. The officer hallooed and the object rose up. Her dress showed that it was a woman. He sprang upon his horse, swam the river and when he reached the woman he drew her upon his horse behind him and took her over and brought her little child along too. Capt. Rinehart was the officer.[7]

At Deer Creek was a post where soldiers were encamped for protection of the route of travel.

Mrs. Kelly's book shows that certain ones who were brought in when she was delivered to the military, were hung at Fort Laramie.[8] Mr. Mousseau gives the following account:

John Calico was a scout under General Sanborn who was fighting Indians in the south. John Calico's father's name was Two Face. The latter and another son were brought to Laramie, or came in, with Mrs. Kelly, and the two were hung there.[9] John Calico arrived from the south while his father and his brother were still hanging. Black Crow, a Cheyenne Indian, was accused of capturing Mrs. Kelly, but it was proved that he did not, but that he had done what he could to secure her release; nevertheless he also was hung with the others.[10] John Calico determined that he would revenge the death of his father and brother, and the number of soldiers that he picked off at various times afterwards was not small. He had a paper of recommendation from Gen. Sanborn; but when he came to Laramie and found his father and brother hanging by the neck he burned his paper and swore in his heart to be avenged.

Mr. M. says the whites are worse than the Indians, and instances the barbarities committed by Quantrell and his men in Kansas by putting the inmates of houses on the roofs and burning all together. Indians are wild and raised to acts of outrage, but white people have been taught better things yet do even the worst.

Mr. M. says that the misery and mystery which would be revealed if only the ground around Fort Laramie could speak would be a shocking recital. Murders and other crimes were numerous and unexplained. One time he was going along a little way from the Fort and came to a place where a white man was hanging to a tree. No account was ever given of the tragedy.

Another man was taken into the cellar of the post trader's store and stripped naked and tortured to death by burning him with wax tapers. His body was thrown into a hole just outside of the building and covered over with earth. His tortures were inflicted to make him confess to certain knowledge which he protested he knew nothing about.

If frontier posts and lonely places elsewhere could give up their secrets there would be a horrible record of crime revealed.

Bridger was blind for several years, and at time of his death. Says Bridger sold his fort to Gov't. for $2,000 a year for 99 years and his heirs at Weston, Mo. are receiving the money. Weston is just below St. Joe.[11]

Mr. M. does not know exactly when Fort Casper was abandoned.

1865–1866. Generals Connor and Moonlight—Jim Bridger

The Arapahoes were on the head of Powder River. An expedition was sent there, Moonlight in command.[12] Jim Bridger, who received from the government $7.50 a day as scout, was the guide. He came upon recent Indian signs. He saw pony tracks. A light fresh snow had fallen. Bridger dismounted, blew off the snow from the tracks, and said to Moonlight that these tracks had but just been made. He also noticed the green horse dung. He told the general that the Indians were only a little way off. Moonlight did not believe him, but said that what Bridger said was only imagination. Bridger said that he would show him; and he went up to a hill in advance and crawling along the summit till he could see over, he discovered the Indian village down in the valley. He reported to the general who refused to take his word for it. Bridger, who spoke with independent directness and candor to everyone, replied: "You are a damned fool; you know everything; I know nothing; you have no need of me; I quit now;" and so saying he pulled out for Independence Rock. From there went down to Fort Casper, and thence he telegraphed to General Connor at Fort Laramie, advising him of the state of affairs. He then went down to Laramie and imparted the whole story to the General. When Gen. Moonlight came back without having accomplished anything, he met Gen. Connor and extended his hand. Connor turned his back for a few moments. Then he opened out on Moonlight with a torrent of criticism. Referring to Bridger he said: "Bridger knows more asleep than you do awake!"

After Mr. M. left Fort Casper he lived down at Laramie 7 or 8 years. He worked for the government at Fort Laramie. When he left there he went up to Twin Springs 37 miles above, where he made a ranch and kept his stock and put up much hay. Three miles farther up he kept a store at Horseshoe Creek, a big stream all the time. He had this store up there a little over a year and then sold his buildings and moved his goods down to the ranch at Twin Springs where he concentrated all his interests. There was a blacksmith shop there too. He lived at these two places 26 months, and in this time they sustained

24 attacks from Indians, and finally it became so hot for them that he moved back down to Laramie. The people came in from around and huddled up in a hundred lodges (made, he says, of poles and buffalo robes) for three years till peace was made again. This was in 1871 when they collected at Laramie — three years after the treaty of 1868. But the Indians kept breaking out. He was there till 1874. After this Mr. M. moved to Bates' Forks and settled on the main stream, there being three streams. Here he and his family spent the winters, but in summer they traveled with ox wagons along the line and sold goods to settlers and emigrants and residents at the posts.

Beginning at Chimney Rock Mr. M. states according to his memory the streams and notable places as far up as Casper.

Scott's Bluff got its name from a man name Scott (first name unknown). He was bookkeeper for the Am. Fur Co. and was journeying to Fort Laramie. Was sick and died and was buried there.[13]

Camp Mitchell was on the south side of the Platte and a day's drive with ox team above Chimney Rock.

Horse Creek, called 40 miles southeast of Fort Laramie and Laramie River. There is no stream between Horse Creek and Laramie River, but there was Beauvais Spring 8 miles below Laramie River.

Going north yet, and all the time on the south side of the Platte, we have next Laramie River. Next are Warm Springs; water is warm, winter and summer. Next Big Bitter Cottonwood Creek; Little Bitter Cottonwood Creek; Twin Springs; Horse Shoe Creek; Elkhorn Springs; La Bonté Creek; Wagon Hound Creek; Bed Tick Springs; Laparelle Creek; Box Elder; Deer Creek; Cottonwood Springs; Big Muddy Creek; Richard (Reshaw) Creek; Willow Creek; now Casper.

Mr. M. says there was a road up the Platte River on both sides.

Starting now a little below the mouth of the Laramie on the north side of the Platte is a creek for which he knows no English name, but the Indians called it, The Creek that Smells Good; next above he cannot remember the name of (after thought Keene Creek), the third is Shawnee Creek; Devil's Dooryard Creek, so named by the Mormons, and called by the Indians Stinking Water Creek; the next and last creek before reaching Casper he has forgotten name of. There is a creek on the north side close to the old bridge at Fort Casper which is called Sage Brush Creek.

He had lived at Casper two or three times before now but had retired down the river when the Indians became warlike.

In 1895 he was on the Big Muddy in Wyoming with his whole family; stayed there a month closing up business and visiting. From there the family moved to Medicine Root or Kyle and settled, and has since moved several times on the east part of the Pine Ridge Reservation. He is now living in Buzzard Basin at the age of 76. He has four sons, namely Louis, James O., Joseph Alfred, Alexander who is the oldest; also has two daughters namely Sophia Munroe, Julia Garnier, widow of Baptiste Garnier. (In French the p is silent, so it is pronounced Batteese.)

Baptiste Garnier

Mr. Mousseau knew Baptiste ever since he was a little boy; knew also his father and mother; knew them first at Laramie. The country was good then and the Indians were not troublesome, and they left Laramie, and the next time he saw them was up near Casper. Four miles below where the town of Casper is was Richard's (Reshaw's) bridge across the Platte.

Bat's father, name was also Baptiste. ~~was killed in this way~~ The people were collected at this bridge in a little settlement, owing to the hostility of the Indians. Bat's father was working for Richard (Reshaw) and was up at the foot of the mountain chopping timber to repair the bridge; this was in the spring while the water was low. The Cheyennes, about 150, came to the bridge and there was a fight between them and the whites. The Cheyennes had a spite against the bridge people, because two of their number got into trouble there at one time, and the whites took them into the blacksmith shop to iron them. One submitted and was ironed; the other broke away and jumped into the river. He was shot at and wounded, but got away and went over on the Sabine which emptied into the south fork of the Laramie, and there he died. His people harbored revenge, and this was the cause of the present difficulty. (Here Mr. M. says that the whites have begun every war since he has been in the country.) It was Saturday and Baptiste Garnier Sr. had been out and shot a deer to take home to his family from the working camp at the mountain, and as he was going along with his game on his back he met the infuriated Cheyenne and they killed him. Nothing was ever found of him but one leg which was taken and buried.

Mrs. Baptiste Garnier now moved with her only son Little Bat and her three daughters to Fort Laramie. Five or six years afterwards this woman and her two daughters were burned to death at Laramie. She was lying in her lodge too close to the fire (it being late in the fall when the weather was cool) and she and two of the girls caught afire and all of them ran out into a high wind and were quickly overcome by the flames from their clothing and fell to the ground. Next day they were all dead.

A man named Witcomb who lived at Fort Russell took the two orphans, Little Bat and his only sister living, to care for and raise.[14] After awhile he got a small rifle for Bat to hunt chickens and rabbits. Bat began on these, but after awhile he concluded to try his hand on bigger game; so one day he was out not far from home and shot an antelope in the forehead; he went on a little farther and came upon another; he put a bullet in this one's body. He had to go to the house and tell his foster-father who was scarcely able to believe what he had heard, but on going out with Bat he found the two antelope which were brought to the house.

From this time Bat kept on hunting; a larger gun was put into his hands, and his progress as a marksman was sure and rapid. He finally went to Laramie and engaged in hunting with success and profit. The game he brought down with his rifle was sold to the soldiers at the Fort. Finally, in _ _ _ _ Bat's sister got after Mr. Mousseau to let Bat have his daughter Julia. He told her to go to the daughter and see her about it. Her reply was that she was willing to have Little Bat if her father and mother were willing. No objections being found, the two were married by a justice of the peace in Cheyenne, and after there was a Catholic church at Pine Ridge they had their nuptials performed by a priest. This marriage was just after the U.P.R.R. passed Cheyenne; so it was about 1868 or 1869. ~~They came back to Mr. Mousseau's place on Wolf Creek four or five miles from Pine~~

He then went to the Chug Water and then to Box Elder Creek where he was hunting and selling the meat that his gun brought down. While here he received a letter from Frank Gruard inviting him to come up into the country where he was at Fort McKinney, (where Gruard was getting $5 a day) stating that he could do well there killing and selling game. He then quit where he was and moved to that place. Here his first child was born, this being several years after the pair were married. He did exceedingly well there at hunting.

One day when Mrs. Garnier was washing she filled her tub with hot water and ran off for a draught of water at a nearby well at the Fort and when she came back the boy had climbed up and fallen into the scalding water and was dead. This sad event nearly broke Little Bat's heart; he could not bear to live at Fort McKinney longer and so they came down to Mr. Mousseau's on Wolf Creek about 4 or 5 miles from Pine Ridge Agency. Colonel Gallagher was now the Agent at Pine Ridge. Gen. Hatch was in command then at Fort Robinson.[15] Bat was asked for by General Hatch who wrote to Agent Gallagher and offered to pay him $60 a month and to furnish him rations. He moved over and was given commodious quarters. He afterwards came back to Pine Ridge (not long after) to hunt mountain sheep in the bad lands close by his father-in-law's house at Medicine Root. While there he prevailed upon Mr. and Mrs. Mousseau to go over and live with him at the Fort. The reason for his being employed at Fort Robinson was on account of his reputation as a hunter. Mr. and Mrs. Mousseau lived with Bat at Fort Robinson four years. Bat finally got tired of working for $60 a month and at last had his father-in-law (Bat could neither read nor write and was opposed to learning to do so, saying that if he was to learn these arts he would be killed) write to General Brooke in Omaha that if his pay was not raised to $100 a month he would quit and go north where he could make a great deal more at his business of hunting. His demand was acceded to and ever after he was paid this sum.

He was foully murdered in Detrich's saloon by the bar-tender _____ in Crawford, Neb. (date   ).[16] It was a cowardly and cold-blooded murder. His murderer was tried in Chadron, before "a Dawes County jury" which acquitted him. The term "Dawes County jury" was once spoken by a county attorney of the county in derision, and it is pregnant with significant meaning.

Baptiste Garnier had first and last 14 children — 8 sons all of whom, except one, died in his lifetime; and six daughters who are living.

He was about 50 years old at his death. His remains lie in the military burying ground at Fort Robinson. His widow and his sister Eulalie live on Pine Ridge near Holy Rosary Mission.

"Little Bat" was a dead shot either on foot or on horseback. His powers of endurance were almost beyond belief. His hunting faculties were as acute as were ever known to be possessed by any man. He could track an enemy or an animal traveling at high speed, where the ordinary man could not detect sign of foot-print.

Mr. Mousseau says La Bonté was not in the country when he came there. He says that Red Cloud was well acquainted with La Bonté; that he told him the following about La Bonté:

La Bonté had a camp below the mouth of La Bonté Creek. He stopped there to trap beaver. His companions went beyond up to Elkhorn which ran up to the mountains where there was plenty of timber, and it was agreed between them that he should wait at his camp when the season closed till they passed down, and he would fall in with them. They never appeared, and he tarried for them till it was too late for him to start; so he prepared to stay alone through the winter (they trap till in June for the water is cold as it comes down from melting snow). Red Cloud and his tribe were moving up the Platte to find buffalo plentier, and he had a friendly conversation with La Bonté. He left him and went on. Some of his warriors asked him why he did not take his scalp. He said he LaBonté was his friend. But after he had gone away some of the young Indians coming up behind killed him and took his scalp. He says this is the Indians' way.[17]

~~The Richards (Reshaws)~~

John Richards Sr. was killed near the head of Running Water between Lusk and the old road from Rawhide to Running Water. He had a nephew killed at same time; both killed by Cheyennes.[18] Joe Richard, the youngest son, died in Denver where he had land which is now in the city limits. Died after a spell of hard drinking on the 4th of July, with Jim and John Baker, died next day, the 5th, & was buried there. Jim and John Baker could drink liquor heavily without appreciable effect on them.

Peter Richard died at Baptiste Poirier's (Big Bat) on Wounded Knee Creek. A natural death.

John Richard Jr. was killed on the Platte — across the Platte — close to Fort Laramie. He was in Yellow Bear's lodge (a Sioux) and shot Y. B., nobody knows why only that he was drunk; when he had done this he received a butcher knife wound on each side of his neck; he sat there as though unhurt, and then two of Yellow Bear's sisters struck him in the head with clubs and opened his skull and tore out his eyes and threw them in the fire.[19]

Louie Richard was a fine man. He died on Lake Creek 25 miles northwest from Cody. He has given me a great song and dance about President Grant's sending from Washington for him for an interpreter — sent through John S. Collins at Laramie, and a special train carrying him, and that he was there a month, and a year afterwards he received a check for $1,600 signed by Grant.

His death was on 4th of July.

John Richard Sr. was an old rascal and all his sons except Louie who was well respected.[20]

Charley Chadron from whom Chadron Creek took its name had his trading post at the point where the road crosses the creek below the Half Diamond E ranch. Mr. M. did not know him, but he heard people speak of him who did. They said he was a very good man.[21]

The Bordeaux

Mr. Mousseau got acquainted with Jim Bordeau in St. Louis in 1850. He came down from the Platte after goods. He was a trader among the Indians. His station was on the Platte ten miles below Fort Laramie where he had men employed. Afterwards he went across the country and settled on the north side of the Missouri River at Bijou Hill, a level stretch overlooked by this ridge which took its name from an old French trapper from St. Louis by the name of Bijou, but signalized more properly as being the place where many unfortunate wayfarers have at different times been caught in deathly storms and surrendered to their fury. Old Jim was a hard drinker. There was a heavy emigrant travel up both sides of the Missouri. Bordeau did a swelling business, exchanging goods and alcohol for horses, mules, buffalo robes, and peltries, and money. All those traders handled firewater.[22] The bulk of this came to them in the form of alcohol, especially for Indian consumption. The standard rule of reduction of these fiery spirits ~~was 3 to 1, that is, three parts water to one part alcohol. A few draughts of this compound would land an Indian upon the unconscious hunting grounds; but before he had arrived at that point of independent happiness, the trader usually dosed it out to him in a mixture of two parts water to one of~~ was about three parts water to one of alcohol; but when the dealer started in with a sober crowd he fixed it up stronger to make the effect speedier, so that trade would not drag but become brisk at once; then when his patrons were drifting on towards the unconscious hunting grounds he added more water to delay their progress in that direction, to extend the time that they would be able to do business, and not least of all to increase by several fold his profits.

Bordeau's wife left him over there on the Missouri because of his drinking habit and came over to the Spotted Tail Agency where Rosebud now is, and where their son Louie was living.[23] Louie was raised by his mother's sister. He never went with his father. He was Boss Farmer on Rosebud for years. After awhile old Jim came over to Spotted Tail and got the government contracts for wood, hay and charcoal. In this business he prospered. Before he came over from the Missouri with two trains, one of horses and mules, one of oxen, nearly 30 teams in all, he had quit drinking. He had put in his bids and got his contracts before his departure. He did not live very long at Spotted Tail; he had quit drinking so suddenly after such immoderate use of the stuff that my informant says it killed him. It was like the Irishman's fall which did not hurt him; it was the stopping so quick which did it.

It was when Jim Bordeaux moved from the Platte to the Missouri that he built a saloon on the Big Bordeaux where the Nelson place is. He was succeeded in that location by Peter B. Nelson. Bordeau's bartender was shot behind the bar by an unknown man who rode up and accused him of saying something derogatory of him to some officers who were close by with troops. The man rode away on a fast horse. Mr. M. says "it was nothing to kill a man in those days." The creek got its name from Jim Bordeau because of his making a trader's place on it. He kept other goods there for sale; it was a trader's store. The Little Bordeaux was settled by a French Canadian named Boucher who had his cabin somewhere below where the station now is, presumably on what is the Messenger property. His wife was a daughter of Chief Spotted Tail. She died there, and the Agent at Spotted Tail, a military officer, would not allow him to remarry. He went away.[24]

Major Frank North

Mr. M. knew him; says he was a fine gentleman, universally respected. Mr. M. says he himself never went with expeditions. But he used to see Major North[25] at Fort Laramie in command of the Pawnee scouts when expeditions were going out. He was a very fine man; a common man, saluted and chatted with all men alike; would sit down on a log and talk with a teamster or a roustabout with the same freedom and indifference that he would with a general officer.

Jim Beckwourth

Mr. M. knows nothing of him only this: He was at Fort Laramie when Beckwourth was passing on his way to the Crow nation. Some one asked: "Who is that nigger?" Answer by a bystander: "That is Jim Beckwourth, mulatto, he is going back to his people, the Crows."

Mr. M. says a trader by the name of Jim Saunders told him how Beckwourth died. The Indians told Saunders. They were so glad to see him return that they gave him the best horse they had. When he mounted him the horse pitched and threw him and broke his neck. He had just sold out at Denver.[26]

Jim Saunders was an old timer who died at the foot of the Black Hills where he had a good ranch, some ten years ago.

Mr. M. saw Kit Carson and his friend Maxwell from Texas who had thousands of cattle, and he offered to stock Mr. M. with 1,000 head on the halves, but M. was young, Indians were troublesome, and he would not undertake it. He saw these men on the Sweetwater.[27]

Buffalo Bill

Mr. M. never saw Bill, but he says he was the biggest liar he ever heard of. But he was a sure shot; that was his chief merit.

Colonel Fitzpatrick

He was the best man who ever came to this western country. He came up the Platte in 1851 to make a treaty with the Indians with 275 wagons hauled by three yoke of oxen to each wagon, loaded with bacon, flour, sugar, coffee, fire-arms, ammunition, in short groceries, dry goods, hardware, hammers, hatch-ets, axes etc; and these goods were boxed up and marked for each tribe, and the Colonel distributed them to the several chiefs without opening, and told them to make the division among their own people to suit themselves, that he would not undertake that. All the tribes were represented at this council except two that were in the Oregon Country; they said the government could send their goods to them by ships, that it was too far for them to come. Fitzpatrick had resigned from the army and was wealthy. He returned to Washington and was called before Congress (sic). They wanted him to go out west and take an Agency. He said "No; no man who considers himself a gentleman will be an Indian agent. The temptation is too great for him not to steal like the devil." And he would not accept the tender of office.[28]

Old Man Laramie

Mr. M. says in the early days of the American Fur Company he came up with a party of 75 beaver trappers to the Laramie River. He was not in the employ of this company but was on his own hook with these employees. He built a post and afterwards sold out to the Am. Fur Company and became their agent at that place.[29]

Speaking of beaver skins Mr. M. says that 100 made a pack. In those days the beaver skin was worth $10, a pack $1,000. But now they are not worth trap-ping; he says furs are now manufactured in imitation which sell well, look better than the genuine, but are not so durable.

Mr. M. says that a great many persons have been killed in the vicinity of Laramie by Indians who picked them off at different times, and many have fallen at the hands of the white men themselves.

California Joe and his Slayer

Tom Newcomb was the murderer, but Mr. Mousseau knows nothing about that. He says that he lived at Fort Robinson with Little Bat four years, and was there quite awhile after the W.K. fight. While he was living there two well dressed men, bright, well educated, claiming to be sons of California Joe, came to Fort Robinson and inquired of him if he knew where "Joe" was buried; but he did not so asked an officer who told him that his remains were in the cemetery at that place marked by a headboard. They talked of removing his body, but don't know whether it was ever done. California Joe was very jovial and a favorite among the officers.

These men intimated that they wished to find their father's murderer. Mr. M. says they traced him to the Pacific coast. He saw them afterwards and they told him that they "accomplished their mission," from which he inferred that they got his life.

Mr. M.'s dates are totally unreliable, especially the later ones, as is usually the case with old men. I have more confidence in his earlier ones.

Mr. Mousseau says William Shangrau who lives at Cody Lake, 8 miles from Cody, has paid $900 per capita tax on live stock. Mr. M. does not know what is done with this; he says the clerks at the Agency know nothing about this tax money; they say there is no account of it on the books. Someone else has told me the same thing about what the clerks say.

Mr. M. prefers civilian agents to military; he is very hard on Agent Clapp whom he accuses of corruption and villainy. I understand this. Clapp was not a Catholic and once called in Father Busch who was going about the Reservation with a picture of Heaven and Hell and of the roads leading thereto; and he was telling the Indians that there was but one church — the Catholic — and that those who did not belong to it took the road to Hell, etc. Clapp told him that he did not like this; Father Busch retorted that he did not care what he liked; that it was his duty to do this and he should do it. This ended the interview. R. O. Pugh told me of this circumstance.

Clapp extended the school system here.

Mr. Mousseau, notwithstanding his enmity toward the Indians, says that ever since he has been in the country the whites have brought on every war. I think that his feeling against the Indians is due to his hardships and loss of property on their account.

Mr. M. says the early days were hell. Whisky was the staple article. Men's lives were not worth much. We hardly ever reckon what a stirring factor whisky has been in the subjugation of the country and in the closing up of men's earthly accounts.

Mr. Mosseau says the old Choteau Co. and afterwards American Fur Company was heartless, cruel and brutal to their men, and that it committed murders without hesitation. Henry Picott, chief agent on the Missouri River for all the trading posts on the river, (thinks there were seven of these) (All these posts were finally sold out to the War Department) was a hard man. When employees had worked until they had large sums due them old Picott employed Indians to kill them. When these posts were sold to government Picott went crazy over his murders and his wife [blank] who was a Choteau, took him to foreign lands in the endeavor to restore his reason. He got very rich in the fur trade. His salary was $5,000 a year and perquisites.[30]

Mr. Mosseau says the Choteau company was an iniquitous concern. The men composing it were Pierre Choteau Sr., Pierre Choteau Jr., [John B.] Sarpy, Lamye, James Lorette. There may have been some silent partners.[31]

Lorette drew out and took his share of the proceeds. He went up somewhere about St. Paul (on the Mississippi) and erected with his private funds a school to manufacture priests and monks and nuns and to Catholicize the young Indians. But he could not fill his houses, as his name, associated with the Chouteau Company, was rank and monstrous. So he shipped prostitutes from St. Louis to occupy these quarters, and he went back to Canada to live.

I called his attention to Chittenden's History of the American Fur Trade, and he remarked that it would not tell half the truth; that he is acquainted with such books, and that they conceal more truth than they record.[32]

Mr. Mousseau says that the Indians dreaded to fight the western settlers because they were tough, hardy, and trained by experience to Indian warfare, fought the Indian in his own style, and living so much by hunting as they did they were sure shots—the Indians were chary of these men; but to fight the soldiers was more in the nature of a picnic; they said they could kill them with clubs.

The Indians also feared the infantry more than cavalry which could run away; but infantrymen could do nothing but stand their ground and fight, and they were therefore far more dangerous.

Mr. Magloire A. Mousseau, speaking of the Indian ring, says it is doing everything in its power to keep the Indians from realizing on their intellectual and moral improvement. This ring, not being able to prevent the national effort to educate and civilize them, is successful in keeping them from making any progress after they quit school and are turned out with sufficient knowledge to become good artisans and mechanics and teachers, by closing the avenues of employment to them and giving the places to others, and when they are accepted their services are compensated with such paltry wages as to discourage and drive them away. The following cases he cites: A young man who had spent full time at Carlisle came back to Pine Ridge and was employed by Colonel Gallagher at the trade of harness making and saddlery. He was a good workman. A special agent came in one day where he was at work in the Agency shop and asked the young man his name and where he learned his trade. The young man replied at Carlisle. The Indian was sitting facing a large window at work and with his back to the door where the special agent entered. The agent came up behind and the Indian failed to observe who he was. In answer to his inquiries he told the agent that he went to Carlisle when very young and was there 12 years. He also said that he was now working here; his boss told him in the morning what to do that day and then he went away to his ranch to attend to his private business and returned at night. At the Agent's request he told him the name of his boss. "How much a month does your boss get?" "Seventy-five dollars, I am informed." "How much do you receive?" "I get fifteen. I shall have to quit if I do not get more. I cannot live and clothe myself at that." The special agent then said, "I want you to have forty-five dollars a month. I will see the agent about it; and I will see that you get it. When I leave here I will give you my address, and if the Agent knocks down your wages you let me know and I will see that they are restored." The increased wages were paid to him for six months and then he had saved enough money to buy some leather and he started into business on his own account out on Wounded Knee Creek. This Indian was Calico's son. Forgotten his own name.

Mrs. Mosseau's own son, James, learned carpentry at Pine Ridge Agency. He asked several times for work at the Agency from Mr. Brannan but was refused. The time came when he went to Brannan for a pass to the Arapahoe Agency (which is in Wyoming near Fort Washakie) and the Agent asked what he was going there for. He told the agent to get work; said he could get all the work there that he wanted. He had worked there before and knew. Mr. Brennan said, "You can have work here." Jim Mousseau answered, "No, I don't want it; I applied several times and you refused me work, and now I am going where I can get it and have it all the time."

Mr. Mousseau speaks in great praise of Major Brennan; says he is the best agent ever here; stands next to Fitzpatrick of 1851 fame. Brennan is a good and upright counsellor; does not magnify difficulties or pecadilloes or offenses, but carefully investigates and advises and excuses as far as possible, aiming always to do justice.

When the Protestants attempted to have the funds withdrawn which the Catholic schools receive, Mr. Brennan actively interested himself to defeat the plan. This, it is evident, has its influence on Mr. Mousseau as he is a Catholic by education in youth and life long practice.

Mr. M. A. Mousseau says he has heard General Sheridan say that the only good Indian is a dead one, and he himself seems to have about the same opinion. He certainly has no good opinion of them, and this he distinctly says. He says they ought to be killed and burned as the whites were by them. He scouts the Indian Rights Association.

[George W. Colhoff's Interview]

George Colhoff had a varied career in the West. He was an unem-ployed store clerk when Charles Allen met him near Fort Laramie in the early 1870s. He had a temporary job reading books to Nicholas Janis, an illiterate but moderately wealthy trader. Later Colhoff clerked in a store near Fort Robinson.[33]

[Tablet 17]

~~Interview with George W. Colhoff at Pine Ridge, Nov. 22, 1906.~~

He was a member of the 5th U.S. vols., the "galvanized" regiment which was composed of some ex-Confederate soldiers & a good many Union men who had been taken prisoners, generally from the Army of the Potomac, and having little hope of being exchanged in any reasonable time enlisted in Confederate regiments and as soon as opportunity presented deserted and came to the north; after which they became alarmed fearing what might be the consequences, and allowed themselves to be treated as Confederate prisoners, and afterwards enlisted in this 5th U.S. volunteers.

There were six of these "galvanized" regiments, namely, 1st, 2d, 3d, 4th, 5th and 6th. Mr. Colhoff belonged to the 5th, which was composed as follows: 2 companies from Camp Chase, Ohio; 4 from Camp Douglas, Chicago; and 4 from Alton, Ills. He thinks the first four were sent up the Missouri river. The 5th & 6th were sent out to protect the U.P.R.R.

Mr. Colhoff came out west in the 5th in 1865, landing at Fort Laramie Nov. 14th.

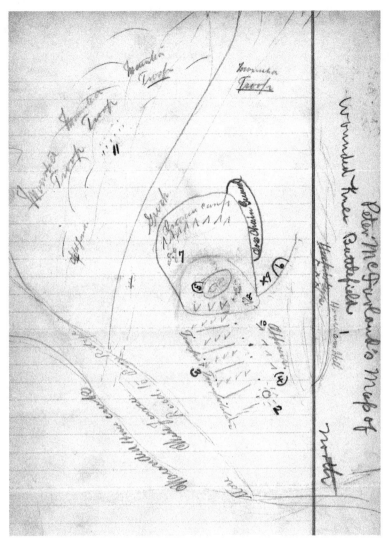

Peter McFarland's map of Wounded Knee

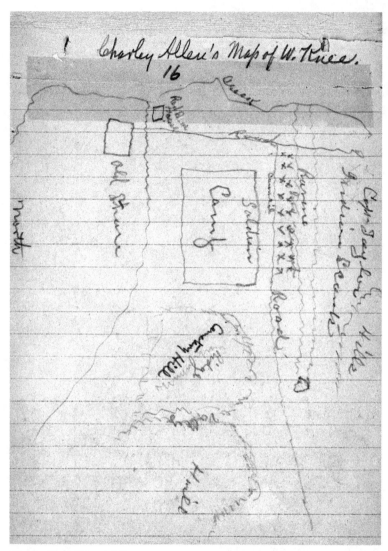

Charles Allen's Wounded Knee

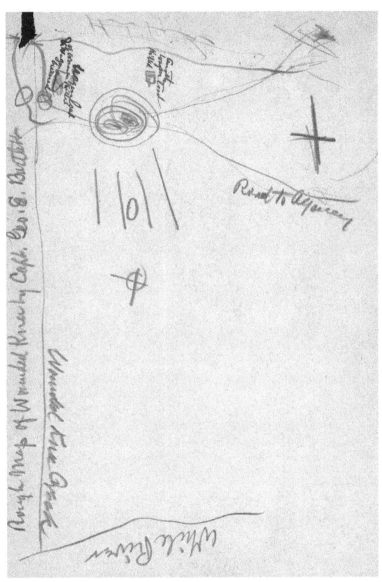

Rough map of Wounded Knee by Capt. Geo. E. Bartlett

The Comanche people and some other tribes have them like this. — — — I am going to send one to Esther for Christmas if I can find a pretty one. The Apache cradles are more like this, and the baby lies on the lacing, covered with buckskin or blanket. Of course this is not Apache country, but there are some Apache prisoners of war near by; Geronimo the chief is down in history as the most cruel chief that ever lived. I met him yesterday and talked to him through an interpreter. When asked

Ricker copied Mabel Gould's sketches of Comanche and Apache cradles.

Isaac Robins's fight on Lightning Creek

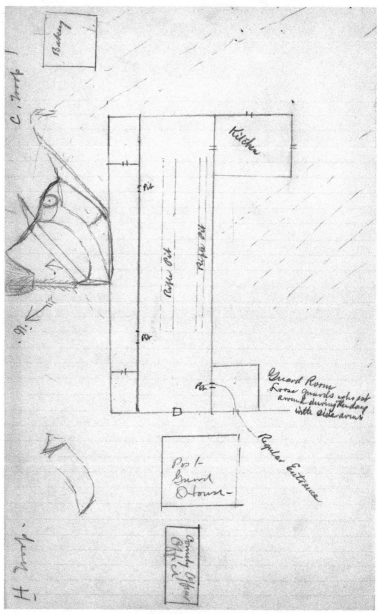

Carter P. Johnson's sketch of the barracks at Fort Robinson, where Dull Knife's Cheyenne were imprisoned in 1878

2,0

Beecher Island 2nd Monument.

The shaft is larger than shown here to harmonize with the base. Fine monument & not defaced a particle. Iron fence six feet high incloses monument.

Inscriptions as follows:

On north side:

Battle of Beecher's Island
Fought Sept. 17, 18 and 19 A.D. 1868
between Col. Geo. A. Forsyth's Company
of Citizen Scouts numbering 51 men,
and a large party of Indians comprising
Northern Cheyennes, Ogallalah Sioux
and Dog Soldiers commanded by the
noted war chief Roman Nose.
The Scouts were surrounded and
held on this Island for nine days,

Eli Ricker's Beecher Island

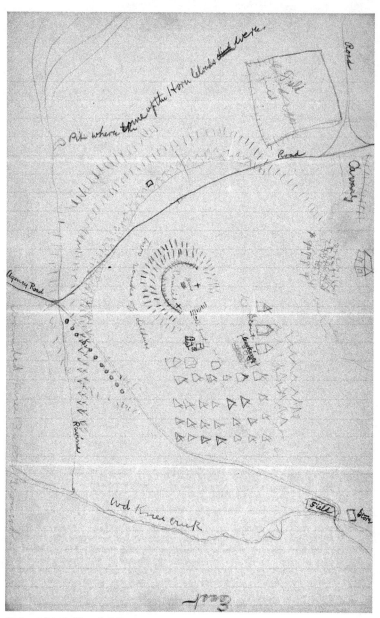

Richard Stirk's Wounded Knee

ooooooooooooo These are the troops placed by Stirk. I think
Horn Cloud put soldiers there thus ////////

Description of Battleground

This house was on the summit of Cemetery Hill and occupied by Eagle Bull. There were two houses there, as Louie Mousseau says.

Guards kept ~~trenched~~ at the foot of Cemetery Hill from whom the Reliefs were sent out during the night. Had no tents. Sat and talked.

Hotchkiss Cannon. Joseph Horn Cloud who made this map does not know the number of cannon. Louie Mousseau says there were four.

△ △ △ △   Tents of the Soldiers

Big F. slept. This is the tent in which Big Foot slept that night. He was carried out of this tent to the Council. He was placed where the boxes is in this row. The one to the right of Big Foot is his brother, the one to the left is Joseph Horn Cloud's father ~~Horned~~ Cloud. The others are officers, interpreters, etc.

Indian Tents. The ☐ is where Big Foot's own tent was where his family spent the night.

These are Soldiers in rear of the Indian camp. The inner line is the camp guard that was maintained during the night and was on duty when the fight began. The guard had been relieved in the morning. The outside line is composed of the Taylor scouts. The two small half or three-quarter circles are soldiers in two ranks around the Indian council which is indicated by this ℭ.

Indians in Council

= Pile of guns

+ This figure in the upper part of the Council is the Medicine Man who was gesticulating by swinging his arms.

+ This figure at the right extremity of the Council is the deaf man who stood a little in advance of the Indians in council. He it was who had the struggle with the three sergeants for possession of his gun, and it was this gun which was discharged by accident and set off the fight.

These tents marked "Scouts" were those belonging to the scouts who were with Major Whiteside at the advance. Capt. Taylor's scouts came out from the Agency about 11 p.m. on the night of the 28th, and they camped half a mile or more back on the road toward the Agency. Philip F. Wells was with these.

Mr. R. C. Stirk says (and I adopt the statement) that the Indian tents did not cross the agency road that led to the store, but they came to or nearly to it on the west side.
The white horse troop of cavalry was dismounted, holding their horses and facing toward the west and standing on the east side of the agency road leading to the store; this troop's left flank rested on the ravine and extended along the road the length of the troop. This must have been Wells' Troop K. The Indians broke from the circle toward this troop as if to go down the ravine to W. K. Creek, but these soldiers drove them back up the ravine when they took shelter under the banks. He says Horn Cloud's half circle should be screwed round so the west end would be more in the north and the east end more in the south. He pronounces this a good map.

He says that at this time there were Indian districts and each had a superintendent of Indian Affairs. At this time E. B. Taylor (Editor & prop. of the Omaha Republican) of Omaha was the supt. for Nebraska.

He was stationed at Fort Casper 2 months in 1866. He thinks this fort was built in 1863. It was made wholly of logs. When Fort Fetterman was established in 1867, Fort Casper was abandoned. Fort Fetterman was built by Capt. Kellogg (bvt. major) who began it and did a good deal of the building which was of logs except the sutler's store which was of adobes. Major (bvt. Colonel) Dye (of Iowa) came later and took command of the post over Kellogg, who was lower in grade, and finished the work.[34]

The Overland stage and Western Union Telegraph used to run through Fort Casper. Operators who were not very competent were stationed along this line 20 miles apart, more to work each way from their several stations and keep their lines in repair than for anything else.

In the fall of 1865 the 5th U.S. Vols. arrived at Fort Laramie (Nov. 14th). The officers of this regt. were men who had been officers in the regular army. The Colonel was Henry E. Manydier (I have in some places contradicted people who spoke of Manydier & told them it was Manypenny). In the fall of 1865 he sent out two Indian messengers to all the bands of the Sioux nation who lived off to the north at that time — Spotted Tail, Young Man Afraid of His Horses, Red Cloud and others. These Indians came in abt. May or June, 1866 and a commission was there to meet them.[35] Spotted Tail made a treaty at this time and was quiet ever after this. Red Cloud would not make a treaty but told the comrs. that they must abandon the three forts — C. F. Smith, Reno and Phil Kearny — before he would make a treaty. Spotted Tail was the only one who made a treaty at this time and he always kept it.

There was a chief Roman Nose, a Sioux who belonged really at Standing Rock but happened at the time to be over where "Spot" & the others were and he came in with these; he was a mean fellow, etc.; he brought in one hand a pipe and in the other a bundle of arrows, and holding these out to Colonel Maynadier asked which he wanted. The Colonel replied that he had sent for him to make peace, and he took the pipe and asked the chief to come and smoke. They went in and had a talk which amounted to nothing.

When Spotted Tail came he bore the dead body of his daughter on a horse. The military and all (not under orders) but voluntarily turned out and paid their respects to the dead and the old Chieftan. Colonel Manydier took a leading part in the preparations and ceremonies and bore most of the expense of the burial. The usual scaffold was erected; on the two posts facing east were placed the heads of two beautiful spotted ponies which were killed by the Indians for the purpose, and the two tails were nailed at the top of the other two posts. The coffin was laid on top of the scaffold and covered with blue Indian cloth nailed on the box.[36]

Mr. Colhoff says it was told and published afterwards that this girl fell in love with an army officer and he cleared out; but he says that nobody who was acquainted with the parties ever knew of it, and that it was a fabrication.

Fort Laramie was the center of the long-time gathering of trappers, freighters, pioneers, emigrants, traders, scouts, mountaineers, hunters, soldiers, warriors, travelers and every description of western life and living and employment. Its neighborhood was a great resort for the French.

Mr. Colhoff says the Laparell Creek empties into the Platte at old Fort Fetterman.

In 1870 he was up at Fetterman working on a hay contract; came down to Laramie after haying and went to work in a store; the next spring or summer work was begun on the "Sod Agency," as it was called, but which was really the Red Cloud Agency, built on the north side of the Platte River, 30 miles below Fort Laramie and some 6 or 7 miles above the mouth of Horse Creek.[37] An incident follows: A Major Joseph W. Wham, an Illinoisan, was the first agent appointed to that agency under the 1868 treaty.[38] Orders from government sources came directing that no more rations be issued to Indians on the south side of the Platte. Red Cloud hearing of this gave notice that he would kill any person who should make the attempt to issue on the north side or go over to receive rations. Chief Red Dog (long since dead) and John Richard Jr. a half breed, getting Red Dog's band together and some of the Loafer Indians, and scattering ones besides, went over the river and gave out that the rations should be issued over there and that the agent and his employees should be safe from harm.[39] This accomplished the design. So the "Sod Agency" was built away down on the north side where it remained two winters, and in the fall of 1873 it was moved to the White River and in the fall of 1877 to the Missouri.

In 1867 Gen. Sherman and other commissioners came out to Fort Laramie to make a treaty but they could not get the Indians in. The next year (1868) Gens. Harney and John B. Sanborn and others came out but Gen. Sherman was not there, and this time a treaty was signed.[40] It was provided in this treaty that the Indians should go to the Missouri, and as soon as those who had signed the treaty had done so they went to the Missouri, but they did not remain, some stayed that winter and began drifting back, together with some white men, in 1869. Red Cloud did not come in to take part in this treaty, and he has always declared that he did not sign it, and Mr. Colhoff knows that he did not come in till October, 1868; for Charles E. Geuren, special interpreter, a native born Frenchman, was left behind with beef cattle and rations for Red Cloud when he should come in to accept the terms of the treaty.[41] But he did not come and these cattle were driven to the Whetstone Agency on the Missouri. Mr. Colhoff went with this stock. Young Man Afraid would not stir, but some of his Indians went to Whetstone; and scattering ones from other bands, so that there was a large concourse of these altogether. These, in going, swung down on the Platte to North Platte and took in Spotted Tail's band, but this chief would not go to Whetstone, but did settle down on the White River some distance above the forks of the White River, and being obliged to adapt to circumstances, a sub-agent, Tod Randall, was sent out to act for the government in that locality.

The treaty of 1868 is one of unusual importance, and has been held by many Indians and mixed-bloods who acquired privileges of equality with Indians under it, has been held with reverence. ~~There can be no just pretense that Red Cloud assented to it, though~~ (the name of ~~General~~ Major Cain, 4th Infantry appears upon the treaty as a witness to Red Cloud's signature;) ~~for Mr. Colhoff personally knows, being himself connected with the care and removal of the property left behind for Red Cloud, that he did not come in to receive it as he would with all certainty have done if he had come and agreed to the treaty.~~ There was some question whether Red Cloud signed, it being claimed that he had not come in.

The bounds of the reservation under the treaty of 1868 were not and could not be clearly defined so as to escape the danger of subsequent dissatisfaction by the Indians. The west boundary was the 103d degree, the north the Cannonball river, but the south line was indeterminate, the white commissioners supposing it would be along the Niobrara River and the Indians understanding it was so, have never been satisfied with the occupation by the white settlers of that part of their reservation which they claimed as lying in Nebraska.[42]

A line was run by Col. Sawyer in 1865, who was escorted by two companies of the 5th U.S. Volunteers; he started at the mouth of the Niobrara River and followed up this stream and he ran to where Fort Connor was established in 1865. These two companies of 5th U.S. Vols. was ordered up from Fort Leavenworth. Mr. Colhoff does not know what this survey was for.

Mr. Colhoff and others came back from the Whetstone Agency in June 1869 to Laramie. Crazy Horse ran some men into Laramie soon after Mr. C. got back. There was really little peace and safety around that country at that time; the Indians were stealing horses and killing people. It was in the fall of 1869 (he is pretty sure) that a delegation of Indians, including Red Cloud (this was before Young Man Afraid had become much) Old Man Afraid was the main one of the Afraids in those days.

(Mr. Colhoff says that Old man Afraid abdicated in favor of Young Man Afraid a year or two before his death which was about 1886 or 1887. He was getting pretty old.)

Twenty-five or thirty Indians were taken to Washington and New York and other places. Young John Richard, Jules Eccoffey, and Nick Janis went with them, perhaps others also.[43]

Young John Richard had a little while before wantonly shot a soldier who was sitting out in front and eating; John was drunk & riding by on horseback and murdered the soldier & skipped. He was said to be influential in getting the Indians together & to consent to go, and for this service he was pardoned or let off in some way from prosecution for his crime.[44] He was subsequently killed about the summer of 1872 between Fort Laramie and the Sod Agency. The circumstances were: when he murdered the soldier he had a wife, a daughter of Joe Marrivall, father of Charles. After the murder he fled north among the Indians and was there a year or so among them, and in the meantime took a wife up there and had a child by her; when he got back to Laramie he saw Nick Janis' daughter (now Mrs. Tibbitts) and married her according to Indian fashion. John Richard later started down the Platte with Wm. Garnett and others, going in a wagon, and when they got down on the north side of the river 14 miles below Fort Laramie he went into the tent of Chief Yellow Bear, and he told the chief that he wanted the woman he had taken when he was up north and Yellow Bear told him he had now married the Janis woman and could not retake the other, and in the dispute Richard shot Yellow Bear dead, and the Indians present stabbed Richard and killed him.

The old man Richard was killed with a man named Palladay at the upper crossing of the Niobrara. California Joe was accused of the crime, but it was afterwards ascertained that he was innocent; it was found that a party of Cheyennes did it, two of them wore highheeled boots which led to the supposition that the deed was done by whites, but two of these Indians had obtained them and wore them. The Richards were a pretty hard lot.[45]

Red Cloud Agency got to be a mighty tough place, being a rendezvous for road agents — such men as Black Doc, Fly Speck Bill, Paddy Simmons, Tom Reed, Herman Leisner and many others who infested the Sidney road, and the Black Hills route through Hat Creek, and farther west; a lot of them worked off into western Wyoming, some got killed; they operated over a wide territory, some got into the penitentiary both east and west; they all gambled, stole horses and other property, held up stage coaches, committed murders and were just about as versatile in crime as practice could make them. Lame Johnnie was another.

Mr. Colhoff says Charlie Allen is the friend of Red Cloud while he himself is not a Red Cloud man, though he respects him for his age and because he has always been faithful to his people. He has never betrayed his race. But he has always opposed the whites and all their propositions for the benefit of the Indians. When the "Sod Agency" was moved over from the Platte Red Cloud opposed it and refused to move his band, but the agency came over nevertheless, and he was compelled by necessity to follow. When the removal of the Indians was made in 1877 Red Cloud again was in opposition and went down the White River with strong reluctance, and when they came to the mouth of Black Pipe he declared that was the forks of the White River and he would go no farther. A stop was made here and work begun on some log buildings which were raised to the height for roofing when it was found out that they were 40 miles above the forks of the river, and they had to tear up and go farther down. Colhoff says there was a detention here about ten days.

Mr. Colhoff knew Frank Gruard well. When he was first at Red Cloud Agency he wore a G string. This is the statement of others. He wore a blanket the same as other Indians. Mr. C. thinks he came over to Red Cloud from Standing Rock. Says he was an inveterate gambler and always out of money. Mr. C. sent him up to the Fort when he was employed by the military who asked Colhoff if he knew where Gruard was. He was paid $10 a day. Both Big and Little Bat told Mr. Colhoff that Gen. Crook told them to watch Gruard and if he attempted to betray his companions to shoot him. This was before he had been on service and proved himself. But he was found to be most faithful. The Indians were very sore at him and complained that they had raised him and that he had quit them and joined their enemies and giving them the benefit of his knowledge. In his knowledge of the northwest country he was not surpassed by that prince of scouts, Jim Bridger. He could tell exactly in what direction & how far it was to any particular spring, or stream, or to grass or wood and how long it would take to reach the desired point, and it would be reached not far from the time that he had stated.

The Northern Cheyennes and Northern Arapahoes belonged to the Red Cloud Agency till about the time the Oglalas were taken down to the White River and the Missouri. The Arapahoes by some arrangement went west to the Shoshones and got part of their reservation. The Cheyennes — Living Bear's, Little Chief's, Wild Hog's and Dull Knife's bands — were taken south to Indian territory in 1877.

There are Northern and Southern Arapahoes as well as Northern and Southern Cheyennes. Colhoff does not know how they came to be divided.

In the summer of 1878 Gen. Stanley, Stephen R. Riggs and James R. O'Burn (O'Bierne) (the latter was afterwards Commissioner of Immigration in New York) and Red Cloud came up to Pine Ridge and located this Agency. Red Cloud would have been glad to go farther west and really desired to have a location in the neighborhood of Raw Hide, but these commissioners told him that this was as far west as they thought they could go, and a stop was made at this place. The old commissary at Red Cloud was moved over to Pine Ridge; it used to stand where the new Agent's office now does. The good lumber in the stockade and some other buildings was hauled over to P. Ridge.[46]

The building that I saw standing at Red Cloud, being of sawed logs, was Frank D. Yates', a brother to Capt. Yates who fell with Custer. Yates was a trader at Red Cloud.

Colhoff was clerking for Frank D. Yates at Red Cloud when the Custer battle took place. Some Indians in the store one morning were overheard talking among themselves and saying that they had killed Custer and all his men. Colhoff went in and told Frank D. Yates what had been heard & Yates drove up to the Fort and told Capt. (Bvt. Major) Mayer, commanding officer, of the rumor; he pooh poohed the statement and remarked that when they killed Custer they would know that they had been having a matinee among themselves. Yates asked the officer to telegraph to Ruggles, Adjt. General of the Department, at Omaha, for news; but no word had been received there of the disaster. However, in about [?] confirmation of it came from headquarters.[47]

Mr. Colhoff speaks of the signalling by the Indians by means of glasses, and adds that in those days when he was around the Agencies that nearly every Indian had a glass hanging to him. These glasses were set into a solid wooden back with a handle. The glass proper was about four by six inches. He does not know how the Indians communicated the news of the Custer battle so quickly, but thinks they were expecting a fight and had signaling couriers stationed along from the Big Horn country to the agencies.

He says that Boucher had a trading post somewhere on Chadron Creek (doesn't know where) wherefore the Indians always call it Boucher Creek, and until recent years they used to speak of the City of Chadron as the town on Boucher Creek.

It was thought that Boucher was supplying the Indians who drew supplies from Red Cloud, with ammunition and arms. These Agency Indians were drawing rations on an excessive enumeration. They received a beef for thirty persons every ten days. They used to empty the flour out on the ground to get the sacks. They were drawing much more than they could use and were sending the surplus to their hostile friends in the north who were fighting the troops.

Mr. Colhoff says that Sword, son of Brave Bear and brother of George Sword, was the principal young man who headed the decoy party with American Horse at Fort Phil Kearny. He says that he has always understood that there were six or seven men in this decoy party. This old Sword died and was buried over about Ash Creek.

Colhoff relates an incident in the life of Jim Bridger which came near costing him his life. He was guiding a party of men up into the Montana country and was as usual pestered beyond endurance by their inquiries, and particularly their demands for information about gold. To make an end of their annoyance he thought he would tell them a story so improbable that they would take the hint and let him alone. But they were gold-mad, and when he told them that he knew of a place where they could back wagons up to it in the mass and break it off like icicles, they must have thought that he knew where there were fabulous quantities of the metal stored in the earth and did not want to reveal its location. His answer so incensed them that they were about to hang him, when Joe Marrivall (father of Charles) and another, believed to be Nick Janis, who happened to be with the party, interceded and told them that it would be suicide to take Bridger's life, as they could never find their way out of that blind country without his assistance.

Mr. Colhoff says that Little Bat was Gen. Crook's favorite hunting scout. Crook said Bat was the nerviest man he ever saw. One time Little Bat was out with a party and Crook was along and had wounded a grizzly. Bat jumped down into a hole in the ground and the bear was coming toward him. Bat jerked out his paper and tobacco and rolled up a cigarette and lighted it coolly while bruin was approaching and had his gun in hand as the monster was at the edge of the pit. Bang! and the top of the animal's head was off!

Another time they were out on a hunt and a fine black bear had been shot and fallen into a deep place. The General was eager for the bear skin, and Bat said he would jump down and get him. The General expostulated telling Bat that he did not want to lose him, fearing the bear might only be wounded. Bat replied that the bear was dead, and went down and put a rope on him so the others could draw him up.

Colhoff says that Little Wound's cutoff band and Young Man Afraid hunted down on the lower Platte, while Red Cloud and Spotted Tail and most of the others ranged up in the Black Hills and off on the Tongue, Powder, Rosebud and the Big Horns.

Indian Billy [?] Colhoff and Sammy Deon say, killed Big Mouth at the instigation of Spotted Tail. They think Mrs. John Farnham was a daughter of Big Mouth. Big Mouth was a mean, lazy Indian who laid around the agency. when he got full of bug juice he always wanted to kill a white man.

Colhoff and Deon say that the Fort St. John which belonged to the American Fur Company was sold to the government in 1849 and became Fort Laramie. Mr. Colhoff understands that it was an army officer, Col. Laramie, who negotiated on behalf of the government for the purchase of Fort St. John; and hence after the transfer the fort and the river and the mountain were named Laramie.[48]

Crazy Horse's widow was a daughter of old Joe Larrabee. She was a half breed.[49] Colhoff says the only act of bravery he ever saw in an Indian was when Crazy Horse chased [blank] into Fort Robinson [Laramie] and shot him before all the soldiers looking on.

[Tablet 25]

George W. Colhoff says, in my interview with him at his home on White Clay Creek, Sunday, November 25, 1906.

Speaking of Red Cloud he says: That the old man was not democratic but autocratic; he was not willing for the majority to rule, but was insistent that the minority, with himself at their head, should have things their way. If he had had the majority with him McGillicudy would not have stayed here six months. But he got the Indians divided, as a good politician would, though Mr. C. says he had an actual majority of the Indians on his side.

Young Man Afraid of His Horses who had a considerable band, and Little Wound and his large band to a man, and part of White Bird's band which was also large, were the supporters of McGillicudy. American Horse and Three Stars, (uncle to Clarence) both of whom had a few followers of some eight or ten lodges each, were nominally if not genuinely supporters of the Agent. He thinks Three Stars was genuinely true to McGillicudy: but he says he does not know how American Horse really felt, but as a policy man he of course appeared to be on the side of the man in power.

Dr. Irwin had been agent for the Shoshones (I think he was the one who made complaint about the Indians starving and some action was taken by Congress. Some beans intended for the Inds. got snow bound & when the doctor was asked what had become of them he reported that they "had wasted their sweetness on the desert air," and for this impertinence he was summoned to Washington upon the carpet for explanations.)

Dr. Irwin was appointed Agent for Red Cloud Agency before the removal to the Missouri in 1877; he relieved Lieutenant Charles A. Johnson, 14th Infy. He was agent till after the Indians came to Pine Ridge. He did not hold after the return quite a year. He was relieved by McGillicudy. McGillicudy was relieved by Major Bell of the 7th Cavalry.[50] He was removed because of a foolish break. A committee of Congress consisting of Holman of Indiana, Ryan of Kansas and Cannon of Illinois came out to investigate Agency affairs, and Holman did not accept the Agent's hospitality but went to the hotel for entertainment; the others threw themselves into McGillicudy's arms. At length McGillicuddy sent Donald Brown, who held some position as employee at the Agency under the Agent, to invite Holman to his office. Brown went to Holman and delivered his invitation and Mr. H. told him that he was on the ground charged with official duties as a congressman and he did not see his duty clear to go. Brown had told him that the Agent wanted him to report at his office. Brown now said to him that his orders from the Agent were that if he did not come to bring him. Holman said he was not in the habit of receiving such treatment, but to avoid trouble would go, and he did so. In a few months, as a result of this insolence, Major Bell was sent to relieve him.

Bell was in as Agent about six months and was supplanted by Col. Gallagher of Greensburg, Indiana. Gallagher was an easy man like Dr. Irwin, and satisfied with drawing his salary if affairs went along in orderly fashion, and it did not give him so very much concern if the Indians did not get ahead so very fast.

When McGillicudy was appointed Agent Red Cloud came over and greeted him with the information that he had heard he was now to be their agent, and told him that when he received anything from Washington he wanted him to send for him and read it to him so that he could keep informed of the course of affairs. McGillicuddy told him that when he received anything that concerned Red Cloud he would do so, but otherwise he should not; and furthermore he wanted Red Cloud to understand that he himself was going to be the Agent.

This was the beginning of the strife between the two. Red Cloud could not control the Agent, and this was enough for the domestic war which raged between these men as long as McGillicuddy held his place. McGillicuddy took charge early in the year 1879. He filled one full term and was serving his second when [Pres. Grover] Cleveland came in. There were no charges against him as an Agent, but a pretext was found for his removal in his overbearing treatment of Mr. Holman.

Senator Pettigrew of S.D. was godfather for Agent Royer, who had been a member of the legislature and done the Senator some service in securing his election as U.S. Senator. Royer was backboneless. There was no need of troops.

Post trader Finley had a Missouri U.S. Senator for godfather. When the die had been cast by Royer, Finley, for whom Colhoff was clerking in the store, called Colhoff to one side and told him that it was not his night to go home, but there was something about to happen and it might be well for him to go home for the safety of his family; then he told Colhoff that the troops were coming and were likely to reach the Agency that night. Colhoff said he should certainly go home in that event to look after his folks. He did so. His place then was where it is now 1½ miles north of [the] Agency but he was living in a log house nearer the creek than at present. Next morning he returned to the Agency.

When Mr. Colhoff got into the Agency he saw the Ninth Cavalry in front of the Agent's office.[51]

The proceedings at the Agency were from this time on lively in getting wood and hay for the troops, and there was some enlisting of Indians for scouts, there being, as he states about 200 of these enlistments (This may be high).

Mr. Colhoff says that Red Cloud and Nick Janis were close friends. That it was through the influence of the former that the old sod Agency on the Platte was given to Nick.

Red Cloud's band, he says, was composed of the renegade Indians, and so says Clarence Three Stars; that they were called Bad Faces.[52]

Old Man Afraid was a chief of great worth, but Three Stars says Red Cloud has had greater reputation as a brave fighter than any other.

Mr. Colhoff says that Father Jutz was coming to the Agency and got up on the ridge near Colhoff's place and the Inds. would not let him go any farther but turned him back telling him to go the Mission and remain there within the premises and he should receive no harm nor any of his people there. So he returned and it was as had been promised.[53]

Mr. Colhoff says that the Indians when they went down to the Missouri River in 1868 did not stay very long; he remembers that he and the others with whom he was [with] came back around by the U.P.R.R. and up from Cheyenne in the fall of 1869, and that the Indians were sifting back at that time.

He also says that the issuing points were shifted about up in this White River country as different contractors got the contracts, the incentive being to secure the fat allowances for transportation, they being paid two cents a pound for one hundred miles. They let the contracts in those days by the hundred miles. Miles were pretty short. The issuing station was once at the mouth of Beaver Creek for Spotted Tail's band, and it was moved from there up to where Camp Sheridan was. The issuing post was for a period on wheels, so to speak — six months or so in a place.

Mr. Colhoff says he does not blame the Indians for not staying down on the Missouri; it was a poor place; but it was all right at the forks of the White River.

Frauds

He says that J. J. Saville belonged to Omaha and dabbled somewhat in politics. He came up for office and Rosewater sprung the beans and sugar incident on him at old Red Cloud Agency and Saville was knocked out. The incident was this: This agent receipted to the contractor for sugar and actually received beans when the difference in price [was] three to one for sugar against beans — sugar $12 a sack, beans $3 or $4.[54]

Mr. Colhoff says in those times some 500 head of cattle were issued every ten days. He remembers one lot had not been branded, and in the night 200 head escaped. The contractor was fair enough to all appearances; he said if the Agent could identify the cattle he was welcome to take them from the contractor's herd. Of course he could not do that. Of course his interest did not lie in identification but rather in the failure of it. But Colhoff saw numbers of these same cattle pass in the second time for issue. Why should the agent receipt for sugar and take beans? And when beans were not half so expensive as sugar. Everybody but a lightning calculator would have to give it up, unless he was impious enough to suspect that a man in the Indian service could he corrupt enough to steal.

Yet Mr. Colhoff says that stealing was the rule and honesty the exception.

I have yet to find one person who was on the frontier in those days, and I have talked with hundreds of them, some of whom were helping to handle the Indians' property in clerical and menial positions but who needed only eyes and ears to know the truth of what they aver. I have yet to find one who has not said that stealing from both Indians and government went on daily, glaringly, wastefully and by wholesale. No man with knowledge and with eternal consequences staring him in the face would think of raising any question on this point. If the service has improved in more recent years it is not because human nature has changed and the desire for gain diminished in men's hearts, but because opportunities are less open and easy, though experience has shown that in such cases the corruption and crime are as rife as ever, while only the methods change with varying conditions by becoming more insidious and exquisite, the rascal studying how to load his pockets and at the same time slip by, though rubbing incautiously hard the doors of the penitentiary. Happy age—for speculators and robbers! There have been some notably honest Indian officers. Capt. John Bourke records one which is worthy of notice in this connection, etc.[55]

More provisions were issued than the Indians could use. So much beef was cast away on them that they frequently made use of only the choice parts. ~~The Oglalas and Cheyennes were reckoned at one time at about 14,000, but when later 10,000~~ The Sioux, Cheyennes and Arapahoes at one time, and this when Major Wham took control on the Platte, were returned at 14,000. Nick Janis was employed by the Major to count these Indians and give each family a ticket certifying the man as head of the family, together with the woman or women who were wives, and the children (the same method being used to this day). Nick's tickets when footed up amounted to 14,000 persons entitled to rations. Major Wham asked Nick after an issue had been made on his tickets, to certify that this number of rations had been dealt out. But Nick balked—flatly refused to do it; for while he was a man of the Big Heart and took pleasure in doing the Indians a good turn, he was the last man to make a false certificate! Wham accused Nick of repudiating his own figures and complained that by his off-hand generosity he had put him in a squirmish situation, and wound up his protest by ordering Nick out of his office. Then he appointed Nick's brother, Antoine, to the vacated position of census taker.

Indian families were truly patriarchal in those days, the progeny numbering from a dozen to a dozen and a half to a lodge with as much ease as regularity. It was never any trouble for children which had been counted in one tipi to stand ready in another to do good service there when the Big Hearted enumerator got around. This is a species of accommodation in the form of loaning not of exclusive Indian acquaintance and probably not of Indian origin. However, the Indians never forget this padding of the census and it served them well till McGillicuddy became Agent, when he effected some reforms. One of these was the cutting down of chiefs' rations. A chief, besides drawing for the actual number accredited to his lodge, also drew some 15 and others 30 as he recollects, rations every ten days on account [of] his chieftainship, the reason therefor which was recognized and allowed, was, that his official position in the tribe compelled him to do extra entertaining. Mr. Colhoff says they issued tickets once a year, as they do now after taking the census.

Major Bell who was the Agent about six months between McGillicudy and Gallagher, was the first to cause a rigid and correct census to be taken. He had them lined up and Indian police so stationed as to detect and prevent repeating. This proceeding reduced the number of rations some 1,000 to 1,200.

The effect on the Cheyennes of dropping from some 600 to less than 400 was especially pleasing to McGillicuddy who had once had an "incident" with these people. When they were living at the mouth of Beaver Creek the early settlers in northwest Nebraska were losing stock and accused the Indians of stealing it. The Agent, satisfying himself that there was probable truth in it, ordered the Cheyennes to move on to the Reservation behind Wolf Creek and the Agency but they would not do it. When issue day came the gates of the corral were opened and animals for the Oglalas turned out to them. Then the gates were closed and the Cheyennes told that when they complied with his order of removal that they could obtain their beef and not until then. Then the work oxen were brought and put into the corral so the discomfited Cheyennes could not slaughter these, and then they moved off sullenly, not daring to offer any violence. In a few days they came stringing into the Agency in obedience to orders, and the Agent gave them the cattle.

Mr. Colhoff thinks the Indians did not make their numbers appear large for any other object than to impress the whites with their great numerical strength and power; and the reason he gives for this opinion is that the Indians made no disturbance when they were cut down.

George W. Colhoff says: That on the morning of the battle of Wounded Knee he was coming up from his ranch to the Agency when the distant sound of battle could be heard. The Indians were in commotion on the ridge north of the village; some were throwing stray shots into the Agency; some were starting toward W.K., and the excitement was universal. The Indians told Colhoff to go into the Agency and stay there. They did not say what they were going to do.

[Tablet 13]
March 13, 1907

Mr. Colhoff says that Rev. John Robinson, representing the Episcopal Church was the first missionary to the Oglalas. Rev. Cleveland was missionary to the Brulés. Robinson is still living at Sisseton Agency. He was followed by Charles Smith Cook, a full-blood Indian educated by Bishop Hare. Cook died at his post at Pine Ridge.[56]

He says that he thinks it was abt. 1873 when the Pawnee young men were out on a hunt & the Sioux jumped their village & killed the old men, women & children who were there. After this, it is his recollection that Col. Carr organized an expedition, and taking the Pawnees with him, went after the Sioux. This must have been when the Tall Bull fight took place and Tall Bull was killed.[57]

Colhoff says that it was Col. Mills who opened the Slim Buttes fight who burned the train southeast of Gordon, that was heading for the Black Hills.[58]

He says also that it was Guy V. Henry who made the winter march to the Hills & returned to Fort Robinson with his command nearly frozen. He made his men lead their horses to keep from freezing in their saddles. Henry lost two or three fingers.

It was he who commanded the Ninth Cavalry (colored) at Pine Ridge in 1890–1, and his were the last troops to depart from the Agency when the disorders were over.[59]

[Carter P. Johnson's Statement]

Carter Page Johnson enlisted in the army in Virginia in 1876. He was a sergeant at the time of the Cheyenne outbreak. Johnson was promoted to the rank of lieutenant in 1882. A year later he was assigned to the Tenth Cavalry and sent to Arizona. Major Johnson retired from the army in 1909. He came out of retirement in 1916 to command Fort Robinson briefly, before his death the same year.[60]

[Box 26]
Captain Carter P. Johnson's Statement In Relation To The Cheyenne Outbreak.

The 1st day of June, 1877, the following troops left Fort Laramie, Wyoming, for the Black Hills, Major Carleton commanding the Cavalry composed of five troops of Third Cavalry: Captain Gerald B. Russell K Troop, Lieutenant J. B. Johnson B Troop, John B. Thompson, Lieutenant D Troop, A. B. D. Smead F Troop, Lieutenant George S. Chase A Troop, and four Companies of the Ninth Infantry commanded by Major Townsend; the expedition commanded by General Luther P. Bradley (who was in command of Fort Robinson when Crazy Horse was killed).[61] This command was assembled at old Fort Laramie, Wyoming, and composed a part of the line of troops that was established along the Canadian border with a view of preventing the return of Sitting Bull to the United States territory from Canada. This line of troops extended from Fort Assinaboine, Montana, Fort Meade, Dakota, and when removed this line was replaced by the Forts Assinaboine, Custer, Keogh and Meade.

The Sioux Indians in Canada under Sitting Bull had sent runners to the United States to all the large Sioux agencies Red Cloud, Yankton, Standing Rock and others notifying the most influential chiefs to come north and join him in the annual sun-dance with a with a view to persuading them to take up arms against the United States.

This sun-dance usually takes place about the 20th of June, depending upon the June moon.

To prevent this junction troops were hurried out on this line early in June. General Bradley's command moved north by the old Cheyenne and Deadwood stage road, moved from the Black Hills to the Belle Fouche ridge where the town of Belle Fouche now stands, to the Little Missouri River where the permanent camp was pitched and remained until the [blank] remained until all danger of an alliance being made between the reservation agency Indians and hostile Indians had passed. When the camp was moved back to Spearfish it might be mentioned here that the troops who had expected a hard Indian campaign were greatly surprised to find their camps surrounded by opera troups, gin sellers, and all civilized appurtenances of Deadwood moved out to these large camps in a body. There were two theaters in General Bradley's camp, from two to three hundred feet long—canvas theatres. The troops were so much demoralized that the General moved his camp three times but the Deadwood citizens kept such good scouts out ahead that in the last camp made by General Bradley he found all the claims were taken up and when he ordered certain parties to leave his camp he was informed that he was camping upon private territory and had better leave himself. He finally gave the thing up and gave them permission to have their shows under certain restrictions. The camp was very much like what we read about of some of the French encampments in Napoleon's days. This camp was seventy miles from Deadwood. The troops were used to build a telegraph line from Deadwood to Fort Keogh, the first telegraph line in that portion of Dakota.

In September the camp had broken up and headed on their return trip to Fort Laramie. The wagons were packed and started out on a march to Deadwood but were stopped and rumors reached the troops that there was an immediate outbreak in the Indian Territory and that some of them would not go to Fort Laramie. It was treated as a joke until the Infantry received orders to proceed to Fort Laramie and the Cavalry to proceed by forced marches to the present site of Fort Meade, which was a cantonment occupied by the Seventh Cavalry. It was finally learned that the Northern Cheyennes, Dull Knife's Band, the same band which participated in the battle of Custer and according to the earliest reports were the first Indians to come in contact with Custer's portion of the column in his charge.[62] These Indians had been taken to the Indian territory from Fort Robinson in '77 having come in through Red Cloud's Agency and surrendered in the spring of '77. They were moved to the Indian Territory under a treaty which they claimed permitted them to return to the North within two years, provided they were not satisfied with the Indian Territory. These Indians had been badly whipped by General McKenzie's command in (December) (Nov.) '76 and their tepees and supplies all destroyed in the Big Horn Mountains, which caused them to come to this agency for food and shelter.[63] In this fight (at Crazy Man's Fork) the command was composed of the Fourth Cavalry, two troops of the Third Infantry, several troops of the Fifth Cavalry and four companies of the Artillery. Lieutenant McKenny was killed in this fight.[64] (Old Fort McKenny was named for Lieutenant McKenny.) These Indians, I understand, had never before submitted to confinement upon an agency. The Northern Cheyennes had determined to return to their Northern Hunting Grounds, with or without permission from the government. They were being pursued from the Indian Territory by troops stationed there and were heading due north recamping through Colorado, Kansas and Nebraska, either eluding the troops sent out to intercept them or defeating those in pursuit. Colonel Lewis of the infantry was killed in this pursuit. As it was plain they were making their way to the thinly settled country of the Dakotas, unless at once stopped, most all available troops were ordered in the field in the Department of the Platte, and Colonel Carleton's command with five troops of cavalry was ordered to Fort Robinson. Upon reaching Fort Robinson they went into camp a few days, and early in October took midnight marches down the Sidney road as far as Snake Creek Ranch. At this place information was received that the Indians were crossing the Union Pacific Railroad at Ogallala station heading due north. Major Thornburgh of the Fourth Infantry, who was afterwards killed in the Ute Campaign, left Sidney with four companies of the Fourth Infantry, proceeded by rail to Ogallala and took up the pursuit.[65] This command was mounted on broken down cavalry horses and quarter-master mules and without saddles. They pressed the Cheyennes as rapidly as they could due north. Colonel Carleton's command was intended to intercept them and thus place them between two bodies of troops. With this object the Third Cavalry command proceeded into the Sand Hills of Nebraska, moving due east from Snake River Ranch. The guide in the Frontier's men by name Hank Clifford marched three days to the east. His command found themselves without water except such as could be procured from alkali lakes, which was totally unfit for use. When about due north of Ogallala station, where the command should have stopped and waited for the Indians to approach, it was compelled to move on in order to procure water. Pickets were left at this point and the command moved on east under the guidance of Hank Clifford in search of fresh water and after a long and tedious march of over forty hours and a change of directions to the northwest camped on the Snake River. The following morning news came in by courriers that the Indians had crossed the trail in the rear of this command and had scattered upon seeing evidences of approaching troops in force. Courriers from Major Thornburg reached camp the following day requesting this command to furnish them with supplies as his command was without food. About the same time a soldier of the Third Cavalry by the name of Johnson, belonging to C troop, brought dispatches from Fort Robinson to Major Carleton directing him to abandon the pursuit of the Cheyennes and to notify Major Thornburg to do the same and all other troops that he might meet up with, to do the same, and to proceed as rapidly as possible to old Fort Sheridan as an uprising of the Ogallala Sioux under Red Cloud was imminent. The Northern Cheyennes in this manner easily escaped the trap which had been set for them and which, but for this intervention, could scarcely have failed to capture or exterminate them, as the cavalry was in good condition and numbered five hundred men, and notwithstanding Major Thornburg's command was full four companies of Infantry and the Cheyennes were greatly exhausted, that is to say, their women and children and animals were so by reason of their long march from the Indian Territory and the numerous engagements they had been forced

227

into by both the citizens in Colorado and troops enroute. It was estimated that they killed upwards of eight hundred people in Kansas and Colorado.[66]

I have always understood that the Northern and Southern Cheyennes were the same people and that this immediate section, the Laramie River and the Platte River country and on across to Kansas were strictly speaking, the Cheyenne country; that the Southern Cheyennes and the Northern Cheyennes were one great nation and roamed and hunted from as far south as the Pawnees would let them go to as far north as the Crows would permit. That they were ancient enemies to the Pawnee and Crow, and as the country settled up through Kansas, aided by the building of the U.P. railroad, that the band drifted, one portion South and one portion North: that those that were further south were the first to be placed upon an Indian reservation by the government and were assigned the Indian Territory and made a treaty to remain there: that the band remaining north never submitted to agency rule or made any agreement to go upon an agency until they voluntarily came to Red Cloud Agency in Nebraska in '77. It is recorded that they had frequently accepted certain annuities in the shape of gifts and presents from the government agency as friendly gifts and so on.

I was told by Colonel Bullett, who lived on the Chug Water by old Fort Laramie, that he had been trading with these Indians for many years and had always found them the most reliable and honest Indians on the plains but at the same time were the wildest and most uncontrolable.

These Indians after being separated from the Southern Cheyennes were numerically weak compared with the Siouxs, but they were feared by the Siouxs, the Arapahoes and the Crows, owing to their war-like nature and are considered by the Indians themselves as a very superior race. The Sioux Indians considered it an honor to marry in among the Cheyennes while on the other hand the Cheyenne Indians seldom took a wife from the Sioux Nation. This was a strong principle with the Cheyennes. The Cheyenne Indians have been engaged in almost every noted fight in which the Ogallala Siouxs and the Standing Rock Siouxs have been engaged. The Yankton Sioux living on the river first came into civilization and are not so warlike. The Sioux Indians obtained the credit for a great many fights in the Northwest with troops and citizens in which the greater part was borne by this band of Cheyennes, who were their allies. The Cheyennes finding themselves numerically less than their enemies naturally became allies of the Siouxs and were frequently found joined with the Siouxs in a tax [attacks] upon the Crows and Pawnees and troops.

It appears that the Cheyenne's natural country was between the Siouxs and the Crows' country and as they were continually at war with the Crows, who outnumbered them greatly and were better armed, having obtained their arms from the early trappers and often left by the fur traders and the ancient trappers, for many years they waged successful war against these Cheyennes, hence it was natural that they should ally themselves with the Siouxs living east of them, against the Crows, who were finally pressed back by these combined tribes to the Big Horn Mountains, and but for the aid given them by the trappers who traded them arms and ammunition for furs they would have finally been overcome by the Siouxs and Cheyennes.

Upon arriving at Sheridan they found a great many troops assembled there and council was held and Red Cloud, who came to the Fort with a hundred chiefs as his escort, promised to keep the Siouxs in order and to prevent them from taking a hand in the Cheyenne outbreak, provided the troops were moved without delay from the vicinity of his village. He stated that many of his young men were very much excited by the rumors of the war that was going on between the Cheyennes and the troops: that many of them had inter-married with the Cheyenne band that was then in the field and were firm friends and that he did not deny that there was danger, some of them would desire to side with the Cheyennes, but that the presence of so many troops only served to further excite them and render them less easy to control, and that he did not doubt his own ability to handle them provided this large encampment of regulars was disposed of, or at least moved to a greater distance. He asked to have his views on this subject wired to General Crook at Omaha. It would appear that this must have been done since a few days after his departure for his camp, which was situated about fifteen miles east of Sheridan, on White Creek (where Pine Ridge Agency now is). (It may be stated here that Thornburg and Carleton left Newman's Cattle Ranch in the Sand Hills as one command enroute to Sheridan, that there was much speculation in regard to Red Cloud's whereabouts as the last we had heard of these Indians located them at Rosebud Agency — Yellow Medicine — hence as the command arrived on the bluffs looking into the White River Valley at the head of White Clay Creek it was greatly surprised to see an immense Indian village extending for miles and miles in the valley below, and it was at once surmised that Red Cloud was already on the war-path, and the command circled around to the southwest giving the village a wide berth in order to reach Sheridan. The last day's march was through burning grass; the prarie was on fire in every direction and it had been supposed that the Cheyennes had set fire to the grass to embarrass the troops, but upon the sight of this Indian village, decided that Red Cloud's Indians were firing the grass between us and Sheridan to prevent a junction of the troops and every precaution was taken to prevent a surprise.) The troops were dispersed in pursuit of the Cheyennes and were vigorously kept up until the latter part of October. (At the time of these occurrences Captain Johnson was a sergeant of Troop F, 3d Cavalry.)

Lieutenant J. B. Johnson's command consisted of B and D troops of the 3rd Cavalry, D troop commanded by John B. Thompson came upon Dull Knife's band on the table land between Running Water and White River, fifteen or twenty miles from the crossing of the Chadron road (Sidney trail) and Chadron Creek. These Indians were camped in a dry gulch, I think called Willow Creek, and allowed the troops to come within half a mile of them before they discovered themselves. The ground was covered with snow. They had been in there for several days and there were no trails on the outside leading to them and horses and all were concealed in this gulch. Several Indians came up and signalled to the troops to have a talk. Dull Knife, Wild Hog, and several others claiming to be chiefs, met Captain Johnson half way between their men and the troops. Lone Wolf was perhaps one of the council but had never been verified: he nevertheless was with Dull Knife's band. Dull Knife stated that his entire band, or all of it that had left Indian Territory, was with him and that they were out of rations, nothing to eat, and that it was very cold and that he had reached the country that he started to come to; was ready to surrender himself on good terms. His conditions were that he would be carried to Red Cloud Agency. Red Cloud's Agency had been at Fort Robinson when he went to the Indian Territory and he presumed that it was still there. At any rate he agreed to surrender and give up his arms and submit to the government with the sole condition that he should be taken to Red Cloud Agency. He was told that he would be taken to Red Cloud's Agency and he then agreed that he would follow in, that he wouldn't surrender on the prairie, but that he would follow in to the first camp for the night, camp to be selected by Captain Johnson, and there he would formally surrender. He was requested to complete his surrender on the plains (Table) where he was, as Captain Johnson had but two troops with him and they were not up to their full quota, there being about eighty-nine men present. Up to the present time it had been rumored that there were eight hundred Cheyennes in the party. Captain Johnson was very anxious to have him surrender there, turn in his arms; promised to feed him and take him to Red Cloud. The Indian warriors in the meanwhile had come out of the gulch and were circling around the troops and over the hills and galloping up to within fifty or sixty yards of the troops and wheeling their horses back again, after a custom they frequently practiced in those days; this while the chiefs and officer were in consultation, and from their appearances as they came in and out of this gulch they appeared to number three or four hundred. I have heard some of the men of the command say there were five thousand of them. (This is facetious.) The Indians declined to give up their arms, claiming that they never surrendered their weapons on the prairie for fear of treachery, but would faithfully perform their promise when they got within camp for the night and both troops and Indians camped, their arms to be delivered. They then requested that rations be left for their women and children who were very hungry. Captain Johnson very wisely decided to accept this condition of surrender rather than to force a fight, as the result would be very doubtful, and even if the troops were victorious, a greater part of the Indians would escape and then the work would have to be done over, so he gave them bacon and crackers and moved on with his command and stopped within half a mile and allowed them to divide their rations among themselves, and as soon as they took up the line of march to follow he proceeded down the bluffs following down Chadron Creek to the crossing of the Chadron road, or Sidney trail—below Price & Jenks, afterwards Half Diamond E Ranch. This point he reached a little before dark and went into camp in a heavy snowstorm. The Indians following on, it was not discovered that they were not all coming. Owing to the heavy snow it made it impossible to see but a short distance back, and as they filed into the Chadron Creek bottom and began to pitch their tepees it was getting dark and Captain Johnson decided not to ask them for their weapons that night. It was noticed that not more than half of them came in. Dull Knife said that the snow prevented the others from coming, they would all be in the morning. In the meanwhile, Captain Johnson sent out word to other troops, to Sheridan and to Robinson, the band had surrendered on Chadron Creek but that his command was small; thought it advisable that other troops be moved up in order to disarm them, as they might fail to give up their weapons when demanded in the morning. The next morning no other Cheyennes arriving, inquiry was made and it was found that Lone Wolf, or Little Wolf as some call him, had remained behind with a considerable number of the band. The Sioux scouts arrived during the day and several other troops of cavalry. The Sioux informed Dull Knife of Red Cloud's change of agency from Fort Robinson vicinity to Rosebud (Yellow Medicine. But he was now at Pine Ridge), but not before he had volunteered to turn in his arms as he had agreed. He presented himself to the commanding officer, Captain J. B. Johnson with a half a dozen warriors and half a dozen old broken weapons of all descriptions and said these were all the arms they had and if they had had any more they would not have surrendered. Captain Johnson saw at once that there was something wrong and urged the hurrying up of reinforcements. Meanwhile he informed Dull Knife that he was ready to proceed to Red Cloud and had his troops saddled and the wagons packed and told the Indians to come on. The wagons were headed to Fort Robinson, however, instead of to Red Cloud Village. Finally Dull Knife called for another talk and asked him what that meant; that wasn't the direction he wanted to go. He was told that was the direction of Red Cloud and that was where he said he wanted to go. He said he didn't care anything about Red Cloud Agency; he wanted to go to Chief Red Cloud he didn't want to go to Fort Robinson at all and he wasn't going to go there; the troops could go if they wanted to but he would stay where he was. When told that in that case the fight would begin, he said he was ready; ready to fight it out there. The troops went back to camp, the Indians back into the bushes and both sides began to dig rifle pits. The troops dug theirs on the edge of the banks and the Indians down in the creek and under the banks and one Indian had his dug in a hollow tree. Meanwhile troops were coming in every few hours or so from different directions and Colonel Carleton arrived with three troops of the Third Cavalry and a troop of the Seventh Cavalry and a six pound gun from Sheridan. Colonel Carleton took command and demanded surrender at once and received an answer that they had been deceived, that they wanted to go to Chief Red Cloud and not to Red Cloud's old agency, and they didn't want to go any where else and they wouldn't move from this decision for twenty-four hours; they stood on this decision. The troops were cutting down the willow bushes in the bottom of the creek to make way for the fire and the Indians were picking them up and carrying them in and making entrenchments with them revetting the banks of the creek. They also dug what you might call a bomb proof, a large cave in the side of the camp and bank of the creek in which they put their women and children; and there is no doubt but what they would have fought the matter out but for the influence of the Sioux scouts who went among them telling them that the country was alive with troops, that those in sight were no portion to what were in the surrounding country and that they needn't expect any assistance from the Sioux Indians as they had decided not to help them. Major Carleton then gave Dull Knife until his, Carleton's tents, could be pulled down to decide whether to go or not, telling him that when the last soldier's tent was struck that the six pound gun would open up on them and the troops would begin to fire. The old Chief held out until only the commanding officer's tent was left standing when he decided to go with the troops. The women and children were put in the wagons, most of the ponies were shot, as some were unable to travel and it was not desired that any of the warriors should go mounted, and the wagons were started in with the Indian warriors walking beside the wagons and the troops on either side of the column, and they were brought to Fort Robinson, Nebraska, and placed in an empty troop barracks. [Figure 6] As they filed into the quarters, Little Bad Man, [Little Big Man] the Sioux who figured in the Crazy Horse trouble, was one of the scouts for the command, reached up under an Indian's blanket as he went in the door and gave a sudden jerk and pulled off from his neck a rifle, a brand new Winchester, which had been taken apart and hung by a buckskin string around his neck. He had marched all the way from Chadron Creek with that gun under his blanket and nobody saw it. Little Bad Man's companion waited awhile and did the same thing to another Indian. When this was reported to Colonel Carleton he ordered an immediate search made throughout the quarters for arms. This search was made but the women and children and the men were crowded into this small quarters [in] such a dense mass that it was impossible to tell whether they had anything or not. It was afterwards learned that they had weapons, that some were carried by the women in their bundles and others were about the persons of the Indians and as soon as they learned that this Sioux Indian had taken a gun from one of them they expected a search would be made, so they ripped up a plank in the floor and put their guns under the floor. It was afterwards reported that the Sioux Indian and half-breed sypathisers conveyed arms to these Indians while they were in confinement. This is absolutely false, because there was a guard kept inside the house, walking up and down the centre of the floor, night and day, from the time they were confined until they broke out, and nobody was allowed to enter their building without being searched, and it would have been impossible to convey arms to these people after they were confined. I have been in charge of the guard myself a dozen or more times and I know that it could not have been done, but it was easy for the women to carry in anything they pleased when they first went in; and many of their weapons captured after the final escape of these Indians from this building, were tied together with buckskin, owing to the loss of certain screws that held the barrels and stocks together. The fact is these Indians were never fully disarmed, though it was believed they had cached their guns somewhere in the creek bottoms in the Chadron creek when none could be seen about their persons when they came out of their rifle pits; none could be found when they came out.

There was a board of officers assembled here to investigate that subject. Their finding didn't amount to anything and they exculpated the commanding officer.

After this the troops of this command that I have been spak [speaking] about, assisted by L troop of the Third Cavalry under Major Broom, E troop of the Third Cavalry under Captain Lawson, C troop of the Third Cavalry Captain Van Vleet and H troop of the Third Cavalry Captain Wessels, continued to scout the country for Little Wolf's band which it turned out never joined Dull Knife after the rations had been issued to them by Captain J. B. Johnson; but it was still in the immediate vicinity of Fort Robinson and communicated on several occasions with this band of prisoners from the surrounding bluffs by signals and on several occasions by sending in messengers, to try and make terms of surrender, but was so suspicious of foul play that whenever a troop of cavalry went out to get him to surrender he would disappear. One of his messengers came to Arkansas John's house and asked to communicate with the post commander. Little Bad Man of the Siouxs was sent out by the post commander to communicate with this man and persuade him to come up and talk with the commanding officer. He refused to come. Bad Man persuaded him to get on the horse with him and come up near the garrison and he could talk to Dull Knife. When he got him up on the horse he put a knife to his throat and rode him in to the commanding officer. This was a very impolitic move and resulted in Lone (Little) Wolf taking the alarm and going for Montana, where he surrendered to Lieutenant Clark of the Second Cavalry with his entire band. About the 1st of December he started for the north from here.

About this time orders were issued recalling the Third Cavalry to their proper stations, C and H troop to garrison Fort Robinson, D and B to Fort Laramie, M and E to Sidney, A and F to remain in McKenzie's old camp a short time longer, on the flat N.E. of where the sawmill is at Fort Robinson. On Christmas day, December 25th, A and F troops started up White River enroute to Fort Laramie. December 26th they were countermarched and returned to Fort Robinson or went into camp in McKenzie's old camp. A few days afterwards M and E troops returned from Sidney route, took up camp in McKenzie's old camp, leaving the troops now stationed around Robinson as follows: H troop commanded by Captain Wessels, who was the post commander at this time, M troop in command of Major Boom, E troop Captain Lawson, F troop Lieutenant John Baxter of the Ninth Infantry, A troop Lieutenant George Chase, Captain Wessels in command of the post and Major Broom in command of the camp, a mile from the post. It was learned that the sudden recalling of troops was due to the fact that a plot had been discovered by which the imprisoned Cheyennes were to break out of the prison at stable time and rush to the quarters of C and H troops and procure their weapons and attack the troops while at the stables and destroy the post. This plot was discovered. The official interpreter was a young half-breed about twenty-three or twenty-four years old. This plan would have been easily accomplished had it not been discovered. This interpreter slept with the special Indian guard quarted [quartered] in the same building with the Indians but in a separate room. He had removed the plastering from between the logs and was in the habit of listening to their conversation at night through this hole. On Christmas morning he informed the post commander of what he had learned and the post commander, Captain Wessels of the Third Cavalry, dispatched an order at once to Captain Chase, who was enroute to Fort Laramie in command of F and A troops to return to the post at once. When they returned the plan was abandoned by the Indians for that night. L and M troops were recalled from Sidney. Seeing the garrison reinforced this plan of escape was abandoned. From this time on the Indians gave up the plan of escape. Orders then came from Washington to move them to the Indian Territory. They were notified by the commanding officer of the decision from Washington and were requested to sign an agreement to return, which they refused to do, and said that if they wanted them back to the Indian Territory they would carry them there; they wouldn't make any more treaties. The post commander was directed to take them to the Indian Territory, to get them ready to go. He notified the Indians that they were to go but they wanted them to consent to go of their own free will. They refused to give any such consent. Orders were issued to give them nothing to eat until they consented to go. Where this order came from I do not know. They had been fed by a detail of soldier cooks who had been cooking their rations in the kitchen of the quarters and distributing them to them. This ration was stopped several days and the water was stopped on the third day. The Indians then demanded that the sentinel be taken out of the house and if they didn't take him out they would kill him. A old Indian who was considered half crazy attacked the sentinel in the quarters with a knife but was overpowered [by] the Indians themselves and prevented him from doing any violence. They again demanded that the sentinel be taken from the quarters. At this stage of the game Captain Wessels sent for Wild Hog to come into his office. Dull Knife was very sick and Wild Hog was exercising the command. Wild Hog came to the commanding officer's office and was given the ultimatum of going to the Indian Territory freely or by force. He told them he wouldn't consent to go. By prearrangement soldiers had been dropping in to the commanding officer's office and by a signal from him, the guards in the meantime having been doubled and H troop put on entire to guard these Indians and drawn up in line between the barracks and the commanding officer's office, the soldiers attempted to hand-cuff Wild Hog and threw him to the floor. He drew a knife and drove it into the breast of a soldier of A troop. Owing to a heavy blanket shirt he had on the knife didn't do any serious damage. Wild Hog was overpowered and shackled. He gave his war-hoop and the Indians rushed out of the quarters heading for the commanding officer's quarters but were driven back into their quarters by H troop, which was drawn up in line. Wild Hog was then taken to the camp below the post and placed under guard. Old Crow and Medicine Man who came out of the building to investigate affairs were taken down prisoners to this camp. The sentinel was taken out of the building and the Indians commenced at once to tear up the floor and barred their windows and sung their war dance. They kept this up all day. They made wooden clubs out of the timbers and drove spikes into them out of the floor and shook them through the windows at the soldiers. There were two troops of cavalry on guard, dismounted, around among them for several days, night and day. Meanwhile nothing was given them to eat or drink and nobody could go in the quarters. They threatened to kill anyone who came in. They dug a trench under the house and made a fortification of the place, notifying the soldiers through the windows to come and take them to the Indian Territory, they were ready to go. All kinds of threats were made. A battery of six pound guns were turned on the building they were told that they were going to fire on them. It made no impression. The commanding officer's hands were tied, he didn't dare fire and he didn't know what to do so he kept the building heavily guarded and reasoned with these people. Finally he sent them word that if they would let the women and children come out of the building he would feed the women and children but wouldn't feed the bucks. They told him that they didn't intend to let the women and children come out, when they got real hungry they were going to eat their babies first and then they would go to eating the women next, they couldn't spare them. Wild Hog was interviewed and asked to do something, to go up there and persuade the women and children to come out. He was carried up to the quarters by a heavy guard. He talked to the Indians through the window and he told the commanding officer that all the women and children would be coming out. The commanding officer told him he could get out any of his particular friends. He took out nineteen Indians, his wife and couple of children and all the old and decrepit women that were in the lot and carried them to his camp. He made no effort to get out any able bodied Indian. On the morning of the 9th of January the garrison was astonished by the smell of meat cooking in the quarters and the Indians sent out word that they had begun to eat their first baby and were cooking it then. It turned out afterwards that it was nothing but a dog that they had saved for this purpose. In the afternoon it was understood that they sent word to the commanding officer that upon the advice of their chief, Wild Hog; Dull Knife was nearly dead at that time, was carried out on the snow every night for an hour or two with nothing on to recover. Wild Hog, was looked upon as the Chief then and he stated to the commanding officer that the Indians had decided to go to the Indian Territory and would be ready to go with him in a day or two more. The authorities believed that the trouble was all over and the guard was reduced to its usual number and the men of C and H troop, who had been required to sit up all night for several nights past were told that they could go to bed that night. Just after tattoo, between nine and ten o'clock, rifle shots were heard in the post by the camp below and the camp turned out and came up to the post on double quick time to find C troop and H troop in a redhot battle with the Indians on the parade ground. The women had gone through the windows and the back part of the quarters and had headed for Soldier Creek to the south at the junction of the White River at the old saw mill. The men had broken out of the front part of the building and had surprised the guard in the guard room, shot two men in the arm and one as he went through the window, chased the corporal of the guard to the bake house and shot him through the arm, two of them being killed by him in his run from the quarters to the bakehouse. One troop had turned out in their night clothing and had driven the Indians back down to the Soldier Creek. H troop was attacking them from the right. A running fight continued from a junction of Soldier Creek up White River to Cramblett's Lake. It was a bright moonlight night and the snow was on the ground and everything was very clear, almost as clear as day. The thermometer was down 15 to 20 degrees below zero. Major Broom's troop had remained in camp and came into the fight mounted, at Cramblett's Lake and pursued the Indians to the bluffs. Finding they were followed by horsemen they made straight for the bluffs and went up the most inaccessible places to the bluffs just west of Cramblett's Lake, where they made a stand on the bluffs, and fought M troop until daylight. The other troops were sent back to their quarters to get their horses, and from that time on, the 10th of January until the 22nd, the Indians were pursued through the bluffs making stands and ambushing in the daytime and escaping at night to a new position. Six troops of the cavalry took turns in the field, one troop going out being relieved by another, one half working all day being relieved by the other half at night.

The first night's fight twenty-six warriors were killed in the vicinity of the post and old saw mill. Eighty of the women and children were captured, a great number of whom were wounded and some of them killed. Eighty women were brought in prisoners, some were badly shot up. The effort on the part of the soldiers to spare the women was all that could be done. Only one or two cases in which a woman was killed intentionally or through excitement, and many were killed as they ran through the bushes, not being able to tell the women from the men; but considering the confusion there were a great many more captured than one could have expected under the circumstances, as they were very suspicious about surrendering. Dull Knife's eldest unmarried daughter, who was a woman of great intelligence and had been very kindly treated by the officers and men, thinking that she could save some of the women, came up and signaled the soldiers, indicating to them that a certain bunch of Indians under a tree were all women, and if they wouldn't fire on them she would have them come in and surrender. Thirty or forty came in this bunch and were being brought to the guard house by the soldiers when another party of soldiers coming out of Soldier Creek firing at a running Indian, stampeded these women. They start to run and this girl in trying to stop them ran towards the soldiers. They didn't understand her and she was shot dead and the other women then ran into the bushes and this squad of soldiers taking them for bucks fired on them, otherwise there would have been very few women killed that night. There were thirty or forty in this party and most of them were wounded. After this was discovered by the men they took a great many chances and several men were killed before the fight was over, trying to save what they took to be women and who turned out to be bucks. The Sargent of H troop was killed stopping a number of men firing on what he thought was a woman and turned out to be a buck who killed him. But after that night's fight was over there was no women wounded or killed until the final fight on Indian Creek when they were firing into a rifle pit, and everybody that was in there was either killed or wounded.

On the morning of the 10th small parties of troops were coming in all day long bringing in two or three women and children as prisoners and this kept up almost daily until the last fight. The Indians came together again on the 11th or 12th at the head of Soldier Creek and made a stand on a bluff near where Holdorf's mill is now, and pieces of wild timber was taken from the post to dislodge them, but after killing a soldier and a soldier's horse, they slipped out that night and cut the horse up into steaks, which as far as anybody has been able to find out was the first they had to eat after they got out of prison except parched corn which we found they had tied up in their dresses. Most all the women had a little corn. All of the Indians captured from that time on were badly frozen. The following day about the 13th, a scouting party overtook the Indians in the rocks and firing killed one of them; the others taking cover under a ledge of rock and opened fire on them but before they could get their guns in play two of the Indians had jumped out of the rocks and scalped a soldier who was a recruit; got his gun and his pistol. On the 14th they were corraled on War Bonnet, north of this range of bluffs, what is generally known as Hat Creek valley; those days the creek was called War Bonnet. The Indians were in rifle pits and surrounded by M, H, F and A troops. They fought all day and used a six pound gun on them all day without any effect. They were so well concealed in the rocks that no Indian was hurt this day. I think there was over a hundred shells thrown among them. The ground was frozen hard and the shells did no harm. A day or so after this, about the 19th or 20th, these Indians escaped from the four troops and ran into B troop under Captain J. B. Johnson and D troop under John Thompson, commanded by Major Evans, who had been sent from Fort Laramie by General Crook to take command of affairs here and wind up this business.[67] These Indians served him like they had served us; they killed several of his men and killed Major Evans horse under him and left two boys on top of the hill to represent the band and stole out on him that night and crossed the Hat Creek Valley. A trail was discovered by Major Wessels and followed by him and a full blood Sioux scout, called Woman's Dress by some people, and a half-breed who was with Buffalo Bill, Louis Mosseau, at the World's Fair. This scout who was riding a mule in [and] Woman's Dress and a soldier of the Third Cavalry of the advanced scouts, found the Indians entrenched on Indian Creek, sometimes called Antelope Creek. This half-breed received a bullet on his pistol holster, Woman's Dress was shot through the arm and the soldier was shot through the breast and killed.[68] Captain Wessels sent back to collect his command, F troop, under Lieutenant Hardee, now Lieutenant Colonel Hardee,

John Baxter of the Ninth Infantry, A troop with Captain Chase, E troop with Captain Lawson and H troop Captain Wessels and John Baxter, afterwards governor of Wyoming; surrounded the Indians in this rifle pit. F troop was directed to charge their fire, H troop was to come in from the right, A troop from the left, and E troop from the north, closing in on this rifle pit and winding it up. The troops in those days were a hundred strong, but owing to the many scouts, attacking parties and men on detached services; the scattered condition of the command that morning, there was about eight [eighty?] men in the actual fight, upon an average of twenty men to the troop. F troop had only nineteen. They closed up on this rifle pit within nine feet on one side and continued to fire into the rifle pit for two and one-half hours. Captain Wessels was shot once through the blouse and once above the eye, the only officer wounded. The Indians were asked to surrender three or four times; they refused to do so. One girl who was taken out of the rifle pit afterwards with her throat cut slightly but not to an artery, said that when the soldiers asked them to surrender she had raised a carbine and motioned it as a signal to talk, but her mother had caught her by the hand and cut her throat and told her to make no more motions to surrender. Her mother was afterwards shot in the back of the head and was the last one who kept up the fight in this rifle pit, when it was nearly over. Three Indians began to sing a war song; jumped out of the hole and into the ranks of the soldiers, one armed with a knife and the other with a six shooter and the third one, as far as I can remember, had nothing. He went over the bluff and was shot in the head as he jumped over the bluff. The other two flew into the ranks of the soldiers, one of them killing Private Nelson of A troop as he fell. As he fell he fired his pistol and killed Nelson, fell up against him almost. The old woman who was said to be the mother of this girl, kept up the fight with this carbine until she was shot in the hand and the carbine knocked out. When she was taken out she was laid on her back on the outside, and Captain Chase trying to do something for her, thought she was suffering so and to relieve her by changing her position, stooped over her to change her position and she reached out and took his hand and spit in his face. She died that night. There were ten live people taken out of that hole; one warrior who was shot all to pieces and died that night, nine women and children. Two of the boys were the two little boys who had been left behind the day before to decoy Major Evans and had found their way across the country and joined these others in this fight. One of the little boys died before he got home. They were brought in to the post here.

The night after the fight Major Evans and his two troops joined the command that marched towards Fort Robinson. When we got to the old telegraph line that runs across the valley to Hat Creek Station, the wire was tapped to communicate with the department at head quarters and received orders from the Indian Agency from General Crook to stay together that Little Bad Man had gone on the warpath with five hundred Minneconjous and was coming to help the Cheyennes; and Major Evans was ordered to stay with our fort troops and all to come back to Fort Robinson together and keep a lookout for this Indian, and we supposed we would be attacked as we came down Soldier Creek. When we got out at the Five Forks Colonel Evans was ordered to return to Fort Laramie, that the Minneconjous had returned to the agency; had learned that the Cheyennes had been cleaned up they had come out to help.

Wild Hog remained a prisoner in the camp and was not in any of this trouble. His son, White Antelope, was leading these Indians from the time they broke out until they were cleaned up. There was one Indian warrior of this band that got to Red Cloud Agency in some manner. Dull Knife himself escaped by laying in the old saw mill all night long with his wife, and found his way to Pine Ridge Agency many days afterwards. Wild Hog was taken to Denver, Colorado, and tried for the murders committed in Colorado when they came up from the Indian Territory, and was acquitted. Old Crow and the Medicine Man being prisoners were unhurt. There was one buck that was found back of the bluffs here badly shot up and was brought in. There was an Indian buck that I captured that was unhurt. As far as I know these were the only male members, full grown warriors of this band, that escaped; the rest were all killed. Wild Hog went to the Indian Territory and in '83 came back to Sidney with Red Eagle's band of Cheyennes, the remnant of the band that had been carried to the Indian Territory. Old Crow was with him and they went up to Custer and it was from that band that Casey reorganized his scouts that figured in Wounded Knee Campaign. While he was prisoner in this camp, down here I had a great many talks with him, I could speak Sioux then and the sign language some. He told me the reason he left Indian Territory; be showed me his hands which were blistered, hardened, which he said he had gotten by trying to learn to work. He was a great big powerful Indian, the most powerful and strongest Indian I have ever known. His muscles were like a white man's. It took six or seven men to throw him in the building, and they were strong men called in there for that that purpose.

One of the women taken out of this pit was Wild Hog's daughter Blanche, a girl twelve years old, who had learned to read and write in the Indian Territory. It was the special request of Wild Hog, made to Sargent, now Captain, Johnson, to bring his daughter in. Wild Hog had two or three sons and two or three daughters. He made no request to have any of the others brought in, and when asked if he wanted the others brought in, he said they were old enough to take care of themselves, that his sons would die fighting. The girl Blanche had a wound in her arm, shot through the arm, and a few days afterwards it began to mortify and he wouldn't send for any doctor. She was carried down to his tent, let her go with him. I examined it and found that a red piece of calico punched in there had stopped the bleeding and of course the dye in the red calico was affecting the wound. I pulled it out and dressed it. I met him in Sidney in '83 was on his way to Fort Custer via Fort Robinson. I heard that the Cheyennes were encamped, and feeling a curiosity to see if Wild Hog was there I went over and visited the camp at night. I found Old Crow and he told me Wild Hog was there and took me to Wild Hog's tent. He came out and sit down on the outside. I tried to talk to him but he wouldn't talk to me, just grunted. As he had often thanked me for taking care of his daughter's arm I want away feeling very disgusted. Next morning as I was standing at the hotel there in Sidney I saw an Indian coming up the street highly decorated, and a woman following him, two or three girls, one little boy and the interpreter. They soon crossed the street and headed for me, making all kinds of gesticulations. When they came over to me I found it was Wild Hog. He was delighted to see me and took great pride in showing me this Indian woman whom he informed me was the girl Blanche. The interpreter then explained that Wild Hog was in bad repute with his people by having been in prison when all the band was killed, and that while he was glad to see me and wanted to talk to me, he didn't want to talk or mention the subject in the camp where the other Indians were, and for that reason he didn't show me any cordiallity. His esteem seemed to consist of the fact that I had bandaged his girl's arm, and nothing else, and from the fact that he was under the impression that I had made some effort to have her spared and brought in.

The Minneconjous were Crazy Horse's band. This band were with the Ogallala Siouxs and are with them yet. Every band had a separate name.

Keox means cut-off. This was No Flesh's band. He was shot at Custer in the Hills in '75. They got this name for drawing away from the band and following No Flesh, but afterwards went back.

In '75 when Custer was going through the Black Hills and making inspections, he had a conversation with No Flesh and No Flesh got in a passion and fired direct into his face but the gun was knocked up by one of Custer's men or one of the guides or one of the Indians. From the time those Indians broke out here, there was a daily fight between them and the troops in detachments from one to two on a side to four troops of cavalry and all the Indians on a side, from the time they broke out until they surrendered. Part of the time it was bush-whacking and part of the time it was all together.

F troop of the Third Cavalry were stationed at Bowman's Ranch in the spring of '77 commanded by Alexander Moore and Second Lieutenant R. B. Reynolds. This ranch is on the old Cheyenne and Deadwood stage road and was called Hat Creek Springs in those days. It was supposed to be the head waters of Hat Creek but is not. If you followed up the stream now called Hat Creek to its head waters you will come to a divide. On the west side of this divide Hat Creek Springs will be found and they consist of a string of small lakes, fresh water lakes, which are really the head waters of what is called Old Woman's Fork, which empties into the Cheyenne River. This troop was stationed there to protect the United States mail line and when the stage robbers became bad orders were issued to place a guard on each stage going and coming, whenever there was room on the stage. Two soldiers were detailed for this purpose. They rode as far as Jennings' Stockade on the Cheyenne River and returned on the morning stage. This, being the night portion of the drive, was the section most frequently taken by the robbers to attack the stages. It was on this road that the first iron-clad stage coach was run. It was afterwards moved to the Sidney route. This coach was iron-clad and bullet proof and was used only to carry the treasure when they had a large amount shipped from Deadwood or from Cheyenne. It ran once a week only and was guarded by paid citizen messengers, sometimes by soldiers. The safe was a circular safe, was wound up and locked at Cheyenne and, owing to its construction, could not be unlocked for eight days, the end of its journey. No passenger was allowed on this coach and it was understood that this burglar-proof safe was insured for one year. This coach was finally captured by stage robbers at Coal Springs. Will give the instance later on.

Before this coach was put on the road, the stage coach was attacked frequently almost every trip and passengers robbed, except when soldier guards were on the coach; and it was very singular that during the entire summer the soldier guards riding on two of the five coaches that went by Hat Creek were never attacked but once. The road agents would attack a coach coming up or going down without a guard; and would instruct the driver to deliver the coach coming up; to get ready; they were going to take their men; and would tell him to advise the soldiers not to make any resistance. I rode, myself, on this coach frequently and often received that message but fortunately was not attacked. The treasury coach that preceded the iron-clad (that is to say, the one that was used prior to the iron-clad) was attacked about August, '77 with Scott Davis, citizen messenger, and a man named Smith, his assistant, and two soldiers of F troop, Tenth cavalry. This coach was attacked at a point south of Jenning's Stockade, called Robber's Nest. The name was given to the place owing to the fact that they (the bandits) had dug small rifle pits in the side of a small bluff and had at this point frequently attacked the stage. These holes that they dug in the side of the hill had the appearance of a hawk's nest and originated the name. They became so daring that they often told the drivers where to tell the passengers to give up their treasures as they came along. These citizen messengers were in the habit of sitting in the rear boot of the stage so they could readily jump to the ground when attacked. On this occasion Scott Davis, who was a very brave and noted frontiersman, and his man Smith were in the boot as usual; the two soldiers were in the coach. When the stage was held up by these robbers Scott Davis and his man Smith jumped to the ground and the soldiers jumped out of the stage coach. The robbers opened fire. The evidence before the courtmartial that tried these soldiers and sentenced them, indicated that Smith called to the soldiers to follow him and all three of them ran down the road, while Scott Davis returned the fire of the robbers and kept it up until a cartridge hung in his Winchester rifle and he was shot in the leg; and then, I understand, he discharged his revolver afterwards. He refused to surrender to these men but they rushed on him when they found his gun had stopped working and captured him. They called for the other messenger and the two soldiers to return and hold up their hands. Smith threw his shotgun in the sage brush and brought the soldiers up, who it appears had left their carbines in the stage. They said they were asleep at the time and at the first alarm jumped, leaving their guns in the stage. They were sentenced to the penitentiary for this. Scott Davis afterwards captured both of these robbers, one by the name Joe Blackburn, Joe. I have forgotten the other's name. Up to this time the coach had generally been attacked by five or six robbers. At this time it dosen't appear that there had been but two. The travelers were so frightened by the frequent holdups that at the first summons to surrender they invariably did so.

A boy living at Cooney ranch, the same boy who killed Mr. Cooney near Fort Laramie, held up the stage coach near Fort Laramie with a broom stick and robbed the passengers. He was captured immediately afterwards by Lieutenant Chase with a detachment of the Third Cavalry. He had killed Cooney at the ranch and had started to get away; walked up the road to Cheyenne and met the stage coach. He carried a broom stick out of the ranch to walk with and this was his only weapon. He was tried in Cheyenne. (He was a young man about nineteen or twenty. The records at Cheyenne will show the boy's name.) The Company paid the soldiers a reward for capturing the boy.[69]

To return to the Hat Creek neighborhood, these robbers after examining the treasury box, which was the same I described and was afterwards carried on the ironclad, said that they only wished to examine it, as they heard they couldn't break it open; and after taking the Wells-Fargo Express box, which had nothing in it, they said, they told Scott Davis they intended to take that safe some day and be prepared to open it. These two men, Blackburn and his companion, stole a bunch of stage horses at Lightning Creek stage station a few months afterwards and were pursued by Scott Davis with a detachment of F troop and followed them as far as Green River City, Wyoming, and captured them just outside of the city.

The heavy loss of treasure on these coaches decided the Company to put on an iron-clad, which ran for many months without disturbance until sometime in '78 when it was attacked at Coal Springs by a large band of road agents. The attack occurred as follows: As the stage drove up, about daylight, to the stage ranch, the hostler was in the habit of coming out and changing the horses while the messengers and drivers went in to get their breakfasts. On this morning, as usual the driver halted, wrapped his reins around the brake and got off of his coach and called to the hostler. The messengers who consisted of four men headed by Scott Davis, I do not know the names of the others, and a telegraph operator by the name of Campbell, got out of the stage and started toward the ranch house. Instead of the hostler making his appearance as usual, they received a volley from the house. Some of the shots were fired at the horses and stampeded them. They ran off with the stage, the robbers chasing the messengers into the bushes killing Mr. Campbell the telegraph operator and I think wounding one or two of the messengers, I am not sure. They then left the house, where the hostler was found and gagged, and followed the stage and found that it was turned over a little distance from the ranch, and they were in strong enough force to set the stage up. Being very heavy it took quite a good many men to do it. They drove it up into the mountains and succeeded in opening the safe and got away with all the treasure. I have been told that this occurred just a few days after the year (for) which the Safe Company insured the safe had expired, and prevented the Express Company from getting damages. A few days after this Colonel Henry of D troop of the Third Cavalry was scouting around Indian Carra, [Inyan Kara Mtn., Wyoming] a mountain in the Black Hills, when his troop was fired upon by a band of men and he dismounted and attacked and drove them into the mountains and pursued then until they scattered. He not knowing of the robbery of the stage was at a loss to account for the attack upon his troops. It is evident, however, that the robbers thought that he was in pursuit of them and fired on him from ambush. This was Colonel Guy V. Henry. This stage coach was afterwards moved to the Sidney route and I believe this was the last time that the stage was attacked on the old Cheyenne and Deadwood route, though several attacks were made on the Sidney route afterwards. (end of staging account.)

In the fall of '77 F troop received orders to proceed to Fort Robinson at once and they marched from Hat Creek Springs to Fort Robinson during the night, arriving at this place at daylight, a distance of fifty-five miles. We came and reinforced the garrison which was threatened by Indians, owing to the killing of Crazy Horse who had been hurt by a member of the guards in his attempt to escape from the guard house at Fort Robinson. The Indians were all very much excited and threatened the post for several days, during which time reinforcements were pouring in from every direction, and the death of Crazy Horse had been kept a secret from them, they being informed by the Sioux Indian Little Bad Man that he had been stabbed by Crazy Horse, that he, Crazy Horse was unwounded. When the garrison became strong enough to defend itself Colonel Guy V. Henry moved across the bluffs to Crazy Horse's camp where his warriors were awaiting his return with the avowed intention of going on the warpath. This camp was quietly taken possession of by Colonel Guy V. Henry and the Indians informed that their Chief was dead; they could come to the post and get his body which they did. During this week the post was in fearful predicament as the garrison was not strong enough to defend itself against the number of Indians camped around the place, had they made an attack upon it, which attack they most undoubtedly would have made but for the influence of Red Cloud. He informed the post commander that he would not allow his men to attack the post and all that he would have to guard against was Crazy Horse's particular band and the Minniconjous over whom he had no influence.

Fifteen hundred Arapahoe Indians camped on Soldier Creek were moved into the post and stood by the troops, promising to assist in case the Indians attacked, which was of great assistance to the small garrison; and Red Cloud's loyalty at the time no doubt prevented a massacre of the troops.

This Indian Crazy Horse became separated from his band and his capture brought about in a peculiar manner, which will show how often troops in small garrisons in this country owed their existence to the loyalty on the part of some particular Indian Chief or band, in times of excitement. The Brulé Sioux under Spotted Tail, numbering about six hundred young warriors, who were more or less restless at the time and were held in check by old Spotted Tail's influence only; and Crazy Horse wishing to increase his force as much as possible and to involve other tribes in his premeditated war, moved his camp into the neighborhood of Cottonwood, left them there, and proceeded to Spotted Tail's Agency and secretly excited and endeavored to increase his force from the Indians from that place. Spotted Tail, hearing of his presence in his camp for this purpose, managed to get him secretly to his tepee, where he bound him and sent his couriers to Sheridan for a government ambulance which was sent him; and without making any disturbance he placed this Indian in the ambulance and alone guarded him to Fort Robinson and turned him in here to the guard house a prisoner. It was while in this guard house that he was killed. Little Bad Man then employed as a scout by the commanding officer was conversing with Crazy Horse in the guard house when Crazy Horse insisted that he was going to leave the guard house; he was not going to remain in the guard house. His warriors were riding around the post in squads and making demands upon the commanding officer to turn him loose or they would fire the post, and he depended upon them to rescue him. Little Bad Man tried to persuade him from any such attempt, when he got up and started for the door with the avowed intention of going out. Little Bad Man jumped to detain him, told him he would be killed if he went out, tried to hold him back. Little Bad Man was a Minnicojou Sioux and belonged to his band. Crazy Horse was then the most influential among the Ogallala band, save Red Cloud, and was fast acquiring even greater influence than Red Cloud, owing to the fact that he belonged to the war element and was desirous of resisting the white man to the bitter end, while Red Cloud at this time had been advocating peace upon his people. He insisted on going out and Little Bad Man threw his arms around him to detain him by force. He drew a knife and stabbed Little Bad Man in the arm and rushed out of the door. The guards had drawn up in line on the outside, attracted by this disturbance inside and met him at the door with bayonets at a charge. He walked into the file of soldiers and threw the bayonets [to] one side with either hand and gave his warhoop as a signal for his men to rally round him. One of the guards drove a bayonet into his body and immediately carried him back into the guard house. He died three days afterwards. Little Bad Man went among his Indians and told them that he had been compelled to stab Crazy Horse to save his own life but that Crazy Horse wouldn't die. He received a silver medal for this action of his.[70]

An Incident

While stationed at Hat Creek this troop F had rather an exciting episode with the Sioux Indians. Lieutenant Lemley, afterwards of the artillery, with a detachment of soldiers was making a government survey on Spearfish Creek in the Black Hills. When about fourteen miles from his camp he sent word to the camp to move, to come to him on Spearfish. The wagons consisting of three or four mule teams, were put in motion, guarded by seven soldiers of F troop, and when passing through the Black Hills somewhere on the stage road between Deadwood and Coal Springs, were attacked by a band of Sioux and several teamsters were killed and two soldiers wounded, five dashing off in different directions, two men (went) to Hat Creek Springs and gave the alarm. One galloped into Deadwood and the other, Private Meyer, whose horse had been shot through the neck behind the jaw, headed for Lemley's camp and reached there, fourteen miles away, on his wounded horse. The old horse lived and was a pet in the troops from that time on. F troop was immediately put on the march to go to Lemley's assistance and as it had been wired from Deadwood that the wagon-train was entirely destroyed, it became necessary to carry supplies to Lieutenant Lemley. Eighteen mules were taken with one six mule wagon, hitching six mules and relieving them as they got tired, hitching on six more, that were driven in a herd behind the wagon; twenty men of the troop commanded by R. B. Reynolds, and proceeded at a rapid gait to the Black Hills and in forty-eight hours, traveling night and day with only short pauses, reached a point about thirty miles northwest of the town of Spearfish where they found a large wagon-train of two hundred people who had left Deadwood for the Big Horn Mountains on a prospect mining tour. These people were corraled and engaged in a desperate fight with the Indians, who, as far as could be seen, numbered about seventy-five. Lieutenant Reynolds rode into their corral unmolested by the Indians, who were riding around on the bluffs, and took charge of the defense and after exchanging a few shots with the Indians it was discovered that the Indians were moving off. The citizens were very much enraged with Lieutenant Reynolds for not pursuing this band of Indians, and allowing them to go off in peace. He told them that his duty required him to find Lieutenant Lemley, who with a handful of men were cornered by some of these people perhaps, and had been without rations for some days; but as there were two hundred of them he offered to give them all the ammunition they could use if they would go after the Indians themselves. They decided that they would return to Spearfish, and he very wisely decided that his command was too small for any such number of Indians, as they would probably be led into ambush, and he proceeded to hunt up Lieutenant Lemley and found him two days afterwards, the Indians not having discovered him, and he was very destitute of food. These Indians immediately returned to this reservation after this episode, and on their way back attacked a wagon-train escorted by infantry, in Red Cañon. They didn't do much damage, the infantry stood them off. They brought the mules here, turned them into Red Cloud's herd, which indicated that they belonged to that band. Lieutenant Lemley was in the habit of marking his name on the back of his shirt on his shoulder, and his shirts were paraded around the reservation for a year afterwards. You could see a big Indian with Lemley written across his shoulders.

Apache History

In 1877 in the month of June Apache Kid, the First Sergeant of the Apache scouts in San Carlos, Arizona, and four scouts of his company killed another Apache Indian in revenge for the killing of their chief several years previous.[71] Fearing punishment by the agency authorities they fled to the mountains and through their friends negotiated terms with Captain [Francis E.] Pierce of the United States Army, then Agent of San Carlos, and agreed to come back and surrender and take their punishment, which they did so far as coming back and surrendering themselves was concerned. They walked into his tent and turned in their arms, which were taken and stood in the corner of the tent, by the Chief of the Scouts, Al Sieber.[72] For fear of an attack being made upon them before they would get to the agency, by the friends of the Indian they had killed, they were accompanied by a large number of their band. These men remained on the outside of the tent engaged in conversation with a Mexican interpreter, who very foolishly informed them that the Kid and his companions would be sent to Florida and the rest of his band would probably follow him. The Kid's friends determined that if that was the case to make a rescue and go on the warpath. They were out about one hundred yards from the tent sitting on their horses when they came to this conclusion and they dismounted and without any warning opened up a fusilade upon Captain Pierce's tent. As the first shots were fired the Kid and his people appeared as much surprised as Captain Pierce, and broke out of the back of the tent and ran off. Sieber sprang to the door of the tent with a rifle in his hand and received a bullet in his leg, which knocked him down! The Indians then undertook flight and left the post before any effort could be made to stop them and went to the mountains where they began to attack such whites as they came across and killed several miners and started on a warpath heading for Old Mexico.[73] The troops from Fort Grant were all turned out in pursuit. So were those in San Carlos. With a detachment of L troop of the Tenth Cavalry I proceeded to Dunlap's ranch in Arivapa Cañon, thirty-six miles from Fort Grant. The command left Grant at sundown and reached Dunlap's ranch at daylight. Just before I got to the ranch I crossed the Indian trail within a mile of the ranch, leading south, but I stopped there and went over to the ranch to gather any news I might hear and found Tom Horn, the celebrated scout and guide, and fifteen or twenty cowboys and miners were congregated in this house for self defense.[74] From them I learned that the trail I crossed was the hostile Indians' trail. I also learned that it was three days old. They also informed me that Lieutenant Hughes with B troop of the Tenth Cavalry and five Indian scouts were down in the cañon trying to work the trail out.[75] I went into camp and sent for Lieutenant Hughes, requesting him to meet me so that we could talk the matter over, which he did. He complained that his Indian scouts wouldn't run the trail and that he had been four or five days in making headway when they reluctantly refused to go ahead. These scouts were headed by a man named Oliver Eaton, a graduate of the Hampton Indian School. This fact is mentioned because newspapers stated that the Kid was a graduate of Carlyle. The Kid was never anything but a wild Apache Indian belonging to the wildest band of Apache Indians, save one in Arizona. From his youth until he was placed in the penitentiary he was a very reliable Sergeant of scouts for awhile and extremely trustworthy at that time. He could speak no English, and the story that he was a Carlyle graduate, often repeated in the newspapers, was false. They confused the scout with the man he was pursuing. I put my men in camp to rest and at Lieutenant Hughes's request traveled with him until noon and got him well started on this trail, telling him that I would follow and render him any assistance he might need, and then returned to my camp. That night a courier came from him asking me to join him at once. I broke camp at twelve o'clock, reaching him at daylight in the morning, and found his scouts had expressed reluctance to go further, because they said the trail was leading into a desert country; and besides that Lieutenant Hughes's command was nearly out of rations; that the scouts horses were wore out; and they wanted to go home. These scouts were Mojave Indians. Giving them fresh horses and orders that if they didn't follow the trail to the best of their ability they would be considered as hostile themselves and sent back to the post in irons, we proceeded on this trail and from that time on these scouts did such good work that Oliver Eaton, and one commonly called Roudy, became quite famous scouts in Arizona. Roudy afterwards won a medal for gallantry under Captain Watson.[76]

An Apache scout is peculiar in his disposition and if not handled properly by an experienced man is utterly worthless. When properly handled by a man in whom they have confidence the sterling ability they show and the risks they will take are wonderful. They can travel on foot a hundred miles a day, have been known to do it on several occasions within twenty-four hours, and of all the Indians I have ever known they are by far the best travelers, and I think equally as trusty under favorable circumstances, at least, as any others. This band of Mojave are called Mojave Apache, having been closely allied with the Apaches for years. They are distinct tribes possessing many of the same traits.

That night we reached Diel's ranch and found that he had been killed by the Indians. From this time on we found that every ranch had been raided, horses run off and other depredations committed. Pursuing these Indians to Pantana, we located them either in the Whetstone or Patgonia Mountains. I sent dispatches to the department indicating probable whereabouts of the band and direction they were heading. This information turned out to be so correct that the troops turned out from Huachua commanded by Captain Lawton [?] cut them off from Mexico and headed them back from that direction. I opened communication with Captain Lawton who drove them north, while I attempted to form an ambush for them, which failed owing to false report brought in to me a little before dark, which caused me to make a ride of thirty six miles between that and daylight, and I found myself back at my original camp, the Indians having passed through my camp, and Captain Lawton with his command in my original camping place. The next morning Captain Lawton and myself followed the trail into the Rincon Mountains this side of Tucson, and there we separated around the mountains in order to head them off, I following the trail into the heart of the mountains. The next day at noon I surprised the camp and recaptured all the horses and scattered the Indians afoot. For three days we were compelled to follow them afoot owing to the inaccessible parts of the mountains they went into; succeeded in chasing them out of the mountains and across the valley of the San Pedro where I found Captain Wint's troop of the Fourth Cavalry, who had just struck the trail and was pursuing it into the next range of mountains.[77] When I overtook Captain Wint's command I had only the five Indian Scouts and five soldiers with me. The rest had given out and had been left behind, picked up by the mounted men as they came along. At night, however, all of my command got into camp with a few exceptions, and the next morning Captain Biglow's command arrived and followed Captain Wint's trail.[78] I decided to make a chase and try to make a flanking movement to cut the Indians off, suggested to Bigelow to go northeast and I would go northwest, and if they turned either east or west, which they were very liable to do, that one of us would be close behind them or in ahead. As I was very familiar with the mountains into which Captain Wint was forcing them, I knew they would be compelled to turn either to the right or the left within a day or two or run into the settlements and into other troops who I knew were in the north valley of the Sulphur Springs. My command was very much worn out at this time, as we had been riding night and day in a very mountainous country without grass and scarce of water. My course took me back to Dunlap's ranch. While there I made an ambush in the valley, expecting them to cross pretty much the way they had crossed making south, if they passed through there at all, and I remained in this concealment all day. Unfortunately Captain Wint had been somewhat delayed by the rough country that they led him into, and the Indians had been able to avail themselves of twelve hours rest, and they had concealed themselves in a cañon a mile north of my ambush. Had they been forced out that day they would have come within sight of me and we would have captured them or destroyed them. This twelve hours' delay enable them to remain concealed all day, and they crossed the small valley that I was guarding in the night. The next morning at daylight I discovered their trail and pressed on and surprised them again at noon in a small cañon where they were cooking some fresh beef that they had procured, and they had such large quantities of it on the fire that my men got a good breakfast. I followed this trail until two o'clock in the morning when the country became so rough that we had to stop until daylight. I then selected my best horses; these horses were taken from a command which had reached me the night before from Fort Grant, from thirty men who, owing to a dispatch sent in of my probable direction and the broken-down condition of the command, were sent to me by order of General Miles who was then at Fort Grant, and they came to me comparatively fresh. With these fresh horses

I pressed these Indians out of the mountains onto the Gila River and at sun-down that night had pressed them into the wheat-fields of the friendly Indi-ans around San Carlos where they hid themselves; but for want of sufficient forces I was unable to take advantage of this and surround and capture them, as when they disappeared in the grain fields. I had two scouts and four men left with me out of a command of ninety odd soldiers who had started with me in the morning. This pursuit, as soon as we had gotten out of the mountains and found favorable ground was conducted at a trot and a gallop for hours. From day-light until dark we had ridden what has been estimated by the best judges time and again to have been not less than seventy miles. The Indians had not as long a run as this, because they cut across Turnbull mountains. I left a few men to follow and keep them going and made a wide circle around the base of this mountain, and got their trail again at the river road. My men coming up during the night I surrounded these wheat-field[s] but was too late to cap-ture them as they had again slipped into the mountains, and for several days we continued this pursuit, the Indians twisting and turning and coming back on their trails until I received a letter from General Miles directing me to come into San Carlos, I being fourteen miles from that place, to put my command on rising ground, so I could be seen coming to the post; that the Indians had sent in a courier stating that if the pursuit was stopped they would surrender. Getting my men together I carried out these instructions. The next morning all of the Indians except Kid and his four companions came in and surren-dered. Kid remained out trying to make terms for his life, and I was instructed personally by General Miles to keep myself informed of his whereabouts. He moved his camp every night from one place to another, closely watched by my scouts, so that I received information every morning where he had camped the night before. I was ordered not to move any way to frighten him off until the negotiations, which were carried on through an old women, either failed or succeeded. On the fourth day he came in and surrendered to General Miles. This pursuit lasted seventeen days, in a very mountainous country, and in por-tions of which had been considered before this time impassable for Cavalry, and we had itinerated seven hundred odd miles.

The Kid was tried for mutiny by a courtmartial, sentenced to the peniten-tiary for ninety years; he and his four companions. Some of the other Indians were tried by civil courts and sentenced to be hung. They committed suicide in the Globe jail the night before they were to be hung, by placing their G strings around their throats, each one taking hold of an end belonging around another man's neck and all twisting and pulling until the succeeded in chocking [choking] each other to death, where they were found by the Globe jailer the next morning. After a lapse of two years General Howard pardoned the Kid and his four companions and they returned to the reservation. The United States Federal Court indicted and tried them over again for the murder of this man Diel and others, and they received various sentences, the Kid's being twenty years in the penitentiary. He was returned to the penitentiary under this sentence.[79]

The Supreme Court of the United States rendered a decision about this time in a case of some Ponca Indians, who had been sentenced in Nebraska for various crimes, to the effect that the United States Federal Court had no jurisdiction over the Indians where there was a territorial court established. This decision was more wide-reaching than was intended by the people obtaining the decision for the Ponca Indians; and affected all Indians who had been tried under various circumstances in the territories and states, and in Arizona Indian criminals serving sentence in prison, were turned loose in large numbers; the Kid being among those liberated by this decision. He returned to the reservation at San Carlos, only to be arrested again by the territorial courts and tried the third time for the same offence. He was tried again at Globe, Arizona, and given a ten years sentence. They were carrying him to the penitentiary with ten other criminals, not of his band, but those who had escaped under the other jurisdiction and had been tried over again for their crimes. There were nine Indians and one Mexican in the gang. The Indians were chained three and three and were guarded by sheriff Reynolds and one man. They got out of the stage at a steep hill to lighten the wagon. The sheriff was walking behind them when they wheeled suddenly three of them taking charge of the sheriff and the other three men twisting him up in their chains and hammering his brains out with the shackles. They did the same with the other man, the other three took charge of the driver with the sheriff's pistol shot him through the shoulder and he rolled off into the road and was insensible. They thought he was dead. He recovered and gave this version of the affair.[80] These nine Indians terrorized Arizona for several years, committing murders everywhere. They were finally broken up to some extent by Captain Watson, Tenth Cavalry. We got two other Indians by the name of Josh and Nosy who were renegades from my command, I being a sub-agent in the command of Scouts at Fort Apache at this time, to betray these Indians under a promise of a pardon to them for their influence.

While five of them were sitting around a camp fire Josh and Nosy, companions of theirs at the time, who had joined them in the mountains, attacked them suddenly and killed two and wounded one and the other got way. The wounded man, by the name of Sayers worked his way into San Carlos under the promise of pardon to him to betray some of the others.[81]

It has been reported that Kid died in Old Mexico. But there is one thing that is certain, he has never been killed or captured to this day to anyone's knowledge.

Many claim the capture of Kid's first surrender and no doubt they may have had some share in it. General Howard in an official telegram congratulated General Nelson A. Miles, the department commander and Lieutenant Carter P. Johnson, and all other officers and soldiers engaged in the campaign for the speedy quelling of this outbreak. If the division commander was correctly informed when he wrote this dispatch, I am justified in taking the credit of the surrender to myself so far as credit is attached to a line officer.

General [Benjamin] Grierson estimated and stated that my presence in this outbreak had cost the government over two million dollars.

[Baptiste Pourier's Interview]

Baptiste "Big Bat" Pourier went west in 1858, and became a freighter and trader. He married Josephine Richard, who was part Oglala Sioux and part French-Canadian. He was an interpreter and guide by 1869, and was hired as a scout for Crook's force in 1876. Bat died in 1932 at the age of ninety-one.[82]

[Tablet 15]

~~January 7, 1906.~~

Baptiste Pourier (Biog.) was the second son of Joseph and Mary (Obeshome, French; this is spelled to sound as Mr. P. speaks the name & I should try for the true orthography) Pourier, and was born in St. Charles, Mo., July 16, 1843. His parents were both of French parentage. He had an elder brother Joseph who died at the age of 21. He had a brother two years his junior, named Emile. He had one sister, Elizabeth, who was between his brother Joseph and himself. His father died when he was two years old. His mother died in 1876; she came to Wyoming in that year after his return from the Crook campaign, to visit him and spent two weeks with him. She returned to St. Charles and sickened and died. His father used to come out into this White river country and travel in Colorado and Wyoming and Montana and Dakota and follow trapping. But this was before Bat's recollection. His brother Emile and his sister are living in St. Louis.

Bat knew John Richard Jr. in St. Charles where John went to school and afterwards clerked in a store and Bat bought goods of him. John told Bat of the fine country in the Great West and urged him to go to it.

Bat's wife is a daughter of John Richard, Sr.

When he was 14 yrs. old he left home. He hunted up John Richard Sr. at his home in St. Charles, and asked him if he wanted to hire a man. "Yes," said Mr. Richard eyeing the youngster, "I want to hire a man but not a boy." The spunky boy spoke up with his native spirit and earnestness, "I can do a man's work!" "Whose boy are you?" was the inquiry. "I am John Richard's (?) boy." "You are! I'll hire you." The boy went to his mother and told her that he had hired to Mr. Richard and was going out west. The mother's eyes filled with tears, and she said to him that she could not let him go; that he was the one who helped her to support the family, and she could not give him up. But he was persistent, and she yielded and told him to bring his clothes and she would see that they were in good order before his departure. Another boy about his age, Henry Bashmere, (this is written to represent the sound Bat gave it) a half-blood Indian, hired at the same time to Mr. Richard. That night the Minnehaha came up the river and the two lads went aboard. They came up to Fort Leavenworth. Here a man named John Baker came aboard and asked if any of John Richard's men were on the boat and Bat Pourier answered that there were two. They went with him to a hotel and remained there till Mr. Richard came up on the next boat. After his men had all assembled at that point they went 25 miles back into the country to his corral where his oxen and wagons were assembled. This was in May or June 1858, probably in the latter month, for the grass had started. Next morning the oxen were yoked and put to the wagons, and they all went to Leavenworth City to load up with goods. This took three days. Then they began their long journey for the Platte bridge which was owned by Mr. Richard, where they arrived in October in a snow storm.[83]

The teamsters unloaded their wagons and took off the wagon boxes and went to hauling wood for winter. They made a wood camp six miles from Platte bridge. This bridge was only a few rods above Fort Casper when it was afterwards built, and in September, 1906, I saw some of the posts of the old bridge still standing in the channel.

Every other day the teams made a trip to the wood camp. They hauled about a month.

Then, after Bat had worked awhile at this, he and another were detailed to go with the (1858?) trader sent by Richard to Red Cloud's camp on Wind River, with eight pack horses loaded with goods for traffic among the Indians. About eight days' travel brought this party to the village through snow knee deep. The goods were unloaded and placed in Red Cloud's lodge. Bat was given charge of the horses; these he turned out in the morning and hunted up at night; he gave them water, then loosed them again to graze till the next day—making it his business to see them twice a day. The other man assisted the trader in the handling of the goods. Their stay here lasted a week when Bat and the man were dispatched to Platte bridge by the trader, John Floreseur (right spelling not known) with buffalo robes, twenty packed on each horse, and for more goods. In five days these men had reached Deer Creek, to which place they came. Here he fell in with Charles Carbonneau who offered him $25 a month to take care of his horses and get fuel for his family. In addition he lent him a horse to go next day to Platte bridge and get his bed and clothes, at which place he met Mr. Richard and received his pay. The following day he returned to Deer Creek. He was with Carboneau all that winter.

In April next (1859) Carboneau, in company with Joseph Bissonnette, Ben Claymore, and another he calls Cuddyfail, went to Oury which was before Denver, but on one side of Cherry Creek. Bissonnette had two wagons loaded with goods, his drivers were John Obershone (?), a cousin to Bat, and Cuzzeme (?). Claymore drove his own team and had his family with him. All drove ox teams, and the traders had some horses and cows with them, and it required a month to make the journey. After Bat had been there awhile he met his cousin, Alexander Woods who asked him to go with him prospecting. He quit Carboneau and joined Woods who had a pack horse, and they started for Gregory which was then a mining camp near California Gulch (not far from the present Leadville). Here he spent the summer. At length Woods received a letter from Bat's mother imploring him to send Bat back to St. Charles. Woods let him have a horse to ride and placed him with a man who was returning to St. Charles. They reached Denver where Bat met John Richard Sr. who asked him if he did not want to go back to Platte Bridge and offered him $45 a month to drive a team through. Bat accepted and left the horse he was riding in Denver, and he went to work for Richard. At the end of 25 or 30 days they reached

Platte bridge with goods which was mostly flour. Bat worked here all winter hauling hay. In the spring he returned to Denver on horseback with his own horse and saddle, in company with two men with like outfits. They made the trip in about three weeks. There he met Alexander Woods who now had a partner in one Capt. Bassett. He hired out to them and was sent to the woods 4 or 5 miles up the Platte to hauling cottonwood logs for a building on Laramie [Larimer] Street in Denver. This was the first building erected in Denver. One evening when Bat was unloading a load of logs, Bassett was working at the building when John Scudder, the postmaster came up and called out to Bassett to come out there where he was, for he wanted to talk to him. Bassett went out and Scudder asked him if he said that he had opened and read one of his letters. Bassett answered that he had so said, and that he had so done; whereupon Scudder shot Bassett in the breast and he fell. Scudder was about to go when Bat said, "Hold on, John, let's load him on the hounds and I will take him to the house." The two put him on the running gears and Bat took him to Bassett's home where he died next morning at 4 o'clock. Scudder immediately left the place and never returned. No effort was made to capture the murderer.

Bat worked on with Woods till fall when he quit and hired to Joseph Richards, a brother to John Richards Sr. He was going to run a store and was about the first to start a store. He went to work hauling lumber with a bull team till cold weather, to build the store on Elephant street. His employer had a ranch near the mouth of Clear Creek which empties into the South Platte about 5 miles from Denver. Here Bat was next sent by Richards to this ranch where all he had to do was take care of the horses and work cattle. He worked here about a year. One morning when Bat went out to hunt up the horses there was only one old mule to be found. In the night a war party of Utes had taken a hundred head. A small party tried to follow and retake the horses, but all they recovered were some that had given out and were left by the Indians, some twenty altogether. He passed the winter of 1861-2 in this place. In the spring, having fallen to drinking hard and being about broken up he started with his family and what stock he had left for Platte bridge; but he stopped at Thompson near where Ft. Collins now is, the same being a little creek, and Bat meeting John Richards, Jr. who had come from Platte bridge, he went back with John to the bridge. Bat, when he had arrived there, hired again to John Richards Sr. He was now kept traveling with John Richards Jr. to the Indian camps trading goods for buffalo robes and skins of all kinds.

In March, 1863, John Richard Sr. moved down from Platte bridge to within

25 miles of Fort Laramie; but Bat and Louie Richard and an Indian were sent on ahead with a four-mule team to Fort Collins with a load of buffalo robes to exchange for goods but mostly provisions. When they reached Cheyenne Pass on one prong of [Lodge] Pole Creek which empties into Crow Creek on which Cheyenne City is situated — Cheyenne Pass being where in early times a little fort stood and a company of soldiers was stationed — they were assailed by a severe snow storm which lasted five days and nights and impeded all travel when over. These men had nearly run out of provisions when the storm set in, and it was five days before they tasted anything again. As soon as the storm ended they each mounted a mule, and followed by the fourth, they started back to Rocky Bear's camp on the Chug, where this Indian was taking care of John Richard's Sr.'s horses, a distance of twenty-five miles, and which place they reached at the close of day. Some six or seven miles back from the camp they came upon one of Whitcomb's bulls running at large; this they slaughtered, and taking some cuts broiled them over a fire, but Louie and the Indian overloaded their empty stomachs and were made sick whereupon they parted company with every ounce of that insurrectionary or refractory bull while Bat, though a little sick, held the mastery over his portion. When they got to the camp Rocky Bear doled out victuals to them in sparing quantities till they could eat their customary ration without ill effect. Afterwards they notified Whitcomb what had been the fate of his bull and paid the price he charged — $45. When they had come to the Chug they were entirely past the snow belt and found the ground bare.

Afterwards when they returned to the abandoned wagon the party was composed of Louie Richard, Big Bat and Buckskin Jack (Jack Russel).

In abt. May, 1864, Jim Bridger from the Platte bridge, as it was called, at Fort Casper, being the bridge built by John Richards Sr. Bridger must have come through from Leavenworth, Kansas; for he was in charge of a large train as guide. It was now on this trip he made the trail to Virginia City, Montana, where the new gold diggings were. Bridger ran his trail (which bore his name) west of the Big Horn Mountains. Casper and Bozeman are two towns on this famous road. Bozeman ran his trail on the east side of the Big Horn Mountains.[84] Sheridan Wyo., is on that trail.

John Richards Jr. started from Platte bridge with a load of goods for Virginia City, and Big Bat hired to him to drive a team. They overtook Bridger's train on the Stinking Water, a very swift stream. The river was high and they all had to wait a week or two for the torrent to subside so they could cross.

They reached and crossed the Yellowstone on the evening of the 3d July, and that night an inch of snow fell to greet their eyes on the morning of the national holiday. They traveled about 20 miles a day and arrived at Virginia City early in August. Richard sold his goods & returned, Bat coming with him. They got back to Jefferson's Fork (mentioned by Irving in Astoria in his account of John Colter)[85] and stayed there at a ranch belonging to Slade who was now dead, for a week or two to rest. From there Bat came back to the Platte bridge in the fall of 1864 with Joe Knight who was a Canadian and a trader in this country. He was married to a daughter of John Richard Sr. John Richard Jr. had, on the outgoing journey sent Bat to Joe Marrivail and his wife to ask for the hand of their daughter Louise. They consented, and the two went together as man and wife and on the return this newly married couple stopped and made a home at Bozeman.

Joe Marrivaill was a Spaniard. Joe Larrabee was a Frenchman from St. Charles, Missouri.

Bat stayed at Platte bridge all the winter of 1864-5 and worked for John Richard Sr. In the spring Richard who had a store there sold it out and he went back to Laramie. Thence in the same year (1865) Richard settled on Rock Creek at the foot of the mountains about 20 miles west of Laramie City (there was no Laramie City then). When he got camped there, Joe Knight came up with an ambulance and six wagons of goods. Knight hired Bat at $35 per month. Louie Richard accompanied, & they went to Virginia City where they arrived from Rock Cr. in 35 days, arriving in August.[86] They both quit Joe Knight there and the two went on horseback to Bozeman, where John Richard was living. Bat went to work for John Richard and Mike McKenzie and Al Long, all three being in partnership, at $25 per month. This firm was trading with the Crow Indians, John going out among them with goods which were exchanged for furs. Once they went out on the Mussel Shell and got a wagon load of furs & robes. The party was composed of John Richard, Bat, Mitch Boyer, & Louie Richard. A war party of Sioux came upon them & they cut their horses loose from the wagon and escaped [on] horseback to Bozeman. A month afterwards they went back and got a part of the robes and furs, such as were not cut up or spoiled by rains. This was in the spring of 1866. They stayed at Bozeman all summer at work. It was either this year (1866) or 1867 that flour rose to $100 a sack in Virginia City, and John Richard, McKenzie, Bat and another man went to Salt Lake, each driving a four mule team, and brought back flour which was sold at high price in V. City. They got back in October — there was some snow. Then they returned to Bozeman.

Bat thinks it was in 1865 that provisions got short at Fort. C. F. Smith and John Richard sent several loads of potatoes to that place, Bat going along, also Louie Richard and Mitch Boyer. They had to leave three loads of potatoes which were frozen on Clark's Fork. They started for Bozeman, but to save their mules had to stop with the Crow Indians on Rosebud river. The night they camped there the Blackfeet came and stole 10 of their mules. Next morning John Richard and Mitch Boyer gave chase and at the foot of the Big Horn mountain recovered the mules, but they were so injured by the Indians by stabbing when they saw they could not hold them, that the mules afterwards died in the Crow camp. John went to Bozeman after goods to trade with the Crows. The Indians were starving, there were no buffalo, the whites had no provisions, so they all moved to the Yellowstone, 35 miles, & it took 3 days to journey thence. Snow was four feet deep on the level. As soon as they reached the Yellowstone a chinook wind rose and took off all the snow. Game was plenty; the Indians went to slaughtering it; John Richard came up with the goods and met with a good trade. In April 1866 the white men, taking a wagon, and some horses bought from the Crows to pack, they returned to Bozeman & sold the robes in Virginia City.

Bat now thinks it must have been in 1865 that the trip was made to Salt Lake for flour.

They came back to Fort C. F. Smith. Bat seems somewhat mixed on dates. But he says that before Fort C. F. Smith was built he and Mitch Boyer, Lew Wahn, Louie Richard and John Richard Jr. built a ferry across the Big Horn River for the emigrant travel. The charge for a team — 4 horse team or 2 yoke of cattle — was $7.50. No charge for footmen, as these were required to help at the landings.

This ferry was built before the fort was — Fort C. F. Smith was afterwards erected right there. While they were operating the ferry a train crossed and camped there. In the night Red Cloud with his band dashed in and captured the horses; the man who was guarding them was wounded and died next morning. They had to go to Bozeman and Virginia City to get horses to move their wagons. They bought the ferry from Bat and his friends who now went back to Bozeman.

Bat does not know when Fort. C. F. Smith was built, but he and John Richard Jr. reached the fort about one or two days after the fight took place in the hay field. John Richard Jr. then took the contract to finish the haying.

The Indians attacked the haying party which was out a mile from the Fort, the attack being made about daylight. This was done by Red Cloud's Indians. The fight lasted till about noon. Something like two or three white men killed and some wounded. The Indians were trying to dislodge the whites who had their wagons corralled, and had limbs of trees and brush put up on the inside so as to conceal themselves from view. The Indians set fire to the hay and tried to burn the whites out. Some of the wagons were burned up, the brush got on fire, and the smoke and heat were intense which made the situation of the whites extremely critical; for they had to remain inside as to go outside was sure death from the shots of the enemy. There was a small military guard there from the fort. At last a white man volunteered to go to the fort for help. He mounted a horse and dashed among the Indians but succeeded in getting through them without a scratch, and reached the fort. A company started from the fort but were driven back by the Indians. The Indians at length withdrew abt. noon. There must have been, Bat says, judging from what the Indians say themselves, 7 or 8 Indians killed and quite a number wounded. After this the hay party moved to the Fort.[87]

Next day John Richard came and took the hay contract off the hands of the contractor who had lost a part of his horses and was otherwise crippled in his outfit.

Following the completion of the hay contract John Richard Jr. took the wood contract and Bat worked for him all winter as a hunter for the outfit to keep the men supplied with meat. In the spring of 1868 Little Big Man made a dash and captured 10 head of cattle and about 35 mules and 5 horses including one of Bat's. During this attack the cook, a white man who had gone for water, was shot and wounded by an arrow, but being only a flesh wound he recovered. A part of the stock was regained, but those lost numbered as above stated.

After the wood contract was finished in the spring of 1868, John Richard and Bat left Fort C. F. Smith in May to go back to Laramie. Arrived there and camped with his teams at his father's. John Richard then went to Cheyenne & afterwards returned to his father's. John now got a letter from his partners McKenzie and Story, advising him that they had bought the junk belonging to Fort C. F. Smith and telling him to put his freighting outfit in good order and to come up there and move the property to Helena. Some men were hired for the work. The Fort was on the south side of the river. The troops moved off south towards Fort Laramie. Bat thinks there were four companies, the Fort was being abandoned; the soldiers were withdrawn to the south, he says to Laramie. John Richard et al. crossed to the north side with their goods. The Big

Horn is about 100 yards wide at that point. About sunrise next morning Red Cloud attacked. The soldiers had gone, but John Richard, McKenzie & Story were yet on the other side. Red Cloud set the fort on fire. It was a big conflagration, for some of the buildings were made of sawed stuff—sawed logs, sawed boards, adobe, &c. The fire reached some ammunition which had not been removed and there were some lively explosions of shells. Bat was there & saw all these things. There were about 20 men in the Richard Jr., McKenzie & Story party, and Bat thinks if it had not been for Red Cloud that all of them would have been killed. Afterwards Red Cloud and his brother Spider told these men that they had saved their lives. Red Cloud and Spider crossed below and came up where the wagons were and stayed there. A few Indians crossed over to the white men's camp, but Red Cloud told them that these men were his relations and he did not want them harmed, or their property molested & so these were left except that a few blankets were taken and a part of a California saddle. Richard sent some tobacco & provisions across to the Indians. The Indians had thrown some of the movables in the fort into the river, such as stoves and the like. Richard & his partners claimed to have bought the fort and all the property left behind by the soldiers. This firm filed a claim against the government for $50,000. Bat says this claim was for the fort itself; but these partners were allowed and paid $1,250 for the personal property which the Indians destroyed.

The partners now moved to Helena, where John Richard turned over the outfit and the goods to McKenzie and he and Bat, ~~Peter Richard~~ Speed Stagner, Pete Janis, Charles Janis, Joe Richard, and Louie Richard (Joe Richard was a cousin to John & Louie) and Touissant Cancellor all came in a party to Laramie.

In 1869 John Richard Jr. and Hi Kelly took the wood and hay contracts at Fort Fetterman.[88] They outfitted with mules and oxen; Bat ran the mule train and another man handled the oxen; these hauled wood all summer, & next hauled the hay. About election day in the fall Bat was sent as a messenger to Fort Laramie from Fetterman, 120 miles, to carry the votes which had been cast.

When Bat returned from this trip [there] occurred the killing at Fetterman of the corporal by John Richard Jr. John had gone out on his last trip for hay, and in his absence the military went out to his camp, about 3 miles, where his father & mother & his sisters and Hi Kelly's wife, and where John had a lot of Indian goods, all were there, and the soldiers moved the whole in, & in coming in tipped the wagon over and some of the goods were lost or injured & the soldiers stole some, and when John came in he found the condition of his camp and property where it had been made down on the bottom by the fort, he was angered.[89]

Prior to this he had been in a house where a loose woman held forth; a corporal was there with arms while John was unarmed; the soldier drove him out, but John told the soldier that he would get even with [him] some time.

So next morning after John came in with the hay he asked Bat not to interfere with him that day, saying to him that he had stopped him a good many times; so Bat assured him that he would not interfere with him, not suspecting that anything was going to happen. John had bought a horse that morning from Speed Stagner for $150; he went up to the sutler's store where this offending corporal was sitting out in front; he raised his Winchester and shot the man through. He then went down into his camp and remained an hour before taking his departure for the north. No attempt had yet been made to arrest him. He left behind a large amount of property and a good deal of money in his trunk. The military took all this and Bat says that nobody knows whatever became of it. John went to Red Cloud's camp on Powder river. He remained there a year. During the winter of 1869–70 John came down to Bat who had in 1869 married John's sister and was now living on the Chug, twice for things he needed & Bat went to Laramie and got them for him. It was arranged by Colonel Bullock to have John to get certain leading Indians to go as a delegation to Washington.

John did this, and the following are the ones who went: Red Cloud ~~Man Afraid of his Horses~~ (the biggest chief at that time) Red Dog (the father of the Red Dog at present on the Reservation), Sword (brother to George Sword Jr.) Rocky Bear, Yellow Bear, (the one killed by John), Black Hawk, Red Shirt and Face, and Jules Eccoffey and Standing Bear (Woman Dress's brother) (Man Afraid, Bat says backed out from going). James McClosky (brother to Joe Kocher's wife) went as interpreter.

Colonel Bullock was not an officer, but he kept he sutler's store at Laramie. He went along with the delegation. General Smith who was in command at Laramie also went with the delegation.[90]

Red Dog spoke first. He said substantially (this part is told me by Mrs. Pourier) to President Grant, "Your people are coming into my country and overrunning it, and unsettling everything; doing as they please with every-body, taking a man here and a man there and doing just as they want to with him; now here is a young man, and I have brought him to you to do with just as you will; he got into some trouble with one of your men and killed him; now here he is and what are you going to do with him; will you cook him and eat him?"

The President answered Red Dog & told him to take the young man back with him. And to John he said he warned him to keep our of further trouble and to use his abilities to help the Indians to attain to higher conditions. There was further talk on various matters including the subject of agencies. (It is believed that the subject of the Sod or Red Cloud Agency was discussed.) (The President was inaugurating a new Indian policy, and his main design was to assemble the leading Indians and have a talk with them. The pardoning of Richard was a side-matter; he used this incident to get the Indians in, and Richard's pardon had been promised if he would do the service to bring the Indians.)

After John had killed the soldier John Richard Sr. & family & Bat and Hi Kelly & wife moved back to Richard Creek which empties into Chug. After arriving there old man Richard & family and Antoine Reynolds & Bat and a hired man named Joe Hornback & an old Mexican and another Mexican & his family; these were all camped on Richard Creek. Louie Richard went in October, 1869, also Bat Pourier to Fort Laramie and were there married by Frank Yates (who was trader afterwards at Red Cloud near Fort Robinson). Louie & Bat were both married, & then they returned to their camp. About a week after, Bat went out to shoot some game. He had taken only a muzzle loader; he shot an antelope & wounded it; he sent his dog after it; he was on a mule and 4 or 5 miles from camp; suddenly he saw a Cheyenne war party of 35 or 40 going along the ridge above him, but there was a deep ravine below him, and he did not suspect that there were other Indians in the vicinity; but it was only a moment till his mule shied and he saw eight Cheyennes charging on him. He instantly dismounted and began singing in Indian and dodging from side to side of the mule. Frank Yates was passing not far off in the road in a buggy & he counted 40 shots at Bat. The mule was slightly wounded and fell into the hands of the Indians. Bat talked to these Indians by signs & invited them to ride up on him & kill him, & otherwise showed his contempt of them & his bravery. He shot once from his revolver at them. The Cheyennes got afraid of him and would not come closer to him than 300 yards. Espying the horses at the camp they drew off from Bat and made for them and got them, 6 head.

About a week after this a party of Sioux charged on their camp and took all their horses and mules, about 25 head. The men in the camp followed them and retook all but 2 horses, and got one horse belonging to the Indians, and a war bonnet.

When Bat and others were recovering their horses from the Sioux he says that Woman's Dress was among the Indians who were driving off the horses, and he helped the whites to get them back, by cutting them out. Bat says the Indians threatened him [Woman's Dress] and said while he was doing this that they would kill him, but he replied that he was going to help his friends to get their horses.

After this these people were afraid to live so far up in the country, so they moved down on the Chug close to the station where there was a squad of soldiers. Again, 3 or 4 days after camping there, the Cheyennes made a dash on them and got all the horses & mules, but the latter all ran back to the bell mare. The men got out with their guns & killed two of the attacking party, and recovered their horses all back.

In the spring of 1870 Bat was employed as scout and interpreter at $100 a month, and was in the government service continuously for ten years. He stayed all this summer with a company of the 5th Cavalry, Major Hart comdg.[91] When this company which had been stationed all summer on the Chug, went in to the Fort Laramie in the fall, he was discharged. He went at once up to Fort Fetterman. On arriving there he found a letter asking him to come down to Laramie and accept service as scout and interpreter, as Jim McClosky, who had been the guide and interpreter there, had been killed by Johnny Boyer, a half brother to Mitch.[92] Bat went right down and went to work.

Bat continued in service at Fort Laramie till 1876 when General Crook employed him for the campaigns of that year for $150 a month.

Passing on now to the battle of the Rosebud, Bat says that when Crook arrived on the scene where the battle took place, the General ordered his cavalry to dismount; Little Mountain Sheep, one of the Crow scouts told Bat to tell the General not to dismount his men, as the Sioux were charging on him.[93]

The Sioux were charging and Bat says the General would have lost his horses, for they would have scared them off. Immediately the Crows and Shoshones made a counter charge; Colonel Guy V. Henry charged to the left; Bat was with the Crows, he was the Crow interpreter; the Sioux were driven back; Henry was fighting Cheyennes, and Bat's party were fighting the Sioux. This was when the battle began. This charge on the Sioux gave the cavalry time to get ready for action.

After Col. Henry was wounded there were two of his men who were killed by Cheyennes.[94] They were dismounted and their horses had got away from them. Two Cheyenne warriors charged on them. The Crow Indians started to charge on these Cheyennes and save the soldiers' lives, which they would easily have done, but General Crook told Bat to call them back. Bat did so. The Cheyennes rode on to the soldiers who gave up their guns from their hands to the two Indians who instantly shot the two men with their own guns. The Crows were angry because Crook had called them back, and they inquired what was the use to fight if the General would let his men be killed that way right in sight & would not let the Crows go to save them. As soon as the Indians had shot the two soldiers they jumped from their horses and struck them with their knives.

Where the infantry fought Bat had noticed that the men had left great numbers of cartridges on the ground. They would lie or kneel down to fire; in each case they drew from their belts a handful of cartridges and laid [them] on the ground handy for use. When they advanced they did not think to take these cartridges, but left them.

The Indians all fell back out of sight. This was a decoy. When the Crow scouts came to the Rosebud cānon they refused to go into it. One of the headmen named White Face was spokesmen. He told the General they wanted to go back. The General asked them what for. He said they did not want to get killed, as they all would be if they went into the canyon. The Crow, having in memory that the Crows had been called back from saving the two soldiers, asked why he had not let them fight back there when the two soldiers were killed. The General said he wanted to get to the Sioux village and fight them there. White Face answered and said that the force you have been fighting is only a little war party; if you go to the village you will find as many Indians as the grass. If you go down there you can never get out of the trap; you will all be killed, and the knowing Indian rubbed the palms of his hands together in imitation of grinding stones, which is the Indian sign meaning complete destruction. He added that he was going back; that he had a lot of wounded men. Bat had been interpreting all this. He now spoke to the General and told him what he had observed about the ammunition, and added that the Indians had told him that they had seen the same thing. So the General dispatched an orderly to the officers to inquire about the ammunition supply among the men, and word came back showing that it was very short. Then the General said there was not ammunition enough to advance, & he would have to go back. The command was withdrawn to the camp where the battle began. The soldiers killed were buried on the field. The column remained at that camp till next morning, the wounded being attended to in the meantime; next morning he began his movement back to Goose Creek. It was the second morning that the Crows quit Crook and went home—the second morning after the battle. The reason the Crows wanted to return to their camp was that they saw a roan horse among the Sioux which they had left at home, and they were afraid that the Sioux had been at their village and killed people and taken horses. But the real reason no doubt was that the Crows were disgusted with the way the fighting had been done that day, and they so told a certain infantry officer, Capt. Burk or Bourk.

Bat says that a prospector was along who took down all this talk and wrote an account of the battle; his name was something like Toneburg; he was a tall man; he had a store afterwards in Deadwood where Colonel George lives, & Col. G. can give his whereabouts. He sold his store and went east.

One morning when Crook was following the Indian trail, after he and Terry had separated, and he was down on the Little Missouri, Bat and Buckskin Jack, and Louie Richard, Little Bat and a Shoshone half-breed were sent out in advance on one side of the command to see if they could discover any trail. Stanton (who was paymaster) and newspaper correspondent also went out with about a dozen other scouts under his command.[95]

Bat says they struck a trail & were following it when two (continued in Tablet "Big for 10 cents, p. 29) [Tablet 13] Indians turned into the trail ahead of the scouts. Bat cried to Stanton telling him that "here are the Indians; let's go after them!" The scouts burst after them, spreading out somewhat as they went; they raced about five miles when the pursued Indians came up with their party ahead; and now the whole body of Indians turned back upon the scouts in a charge; the scouts began to retreat. Bat fell back 100 yards and dismounted, his horse being played out and unable to make any time. Buckskin Jack (Jack Russell) called to Bat and asked what was the matter; he answered, stating that his horse had given out. All the rest were fleeing for safety; but Buckskin Jack said I will stay with you; Little Bat said the same, and both jumped from the saddle; these three exchanged a dozen shots with the enemy, and then the Indians retired leaving the three scouts alone. These kept their position, and in about 20 minutes Stanton came up with the other scouts, and inquiring where the Indians were Bat said they were falling back. Stanton says "Let's go after them!" Bat indignantly replied, "If you want to go for them, go on; we are not going;" and the three would not go. Stanton and all the scouts returned to the command. Stanton told the General that Bat had "gone back on himself," but when the General spoke to him about it & he explained how he had been deserted to his fate & would have been killed if it had not been for Jack and Little Bat, the general expressed his pleasure at Bat's conduct.

It was next morning that the troops had to cross Hart river, and it was here

where the bridge was made of boxes of ammunition. (See Uncle Dave Mears'
statement.)

Next morning after this bridge had been built, Gen. Crook started 50 men
on ahead for Crook City in the Hills to obtain provisions. Frank Gruard was
sent as guide.

The following morning after they started, a courier arrived with a message
to Gen. Crook saying they had found an Indian camp of 30 lodges and that they
were going to attack. Crook moved forward with all speed. When he arrived
there had been some fighting, but there were Indians in the hollow. Bat says
that he and "Buffalo Chips," (Charley White) and Little Bat were together on
the bank at the verge of the little gulch which was about five feet deep and abt.
300 yards long and ten feet wide and was grown up with willows & bushes.
He was on one side of Charley White and Little Bat was on the other. These
three were on the opposite side of the ravine from the General and the soldiers.
White was bound to take a shot into the ravine but Big Bat kept remonstrating
with him and telling him he would get shot if he raised up; but he could not be
kept down, and raising a little too high to get aim, he exposed the upper part of
his body and received a bullet in his heart, and with an Ugh and an "Oh! God"
he fell and rolled over dead.[96] The General kept directing Frank Gruard who
kept back by the wagons to tell the Indians in the ravine to come out, and he
did so, but they would not do so. Gruard never got up to the ravine. General
Crook and the soldiers was on the opposite side of the ravine from Bat, & so was
Gruard when Bat first engaged in the fight. Buffalo Chips was killed within half
a minute after these three had stationed themselves on the bank of the ravine
which was depressed and descending where they were, and not high and rising
as by some stated. In a few minutes more Bat heard the cry of a little child in
the ravine. He shouted to the General that women and children were in there.
Then he ordered the soldiers to cease firing, and there was no more firing by
soldiers after this. When the firing ceased Bat jumped down into the ravine; a
woman in great distress of mind, wet and numb and shivering grasped hold of
him and said she wanted to live. Bat told her if she wanted to live, to come out of
that place. At this moment a young warrior leveled a revolver at Bat who jerked
it from him and threw it to a captain. Now Bat went up out of the ravine, taking
with him this woman who had spoken and another woman who was wounded
in the legs and breast, and the young blood who had drawn the revolver on him,
and a little girl some ten years old. An infantry company was right up close to

the ravine, & these four captives were turned over to the troops. On the other or north side of this same gulch there were no soldiers close up. When this was done the General spoke to Bat as the latter was descending again into the ravine cautioning him to be careful or he would get killed. Bat went down with cocked gun in hand and saw a man on his knees with gun in hand. Bat ordered him to drop the gun and he instantly obeyed. Bat told him to get up and walk up to him, & he did so. He got up on the bank and shook hands with the General. American Horse was lying in a hole which he had scooped out with a butcher knife. He was the last left in the ravine. Bat went up to him. The General came down into the ravine, and he & Bat assisted him out; he was holding his intestines with his two hands. The doctor took charge of him and gave him all possible attention, but nothing could save him and he died at four o'clock next morning.

This man said his name was American Horse; Gruard knew him and he said this was his name; and the General told Gruard to ask his name and he said "American Horse." Bat heard all this. He says that this American Horse belonged on the Cheyenne River Reservation, and he thinks he was a Minneconjou. These Indians were returning to their Agency from the campaign. The bands of Indians were separating and scattering to their several reservations.

It was three days after the battle of Slim Buttes when a convoy of provisions arrived for the army. Men had been suffering horrible hardships. Horses were exhausted and falling everywhere along the line. The mud was a foot deep. Rains had been incessant. The starving soldiers sometimes when a horse fell from weakness, would take out a knife and cut out a piece of horseflesh and eat it raw.

[Tablet 13, continued]
~~At Baptiste Pourier's, March 6, 1907.~~

Crazy Horse

Bat Pourier says: He was in Lieut. Clark's quarters at the northwest corner of the square when Crazy Horse was wounded, and did not see the tragedy. He says that he himself and Touch-the-Cloud, Dr. McGillicuddy, the soldier on guard, and the father of Crazy Horse (whose name was also Crazy Horse) were with him that night of his death until he died. Bat was the first to discover that Crazy Horse was dead. He remarked to the doctor that he was dead. The doctor said he guessed not, but on feeling of him found it was so. Then they feared to announce it to Crazy Horse Sr. on account of his grief. So Bat suggested giving him a drink of grog which was done, Bat getting his portion also. The old man expressed his satisfaction, saying it was good. Calling Bat his son, which he usually did, he said "it was good, that will open my heart." Bat says: "Don't take it hard; your son is dead." The old man's outburst of grief and remorse was explosive. His expression: "Hengh" (a grunt like a bear when he seizes & squeezes, & is just an exclamation). "Micinci watoye sni te lo" (My son is dead without revenging himself!"). Crazy Horse died at 4 o'clock A.M. [97]

(Heugh! Micinksi watogye sni te lo. my son. The above is given me by Rev. W. J. Cleveland as correct.)

Bat says: Crazy Horse was wounded this way (although he did not see it). When Crazy Horse entered the guardhouse, Touch-the-Cloud was the first to speak and warn him that he was going into confinement, that he was in the guardhouse, as he saw and heard balls and chains. Crazy Horse sprang back and drew his knife; Little Big Man seized him, but Crazy Horse cut him across the base of the thumb and base of forefinger—a slight wound only—but Little Big Man howled and cried and acted the baby as though he was half killed.

Bat says that when Crazy Horse was wounded there were orders to take him to Laramie in an ambulance, and from there to Omaha. Bat was to go with him, also Yankton Charlie and No Neck, and another, and an escort of officer and soldiers.[98] Bat's understanding is that Crazy Horse was purposely stabbed.

Crazy Horse was a slim, light man; weight about 140 pounds. Little Big Man was very short and stout, weight in his prime about 140. Bat says Crazy Horse was as fine an Indian as he ever knew. When Crazy Horse stole two blooded mares from him at Fort Laramie (when Billy Garnett was herding his horses for him), Bat went to him and asked for them, and Crazy Horse told his wife to get them, but she did not want to do it—did not want to give them up—but he ordered her again to get them, saying they belonged to Bat, and she delivered them. Bat says he was the only Indian who would have given them up. Crazy Horse fought only for his country, and was not a bad man at all. He was slow of speech. (When C. Horse fled to Spotted Tail Agency he took his original full-blood wife & left the Larrabee [Laravie] woman, Bat says.) Bat says that Crazy Horse's second wife was the daughter of Joe Larrabee, and that Lieut. Clark had got Crazy Horse to take her to wife, thinking that this chief would regard it as a favor and that it would have the effect to mellow his feelings and make him more kindly disposed toward the whites. There may be a mistake about this.[99]

Bat says it was bad policy to arm Crazy Horse and some of his men as scouts.

When Lt. Clark wanted him to go against the Nez Perces Crazy Horse taunted him by saying that he (Crazy Horse) had given up his arms as an act of peace, and "now," he says "you put guns into my hands again to go to war!"

Bat does not know anything about the councils between Gen. Crook and the Indian scouts over the Agency question.[100]

Bat says that Garnett is in error about his being in the room with him at Lt. Clark's headquarters on the night of C. Horse's death and being awakened in the morning by C. Horse Sr. Bat sat up that night with C. Horse.

[Tablet 15]
Interview with Baptiste Pourier ("Big Bat"), began Sunday, January 6, 1907.

The Sibley Scout[101]

General Crook and his army was camped on the south fork of Goose Creek, about a mile above the junction of the north and south forks. Where they unite is the beginning of Tongue River. They form Tongue River. Tongue river has 3 parts, 2 are called Goose Creek.

When Gen. Crook was contemplating employing some Crow Scouts to accompany him on his expedition north, he called Frank Gruard and Big Bat and told them he wanted them to go to the Crow village, and he asked them how many men they wanted to go with them, & they replied that they wanted 30 of the best men with good horses, and these were given them under the command of Lt. Sibley. Among these was one packer who went just as a volunteer without carrying any pack. Bat thinks he may have made 31, but is not sure. See Finerty's and Bourke's books.[102] They started a little before sundown — went north to a little dry creek on the north side of South Goose Cr. & which empties into Goose Cr. At this place they stopped just as the sun was going down and made a cup of coffee; & soon after this they started & arrived at Tongue River at dark and Gruard suggested to Bat that they stop there for the night, but Bat resisted this, saying that they were probably being watched by Indians who had observed their movements & were aware of their location, and that it would be better to move off a few miles since it was now dark, & thus avoid the Indians who might now know where they were. Gruard saw the reasonableness of the suggestion, and they moved about two miles north toward the foot of the mountain. There they found a basin about 50 yds. across, & here they camped for the night without unsaddling their horses; the men laid down to sleep and held the bridle reins of their horses in their hands.

They were up in the morning before break of day and without taking any refreshment moved forward. They had gone but half a mile when they came near a high hill with very steep sides, too sharp for horses to climb, when Gruard said to Bat you and the Lieut. go up to that ravine (pointing) and I will go to the top of this hill and look with the glass. Gruard left his horse at the bottom of the hill & went up. Before this, however, he told Bat that if he swung his hat that he (Bat) should at once come up to him. Bat and the Lieut. and the party moved to the head of the ravine & stopped. Presently Gruard swung his sombrero. Bat spurred his horse up to the side of Gruard's horse, dismounted and left the two horses together, & he was soon by G.'s side. G. said: "Take this glass and look and see if those are Indians or rocks over on that hill." Bat took the glass & looked. Then he said "Those are Indians—a war party of Indians." "Of course they are," said Gruard, "They are Crows, I believe." Bat replied: "I believe they are Sioux; but hold on: I can tell whether they are Sioux or Crows when they start." (They were dismounted and all in a bunch holding their horses when these scouts discovered them.)

This is a rule among the Sioux and the Crows:

When the Sioux are moving on the warpath or at any time they observe no regularity but pass and repass one another even the leader or headman; whereas the Crows move as our cavalry do, none ever go ahead of the leader and fall back at will.

As soon as these Indians were seen to mount, they began to pass one another without any orderly movement, at the same time dashing toward Tongue River where they expected to find the soldiers who, it was now plain, had been discovered the night before, and who, but for Bat's knowledge and judgment, would now have been attacked. There were about 50 Indians. The Indians failing to find the troops on the river had no difficulty to take their trail which they followed up in the direction of where the soldiers now were at the head of the ravine. The troops were now at the head of the ravine & on the top of the mountain which is in the Big Horn range. From this place the scouts had seen the Indian village 4 or 5 miles distant, in a northeasterly direction and on the head of the Box Elder Cr. east of the wickiups were standing. The command was on a big Indian trail where the natives were in the habit of going & cutting lodge poles. Bat told the Lieut. to hurry up, for the Indians will cut us off if we do not hurry. Gruard rode in front with the Lieut., while Bat took his place in the rear to watch from that point.

Bat was in a desperate hurry, knowing how much at this moment speed meant. He kept urging those in front to "hurry up, or the Indians will overtake us." Gruard yelled back: "We can't go any faster. The Indians haven't seen us."

The command soon filed down the hill and were in the mountains on Tongue River in a little park. Here, all stopped. Bat said: "What are you going to do?" The Lieut. answered, "We've got to make some coffee for these men." Bat yelled back to Gruard: "Frank, you know better than that. We'll be jumped sure." Bat screamed again: "What are you going to do? Going to take the saddles off, too?" [The] Lieut. said: "Yes, we are going to unsaddle." Bat answered: "Well, my horse is going to be tied to this tree," adding that he was not going to take the saddle off from his horse.

Coffee was made and quaffed, then the men saddled up and started to ascend another hill. While the coffee was making Bat could not repress his disposition for fun-making; so, as John F. Finerty had gone on this scout for adventure and to enlarge his knowledge, Bat who knew that the Indians had accomplished their design to get ahead of the scouts to prepare an ambuscade for them, and that there was a warm time coming, began to rally Finerty by saying to him that now he would have something to send to his paper meaning the <u>Chicago Times</u> for which he was correspondent. Finerty said "Yes, it was the last scout he would accompany for the sake of news; and he hoped nothing more serious would occur than had already happened." Bat then told him to look out for things of stirring interest to come.

Soon, they were on the top. ~~of the hill.~~ Here Bat saw two coup sticks which the Indians had ~~stuck into the fresh horse tracks which they had discovered~~ left lying on the ground. This was a sign which was unmistakable that the Indians had discovered the scouts and had got ahead of them. Now was Bat's turn to speak: "Oh! no; they didn't see us! Here are these sticks; they are ahead of us now!" These sticks were coup sticks which had been left or dropped by the Indians in their haste to move off into the pines probably when they saw the troops advancing. There were fresh tracks of their horses also. This stop for coffee had given the Indians time to get on ahead of the troops. Bat dropped back to his place in rear and the column moved forward. (It should be observed that at the time when they stopped for coffee that Gruard was sick on account of a venereal disease, and when the horses were unsaddled, Gruard laid down and rested on his saddle, and when they were ready to go Bat had to go and rouse him up and urge him to get his horse ready &c.)

The sticks were seen on top of a hill. At this point it was where Bat said: "Go on ahead; I'll drop back." They moved on & were soon in the thick pines. Bat now looked back and saw three Indians coming behind. When he saw these he rode up to the Lieut. and Gruard and said to them: "They are right behind us." Bat loped on ahead and saw a lot of Indians in front looking for the trail of the troops. Bat was now right on the lead with Gruard and the Lieut. as they advanced. They were now in a park. On the right of the soldiers was a ridge covered with big rocks.

Just as the column got opposite the rocks the Indians who were hid behind the rocks, rose up. Bat shouted: "Look out. They are going to fire!" Instantly the Indians began firing at a range of not more than 100 yards. The scouts broke for the pine timber on the left, not more than 20 yards away. Bat said to Frank: "Let's dismount and tie our horses." Bat was the first man to act, he was about 50 yards from Gruard & the Lieut. when he dismounted. Gruard said to the Lieut. that it was necessary to dismount and tie the horses, and the Lieut. gave the order.

When the firing began the mare which John F. Finerty, the correspondent of the Chicago Times, rode, was wounded. This was the only damage done.

The men hid in the brush and behind rocks and trees.

The Indians kept their places behind the rocks and did not cease firing, and re-inforcements were continually arriving, and the Indian fire steadily increased in volume. When the troops took their present position in the timber it must have been two or three o'clock in the afternoon. (See Finerty & Bourke.)

Bat thinks they were here several hours; he is sure it must have been close to night when they stole away.

Bat was studying the situation all the while that the troops were lying in the woods without firing. The soldiers remained doggedly silent—not a voice was heard—not the crack of a gun on their side.

Once during this one-sided conflict an Indian named Painted Horse (who is living now on White Clay Creek on Pine Ridge Reservation) called out: "O, Bat! Come over here; I want to tell you something. Come over!" This he repeated; but Bat knew too well that this was no time for friendly converse, and that it was only a ruse to ascertain whether he was in the party, and if he was to gain some advantage over him, if it be only to put him out of the way; for Bat was well known to these Indians, and they realized that he was a shrewd and energetic antagonist. (It has been published that this call was made to Gruard. This is fiction.)[103]

Bat reasoned that they could not hold out indefinitely. They were not more than seven miles from the Indian village they had seen in the morning. This was

a Sioux and Cheyenne village. He knew that their position was untenable—
that the Indians were hourly increasing in numbers and that they would in time
be numerous enough to surround them; he saw that the pine leaves and cones
and the decaying brush and trees and the dead limbs which were thick on the
ground would make a terrible holocaust when the time should come when the
cunning Indians would apply the match to these highly inflammable materials. When that time should come, as it was sure to, the troops would be in a
roaring furnace. The end would be there. No man would escape incineration.
If he should attempt it the foxy Indians would see him and he would fall before their rifles like wild prey. There would be no hope and no escape. The
only chance for safety was in prompt and early action. Bat was reasoning it out
all alone as he sat behind that large pine tree cogitating, where he had already
escaped a wound in his knee by the timely withdrawing of his leg a moment
before the missile swept down a twig within his reach. Bat said to himself this
horse I ride is my own. To stay here is to die soon and miserably. I can leave
the horse—he will be sacrificed at all events—and there will be some chance
for me to get away. The only sensible thing to do is to take that chance and
make the most of it. What is good for me in this respect will be equally good
for all the others. It is my duty to save this command. So reasoning, his resolution was quickly formed. He was lying in the extreme front on the right and
Lieutenant Sibley, Frank Gruard and John F. Finerty were on the left. Crawling on his belly to where these men lay, Bat said to the Lieutenant: "What
are you going to do?" The officer replied: "There is nothing to do; we can't
do anything." Bat said: "We can do something; let's leave our horses tied and
get out of here. I've got my horse tied; he is my own private property, and he
will stay there. If you were wounded, Lieutenant, we would pull out and leave
you; if I was wounded you would pull out and leave me; therefore let us leave
our horses and get out of here before any of us are wounded." The Lieutenant said: "That is all we can do. Go and tell Frank about it." Bat now crawled
in the same manner to where Gruard lay a little farther to the left. He said to
Gruard: "Frank, let's get out of here," and he explained his view of the matter over again. Gruard replied: "That is the only show we've got." While Bat
and Gruard were talking, a Cheyenne Indian costumed in a gaudy war-bonnet,
who had been cantering up and down in the open space between the troops
and the Indians offering a challenge to the scouts to fire so they might betray
their places of concealment, came down at this moment and Gruard said to
Bat, "Let's get ready and shoot that Indian when he comes again." The two

men brought their pieces into position for use. When he was opposite of them they both fired and the bold rider fell to the ground dead. These were the only shots fired by the scouts during their stay in this position.

Lieut. Sibley was a young man, just out of West Point, about medium height, spare as young men usually are, of handsome features, fine figure, intelligent, gentlemanly, refined, brave and at all times as cool as if on dress parade. If he had not been a man of sound practical common sense and taken the advice of the rough frontiersmen who were sent to guide and serve him, he would have lost his command and his own life.

Having dispatched the saucy Indian, Bat now renewed his urging on Gruard for immediate action. He said: "Now hurry up, Frank, let's get out of here. Let's go to the Lieut., and let's get out of here!" Both then crawled to Lt. Sibley who spoke up when they had reached him, and said: "Frank, what will we do?" Gruard replied: "What Bat told you. It is all we can do." The Lieutenant gave the command to the men which was passed along from man to man, to get their ammunition from their horses, concealing themselves as much as possible while doing so, and to assemble on the left, so that the whole party might withdraw in a body without straggling. This was done in a few minutes' time. Bat said to Gruard, "You go ahead and I will go behind and see that all keep up." All moved out as noiselessly as could be. The Indian fire did not slacken. The horses were behind to keep up the delusion among the enemy that the scouts were still in their old position, and these poor animals were painful targets for bullets. Some of them were groaning with pain from wounds when the men secretly withdrew. The men had gone but a short distance when they emerged into a glade, miniature in size. A few steps, and they were beyond it and into a motley forest where fire had once done havoc, and the leaning dead trees which were held up by the living ones marked every possible angle and interlaced the standing timber, while the ground was strewn with blackened trunks and limbs, the whole forming an entanglement which required the utmost patience and labor on the part of the fugitives to overcome, and rendered their progress most difficult and slow. They toiled on until they came to Tongue river when they had to cross on a fallen tree which spanned the stream.

Bat kept advising the men to step on the stones and not on the soil, so they would leave no trail for the Indians to follow; and sometimes this advice was communicated in Bat's nervous, energetic, and explosive style of speech which could not be heard without leaving an impressive effect for immediate good to all.

The Lieutenant who was in the lead just behind Gruard, had a mishap in making the passage over. He slipped and went into the water, and the men had to fish him out. It was now dusky from nightfall and the ascent of the Big H. [Horn] mountain was begun. When the top was attained night had fully settled down. The men had had nothing to eat since the day before; they had had just a cup of coffee before their encounter with the Indians; now hunger was oppressing them; the excitements of the day and the strain of care and exertion had told on their strength and they were nigh exhaustion. The men halted to rest and soon sleep had disarmed almost all of them of the slightest concern. The scouts had only light clothing, and Bat had not even his blouse, for this had been left behind on his horse; so he started a fire under an overhanging ledge of rock; but while he was doing this, the sergeant came to him and remarked that he should not kindle a fire, that it was against orders and was dangerous as it would show to the Indians where they were. But Bat adhered to his purpose, saying that it would do no harm; and moreover, he would rather be killed by a bullet than by frost, and with an expletive ~~which was an index of his determination~~ as strong as his proper determination, the interview closed between the two, when the sergeant said he would have to rouse the Lieutenant and let him know, and Bat said, "Go and tell him; I am going to have a fire."

The Lieutenant came forward and in his accustomed kindly way asked Bat if he did not think it was dangerous to have a fire. Bat said, "No; look at this rock above us and the timber all around us; the Indians cannot see this little fire; besides, I am cold and must be warmed." Sibley said: "All right, Bat. I am awfully cold myself," and being soaked from his immersion in the river below, he hovered close to the little blaze which Bat had so firmly produced, and spread his arms out over it, and in a little while was feeling much better. Another circumstance went far toward making this fire a wonderfully grateful source of satisfaction to the tired men. Snow and rain were falling in about equal proportions; it was dark as pitch; there was no moon and the clouds were dense and ominous. It was but a few minutes till all the men were crowding around to receive the welcome warmth. Gruard crawled off and sought rest lying up against the granite wall. The men overcame their shivering and then threw themselves down upon the ground to drown their consciousness in slumber. A guard was kept in proximity to the camp fire during the night, and was changed at regular intervals, so that there was not a man who did not become refreshed with sleep and relaxation.

When daylight came the party resumed their perilous journey toward Gen.

Crook's camp. They had gone a few miles, possibly six or eight, when as they were trailing a small wild game path at the summit of the mountain they came into a spot where the timber was light and thin, and Bat discovered a war party of thirty-two Indians trailing along at the base of the mountain. He informed Gruard who was now in the rear, it being difficult for him to keep up, owing to his disability, Bat now being the active guide in the lead. Gruard said that as these Indians were ahead of the scouts and going in the direction of their camp it would be necessary for the scouts to fall back into the woods and keep themselves concealed during the day from discovery by the enemy. They retreated a hundred yards or so and laid down under the pines and waited for night.

Here the men, because their strength was overtaxed, lightened their loads by depositing some 250 rounds of ammunition under a stone and left it there.

The weather was clear and warm and the shade was as welcome as the fire had been only a few hours before. The men were hungry and sore. Every now and then some one of the luckless scouts would voice his cravings in expressions like this: "Oh! if I only had something to eat I would be all right!"

This party of Indians that had been seen on the flank of the mountain at the foot went on to spy about Crook's camp and steal and drive off any livestock that they could get. They got two saddle horses which belonged to Bat & were left at the camp when he started on the scout. They took 3 or 4 head of horses besides — some that belonged to some miners who were with the expedition. These Indians started fires to burn Crook out, but they failed in the design.

While lying in the pines this day Bat nudged Finerty again when he said to him: "You will have lots to send to your paper when you get back to camp." In his position this was irritating, especially as no man in the party could be supposed to cherish at this stage of the war-game the most amiable feelings. Finerty remarked once more: "I'll never go on a scout again for news. Damn you, Bat, you are always making fun of me!"

Finerty wore a very large boot that turned up at the toe like a prairie schooner at either end. This was an unfortunate design of the Irish shoemaker for the correspondent on this occasion, as it was continually hooking the brush and grasses and causing him to fall, which was a trying annoyance.

When the darkness of night came the march began again. It took about eight miles' travel to bring them to middle Goose Creek, but in journeying this distance Bat had his hands full to keep Gruard moving. Twice before they got to this stream he had to go back to rouse him up and get him on his feet and to encourage him with pleadings and drive him by cursings to maintain his place in the column and not oblige the party to wait for him. He protested that he was sick and distressed and without strength, but took Bat's urgings and imprecations in the best of good spirit, for he was a good-natured man, and felt that Bat had nothing but his welfare at heart, and then he would renew his promises to do the best he could. When they had come to the stream the men severally made their choice whether they would strip themselves of clothing and carry it in a bundle over their heads, or whether they would wear their clothes while wading through, and have to suffer with them wet when they were over. While going across two of the men slipped on stones and lost their guns. Others slipped in the same way and fell in the water and got their clothing that they were carrying well soaked. The water, of course, being from the melting snow on the mountains, was desperately cold. At this place one of the men who had thrown away his shoes before they had arrived at the place where they rested all day, and whose feet were terribly swollen from wounds by prickly pears and sharp stones, was so disheartened and indifferent to his safety that he refused to cross the creek and follow the party farther; and he stepped aside and laid down in the thick bushes to welcome fate, be it what it might—rescue by fresh soldiers, or destruction at the hands of the enemy.

The passage of the stream having been accomplished, Bat started another fire, but not without a query from the Lieutenant as to the safety of the proceeding; but being assured by the scout who thought if there was any danger, which he did not believe, it was better to take the chances than to suffer from cold and still further weaken and debilitate the men, that there was not a particle of danger, and so the fire was made and the men dried and warmed, and the result justified Bat's judgment.

After the men had become comfortable the march was continued, but it could not be kept up steadily, for every mile or two they halted for rest; and so the night passed away marching and resting by turns till morning dawned. The sun rose clear and warm and shed its bright beams down on the straggling party of men who were lame and weak, and faint in body but strong of purpose, whose stomachs were empty and whose eyes had a strange, unnatural look. Constantly they turned their heads looking in all directions; this was a precaution which the first law of nature enforced by instinct; for no prescience could give warning of the moment when a party of the enemy would burst upon them from some quarter and "rush" them to instant death.

Bat explains here that the Indians watch from high places; they can tell if any persons are in the vicinity if they see the wild game running; he used always to observe this sign; if men "wind" the game (that is get on the windward side) the animals take the scent and flee; so the Indians act intelligently and surely by this sign; and in dangerous times men move in the Indian country in momentary liability of being discovered and attacked by the redskins.

It was sometime this morning that Bat saw Lieutenant Sibley seize a little bird that was hopping in the grass and devour it. He remarked to the officer: "That is pretty rough, Lieutenant." "Yes, Bat," replied the starving man, "but I am so hungry that I do not know what to do." Afterwards he saw a soldier do the same thing. How many more surrendered to their ravenous appetites in a similar way he does not know; but for himself he says that he had been going along that morning uprooting with his hunting knife an occasional Indian turnip that he found, and eating it, and through it gave but little nourishment, it contributed something to sustain him in his weakness.

How aggravating to these famished men it was to see wild game sporting in the air and on the plains, and yet they dare not shoot from fear that the report of firearms would attract the Indians and lead to their own certain destruction.

About the middle of the forenoon joyful evidence of rescue appeared. A mule belonging to the pack train had disappeared, and Dave Mears, the assistant chief packer, had gone out a mile or more to see if he could get any trace of it. In the distance he saw a man, but supposing he was an Indian he did not advance toward him but waited and watched his movements. When the man saw him he made signs which were unintelligible, and kept on coming toward Mr. Mears who remained in the one position till he was convinced that it was not an Indian but a white man in distress, when he went toward him till they met, and he learned from this abject man the situation and whereabouts of the returning scouts. Uncle Dave went back to the camp with the information, and men were speedily sent to their assistance; the first to reach them was a packer riding a mule; then horses came for all the men to ride into camp which was now in sight. (What is given here of Uncle Dave's part I have obtained from himself.) [Tablet 24] A company of cavalry was sent out on the trail of the scouts to recover the man who had been left behind on the opposite bank of the Middle Goose, and he was found and brought into camp.

[Tablet 13]

Speaking of the Sibley scout, Bat says that when the Indians fired on the soldiers, they raised up from behind the rocks, and he judges that the number he saw was about fifteen—there might have been twenty; but he puts it finally at fifteen. Says they heard the firing kept up after their departure until they got on the mountain after dark. Has talked with some of those Indians since; they said they stayed in the vicinity of the attack that night and next morning charged in among the horses and found them abandoned & took them. He says these Indians were being reinforced after the attack began. It looks as though the scouts, if they could have remained till in the night and at that time have picked their way out, they could have escaped with their horses. But the country may have been such that they could not get out with their horses in the night. Billy Garnett says that Indians who were in this attacking party have told him that there was only a few of them—half a dozen or so, and that they went away after the fight had lasted awhile and came back next morning and found the horses there hitched to the trees. These Indians said the scouts could have taken their horses with them as well as not; but they did not know that the scouts left before dark.

Little Bat

Bat in speaking of Little Bat says that once he was with him when seven mountain sheep were scared up and started to run at their highest speed. Little Bat shot every one of them before they could get beyond the reach of his gun.

[Richard C. Stirk's Interview]

Richard Stirk came from Indiana in 1870. He trailed cattle from Texas, hauled freight between Sidney and the Black Hills, and campaigned with Gen. George Crook. Stirk died in 1942 at age eighty-seven.[104]

[Tablet 8]
Interview with Richard C. Stirk at his home north of White River in South Dakota, November 10, 1906.

He says he came out into this country with cattle in 1870; came to Fort Laramie in 1872, and after the Old Red Cloud [Agency] was moved from the Platte to Robinson he came down in the spring of 1874 from Fetterman to Red Cloud and was employed there in 1874 and 1875.

He does not remember much about the conference for the sale of the Black Hills.

He says he was at the Agency when the trouble occurred about the flagpole. Two or three attempts were made to get a pole up before it was accomplished. The Indians threatened to burn the Agency, and the soldiers were sent for and came down, led, he thinks, by Capt. Crawford. This officer assisted by Young

Sitting Bull made the Indians open or clear a way for him and his men to enter the gate. There was an Indian there called Young Sitting Bull who had a big knife—a long handle about 3 feet long, with 3 blades in it—he was a kind of head man whom they all feared, and he cleared the way for the officer who pushed right in through the Indians.

He was herding beef herd in 1875 at Red Cloud. The Cheyennes used to come and take cattle when they took the notion. He says the Cheyennes were the bravest Indians; they led and the Sioux followed.

In the spring of 1876 he left the Agency with 5 or 6 others and went to the Black Hills prospecting. They had no success to speak of, and as Gen. Crook was around Fort Fetterman they went over there to get work but could find none so he came back to Red Cloud Agency, and the others went robbing stages and some of them were sent to the penitentiary. Says it was a pretty hard crowd at Fetterman.

He speaks of the tough gang of stage robbers who were operating at that time. Dunc. Blackburn and Fly Speck Billy were two of the worst. The former went to the pen. Also Bivens. Stirk used to night herd at Robinson with Blackburn before he went to the bad. Bivens [was] one of his party to the Hills and to Fetterman.[105]

Some independent scouts went with Crook from Fetterman. They received rations from the gov't. and were to have for pay whatever they could capture. They got a lot of Indian ponies at Slim Buttes, but these were taken away from them to feed the soldiers. Two of these independent scouts and some others followed behind picking up the abandoned cavalry horses. They brought them along and got them pretty well recruited up. They would come up within about a mile of the troops at night and leave them and come into camp and stay till morning and then go back to bring their horses along. At Slim Buttes the Indians got these horses which were now in pretty good condition. They put up their tails and ran off in style.

He went as a scout with Crook on his summer campaign of 1876. (Didn't go in March.) This should be corrected. He was with Carr and Merritt; went out from Fort Robinson, and was in the camp when Buffalo Bill is said to have had his fight with Yellow Hand. He did not see this; but says some of the men claimed that they killed the Indian and that Bill merely took his scalp.[106]

Stirk made the trip around with Crook, and gives an account of the Slim Buttes fight to agree with Captain Bourke.[107] He tells one new thing worth recording and it was the way the Indians in "American Horse's" pit were overcome.[108] The soldiers at first would advance on the pit and fire, then the Indians delivered their fire and the soldiers would run back. This was done a few times till several soldiers had been killed. It was then planned to have the soldiers advance in three ranks; when the first rank fired it would lie down and the others advanced a little distance and the second rank would fire and lie down; then the last rank would advance and fire and lie down; by that time the rank which first fired would be ready now to advance and fire; and so this was continued, keeping the Indians all the time under fire. In this way the soldiers got up to the pit. He describes this pit thus. There was a dry creek running east. On the south side of it was a ravine or coulie about 50 yards long. On the east side of this coulie the bank was 25 or 30 feet higher than the other and was skirted by timber. In each bank of this coulie the Indians had cut holes for shelter, with their knives or other implements, and protected themselves in them. The soldiers advanced from the west to the east along the south side of the dry creek. The holes the Indians had cut into the banks were small and it was a tight squeeze for the Indians to get into them. He says that the Indian who had his intestines shot out was called there American Horse.

Buffalo Chips was killed on the east side of the gully or coulie at a high point covered by trees and next to the dry creek. Stirk was within 10 feet of him when he was killed; he had warned him several times not to expose himself so, or he would get killed. Chips went to an officer and borrowed his Sharp's rifle, and was bound to get an Indian. Stirk says some of the men kept holding up a hat on a stick for the Indians to shoot at till they learned the ruse and quit. Chips went to raising till he exposed the upper portion of his body, and at length he received a bullet in the chest, and with a grunt rolled over and down the bank some 25 feet. He was rolled up in a blanket and buried in the camp, and then the horses were led over his grave to obliterate the burial to protect his interment; but Stirk says that Indians have since told him that they were on the hills and saw him buried and afterwards they opened the grave and took his scalp.[109]

Stirk says that the last two days of the march of the army were very trying on account of famine, and the soldiers were becoming sick. The Indian ponies captured at Slim Buttes, some 500 head, were killed and eaten. A good deal of dried meat was found in the Indian camp.

A part of the 5th Cavalry, several companies, came off in a southeasterly direction on a scout and rejoined the rest of the regiment at Fort Robinson after its arrival there. It was right away now that Crook disarmed Red Cloud and Red Leaf—took their horses from them and drove them to Fort Laramie and sold then at auction for $2, $3, and $4 apiece.[110] The herders are understood to have sold a good many on the sly to buyers. Claims have been filed against the government for these horses and they have been getting $40 a head—the Indians have been getting this.

In 1879 he was putting in hay at $35 a ton and hauled it 28 miles. This was at old Fort McKinney on Powder River. This fort was afterwards moved to Buffalo, Wyoming. After haying at Fort McKinney he was down here hauling lumber from Red Cloud Agency to Pine Ridge; the old buildings were moved over to build this Agency.

He used to freight from the Missouri river to Pine Ridge—from Rosebud landing, and got two cents a pound. When the Northwestern was first built hauling was done from Valentine to Pine Ridge, and later from Rushville. Freighting was done by contract.

In 1893 he went into the Indian trader business and has been in it ever since—6 years at Pine Ridge—7 years at Manderson, and now at Pine Ridge.

This year (1906) he has the contract to supply the Indians with beef.

Wounded Knee

[Figure 7]

When the troubles of 1890 came to a head all the people on the Reservation were ordered into the Agency, and after they got in there the authorities would not let them come out. Stirk says he was living about 2 miles below his present residence on White River & didn't know there was any trouble at the Agency. They received orders to go to the Agency, but did not know for what reason till they reached there and found soldiers occupying the place. He left everything at home and the Indians helped themselves, ransacking everything. He got about 50 cents on the dollar for his losses. Other people suffered likewise. But all the people thus treated suffered less from depredations by Indians than by the whites. The soldiers hired remote citizens to furnish transportation to them; these whites when returning to their homes, pillaged houses of their contents, taking sewing machines and other valuable property, and Mr. Stirk had a two-seated buggy taken from under his shed. The Indians contented themselves with taking live stock. During the trouble, Stirk slipped out from the Agency to his ranch and took 40 head of horses into the Agency for safety, and these were stolen from him there and taken to the sandhills for shipment east, but two friends gave him aid and he recovered them. White men were doing this; Doc Middleton did it, having Tom Batchelder do the work. They were taken down on Snake River, a hard place to find them. Bennett Irwin and John Riggs had seen the horses go by and they knew the country and posted Stirk who recovered them.[111]

There was one company of soldiers stationed on the east side of the Agency road and north of the Ravine, and a lot of the Indians made a break in that direction and for W.K. Creek, and these soldiers drove them back, but quite a number of these soldiers were killed.

He says there is no doubt but the soldiers killed one another. When the Indians were defeated in the attempt to go to W.K. Creek they then made a break up the ravine.

Stirk says there were some newspaper men at the Agency, and Whiteside was out at W.K. with the troops, and these men wanted to go out, and Stirk took them out; this was the day or two before the battle. They found that the scouts had reported no Indians in sight. Two of the correspondents remained and Charley Allen and Stirk went back to the Agency. That night a courier arrived stating that Big Foot was captured with his band and [was] at W.K. So Allen wanted to go back, as also others, and Stirk took them out that night.

Next morning the Indians were told to come together into a circle and to bring all the arms they had with them. The circle was formed as Joseph Horn Cloud described it [Tablet 12]. He says it was open on the east side, and towards the hill. There were two ranks of soldiers around behind the Indians. The circle was just about a quarter circle. On the north side there was just one soldier guard walking.

The old Indians urged the young Indians who hesitated to come out into the circle to come forward and to bring their guns. A sergeant and two or three soldiers with him began at west end of the segment of the circle to search the seated Indians. As often as they searched one they moved him over about ten feet to the right and he sat down. There was one Indian painted black who was a hateful looking man—mean looking—when the searchers came to him, the trouble began.

After the searchers had examined a few Indians and obtained nothing but a few worthless guns like squirrel rifles and guns out of repair, they were convinced that the Indians had not brought out their good guns; so an order was given for the tents and wagons to be searched. The Indians had some of their wagons nearly loaded at this time and their horses harnessed, and some teams were hitched up. Some of the hitched up teams ran away when the firing began. A detachment of soldiers went about the tents and found guns in wagons, in tents buried in the dirt, and some were concealed by the women under blankets. This searching party was thus occupied about half an hour and while they were busy the searching of the circle ceased. While the searching was going on, a certain Indian was making medicine — telling them to be brave, that the soldiers' bullets could not pierce their shirts; he was gesticulating with his arms, making signs over their heads and passing his hands toward the sun, etc. Stirk thinks he should have been made to keep still.

When the party searching the circle began again their work and reached the black painted man he rose up and hesitated about being searched, and when the sergeant opened his blanket he brought his gun down on him and shot; the Indians were expecting him to make some trouble, for he was a single man and said he was willing to die, & he was a bad man, and had been making some talk before. When he got up and a little scuffle ensued between him and the sergeant, several of the Indians in the circle rose up. When this black painted warrior fired he shot the sergeant.

Before the party searching the circle resumed the search, an officer asked an officer in charge of the search in the tents how many he had and he replied 57, and added that he guessed he had them all. (Mr. Stirk says he thinks there were 63 warriors counted in the circle.)

When the sergeant was shot the next thing was the general fusilade, soldiers firing, Indians running toward their lodges, etc. He thinks there were not more than 5 or 6 guns in the hands of the Indians when the battle began.

The main firing where most of them were killed did not last ten minutes. But scattering firing and all lasted about four hours. He left for Rushville before the last shots were fired, carrying dispatches for newspaper correspondents for which service he was paid $300.

Before he left, the soldiers were bringing in prisoners. The first he saw was a woman brought in leading a horse with her little child on the horse.

Mr. Stirk says he did not see any particular barbarities committed against the Indians, but he has heard of them and knows that they were true; such as rushing up on them when they were lying down in pockets in the ravine, and killing them indiscriminately without offering to take them prisoners.

When the fighting began soldiers and Indians were commingled and running together. It was all uproar, shooting, yelling, smoke and flame.

Stirk saw all he has related; he had no business there; he was an onlooker; and watched everything closely. His attention was not distracted by any duties to be performed.

He says there need have been no trouble at all if the Agent had had any backbone; says the ghost dance was dying out, some of the Indians beginning to drop it.

There is substantial agreement, I find between Stirk, Wells and Horn Cloud as to the discharge of the first gun and a scuffle, except that Stirk says a sergeant was killed.

Stirk says positively that the sergeant was killed at the first fire, for he saw him fall. They were standing pretty thick in & round there at the time. He thinks there were three soldiers with the sergeant. I am satisfied that it was a squad with a non-commissioned officer that was searching. Stirk says there were other soldiers within five feet of them. Stirk stood within 20 feet of the scene & he thinks he knows as much about it as anyone; he had nothing to distract his attention and was there doing nothing but look[ing] on. Thinks Wells was pretty badly rattled, knowing that something was coming. Horn Cloud was young and not familiar with official insignia.

I have called his attention to the scuffle mentioned by some between the Indian and the officer — of the swinging up and down of the arms — the lowering of one end of the gun and the raising of the other and vice versa. He says it was not so, that the black painted warrior stood up holding his gun under his right arm, and in his right hand with the muzzle pointing down to the ground, the butt pointing upwards behind his right shoulder; his left arm extended across his breast, his left hand holding his blanket which hung over his gun. The sergeant had some struggle to open his blanket to get the gun; while this scene was transpiring the Indians in the circle began to rise up here and there; the black painted Indian finally swung his gun up on the sergeant and let it off killing the sergeant instantly. Stirk stood at this instant within ten feet of Forsythe, and he heard no command to fire by anybody. The firing began almost in an instant after the killing of the sergeant.

After the soldiers were stationed round the circle and before searching began the soldiers were ordered to load their guns right in the faces of the Indians. Stirk says the Indians did not know what was going to be done to them or where they were to be taken, and this loading in their faces was calculated to set the Indians to reasoning and to make them uneasy and fearful.

The medicine man frequently used the word ŏb e lēch ĭ ō, meaning "be brave, stand up and be brave."

Stirk says that Jim Asay was keeping a trader's store at the Agency. He was at W.K. with a barrel of whisky. Stirk says that whisky was very abundant the night before the battle; he saw this and was invited to partake; the officers were passing from tent to tent and drinking and congratulating Forsyth on his capture of the Indians. He says he did not see that the officers were boozy next morning, but he knows that whisky was plenty. Doesn't think the soldiers had any. He does not think the officers were intoxicated next morning. Stirk had a good deal of freedom, was acquainted with several of the officers and had access to their tents, and knew considerable on the inside. The only blunder he could see in the morning of the battle was that the medicine man was not hushed up — suppressed; says this fellow was talking and exhorting from half an hour to an hour.

He did not hear any hushing up of the affair.

The Cheyenne Outbreak

Mr. Stirk was camped at Arkansaw John's at the time of the outbreak.[112] He was up at the barracks where the Indians were confined, just before sundown, and they were having a great hubub; the women were singing in their way and some crying, and he said it looked as though there was going to be trouble, and he thinks the officers were apprehensive of something, though they never expected the Indians to take such desperate resolution as they did.

He visited the barracks after the outbreak and saw the floor torn up and lying there. He does not credit the statement that they were burning the floor; says fuel might have been withheld for a day. Saw no rifle pits inside and under the floor. He says there were small places digged in the ground where they had things buried; he believes arms buried.

He was freighting at this time and had nothing to do with the public service.

He was playing billiards that night when the outbreak commenced. When he got up to the Fort the Indians had got to the creek. He stayed up there till about 11 o'clock that night. He was up at J. W. Deere's store at the old Red Cloud Agency when the outbreak occurred.

Next morning he was up at the fort and saw a wagon sent out to bring in dead bodies of Indians. The saw mill at this time was at the mouth of Soldier Creek which empties into White River just behind the horse stables at the fort. He saw there 4 or 5 Indian men and 4 or 5 Indian women dead, and between the barracks and the mill were also 4 or 5 men lying dead and scattered along the route. At the mill two women were lying beside each other with their dresses thrown up over their heads, their naked bodies exposed and sticks run up into them. This was supposedly the act of soldiers; if not it must have been of white employees or other civilians at the post.

Stirk saw two women dead that he knew; one was a comely daughter of Dull Knife. He thinks there were 15 or 20 Indians killed — he saw about a dozen. The night of the fight an Indian and two women came to Arkansaw John's and were kept there by him in concealment 3 or 4 days and then they came to Pine Ridge.

Mr. Stirk says it is reported that Minnie, wife of George Ball, daughter of Arkansaw John died a few days ago. She lived on Potato Creek, towards the mouth.

Mr. Stirk is an intelligent, clear-headed man, not excitable and I think he saw the W.K. battle dispassionately. He had no position and therefore was disinterested.

Mr. Stirk says he knew an outsider to come in [to the reservation] to buy horses & he offered an Indian $10 for one; the Indian went to the Farmer for a permit to sell & he would not give it for the reason, the Farmer said, that the horse was worth more. Next day the Farmer's secret buyer went to the Indian who wanted money & bought the same horse for $8. This is common.

[Ben Tibbitts's Interview]

[Tablet 8]

Interview with Ben Tibbetts. At his home north of White River and 18 miles above Interior, S.D. November 12, 1906.

Ben Tibbetts says: He came west from Washington after the grand review and came with the quartermaster's Dept. to Louisville Ky. with one of the six big trains of mules and wagons. He came thence to Leavenworth. He was with Custer on the Washita campaign, was wagon master.[113]

Major Bell belonged to the 7th Cavalry, was quartermaster; and in recent years was Indian agent at Pine Ridge.

He says Custer was a stern man, overbearing, but he "got there." He ordered reivelle to be sounded at 4 o'clock, A.M. on the Washita campaign, and the troops to be ready to move at 6 A.M. He saw him burn the tents of some of the officers who were tardy in getting ready to move. After that there was no tardiness.

He had been court martialed before this for some trouble he had had with some citizens, and was suspended from duty and pay for a year.[114]

Gen. Sanborn had been in command & had charge of the expedition against the Indians till Sheridan and Custer came to Fort Dodge. He says Sanborn would never have got any Indians.[115]

After the Washita battle the soldiers, a few days after, found the white woman that the Indians had killed and the little boy whose brains had been dashed out.[116]

After the battle, quite a little while, Custer marched 25 miles a day to a Cheyenne village, but on reaching it the Indians were gone. Through the interpreters some 20 or 30 of the Indians came in, but a soldier accidentally discharged his gun which stampeded the Indians all but 2 or 3. These Custer held as prisoners until through the interpreters the Indians were induced to bring in the two captive white women which the Cheyennes had. These two women were first captured by the Sioux up on the Saline and the Solomon and were sold to the Cheyennes. The Indians brought them in; but instead of the Indians who were held as prisoners being released, Custer brought them back to Fort Harker, Kansas. He was holding the Indian prisoners there that were taken in the Black Kettle fight.

There was a young man with Custer's command to meet one of the rescued white women, his sister; he shook hands with his sister and did not recognize her and went right on and the soldiers had to turn him back. These two women were dressed just like squaws and had their appearance. On this campaign there was a good deal of snow, rations were short and so was forage. Many horses and mules perished from weakness and fatigue. Gen. Custer wore out two of his thoroughbred horses. The infantry became able to out march the cavalry.

Mr. Tibbetts after this went up into Montana and spent a winter there. Then he came to Cheyenne, Wy. He went to work at the Agency about 30 miles below Laramie, on the Platte when it was first established for these Sioux Indians. But he does not remember the year. He went to work under Major Waud [Wham]. The Agency was moved over to Robinson on White River. Tibbetts came over with the Agency. He went down with the Indians to the forks of the White River and stayed there with the Indians through the winter and issued the beef to them. He drove down a herd of 1,000 head. A number of the Indians stayed at the forks of the White River, but the most were down at the Yellow Medicine Agency 60 miles below on the Missouri. They had to draw rations and annuities down at Yellow Medicine. The Indians did not like it down on the Missouri.[117]

Major Irwin went to Washington with a delegation of the Indians, and they were promised that if they would remain at the Missouri that winter (1877–8) they might have the Agency where they should select a place.[118] They brought back a pamphlet with them on which they based their privilege. The next fall they moved up to Pine Ridge — came in great haste. Ben continued at the Agency issuing rations to the Indians as long as Dr. Irwin was Agent and McGillicuddy came in to succeed him. He says Irwin was a fine gentleman. Pete Nelson ran a restaurant down at Yellow Medicine Agency. [See Nelson interview, Box 19.]

Mr. Tibbetts was at Fort Robinson from the time of the removal of the Agency on the Platte till the Indians were sent to the Missouri.

He was there when the trouble arose over the flagpole; J. J. Seville who was afterwards dismissed. Seville was an Omaha man.

He says the soldiers were in luck that no one fired a shot. One shot would have set the trouble to going and the Agency would have been burned. Does not know who the officer in command of the soldiers was. He says that Red Cloud was in the stockade during all the trouble and stood by the whites. (I question this.)

Young Sitting Bull was very influential in preventing an outbreak. He used to carry a long knife — 3 or 4 blades in a long handle. The Indians were afraid of him. Ben says there is no mistake about Red Cloud being in the stockade; for he sat on a pile of lumber by Ben's side and stayed right through the scene.

Wounded Knee

Ben Tibbits (this is correctly spelled for he spelled it for me) and his family stayed right here on his place during all the troubles, though they were ordered into the Agency. Hank Clifford, Monte Clifford, old man Black, Nick Janis and his folks, and enough to make 25 or 30. They all stayed at Ben's. They wouldn't go to the Agency.

The old man Black was living close to where Big Foot's band passed after descending the wall; Black was within a mile of where they passed, and had no arms except an old gun that could not be used, and the Indians offered him no harm. Tibbitts says that the people over where Big Foot came from tell him that his intentions were peaceable; that there was a corral of horses over there where his people started from which were in charge of two young men who went off and left the horses. The Indians watered and cared for these horses 3 or 4 days after the boys left.

Young Sitting Bull who behaved so well at Red Cloud, was afterwards killed down on the Missouri when entering a post. There was no war at the time. Does not know how it came to be done.

Spotted Tail Killed Big Mouth. Crow Dog killed Spotted Tail.[119]

Ben thinks that whisky was influential at W.K. He says Jim Asay had a saloon on wheels there, & he had practically a saloon at the Agency.

Ben Tibbits is now 66 years old.

Ben Tibbitts' post-office is at present, Preston, S.D., but when the R.R. is through it will be something else.

[Heber M. Creel's Interview]

Heber M. Creel entered the military academy in 1873. He served in both the Seventh and Eighth cavalry. Creel was a lieutenant when he resigned in 1882.[120]

[Tablet B]

Interview of Brig. Gen. H. M. Creel on Thursday, March 6, 1913, in Washington City at No. 506 Sixth Street, who says:

The Northern Chey. who were associated with the Sioux in the Custer Massacre, shortly after the Custer massacre formed treaty with the whites prior to the return of Sitting Bull in 1881. Gen. Sheridan who was a great admirer of the Cheyennes, thought it would be a great thing to consolidate the Cheyenne nation, & asked the Northern Chey. to go to the Ind. Ter. & live jointly with the Southern Chey. as one people. In his interview with the representatives of the North Chey., notably Little Chief, the headman among them and Iron Shirt, he told them the Ind. Ter. is a desirable country & when you arrive at Camp Supply, in proceeding thence to Fort Reno, 13 miles below this Fort you will find the junction of Wolf & Beaver Cr., forming the North Fork of the Canadian River, with Fort Reno 112 miles below. From here (the junction of the 2 streams) you will have mag. hunting, country abounding with antelope, deer & wild turkeys.

On account of the representations of the General, the band of Northern Chey. under Little Chief, the head man, came from Montana to Fort Lincoln with the 7th Cav. after their campaign (the 7th Cav.) with the Nez Perces, wintering at Fort Abraham Lincoln.[121]

Accompanying 7th Cav. in spring of 1878 to the Black Hill[s] when Fort Mead was located, K Troop of 7th Cav., Capt. Mathey, and Lieut. Creel, officers, escorted this Little Chief's band to Camp Robinson, thence to Sidney, Neb., where the Inds. remained while K troop joined Thornburg's command against Dull Knife & Black Wolf, the North. Chey. numbering 800 who had fought their way successfully from Fort Reno in Ind. Ter., killing Lieut Col. Lewis, 19th Infy., in an engagement a few miles south of Ogallala[122] (He

293

says they whipped the 4th Cav. all the way up from Ind. Ter.). Thornberg's command detrained at Ogallala; it being a cold & very pouring rainy day in late October, 1878. His command consisted wholly of mounted Infy. except K Troop, and were no good because the men were not used to the new horses which were raw, & would have suffered discomfiture had it not been for the Cav. Thornberg followed the Chey. north 12 miles to North Platte River where he was compelled to abandon his wagon train; subsequently, following the Inds. North with no forage for his horses, the men sleeping on the ground with no covering, nothing to eat but fresh meat which they singed with sage brush, until the 7th Troop of 7th Cav. from Bear Butte of the Black Hills met the Inds., capturing Dull Knife and his band, while Black Wolf with his band made a detour, escaping to the west between Camp Sheridan and Fort Robinson, reaching their destination on Tongue River.[123]

Dull Knife & his band were taken to Fort Robinson. Lieut. Creel under detail from the Lieut. Gen. Sheridan returned to Sidney where he proceeded with the Northern band of the Chey. escorted by 4 Troops of 4th Cav. to Fort Reno, Ind. Ter. In going down (this was in the early part of Dec.) he went from Sidney to Fort Wallace, thence to Fort Dodge, then Camp Supply, then en route to Fort Reno, & camped at junction of Wolf & Beaver Creeks, 13 miles below Camp Supply. Next morning it was snowing terribly, Major Mauck, comdg. 4th Cav. (being Bvt. Major, but ranking Capt.).[124] The Indians were camped round in a circle and the Cav. on the outside, Lieut. Creel in the center.

At 4 o'clock in morning Major Mauck handed Lieut. Creel a telegram as follows:

Comdg. Officer

Comdg. 4th Cav. escorting North Chey. Inds. to Fort Reno, upon receipt of this order disarm & dismount these Inds. Interior Dept. refuses to allow these Indians to enter the Ind. Ter. unless this is done.

(Signed) Pope

Brig. Gen. Comdg.

Dept. of Missouri.[125]

Receiving this telegram Lieut. Creel asked Major Mauck "What do you think these Indians will think when you attempt to execute this order? Here they are, most of the guns and ponies now in their possession captured by them when they were fighting in Montana with our troops against hostile Indians? (He says they had been fighting up there with our troops against the Nez Perces and Sioux.) And after the persuasive statement of Sheridan Lieut. General, that magnificent hunting would commence here. How will they hunt without their guns and ponies? What will they think of the word—the reliability of Gen. Sheridan. Why, they will think he lied. If you will wait until I can communicate with him, this order will be countermanded." Maj. Mauck agreed with me but said, due to the isolation of our command, he had no discretion and he proceeded at 7 o'clock that morning to carry out the order. The Inds. donned their war paint the men forming a semi circle facing the Cav. 30 yards distant, the women and children crowded into Lieut. Creel's three tents in the center, the remainder who could not get inside with their babies on their backs held there by shawls as in usual way, sat on the ground in rear of the Ind. warriors singing the death song, which encouraged the bucks to fight. An awful day. Iron Shirt, as the military leader, cried out to the soldiers of the 4th Cav. "You have lied to us long enough; we will not surrender; we do not lie; and brave men do not lie; and take our guns and ponies if you can." He passed up and down the line of Inds. saying to them, "Shiv-e-ta-noth shiv-e-ta-noth." (Stand fast! don't give up! persevere &c.)

The Indians and soldiers all were standing in a blinding snowstorm. The Indians were yelling the war cry most forcefully, shaking hands over their mouths & in other ways; the cavalry was moving some & officers giving commands; the situation was tense and dramatic and critical in the extreme. The soldiers were on their horses holding their guns at "advance carbine," that is holding the firearms in right hand by the small of the stock, the muzzle pointing upwards, the but resting on the leg, the guns loaded with ball cartridges, ready for instant use. The Indians were in battle line, guns in hand pointing at the soldiers ready to shoot at the sound of a single shot. (There were between 250 & 300 soldiers, and about 180 Indians.) This attitude was maintained until 11 o'clock—four hours. During this time Lieut. Creel was with the Indians talking to them, persuading, pleading and remonstrating and advising them not to fire. There was Amos Chapman the great scout who was married to a Chey. woman, and had lost a leg in the service as a scout fighting Indians in Kansas, lying in a buffalo wallow to which he had dragged himself to get water; Ben Clark who was married also to a Chey. woman, another scout, no two braver men ever lived; they had rendered signal service to the government; and Wm. Rowland, son of Wm. Roland of Lame Deer, Montana;[126] all left the Indian encampment, saying to Lieut. Creel that he would get killed, that there was going to be a fight; that there was going to be a hell of a fight, all were going to get killed; these scouts stayed for an hour talking to the Indians and trying to turn them, but failing, and calling to the Lieut. to come with them and save himself, they pulled off, having said with all the earnestness they could that there was going to be a massacre, an awful fight, and right away. Lieut. Creel was in charge and command of these Indians under direct orders from Gen. Sheridan with further orders to keep them at Fort Reno in Ind. Ter. and there to write a dictionary and grammar of their language, and he exerted himself on this occasion to save the Indians and avert a horrible disaster. He continued to try to restrain their war spirit. His staying right among and with the Indians and pleading with the warriors not to do anything to cause their women and children to be killed, and telling them if they would think better of it and give him time to write to Gen. Sheridan (whom they called Three Stars) that it would all be made right for, as he told them, Gen. Sheridan knew nothing of this order, and was not himself breaking faith with them; and in this course he was backed up by Little Chief, who, though not in the best mood at the treatment, was wise and good, and tried to repress any rash action by his warriors and advised them that it would be better in the end to submit and take chances of getting justice, etc. Finally the Indians listened to the joint persuasions, and the proposition of Lieut. Creel who by staying with the Indians and telling them in defiance of the requests of the white soldiers for him to come over to them, that he would stay where he was and be killed with them, which had the good effect to increase their confidence in him, he induced them to agree to turn their horses over to him. As an army officer was not subject to the orders and regulations of the Interior Dept., he could take his own property on to the Reservation, so the horses, except a dozen which were reported as war ponies, were given by the Indians to Lieut. Creel, but the Inds. were allowed to keep the 12 ponies till they reached Fort Reno when these were sold and the proceeds given to the Inds. Lieut. Creel let them keep the horses they had given to him. An inventory was made of the guns, Maj. Mauck invoiced them to Lieut. C. and he loaned the guns to the Inds. without ever taking them out of their hands, and he also gave them ammunition and they hunted all the way down to Reno, and on arrival there they faithfully delivered to him every gun and all the unused ammunition.

The situation which came so near furnishing a horrible tragedy, was caused by the double operation of orders issuing from the two rival departments — Interior and War; the first having sent instructions to General Pope who was in command of the military district, not to allow any Indians to go armed into the reservation. Major Mauck was under orders from General Pope. Lieut. Creel was acting upon instructions received directly from General Sheridan, the commander of the military division. Neither Sheridan nor Pope, nor Mauck nor Creel was cognizant of the conflicting orders which had gone out; and so the danger developed suddenly and naturally as a consequence. That bloodshed and annihilation did not follow the meeting of the two forces was an event akin to a miracle, and to the presence of mind, coolness, courage, steadfastness, and judicious and conciliatory conduct of Lieutenant Creel was due the fortunate termination of the affair.

[William L. Judkins's Interview]

Ricker's notes on this interview are on three sets of numbered pages. Some page numbers are missing and other pages bear duplicate numbers. The editor has arranged the narrative in the most coherent fashion possible without regard to Ricker's pagination.

[Box 19]

Statement of William L. Judkins, December 7, 1905, made at my rooms in Chadron, in relation to the attack on the Cheyennes and some associated Sioux Indians on the 25th November, 1876, by Colonel Randall S. Mackenzie.[127] Mr. Judkins had enlisted in Chicago on the 1st September, 1876, and was sent with other recruits to Fort Robinson, Neb. From there he went to Fort Laramie, thence to Fort Fetterman whence Crook started on his winter campaign. He [Judkins] was a member of Co. D, 4th U.S. Cavalry, and went to campaigning immediately under Crook. The expedition started on the 23d.

The Cheyenne camp was discovered in what Frank Grouard, the scout, calls the Red Fork of the Powder river, at a point where it leaves the mountains in a little open valley. According to the scout the command had camped on the Crazy Woman after the day's march was ended, and Judkins says that the troops were halted there about two hours; and orders having been given by General Mackenzie to resume the advance, the columns started promptly at sundown for a night march of eighteen miles. Grouard says they went over onto the North Fork of the Powder river and from there to the Red Fork, striking it about eight miles below the village, where a halt was made and instructions for the attack were given. ~~Major North of Nebraska had command of the Indians.~~

Major North, with one hundred well-drilled Pawnees who had enlisted for one year as scouts, had reported to General Crook and was placed in command of the Indian auxiliaries. Frank Grouard, the famous scout, who was of the highest value to the service because of his long residence with the Indians as a captive when a boy, and his knowledge of their language, habits and system of warfare, and his acquaintance with the country, who, after a severe illness which prevented his starting with the expedition, ~~had overtaken the column and reported to the general for duty.~~ from Fort Fetterman, had overtaken it at Antelope Springs and reported to the general for duty. At this place a cantonment was made and Captain Pollack of the 9th Infantry was placed in charge. A party of Shoshone (Snake) Indians joined the command with the friendly object to go against the Cheyennes to repay them with vengeance for an attack which these had lately made on their tribe.

Judkins states that the troops did not enter the valley below the village, but that they were escorted by the scouts down a rugged ravine which led into the valley of the Red Fork a mile or two <u>above</u> the village and at this junction the command was halted about 4 o'clock on the morning of the 25th and waited for daylight before beginning the attack. As the use of Indians as soldiers under white commanders was an uncertain experiment, this fact received consideration in the formation of the troops for the assault, in the following order: The Sioux were placed first in the column, the Cheyennes second, the Shoshones next followed by the Pawnees—all stripped to the skin for battle in the ~~piercing morning air and under the command of Major North piercing morning air, mounted upon sleek, war-painted ponies which they had led for this use all the way beside the~~ piercing morning air; astride of bare but sleek, war-painted ponies which had been led for this purpose all the way beside the ones they rode—the whole under the command of Major North. Behind the Indians came first Troop M followed by Troop D, both of the 4th Cavalry, and the remainder of the force in proper disposition.

After the battle the ~~stricken~~ naked, foodless and distressed Cheyennes appealed to Chief Crazy Horse for succor without avail. He probably thought he had no provisions to spare from the mouths of his own people who might themselves have to fight the whites before the winter was over, and who without warfare and with the most favouring circumstances aiding them, were liable to experience the cravings of hunger in their own camp before spring. This cold and unfeeling ~~as this~~ view of the situation, ~~must have been, and though~~ had it even been reinforced by a dislike for these racial kinsmen of another tribe, was shortsighted and impolitic for him at that crisis to turn away in a moment of such extremity his most valuable allies in war. If he listened to the voice of selfishness the Cheyennes must perish, and then no more could he lean upon their aid. But they had one alternative. They could return to the agency and throw themselves upon the calculating humanity of those whom they had fought with barbarity and whose friends they had slain without pause of ferocity or mark of mercy. In this event the same result would follow as if they were exterminated; for, once more in the grasp of the government, these Cheyennes would be sealed from further participation in war with the Sioux. If they turned their faces in despair to their enemies, before they could reach these their numbers would undergo decimation from frost and lack of food. It was just these things which Crazy Horse, if he could have given the relief prayed for, had not the foresight to comprehend but which followed as an inevitable fact.

This will take its place among those instances of treachery to a cause which have so often in the course of history sullied human nature. The inducement of trivial compensation, not less than the smiles of superior power, which smothers the ties of ~~race~~ family, ~~and~~ the hopes, traditions and aspirations ~~and loyalty~~ of race, and loyalty to honorable remembrance and reflection, is truly insignificant and sadly dishonoring.

William L. Judkins

Both Sioux and Cheyennes in Dull Knife's camp

Grouard had a detail Sioux, Cheyennes, Shoshones & Pawnees, detailed out of Maj. North's command of Indians; ~~he was a~~ His Pawnees were well drilled in manual of arms & evolutions

Order for the charge: Sioux in lead followed by Cheyennes, then the Shoshones, next Pawnees; then came Troop M 4th Cav. Troop D 4th Cav. [Troop and 4th were directly below the previous Troop and 4th so Ricker used "] Judkins was in D. Capt. Lee and 2d Lieut. Mason of D. Indians were naked Started from Forks of Crazy Woman & returned to that place See Jerome Parrott Hot Springs. An Indian's G string

Judkins thinks these were the first Sioux & Cheyenne Inds. enlisted. See Grouard p. 324

Coulies [?] [Ricker drew a circle around this word and the following line.]

The Belle Fourche river is the Cheyenne

The expedition returned and reached Ft Robinson about 10th Feb. 1877. In abt. 2 wks. the Cheyennes began to straggle ~~to~~ into Ft Rob. in sorry condition, some with frozen feet, some with froz. hands, others froz. ears &c. They reported that many had died on the way. [Missing page]

There was little snow. Had been some but it was all gone except spots here and there on the north side of hills not exposed to the sun. Weather was not extremely cold at the time of the battle; Judkins says he rode all that night with his overcoat strapped to his saddle.

Judkins says the lodges were made of Buffalo hides and other peltries sewed together.

[David Y. Mears's Interview]

*David Young Mears was born in Pennsylvania in 1833. As a teen-
ager he worked on steamboats on the Ohio River. In 1856 he went
to the West Coast and then to Idaho, Montana, and Nevada. From
1874 to 1879 he was transportation manager for General Crook
on his Indian campaigns. Mears then settled near Fort Niobrara
and then at Chadron, Nebraska, where he served as the town's first
mayor.*[128]

[Tablet 24]

~~Aug. 20, 1906.~~

Statement of Uncle Dave Mears: When the advance man of the Sibley Scout returned Uncle Dave was the man he met. Uncle Dave was out hunting a strayed or stolen animal, and he saw somebody wave his hat in the distance. Uncle Dave approached him & they met. The soldier was very weak & could hardly walk. Uncle Dave approached cautiously at first suspecting he might be an Indian trying to deceive. Uncle Dave gave him his mule which he was riding, & the soldier went to camp abt. 2 miles distant. Before Uncle Dave could get back to camp he met the relief party dashing forward with provisions to meet the re-turning scouts. (Uncle Dave doubts Grouard's story of his visit to the Custer Battlefield. Tell Big Bat.)

When this soldier reached the camp, Gen. Crook was out on a hunt to pro-cure meat for the men; when he returned he had 14 elk.

Tom Moore was really Chief of Transportation. Uncle Dave was also called Chief Packer, for he was always in the field; while Moore would sometimes be away, for instance in St. Louis or Kansas City or Omaha buying mules, etc. Uncle Dave says he was in fact Assistant Chief Packer.

This is abt. the Cheyennes from the Indian territory. Uncle Dave was on the trip with Col. Auger [Jacob A. Augur] who was then (he thinks) a lieuten-ant. He was with the pack train. The expedition started from Cheyenne, Wyo., passed through Laramie & came to Fort Robinson, then to Camp Sheridan, thence via the Hay Springs neighborhood to Newman's ranch on the Nio-brara River, at the mouth of Deer Creek, south of Gordon, Neb.[129] They went on down the Niobrara to Boiling Springs Ranch, the Morehead Ranch. The Newmans had been down to the Morehead ranch and found that 2 men had been killed at the Morehead ranch by the Indians who had stolen some stock.

Stock was also stolen at the Newman ranch. The ground had no snow up to this time & the traveling was good. The troops were under command of an infantry officer (thinks it was Capt. or Major Ferris) who had been sent with the scout instead of the regular cavalry officer who was sick. The troops camped one night at Newman's then went to Snake creek, the men at the ranch in employ of the Newmans going with them. That night at Snake Creek it snowed about 6 inches and covered all tracks. Moved next morning with pack trains, leaving the wagons, as the country was too rough to take them along, and went to the head of Dismal River and Loup Fork. They found nothing but a few cattle belonging to the Olives. Ferris killed some and afterwards had to pay for them. Here the troops turned back and returned to the Newman ranch where dispatches were found ordering the command back to Cheyenne, and they returned to Camp Sheridan, Fort Robinson, & so on to Laramie & Cheyenne. After the snow came on Snake Creek the weather became extremely cold.

Col. Auger said the commanding officer of this scouting party was Major Samuel Ferris.[130]

[Jacob A. Augur's Interview]

Jacob A. Augur enrolled in the military academy in 1865. He was the son of Christopher C. Augur, a former commander of the Department of the Platte. The younger Augur served in the Fourth and Fifth Cavalry before being promoted to command of the Tenth Cavalry at Fort Robinson in 1902. He commanded the fort until 1907.[131]

[Tablet 35]
Col. J. A. Auger says: Major Saml. Ferris with six troops of the 5th Cavalry left under orders from Fort D. A. Russell January 15, 1879, and marched to Fort Laramie 95 miles, thence to Fort Robinson 75 miles, thence to Camp Sheridan 50 miles, thence south into the Sand Hills scouting about 75 miles south and southeast in search of Indians which it was reported were in that country & had killed some Whites. None were found & the command returned to Camp Sheridan & on arrival found newspapers saying that the Indians had crossed the Niobrara east of where the troops were going north the day before the command got down there. It was very cold & six inches of snow on ground. The command returned to Fort Russell arriving there on the 28th of February.

The foregoing from Col. Auger is in relation to pursuit of the Cheyennes from the Indian Territory.

[A. G. Shaw's Interview]

Before he interviewed Shaw, Ricker made the following note.

[Tablet 39]

Valentine. A. G. Shaw. Has photos of Spotted Tail and his assassin Crow Dog, White Thunder & Two Strike, & Sioux history in hieroglyphics from the year 1000 to 1872; & he was on Little Big Horn battleground next day after battle. Came to the west as a soldier in 1862 in 11th Ohio Cavalry & is full of Hist. Mr. Craven says he is reliable. Can tell about Fort Casper. Knows the whys and wherefores of the wars and Agency troubles.

[Tablet 11]

~~Interview with A. G. Shaw, of Valentine, Neb., Sunday, Sept. 1, 1907.~~

Mr. Shaw came into this country in 1862, a member of Co. B, 11th Ohio Cavalry. This regiment had done some service in Missouri in the Civil War. At the time of the Minnesota massacre it was on the road to the Platte country to Fort Laramie to operate to suppress Indian depredations and give protection to the border settlements and emigrants across the plains. Its first duty was to protect the Overland stage line from Fort Laramie to South Pass, 300 miles, and the Reg't. was distributed along this route.

This regiment in detachments was attacked several times by the Indians; at South Pass one of these soldiers was killed—a member of Co. B. These soldiers had 300 mules stolen from them at South Pass, and the teamster (another man) was killed. The mules were recaptured. This regiment was on duty going and returning, 3½ [years] less 12 days.; Co. D. of this Reg't. built Fort Casper, beginning in the fall of 1862 and finishing it in 1863. The Colonel of this Reg't. was William Collins. Second Lieutenant Casper Collins, son of the Colonel, and belonged to Co. L, a recruited company which after the original march came out to join the regiment. When this regt. came out to the plains it consisted of only four companies, the remainder of the Regt. being in service in Virginia. The enlistments were first in the 7th Ohio Cavalry. The recruiting was slow at first, and when 4 companies were ready they being needed were dispatched to St. Louis & thus got into Missouri where they were kept a little while, from abt. Feb. 1862 & did a little service. They being separated from the companies which were afterwards recruited for the 7th, were numbered the 11th and this 11th was subsequently filled.

Fort Casper and other stations along the route were garrisoned by this reg't., and at first the companies were divided into detachments except at Forts Laramie and Casper. These companies and detachments exchanged places at times. This Reg't. quit Fort Casper when the Reg't. was mustered out in the late winter of 1864-5, being about Feb. 1865.

When this Reg't. was filled the Colonel, Collins, who was always its colonel, went over near where Laramie City now is and in 1863 built Fort Halleck. In 1864 Cos. B and C went to Cache la Poudre in Colorado and built Fort Collins. In 1863 Co. H came down to Scott's Bluffs, Nebr. & built Fort Mitchell. Co.'s E, F, & G built Fort Halleck. These are all the forts built by the 11th Ohio Cavalry. To show the industry & service of this Reg't. — It covered with its garrisons a region 400 miles east & west & 100 miles north & south.

The regiment rendezvoused at Ft. Laramie in February, 1865, and marched to Omaha and was mustered out April 1, 1865, & if it had been in service 12 days more the entire term would have been three yrs. & six months.[132]

Fort Casper was named for Second Lieutenant Casper Collins who was killed there by the Indians. The Indians came up to the north side of the river Platte and concealed themselves in ambush; a few showed at the farther end of the Richard bridge. Lieut. Collins belonged to Co. L. which then garrisoned the Fort. The comdg. officer thinking there were but a small number of the enemy ordered Lieut. Collins to charge across which he did, the Indians in sight falling back and he pursuing them. The main body of Indians was concealed by the intervening high ground back from the river, and when the troops had gone out far enough from the bridge they were suddenly set upon and overwhelmed by the Indians. All the soldiers including this officer were killed, numbering according to Shaw's recollection, 23. He has been told by Indians that the plan was to draw all the soldiers (they thought all would go) across the river, leaving the Fort defenseless, while a force of Indians which was concealed on the south side where the Fort was, would attack and capture it. This band seeing that the soldiers did not all go did not show themselves.

When the lieutenant was north of the river fighting, the troops at the Fort could see the overwhelming number against which the lieutenant and his men were contending, and knew that it would be hopeless for the entire garrison to attempt to defeat the Indians.

Another incident in the history of the 11th Ohio Cavalry was the battle the Reg't. had with the Indians at Rush Creek on the Platte above Ash Hollow 18 or 20 miles. The Reg't. first went to Mud Springs (then in Idaho territory, now in Neb., he says) which is east of Courthouse Rock, on the trail from [Lodge] Pole Creek to the Platte, just before and in sight of the Platte. This was in January, 1865. Mud Springs had been a stage station but was now abandoned as such & was at this time a telegraph station. There were several buildings, and rooms connected or a part of the same building. The Indians got behind the hill in the rear of the buildings & would crawl to the top and shoot down into the log building. There were no windows on that side, but occasionally a bullet went through the chinking and penetrated to the inside, but nobody was hurt. The attack was begun at daybreak and kept up with irregular intervals of suspension until sundown. Ceased altogether then. The Cmdg. officer sent soldiers to the top of the hill to reconnoiter the enemy's position, and several were wounded, one belonging to Co. B. fatally.[133]

Next morning the command moved down on the trail to Rush Creek & went into camp on a low bluff overlooking the river on the south side; and the wagons were corralled by bringing the fore wheels up to the hind wheels of the wagon in front till the boxes of the two wagons met, except on the north side of the camp next the river. This was in January [February], 1865.

On the north of the river the country was open and slightly rolling but not sufficiently so to hide a horse. The camp was formed about noon. There was seen what appeared to be a forest of pine trees in the distance. The Colonel examined with his glass and discovered this appearance to be a dense swarm of Indians coming toward the camp. The soldiers were ordered, notwithstanding the ground was frozen, to dig rifle pits within the enclosure and so the men could shoot under the wagons. Before the preparations were all made the savages began the attack. Shots came into the corral from the surrounding hills. Indians came up ravines and got within fifty yards of the camp. The colonel was the first one shot; he was struck by a spent ball on his shin bone. The Colonel asked for volunteers to charge this ravine and drive out the Indians. Charge was made & Inds. dislodged. One soldier was carried by his unmanageable horse in among the Indians and next day his body was found filled with arrows. This was the only casualty among the soldiers. The Inds. escaped across the river on the ice. The mountain howitzer was turned on them and this sunk some Inds. horses and riders through the ice. This occurred about evening and the Indians disappeared. The command hitched up and moved back to Fort Laramie.

This took place when the Cheyennes were raiding and moving from the Indian Territory through Kansas. This is known as the Great Cheyenne with Sioux raid. These troops had been sent out from Fort Laramie to meet the raiders. They were glad to get away from the Inds. He thinks there were abt. 5,000 Inds. & about 3,000 warriors; enough to annihilate the command and if the Inds. had continued a siege.

Mr. Shaw tells about the fight at Horse Creek in the spring of 1866 [1865]. He says they were moving the Indians from Fort Laramie down to North Platte (what is now the town) to what was then called the forks of the Platte. They camped there all night. This was a conspiracy among the able-bodied Indians to massacre the officers. Captain Fouts was in command. They killed him. He and his soldiers were on the east side of the creek encamped; the Indians were on the west side abt. half a mile apart. In the morning when the soldiers were ready he had the Indian camp apprised that they must pack up and go. When the soldiers were ready to start not an Indian tepee was taken down. Captain Fouts went over unattended—no interpreter with him; his interpreter being James McClosky, son of McClosky who lived and died on Pine Ridge Reservation. When he got among the lodges he was murdered.[134]

The Indians were at that moment mostly mounted and some were even down to the river ready to cross. Shaw thinks Interpreter McClosky was knowing to the design of the Indians; he has asked him since why he did not go with Capt. Fouts over to the Ind. camp, but McClosky always said, oh, he was busy about something. Shaw thinks Frank Salaway camped that night with his team on the side of the creek with the Indians, & that Fouts, when he crossed over to see why the Inds. were not moving, asked Salaway the question. About this time Fouts was killed. It is thought that the interpreters knew about the conspiracy but were afraid to say anything. Shaw thinks Salaway knew, and I thought so when Salaway gave me his account of this affair.

The river was very high. Thinks this was in June.

The Indians stampeded toward the river & and when they had got down another Indian rode up and down behind them crying (his name meant Guts and in Indian is Chu pa, pronounced Shupa) to them, "Throw away your heavy baggage. If your horse flounders get off his back and hold to his tail or mane. If you all arrive safe on the other side I will dance the sundance."[135] This was the highest vow that could be made by an Indian. It was as when Joshua vowed to the Lord that if he was successful he would sacrifice the first thing he saw; he was victorious, and the first thing he saw was his own daughter.

All the Indians went over in safety. Sometimes there were two riders to a horse, in other cases a man and two children. Mr. Shaw saw the sundance where Guts kept his vow.

Shaw saw the last sundance danced between Rosebud Agency and the St. Francis Mission in 1883.

Mr. Shaw was at Fort Custer in 1877 working on a hay contract on the Little Big Horn and worked right on the field between the ridge and the river. F. D. Yates of Denver was the contractor, and William H. Brown, formerly a captain at time of the muster out of the Reg't. of Co. A, 11th Ohio Reg't. was superintending the work & was Yates' father-in-law. This F. D. Yates is the one who was a trader at Red Cloud Agency and a brother to Capt. Yates under Custer. This Yates went all to pieces from drink. He sold out to Deere brothers.

Mr. Shaw was up there all that summer; left, thinks, 10th Nov. 1877.

Custer

Shaw says the second covering of the bones of the Custer dead was done in the fall of 1877. The bones were lying exposed as he thought with shameless indifference, and he said so to the officers at the Fort. He says the bones were put into the vault that year. He remembers that the vault was laid up in masonry.

Mr. Shaw read to me from W. P. Clark's book on Indian Sign Language under head of "Crazy Horse," what that author says about the conspiracy of the Indians to kill general officers of the army, Clark evidently believing Woman Dress's story.[136]

Mr. Shaw thinks that the white officers believed this story. He states that there was an almost universal impression among the Indians at the time that something of serious importance was going to take place at Red Cloud. Shaw heard the rumor that general army officers were to be killed, which circulated as an under current of miasma; so he asked Chief Spotted Tail whether there was any truth in the secret reports which he was hearing. Spotted Tail replied in these significant Delphian words of evasion: "Yes there is a conspiracy; but we will be the winners." At first Spotted Tail denied that there was any conspiracy; but when Shaw told him that he knew there was a conspiracy, Spotted Tail then abandoned his secret attitude and made the above acknowledgements.

Little Big Man wanted Crazy Horse out of the way, and he even had hope of supplanting Spotted Tail. At that time Little Big Man had more Indians with him than Spotted Tail had.

Spotted Tail was jealous of Crazy Horse and wanted him out of the way.

It is the fact that Gen. Crook had promised Spotted Tail that he would advance him and make him a bigger chief than he was. Shaw heard among the Indians of this understanding between Crook and the chief and he often spoke to Spotted Tail about it. Spotted Tail was an every day visitor at his house at that time for advice. Spotted Tail said in answer, that Crazy Horse was a weak chief and he (Spotted Tail) wanted to keep friendly with his people. This way of speaking means a great deal among the Indians. He did not brag on Crazy Horse, but he bragged on his people only. He would not thus speak to an Indian, but would say it to a white man who would of course form his own conclusions. Shaw says he could see through the plan then; and he told it to his own squaw who said that was the meaning of Spot's words, namely that he wished to keep (hold) the good opinion of Crazy Horse's people, so that he could personally profit in the hereafter when Crazy Horse should be out of the way. Spot was very jealous of Crazy Horse and did not want him to go to Washington; for, as C. H. was a great warrior and had become world-famous because he was the most notable Indian leader in the Custer battle, he was sure, in Spot's acute understanding, to be the lion of the delegation, and to shadow and efface Spotted Tail in the public mind and diminish his influence as a chief.

There is Indian politics as well as politics of the noble white man. But the Indian way is to kill the antagonist. It is less the way with the "noble white," though he sometimes plans and acts as does the Indian.

Crow Dog, the slayer in after years of Spotted Tail was also ambitious; he had then as now a band of his own, but he itched for more power. The "field" kept knowledge of the conspiracy from Crow Dog; but the telepathic suggestion could not be kept out of the air, and Crow Dog gained a vague knowledge as by instinct of something tragic impending. He came to Mr. Shaw and said: Is not some conspiracy going on? Said Yes; there is a conspiracy to kill the army officers! (Shaw explains that the Indians said all the soldiers were to be killed, but the Chiefs said the killing was to be only of the officers.) Crow Dog replied that that was not so; that it was something else, and he would find out.

Mr. Shaw says that just recently (this is Sept. 1, 1907) he asked Crow Dog why he killed Spotted Tail. Though he hesitated to say, yet he replied that when Crazy Horse was killed Spotted Tail became a great chief, so he thought that if Spotted Tail was out of the way there would be a chance for some other Indians. This would include himself; plainly, this meant himself. This is the way the Indian puts it. He does not say he will kill him who is an obstacle, but he declares that this obstacle ought to be out of the way. His way of insinuating his purpose. An Indian knows what that means — knows what the result will be — a killing by the one who has made the discovery of what ought to be.

Crow Dog has always based his act on a family feud. A long time before,

Spotted Tail's grandfather had killed a member of the Crow Dog family or ancestry. It was in accordance with Indian law for Crow Dog to avenge himself on Spotted Tail. He could do this without injury to his political standing. So he did the deed to improve his hope and chances of promotion, and not to alienate the Indians he said he had avenged the killing of his relation. It was not a woman case at all say Bordeaux and Shaw.

Shaw warned Spotted Tail to beware of Crow Dog only a day or two before his death. Shaw knew Crow Dog was a bad Indian. Spotted Tail in his bland and complacent way turned the subject off by saying with his soft and assuring smile, "I am not afraid; he is not brave; he has never killed anybody; he will not kill anybody now."

There was a council of the Brulé or Spotted Tail band, the same day that Spotted Tail was to start at noon on a journey to Washington at the head of a delegation of Rosebud chiefs. Council was in the forenoon, held about one mile from the Agency. Spotted Tail's house was between the Agency and the place where the council was held, but a quarter of a mile from the road. Crow Dog was at the Agency, and with his wife in a wagon was driving on his way home on the White River. He met Spotted Tail about ¼ of a mile from the Brulé camp. There he halted his team, gave the reins to his wife, jumped out, and got down on one knee with his rifle and shot Spotted Tail who fell from his horse dead the bullet having passed through his heart. Crow Dog jumped into his wagon & drove through the Brulé village on the run. This was seen, and as Crow Dog was passing out of the village, several shots were fired at him by Indians in the camp without effect. He was arrested by Gov't. and confined at Deadwood four years. Once he walked away from there without objection by anybody. After visiting at home he went back voluntarily to his imprisonment. There was no statute at that time to punish the killing of one Indian by another, and when he came to trial he was discharged by the court for want of jurisdiction.

When Spotted Tail was killed Chief White Thunder who had not been put on the delegation to go to Washington now took the place of Spotted Tail on delegation.

I note the tragic end of White Thunder the next year after Spotted Tail's death. He stole another Indian's wife. The offended husband came and took all of White Thunder's horses in the night. White Thunder retook them in the night. Early next morning the husband accompanied by Long Pumpkin and other Indians came to recapture the horses. Long Pumpkin and all got into ambush. White Thunder shot Pumpkin and badly shattered his leg, so that he is a lame man for life. White Thunder was then shot and killed. The horses were then taken again. The Indian police on the Reservation interfered and compelled the delivery of the horses to the woman that White Thunder had taken.[137]

Custer Battle

A. G. Shaw, Valentine, Sept. 1, 1907.

Says: That Thunder Hawk, an Indian (Brulé) went from the Spotted Tail Agency to attend the sundance on the Little Big Horn. (The Indians were in the habit of going long distances to sundances; they would go farther to that festival than to attend anything else.) By this means he happened to get into the fighting mentioned. He was in the battle of the Rosebud and got wounded. He was carried over to the Little Big Horn and was lying in his tent and his two wives were with him. This Indian committed some crime and was confined at Hot Springs where he suicided. At least one of his wives is now living on Rosebud Reservation near Valentine. Mr. Shaw knows her. Thunder Hawk told him that Custer crossed the river at the mouth of Reno Creek east of Calhoun Hill; that he swept down with all his command along the river on the west side and passed his tent, and was shooting into the Indian camp, his men doing so wildly, evidently scared and not trying to hit the Indians. He passed along the camp and recrossed the river at the crossing below the present national cemetery. Shaw says he saw five soldiers graves on the south side of the river where they had been slightly buried, and nearby seven Indian bodies in a low place which were not buried. He says Tom Custer [was] killed down close to the river on the north side. He says some of the Indians tell him that the last fighting was done on the line from Calhoun Hill. This account is sadly mixed. But it appears to agree with Dr. Eastman's statement to me at Allen.[138]

Crazy Horse

Continuation of the Interview of A. G. Shaw.

The primary conspiracy against Crazy Horse originated with the Indians, that is, with certain of them. The object being to get rid of him as an obstacle to personal glory and power of some ambitious individuals, nothing could be more natural than that it should be made to appear to the whites that Crazy Horse was an arch fiend planning to take the life of General Crook and perhaps the lives of other general officers. It would help their secret design to have the army aroused against Crazy Horse, no matter if their suspicions were ungrounded, the effect would be the same, and it is probable that the army itself would do unaided, though in different manner which was immaterial, just that thing which would remove Crazy Horse from the path of their aspirations. There was thus much incentive to inspire the falsehood which was borne to Crook and Clark by Woman's Dress who may or may not have been a mere tool of the combination. It was a shrewd plan, skilfully worked and shamefully successful. Crook kept his word with Spotted Tail when after the disarming of Red Cloud and Red Leaf he deposed the former and made Spotted Tail the chief.

[Peter Abraham Deon's Interview]

Peter Abraham "Samuel" Deon lived among the Lakotas beginning in the 1850s. A French Canadian from Montreal, Deon emigrated to Boston in his early twenties to join his two brothers and find work. That same year, 1847, he accompanied his Boston employer's shipload of ice to New Orleans. From New Orleans Deon continued upriver to St. Louis, where he hired on with the American Fur Company. Joining a crew destined for the company's upper Missouri trading posts, Deon wintered twenty miles from Fort Benton, present Montana, at an American Fur Company lumber camp. He returned to St. Louis the following year. In 1851 he again joined the American Fur Company for another trip up the Missouri, serving as a valet of sorts to Father Pierre-Jean De Smet, S.J.

Deon served the company and its successors many years as an Indian trader among the Lakotas. He took goods to their winter camps and returned to his employer in the spring with robes and furs. He became fluent in their language, and, following the custom of the day, took as his wife a woman from the tribe. He lived with Red Cloud, who became his sponsor, protector, and friend.

Except for the facts found in this narrative, little is known of Deon's life among the Indians, although his association with the Oglala Lakotas spans decades. He hung around the Fort Laramie area for years. In the 1860 U.S. census of the Fort Laramie area he is enumerated as "Samuel Dun," a thirty-five-year-old clerk for trader William F. Lee. Other records show Deon in the employ of Lee's brother-in-law, Geminien P. Beauvais. After leaving Red Cloud's camp before war broke out, Deon suffered the loss of several hundred dollars' worth of horses stolen by Sioux raiders in October 1864. On June 14, 1865, he happened to be present at the Horse Creek fight east of Fort Laramie when Indians, unwilling to be taken to Fort Kearny, Nebraska Territory, escaped from their military escort, killing Capt. William D. Fouts in the process. These set-

backs notwithstanding, Eugene Ware, another army officer of the
time, described "Sam Dion" as "one of the pioneer Frenchman of
the period, a jolly, royal, generous fellow who cared for nothing par-
ticularly, was happy everywhere, and whom the very fact of exis-
tence filled with exuberance and joy."

Later, Deon's name graced the list of witnesses to the Fort Lara-
mie Treaty of 1868. On an 1891 affidavit Deon claimed he had been
a resident of the reservation for twenty-one years, indicating that he
may have followed the Oglalas from their first agency on the North
Platte River in 1871 to the new Red Cloud Agency on the White River
in 1873. His Oglala wife and four children were listed as residing
in the village of American Horse at Red Cloud Agency in early 1877.
Deon probably moved with the tribe to the Missouri River in the
winter of 1877–78 and finally to Pine Ridge later in 1878.[139]

[Tablet 17]

Pine Ridge, S.D. Nov. 24, 1906.

Mr. Samuel Deon, 82 years of age, a French Canadian by birth, came out to this country in 1847 from Montreal, and coming by way of Boston where he had two brothers, and remaining four months, proceeded thence to St. Louis via New Orleans, to which city he had gone with a shipload of ice belonging to his Boston employer, and from New Orleans went to St. Louis by a large river steamer called the Big St. Louis. He arrived at St. Louis in March, 1847, and remained there six weeks, ascended the Missouri in the employ of the Am. Fur Co. When he reached St. Louis he went to a hotel kept by Louie Gowen (the last name may not be spelled right; he spelled it this way but seemed in doubt as to correctness; he pronounced it Gwachk; the man was a French Canadian) and after eyeing him sometime thought he had seen the man, and he got up from his seat and went outside and looked at the sign and saw that it bore the name of the man he recognized as his early friend and companion.

So he went back into the house, and according to the custom of the day (or then in vogue) called for the drinks at the bar for the bystanders, and when the proprietor was drawing the beverages, Mr. Deon remarked to him to pour one for himself, saying that it had been a long time since the two had drank together. The bartender replied that it had been so, without understanding the significance of the other's saying, supposing it to be a jest. Mr. D. then said to the man, "You do not seem to know me." He answered that he did not. Deon replied that the two once lived together in the same village; went together to the first communion and were baptized at the same time, and giving his name was instantly recognized by his erstwhile acquaintance. When the drinks were passed the hotel keeper took Mr. Deon back into the kitchen and introduced him to his wife and told her their common early history, and that they were as brothers, and it was his desire that his old friend be treated in his house as his brother. The woman's eyes grew wet at her husband's warm recital.

After awhile the proprietor told Mr. Deon that the American Fur Company was hiring men for the northwestern service and that it would be a good opportunity for him if he had any desire to go up among the Indians. He said that it was just the prospect which would please him, and asked how he should make the start to get a place. The other told him to go to the office of the company and have his name registered as an applicant, and he added that he would go along with him and introduce and recommend him. They went to the office and the hotel keeper introduced him to Mr. Sarpy as his personal friend, giving an outline of the early history of the two together, and asking Mr. Sarpy to give him a place. They finally agreed on the sum of $200 as pay for the round trip, going up in the forepart of the season and returning in the fall. Papin was the office clerk there.[140]

This was in 1847 that he made this trip. When he arrived at the mouth of the Yellowstone where was Fort Union, the cargo was, owing to the stage of water, transshipped to two keel boats called Mackinaws, and the journey was resumed, taking such part of the lading that came from below as they could well carry.[141] It should be stated that boats did not run at night either ascending or descending these rivers. It should be said that the men who embarked on the Mackinaws up the river had to haul them by ropes, (cordelling), the men walking on the river bank. In places where they could not keep the dry ground, they waded in the water from any depth to their armpits, and some of them would have to swim. At the time of the year they went up the water was cold; often there was ice in the streams, and the men bore great hardships from plunging into ice-cold water and mud. A man stood in the prow of the boat with a pole with which he kept the boat off from the shore. There was also a man in the stern who operated the rudder.

At Fort Union the party which had come up separated and a part went up the Yellowstone, and the other party to which Mr. Deon adhered ascended the Missouri to Fort Benton. They wintered at Fort Benton. The party went out to Sash Mountain, 20 miles from the fort, and worked in the timber getting out logs for lumber to be used at the fort. Besides the chopping, a part of the men ran whip saws cutting the logs into boards. These boards were about an inch and a quarter in thickness. They were cut by two men running one saw, one above the log and one below it. These saws were seven or eight feet long and about six inches wide. The boards were mainly used in making boats to carry peltries down in the fall, and the company generally sent down four or five boats. The manufacturing of lumber was carried on out there at Sash Mountain till in March when bull teams were brought into use to transport the product of the winter's labor to the fort.

Mr. Deon returned in the year 1848, the year of the cholera contagion, reaching St. Joe in July.[142] St. Joe was then just starting. There they unloaded three Mackinaws to a steamboat.

When Mr. Deon made this first trip up the Missouri the LeBarges were running the boat on which he went up from St. Louis. One of the LeBarges was the captain, one was pilot, and the father of these two helped on the boat. There were three LeBarge brothers.[143] They ran this boat up to Fort Benton.

It was on this trip that Mr. Deon befriended Champaign who was the company's Blackfoot interpreter. He had married a Blackfoot woman and had several children.[144]

From St. Joe the returning party came down to St. Louis. Mr. Deon wants to add here that after discharging cargo at Fort Benton the LeBarges returned to St. Louis, while Mr. Deon and the other company employees ascended the Missouri 20 miles in four Mackinaws without, however, any goods aboard except what was needed to make the winter camp and provide for the work. Sash Mountain was close to the river, but bull teams were used between the river and the mountain.

It should have been stated before in connection with Mr. Deon's contract for service that one part of his compensation was his provisions which were stipulated to be "according to the custom of the country," which meant that they sometimes would have something to eat and at other times might have nothing; and when they had something it might be nothing more than corn which he says was their diet on the journey from Benton to Sash Mountain.

Mr. Champaign was a half-blood interpreter who had come from some of the lakes — Erie, Michigan or some other — and had his family at Fort Benton. It was the year 1848 when the cholera was so bad from New Orleans to Fort Benton. Champaign got it and Mr. Deon tended him and he recovered.

Mr. Deon went up to the Wisconsin River and tended bar about a year. When here he received a letter from his father asking him to come home and see his folks, and offering to send him money if he needed it. Since he had seen the family they had all moved to Wisconsin and settled not far from Milwaukee. He confessed to his employer that he did not know the way, but the former gave him full directions how to go, and he performed the journey with a horse team and brought back a load of liquors and tobaccos from Milwaukee. He was working for another man on this trip. He found his father and mother and the rest of the family. His brothers had a saw mill, and all of them were in possession of land. He found a brother of youthful size that he did not recognize. He spent one week at home and then returned to the West. He never saw any of his people afterwards.

In 1851 I started up the Missouri in the employ of the Am. Fur Co.[145] The big treaty of 1851 was to be made this year and we had to stop at every trading post along the river to get representative Indians aboard.[146] The first place where we took any Indians — and we took headmen — was at Vermillion (now South Dakota). The next place was Fort Pierre. While on the way up on this trip Father De Smet made known to Champaign that he wanted to exchange for another man.[147] The one he had was bloody in the face along with others, who had had too much drink the night before and had come to blows, and Father De Smet said he thought it did not look well to have a man who carried a bloody face. Champaign told him of Mr. Deon and said he was all right; that Deon had saved his life by caring for him when he had cholera. Therefore Pignot, the manager of the company, transferred Mr. Deon to Father De Smet merely to serve the priest. The headman of the Indians at Fort Pierre was Drags The Rock, and he was taken along. Then they proceeded up the river. Father De Smet was employed by the company to go around and baptize children.[148] From Fort Pierre they went to the trading post of the company at the Ree village which was quite a smart little place. Here they took on two Rees. It should be stated that Drags the Rock had two of his tribe with him. From the Rees who were on the north side of the river, the boat crossed to the other side of the river and there they found on the south side of the river a camp of the Grovans, and of these they took four, the headman being Four Bears;[149] the next post visited was Fort Union where some Indians were taken on, these being Assinnaboins. At Fort Union they unloaded from the steamboat to four Mackinaw boats the goods of the company. The LeBarges were running this steamboat. There were 15 or 16 of the company's employees to each boat to tow it up the Yellowstone. They pulled up on the south side of the Yellowstone. There is an island in the Yellowstone where it empties into the Missouri. They towed, and part of the time rowed from one bank of the river to the other, diagonally across each time, thus making headway up stream till they reached the mouth of Powder River. They passed the Tongue and Rosebud and stopped below the Big Horn. They crossed the Yellowstone at the mouth of Rosebud & there they left all the boats; but took along their horses and mules. Father De Smet had a saddle horse and a buggy and two mules. The father carried along in his ambulance two or three boxes. This was all his baggage.[150] They contained his clothing and wine and a few conveniences for himself besides a few trinkets like combs, vermilion and rosaries for presents to the Indians.

[Tablet 25]

Peter Abraham Deon (to whom the name "Samuel" attached without fault of his own). (Continued from page 80½ smaller book [Tablet 17])

They met Culberson, the headman of the Blackfeet, an American, at Fort Union & he went with them thence.[151]

Father De Smet was a rather short man, somewhat thick and heavy and inclined to be fleshy; of good features, a Belgian, very sociable, good-natured and inclined to joke.

This party went inland a little distance and made a camp and put out a guard. From this camp they crossed to the Powder River. ~~This was the fur company's party.~~ Somewhere about this time Father De Smet and Culberson and all the party and all the Indians who had been assembled for the treaty, and went to Fort Laramie where the treaty was made amidst much dancing and feasting.[152] Here it was Mr. Deon says that the Crows put all the other Indians to shame with their superior dancing. They were at Laramie quite awhile. There were 27 wagonloads of goods brought to this rendezvous to be distributed to anybody who desired them, red, white and mixed bloods, and they were spread up and down the river bottom for five miles. (Perhaps better say a great distance.)

Father De Smet and Culberson and another person who went on ahead of the general party.

It was by this treaty that the whites acquired a right of way along the Platte on both sides for emigrants to Oregon and California, with room enough for travelers to graze their stock.

The goods were opened and given right and left to all who wanted any.

Father De Smet wanted Mr. Deon to go thence with him to St. Louis to spend the winter; and he gave him some shirts that his sister had made for him in Belgium.

The Fur Co.'s party crossed from Laramie to Fort Pierre.

Mr. Deon says that in three days after the treaty was made and the goods distributed all the people were gone from Laramie.

The name of the Indian who was hung (not meaning Two Face) at Fort Laramie was Blackfeet (think somewhere I have changed it to Blackfoot. Blackfeet is right; his name is from his feet). He was the father of Thunder Bear, one of the judges of the Indian Court at Pine Ridge. Mr. Deon, Thunder Bear and another told me that he was hung, & Thunder Bear said it was his father.[153]

Peter Abraham Deon (by long error called "Samuel") says: He was in the fight at the mouth of Horse Creek. The wagons corraled about half or three-quarters of a mile over Horse Creek. It was Calico who lives just south of the Mission who was one of the Indian prisoners at that time, and he made his escape with ball and chain. These prisoners were made at this time to carry the ball and chain as they marched. Mr. Deon saw one of the prisoners shot down. A soldier proposed to scalp him, but Mr. Deon told him if he wanted scalps to take them himself. After Capt. Fauts (?) was killed a Capt. Wilcox succeeded to the command. One of Wilcox's soldiers told Deon that Wilcox was a coward and he would discover it before he had done with him. Capt. Wilcox made a little talk at the corral to his soldiers in which he said that the squawmen were as bad as the Indians and these ought to be killed. There were numbers of them and their families in this corral. Some of these squawmen asked James Beauvais one of the traders at Laramie & had a store also on the South Platte to give the Captain and the soldiers a talk and tell them [blank] He did so and that promptly settled the matter which Wilcox advised.

Capt. Faut's (?) wife and children had just returned to Fort Laramie from the states.

[Tablet 17]

Old Mr. Samuel Deon of Pine Ridge says that he and Red Cloud were old friends and he used to go and sit with him and talk over old times by the hour from his birth up and then communicate what he had learned to Postmaster _____ Caufield [Coffield] and Chas. W. Allen who wrote what they call his "Life" but this relates only to his early life.[154]

Mr. Deon told me that he [Red Cloud] did not all his life command the respect of other Indians; that they had been known to strike him in the face with quirts and assail him as a cowardly woman. It is to be recollected, however, that it was the part of an Indian to receive such castigations and insults with patience and fortitude as proving the self control of the injured person and his title to be ranked as of superior training and nature, capable of resisting indignity.

[John Russell's Interview]

[Tablet 8]

Interview with John Russell, commonly called Jack Russell, nickname "Buckskin Jack," because he wore buckskin clothes, and was so named by Magloire A. Mousseau, at his home on White River north of Porcupine, S.D., November 13, 1906.

He was born in Missouri, 8th day of November, 1847. Came in 1863 to Denver; driving a bull team of 9 or 10 yoke of cattle to one wagon, for an uncle, Russell having run away from his home. When he got to Denver he gave his uncle the slip so as not to return with him. He went to Boulder and Tarbox & Donnelly having bought a lot of cattle, he and a man he called Sailor (real name he does not know but the man had been a sailor) hired to these partners to tend the cattle the winter of 1863-4 on Crow Creek. In the spring of 1864 Russell came over to Fort Laramie with Jim Green and soon after he went up to old man Richard (Reshaw) John Richard Sr. on the north fork of the Laramie. He worked for the Richards all that summer and winter. John Richard Jr. took such a liking to Russell that he adopted Russell as his brother after the Indian fashion.

Early in the spring (he says it was in 1865 and it cannot be changed from the circumstances he gives — one winter on Crow Creek, next winter with Richard on the north fork of the Laramie, then next spring he went with John Richard Sr.) of 1865 and was with the old man Richard who had a bridge across the Platte 5 miles below Fort Casper, and about where the town of Casper now is. He spent 3 or 4 months there with the old man, until the river fell, then they went back (they tended bridge only during high water); Russell stopped at Deer Creek and went to work for Jules Eccoffey and Adolph Cooney, and the old man came on down to his ranch on the north fork of the Laramie. These Richards were French, squaw men, and Indian traders — trading was mostly in the winter. The Indians traded robes and ponies. Eccoffey & Cooney stayed at Deer Creek two years and then moved down to Fort Laramie.[155]

(Mr. Russell now admits that it must have been in 1862 when he came to Denver; this brings his dates right to correspond with the Larimer-Kelly-Wakefield affair.)

He was at Deer Creek and saw Mrs. Laramie and her little boy on the oppo-

317

site side of the river when she came in escaping from the Indians. He says she was brought across in a skiff or canoe.

There had been an emigrant train attacked and destroyed at Plum Creek, Neb. Two women were taken prisoners (he says it was the same year as the Larimer-Kelly affair). The Indians got into trouble over the women and old Two Face brought them in and Blackfoot came with him. These two Indians and Calico were put into the guardhouse. Then four Indians were hung, he remembers that Two Face and Blackfoot were two of them; and he saw all four hung.[156] ~~He saw Mrs. Kelly brought into Fort Laramie.~~

He is a little mixed on the Plum Creek women & Mrs. Kelly. Joe Bisnett [Bissonette] and a man named Kensler were sent out by the officers away north for two white women; they made two trips; the first time the Indians took away the things that had been sent out to pay them for the women. A second effort was made and was successful, a Cheyenne Indian coming in with them was thrown into the guard house & was hung, making one of the four.[157] He says the military did wrong in hanging these Indians. The military was often rank [?].

In 1865 Eccoffey & Cooney went down 5 miles from Fort Laramie and built ranch which was a trading house, saloon and billiard hall. Russell stayed with these employers till 1868. The government had got all the squaw men in the country to go to the Whetstone Agency on the Missouri River about 20 miles above Fort Randall, in order to induce the Indians to go over and settle there. These were the Oglala Indians. In 1868 these all went to the Missouri River. These white men were by the terms of the treaty given the same rights as Indians as an object to them to influence the Indians to move to the Missouri. This is what brought the Janises and Jim Bordeau who had charge of the rations in the removal, a man named Raymond, Pete Decorah, Joe Brown, old man Duval, Pattent, Bill Fielder, Chat DeBray, old Iott, Adolph Cooney, Jules Eccoffey, Rulo, John Kalome, Talt Gillespie, Dave Kocer, John Russell.

This Reservation was called Whetstone after the creek by that name; the Agency was at the mouth; the creek was on the west side of the Missouri.

In 1870 Russell went from this Reservation where he had lived till now to Texas for a man named Jim Hines who had the beef contract for these Reservations and drove a herd of cattle up to the Grand River Reservation which was at the mouth of Grand River above & on west side of the Missouri. He returned to Whetstone Agency in following winter, and in spring of 1871 he came over to Columbus, Neb. for Cooney & got a bunch of cattle and drove to Fort Laramie and beyond to Sabille on south side of the Laramie River, right under the mountain. The Chug Water was right in west of this. He worked here for Cooney till 1874 when he came to Spotted Tail Agency, just below where Crawford is and at the mouth of the creek and close to the buttes.

(Mr. Russell knew the house which it was said LeBonté lived in on the creek of same name.)

Mr. Russell says he knew Jim Bridger well. Bridger could not remember the name of his son-in-law who lived in Kansas City. Charley Geren (?)(this is French and I cannot spell it) who was the trader's clerk (Col. Bullock) at Laramie used to write his letters for him.[158] When Bridger was not at work he stayed at this store a good deal. When he wanted a letter sent to his son-in-law he would go to this clerk; the clerk would ask the son-in-law's name; Bridger could not give it and the clerk would have to tell him. But if Bridger ever once went over a piece of country he knew it by heart—every hill, stream &c. He had his headquarters at Fort Laramie when he was in the service of the government.

He saw Major North when the Pawnees came up to Laramie and his Pawnees were set to cut down the four Indians who were hung, and bury them. He saw North again in the fall of 1875 [1876] when Crook disarmed Red Cloud and Red Leaf; saw him at Red Cloud Agency in the night. He heard North spoken of as a great man among the Pawnees, as scout, guide and interpreter.

In the summer of 1875 Gen. Crook sent word to Russell to report at Red Cloud Agency to report to Big Bat and Little Bat. They showed him a paper stating that Crook wanted the three to go north as scouts for the troops, and to bring others with them. When they got to Fort Laramie they found the troops all camped there, and after awhile Crook and all went off hunting Indians. He describes the scout that John Shangrau described when they were out together scouting in the night and they saw flashes of light and knew Crook's camp was attacked & they went back. Russell says one or two were slightly wounded in the camp.

He also tells about the night herder being killed.

He admits that this campaign was in March 1876 when it was hard winter.[159]

He tells about the two soldiers and two Crow Indians whom Terry had sent to meet and communicate with Crook. Crook had just before ordered Little Bat and Russell to go and look for Terry's soldiers; they were packed and ready to start when the four were discovered coming. By aid of glasses the four were identified as two soldiers with uniforms and two Indians. These came and reported Custer's disaster, so Bat & Russell were relieved of this trip.

He says the Sibley scout occurred after the Custer battle, and sustains "Respects Nothing" in his statement that the Indians who got the Sibley scouts' horses were those who did up Custer.[160]

After the return of the Sibley scout Russell, Big Bat, Little Bat, Frank Gruard and John Shangrau (?) (does not know exact number) were sent by Crook to see which way the Indians had gone. When these scouts struck the Rosebud they struck their trail. It was a big wide trail on both sides. The Rosebud up there is only a creek; no more water in it than in Wounded Knee Creek. They knew that the Indians would take the Rosebud in preference to any of the other streams for it is a fine valley, smooth, not so very wide, but nice. After they met Terry and was with him awhile, Crook said they would pull for the Black Hills. It was rain and mud and cold, and the soldiers ran out of rations. It was a terrible march.

Mr. Russell says that American Horse who was wounded at Slim Buttes gave his name as American Horse; he was a Sioux, talked Sioux, had two Sioux wives, that is, they both talked good Sioux and he did not hear them talk any Cheyenne. This Am. Horse would have lived if he would [have] allowed the doctor to replace his intestines for they were not injured. He said he wanted to die.

Skipping all details for want of time to write them, Russell says that Mackenzie who was in command at Fort Robinson sent a dispatch to Crook in the Hills and informed his superior that Red Cloud was ugly, etc.,[161] and so Crook at once dispatched Russell, Grouard, the two Bats, thinks John Shangrau was one and says there were 5 or 6 of the scouts sent to Fort Robinson to report to Mackenzie who sent all these scouts and also Billy Hunter or Garnett was sent along too. They asked him [Red Cloud] to move up to the Agency; for it was understood that he was trying to work off to some distance from the Agency where he could not be watched so well, and then break off for the north with his tribe. They gave him the privilege to move up to the creek about three miles down from the Agency, when he had told them that he would not go up there, but if he moved at all it would be lower down. They returned & reported. Next day Mackenzie sent the same scouts to Red Cloud with the same message as before. He gave no better satisfaction. They went back again. The following day Crook arrived at Fort Robinson. There was a gathering of officers and the scouts in the club room & Russell heard [Tablet 26] Mackenzie say "He will move!" meaning Red Cloud. At ten o'clock that night the scouts left the post; Russell was sent up White River by Crook to meet the Pawnees under Major North; he went 6 or 7 miles and met them coming down, having come (he supposes) from Laramie; he escorted them around the Agency to avoid encountering any of the Indian camps around Red Cloud. Russell escorted the Pawnees clear down to Ash Creek where Red Cloud and Red Leaf were encamped. Then he returned with a message from Mackenzie to Crook, & remained at the Fort till next day about 10 o'clock when he went back to see what was going on, & he met them all coming to the Fort in charge of the military, the Pawnees were driving the horses. The two chiefs and a lot of other Indians were put into the guard house for a few days and nights. The Indian families were camped right round there and a guard was kept over these for a short while.

After a short time the Indians' horses were driven to Cheyenne by the Pawnee scouts, where they were sold. (This was the disarming of Red Cloud & Red Leaf.)

After a month or two Russell was sent to Fort Fetterman where he stayed abt. 7 months; then he was ordered to Fort McKinney on Powder River right near old Fort Reno. He did not do much here; went out once in awhile with soldiers; but he received his $150 a month right along. This was the way [of] the regular scouts.

He was ordered by Crook to guide seven companies of troops from Fort McKinney to Rawlins; thence across the summit or range of mountains to White River in Colorado. The Meeker massacre had taken place, but the Indians were camped out among the settlements of white people about 20 miles below the Agency, but would not come in to the Agency. The Indians said they did not want to fight. Thornburg had been killed and the Agency burned before Russell moved from McKinney. The Indians moved up after Russell got there, within three miles of where the Agency was, and the military went to building a post where the Agency had been.[162] Russell stayed there till fall doing little. He got a pass after snow came to go to Fort Laramie. He did not go back any more. He now began working on cow ranches and followed this till 1894, when he became Assistant Farmer on Porcupine under Additional Farmer Gleason and was under Gleason abt. 9 yrs.; Gleason resigned & was followed by George Dawson, brother of H. A. Dawson, and was under him two years. Since that time, beginning in 1905, he has been and still is handling working parties on the roads on the Pine Ridge Reservation.

Wounded Knee

Russell says that Royer sent some Indian police to arrest an Indian, he thinks it was Moccasin Top for killing a beef, and the Indians around the Agency would not let the police put him in the guard house—bluffed the police—and this was the disturbance which upset Royer and sent him flying to Rushville for troops; Russell says this is hearsay. He adds that the ghost dancing was quieting down, and he did not see anything for anybody to leave the Reservation. There would have been no trouble if there had been a good Agent.[163]

Russell says he was with Cody's show altogether four years; had been in Europe two years before the 1890 troubles, and the show Indians and he returned from Europe the next day after the troops arrived at the Agency.[164] He heard before they got here that there was likely to be trouble on account of the ghost dance; but he says this dance amounted to nothing, the Indians did not mean trouble.

Some of the Indians, probably 400 or 500 Indians had already stampeded to the Stronghold and when they went they took any body's horses; they were killing & eating cattle, for they had to have something to eat. They had got over the Cheyenne River and stole some horses and got into a little trouble with some cowboys, & did a little shooting; it was claimed an Indian or so was shot; but it all did not amount to anything. Then the attempt was made at the Agency to get this camp to come in; thinks 30 or 40 went out. First trip did not accomplish anything. Second trip they got the Indians to cross White River, and they camped there a day or two, then they came up on White Clay. There were some friendly disposed Indians camped on Wolf Creek between the Slaughter House and the Agency.

On the morning of the battle Russell had his horses at the beef corral and he went up to turn them out to graze. While there he heard a cannon at Wounded Knee. He thot at first it was a signal. But the cannon discharges began to increase and he thought there must be trouble over there as it was known that Big Foot was off in that country somewhere. So he saddled up and rode over from the beef pen to the hills near Wounded Knee and he could see shooting going on; so he came back to the Agency, and the Indians on Wolf Creek were tearing down their tepees and he told them they better go and camp with those Indians who were camped on the White Clay above the Agency about three-quarters of a mile. These were the Friendly camp. But the moving Indians were in haste and said they were going down and camp near Red Cloud's. He urged them to go to the other place. They would not. They moved down below the Agency and just as they had got over the White Clay an Indian shot into the Agency. A soldier was shot & it was claimed this shot did it. This Indian who did the shooting shot from the hill right north of the Agency; he was on the road that goes to the Mission. As soon as this was done this camp that was moving stampeded and went right down the White Clay to the Mission; these ran into the camp of Kicking Bear and Short Bull who were coming in, and this stopped them from coming on into the Agency, but all went together back north and camped on a little creek that comes down from the east and empties into the White Clay.

Buffalo Bill

Russell says Buffalo Bill was made by the generals and the newspapers. Major Bourke is a nice man.[165] He has done the later advertising of Bill.

When Bill went on the campaign in 1876 with Crook, the general told him if he wanted to go and be under his chief of scouts Frank Gruard he might go. But Bill when he struck the Missouri he hopped into the first Mackinaw that came along, seeing there was no glory for him the way things were going.

Russell says he thinks Fort Casper was built about 1863. When he went up there it looked new.

The Stronghold

The Stronghold and Sheep Mountain are north of White River nearly opposite the mouth of Porcupine Creek and about eight miles from it.

[Augustus W. Corliss's Interview]

[Tablet 24]
Denver, Colo., Oct. 29, 1905.

General Corliss was born in North Yarmouth (now Yarmouth), Maine, in 1837 (March 25) of a long line of venerable Revolutionary ancestry, and including 1812; himself entering the U.S. Army in 1862 first as major of the 7th squadron of Rhode Island Cavalry of 3 mos. men; next was made Lieut. Colonel [of] 2d Rhode Island Cavalry, then was appt. 2d Lieut. and 1st Lieut. 15th U.S. Infy.; then was transferred to the 33d Infy. and afterwards to the 8th Infy.; and in 1873 was promoted to Captain in [the] regular service and served as Captain 24 years, and was then made major of the 7th Infy.; and in the first day's fight (July 1, 1898) at El Caney in Cuba he was severely wounded; in September he was in command of his regiment at Montauk Point on Long Island, N. Y.; in 1899 he was promoted to Lieut. Colonel of the 2d Infy. and joined the regiment in Cuba and was in command of it. He was promoted to Colonel of [the] 2d

Infy. in 1901 and was retired March 25, 1901; and was promoted Brig. General April 23, 1904, by act of Congress which advanced one grade all officers of the regular army who had served with credit in the volunteer service, one grade.

Served in Shenandoah valley in a detached brigade commanded by Gen. Julius White (this brigade belonged to 3d corps, but was detached); afterwards went to Louisiana and served under Banks & was on the Bayou Teche expedition.

(He resigned from the 2d Rhode Island Cavalry and was app. Lieutenant in the regular service.)

Was at the taking of Port Hudson; and at that place he received notification that he was to be app. in the regular army, and there he resigned and was ordered north & spent most of his time in Washington in service of the government, and in spring of 1865 he went to Lookout Mountain & was there till October & then went to Mobile. Remained in the south 5 yrs. & was then taken to N.Y. to go to Santo Domingo in expectation that Grant would get the island, but Chas. Summer defeated the treaty, and then in 1872 he went west and was on the Yellowstone Expedition of that year and on that of 1873; thence to Arizona in 1874 from there [to] Spotted Tail Agency; from there in 1878 he went up to Oregon and Washington to Territory, called there by the Bannock disturbance which was suppressed with more chasing and a little fighting; (the second Bannock disturbance was in 1895 and was more a white man's uprising than anything else). Went thence to Nevada and California where his station was, but was sent every year down into Arizona to follow and subdue Apaches; in 1886 he was ordered to Fort Robinson where he remained till 1894; thence went again to Fort Russell; in 1895 he went on the 2d Bannock (so-called) campaign, but he calls it the settlers' campaign (the settlers kept encroaching on the Indians to drive them to hostility for a pretext to kill them). He was sent from Ft. Robinson to Market Lake Idaho, & then they marched over into the Teton country and stayed there all summer. Six companies of the 8th Infy., a part from Robinson & a part from Fort Niobrara, went out there and served with other troops. One day some of the Indians came to Capt. Corliss and asked him for protection. He told them to come and camp close to his own camp and he would take care of them. They did so. Then the whites came and asked if he was going to protect those Indians, and he told them he was; they remonstrated, saying they wanted to kill them. Then he told them that if they attempted to harm them he would kill every one of the white men. And so the Inds. were let alone.

In 1900 Lieut. Colonel Corliss in command of the 2d Infy. went from Cuba to the Philippines, arriving Oct. 1st & left there 17th Feb. 1901 being ordered home for retirement, returning via Japan.

Gen. Corliss says that the 1st and 2d Infantry and his company C of 8th Infty. and the 7th and 9th Cavalry were at Pine Ridge. Colonel Shafter (afterwards General) commanded 1st Infty., Gen. Wheaton (Frank) commanded 2d Infty.[166]

Gen. C. points out in the artillery picture his own Hotchkiss guns on the right of the long guns of Capt. Allen Capron who had 3.2 field guns;[167] General says Capron had 6 guns, but 2 of them were out somewhere else; had 4 at agency; General thinks he had 3 or 4 Hotchkiss guns himself and one Gatling gun as stated by McFarland on back of artillery picture. In this picture his company tents can be seen to the right and rear of the artillery line. Corliss' battery is to the right of Capt. Capron's guns.

Says he went to Brooke and asked him if he might not fire on the Indians as they were over back of Red Cloud's house & he told Brooke he was tired of having them firing on his Co. as they were doing, without replying. Brooke replied, "No! No! If we fire on them what will the people in the east say?"

Two or three days after battle Wounded K. Capt. Mills of 2d Infy., a brave soldier, one of finest he ever knew & who was a Civil War soldier in the 16th Infy., spoke to Corliss & told him he was feeling very bad & Capt. C. said he could see that he looked so; and Corliss told him to go to Corliss' tent where he would find some whisky under his pillow; he did so and took a potation. Capt. Mills was then ordered out on the ridge north of the Agency with his Co. to make breastworks, and after awhile was relieved by another co. which he was in turn to relieve. That evening a party of the officers were singing the dirge-like song composed by an Irish officer in the British Army in India at the siege of Lucknow or Delhi when all the besieged expected to be slain (Dinna ye hear the slogan). Capt. Mills seemed to be very much affected by it and he asked Capt. Corliss to have it repeated, which was done. The closing lines of the chorus were:

> Here's a glass to the dead already
> Hurrah for the next that dies!

(The officers were in the habit of meeting at night and drinking rum and singing this song.)

The title is "The Revelry of the Dying." It is a popular college song in all colleges.

Capt. Mills laid down, he was to be called at 2 o'clock A.M., and when the striker went to call him he was found dead, in a kneeling position in front of his bed & his head on the bed. If McFarland said he was dead in his chair he was mistaken. Capt. William Mills.

Major Dean Monahan entered the army in 1856 as a trumpeter.

Capt. Augustus W. Corliss went to Fort Robinson in 1886 and was there till 1894. The first time he was up in the Fort Robinson country he came in February, 1874. Capt. Corliss was on the 1st Yellowstone expedition and on 2d. The 1st was in 1872 & 2d in 1873, Gen. Stanley commanding each time. Gen. Sully had been out before either of these but don't know when, but he did not go so far. Custer went in '72 & in '73. In '73 a hail storm stuck the troops and in a few minutes the wagons were in aroyos and creeks, overturned, and provisions gone. Stanley ordered Custer to go over and take commissary stores to them & to stay with them until they were all right. The cavalry all ran away and the command scattered and broken. There were abt. 30 cavalry, and the bulk of the command was infantry. All this was on the north side of the Hart river. The bulk of the command was on the south side of [the] river, and Custer was there too. A bridge was formed across [the] river with wagon boxes & Custer was sent across to relieve & assist those who had been smitten by hail, their hands being beaten black & blue &c. Custer crossed & took over supplies, but instead of remaining with the infantry, he went 12 or 15 miles beyond and for this disobedience of orders was put under arrest by Gen. Stanley & kept so a long time, until they got over to Yellowstone river, at least 2 wks.[168]

Custer was brave as could be—feared nothing—reckless & without judgement. Needed to be under control of a stronger will. In this same expedition (1873) Custer got into a fight & would have been cleaned out badly but the infantry came up and he withdrew around the flanks to the rear of the fresh troops and reformed. The Indians on seeing the Infy. at once retreated.[169]

After this expedition Capt. Corliss with part of the troops under Stanley went back to Omaha and in Nov. 1873 Corliss was sent to Fort D. A. Russell. From there in Feb. 1874 he went up to Fort Laramie and thence across to Red Cloud. When they went over to Red Cloud Col. John E. Smith was in command.[170] Red Cloud drew up his braves in skirmish line then Smith threw his troops into line and kept moving on to the Agency, the Indians falling back as he advanced. At length Red Cloud came over to Smith & told him that his young men wanted to fight & Smith asked him why he didn't do it. The bluff didn't work.

There was no Fort or Camp Robinson at this time. Smith moved right on to Spotted Tail Agency, after leaving the main body of the troops at Red Cloud. Corliss was at Spotted Tail from 10th March till Aug. when they went down to [the] R.R. & went to California and Arizona.

Spotted Tail had a white man named Quigley living with him & who kept him well posted on all that was going on in the U.S. Took papers. Quigley was a well educated Irishman.

General C. remembers "Old Spot" and Black Crow who afterwards killed Spotted Tail.[171]

Two Strike was a very keen Indian & knew much more than he ever got credit for. A sharp old Indian.

Swift Bear was a shrewd, good natured pleasant and very good Indian.

White Thunder was the handsomest Indian Gen. C. ever saw, a particular friend of his, would attract attention anywhere. All these Indians were at the Spotted Tail agency.

There was another named "Ghost" who had white eyes.

Spotted Tail struck General C. as a man of mighty good brains. "Spot" had judgement & was friendly & peaceable; he said it was futile for the Inds. to fight the whites; that he could go on the warpath and kill a few settlers, but that no good would come of it and he and his would suffer and get the worst of it in the end.

[John C. Whalen's Interview]

[Tablet 13]

~~John C. Whalen, Pine Ridge, March 12, 1907.~~

He says he was in "D," 16th Kansas Cav. left Ft. Riley, Kansas, April 1865. Started for Fort Laramie; left there in August for Powder River. The regiments that went were two from Missouri, & one from Kansas, the three under command of General Cole; Fred Woedel (?) (spelling not certain). The orders were to be out 60 days. They built a stockade called Fort Conner away up towards Powder River. After this was built they went on and two days after, the whole command got lost. Were expecting to meet or join Connor every day, but did not see him. They had a party of 50 men in advance making roads for artillery & wagons and some of them were killed every day by the Indians. The officers held several councils. They were lost & the guides Nick Janis, Wm. Tucker and Henry Iott could not pilot the troops out. Jack Whalen says that the guides were not lost, but that the officers had maps and could not agree and had no faith in the guides and refused to follow their directions, so that the guides quit the employment and merely kept along with the expedition, while the officers moved about blindly. (I have heard this spoken of before.) The officers were angry with each other; they disagreed, but kept moving north down Powder River. The mules began to die & the rations got short, flour being all gone, so that 50 men were detailed from the 3 regiments to kill game for the command. They had to give up hunting because the Inds. killed the men & would not let them get game. Many of the mules were slaughtered and issued as rations every evening. Many of the men were sick with diarrhoea on account of the Powder River water which after the great rains they were having, was muddy & unwholesome; besides it was mineral or alkali. There were great quantities of buffaloes and other game but they could not get it for the Indians. The Inds. could go anywhere on their little ponies where the cavalry horses would mire down.

The troops had several severe fights with the Indians—the Cheyennes, Sioux and Arapahos.[172]

As long as the troops used only light arms the Inds. would come right up close to the soldiers in constantly contracting circles. This was in Sept., but was very cold, & being out of rations for the men & no feed for the horses, the distress was very great. On the night of the 17th of September many horses froze to death on the picket rope, but Jack thinks there were not 300 that froze. One evening while the troops were in camp two Winnebago Inds. & a white man were noticed coming toward the camp with a flag of truce. They bore a letter from Gen. Conner addressed to Col. Cole, the commanding officer, who belonged to the 13th Missouri Cavalry. This letter ordered this expedition back to Fort Laramie. The 16th Kansas Cavalry had but very few wagons, as they depended on a pack train or pack animals rather. The orders directed that the horses that became too feeble to be ridden should be turned loose & shot. The command turned about next morning & moved back to Fort Connor, several days on this return march being required. This command did not see Gen. Connor during the campaign.

It was this command that cleaned out the Arapaho village and found stacks of dried meats. These troops also had a fight where they & the officers took to the rock for safety and had a hard fight.[173]

Mr. Whalen says that the Arapaho village was held only by old men & women & children and it fell an easy victim to the soldiers. The warriors were at the time away on a hunt. On their return they were incensed at finding their village destroyed.

Then they made the attack on the soldiers later, and it was furious because inspired by bitter revenge. The soldiers and officers were glad to find shelter behind the rocks.

They drew rations at Fort Connor & stayed there a day or two. An ox train was waiting for these troops to go back to Laramie. Many of the soldiers who were now on foot were put into the wagons.

There were several hundred of these whose horses had died, and being with the wagons they acted as an escort. The cavalry reached Fort Laramie abt. a week ahead of the ox train. While waiting for this train to arrive these soldiers were put to making an extensive ditch & breastwork around Fort Laramie for its protection. The Missouri troops were turned off before Fort Laramie was reached, he thinks; for the Kansas Regiment went in alone & the others did not come as long as he was there.

At Laramie, when they were ready to move to Fort Leavenworth, the officers were given picked horses out of all in the command, and each soldier was mounted on a mule. Many of the mules had never been ridden, so the men walked the whole distance to Leavenworth; some trading of[f] their mules for a trifle or a jug of whisky. They got to Fort Leavenworth abt. November 16, 1865, & remained there till the 6th day of December when they were mustered out. Col. Samuel Walker was colonel of the 16th Kansas Cavalry.

About this same period quite a number of soldiers were mustered out of the service.

There were out in this country at this time on service 21st New York Cavalry, 11th Ohio Cavalry, a part of the 6th Michigan Cavalry, several batteries of artillery & 16th Kansas Cavalry & two Regts. of Missouri Cavalry.

General Connor was in the country with California soldiers.

Early in 1865 a part of the 6th Michigan Cavalry was at the Platte River bridge (Richard bridge); a part of the soldiers passed over & the others were waiting to go over; the Inds. attacked those who had crossed, got between the two parts & killed those who had crossed. Eleven soldiers were buried in one grave.

Casper Collins was in command of these Michigan soldiers, & it was from him that Casper got its name.[174]

On the south Platte Spotted Tail was raiding along in the vicinity of O'Fallon's Bluffs & attacking freighting trains & burning wagons, emptying flour in heaps on the ground to get the sacks, & plundering & carrying off goods & killing the men with the outfits. This was in 1864.

John C. Whalen went to Laramie, after he was out of the military service, in 1867.

The treaty of 1868 was made after holding many crowded councils; the chiefs would listen to the commissioners, and then go and counsel with the white men, such as Nick Janis, Antoine Janis and others.

In 1868 Spotted Tail's band went to Whetstone, going in two sections, the first started from Fort Laramie in June under Todd Randall who was sub-agent at Whetstone. The second section started in October and arrived at Whetstone in November. These followed down the Running Water River. The first section followed the Platte a part of the way, passing the Turtle Butte. Nick Janis was guide for this second section. The Indian agent at Whetstone was a man named Chambers. A man named Raymond and selected by the white men living among the Indians, but he held the place only a very short time. Raymond was succeeded by Neighlet (?) (spelling unknown). This man was relieved by a military officer, Major D. C. Poole. He was relieved by G.[J.]M. Washburn of Yankton.[175] In the meantime, in 1870, Spotted Tail went to Washington with the first delegation accompanied by John Richard Jr. Major Poole took the delegation to Washington.

Spotted Tail told President Grant that he did not want to live down at Whetstone & gave as a reason that his people were destroying themselves with whisky & having drunks & brawls and fights & murders in consequence.[176] Grant told Spotted Tail he might move to White River. So on June 1, 1871, all the Brulés left Whetstone which was on the Missouri & 30 miles above old Fort Randall, for this upper country and camped on the White Clay Creek five miles south of the present Pine Ridge Agency, arriving in July. Here they built a small Agency and put up a sawmill, & one store. The Indian trader at this time with this band was John W. Smith, & he was the guide for this march. The Agent for this time was J. M. Washburn. J. M. Washburn was relieved abt. 1872 by D. R. Risley, he by A. E. [E. A.] Howard & he by the military.

Late in the fall (being 1871) Spotted Tail moved up on White River, 12 miles this side of Robinson—where Robinson now is. Another small Agency was built, consisting of Agent's office, small warehouse, and a trader's store, in the bend of the river where the three round knolls are on the northwest, and due north from Crow Butte. They remained here till and during the winter of 1872–3. The saw mill was set up around and south of Crow Butte. In the summer of 1873 this agency was moved down to the mouth of Beaver Creek. At that time a commission was sent out from Washington, with whom was Bishop

Hare, the Rev. Hinman, S. S. (Sunset) Cox and two others, whose names he can not name. These commissioners told Spotted Tail to go with them and to take some of his Indians along, to look out a satisfactory location for his people, & that he might have any place he wanted, even anywhere in the Black Hills, & they would establish him at the place of his choice. Bishop Hare was taken sick & did not go. Spotted Tail refused to go himself, but said any of his people might go who wished to, and several did go.[177]

They went, but the Indians could not find a place which gave them better satisfaction; so the commissioners went to Fort Randall & and telegraphed the Dept. that they had failed to find a better place than they were in. The Commission had been sent out to locate & settle these Indians. In 1874 they moved up the Beaver about eight miles, and built an Agency which ever after went by the name of Spotted Tail Agency. Camp Sheridan was established there [the] same year, being farther south, up in the pines where they built houses; but [the] next year the military were dissatisfied with their ground, as there was no good drilling ground, & they came down to where the Agency was & established themselves there (where I viewed the ground) and sent the people who hung round the place, up to take the buildings they had vacated. The military came down & occupied ground where there were some scattering houses, & and this was a half a mile below and north of the Agency. Here was built a strong post which was maintained till after 1880. From there these Indians went to the country taken from the Ponca Indians. (See President Hayes' speech to the delegation in 1877).[178] Thinks it was in 1877 they went down, [the] same year the Oglalas went to the Yellow Medicine. Thinks they came back in 1878 & settled at Rosebud where they now are.

Commissioner of Ind. Affairs Hayt came out to Yellow Medicine & told the Oglalas he would give them 500 cows when they got located, & Whalen saw the cows delivered, but the Inds. did not get them till abt. 1880 (he thinks it was).[179]

Jack Whalen says that the Spotted Tail and Little Wound Indians used to go down from Laramie into the lower country on the Platte and on the South Platte and the Republican and all over that country and hunt. They waited till they had drawn their annuities in the fall, then they moved away and were gone till the next summer when they would come in with their hides to trade, and they remained around again till autumn.

Their migrations through that country brought them into contact and conflict with the Pawnees and other tribes; and the government wished to put an end to their visits & roaming in that quarter and to promote peace not only among the Indians, but to spare the constantly increasing tide of travel across the plains the dangers and annoyances to be apprehended from the presence of these predatory and warlike people; and to this end they were solicited to alienate their treaty privilege to hunt south of the Platte, for a consideration. He says they received $25,000. He also states that for the other $25,000 which they always claimed, they were given some wagons and other property, government officers claiming that they could find nothing to show that an additional $25,000 was to be paid, but to appease these Indians they gave them this property. (Be careful on this point. Jack refers me to Mr. Cleveland who, he says, knows all about the matter, and who, he further says, was the one that prevailed on Spotted Tail to sign the agreement, by assuring him in the most solemn terms that he would positively receive the $25,000. Mr. Cleveland was the missionary to the Spotted Tail Agency and came in 1873, and was held in high estimation by his dusky spiritual children. After their removal to Rosebud he was there sometime before he came to Pine Ridge.)[180]

Jack Whalen says that the Wounded Knee and 1890 troubles originated in starvation. That the commissioner and Col. Gallagher cut down the rations. The beef was decreased from 6,000,000 to 4,000,000 pounds. Instead of issuing every 15 days as formerly, they issued every 20 days. The flour ration was cut down from four ounces daily to two ounces.[181] The clerks claimed to issue rations when they did not do so at all. One time the Chief Clerk came out to the commissary and asked the commissary clerk if he was issuing and he answered that he was. Whalen spoke up and said "Why do you say that? You are not issuing!" Under his breath the clerk said knowingly "We need this!"

Of course the rations were carried on reports as issued, but the Indians did not get them. Perhaps the rations were never sent to the Agency, and there may have been collusion and division between contractor and Agency officers. One time a lot of bacon shipped to Sidney got away off up into Wyoming—found up there. Why up there?

The Indians took whatever was given them without a word; they complained after they got home; if they received only a mite they said nothing when it was handed out; that was their way; they go home, and if not satisfied, or if they wish to beg for more they come again. They take from the traders whatever is given them; as they know nothing of scales and weights, they go away with whatever is parceled out to them, not knowing whether they have been defrauded or not. The chances to swindle them have been most broad and tempting, and if they have not suffered woefully and outrageously through the broad opportunities which white traders have had, it is because all the Caucasian rascals have remained at home while only the saintly and honest have scrambled for and obtained the lucrative frontier positions.

[John W. Irion's Interview]

[Tablet 20]

John W. Irion of Thomasville, Colorado, being in Grand Junction, April 14, 1908, in answer to my interrogatories, says:

That he came from Indiana to Council Bluffs in July, 1857, and on the 2d day of August he arrived in Fremont, Neb., where he made his home a little over a year, though he was in Omaha cutting cord wood in the following winter & spring. During October & Nov., 1857, he worked on the government bridge then building at the Elkhorn crossing.

From the ferryman at this Crossing, Fifield (called Capt. Fifield) who was running a ferry there at the time of the tragedy, he learned the story of the skinning alive of the white man by the Indians.[182]

Mr. Irion had previously read an account of this affair in a Cincinnati paper —read it in the winter of 1850–1, and it is his understanding that the tragedy was in the spring of 1850. He says it may have been in 1849; that when the emigrants got through to California they sent word, possibly, back by mail telling of what had taken place, and then it got into the papers.

The emigrant party crossed the Elkhorn River on the ferry near night and went in the direction of the Rawhide Creek where it was then crossed by the trail. There was a camp of Indians north of the Rawhide and on the south bank of the Elkhorn. This murderer and a companion were together when the latter reminded him of his vow made awhile before that he would kill the first Indian that he should see. The fellow said he remembered what he had said, and he would keep his promise, and drew up his gun and shot a squaw who was sitting on a log. The party went on about three-quarters of a mile and camped on the Rawhide without crossing it. (It was only about 1¼ miles from the Elkhorn crossing to the Rawhide crossing.)

The main village of the Pawnees was about 13 miles west of the Elkhorn crossing & about 12 miles west of the Rawhide Crossing and on the south side of the Platte River.[183] Just a little hunting or fishing party of Indians, (Pawnees) was down on the Elkhorn, perhaps they were visiting the Omahas. When their squaw was killed runners were dispatched to the main village, and next morning the camp of the emigrants was surrounded by about 500 Pawnees who demanded the delivery of the offender. The whites parleyed and refused. The Pawnees told them they could have their choice, to give him up, or all of the party be killed. They gave him over to the Pawnees.

Mr. Irion says Fifield told him that the Indians carried the white man's skin away to the Indian village; and in 1858, he was told by a young Pawnee, John Rogers, who had attended school at the St. Mary's Mission about 15 miles below Council Bluffs & on east side of the Missouri, who was a friend and associate of Mr. I., that the Pawnees carried the man's skin to their big village. Mr. I. does not believe that the skin was taken off in strips as has been stated. He does not recollect that Fifield said he was present at the skinning, but he thinks he was present, for Fifield said he visited the white camp, & he told the story just as though he had seen the full performance. Mr. I. had the story from the lips of this ferryman. Mr. I. and others who were working on the government bridge went together to the scene of the tragedy and saw the grave, & Mr. I. thinks he could locate the spot now. The grave was plain. Mr. I. says that Capt. Fifield told him that after the Indians left the skinned man he got up and walked to his father's wagon but soon died from pain and loss of blood. The creek took its name—Rawhide—from this incident and tragedy.

The St. Mary's Mission was 5 or 6 miles above Plattsmouth, but on the opposite side of the river. It was also from 5 to 10 miles from where Glenwood, Iowa, now is.

The Mormons going to Salt Lake collected at Council Bluffs. They usually crossed the Missouri and went up to Florence, about six miles (then) above Omaha. Florence is probably now a suburb.

In October and November, 1857, Mr. Irion worked for the government on the bridge over the Elkhorn.

Reagan and Stores were the contractors. They built the bridge and a high grade leading from it west nearly half a mile, in places the grade was six feet high; for here the bottom overflowed. The Elkhorn at this point made an ox-bow bend, and the military and emigrant road traversed this low neck or stretch of bottom between the two arms of the Elkhorn. The government used this road for hauling to Fort Phil Kearny, Laramie &c.

Mr. I. says that the real original "Buffalo Bill" was William Richards with whom he was well acquainted. He was a carpenter working on the government bridge at the Elkhorn Crossing in 1857. He was known as early as 1856 as "Buffalo Bill" and he was familiarly called by that when Mr. I. worked with him, and he went by no other name. W. F. Cody hunted for Fort Phil Kearny and for the U.P.R.R., & having killed great numbers of buffaloes, the name also attached to him. William Richards is still living in southeastern Kansas, not very far from Wichita. Mr. I. can get the address of a man named Ailey who can give Richards' post-office address. This Buffalo Bill was also a great hunter and killed a good many buffaloes. Mr. Irion says that the man skinned alive was buried within twenty feet of the road, on the north side of the road, and on the east side of the creek, about 12 yards from the water in the creek & not more than 25 feet from the bank of the creek which was then high, possibly ten feet high.

Where this man was skinned alive is about 12 miles east of Fremont. A bridge was built across the Rawhide something like a mile above the old cross-ing where the tragedy took place, a few months before the bridge was built over the Elkhorn. Before the Elkhorn bridge was built the trail was changed so that it missed the spot of the tragedy, going farther up the stream—northwest. See Mr. Irion's map.[184]

Referring to the locations of Nebraska Indian tribes in 1857, Mr. Irion says that the Pawnees were settled on the Platte near where Fremont now is, this was in 1857 and 1858. He thinks it was in the fall of 1858 that they were moved to their reservation up on the Loup, north and west of Columbus. Columbus is at the mouth of the Loup Fork.

The Omaha Indians were in the Blackbird Hills, N.W. of Omaha; thinks they may still be living there.

The Otoes were south and west of Nebraska City—were on the Blue River; is not certain as to exact location.

The Poncas were immediately west of the Omahas, he thinks—is not posi-tive; knows they were not far out; for all these tribes were ever at war with Sioux and the Cheyennes.[185]

Speaking of what some have called Masonry among the Indians. Mr. Irion says:

The American Ranch was abt. 156 miles from Denver by the river road, and about 116 miles [by] the stage road as traveled in January, 1865; this was down the Platte river and was abt. 36 miles below Fort Morgan. This ranch was destroyed in January, 1865. Capt. Joe Davidson and his company of the 1st Colorado Reg't. were the first persons to arrive after the people there had been killed and the place destroyed. Davidson told him that all had been killed but the woman, Mrs. John Norris and one or two of her children. Thinks there were two children, and that one was separated from her and never seen again, and that one was left with her, & this soon died. Three or four men were killed he thinks, Tom Norris being one. On his body was found a Masonic emblem; he was carried out and laid by an adobe or sod wall; he was not scalped or mutilated in any way; and a Masonic apron and other articles pertaining to the order were laid on his body. He was found in this condition.

The buildings were burned so far as they were inflammable, the walls were sod; these did not burn. Mrs. Norris was ransomed by an officer of the army and sent to her folks at Granville, Indiana, a place about 24 miles from where Mr. Irion's father was then living.

It was the opinion of Capt. Davidson that these Indians, the Cheyennes and Arrapahoes, possibly some Sioux, had knowledge of Masonic emblems.

Mr. Irion says further on same subject: That a man T. N. Evans, either in Southern Colorado or New Mexico, at any rate near the Dry Cimmaron (he pronounces it Sim ma rōne) (He says there is more than one Cimmaron, but this is the Dry Cimmaron) Evans with a small party was traveling through that country. He went hunting one day & after walking several miles without killing anything he returned to the road quite a way in advance of the outfit, walking slowly along the road when he saw five or six Indians approaching from an opposite direction. Knowing it to be a hostile country he felt ill at ease and finally concluded to give a sign, he having heard of something of this secret knowledge among the Indians; he had no more than given the sign when the leader of the party rolled off his horse and as he struck the ground he gave a sign, and he kept on with his hand springs and antics, and every time he struck the ground on his feet he gave a sign. He gave all the signs that Evans knew and more than he knew. These were all Masonic. The Indians came up to him and shook hands and deported themselves in a very friendly manner. The Indians stayed with him till his friends came up; then they sent an escort with the whites through their country.

Sand Creek Massacre

Mr. Irion says that Adam Smith who is living at Meeker, Colorado, has given as good an account of this as he has ever heard.[186]

Smith says that the expedition was composed partly of the First and partly of the Third Colorado Regiments (both Cavalry); Col. John M. Chivington was colonel of the 1st and Col. George L. Shoup was colonel of the 3d; but Chivington being the ranking officer, was in command of the expedition. They started about night from Fort Lyons, near old Fort Bent, and they arrived at the

Indian camp at the Big Bend on the Big Sandy. They dismounted & a detail was made of horse-holders; and the main body of fighting men approached the Indian camp as near as they could when it was daylight, and attacked the camp when the first smoke was started, which was the signal to begin the attack. The camp was attacked on about three sides, as it was nearly surrounded. A few Indians made a dash for their horses and got away. All the Indians remaining were killed except two children. After the fight was over Smith saw a brush pile move. He and a few others went to it, and finding a living Indian concealed in it, killed him. They scalped the Indians altogether, but with a few exceptions did not otherwise mutilate them. They destroyed the camp completely and captured several hundred horses.

After this drastic remedy for Indian horrors there was peace for sometime, except what occurred during the succeeding two months when the worst and most horrible hostilities took place that ever did. Following Sand Creek massacre, the Indians appeared to concentrate on the South Platte, and their depredations and atrocities were in the neighborhood of the 2 American Ranch, 1 Godfrey's Ranch, 3 Wisconsin Ranch, 5 Moore's Ranch, 4 Valley Station, 6 Lillian Springs, 7 Buffalo Springs and many other stopping places. These were all near together covering a distance of 50 or 60 miles, beginning with Godfrey's Ranch which was highest up, and running down stream in the order in which these places are numbered above.

Mr. Irion never heard of Charles Bent being a hard character.

Mentioning James R. Beckwourth with whom Mr. Irion was acquainted, he says that in his estimation Beckwourth spoke the truth in his narratives concerning other persons, but when recounting his own adventures he thinks Beckwourth had some inclination to exaggerate. Beckwourth, he says, did not live, as has been stated, on Cherry Creek near Denver, but up on the Platte, on the south side about three miles (at that time) from the city. (Mr. Irion told me the identical spot but I did not get it down at the time.) He kept a road-house there — an inn, or place of entertainment, with feed and stabling for animals, and liquors for sale. He had a colored woman for wife. He left this woman when he went north to the Crows. Mr. Irion cannot give the authentic facts of his last days and death.

Beckwourth had some negro blood; thinks he was a quadroon.

Mr. Irion says that it is his recollection that the trailing of cattle from Texas to the north began in 1868. This the date given by J. H. Cook on May 23, 1907.

[A. W. Means's Interview]

[Tablet 13]

A. W. Means of Pine Ridge says that Col. Chivington was not in the battle of Sand Creek, but was not far off, & he it was who gave the order to fight this battle. Major Wynkoop of the 1st Colorado was in command on the field. Thinks that the 1st and the 3d Colorado were the only troops at Sand Creek, and doubts if the 3d got there in time for the fight. There were only six companies of the 3d Colorado & these were infantry. The 1st and the 2d Colorado Cavalry regts. were not full regts., but were down in New Mexico and fought & drove back the rebels in 1861 at Fort Union. Afterwards at Benton Barracks, St. Louis the 2d Colo. and these six companies of the 3d were consolidated and called the 2d Colorado Cavalry.

[John M. Comegys' Interview]

[Tablet 7]

John M. Comegys says he left Chester River at a place called Chestertown, Kent Co., Md. in 1856 and came to "bleeding Kansas" when Jim Lane was there killing people, and he reached this country in 1862.

He knew James P. Beckwourth, got acq. with him in the 60's down in the Platte River country and the Medicine Bow Mountains—down about Denver. Doesn't know any of Beckwourth's history; he had run his race before. He was a man of truth and honor.

Knew Jim Baker and his brother John, and _____ Brown (they called him Big Mouthed Brown—all had nicknames)—all these had Sioux women for wives. They settled over on the Stinking Water in Wyoming; this is quite a stream and is a tributary of the Big Horn.

John Baker killed a man and they all went back among the Sioux. He was not with Baker much; Baker was too old and broken to pieces when he became acq. with him.

He knew Bridger but not so very well. Fort Bridger was at the confluence of the Laramie and Platte rivers. Had a big stockade made of logs and adobe bricks; the location was nice; the government bought it from Bridger; it was east of Echo cañon & 113 miles from Salt Lake. Fort Bridger was on Ham's Fork on the other side of South Pass & this side of Salt Lake.[187] Thinks the Mormons had great nerve and did a great thing & that Brigham was an able man. The worst feature of their operations was the robbing & killing of immigrants, & the Mountain Meadow Massacre.[188]

He says the Indians were not troublesome in the early days as later; they were more peaceable; people could go and live among them.

Mr. Comegys is 82 years old; has lived on the Crow Reservation 22 yrs. He helped to survey the Elkhorn valley. Albert Sidney Johnson wintered at Fort Bridger.[189]

Mr. Comegys says he stayed with Gen. Albert Sidney Johnson's train of 175 wagons camped at O'Fallon's Bluff on Platte river. Johnson asked for volunteers to stay with the train and stock. He and six others volunteered and remained. Johnson got as far as Fort Bridger where the army camped for the winter and subsisted on half rations. They killed their oxen at Bridger and hung the meat up for food. Johnson was relieved (he says) by Hoffman without going to Salt Lake. He returned to Laramie and resigned.[190] Mr. Comegys says that he and his companions got along nicely with the Indians that winter. They gave a feast to the Indians which pleased them very much and created a friendly disposition among the natives. He says they cooked provisions ahead for several days and told the Indians to come at a stated time. The remnants of the feast were given to the Indians to carry away. They fed them on flour, bacon, coffee and sugar. There were abt. 4,000 Indians. The chief was High Buck Bear. They were Sioux. The chief told these men if they were molested by any of his tribe to let him know and he would give them redress, but there was no trouble at all; the white men would go over to the Indian village and the Indians would come to their camp where they had built a house, and they would play games. When they first halted at this place they were forced to do so by snow of which two feet [fell] in one night. The winter was severe in the forepart and most of the mules were frozen to death, but afterwards the weather grew milder and the winter was comfortable. They were on the Platte river. In the spring the men were relieved by troops and trains arriving; these took into their own wagons the stores which the seven men had guarded and the latter went back to Fort Leavenworth with empty wagons.

It was this winter that the Mormons burned Johnson's wagons. Johnson had 75 wagons burned. One train was found at Ham's Fork (Bridger's stockade was on this) and the Mormons destroyed it; two other trains they found and burned on Green River.

Mr. C. after returning to Leavenworth came back the next spring to Bridger.

These wagons burned were in rear of the army, and the general not aware of the presence of the Mormons in that country lost his wagons which were guarded only by the teamsters. The wagons that Mr. Comegys was with were still farther back on the plains.

[William H. Taylor's Interview]

[Tablet 3]
This is "Cheyenne Bill" Taylor of Interior, S.D. Cornelius A. Craven, commonly called "Gus." Craven of Interior, S.D., says Taylor is reliable and his judgement good.

Mr. Taylor says he came into this region of country in 1872. He was not a scout, but a teamster, as he says, a mule skinner.

Wm. H. Taylor October 13, '06. Says: He was with Crook in March, 1876, & says he stayed back with the pack train & sent Major Reynolds ahead. Blames Crook & thinks he should have been court-martialed instead of Reynolds.[191] Says Crook had Reynolds court-martialed. Reynolds was 60 years old — too old to be put in charge. Has no high opinion of Crook; says he has talked with a good many officers & men, and they all condemned Crook, and these were with him in March 1876. Says 2 men were killed in the fight of March 17, and they were put under the ice, one of these was killed after the battle was all over, he was shot in top of head by an Indian up in the rocks.[192] The Inds. scattered, being driven out of their village and took to the high cliffs surrounding. Their camp and village were destroyed, robes, guns, supplies and all burned up. Crook fell back to his base losing a lot of horses. Capt. Egan who charged into the village back & forth was next to Custer. Noyes was ahead of Egan up to this time, but he dismounted his command behind a hill & stayed there.[193] After this Egan went ahead of Noyes. This battle was on Powder River, and not on any tributary. Thinks if Crook had done his duty there would not have been such odds against Custer. Says Crook was slow; that when he got up to where there was something to be done he sent somebody else ahead to do it. Thinks Crook showed cowardice March 17. Says Reynolds was also afraid. Thinks Custer was the great fighter. Thinks Col. Mackenzie was better than Crook.

[Mr. and Mrs. William M. Robertson's Interview]

[Tablet 12]

Near Allen S.D., Oct. 26, 1906.

Interview with Mr. and Mrs. Wm. Robertson, Day School teacher and house-keeper at No. 21. Mrs. Robertson was Augusta Brown, daughter of Hon. Joseph R. Brown.[194]

Mr. Robertson told me of Mrs. Iron Road, an old woman living at Lipp's camp, who was present at the Bear Chief affair and saw it all. She told him the particulars as follows:

Bear Chief and his band met some white people who were travelling west. These proved to be Mormons. They told him that they had left a cow behind on the road; that she was footsore and could not travel; and that he might have it. He went on and found the cow and slaughtered her. It was reported to the military that Bear Chief's band were killing stock belonging to emigrants. A lieutenant with a party of soldiers came to Bear Chief's camp and demanded the man who had killed the cow. Bear Chief said they might have him, and he pointed out the tent where he was and said to the officer that he might go and get him. The lieutenant told the chief to go and bring him. He went to the tent and came back and said that the Indian would not go, and that the lieutenant might go and get him. The officer told the chief to go again and bring him out. He went again and saw the Indian who replied that he would go but would not do so then. The Chief returned and told the officer what he said, and further said that the soldiers might take the Indian out if they could; whereupon the officer ordered the soldiers to kill the Chief, and they filled him with bullets. This so incensed the Indians that they fell on the soldiers and killed the whole party, the interpreter, who was an Indian, being the last one dispatched. He pleaded for himself to be spared by saying he was an Indian; but they told him he had discovered this too late, and so he met the same fate as the others.[195]

[Tablet 28]

Mr. William Robertson said that the Indians have a more passionate appetite for strong drink than white men, and that the introduction of the drinking habit among them has had a great damaging affect.

He further said that he thought one reason why the Indians' rations were decreased before the 1890 outbreak was the reports sent in by the farmers giving exaggerated accounts of the prosperity of the Indians; their success in productions of the soil and of the range.

[Allison J. Pliley's Letter]

[Box 19]

K C K, Nov. 6/1912

Mr. E. S. Ricker

Washington, D.C.

Yours of Oct 18th at hand. Enclosed find a short act. [account] of this fight on Prairiedog Cr. in what is now Phillips Co. Kans. You may infer the truthfullness of it by seeing Major Armes who is I believe a resident of Washington City in the real estate business the last I heard of him.

I have no photos on hand but have an enlarged one taken at Ft. Sill in 69. I took it to a photographer and as he would not take less than 6 copys of it after showing him your letter he took them and wrote you at the time and as you have not ordered them sent on I have assured him my friends will take them off his hands so he will not be loser.

Yours respectfully

A. J. Pliley

501 Stanton Place N.E. Washington City, Nov. 23, 1912.

The foregoing [following] sketch was received to-day from Captain Pliley to whom it was submitted for correction after it was typewritten from his original notes, and is thus authenticated. In his letter to me he states that he "was engaged with the Indians on Prairie Dog Creek Sept. 22, 1867. Major Armes was engaged at same time 5 or six miles in our front. We were also engaged at the train the next day, Sept. 23. With the one correction the copy is correct." E. S. R.[196]

The Battle on Prairie Dog Creek in September 1867

By Captain A. J. Pliley

A scouting expedition composed of two companies of the 18th Kansas Volunteer Cavalry and two of the 10th U.S. Cavalry under command of Major George A. Armes, moved out of Fort Hays September 20, 1867 on a scout to Fort McPherson on the Cottonwood; on the night of the 21st we made a night march over to Prairie Dog Creek. I will here explain that I was scout and guide for the 18th Kansas, and was assigned to this expedition, and on this night march I had orders from Major Armes to keep out on the left front of the column about a mile in advance and if I saw any indications of Indians to turn to the right and join the command which was moving due north by the north star, and report. About three o'clock when near the breaks of Prairie Dog Creek I saw signal arrows going up off to the northwest of my course, and went in and reported to Major Armes. He then gave orders for our wagon train of eight wagons with an escort of 65 men under command of Lieut. J. M. Price to move over in a northeast direction to the creek and go into camp and await orders to move forward. My order was as before, with the assurance that the column would continue to move north as before. About five o'clock, after getting down to Prairie Dog Creek I seeing fresh Indian signs turned to my right to join the command and report; but alas, from some cause, Armes, instead of moving north, had taken a sharp northwest course, and had cut into my left so I missed him and kept on going until I reached the train. While at the train awaiting my breakfast a detachment of 10 men of the 10th Cavalry from Fort Hays rode into camp with a message to Armes to return at once with his command to Fort Hays. Taking charge of the party I moved up the creek to the point where the command had crossed Prairie Dog Creek. It was about ten miles from the train. At this point I began picking up stragglers from the command and found my party had grown to 27 men. I also learned that the command was about five miles ahead. Taking up their trail, I followed it up a tributary of Prairie Dog Creek until about 11 o'clock. The trail deflected slightly to the right. Halting here to water our horses, and while waiting for the men to reform, I discovered a large body of Indians coming from the northwest about a mile distant. They had evidently discovered us, for they were coming full tilt for us, about, I judged, 300 strong. It was the most forlorn hope I ever took part in. Dismounting the men and forming a hollow square around our horses, and following Armes's trail out on to the high open ridge, we met the terrific charge. Our hope was that Armes would hear our firing and come to our rescue. At the first onslaught five of our men were wounded and had to be assisted, 2 among the horses out there hanging on to the stirrups of their saddles hobbled along, those who were able firing on the enemy when they could. The Indians soon showed a wholesome respect for the fire of our men. The ridge was fast becoming spotted with their dead and wounded. Our ranks too, were becoming distressingly thin; and still no sign of Armes. And so the unequal struggle went on for at least 3 miles, when off to the northwest some distance a great cloud of dust met our view, and every one became hilarious. Help was coming. Armes! Armes! And a great shout went up. But great God! it was answered by the blood-curdling yell of more Indians, a larger party who had attacked Armes at the time we were first attacked, and whom he had repulsed but failed to follow up. Quickly reversing the line of action we fought back over the same ground to avoid the impact of this hoard of yelling devils in our front, still hoping that Armes was following them; and so the fight went on. Learning the original course, I bore off to the southeast in an effort to reach the train. At this point we lost heavily; our loss up to this time was 2 killed and 12 wounded, including myself. I had received two severe wounds in my right leg, which necessitated the assistance of one man on my right side for support. Just before dusk the Indians began to close in on us, and it became evident that they intended to make a final effort to get us. To divert their attention we selected three of the best horses, and mounting 5 of the most badly wounded on them, we turned the rest of the horses loose; and while the Indians were taken up capturing them, we got the wounded down into a canyon on our left, and formed our remaining men on either bank and pushed our way toward the train. Darkness coming on, the Indians left us. Our loss was now 2 killed and 14 wounded, together with all of our horses except the three which had saved the wounded. Here we had the first opportunity to give attention to the wounded men. Three were mortally wounded and died the next day. We were then about four miles from the train; the Indians had left us and gone down to that and invested it for a daylight attack the next morning. After resting and doing all we could for the wounded, we made a wide detour and crossed Prairie Dog Creek about a mile below the train. Going across the narrow valley, back of the sand ridge, and up as nearly opposite the train as it seemed safe to go, I hid the party away. At daybreak we heard the firing commence around the train. Here it became necessary for some one to go to the train and get an escort to take the party in before the Indians discovered us. Being helped upon the back of one of the best horses, I rode up behind the ridge to the wagon trail, and waiting there until the firing ceased I went to the top of the ridge and came into full view of the train and the Indians, but was nearer the Indians than the train. Now occurred an incident which confirmed my most religious belief, namely, that you cannot kill a man until his time to die has come. Fully 500 Indians made desperate effort to cut me off; every one of them gave me a shot or more before I gained the train without a scratch. I got an escort and got the party in. Major Armes arrived about an hour later.

This ended the battle of Prairie Dog Creek. The total casualties of the whole command was 2 killed, 47 wounded.

Captain Pliley was born in Ross County, Ohio April 20, 1843, of German and Scotch parents. His paternal grandfather came from Germany and served as a soldier in the Revolutionary War under Gen. Greene. His mother was a native of Edinborough Scotland. His family emigrated to Kansas in the year 1857.

[William Holdaway's Interview]

[Tablet 40]

~~Salt Lake City August 13, 1909.~~

Interview of Mr. William Holdaway of Provo, Utah. Says he was born in Utah, about 50 miles south of Salt Lake City, in 1851.

In 1867 he and a party of men started from Salt Lake City to go to Cheyenne, to work on Union Pacific R.R. & arrived in Sept. Started in to work on the road, but it was soon discovered that they were good herders, and were employed by a man named Moore who put them to night-herding of Texas cattle. During the winter they fed the stock more than they grazed. This was stock kept and used for feeding the graders. When spring came they went to work for government, the first few weeks being engaged in chopping wood on the North Platte river bottom and hauling it up to the fort—Fort Steele—situated on the south side of the river, about 30 miles from Rawlins. After the wood contract was filled these men began hauling hay, abt. the first of July.

On the morning of the 4th of July (thinks it was the 4th) the Indians raided their stock and got away with it, but it was recovered. Later the Inds. dashed into Rawlins, killed the sentinel, filling his body with arrows. This was then a R.R. camp at Rawlins Springs as it was called.[197] They killed the two guards before they got to the sentry. When the sentry was killed no alarm could be given. A boy was killed—with 17 arrows in his body—before the sentry was slain.

After this [a] squad of men received orders to follow and keep track of the movements of the Indians. At Whisky Gap is nearly due west of Rawlins, abt. 40 miles. One day after the running off of the stock at Rawlins Holdaway saw Gen. G. M. Dodge come in chased by Indians, himself and steed nearly exhausted.[198]

These scouts went from Rawlins to Whisky Gap where they met Gen. Connor; from there they proceeded to Devil's Gate; thence to Chimney Rock; thence to Church Butte (where the river starts to break through the range of mountains). This winter of '67–68 there was a big camp of Indians of some 2,000 on the Platte—wintered there—2,000 or more—these scouts were watching them; when these Inds. broke camp in the spring they started north &

west. The scouts then started N.W. around the head of the Stinking Water, then around the base of the Big Horn Mts.—around S.E.—swung to the Sweet-water—Mr. Holdaway and 3 others held back in the morning while the rest went on, and while examining some specimens of copper ore, the first ever found on the Sweetwater, the Indians nearly captured them. From the Sweet-water the scouts went to the Platte, passing up to Fort Steele where they were disbanded, & Holdaway & 2 or 3 others came to Salt Lake with a Mormon emigrant train. These scouts had a leader they called Sergeant Smith; he does not know whether he was a military man, wore no uniform.

At Provo call for Mr. Holdaway at the office where one of his boys is—a dentist—with sign, "Utah Dental Ass'n." 32 West Center.

[John Burdick's Interview]

[Tablet 13]
Pine Ridge, March 13, '07.

John Burdick says: He was on the 1873 expedition under Gen. Stanley with which Custer was connected up on the Northern Pacific in the preliminary survey.

(Write to Lieut. Charles A. Braden, West Point, New York, who was wounded on the expedition and carried three hundred miles on an old ambu-lance cut down, and who teaches officers' children at West Point.)

(Burdick whose frontier name is "Slim Jim" made this conveyance.) "Slim Jim" says when I write to Braden to mention that Slim Jim gave the address. Slim Jim was chief of Dog Scouts for Custer and Stanley; he was supposed to be a beef herder, but he was the one who took soldiers out to hunt up the dogs after a hunt, as they would get scattered & left behind.

He relates about Stanley putting Custer under arrest. Stanley sent Custer from Fort Rice with orders to overhaul Rosser & hold him at Hart River Butte till the main command came up. He overtook Rosser in time, but the two put their heads together to go on, & Stanley did not come up with them till he got to the Beaver Creek, just before entering the Little Missouri Bad Lands, & they would not have been caught then if it had not been that they were caught in a big hail storm and lost all their stock.[199]

Besides, there were orders that no women should be taken & no cook stoves, but in defiance of this order Custer took a wench to cook & a cook stove in his wagon.

Custer was put under arrest at Beaver Creek & was not released till (thinks) they reached the Yellowstone.

(Write to Major H. L. Scott, West Point, N.Y. who knows a good deal about the 1873 expedition under Stanley, although Scott was not on that expedition. He has been sent out by Gov't. & has written books. Mention "Slim Jim.")

[William A. Coffield's Interview]

William A. Coffield came to Pine Ridge in the 1870s, and was em-
ployed as a telegrapher and later as a farmer. In 1883 he married
assistant teacher Luella D. Melvin.[200]

[Tablet 13]
Pine Ridge, March 13, 1907.

W. A. Coffield, Postmaster says: The Pine Ridge Agency was first connected with Rosebud & the [telegraph] line ran out to Camp Sheridan. Camp Sheridan was abandoned in 1880.

Mr. Coffield was at Fort Robinson as manager of the Cheyenne & Black Hills Telegraph line. In 1881, July 15, Pine Ridge Agency and Fort Robinson were connected by telegraph with the outside world.

Mr. Colhoff [Coffield] was followed at Robinson in 1881, he came to Pine Ridge in November, 1881, & took charge of the office there.

[James H. Cook's Interview]

James H. Cook began his long career in the West as a ranch hand
in southwestern New Mexico. He was a professional hunter before
returning to ranching in western Nebraska. Cook became a friend
of the Oglalas and Cheyennes at the Pine Ridge Reservation, who
often visited him at the ranch.

Cook found Miocene epoch fossils on his ranch, which he brought
to the attention of paleontologists. This discovery led to the creation
of Agate Fossil Beds National Monument in 1965.

Cook published his autobiography in 1923.[201]

[Tablet 3]
James H. Cook, Agate Neb. was born in Kalamazoo, Mich., Aug. 26, 1857. Common sch. education. Raised in an atmosphere of noble Christian living, exactness and purity. His mother died when he was 2 yrs. old & his father put him in a family named Titus. This man was a good hunter, trapper and fisher-

man in those days. He was of the old type; a mechanic of excellent parts, conversant with high models and extensive practice; made the first cotton gin in the south. Jack was an older brother. He was in charge of a family of different tastes who had no moral ideas—nothing only to make money.

James H. removed to Texas in 1870 when there was only the old Chisholm trail running to Wichita and Abilene which was practically the end of the trail. He helped afterwards to make all the other trails from Texas north. He worked in southwestern Texas gathering wild cattle in winter and driving them north in summer over the trails which he had, excepting the first which ended at Abilene, Kansas, helped to establish. This employment lasted until about the year 1877.

He next engaged in hunting.

[Tablet 13]

James H. Cook at Agate, May 23, 07, says:

Thinks Cody would not be a nature student—a plainsman would not know the call of one bird to another—of one animal to another—would not know the nature of plants, of the changes they go through on account of the changes of weather. etc.

The engineer lying in bed at night hears the engine passing utter its whistle scream, or he hears the bell ring, and he rouses up and nudging his spouse and says there goes Engine 49, Bill Smith is on to-night, I know his tune, so the old trailer—the natural trailer as opposed to the artificial—finds his chief enjoyment in hunting and seeking in solitude; he can little bear the presence of men; he does not need the excitement of company; his excitement is with natural objects.

Men like Boone could not feel at home with men; as these crowded up to them they withdrew to remote parts far from the haunts of civilization. Their love was for nature—the hills, the streams, the forests, the plains, birds and wild animals; then came the call to adventure which was followed by strife with these and with the higher animal known as man—little difference whether the latter was red or white. Not necessary that he should see many men; so well settled communities were an idle fact to him—a revulsion. He could study the race of man from a single specimen, as he studies any species of the wilderness by a single member. Strife with men is repugnant; civilized life forbids it and visits upon it pains and penalties; therefore our Boones go west and lose themselves in the solitudes where the craving for conflict can be gratified by contact with wild animals, with hardship in overcoming the sterling and strenuous features of battling with rivers, and mountains, and storms and hunger and thirst.

Mr. Cook thinks Cody was not — could not be — a trailer; he was an actor. His place was among men; his happiness was not drawn from solitude and the profound and shrinking contemplations inspired by it.

The Texas Trail[202]

At Agate, May 23, 1907. J. H. Cook says:

The trailing of cattle from southern Texas to Kansas and Nebraska began in 1867? 1868. Immense herds were, during the existence of the industry, driven through to the north, the first destinations bring Abilene, Wichita, Great Bend, Ellsworth, Baxter Springs, Fort Hays, Ellis, Fort Dodge (April 14, 1908. J. W. Irion says the date was 1868.)

Finally Ogallala became the northern point of destination, and Plum Creek was earlier a distributing point. At first drivers came up only as far as Kansas. In the beginning there was no market down in Texas, and southern men started to running their stock north to find a market. It had been discovered from the fact that bull trains which had been caught in crossing the plains and compelled to winter, that cattle could subsist on the plains grasses and do well and come out in spring in good flesh; and this suggested the grazing of southern cattle on the northern ranges. The above named Kansas towns were called "cow towns" by the men who followed the business; for here it was that markets for sale of the driven stock were established. Buyers came to these places to make their purchases. Sometimes the seller, as a part of his contract of sale, drove the sold cattle to the buyer's ranch, a hundred or two hundred miles distant. After an acquaintance had been created between the southern sellers and the northern buyers, the latter frequently ordered from the southern men such stock as they desired and it was driven north to them. Ultimately it was no uncommon thing for the northern men to go direct to Texas and make their purchases, and afterwards the cattle were driven. The owners of stock did not usually go along with the drive; they were not themselves drivers — did not understand the art of driving; some of them, however, lived on ranches and knew something of the business of raising and branding. It should be observed that the trails did not remain stationary during the whole of the period covering the life of this industry. These thoroughfares were gradually crowded westward, one route after another being formed, as circumstances made it necessary for herds to be taken north on a line farther west from all prior ones. At first it was necessary for Texas stock growers to find a market for their stock cattle, but after this business had been established and buyers and sellers had formed what may be termed a commercial acquaintance, the animals were frequently marketed at home.

A drive always occupied the season—never but one drive was made the same year.

The method of driving was something that had to be learned; it required special training to qualify the men who performed the arduous labor of transferring these large herds from the gulf country to the northern selling points. Like all other occupations, this one was not to be taken up as a light employment to be learned in a few days; a rare few would, as if designed by nature for it, embrace it with a natural aptitude showing fitness by endowment, while others were slow to learn, and some could never learn. It was a business which required the utmost circumspection at all times, because the risk was ever great owing to the values involved in the cattle, and the losses which might from want of care be run up to high percentages. One mode of driving would regulate the profit and loss balance with a comfortable margin in favor of the seller, whereas an opposite mode would change the balance to the other side of the account with disastrous results. The cattlemen had their foremen for the drive, and under these were all the other employes. Exigencies and emergencies were numerous and striking during a drive of a thousand miles to 1,800 miles, covering a whole season of six months. The drive began usually about the first of March from southern Texas. Frights and stampedes of the cattle at any moment were not the only difficulties that were reasonably expected and which kept the men alert and under strain; but this business was carried on in the Indians' country and was subject to the alarms caused by knowledge of their proximity, varied by their frequent attacks and skirmishes.

Mr. Cook has furnished some sketches showing the right way and the wrong way of driving cattle, the former of which was evolved by long experience, and the principles of which will always be useful to any who make a study of them for use in actual practice.

It took about 12 men to handle a herd. There were the Caporal or Foreman or Boss, the Cook, the Horse Herder or Wrangler, the Point Drivers, the Swing Drivers, and the Drag Drivers. When on night service they were divided into three watches. When all was quiet, the cattle were easy and contented, and there was no danger from the outside, three men stationed around the herd-circle, were enough to control the herd through the night, but if the cattle were restless, were lying upon their briskets and sniffing the air as if there was something in the air to disquiet them, and they were by instinct smelling trouble or excitement, then it might be that the whole force would be required to be on their horses, riding around the cattle and keeping them well in hand, and in position to act instantly if they should break away. From six to ten horses to the man were used; these were furnished by the owner, for experiment had shown that when the rider owned his horses he had such a personal interest that he would not ride hard enough, when sometimes it was necessary, to prevent the cattle from getting away. There was always a wagon in the outfit, drawn by a four-ox team; occasionally six oxen were used.

The right way to drive these cattle was to run them in a long, narrow column which tapered toward the front end to half a dozen in width. On each side and some distance in rear of the leaders, or "pointers" as they were called, was a single driver, and these two foremost drivers were called respectively right and left "point" drivers. Behind these on either side and nearly midway of the column were the right and left hand "swing" drivers; in rear of these at the proper distance were two more "swing" drivers, and in rear of the column were two "drag" drivers whose duty was to bring up the laggards. The drivers kept the cattle in column by riding from their stations rearward till they reached the driver next behind. Two opposite drivers riding backward and pressing in toward the center overcame the tendency in the stock to spread out and kept the procession in narrow width. When these riders had gone the length of their beats they swung out boldly and riding back in a more distant line from the column toward the front, then turning inwardly, rode again rearwards a short distance and recovered their proper positions. In this way two thousand cattle could be held in compact line extending two or three or more miles in length. These cattle, when the drive began, were a very wild and ferocious lot of animals; but as the run progressed they became more and more disciplined to the conditions until they were quite docile and tractable, and would take their places in the line of march and move forward with half-closed eyes and admirable regularity, realizing what was required and what they had to do.

At some distance in advance rode the caporal or foreman who was the general guide picking out the trail and on the alert to take the advantages and avoid the disadvantages — to discover grazing spots, find water holes, cross rivers at proper places, and this personage was carefully followed by the point drivers who had the direction of the herd.

When it had been decided by those in front to give the cattle a spell of grazing, supposing the grass was on one side of the trail, the point driver next the grazing plot swung outwardly, giving room to the cattle, while his partner on the opposite side of the line pressed in upon them riding up and down, thus changing their direction to the desired point; and the swing drivers pursuing the same method, the whole line was gradually turned toward the place where they were to refresh themselves. As the hindmost ones came up they all spread out to feeding.

In starting out from one of these places or from the bed-ground at daylight in the morning, the way of putting the herd in motion and stringing it out into a tenuous thread of animated life, was to relax the cordon of drivers on the side whence the cattle were to move, and let them graze out slowly in the direction of the day's drive. It was a placcid and interesting spectacle when these strange animals, tall and gaunt, tapering from head to rump, with frontlets surmounted by spear-like and threatening horns extending from three to nine feet, with noses to the ground, sent their rough, spine-covered tongues out into the rich, juicy grass, gathering in a mouthful to be severed from the roots by the nippers in their under jaws, at every step. Then, raising their proud, imperious heads, here and there one would stride forward as few steps to fresher picking, grinding his jaws as he went. Two or three hours in the morning spent in this way filled their bellies and braced them up to stand the travel, as well as to maintain their accumulated flesh and to lay on a particle more. At an early hour usually by seven o'clock, if conditions were ordinary, the herd was in full swing along he trail, fresh in feeling and with the appearance of brute ardor in their brilliant eyes and their strong limbs.

Always were to be found a given few, just the same as among the higher animals known as men, who were in the lead, because they were swifter steppers, and were born, no one knows why, to be there. These were the pointers, the important leaders, whose magnetism was so effective in guiding and influencing their trailing congeners. The "point" drivers were the heroic figures of the beef procession; for by their reason, their energy, their skill, was the enterprise of moving these valuable droves brought to successful financial issue.

Let us suppose that we have reached one of the large rivers which smite the season's pathway with high and distant banks between which rolls a deep, swift flood. How helpless are a dozen men and a few horses against thousands of these fierce brutes liable to go at any moment like the wild wave of a mighty tide beyond all control only to be followed and coaxed into partial obedience, save for the quick intelligence, the high training and the electric sinews of these same horses, and the tact, the judgement, the courage, the lightning eye, the instant action and the supple strength of the faithful riders who love their work.

With all due prudence the caporal has selected the crossing; but why did he mark a point just at a bend in the stream—a little above it—where the suspicious animals are to be decoyed down to the brink and into the water? When I asked one of the experienced representatives of the forgotten art of trailing, he replied like this: "Don't you know that swimmers cannot make a straight course across a wide swift current, and that they invariably come out on the opposite side lower down the stream than where they entered it?" So it was with these cattle. Often, in spite of all exertions of the drivers concentrated on the lower side trying to keep them headed and struggling up stream, they would land half or three quarters of a mile below the starting point. The passage was fraught with an ever-present danger which caused the drivers to draw a consciously freer breath when it was completed. The force of the stream and the inclination of the cattle conspired to create this danger. As the water bore the beasts down it would have been an easy matter for them to turn back toward the bank from which they started and land on that side, and this was what they would have been glad to do; and the results would have been a misfortune, if not a disaster. Because, in the control of all brute nature, the master constantly keeps his victim in ignorance of what the victim can do. Had the drove come out on the side from which it started to cross, the danger that it would become unmanageable was strong, and the difficulty of getting the cattle over after such an occurrence would have been multiplied many times. When the crossing was made the head of the line was guided so as to bring the whole of it back upon the trail. These trails, it is worthwhile to remark, were such deeply worn tracks that traces of them will remain to distant years. In some fields the plow, after decades of cultivation, has not succeeded in obliterating them.

The restless and furious nature of the Texas steer was an element against which the drivers were always on guard, and which gave them little respite from every grade of excitement and adventure, to say nothing of the imminent perils which many a hardy and brave man did not survive.

By eleven o'clock the inclination of the cattle to graze would be apparent, and they were allowed to slacken their pace and swing out into the grass skirting the route of travel and fill up. The cook with the wagon continued on the trail to a point a mile or two in advance where he halted and prepared dinner. A part of the men perhaps trailed along with him, and while the cooking was going on, they were catching a little rest and their horses were out on grass. As soon as they had their dinner they were off to the herd which by this time was in the vicinity of the wagon; the other men were set free and came up for their

353

repast, and when that was over, and they had helped the cook lift any heavy articles into the wagon and to hitch up his team, if any of the oxen happened to be ungovernable, they too made a brisk dash for their places in the column which by this time would be about ready to take up the afternoon march. Some two hours were generally given to midday grazing. Towards six in the evening the cattle would be turned again upon the grass to fill up before winding up the bunch on the bed ground. Two to three hours sufficed for this; and then the process of putting the cattle to bed, which was no part of the vernacular, followed. This feat consisted in the drivers, who were on all sides of the herd, riding round and round in a circle, gradually contracting the circuit until the cattle were in a compact body with just enough room to lie down. It was their habit to be quiet till about eleven o'clock when there was some stir by getting up and lying down again in new and restful positions. If nothing happened to cause an outbreak, there would be little movement among them before the break of day. The three reliefs or watches have been mentioned, but it is in order to explain that these went on duty successively at regular intervals, the division of the night into three periods giving opportunity for all to obtain needed sleep. The riders' horses were hobbled and turned loose at a little distance from the herd of cattle, the wagon most always standing between. One man kept watch over the horses, but in the course of the night two changes of the guard took place.

The last of these guards, when he saw the light coming in the east, threw the saddle on his pony, drew the cinch, and in the twinkling of an eye slipped the bit between his pony's teeth and the bridle over his ears; and when he had brought the other horses in and tied them to the wagon, he vaulted into the saddle and was off to the herd to assist the last relief in spinning the stock out for grazing in the main direction of the final destination of the season's drive. There was first acquisitiveness, and then beauty, and, maybe following this, a more delicate sense in the design of the drivers that whenever a steer took a step he should be one step nearer the ultimate destination. [Large Xs were drawn across this paragraph.]

The horses required in these picturesque enterprises formed a herd of seventy-five or a hundred; five or six, and sometimes more, being the quota for each rider. One horse for every man was always under saddle for instant use and these were kept picketed when not on duty. There were supreme occasions in the remarkable life led by these remarkable men. Not every day, not every night did they come; yet they were daily and nightly occurrences. The bow was always drawn with arrow in place, to use a metaphor, and at the first ominous sound of a break by the herd, the twang was sounded by each of a dozen headlong men dashing at desperate speed, heedless of darkness, danger and death. The strain of high tension to meet and overcome all manner of surprises, under which this class of humanity passed many years for small emolument, shows at once how wonderful are the resources and endurance of the human constitution, and how small are the needs of mankind when they are limited to the minimum.

The last of these guards among the horse wranglers, when he saw the light coming in the east, was the archangel of the new day and announced its approach with great freedom of voice, usually with this proclamation: "The bulls are in the pen! Arise and shine! Give God the glory!"

At other times when the enthusiasm of the wrangler had soared to celestial or anti-celestial pitch the form of words and the utterance were such as would have melted the type in which these sentences are printed. We must decline to publish them. It is an immense relief to us that under our constitutional guarantees we cannot be compelled to send them thundering down the ages to our unprotected posterity. Then uprose all the stalwart cowboys. The horses had to be brought in and have their hobbles removed. This was something of a task and took a little time—ten or fifteen minutes. Ropes were run out from the wheels of the wagon, and a man at each end drew them taut and flaring to receive the horses when the wrangler drove them into this improvised corral. Others stood and closed the mouth so none could run out. The rest of the men took off the hobbles. These hobbles were made of strips of rawhide and were three and one-half feet long. They were so fashioned that the parts were flat which wrapped the fetlocks and those coming between the feet were twisted.

The cook was busy meantime, and soon part of the men had eaten their breakfast and gone to relieve those who were attending to the herd. By seven the cattle were strung out in a grand line and moving majestically northward at the regular pace.

The ordinary routine furnishes themes of more easy description than do the irregular events which bring endless anxiety, labor and distress. Slight things threw the cattle into confusion and then a hurly burly scene followed. A horse wearing his saddle lies down to roll; when he rises the stirrups fall, and striking him in the sides give him fright; he springs to the length of his tether, snaps it and dashes into the herd. Up jump the steers in alarm; every one that comes to his feet causes a dozen others to bound to theirs; and now, as if by electric impulse—quick as lightning—the whole herd shaken with terror, plunges in one direction. Terrible is the thunderous roar of trampling and charging squadrons and divisions of this mad animal life. Better to face a cyclone than this awful machine of fright and fury. The alarm has brought every man to his feet. Stopping for nothing, caring for nothing but the one supreme object of overtaking, following, and at the first practicable moment turning and controling the stampede, those quickest to think and act, seizing their saddled horses, and if no bridles be on them, taking a short-hitch on the lower jaw or the nose, with the rope that holds them, are instantly off, followed by the slower starters as fast as they are ready, each going at break-neck speed in the darkness, following the sound of the panic-stricken mass. The flight is so swift that some of the riders lose the herd entirely. Others overtake them; and then these begin that slow, soothing, reassuring wordless song with its long sustained notes peculiar in quality of sound, known to every cowboy on the Texas trail. It is as follows: [blank space]

The results of the chase are various. Sometimes the cattle are brought under control in a short while. The advance drivers head the foremost steers, turning them in their course so as to describe a circle, and presently the whole herd is running round and round; and this is continued till the crowding by the drivers on the outside has so compacted them that they wind up in a close body and come to a standstill. Daylight may find them several miles from where they started. But a single stampede may not be the extent of the night's disasters. After having been once brought to bay a second, a third, a fourth outbreak and race may take place before morning. A cheering circumstance which filled the thoughts of these men with a touch of rejoicing was when the voice of comrades were heard in the distance after the commotion was over. "There's Bill Jones," says one. "Yes; he's alive yet," adds another. And thus was ever present the feeling that the lives of any of these men were a slender possession holden in the issue of frail circumstance.

Another character of the very highest importance upon these cattle driving trips was the cook. He was the keystone of the arch. The hardest worked of all the men. His hours of service were generally from three in the morning till eleven or twelve at night. Good natured, patient, experienced, long suffering, addicted to strong drink, nevertheless feeling his dignity as a man for all that, allowed no liberties to be taken therewith because of the service he performed. His high spirit will brook no insult, and a gun-play is a little thing when his honor has been infringed. This man of the menial position is a factor of such consequence to the business that the caporal has given more time to his selection than to that of any other one connected with the drive. He is the central figure of the group for six months and many hundreds of miles. Throughout the long journey peace and harmony prevail if he so wills; otherwise he may have all the men by the ears and discord in every breast, so potent are his tongue, his restraint, his judgement, his secretiveness, his friendships. The creature comforts were in his charge. The incumbent of that office which caters with handsome satisfaction to the thirst and hunger of men, is a king in the little world where he roams. Likewise with the cook on the Texas trail, there were some who would belittle his importance or throw out challenges to his power. He was usually one who had been with long expeditions — had crossed the plains — was sated with manifold experiences — knew the West by heart — was a book of the mysterious frontier and wilderness life. There were worthless as well as excellent cooks; there were poor trailers and incompetent foremen; when a herd went through with an inefficient outfit the experiences were direful; all the affairs went zig zag and haphazard; instead of growing a little better all the time the cattle got thin; some were lost; many died; and when the end of the journey was reached, all were poor. These were wrecking expeditions signalized by losses from beginning to end. But we mention more pleasurably the prosperous trips, such fascination is there ever in success over failure. This is said of those devoted to their duty, that every fissure was stopped against the entrance of chance or neglect. The most trivial details had attention. Fresh water was not passed on the road without the barrels were refilled; it might be forty miles to the next water; it might be farther. Across those expansive deserts the trails wound without sight of tree or wood for hundreds of miles. But the faithful cook, mindful of everything necessary to good cheer, success and comfort, carried a large hide beneath his wagon, stretched between the two axles, upon which he carried a store of cow chips for his fire when fuel could not be picked up in the neighborhood of the camp. Some of the riders would add an armful occasionally to the little store swinging under the wagon, but this was no part of their duty, only a friendly act of helpfulness. It is well to observe that the cook was the highest paid servitor connected with the drive, the foreman alone excepted. There was another distinction attached to his position, more sobering and less alluring; this was his greater danger from the Indians who infested the plains, and because of his frequent isolation from the rest of the party could easily be cut off, and was always an inviting object of attack.

One of the most highly interesting transactions of his ordinary experience was the putting of his culinary department across the rivers which traversed the trail. Every conceivable mode of passage was used to meet the ever changing circumstances. If trees had grown on the banks of streams it would have been easy to make rafts from them. Such rafts as could be made with parts of the wagon were sometimes put together and small weights taken over at each of several trips. Parts of the luggage like a sack of meal would be carried across on the back of a horse that swam high in the water. The wagon went over piecemeal. Ropes were attached to a wheel or an axle which was dragged from bank to bank by the riders' horses. Utensils were transported one at a time. Numerous trips were required to complete the transfer. When it was possible to get the cook's outfit over in advance this was done; it was of some advantage to have the camp across and established so that hot coffee and steaming viands might greet the drenched and chilled laborers when they had brought everything over. The draft oxen swam over with the herd. It was a slow, tedious, and painstaking task to effect this crossing and all sorts of mishaps were to be expected, and they were borne with that fortitude which, with every possible aid, could alone make these arduous trips to the north attractive and beneficial both to the cowboys and the cowmen. On a certain occasion a herd belonging to John and Billy and Charley and their father Ben Slaughter ascended the Frio river in southwestern Texas to its source where it terminated amid such impassible declivities that, though the cattle could scale the barriers, every particle of the wagon, utensils and provisions had to be raised out of the gorge to the summit of the rocks by ropes drawn up by the men to a height of one hundred and fifty feet.[203]

Having spoken of the "smoking viands" it ought to be explained that the food enjoyed by these men consisted of black coffee without sugar, corn bread baked in a Dutch oven, and fried pork. This menu was occasionally varied with fresh meat when an antelope or a buffalo was killed, or more rarely a fat cow which had been picked up along the way and smuggled into the herd, was shot down to garnish the plain ration of these men with abnormal appetites. In their riotous cheer, when they drew up in a little circle around the coffee kettle, sitting upon the ground or resting on their knees, and loaded their tin plates with Johnny cake and grease and long slices of ancient hog meat, they would merrily sing:

"Corn bread is rough
And corn bread is tough

But let us thank the Lord that we have corn bread enough.

Three pieces for four of us.

Bless the Lord there are no more of us."

The drives of stock cattle to the north began in 1868. The first to send a herd was John Chisholm, whose cattle made the first trail from Fort Worth to Wichita, driving north through the Indian nation into Kansas and this was known as the Chisholm trail. Colonel Myers was one of the first to enter into this business. J. W. Snyder was another. John Iliff was another; later he started a big ranch on the Platte River in Colorado. His widow married Bishop Warren of Denver. James Ellison and John Dewees and two brothers of Dewees. The firm was known as Ellison & Dewees.

(If I want the history of the Slaughters, write to Lum Slaughter, a banker at Dallas, Texas)

Others who sent cattle over the trails were: Blocker Brothers, Butler Brothers, Shanghai Pierce, Captain John W. Lytle, Mr. Fant, Bishop & Hallf, Millet & Mayberry, King & Kennedy, Driscoll Brothers.

Numbers of the men who began life on the Texas trail as cowpunchers saved money and grew into stock owners; many become foremen and advanced to cowmen; many of these have succeeded in life and became prominent and wealthy. Among these are Addison A. Spaugh of Manville, Wyo. on the head waters of Niobrara river; R. G. Head, Trinidad, Colorado; these were very early drivers on the trail; James H. Cook, Agate, Nebr. Mr. Cook does not remember others of whom there were many. Spaugh and Head were associates with Cook in early driving.

The cowboy was a product of the Texas trail. Driving from the south preceded the gathering of the big herds in the northwest. He became the hero of the western wilds and was the leading spirit there till the Indian power was broken and the railroads penetrated his domain and immigrants at large came and occupied the broad country over which he had ranged immense herds, and made his occupation impossible. Driving from the south lasted till about 1882.

The average cowboy was paid fifteen dollars a month and was furnished. [blank]

Buffaloes travel in a straight line. When they were moving and encountered a herd of Texas cattle they invariably bored right through the herd, turning neither to right nor left. It was just the same if but one or a dozen buffaloes were on the move—they walked straight through.

[Donald Brown's Interview]

[Tablet 13]

March 13, 1907.

Donald Brown of Rushville, Neb., says he was a member of the 5th U.S. Cavalry, first under Emory and last under Merritt.[204] He says Bill Cody began his scouting at Fort Hays, Kansas, in 1868, and all he had then was a pair of red leggings, a long Tom and a black horse. Says Cody was the best scout he ever saw; he was a man of judgement. He says some people speak slightingly of him but they are not justified in doing so. When Mr. Brown went to Fort Hays Gen. Custer was serving a year's sentence there following a court martial for ordering some soldiers in Kansas to be shot. He was not in confinement; he had his dogs and employed himself in hunting.[205]

Speaking further of Cody Mr. Brown says that he saw Cody kill Yellow Hand [Yellow Hair] and scalp him. He saw Cody ride up to Col. Merritt and hold up the scalp and heard him say "Here is one for Custer!" This was on the 17th of July after Custer's death. He says Merritt did not seem to appreciate the scene but apparently deprecated it. Brown says he does not think Cody wanted to be chief of scouts; he just wanted to go over the country and have a taste of the old life. He left the Crook command on the Yellowstone.

Brown was with Crook on the starving expedition.[206] Three days before Mills opened the fight at Slim Buttes Brown and another man shot a hawk and a prairie dog and tried to cook them in a tin cup, for the only vessels they had was a tin cup apiece; attempting to do it over a fire made of grass. This camp cooking was a failure; the smoke and soot blackened the water and made a sorry mess of the meat, and they were fain to throw it away. They got provisions at Slim Buttes, & some ponies. The general had rations of horse meat regularly issued finally, and Brown remarks that horse meat would have been delicious enough but the trouble with this was that what they received was from the slaughter of saddle-galled, jaded and feverish animals.

He says he never saw men eat as Crook's famished men did, but though they feasted without restraint, no ill effects followed. The soldiers struggled along, stringing out fully twenty miles on the road, weary, sore, half sick and dejected. It is a marvel that none were killed, although one was killed not far from the column, an acquaintance of his. Crook's army underwent prodigious hardships, and no person would have needed to be told it after having a sight of it when it met the train of supplies sent out to its relief. Ragged, sore, dirty and downcast, after its terrible experiences with rain and cold and hunger and scant clothing and no shelter, their courage was not abated. Brown says they started with expectation of returning to the wagons in eight days and he had with him only the clothes on his back.

Brown says when word was received of Custer's death, Gen. Merritt thoughtfully remarked, "Well he hadn't anybody this time to help him out."

Forbush belonged to the 5th Cavalry & Brown knew him well. He says Forbush would know as well as anyone about Cody's killing of Yellow Hand.

Brown saw Big Bat go down into the little coulee which had a growth of bushes in it, where five Indians were taken out consisting of two women, one child, one man who a little later became a scout for our service, and American Horse — saw Bat go into it, & he thinks Bat brought back a scalp. Says Bat in error in affirming that Gen. Crook helped Bat bring out American Horse; for Crook was away back where Brown himself was. Brown says five Indians were brought out as stated by Bat.

[Winfield S. Ake's Interview]

[Box 19]

1st brief interview of Comrade Ake who is a watchman at south door of the Pension Building. See end.

Winfield Scott Ake of Co M. 1st U.S. Cav. went with his regiment to California, leaving New Orleans, Dec. 28, 1865, by steamer for Aspinwall (now Colon), crossed the Isthmus to Panama by rail, thence went by steamer, the Sacramento, to San Francisco, where they landed Jan. 21, 1866. Col. Blake was the colonel of this Regt., but he did not make the trip with his regt. though he joined it at Fort Vancouver at mouth of Columbia river, in the spring of '66. Col. Brackett at that time was lieutenant colonel of the regiment, and was in command on this transfer to the Pacific coast.[207]

On arrival at San Francisco this regiment was sent out to Presidio barracks remaining there till April 5 when it was divided up, a part being sent to Idaho, a part to Oregon, and a part to Nevada. Co. I was sent to Fort Hall Co. M to Camp Lyon, one-half mile from the Oregon east state [line], but in Idaho, south of the Snake river, about 25 miles S.W. of the Snake river and on Cow Creek. This camp was 25 miles S.W. of Silver City, then called "Silver City Mining Camp." About 2½ miles N.W. of Silver City Mining Camp was another mining camp called "Ruby Mining Camp."

Co. M started out from Camp Lyon, Idaho Territory, on July 13, 1866.

(Above was a short interview I had with Comrade Winfield Scott Ake, one of the watchmen at the south door of the Pension Building. Some weeks afterwards I went to the Pension Building on Sunday and interviewed him more fully on the subject of his service in the West. This furnishes some information about Gen. Crook in 1866. Ake lent me the letter, a copy of which is attached.)[208]

1259770

War Department
The Adjutant General's Office,
Washington.
July 15, 1907.
Mr. W. S. Ake,
231 E Street, N.W.,
Washington, D.C.
Sir:

Referring to your letter of recent date in which you make inquiry as to whether there is any map or record on file in this office of an expedition taken by a detachment of Company M, 1st United States Cavalry, under command of Captain James C. Hunt, which left Camp Lyon, Idaho, on July 13, 1866, and scouted in a northeasterly direction to the Snake River, and in which letter you express a desire to obtain a record of so much of the journey as shows the general direction or approximate distance per day traveled by the party after leaving the Snake River and until reaching the Owyhee River, I have the honor to advise you that no map or report of the expedition mentioned has been found on file in this Department.[209]

There is, however, a record of events of the expedition which affords the following information bearing upon your request:

"x x x July 13th the Company left for Sinkers Creek in compliance with S.O. No. 39, Hdqrs Dist. of Boise on an expedition a/Indians, leaving a detachment of the Co. as garrison for Camp Lyon, I.T., marched 22 miles to Reynolds Creek and encamped; July 14th marched 15 miles and encamped near Snake River Ferry; 15th marched 20 miles and arrived at Sinkers Creek and encamped there, awaiting orders from District Commander, Maj. Marshall, 14th U.S. Inf., who arrived July 20th marched to Chatline Creek, distance 10 miles; 21st marched 31 miles and arrived at the Forks of the Bruneau and encamped and send [sent] Packtrain to the depot at Boise for Subsistence Stores for the Command. Aug. 5th broke Camp and marched up the River 10 miles; 6th left the Bruneau River and marched in southwest direction 30 miles and encamped on Cabbage Creek. 7th march[ed] 7 miles up the Creek and encamped; 8th marched 5 miles towards Gooseneck Mountain and encamped; 9th marched 12 miles passed through a cañon and encamped; 10th marched into Duck Valley and encamped near a small creek and encamped; 11th marche[d] 15 miles and arrived at the Middle Fork of the Owyhee River and encamped there 12th, 13th and 14th. x x x"

Very respectfully,

(Signed) E. H. Ladd

Adjutant General

2d Interview.

Idaho, California and Oregon, service there, 1866. Gen. Crook. Interview of Ake.

Sunday, Nov. 5, 1916. Winfield Scott Ake says: Says that when his Reg't., 1st U.S. Cavalry (he belonged to Troop—then Company-M, commanded by Capt. James C. Hunt, and 1st Lieut. Moses Harris—when his reg't. landed at San Francisco it was divided up, part being [sent] to Oregon, Idaho, Nevada, and some into southern California.[210] Head Qrs. of the Regt. was at Fort Vancouver, at mouth of Columbia River. L Company was stationed at Camp McDermitt; Co. I was stationed at Fort Hall, Idaho, Company M at Camp Lyon on a creek called Cow Creek which empties into Jordan Creek which is a tributary of Owyhee.

Co. M left Camp Lyon on 13th day July, 1866. On August 12, '66 his Co. did its first fighting at headwaters of south fork of Owyhee river. In the meantime this command marched to the Big Tuley Swamp in Oregon where on Sept. 21, 1866, they fought about 175 Indians (Paiutes?); then a week or two later they had another fight with the enemy & killed seven of them without loss to themselves. Immediately after the battle of Sept. 21 the company started to return to Camp Lyon going by way of Camp C. F. Smith on White Horse Creek; then after the little fight when they killed seven, they encountered at Stein's Mountain, Idaho, January 21, 1867, a large body of the enemy (82) and killed 54 of them and captured 27 squaws and pappooses, only a few escaping. The loss sustained by Co. M was 1 killed and 5 wounded.

(The Big Tuley swamp had 100,000 acres; these tuleys were what I have known as flags.)

He says the country was infested by what frontiersmen said were 20,000

Indians, Paiutes about 20,000; the Shoshones, the Diggers, and the Snakes. This was northwest of Pocatello. There was another tribe called Warm Springs Indians, living on the Warm Springs; these were friendly to the whites.

When Co. M got back to Camp Lyon the men cut a lot of wood for the camp fires, & hauled it in, & before this was finished an order came to Capt. Hunt to detail a Sergeant, Corporal, 2 Packers and 12 men with rules [mules] to cross the Silver and Ruby range of mountains over to Snake river & follow down on left hand side, & Sergt. Ake was sent out with this detachment and went across the mountains as aforesaid & down left side Snake river, & camped at Little Farewell Bend, then went farther down till they passed Big Farewell Bend, then kept on till they came to mouth of the Malheur, which empties into the Snake, and there they crossed over the Malheur, continuing on left side of the Snake, and then turned up the Malheur & struck into (he thinks) the Malheur Mountains; just at the foot of this mountain they ran into great deposits of isinglass; after just passing this isinglass they camped for the night; next morning moved marching up a deep canyon, etc. not material for my use.

Gen. Crook was to rejoin Co. M at Big Tuley Swamp, but he never returned.

[Josephus Bingaman's Statement]

[Box 19]

~~Narrative by Josephus Bingaman:~~

I was a soldier in the Civil War prior to being in the Service as hereinafter described.

In the Indian campaign herein described I was in Company F, 19th Kansas Cavalry, which was a new regiment organized by Governor Crawford of Kansas, who resigned as governor and became the colonel of our regiment, Col. Moore, of Lawrence, Kansas, being our Lieut. Col. and upon the resignation of Col. Crawford at Ft. Elliott, became our colonel, Col. Crawford returning home.[211]

Under command of Col. Crawford we marched from Topeka, Kansas to Camp Beecher, now Wichita, Kansas, and on the fourteenth day of November, 1868, we left Camp Beecher, which is now Wichita, Kansas, and started out on what was known as the Chisholm trail, altho there was no trail to be seen. Men who followed us three or four days after we had marched over the trail could not find it, as the ground was so hard. We marched in a Southwest direction, had fair weather, and lived on buffalo meat and our horses grazed on buffalo grass. No incident of note happened until we were on Medicine Lodge River.

On Medicine Lodge River we had a stampede amongst our horses and lost two hundred twenty-five head of horses, which left that many men and a few whose horses had died afoot. Then we kept on Southwest until we were not far from Cimarron, on a stream which we called Hackberry Creek, now known as Soldiers Creek, where we had an exceedingly heavy fall of snow, which detained us for several days—do not know just how many days. Our horses were dying from starvation, and our teams were also dying, which left us in a precarious situation. Our guide, Jack Stillwell, was not experienced and Charles Kadero pretended to be a good scout and to know the country, but he led us a half day's march into the Antelope Hills where we could not get out without retracing our steps for a half day. Here we left most of our wagons and most of our horses were frozen to death.

There were ten companies, supposed to be one thousand men. Then we gathered together the remnant of the best horses and marched on horseback, leaving all the wagons and what mules there were and the dismounted men in that camp at that time. The first night we camped in a gulch in very freezing weather—sixteen below zero—with nothing to eat but buffalo meat. We were eighteen days with nothing but buffalo meat, without salt. We gathered the remnant of our regiment together and marched to Camp Supply through deep snow—about thirty inches of snow fell on us. We sent Captain Plyly [Pliley], with thirty men, ahead to hunt for Camp Supply, where we were to meet Gen. Custer, with the 7th Regulars.[212] Meanwhile Gen. Custer had been at Camp Supply several days. Going on further the scouts found the Indians, Black Kettle's Band, located on Washita River, something like sixty miles South of old Camp Supply.

Gen. Custer made a forced march, reaching the Indian Camp about two o'clock in the morning, capturing and destroying Black Kettle's band of Indians; killing about 250; capturing 53 prisoners, and killing about 600 Indian ponies. Gen. Custer afterwards destroyed this band of Indians, and at day light had them surrounded, but other Indians 3,000 or 4,000 came up and they began to rally and come in on them and he had to retreat, losing about 23 men and Maj. Elliott and Mrs. Blinn and her children were prisoners.[213] Mrs. Blinn was shot in the forehead and the children's heads were mashed against a tree. The soldiers had thrown luggage down and the Indians destroyed it and Custer's greyhounds lay on top of the luggage shot; all of which was seen by the narrator personally.

We then came to Camp Supply and after a couple or three days we all started

South again. Gen. Custer had the Seventh U.S. Regulars, his Regiment, and the Nineteenth Kansas after we met him at Camp Supply. We met him at Camp Supply about two days after the battle of Washita, when he came back to Camp Supply, at which time we consolidated and made the brigade.

Gen. Custer returned to Camp Supply after the battle of Washita and about two days after his return the Nineteenth Kansas joined him at Camp Supply and this was my first connection with Custer's immediate command. We then marched back over the same old battle ground, marching on South over about the same trail that he followed when he went out to the battle of Washita. When we marched back over that ground we picked up Mrs. Blinn, her son, and about nineteen men who had been killed, and saw the dead ponies, about six hundred. I saw the carcasses lying there. We then marched on South by way of old Ft. Cobb, stopping there about a week, going on from there to the foothills of the Wichita Mountains, on Medicine Bluff Creek, where the Nineteenth Kansas encamped, the 7th Cavalry going on into the edge of Texas, to the mouth of Katcha Creek, where Ft. Elliott was built during the winter. On the second day of March the remnant of the 19th Kansas, about four hundred, with two hundred Regulars, started South of West across Texas, by way of the Staked Plains, where we struck the trail of the Dog soldiers, a band of Cheyennes, who had Mrs. Morgan and Miss White prisoners, they having been captured the previous August on the Republican River in Northern Kansas.[214] Following the trail thru Texas, in or near New Mexico (we did not know whether we were in New Mexico or not), we took a circuit of nine days' travel, returning within three miles of where we had camped, marching almost day and night, living on horse meat — without salt. The 19th Kansas men were dismounted. The 7th Regulars started with two hundred horses. After several days' march lack of rations caused us to start on the back trail across the country to get on to the Washita River, where we expected to get supplies. On the afternoon of the first day, about four o'clock in the afternoon we ran on to the band of Indians that we were seeking. Gen. Custer captured eleven Indian chiefs. Turning three loose he told them to bring in Mrs. Morgan and Miss White by sundown the next day or he would hang the other eight chiefs.[215] Just when we were ready to hang the chiefs we saw an Indian ride up onto a hill about a half-mile from camp. He went back and pretty soon three of them came back. Then four or five came back in sight. We got the Indian Chiefs in a wagon and got log chains on a tree ready to hang the eight chiefs when we heard the Indians yell and looked over to where the Indians had appeared and we saw two Indians coming horseback with the prisoners behind them. They rode a short distance over the hill and then pulled the women off from behind them and pointed to camp and started them towards us. Mrs. Morgan's brother and a Mexican interpreter, Romeo, crossed a small stream and went and met them.[216] They came to the bank of the stream and we had thrown some poles in and the two men helped the two women to walk in and Col. Moore reached out his hand and brought them safe on the side that we were on. Col. Moore said to the oldest lady "This is Mrs. Morgan, is it?" She said "Yes," and he said to the other one, "This is Miss White, is it?" Mrs. Morgan asked about her husband, but Miss White did not ask about any of her folks; she knew they were all murdered. Col. Moore took off his overcoat and placed it around the shoulders of Mrs. Morgan and I took off my overcoat and placed it on Miss White. The ladies were dressed in what appeared to be one hundred pound flour sacks, with holes for their heads and holes for their arms and an old piece of blanket thrown around their shoulders, with rawhide leggins and rawhide moccasins, and had been terrible outraged and mistreated; this being in the month of March. We tied the Indian chiefs on their horses and put a guard over them and started East for Custer's battle ground on the Washita. After three days the Indians' horses all gave out and all the prisoners were handcuffed and put in wagons.

We did not take any prisoners except chiefs. We surrounded the Indians and went in and picked out chiefs and let the balance go.

We put the Indians in wagons and were several days marching down the Washita, living on horse and mule meat. We started out with about sixty or seventy wagons and came back with about twenty wagons to the supply post and about twenty head of loose stock and the Regulars of the two hundred horses had about twenty-five head left; the balance of the Regulars and Volunteers were dismounted.

Then we started for Camp Supply from Custer's battle ground on the Washita. From Camp Supply, in Oklahoma, we went to Ft. Dodge; then from there to Ft. Hays, Kansas, where we arrived the sixth day of April, 1869; making 632 miles travelled in the thirty-four days marching from Ft. Elliott. Here we were mustered out of the Service on the fourteenth day of April, having enlisted in the United States Army for a period of six months, the Regiment having been raised, clothed, and fed by the United States.

I captured Santanta—capturing him not far from old Ft. Cobb, when we were going out, and the way it happened was that Custer's bodyguard recognized him and Custer told him to arrest him, and Santanta understood what he said, being able to understand English, and he started out to run as hard as he could and I had gone down to the river and was coming back and met him coming and this bodyguard called to me to halt the Indian, and I told him to halt, and he said "How," and rode ahead, and I had a pretty good horse and I rode up beside him and pushed my carbine into his head and captured him.[217] I was a flanker then. I rode as flanker and scout all the way from Camp Supply. Being a pretty good shot I had killed buffalo for the regiment from Ft. Beecher, and at Camp Supply was detailed as a flanker and scout, being on the left flank of the Regiment, which was the left flank of the train. I most always rode ahead.

In 1868 the Comanches made a treaty with the government. Just as soon as we got to them the Cheyennes came in and pretended that they were going to make a treaty, but the next thing we knew they were gone again. That was near Ft. Elliott.[218]

141 civilians were killed during 1867 and 1868, fourteen women were outraged, and twenty-four children were frozen to death, and one woman was outraged by thirteen Indians, and her head split open and the tomahawk left sticking in her head. One woman was captured, with a child a week old. They carried them away on a horse and the child cried. They killed the child and then threw the woman off the horse and left her. All this was in the papers at that time, and I heard about the woman and child from a neighbor. Name was Stackhouse.

Col. Moore wrote a pamphlet describing the campaign, which is in the family of Leffingwells, 1159 Grand Avenue, Grand Junction.

Saw a letter this summer from Miss White, Enoch Culloch, Ft. Dodge (Kansas) (Chief Bugler) has her address. She was thanking him and all of us for part we took in getting her from the Indians.

[George A. Leclere's Interview]

[Box 19]

Interview of Rev. George A. Leclere of Grand Junction, Colo., at his home, December 28, 1909.

He says he was a member of Co. B, 6th Iowa Cavalry, Dewitt C. Cram, Captain and afterwards Major.

I have heard his story in brief outline of the campaigns of 1863 and 1864, and he confirms the accounts I have read in Gue's Iowa, Mrs. Kelly's Captivity and the Minnesota Hist. Soc. Coll. He states that the battle of Whitestone Hill was near, as he understands, the present town of Ellendale.[219]

He says that the dead soldiers at Whitestone Hill were buried in a grave at night, no lights being used, the horses being removed from the picket rope, and the grave made where they stood, and then the horses hitched again to the rope and over the grave so as to obliterate all signs of it. He says the battle of Whitestone Hill was in 1863.

At the battle of Whitestone Hill the formation of the line of battle was as follows:

On the right were the Iowa soldiers, the 6th Iowa Cav., every company of the Regt. (not 11 companies as Lieut. Kingsbury has stated). On the left were the Nebraska and Dakota companies (See Gue's Hist. of Iowa); these were all the troops.[220] Sully was at the head of the ravine and the Indians were in the ravine and his troops were nearly surrounding them; Sully was at the head of the ravine with artillery and could have given the Ind. camp a raking fire, but Mr. Leclere says his orders were to spare the natives as much as he could and not slaughter them inhumanely. He parleyed with them trying to get them to surrender—parleyed rather too long; finally they, having been dancing the war dance while the parleying was going on, at length divided, one party directing its fire into the soldiers on the hills on one side and the other party aiming at the soldiers on the other side, and they delivered a volley and started the action. The horses were fresh to war and this threw them into fright and a stampede ensued and considerable disorder was the result among men and horses. This was about dark. Sully at length got order restored, and the Indians disappeared. Indians were not in sight next morning. He says that the little Indian that was guide through the Bad Lands was wounded in the progress through, so he could not ride a horse & he had to be carried forward in an ambulance while acting as guide. The Little Missouri runs through the Bad Lands. When the command struck the river it moved up the river in the bed thereof, for quite a little way, and when they came to the place where the valley widened out sufficiently they camped for the night. When they moved next morning fighting began and was kept up continuously for two days when they reached the other side of the Bad Lands.

Capt. Fisk's train started from some place in Minn. but did not reach Fort Rice on account of delays, so Sully went off without waiting for their arrival; they picked up some soldiers around Fort Rice and went on their way towards the gold mines in Idaho. Their escort was not sufficient and the Indians surrounded them. They managed to send two messengers back to Fort Rice for help. Mr. L. was with the detachment sent by Sully to Fisk's relief. This relief party was made up of a detail of the 6th Iowa Cavalry, some were volunteers for the trip, he being one. He says he was present when Mrs. Kelly was brought in.

Mr. L. says that the 6th Iowa and the other troops had Fort Rice nearly built when the 30th Wisconsin arrived and finished and garrisoned it.

These Indians which had surrounded Fisk's train were the party with which Mrs. Kelly was at the time she was secretly trying to get a note to the whites. Some Indians came to Fort Sully to see the General & get permission to camp near the fort & trade with the soldiers, etc. Read her own account. He says when Mrs. Kelly arrived at the Fort Capt. Logan of the 6th Iowa Cav. received Mrs. Kelly into his arms. She said as she slipped off the horse, into his arms, she asked in deeply earnest tones, "Am I indeed safe?" and immediately fainted away. She afterwards explained that she was in trepedation of fear, not knowing but the officers were not on the alert, & that the Indians would be permitted to enter the Fort and a terrible massacre ensue, as she knew their plans.

It was at Killdeer Mountain where Brackett with his battalion filed in front of the 6th Iowa and made the charge on the Inds. that the 6th was expecting to make on the right. At this battle the Indians nearly succeeded in cutting off the rear guard by a circuit, but Sully trained a cannon on them & their purpose was defeated.[221]

Gen. Cook who was superceded by Gen. Sully, was an inefficient, spiritless officer, who, having made no preparations for the expedition when he was aware of the projected operations, was removed because of his weakness. Sully was an energetic and brave man, inspiring his troops with the same enterprise and confidence which were his own characteristic traits. His love of justice and his frankness in intercourse led him to be direct with all men and partial to none. The humblest man in his ranks could get his ear equally with an officer, according to the weight of the matter to be considered. Mr. Leclere says Wilson, the commander of his regiment, was another of the effeminate class; that if it had not been for Wilson's inefficiency at Whitestone Hill there need not have been so many soldiers injured nor the stampede. Proctor who was subordinate to Wilson, thought Wilson had withdrawn (as he was not in sight) and as the men were on their mounts conspicuously exposed, and nothing being done to put them in readiness for action, he gave the order to prepare to fight on foot. This brought up Wilson who remarked that he was in command of the regiment, and then he ordered the men to remount; and they were in saddle when the Indians began firing. The command was thrown into confusion, causing more fatalities than would have taken place had proper disposition of the troopers been made.

Wilson hung on to his official position until the next spring, when the 1864 campaign was forecasted, when he resigned and Proctor was promoted to the command of the regiment and proved himself an able officer.

[Mr. and Mrs. John Farnham's Interview]

Ricker wrote a reminder in Tablet 9 to "See John Farnham for Cheyenne outbreak and Arkansas John. [Gus] Craven says he can hold me a week."

Ricker made note of comments, corrections, and disagreements raised by John Farnham in several other interviews. The Farnham interview of only two sentences suggests there are missing tablets.

[Tablet 12]

Mrs. John Farnham says that Red Cloud was taken and stripped of his horses on East Ash Creek, Dawes County, Neb. This was when Gen. Crook deposed him.

John Farnham says these horses were herded out by sergeants and quietly sold at so much per head and taken away in lots by buyers.

Farnham mentioned how goods were brought to Red Cloud and thrown out squanderingly.

[Charles J. Brown's Interview]

Ricker was working for the Bureau of Indian Affairs in Washington, D.C., when he recorded his last interview. Ricker left Washington in July 1919, two months after his talk with Charles Brown.

[Box 19]

Mr. Charles J. Brown, expert accountant, Room #315, Evans Building, Washington, D. C., who was interviewed by E. S. Ricker, on the evening of May 22nd, 1919, in relation to the Sisseton and Wahpeton and the Medewakanton and Wapecootah Indians, said:

The Medewakanton and Wapecootah and the Sisseton and Wahpetons were known originally in the early history of this country as the Sioux of the Mississippi. As time went by they were divided by upper and lower Sioux of the Mississippi. The upper Sioux being the Sissetons and Wahpetons and the lower, the Medewakantons and the Wapecootahs.

This branch of Indians known as the Medewakantons were known for a great many years as the Sante-Sioux. The Medewakantons and Wapecootahs which grew out of the band of Medewakantons instituted a tribe and terminated prior the 19th Century of Santees.

In the Treaty of 1830, the Otoes of Missouri, the Sissetons and Wahpetons and the Medewakantons were to be constituted in that Treaty, but the Medewakantons and Wapecootahs did not sign any of the articles of the Treaty. In 1836 they made a treaty with the United States in which, among other provisions, they were to release all title they had on land east of the Missouri River and south of the Northern part of Iowa, and in consideration of that they were given an annuity bond of $300,000 which was placed in the Treasury to draw 5% interest.

The Treaty had other provisions also, for Educational and Farming purposes, which carried a period of 10 years' appropriation. In 1851 they made a Treaty with the United States in which they sold the interest that they had in their territory in Minnesota and Dakota.

They sold their property to the Government for $1,410,000 and were to give $210,000 in cash to be divided among the Chiefs and Scribes and heads. The balance was to be put in the Government Treasury and at 5% interest.

The stipulations in the Treaty required the Government to pay them fifty cash payments. One each year of $58,000. The fifty payments were to extinguish the entire indebtedness the Government owed.

They agreed to pay them $58,000 a year for fifty years. At first they agreed to pay 5% interest on the month. Further in the Treaty it stipulated $50,000 a year for fifty years, which was to extinguish both the principle and the interest.

An amendment to that Treaty was made in 1858, in which they agreed to pay the Indians so much more for some land that the Indian claimed he never released in the original Treaty. I think that was $96,000 which was added to the original amount of the fund in the Treasury, 5% interest to be paid thereon.

I know the real causes of the outbreak in 1862, but I don't know whether I am justified in disclosing these things, or not!

When the annuity payment to be made in 1862 was sent to the Indian head for distribution among the Indians, said annuity to be paid in gold, the Indian head went to C —. and exchanged the gold for greenbacks at a large discount, and returned to the agency to make payment on the annuity in greenbacks. The Indians refused the [to] accept the greenback payment and insisted upon the payment in gold as a Treaty stipulation.

The agent sought to obtain gold for the greenbacks again to comply with Treaty requirements and satisfy the Indians, but being unable to get that large amount of gold in the commercial channels and unable to get it from the Sub-Treasury, for the reason that the Government was not exchanging gold for greenbacks he was unable to comply with the Treaty requirements. The Indians in the delay of the distribution of their annuities to them, became restless and began the outbreak. (Note: Look up the difference in values of the two kinds of currency.)

The real conditions concerning the outbreak of this Indian Massacre has never been written correctly. The general acceptance has been that the Medewakantons and Wapecootahs were largely responsible and the principle actors in this sad drama.

It is now known by careful investigation that the Sissetons and Wahpetons, which might be termed the Yankee Indians, were the real instigator and prime factor back of this sad page in the History of the Sioux of the Mississippi. They have been able all these years to place the blame on the Medewakantons and Wapecootahs and escape the responsibility themselves.

The Treaty of 1826, 30, 36 and 51, have all been carried out. The amounts that have been charged to them against this Massacre for damages, stipulates for the payment of obligations and for Sundry appropriations. As far as I am able to see, these appropriations have been carried out from the reports, that is, all have been paid. As to the charges under this act, against their right to the annuity of the Treaty of 1836–51, I have not yet determined

After the soldiers were called out, and the Indian saw that it was going to be a losing fight on his part, he surrendered. They had already captured about 250, and the rest of the Medewahkantons and Wapecootahs were scattered.

After a period of some six or seven years running in with the Sante-Sioux in Arizona, they have become what is known as a "Society Tribe," who spend a good deal of their time visiting. Since this it has been practically impossible to keep tract [track] of them.

Like Oliver Twist, the Wahpecootahs put it over on the Army Officers and then hollered, "There's the man who did it!"

Further investigation along this line shows that the Medewakantons were friends of the white man, and you can readily see it would not be policy in the Government officials to make a statement of this sort, which would reflect on their own action.

(May 22, 1919. Mr. Brown expects to be engaged a year or a year and a half finishing his labors upon this case of claims by the Indians against the Government, when he will write out the remainder of the story, dress it all up, and send the whole to me. I gave him a carbon copy of this statement.)[222]

Appendix A

*The number following each fort is the page number from Francis
Paul Prucha,* A Guide to the Military Posts of the United States
(Madison: State Historical Society of Wisconsin, 1964).

Fort Abraham Lincoln, 55. Established June 14, 1872; abandoned November 19, 1891.
Across the Missouri River from Bismarck, North Dakota.

Fort Apache, 56. Established 1870; abandoned, no date. Northeastern Arizona. Originally Camp Ord.

Fort Assiniboine, 57. Established 1879; abandoned, no date. Near Havre, Montana.

Fort Benton, 61. Established October 17, 1869; abandoned May 31, 1881. Left bank of
Missouri River, near present Fort Benton, Montana.

Fort Bridger, 62. Established from a trading post in the summer of 1858; abandoned
November 6, 1890. Left bank of Black's Fork of Green River, just south of Fort
Bridger, Wyoming.

Fort Buford, 63. Established June 13, 1866; abandoned 1895. Left bank of Missouri
River, above mouth of Yellowstone River.

Fort C. F. Smith, 64. Established August 12, 1866; abandoned July 29, 1868. Right bank
of Big Horn River, about thirty-five miles south of Hardin, Montana.

Fort Casper, 65. Established 1864; abandoned October 19, 1867. Right bank of North
Platte River, near Casper, Wyoming.

Fort Cobb, 66. Established 1859; abandoned 1869. At present town of Fort Cobb, Oklahoma.

Fort Connor, see Fort Reno.

Fort Craig, 68. Established March 31, 1854; abandoned September 1884. Right bank
of Rio Grande River, south of Socorro, New Mexico.

Fort Custer, 69. Established July 4, 1877; abandoned, no date. Right bank of Big Horn
River, two miles north of Hardin, Montana.

Fort D. A. Russell, 70. Established July 21, 1867, at Cheyenne, Wyoming.

Fort Dodge, 72. Established 1864 as military camp, formally established September 9,

1865; abandoned October 2, 1882. Left bank of Arkansas River, near Dodge City, Kansas.

Fort Douglas, 72. Established October 26, 1862; abandoned, no date. Three miles east of Salt Lake City, Utah.

Fort Elliott, 73. Established June 5, 1875; abandoned October 20, 1890. Sweetwater Creek, north of Wheeler in Texas panhandle.

Fort Ellis, 73. Established August 27, 1867; abandoned August 31, 1886. Left bank of East Gallatin River, east of Bozeman, Montana.

Fort Fetterman, 74. Established July 19, 1867; abandoned May 20, 1882. Right bank of North Platte River, five miles northwest of Douglas, Wyoming.

Fort George, a trading post occupied from 1843 to about 1847. Right bank of Missouri River, above present Lower Brule, South Dakota.

Fort Grant, 76. Established 1865, near present Bonita, Arizona.

Fort Hall, 77. Established May 27, 1870; abandoned May 1, 1883. Present Fort Hall, Idaho, north of Pocatello.

Fort Halleck, 77. Established July 20, 1862; abandoned July 4, 1866. Near Elk Mountain, Wyoming.

Fort Harker, 78. Established in August 1864 as Fort Ellsworth, then Fort Harker November 17, 1866; abandoned April 2, 1873. Left bank of Smoky Hill River, near Kanopolis, Kansas.

Fort Hays, 78. Established October 18, 1865 as Fort Fletcher until name changed November 17, 1866; abandoned November 8, 1889. Right bank of Big Creek, opposite Hays, Kansas.

Fort John. See Fort Laramie.

Fort Kearny, 82. Established 1848 as Fort Childs, designated Fort Kearny January 31, 1849; abandoned May 17, 1871. Right bank of Platte River, southeast of Kearney, Nebraska.

Fort Keogh, 82. Established August 28, 1876; abandoned, no date. Right bank of Yellowstone River at Miles City, Montana.

Fort Laramie, 84. Established 1834 as trading post, purchased by the army on June 26, 1849; abandoned except for small guard, March 2, 1890. Near Torrington, Wyoming.

Fort Larned, 84–85. Established October 22, 1859; abandoned October 28, 1878. Right bank of Pawnee Fork, five miles west of Larned, Kansas.

Fort Leavenworth, 85. Established May 8, 1827. Nine miles northwest of Leavenworth, Kansas.

Fort Lincoln. See Fort Abraham Lincoln.

Fort Lyon, 87. Established June 27, 1865; abandoned April 27, 1869. About sixty-five miles due south of Nampa, Idaho, right bank of north fork of Jordan Creek.

Fort Lyon, 86. Established August 29, 1860; abandoned June 1867. Ten miles west of Lamar, Colorado, north side of Arkansas River.

Fort Marcy, 91. Established August 18, 1846; abandoned September 15, 1894. Located in Santa Fe, New Mexico.

Fort McKinney, 88. Established as Cantonment Reno October 12, 1876; moved July 18, 1878. Right bank of Powder River, three miles above Fort Reno or forty miles north of Midwest, Wyoming. Moved to right bank of Clear Creek near Buffalo, Wyoming. Abandoned November 7, 1894.

Fort Meade, 91. Established August 28, 1878. Right bank of Bear Butte Creek, near Sturgis, South Dakota.

Fort Mitchell, 92. Established 1864; abandoned 1867. Right bank of North Platte River, west of Gering, Nebraska.

Fort Niobrara, 95. Established April 22, 1880. Right bank of Niobrara River, east of Valentine, Nebraska.

Fort Phil Kearny, 97. Established July 13, 1866; abandoned July 31, 1868. Right bank of Piney Fork of Powder River, twelve miles northwest of Buffalo, Wyoming.

Fort Pierre, 97. Established from a trading post July 7, 1855; abandoned May 16, 1857. Right bank of Missouri River, northwest of Pierre, South Dakota.

Fort Randall, 100. Established June 26, 1856; abandoned December 6, 1892. Right bank of Missouri River, opposite Pickstown, South Dakota.

Fort Rice, 101-2. Established July 7, 1864; abandoned November 25, 1878. Right bank of Missouri River, about eight miles north of mouth of Cannonball River.

Fort Riley, 102. Established May 17, 1853. Ten miles northeast of Junction City, Kansas.

Fort Robinson, 102. Established March 8, 1874; abandoned 1948. Three miles west of Crawford, Nebraska.

Fort Santa Fe. See Fort Marcy.

Fort Scott, 106. Established May 30, 1842; abandoned April 1873. In Fort Scott, Kansas.

Camp Sheridan. Established March 1874; abandoned 1881. On Beaver Creek, north of Hays Springs, Nebraska In the summer of 1875 moved upstream half a mile.

Fort Sidney, 107. Established December 13, 1867; abandoned June 1, 1894. In Sidney, Nebraska.

Fort Sill, 107-8. Established March 4, 1869. Right bank of Cache Creek, opposite Medicine Park, Oklahoma.

Fort Steele or Fort Fred Steele, 75. Established June 15, 1868; abandoned November 3, 1886. Right bank of North Platte River, due east of Rawlins, Wyoming.

Fort Stevenson, 109. Established June 22, 1867; abandoned August 13, 1883. Left bank of Missouri River, southwest of Garrison, North Dakota.

Fort Sully, 110. Established September 1863; abandoned November 30, 1894. Left bank of Missouri River, ten miles below Pierre, South Dakota.

Fort Thompson, 112. Established September 1864; abandoned June 1867. Present Fort Thompson, South Dakota.

Fort Totten, 112. Established July 17, 1867; abandoned November 18, 1890. South shore of Devil's Lake, North Dakota.

Fort Union, 113. Former trading post, used by army, 1864-65. Left bank of Missouri River, just above mouth of Yellowstone.

Fort Union, 113. Established July 26, 1851; abandoned May 15, 1891. Five miles north of Watrous, New Mexico.

Fort Vancouver, 113. Established May 15, 1849; abandoned, no date. North bank of Columbia River, eight miles north of Portland, Oregon.

Fort Wallace, 114. Established October 26, 1865; abandoned May 31, 1882. Left bank of Smoky Hill River at Wallace, Kansas.

Fort Washakie, 115. Established June 28, 1869 at Lander, Wyoming; moved June 1871 to present Fort Washakie area.

Fort William, trading post founded in 1833. Missouri River opposite mouth of Yellowstone River.

Fort Yates, 118. Established December 23, 1874. Right bank of Missouri River at Fort Yates, North Dakota.

Fort Zarah, 118. Established September 1864; abandoned December 4, 1869. Left bank of Walnut Creek, in Kansas, two miles from Arkansas River.

Notes

1. Wounded Knee

1. Ricker made the following comments about battles and massacres in Tablet 22:

> The Indians sneer at the whiteman's conventional reference to the Custer massacre and the battle of Wounded Knee. They ridicule the lack of impartiality of the white's in speaking of the two events — when the whites got the worst of it was a *massacre;* when the Indians got the worst of it it was a *battle.* The Indians understand that on the Little Big Horn they were defending themselves — their village — their property — their lives — their women and children. They understand that at W.K. they were attacked, wantonly, cruelly, brutally, and that what little fighting they did was in self-defense.
>
> The affair at W.K. was a drunken slaughter — of white soldiers and innocent Indians — for which white men were responsible — solely responsible. A little reason and patience & forebearance would have avoided the murderous clash.

2. This was probably Col. James Biddle, who was the commanding officer at Fort Robinson in the mid-1890s. Thomas R. Buecker, *Fort Robinson and the American West: 1874–1899* (Lincoln: Nebraska State Historical Society, 1999), 200.

3. Charles F. Humphrey enlisted in the army during the Civil War. In 1890 he was a captain in the quartermaster corps and by 1903 he had risen to the rank of brigadier general. Francis B. Heitman, *Historical Register and Dictionary of the United States Army* (Washington DC: GPO, 1903), 554.

Lt. Charles W. Taylor, Ninth Cavalry, led the Oglala and Cheyenne scouts. This unit went with Colonel Forsyth and the rest of the Seventh Cavalry to reinforce Major Whitside on Wounded Knee Creek. Robert M. Utley, *The Last Days of the Sioux Nation* (New Haven: Yale University Press, 1963), 197.

Lt. Guy H. Preston entered the military academy in 1884. He was a second lieutenant in the Ninth Cavalry during the Ghost Dance era. Heitman, *Historical Register,* 806.

4. Baptiste "Little Bat" Garnier was born in 1854, the son of a white man and a Lakota woman. He served as a scout for the army on several occasions. In about 1880 he moved to the Fort Robinson vicinity. Little Bat was murdered in Crawford in

1900. E. A. Brininstool, *Fighting Indian Warriors* (Harrisburg PA: Stackpole Co., 1953), 271–79.

Joseph Horn Cloud told Ricker (Tablet 12), "Big Foot was the headman of the Minneconjou Sioux." Big Foot was also called Spotted Elk. His love of traditional ways led him and his many followers to embrace the Ghost Dance. Utley, *The Last Days of the Sioux Nation*, 173.

5. McFarland drew two other maps. One was titled, "Pine Ridge Agency Peter Mc-Farland's map of operations." It appears to be an attempt to show troop concentrations around the reservation prior to the Wounded Knee massacre, but it is crude and largely unintelligible. It has not been reproduced. Another equally crude map of the agency shows the approximate locations of buildings including the "Episcopal Mission where the Indian wounded were placed." Box 28, MS8, Eli S. Ricker Collection, Nebraska State Historical Society, Lincoln.

6. A Hotchkiss gun was a mobile, breech-loading cannon that fired an explosive shell 3.2 inches in diameter. Four of these light cannons were brought to Wounded Knee. Richard E. Jensen, R. Eli Paul, and John E. Carter, *Eyewitness at Wounded Knee* (Lincoln: University of Nebraska Press, 1991), 128.

7. James W. Forsyth entered the military academy in 1851. He served in the Union army in the Civil War. In 1886 Colonel Forsyth took command of the Seventh Cavalry. He retired in 1897 with the rank of major general. Heitman, *Historical Register*, 430.

Maj. Samuel M. Whitside, Seventh Cavalry, was on patrol in search of Big Foot. Four troops of the Seventh Cavalry and a battery of the First Artillery were under his command when he located the Miniconjou band and brought them to a camp on Wounded Knee Creek. Utley, *The Last Days of the Sioux Nation*, 193. Whitside joined the army in 1851, and retired a brigadier general in 1902. Heitman, *Historical Register*, 1031. Ricker consistently misspelled both officers' names.

8. The Lakotas, and most other tribes who adopted the new religion, wore a special Ghost Dance costume. A Pine Ridge Agency employee, Mrs. Z. A. Parker, described the garments:

> They were of white cotton cloth. The women's dress was . . . a loose robe with wide, flowing sleeves, painted blue in the neck, with moon, stars, birds, etc., interspersed with real feathers, painted on the waist and sleeves. . . . The ghost shirt for the men was made of the same material . . . around the neck was painted blue, and the whole garment fantastically sprinkled with figures of birds, bows and arrows, sun, moon, and stars and everything they saw in nature. Down the outside of the sleeve were rows of feathers tied by the quill ends and left to fly in the breeze.

Mrs. Parker accurately described the shirts and dresses, but failed to mention the painted eagle found on nearly all surviving examples of the Lakota garments. The painted figures represented scenes from the garment-maker's vision, rather than things seen in nature. The blue neck was almost always in the shape of a deeply cut "V." Anon., "The Messiah Craze," *Annual Report of the Commissioner of Indian Affairs* (Washington DC: GPO, 1891), 530 (hereafter cited as *Annual Report of the Commissioner*).

9. Philip Wells's nose was nearly cut off. His account of the massacre begins in Tablet 5. His autobiography is in Philip H. Wells, "Ninety-six Years Among the Indians of the Northwest — Adventures and Reminiscences of an Indian Scout and Interpreter in the Dakotas," *North Dakota History* 15 (1948): 85-133, 169-215, 265-312.

   George D. Wallace entered the military academy in 1868. He was under Major Reno's command in the Little Bighorn battle. He was the commanding officer of Troop K of the Seventh Cavalry at Wounded Knee. For a brief biography, see John Mackintosh, "Lakota Bullet Ends Wallace's Life — 14 Years after Little Bighorn," *Greasy Grass* 16 (2000): 21-30.

10. High Back Bone was the only scout killed at Wounded Knee. Jensen, Paul, and Carter, *Eyewitness at Wounded Knee*, 127.

11. Lt. Harry L. Hawthorne, Second Artillery, was wounded. Cpl. Paul H. Weinert wielded the Hotchkiss cannon. Utley, *The Last Days of the Sioux Nation*, 221.

12. The "hostiles" were the Ghost Dancers who had gathered on a plateau in the Badlands north of the agency. The term could also refer to anyone who refused to assemble at the agency in compliance with the army's orders. Those who complied were "friendlies."

   The rumor proved to be true. Capt. Henry Jackson's Troop C encountered about 150 warriors who had ridden out from the Pine Ridge Agency when they heard the cannon fire at Wounded Knee. After a brief exchange of gunfire they retreated. Ibid., 226.

13. Lt. John F. Guilfoyle, Ninth Cavalry, entered the military academy in 1872. Heitman, *Historical Register*, 483.

   On October 24, 1890, Guilfoyle and ten soldiers escorted Maj. Gen. Nelson A. Miles to Pine Ridge. Miles tried to calm Agent Daniel Royer and encourage Indian leaders to give up the Ghost Dance. Buecker, *Fort Robinson and the American West*, 174. Miles returned on December 31 to take personal command of the troops. Jensen, Paul, and Carter, *Eyewitness at Wounded Knee*, 140.

   In 1885 Brig. Gen. Nelson A. Miles assumed command of the Department of the Missouri, which included the Lakota reservation country. Robert Wooster, *Nelson A. Miles and the Twilight of the Frontier Army* (Lincoln: University of Nebraska Press, 1993), 139.

14. The Ninth had been stationed at a temporary camp near the mouth of Wounded Knee Creek. The unit was ordered to return to the agency and help defend it if the hostiles attacked as expected. The wagon train moved more slowly and was left behind. A corporal was killed before the Seventh Cavalry came to the rescue. Utley, *The Last Days of the Sioux Nation*, 236.

   John S. Loud was promoted to the rank of captain in the Ninth Cavalry in 1880. He retired in 1898. Heitman, *Historical Register*, 643.

15. The Drexel or Holy Rosary Mission was about four miles north of the agency. The Seventh Cavalry was sent to investigate, but found only two log schoolhouses that had been burned. On their return to the agency the soldiers were fired upon by Indians commanding the higher ground. Two soldiers were killed and five wounded before reinforcements arrived. Utley, *The Last Days of the Sioux Nation,* 238–40.

16. Brig. Gen. John R. Brooke had overall command of the soldiers on the reservations during the Ghost Dance era until the arrival of General Miles near the end of December. Brooke served in the Civil War. He retired in 1902 with the rank of major general. Heitman, *Historical Register,* 248.

Eugene A. Carr was a colonel in the Sixth Cavalry in 1890, but was later promoted to the rank of brigadier general. James T. King, *War Eagle: A Life of General Eugene A. Carr* (Lincoln: University of Nebraska Press, 1963).

Maj. Guy V. Henry, Ninth Cavalry, entered the military academy in 1856. He was a brigadier general when he retired in 1898. He died a year later. Heitman, *Historical Register,* 523.

Robert H. Offley began his career in the navy. In 1890 he was a lieutenant colonel in the Seventeenth Infantry. He died on October 14, 1891. Ibid., 756.

Almond B. Wells served in the Civil War and in 1890 was a captain in the Eighth Cavalry. Ibid., 1016.

George B. Sanford was another Civil War veteran. In 1890 Lieutenant Colonel Sanford was in the Ninth Cavalry stationed at Fort Robinson. A year later he would take command of the fort. Ibid., 859; Buecker, *Fort Robinson and the American West,* 200.

Offley and Wells were along the White River just below the mouth of White Clay Creek. Carr was farther up the river and Sanford was downstream. Utley, *The Last Days of the Sioux Nation,* 252.

17. Lt. Edward W. Casey graduated from West Point in 1873, and his first assignment was at Fort Sully. He was stationed at Fort Keogh early in 1890, when his proposal to organize a troop of Indian scouts with full military status was approved. Cheyenne scouts were enlisted that spring at the Tongue River Reservation. In December they were sent to the Pine Ridge Reservation. After the Wounded Knee massacre, the scouts maintained regular contact with the hostiles entrenched in the Badlands. On January 7 Casey set out for the Badlands hoping he could convince these holdouts to surrender. On the way he met a small party of Indians who convinced the lieutenant to return to the agency. When Casey turned to leave, Plenty Horses shot the officer in the back of the head and killed him. Katherine M. Weist, "Ned Casey and His Cheyenne Scouts: A Noble Experiment in an Atmosphere of Tension," *Montana, the Magazine of Western History* 27 (1977): 26–39.

18. American Horse was a proponent of acculturation. After the Wounded Knee massacre some hostiles broke into his house and "utterly demolished every piece of furniture the house contained." *St. Louis Post-Dispatch,* Jan. 23, 1891.

19. Rodman cannons, designed by Thomas J. Rodman, were huge weapons intended primarily for use in seacoast fortifications. The three-inch ordnance rifles taken to Pine Ridge were commonly, but erroneously, referred to as Rodmans since they resembled the larger guns' configuration. Patricia L. Faust, ed., *Historical Times Illustrated Encyclopedia of the Civil War* (New York: Harper Perennial, 1986), 642, 755.

20. In the 1870s Two Strike was a chief of the Brulés. Jesse M. Lee, "Spotted Tail Agency, Nebraska," *Annual Report of the Commissioner,* 1877, 67. He was born in 1821 and died in 1914. George E. Hyde, *Spotted Tail's Folk: A History of the Brulé Sioux* (Norman: University of Oklahoma Press, 1961), 31.

Jack Red Cloud was the son of the Oglala chief and a prominent Ghost Dance organizer. Utley, *The Last Days of the Sioux Nation,* 85.

21. Ricker's Book 4 is Tablet 35. He copied the following from the Fort Robinson hospital records:

> Movements to Pine Ridge. Hospital record, November, 1890, pg. 167 says: Troops "F," "I," and "K" 9th Cav., and Co. "C," 8th Infty. left post en route to Pine Ridge Agency S.D., Nov. 18, 1890. Capt. J. R. Kean, Asst. Surgeon, and three privates of the Hospital corps accompanied the command. (62 recruits for the 7th Cavalry and 12 recruits for the 9th Cavalry arrived at Fort Robinson Nov. 30, 1890.) (See book 2 [Tablet 31] p. 137–38 McFarland's Stat., Light-haired recruit wounded in neck.)

22. William Mills enlisted in the army in 1858. By 1866 he had risen to the rank of captain in the Second Infantry. He died on December 30, 1890. Heitman, *Historical Register,* 714. Augustus Corliss, Tablet 24, also mentions Mills's death.

23. The hostiles fired on the agency in the afternoon of December 29. About dusk they retreated to their camp called the Stronghold, a naturally fortified plateau in the Badlands. Utley, *The Last Days of the Sioux Nation,* 233. Red Cloud went to the Badlands with the fleeing Ghost Dancers. On January 9, 1891, he returned to the agency. He said he had been kidnapped by Short Bull's Brulés, who threatened to kill him if he tried to escape. Thomas A. Bland, *A Brief History of the Late Military Invasion of the Home of the Sioux* (Washington DC: National Indian Defense Association, 1891), 22.

24. Emma Sickels was a teacher at Pine Ridge. If Ricker wrote to her, the letter has been lost. She did write to L. W. Colby, describing conditions at Pine Ridge. L. W. Colby, "The Sioux Indian War of 1890–91," *Transactions and Reports of the Nebraska State Historical Society* 3 (1891): 180–85. In her letter Sickels blamed Red Cloud and Father John Jutz for helping foment the discontent that led to the massacre, accused Red Cloud of plotting to destroy the agency and school, and blamed General Brooke and Agent Royer for weakness and mismanagement.

25. Charles W. Allen, *From Fort Laramie to Wounded Knee: In the West that Was,* ed. Richard E. Jensen (Lincoln: University of Nebraska Press, 1997).

26. Alfred Burkholder, an editor of his own paper in Chamberlain, South Dakota,

represented the *New York Herald.* His first report appeared on November 24. George R. Kolbenschlag, *A Whirlwind Passes: News Correspondents and the Sioux Disturbances of 1890–1891* (Vermillion: University of South Dakota Press, 1990), 15–19.

27. Meded Swigert mentioned a Mr. Miller as a correspondent of the *Nebraska State Journal* (Tablet 14). The newspaperman's identity remains a mystery. James Gordon Bennett was the flamboyant owner of the *New York Herald.*

28. C. H. Cressey's stories for the *Omaha Bee* were indeed sensational. In his first report written on the railroad train bound for Chadron, he hinted there was a plot by the Indians to attack the passengers. Cressey continued to file lengthy reports that frequently contained exaggerated accounts of impending violence. Jensen, Paul, and Carter, *Eyewitness at Wounded Knee,* 44. Years later Allen recalled that he and Cressey "decided to work together — one of us gathering items while the other tabulated them." Allen, *From Fort Laramie To Wounded Knee,* 207.

William Fitch Kelley's report appeared on December 30 in the *Nebraska State Journal.* Later he wrote a book about the Ghost Dance era. William Fitch Kelley, *Pine Ridge 1890,* ed. Alexander Kelley and Pierre Bovis (San Francisco: Pierre Bovis, 1971).

Richard C. Stirk was the messenger. He took the stories to the telegraph station in Rushville, Nebraska. Allen, *From Fort Laramie To Wounded Knee,* 209.

29. Frank A. Rinehart had a studio in Omaha from 1885 to 1919. He took many portraits of Native Americans. Royal Sutton, ed., *The Face of Courage: The Indian Photographs of Frank A. Rinehart* (Fort Collins CO: Old Army Press, 1972). Rinehart did not go to Pine Ridge, however, he may have "borrowed" Wounded Knee-era pictures from other photographers. Clarence G. Moreledge and George Trager took the majority of these pictures. On a page in the Bartlett interview Ricker noted, "Clarence Moorledge was the photographer, (a small boy) who took the views at Wounded Knee, & he was the only one who took photos there." Moreledge took many pictures around Pine Ridge and at Wounded Knee after the massacre. He attempted to photograph a Ghost Dance, but the participants destroyed his camera. James Meddaugh, Ricker's Jim Meadows, was more successful. Jensen, Paul, and Carter, *Eyewitness at Wounded Knee,* Plate 3. Ricker wrote another note in Tablet 39:

> Locke, the Photographer, has Indian Pictures. Probably has one of the "Ghost Dance." Ask him if he knows where Jim Meadows is. Meadows had a lot of negatives taken of the Indians and of ghost dancing before the W.K. fight. When A. H. Baumann sold his Rushville gallery to Meadows he let him have these negatives. Meadows was burned out at Lead several years ago. Baumann took these views. He has been in business in Rushville, Gordon, Buffalo, Wyo., and Crawford.

30. After the Wounded Knee massacre, bodies were buried in a mass grave on a hill overlooking the site. Ricker usually refers to it as Cemetery Hill. In 1903 Joseph

Horn Cloud, with help from friends and relatives, erected a monument at the site of the mass grave. Jensen, Paul, and Carter, *Eyewitness at Wounded Knee,* 182. Interments continue to be made on the hilltop.

31. Allen wrote a similar account in the *Chadron Democrat* on January 1, 1891. In his autobiography he admitted he was some distance from the council when the fighting started and did not mention the Indian who "discharged his piece at the guard." Allen, *From Fort Laramie to Wounded Knee,* 198–99.

32. Two other reporters witnessed the massacre. William F. Kelley worked for the Lincoln *Nebraska State Journal* and C. H. Cressey represented the *Omaha Bee.* Ibid., 123.

33. Paddy Starr told Ricker a call was made in the ravine after the massacre ended. His interview is in Tablet 11.

34. Although Allen's accounts are usually reliable there was no Lieutenant Reynolds at Wounded Knee. Utley, *The Last Days of the Sioux Nation,* 213. Allen did not mention the killing of Big Foot's daughter in his book, *From Fort Laramie to Wounded Knee.*

35. Lt. Ernest A. Garlington graduated from West Point in 1872. He received the Medal of Honor for his role at Wounded Knee. His biographers said "despite pain and loss of blood, [Garlington] continued to direct them [Troop A], thus determining the outcome of the fight." David A. Clary and Joseph W. A. Whitehorne, *The Inspectors General of the United States Army, 1777–1903* (Washington DC: GPO, 1987), 422.

36. Ricker interviewed Dr. Charles Eastman on August 20, 1907 (Tablet 11), the day before his interview with Allen. Wounded Knee was not mentioned.

37. Allen may have been prone to defend "squawmen." In 1873 he married Emma Hawkins, a mixed-blood Lakota. Allen, *From Fort Laramie to Wounded Knee,* x.

Maj. Marcus A. Reno was describing the battle on the Little Bighorn in June 1876. He wrote, "I think we were fighting all of the Sioux Nation, and also all the desperadoes, renegades, and squaw men between the Arkansas and east of the Rocky Mountains." Warren K. Moorehead, *Tonda: A Story of the Sioux* (Cincinnati: Robert Clarke Co., 1904), 307.

38. William Garnett named Kicking Bear as Frank S. Appleton's killer in an interview with Ricker (Tablet 1).

39. Allen, *From Fort Laramie to Wounded Knee,* 188, 209.

40. James Asay operated a trading post at the Pine Ridge Agency. *Chadron Democrat,* July 4, 1889. A month later his trader's license was revoked for selling whiskey on the reservation. C. G. Penney to commissioner, Sept. 19, 1893; T. J. Morgan to F. E. Pierce, Jan. 31, 1891, Letters Sent to the Office of Indian Affairs from the Pine Ridge Agency, (National Archives Microfilm Publication M1282, roll 21), Records of the Bureau of Indian Affairs, Record Group 75, NARA (hereafter cited as Pine Ridge Agency letters).

41. This crude map consists of parallel wavy lines, dots, a crescent, and rectangles. They probably represent features at Wounded Knee.

42. William Kelley was the reporter for the *Nebraska State Journal.* Kolbenschlag, *A Whirlwind Passes,* 20.

43. Philip Wells said the man who threw the dirt was "Sto-sa-yan-ka, meaning something smooth and straight." J. B. Peterson, *The Battle of Wounded Knee* (Gordon NE: News Publishing Co., 1941), 19. In the account by Elk Saw Him, another Wounded Knee survivor, the name was rendered Hose Yanka. Wells, "Ninety-six Years Among the Indians," 293. Long Bull, another eyewitness, said the dirt thrower was Sits Straight. *Washington* (D.C.) *Evening Star,* Jan. 28 and 30, 1891. James Mooney probably erred when he identified the dirt thrower as Yellow Bird. James Mooney, "The Ghost-Dance Religion and the Sioux Outbreak of 1890," *Fourteenth Annual Report of the Bureau of American Ethnology,* Smithsonian Institution (Washington DC: GPO, 1896), 868.

44. Louie Mousseau operated and perhaps owned the store. Mousseau's interview is in Tablet 26.

45. The nine-month-old girl was Lost Bird. She was abandoned during the Wounded Knee massacre by her mother, Rock Woman, who believed her child was dead. After the baby was found alive she was taken to the agency and given to Yellow Bird, who located the mother in the refugee camp. Brig. Gen. Leonard W. Colby, commander of the Nebraska National Guard unit that was patrolling the southern border of the reservation, heard about the miraculous rescue and offered to adopt Lost Bird. At first the mother refused, but changed her mind when Colby gave her fifty dollars. A decade later Mrs. Colby petitioned the Office of Indian Affairs to have Lost Bird listed on the rolls of the Cheyenne Indian Reservation and given an allotment of land. Jensen, Paul, and Carter, *Eyewitness at Wounded Knee,* 135. When General Colby published his account of Wounded Knee in 1892, he alleged that the baby was found beside her mother, who had been shot twice and killed. Colby, "The Sioux Indian War of 1890–91," 159. See also George E. Bartlett's interview, Tablet 44, in which he reports finding the child. Ricker wrote a note about Lost Bird in Tablet 45:

> Following is correct way to write her name: Zitkalan-nuni.
> Following is the translation: Bird Lost. Pronounced as follows: Zit ká lá nuni.
> Capt. Bartlett gave me the above.

46. In the summer of 1906, Ricker talked to Sgt. George W. Gaines and made the following notes in Tablet 35:

> Sergt. Geo. W. Gaines, Troop "A," 10th Cav. Says:
> At time of W.K. he was a member of I Troop 9th Cav. (Colored) the following troops of that Regt. were at W.K: A, F, C, D, G, H, I, K.
> Troop C was at Fort Leavenworth but came up in time to participate at W.K. Troop E was at Fort Washakie and B and L and M were at Fort DuChesne. The last four were not over at Pine Ridge during the difficulties.

Units of the Ninth Cavalry guarded the agency at Pine Ridge, but were not at the Wounded Knee massacre. They were involved in the December 30 skirmish at Drexel Mission. Buecker, *Fort Robinson and the American West,* 178–79.

47. When the Indian men were in the council circle they were surrounded on three sides by soldiers. General Miles believed soldiers were killed by their comrades because of this arrangement. He relieved Forsyth of command on January 4, 1891, and convened a court of inquiry to determine whether the "disposition made of the troops was judicious." The case was ruled in favor of Forsyth. *Reports and Correspondence Relating to the Army Investigation of the Battle of Wounded Knee and to the Sioux Campaign of 1890–91* (National Archives Microfilm Publication M983, roll 148), Records of the Office of the Adjutant General, Record Group 94 (hereafter cited as *Reports, Campaign of 1890–91*). Forsyth resumed command of the Seventh Cavalry by the end of the month. Utley, *The Last Days of the Sioux Nation,* 245, 248.

48. Thomas H. Tibbles, a reporter for the *Omaha World-Herald,* was not a witness to the Wounded Knee massacre.

49. Philip Wells (Tablet 5) told Ricker about a wounded Indian who blamed the dead medicine man for the disaster and wanted to stab the body.

50. Thomas W. Foley, *Father Francis M. Craft: Missionary to the Sioux* (Lincoln: University of Nebraska Press, 2002). Statement of Rev. Francis M. J. Craft, *Reports, Campaign of 1890–91.*

Elsewhere in his notes Ricker referred to the priest as Father Croft. Father Craft concluded this letter with a long paragraph, omitted here, explaining the correct spelling of his name.

51. Butler correctly names Wallace and Preston, but Lieutenant Smith was not a Seventh Cavalry officer at the time.

52. James R. Walker, *Lakota Belief and Ritual,* ed. Raymond J. DeMallie and Elaine A. Jahner (Lincoln: University of Nebraska Press, 1980), 6, 33.

53. Rex Beach, "Wounded Knee," *Appleton's Booklovers Magazine,* 7 (1906): 732–36.

Walker may have had a hand in getting the story, but it is highly unlikely that the scholarly doctor would have written the long, fictitious conversations, as well as some questionable details. It was probably Beach who made the changes and additions for a more dramatic effect.

54. Ricker's map shows the general area. Wounded Knee Creek is in the lower left corner. A line labeled "ravine" enters it. The "Lower Agency Road" and "Upper Agency Road" converge at the ravine. "Day Sch. # 7" is at the right center. In the lower left corner of the page is the "commissary" and "Presby. Chu."

55. Written diagonally across this page is "Colhoff scouts [scoffs at] these stories." George Colhoff's interview is in Tablets 13, 17, and 25.

56. The discovery of gold in the Black Hills in 1874 brought a flood of prospectors. The land was part of the Sioux Reservation and was off limits to whites. In September 1875 a commission led by William B. Allison offered to buy the Black Hills,

but the Lakotas refused. The army had tried to keep the prospectors out of the hills, but the patrols were withdrawn after the failure of the Allison Commission. The order to evict whites remained in effect.

A second commission treated for the sale of the Black Hills in September 1876. The commissioners succeeded in large part because they ignored article twelve of the Treaty of 1868 calling for the signatures of three-fourths of the adult males before any sale of land was allowed. James C. Olson, *Red Cloud and the Sioux Problem* (Lincoln: University of Nebraska Press, 1975), 171, 204, 214, 229.

57. Shortly after the Wounded Knee massacre Bartlett did something to anger Capt. William Dougherty, the acting agent. Dougherty wrote a terse letter to Bartlett: "Your presence at this agency being deemed detrimental to the interests of the Indians . . . you are hereby notified and required to depart from the Indian reservation forthwith." Dougherty to Bartlett, Jan. 24, 1891, Pine Ridge Agency letters, roll 21.

58. Ricker copied an article from the *Cincinnati Times-Star* that mentions Bartlett "now playing with 'The Great Train Robbery' at Heuck's Opera House." Unfortunately Ricker did not note the date of the article.

59. Tom Cogle may be Tom Cogill. William Garnett (Tablet 1) told Ricker that Cogill owned a store.

60. In 1890 Agent H. D. Gallagher reported that the store was owned by Robertson and Prescott. After Prescott sold his interest to his partner the store was run by Louie Mousseau. Gallagher to T. J. Morgan, Aug. 13, 1890, Pine Ridge Agency letters, roll 20. According to Mousseau (Tablet 26) he bought out William Robertson and Ephraim Bartlett, who in turn bought the store from George Bartlett.

61. Ricker originally ended this sentence simply with "it was impossible." Then later he capitalized "impossible" and added the second "impossible," the exclamation points, and the quotation marks.

62. The number of survivors and fatalities at Wounded Knee remains elusive. Bartlett's estimate of the number of Indian fatalities seems high. Richard E. Jensen, "Big Foot's Followers at Wounded Knee," *Nebraska History* 71 (1990): 194–212. One officer, six noncommissioned officers, and eighteen privates were killed. Utley, *The Last Days of the Sioux Nation*, 228.

63. This crude map shows towns in western South Dakota, the White River, the Stronghold, and a wavy line representing the route.

64. Capt. Augustus W. Corliss was with the Eighth Infantry at the Pine Ridge Agency during the army's takeover. His recollections of the events were published in the *Denver Post*, Nov. 15, 1903. Bartlett's disagreement was with statements in this interview. Ricker's interview with Corliss is in Tablet 24.

65. Corliss was quoted as saying, "Wallace was not killed by a gun wound, as some of the newspapers have it, but with a stone battle ax." *Denver Post*, Nov. 15, 1903. Philip Wells told Ricker that the captain was killed by a gunshot to the head (Tablet 4).

66. Charles A. Varnum was promoted to captain in July 1890, and commanded

B Troop of the Seventh Cavalry. He received the Medal of Honor for his actions at Wounded Knee. John M. Carroll, ed., *Custer's Chief of Scouts: The Reminiscences of Charles A. Varnum* (Lincoln: University of Nebraska Press, 1987), 15; Heitman, *Historical Register*, 985.

67. Ricker also copied an autobiographical sketch, which he prefaced with a note that it was "Copied by E. S. R. from M S Wounded Knee by George E. Bartlett." This was published by Ralph W. Andrews, *Indians as the Westerners Saw Them* (Seattle WA: Superior Publishing Co., 1963), 33-35.

68. There were 438 soldiers. Utley, *The Last Days of the Sioux Nation*, 201.

69. Monthly School report for July 1880, Letters Received by the Office of Indian Affairs from the Red Cloud Agency (National Archives Microfilm Publication 234, roll 726, Records of the Bureau of Indian Affairs, Record Group 75 (hereafter cited as Red Cloud Agency letters); Allen, *From Fort Laramie to Wounded Knee*, 70-71.

70. The Sixth Infantry was summoned from New Mexico and assigned a sector north of the Stronghold to prevent the Ghost Dancers from fleeing in that direction. After the massacre the Sixth had a brief skirmish with the Lakotas at the mouth of Wounded Knee Creek. Troops from Fort Niobrara were sent to the Rosebud Reservation. The units Kocer saw were probably two troops of the Ninth Cavalry and a company of the Eighth Infantry. Utley, *The Last Days of the Sioux Nation*, 119, 136, 116, 252.

71. Photographs taken on the day the dead were buried do not show any bodies near Big Foot. Reporter Carl Smith saw the chief's body and wrote, "Big Foot lay in a sort of solitary dignity." *Chicago Inter-Ocean*, Jan. 7, 1891.

72. One hundred forty-six bodies were interred. Jensen, Paul, and Carter, *Eyewitness at Wounded Knee*, 116.

73. George A. Stannard's picture has not been found.

74. See the list obtained by Ricker in note 98.

75. W. A. Coffield's interview is in Tablet 13; W. J. Cleveland's interview is in Tablet 29.

76. Eastman's interview is in Tablet 11. Neither this incident nor Wounded Knee was discussed.

77. Clark described the location of Camp Sheridan, occupied from 1874 to 1881. Fort Halleck was in southeastern Wyoming. Leslie was Ricker's son.

78. The stakes, which appear to be slender tree limbs, are shown in an illustration of the site in Mooney, *The Ghost-Dance Religion*, Plate XCIX. A week after the massacre Capt. Augustus W. Corliss visited the site. Years later he recalled "seeing the entire field covered with short sticks flying flags. The Indians had gone there and located the places where their relatives had been killed and marked them with flags." *Denver Post*, Nov. 15, 1903.

79. Short Bull was a member of the Lakota delegation that went to the Walker Lake Reservation and talked to Wovoka, the originator of the Ghost Dance. Short Bull's statement is in Tablet 17.

80. Cpl. Paul H. Weinert rolled one of the guns down the hill to a ravine where many

Indians were hiding and fired several rounds at them. Jensen, Paul, and Carter, *Eyewitness at Wounded Knee*, 128.

81. Philip Wells's interview is in Tablets 3, 4 and 5. His wound was inflicted by a man.

82. The First Infantry Regiment was ordered from California to Pine Ridge on December 1, 1890. Jensen, Paul, and Carter, *Eyewitness at Wounded Knee*, 31.

83. Some of Smith's articles were extremely critical of Agent Daniel Royer. After about two weeks the agent ordered him to leave the reservation. He was replaced by Thomas Tibbles and his wife, Susette LaFlesche Tibbles. Kolbenschlag, *A Whirlwind Passes*, 19-20.

84. James Riley, alias Doc Middleton, was convicted of stealing horses. He spent time in prison and was released in 1879. Shortly thereafter he came to Gordon, Nebraska, and opened a saloon. In 1903 he moved to Ardmore, South Dakota. Harold Hutton, *The Luckiest Outlaw: The Life and Legends of Doc Middleton* (Lincoln: University of Nebraska Press, 1992).

Ricker's reference to "Nelson's Forty Lies" may be his sarcastic reference to Nelson's biography, which was first published in 1889. In this "as told to" book Nelson becomes the main character in many events he may or may not have witnessed. John Young Nelson, *Fifty Years on the Trail: A True Story of Western Life*, as told to Harrington O'Reilly (Norman: University of Oklahoma Press, 1963).

85. Al Dorrington may be F. M. Dorrington, who helped organize Dawes County, Nebraska. Grant L. Shumway, *History of Western Nebraska and Its People*, 2 vols. (Lincoln NE: Western Publishing Co., 1921), 2:550.

James Dahlman was the Dawes County sheriff. In the 1900s he served eight terms as the mayor of Omaha. Addison E. Sheldon, *Nebraska the Land and the People*, 2 vols. (Chicago: Lewis Publishing Co., 1931), 2:324.

John G. Maher opened the government land office in Chadron, Nebraska, in 1887. In 1913 he moved to Lincoln, where he had an insurance business. Ibid., 2:198. Maher has been credited for inaugurating a one-thousand-mile horse race from Chadron to Chicago in the summer of 1893. William E. Deahl, Jr., "The Chadron-Chicago 1,000 Mile Cowboy Race," *Nebraska History* 52 (1973): 191.

86. Lt. Sidney A. Cloman was in command of a troop of Oglala scouts recruited late in November 1890. Jensen, Paul, and Carter, *Eyewitness at Wounded Knee*, 162.

87. C. J. "Clem" Davis resigned as farmer at the Wounded Knee district in 1892, and moved to Chadron, Nebraska, with his family. *Chadron Citizen*, Feb. 18, 1892.

88. Chadron Creek was discussed as a site for the 1875 meeting to negotiate the sale of the Black Hills. Instead the commissioners and chiefs met on the White River about eight miles northeast of the Red Cloud Agency. Olson, *Red Cloud and the Sioux Problem*, 205.

89. This was probably Red Dog. Ibid., 207.

90. Little Wound ascended to a leadership position in the Cutoff band of the Oglalas in the 1870s.

In 1907 Ricker had a brief conversation with Mrs. Charles Turning Hawk, which he recorded in Tablet 38:

> Mrs. Charles Turning Hawk, daughter of Chief little Wound says: Chief Little Wound died in August (George Little Wound can give the year.) He is buried in the Catholic Cemetery at Kyle. Moses Red Kettle says he thinks Chief Little Wound died about six years ago. (This is 1907.)

91. Adam Kramer joined the army in 1857. In 1890 he was a captain in the Sixth Cavalry. Heitman, *Historical Register,* 608. Phillip Wells's interview is in Tablets 3, 4, and 5.

92. Maj. Emil Adam, Sixth Cavalry, fought in the Civil War. He retired in 1893. Heitman, *Historical Register,* 151.

93. Unfortunately the "Scratch Book" is not in the Ricker Collection.

94. Lt. Col. Edwin V. Sumner, Eighth Cavalry, served in the army from 1861, until his retirement in 1899. Heitman, *Historical Register,* 936.

95. Sumner took up the watch on Big Foot's band on December 3. They slipped away on the twenty-third. Utley, *The Last Days of the Sioux Nation,* 173, 184.

96. The "sketch" of Wounded Knee is six lines, roughly conical in shape.

97. Ricker saved the envelope. It was addressed to him at 638 Gunnison Ave., Grand Junction, Colorado. Ricker added a note, "W. A. Ballou. His account of the militia service around Chadron during the Sioux disturbances."

    Ballou's erratic capitalization and punctuation in his seven-page letter have been corrected, probably by Ricker.

98. The bodies of the enlisted men and noncommissioned officers killed at Wounded Knee, the Drexel Mission, and near the mouth of Wounded Knee Creek were buried at the agency. The body of Captain Wallace, who was killed at Wounded Knee, was sent to his home in South Carolina. Lieutenant Casey was killed on January 7 and his body was also returned to his home. In 1906 the bodies at Pine Ridge were exhumed and moved to Fort Riley. On April 17, 1907, Ricker wrote to the quartermaster at Fort Riley requesting the names of the soldiers. He received the following list dated April 22, 1907. The list is in Box 2, Ricker Coll.:

    List showing the names of deceased Soldiers whose bodies were exhumed at Pine Ridge Agency, and reinterred at Fort Riley, Kansas.

Running number.	Names.	Rank.	Troop.	Reg't.	Section.	Number.	Remarks
365.	Oscar Pollack,	Hosp. Steward			D	104	Disinterred at Pine Ridge Agency S.D. and buried at Fort Riley, Kansas
366.	R. W. Corwine,	Sergeant Major,		7thCavy.	D	105	" " "
367.	A. C. Dyer,	Sergeant	"A"	7th Cavy.	D	106	" " "

Running number.	Names.	Rank.	Troop.	Reg't.	Section.	Number.	Remarks		
368.	Henery Frey,	Private	"A"	7th Cavy.	D	107	"	"	"
369.	Geo. P. Johnson,	Private	"A"	7th Cavy.	D	108	"	"	"
370.	Michel Regan,	Private	"A"	7th Cavy.	D	109	"	"	"
371.	James Logan,	Private	"A"	7th Cavy.	D	110	"	"	"
372.	George Elliott,	Private	"K"	7th Cavy.	D	111	"	"	"
373.	H. R. Forest,	Corporal	"B?"	7th Cavy.	D	112	"	"	"
374.	C. H. Newell,	Corporal	"B?"	7th Cavy.	D	113	"	"	"
375.	Jan DeVreede,	Private	"C"	7th Cavy.	D	114	"	"	"
376.	F. T. Reinecky,	Private	"D"	7th Cavy.	D	115	"	"	"
377.	R. H. Nettles,	Sergeant	"G"	7th Cavy.	E	116	"	"	"
378.	August Kellner,	Private	"E"	7th Cavy.	D	117	"	"	"
379.	Abert S. Bone,	Corporal	"I"	7th Cavy.	D	118	"	"	"
380.	Gustave Korn,	Blacksmith	"I"	7th Cavy.	D	119	"	"	"
381.	Daniel Twohig,	Private	"I"	7th Cavy.	D	120	"	"	"
382.	H. B. Stone,	Private	"I"	7th Cavy.	D	121	"	"	"
383.	Pierce Cummings,	Private	"I"	7th Cavy.	D	122	"	"	"
384.	Bernard Zehnder,	Private	"I"	7th Cavy.	D	123	"	"	"
385.	W. T. Hodges,	Sergeant	"K"	7th Cavy.	D	124	"	"	"
386.	J. M. McCue,	Private	"K"	7th Cavy.	D	125	"	"	"
387.	Joseph Murphy,	Private	"K"	7th Cavy.	D	126	"	"	"
388.	Dominick Francishetti	Private	"G"	7th Cavy.	D	127	"	"	"
389.	Herman Grandberg,	Private	"A"	7th Cavy.	K	128	"	"	"
390.	Wm. Adams,	Private	"A"	7th Cavy.	D	129	"	"	"
391.	John Costella,	Private	"B"	7th Cavy.	D	130	"	"	"
392.	R. L. Cook,	Private	"B"	7th Cavy.	D	131	"	"	"
393.	W. S. Meze,	Private	"B"	7th Cavy.	D	132	"	"	"

99. *Chadron Times,* July 30 and Nov. 12, 1903.

100. Charles Marrivall was the trader at Wounded Knee during Ricker's visits. Ibid., Nov. 12, 1903.

101. The *Omaha World-Herald,* June 7, 1903, reported that the dedication was on May 28. Presbyterian minister W. J. Cleveland preached a sermon and Joseph Horn Cloud and Fire Lightning gave short talks. The *Rushville Standard,* May 22, 1903, said the monument was erected on May 28 and cost $350.

The Ghost Dancers tried to convert Fire Lightning. The dancers claimed they had talked to his daughter, who had died recently, and if Fire Lightning joined, he could be reunited with her. The attempted conversion failed. *Chadron Advocate* Nov. 28, 1890.

102. Charles P. Jordan served in the Eleventh Ohio Volunteers in the Civil War. He came to Dakota in 1872, and worked at Fort Robinson. In 1878 he married Julia Walks First. Four years later he was appointed trader at the Rosebud Agency. *Valentine Democrat,* Jan. 18, 1924.

103. The Lakotas had borrowed the so-called Omaha dance from the Omaha tribe in the distant past. Originally it was a ceremony to protect participants from their enemies' weapons. As years passed the ceremony was misused and its power was lost until the Omaha dance became merely a social event. Clark Wissler, "Societies and Ceremonial Associations in the Oglala Division of the Teton-Dakota," *Anthropological Papers 11,* American Museum of Natural History (Washington DC: GPO, 1912), 49.

104. Joseph Horn Cloud gave Ricker the list (Tablet 12).

105. Ricker talked briefly to Edward Truman about the monument and made the following note in Tablet 10: "Below Kyle, Day School No. 29, February 16, 1907. Edward Truman, Teacher, says that Joseph Horn Cloud initiated the movement for the monument at Wounded Knee and it was due to his exertions that it was erected. He should have this signal credit."

106. If Ricker received Badge's list it has been lost.

107. Ricker probably meant Lt. Fayette W. Roe, Third Infantry, aide to General Brooke. Heitman, *Historical Register,* 842. Ricker makes a number of mistakes in this tablet, which he corrected as his research progressed.

108. Later Ricker corrected this error about the number and kinds of weapons.

2. Agents and Agencies

1. *The Oglala Light* was printed by students at Pine Ridge. Ralph H. Ross, *Pine Ridge Reservation: A Pictorial Description* (Kendall Park NJ: Lakota Books, 1996), n.p.

2. Capt. Francis E. Pierce, Eighth Infantry, was named agent on January 12, 1891. He served for about a month, when he was replaced due to an illness. Allen, *From Fort Laramie to Wounded Knee,* 255 n. 13.

3. Rev. Charles Smith Cook was the Episcopalian missionary at Pine Ridge during the Ghost Dance era. Charles A. Eastman, *From Deep Woods to Civilization: Chapters in the Autobiography of an Indian* (Lincoln: University of Nebraska Press, 1977), 85. William J. Cleveland came to Pine Ridge in 1900. Gertrude S. Young, *William Joshua Cleveland* (n.p.: n.d.), 26.

4. Eastman met Miss Goodale shortly after he arrived at Pine Ridge in October 1890. She consented to marry him on Christmas Day. Utley, *The Last Days of the Sioux Nation,* 232.

5. Hampton Normal and Agricultural Institute was founded in 1868 in Hampton, Virginia. Initially it provided training to newly freed slaves. Paulette Fairbanks Mo-

lin, '"Training the Hand, the Head, and the Heart': Indian Education at Hampton Institute," *Minnesota History* 51 (1988): 84.

6. Allen, *From Fort Laramie to Wounded Knee,* 71–72.

7. Charles Allen suggested the interview with Pugh. See Tablet 44.

8. Hugh D. Gallagher arrived at Pine Ridge in October 1887 to take up his duties as agent. Gallagher, "Pine Ridge Agency, Dakota," *Annual Report of the Commissioner,* 1887, 40. When Agent Royer was appointed to the post in 1890, Gallagher made his home in Chadron. *Chadron Democrat,* Oct. 23, 1890.

9. Daniel F. Royer, an Alpena, South Dakota, dentist, was appointed agent for the Pine Ridge Reservation and arrived there in late September 1890. Royer's paramount concern was the suppression of the Ghost Dance, but it was soon apparent that he did not have the temperament for such an undertaking. In a letter to Thomas J. Morgan, commissioner of Indian affairs, he wrote, "I have been carefully investigating the matter [of the Ghost Dance] and I find I have an elephant on my hands." Royer to Morgan, Oct. 12, 1890, *Executive Documents of the Senate of the United States,* 51st Cong. 2d sess., 1891–92, S. Doc. 9:5 (Washington DC: GPO, 1892). By the end of the month he was insisting that military intervention was necessary, not only to suppress the new religion, but to protect whites from an outbreak. He believed a war was inevitable and his actions proved to be a self-fulfilling prophecy. Years later Royer moved to California and by 1927 was "in trouble for using too much morphine." Carroll Friswold and Robert A. Clark, eds. *The Killing of Chief Crazy Horse* (Glendale CA: Arthur H. Clark Co., 1976), 127.

Richard F. Pettigrew of Sioux Falls was a staunch supporter of the Republican party. He was elected U.S. Senator in 1889. Wayne Fanebust, *Echoes of November: The Life and Times of Senator R. F. Pettigrew* (Freeman SD: Pine Hill Press, 1997), 190.

10. Thomas J. Morgan, a Baptist minister and educator, was appointed commissioner of Indian affairs on June 10, 1889. He firmly believed the only solution to the "Indian Problem" lay in the eradication of the native culture and its replacement with white Americans' ideals. Francis Paul Prucha, "Thomas Jefferson Morgan," in *The Commissioners of Indian Affairs, 1824–1977,* ed. Robert M. Kvasnicka and Herman Viola (Lincoln: University of Nebraska Press, 1979), 193–203.

11. L. W. Colby, with the help of George Sword and Pine Ridge teacher Emma Sickels, wrote down thirty-one Ghost Dance songs, including eleven attributed to Big Foot's band. Colby, "Wanagi Olowan Kin: The Ghost Songs of the Dakotas," *Proceedings and Collections of the Nebraska State Historical Society* 1 (1895): 142–49.

12. Royer went to Rushville, Nebraska, on November 19 to meet the troops, who arrived there on the train. Utley, *The Last Days of the Sioux Nation,* 116.

13. Rev. C. G. Sterling founded the Presbyterian mission at Pine Ridge in 1886. He retired in 1890, but remained there at least until the early part of 1891. *Chicago Inter-Ocean,* Jan. 21, 1891; Sterling, "Report of the Missionary, Pine Ridge Agency," *Annual Report of the Commissioner,* 1888, 53.

14. Dr. Eastman wrote about this incident. On November 11 the police attempted to arrest a man named Little accused of killing agency cattle. Approximately two hundred Ghost Dancers intervened and prevented the arrest. Eastman credited American Horse for restoring order. Eastman, *From Deep Woods to Civilization,* 93–96.

15. Young Man Afraid of his Horses was a Shirt Wearer, one of six men chosen to lead the Oglala tribe. In 1877 he enlisted as an Indian scout with the rank of sergeant. Young Man Afraid was considered a progressive Oglala. He died while on a trip to the Crow Agency in Montana. Richard G. Hardorff, *The Surrender and Death of Crazy Horse* (Spokane: Arthur H. Clark Co., 1998), 39 n. 23. Also see Joseph G. Agonito, "Young Man Afraid of his Horses: The Reservation Years," *Nebraska History* 79 (1998): 116–32.

16. Abandonment of the so-called Sod Agency on the Platte began on August 1, 1873. J. W. Daniels, "Red Cloud Agency, Washington [*sic*] Territory," *Annual Report of the Commissioner,* 1874, 243. Stover's interview is in Tablet 26 and Farnham's is in Tablet 12.

17. Henry W. Wessels began his military career as a cadet in the naval academy in 1862, and then enlisted in the Union Army in the Civil War. By 1879 he had risen to the rank of captain assigned to the Third Cavalry. Heitman, *Historical Register,* 1019. Wessels took command of Fort Robinson on December 5, 1878, and commanded during the Cheyenne outbreak. Buecker, *Fort Robinson and the American West,* 198. Lt. Levi H. Robinson and Cpl. John C. Coleman were killed on February 9, 1874, by a Lakota war party. They were hunting deer a few miles from the Red Cloud Agency. Within a month soldiers founded Camp Robinson to protect the agency. Buecker, *Fort Robinson and the American West,* 7–8, 14.

18. Agent J. J. Saville was going to raise a flagpole at the Red Cloud Agency. On October 23, 1874, about two hundred non-agency northern Indians and Brulés entered the compound and destroyed the flagpole. The Indians saw the raising of a flag as a first step in the conversion of their agency into a fort. Lt. Emmet Crawford and twenty-six men of the Third Cavalry from nearby Camp Robinson were called to the agency, and this only added to the tension. In the end it was Indian leaders who persuaded the angry mob to disperse. Saville did not erect another flagpole. Lt. Patrick H. Ray, Eighth Infantry, was at Camp Robinson at the time. Ibid., 24, 37.

19. The Miniconjou American Horse surrendered to Gen. George Crook after the battle at Slim Buttes in 1876. He had been wounded and died the next day. Jerome A. Greene, *Slim Buttes, 1876: An Episode of the Great Sioux War* (Norman: University of Oklahoma Press, 1982), 77, 90.

20. William B. Allison led the commission to negotiate for the Black Hills. Discussions with the Lakotas began on September 20, 1875. The commissioners heard rumors that the Indians might ask as much as $50 million for the land. Olson, *Red Cloud and the Sioux Problem,* 208.

21. The army took charge of the Pine Ridge Reservation as a result of the Ghost Dance troubles. Capt. Charles G. Penny, Sixth Infantry, served as agent for most of

1891. Penny, "Report of Pine Ridge Agency," *Annual Report of the Commissioner,* 1891, 408–10. He was replaced by Capt. George LeRoy Brown, Eleventh Infantry. Brown, "Report of Pine Ridge Agency," *Annual Report of the Commissioner,* 1892, 453–57. Penny was reinstated in 1893, and served until early in 1896. Capt. William Henry Clapp took over from Captain Penny on January 1, 1896. Clapp, "Report of Pine Ridge Agency," *Annual Report of the Commissioner,* 1896, 291–95. Clapp served until early in 1900, and was replaced by special agent James E. Jenkins. John R. Brennan, a civilian, became agent on November 1, 1900. Brennan, "Report of Agent for Pine Ridge Agency," *Annual Report of the Commissioner,* 1902, 363–67.

22. Brown may have encouraged additional school construction, but schools were being built on the reservation at least as early as 1881. Certification signed by John Robinson and F. E. McGillycuddy, Dec. 20, 1881, Pine Ridge Agency letters, roll 21.

23. In Tablet 22 Ricker noted, "Dr. John P. Williamson of Greenwood S.D. Mr. Garvie says can give a great amount of history about the Minnesota Massacre. He is the author of the Dakota Dict. He worked on the Riggs Dict. 2d ed." Rev. Williamson was a Presbyterian who began missionary work at the Yankton agency in March 1869. Williamson, "Yankton Agency, Dakota," *Annual Report of the Commissioner,* 1887, 66.

24. Young, *William Joshua Cleveland.*

25. Cook began his mission for the Episcopal Church in 1869. Joseph W. Cook, "Greenwood, Dak.," *Annual Report of the Commissioner,* 1887, 67. Rev. H. Burt continued his missionary efforts for forty years. He was at Crow Creek in 1910. M. A. DeWolfe Howe, *The Life and Labors of Bishop Hare: Apostle to the Sioux* (New York: Sturgis and Walton Co., 1913), 214. Rev. Henry Swift and his wife were stationed at Cheyenne River at least until 1884. Later he became an army chaplain. Ibid., 132, 203.

26. The Santees were exiled from their Minnesota homeland in 1863, after the so-called Sioux Uprising of the previous year. They were first taken to Crow Creek. Then a reservation was created for them in present Knox County, Nebraska, where they began arriving in June 1866. Roy W. Meyer, "The Establishment of the Santee Reservation, 1866-1869," *Nebraska History* 45 (1964): 59, 72.

27. In 1872 Rev. William Hobart Hare was elected to the post of Episcopal Missionary Bishop of Niobrara. The Niobrara district included present North and South Dakota west of the Missouri River. Reverend Hare visited Standing Rock in 1884. The church opened a mission there the following year. Howe, *The Life and Labors of Bishop Hare,* 29–30, 203.

28. Robert H. Clarkson was named the Episcopal missionary bishop for the territories of Nebraska and Dakota in 1866. George L. Miller, "Bishop Clarkson," *Transactions and Reports of the Nebraska State Historical Society* 1 (1885): 109.

29. The Indian Rights Association was formed in 1882. It quickly became the most

active and influential Indian reform group. William T. Hagan, *The Indian Rights Association: The Herbert Welsh Years, 1882–1904* (Tucson: University of Arizona Press, 1985).

30. John C. Borst, "Dakota Resources: The John R. Brennan Family Papers at the South Dakota Historical Resource Center," *South Dakota History* 14 (1984): 67–72.

31. Frank Grouard's "pedigree" appears in Tablet 1 and he is mentioned in many other tablets. Ricker spelled his name with and without the letter "o." For a biography see Joe DeBarthe, *Life and Adventures of Frank Grouard,* ed. Edgar I. Stewart (Norman: University of Oklahoma Press, 1958).

32. Stover is probably referring to Col. Ranald S. Mackenzie's campaign in 1876. Dull Knife's Cheyennes were routed on the Powder River in November.

33. Kanacke means a native of Hawaii or the South Sea Islands.

34. Thomas A. Bland was the author of *A Brief History of the Late Military Invasion of the Home of the Sioux.* Bland was extremely critical of the government's dealings with the Indians during the Ghost Dance era.

35. William Garnett talked to Ricker about the hazards faced by early mail carriers and mentioned a man named Clark who was killed. Agent E. A. Howard reported that a mail carrier was murdered in May 1876. Howard, "Spotted Tail Agency, Nebraska," *Annual Report of the Commissioner,* 1876, 35.

36. Moses E. "California Joe" Milner was killed at Fort Robinson on October 29, 1876. Joe. E. Milner and Earle R. Forrest, *California Joe: Noted Scout and Indian Fighter* (Lincoln: University of Nebraska Press, 1987), 281–82.

37. John B. Sanborn was a brigadier general in the Civil War. Heitman, *Historical Register,* 858. He served on the commission investigating the Fetterman debacle and was a member of the Indian Peace Commission of 1867. Sanborn could be described as pro-Indian. Olson, *Red Cloud and the Sioux Problem,* 53, 59.

38. Peter B. Nelson, *Fifty Years on the Prairie* (Chadron NE: E. E. Nelson, 1941), 28; Jon Olsen, "Cultural History," *Chadron, Nebraska, Centennial History, 1885–1985* (Chadron NE: Chadron Narrative History Project Comm.), 1985: 81–88.

39. Mrs. Nelson's interview and that of her husband were on typewritten pages. Someone, probably Ricker, edited the material and made minor correctional additions.

40. Dr. James Irwin began his duties as agent to the Oglalas on July 1, 1877. Irwin, "Red Cloud Agency, Nebraska," *Annual Report of the Commissioner,* 1877, 62.

41. Nelson, *Fifty Years on the Prairie,* 31; *Hay Springs News,* Dec. 31, 1937.

42. Employed by James Irwin as his personal interpreter, Leon Palladay was born of French parents in St. Louis about 1830. His experience with the Lakotas dates back to 1845, when he was employed by the American Fur Company at Fort Laramie. Hardorff note, *Death of Crazy Horse,* 41 n. 31. In an 1879 court deposition Palladay said he "talked the Sioux language" since he was twelve years old. Bayard H. Paine, "An Indian Depredation Claim that Proved A Boomerang," *Nebraska History Magazine* 15 (1934): 54.

43. Also known as Charging Bear, Little Big Man was a member of Big Road's (Wide Trail) Oglala band of Bad Faces, which surrendered at Camp Robinson in 1877. Having enlisted as a U.S. Indian Scout, Little Big Man was transferred to the Pine Ridge Indian Police in 1879 in recognition of his valuable service to the military. He was a close ally of Crazy Horse and was said to have been his cousin. A son of Little Big Man, named Bad Whirlwind, and a daughter were living at Standing Rock Agency as late as the 1920s. Hardorff note, *Death of Crazy Horse,* 28 n. 4.

44. Dawson was a storekeeper at Pine Ridge. Tablet 18.

45. General Miles's account was slightly different. The Cheyennes had trapped an army unit on Beecher Island and scout Jack Stilwell slipped away to get help. While hiding from the patrolling Indians, Stilwell discovered a rattlesnake beside him and spit tobacco juice on the reptile, forcing it to leave. Nelson A. Miles, *Personal Recollections and Observations of General Nelson A. Miles* (Lincoln: University of Nebraska Press, 1992), 148. Captain Frank D. Baldwin was not on Beecher Island.

46. Geronimo surrendered to General Miles on September 3, 1886, and was among the 434 Apaches who were imprisoned in Florida. Geronimo was sent to Fort Sill in 1894. He joined the Dutch Reformed Church after he came to Fort Sill. Odie B. Faulk, *The Geronimo Campaign* (New York: Oxford University Press, 1969), 145, 208–9.

47. W. H. Cox, superintendent of the Fort Sill school, complained about the overcrowding at the school and the need for an additional building to house the teachers. Cox, "Report of Superintendent of Fort Sill School," *Annual Report of the Commissioner,* 1897, 235.

48. Ricker copied Gould's sketch, a three-inch circle with "G's' Building" on top, "B's' Building" on the bottom, and "School House" on the right. An arrow points out of the circle on the left with three Xs above it. A square labeled "Bell" is in the center of the circle.

49. Ricker's copy of Gould's drawing is a crude sketch of a tepee with vertical lines in the background to represent the sunflower stalks.

50. Capt. Frank D. Baldwin, Fifth Infantry, was acting agent at the Kiowa Reservation. Baldwin, "Report of Kiowa Agency," *Annual Report of the Commissioner,* 1897, 234. He previously had headed the investigation after the Wounded Knee Massacre. Utley, *The Last Days of the Sioux Nation,* 245.

51. Ricker undoubtedly made a mistake. The letter was probably written on April 11, 1898.

52. Joseph C. Hart was the superintendent of the Cherokee Training School. Hart, "Report of Eastern Cherokee Agency," *Annual Report of the Commissioner,* 1898, 220.

3. Little Bighorn

1. The first line was in Ricker's handwriting. The remainder was typed on legal-sized paper.

2. Brig. Gen. Alfred H. Terry was in command of the Dakota column moving west from Fort Abraham Lincoln. Edgar I. Stewart, *Custer's Luck* (Norman: University of Oklahoma Press, 1955), 132.

3. Grant P. Marsh was the captain and pilot of the steamboat *Far West.* Joseph Mills Hanson, *The Conquest of the Missouri* (New York: Murray Hill Books, 1909), 239.

4. After graduating from West Point, George Crook was assigned to the Fourth Infantry on July 1, 1852. By 1873 he had risen to the rank of brigadier general. In March 1876 Crook took command of the Department of the Platte, which included Nebraska and Wyoming Territory. He died on March 21, 1890. Martin F. Schmitt, *General George Crook: His Autobiography* (Norman: University of Oklahoma Press, 1946).

5. Fort Pease was a trading post on the left bank of the Yellowstone River and a few miles below the mouth of the Bighorn. It was founded in 1875 but harassment by the Lakotas forced its abandonment in March 1876. Clyde McLemore, "Fort Pease: The First Attempted Settlement in the Yellowstone Valley," *Montana Magazine of History* 2 (1952): 31.

6. Curley was a Crow Indian born about 1856. He was a scout for the Seventh Cavalry from June to September 1876. Curley eluded Custer's fate by posing as an attacking Lakota long enough to escape. He carried the news of the defeat to officers on the steamboat *Far West.* Kenneth Hammer, ed., *Custer in '76: Walter Camp's Notes on the Custer Fight* (Provo UT: Brigham Young University Press, 1976), 158–59.

> Ricker wrote the following note in Tablet 22. No source was given. The list is accurate if some allowance is given for the translator's interpretation.

> > The Crow Scouts with Custer were: Curly, White Swan, Goes Ahead, Wool Moccasin and Yellow Face.

> > White Swan died 2 or 3 years ago and Yellow Face died a little over 20 yrs. ago. Daylight who was visiting at Pourier's left Crow Agency January 3, and he saw Curly the day of his departure. Curly cannot talk English but can use & understand a few simple words. He has had two daughters; the older married and died. The other is a little girl and is now in school at the Crow Agency.

> > White Swan was badly wounded, shot in the wrist and several times in the body. Daylight is a kind of leading man on the Crow Reservation. He was one of Crook's Crow Scouts whom "Bat" went after, 70 of them; and he was in the battle of the Rosebud.

7. Maj. Marcus A. Reno commanded three companies of the Seventh Cavalry. His unit was the first to fire upon the Indians about three o'clock in the afternoon. John S. Gray, *Custer's Last Campaign: Mitch Boyer and the Little Big Horn Reconstructed* (Lincoln: University of Nebraska Press, 1991), 245, 272.

8. Col. Custer rode Vic, but the horse was killed. Capt. Miles W. Keogh's horse Comanche survived. The blacksmith was probably Gustave Korn. Korn was one of several men who later claimed to have found the animal. Stewart, *Custer's Luck,* 473.

9. "Rodmans" were likely three-inch ordnance rifles, nominally ten-pounders. If they had Napoleons, they were twelve-pounders.

10. The junction of the two commands occurred on August 11. John G. Bourke, *On the Border with Crook* (Lincoln: University of Nebraska Press, 1971), 350-51.

11. The hunters at Fort Pease sent an appeal for help to Fort Ellis on February 18, 1876. Four troops of the Second Cavalry, with an infantry detachment under the command of Maj. James Brisbin, came to the rescue on March 4. Six hunters had been killed and eight wounded. Stewart, *Custer's Luck,* 85-86.

12. Mitch Boyer was born about 1839 to a French father and Lakota mother. The family moved west to Fort Laramie area about 1850, and by 1864 Mitch was on the Yellowstone River. He was killed on the Little Bighorn with Custer. Ibid., 6-7. Gen. John Gibbon commanded the District of Montana. Ibid., 127.

13. By 1872 Henry Clay Clifford was traveling with the Lakotas, probably as a trader. E. O. C. Ord to assistant adjutant general, Nov. 1, 1872, Red Cloud Agency Letters, roll 716.

14. Capt. Frederick W. Benteen commanded Companies D, H, and K of the Seventh Cavalry. Richard G. Hardorff, *Lakota Recollections of the Custer Fight: New Sources of Indian-Military History* (Lincoln: University of Nebraska Press, 1997) 27 n. 8.

15. Ricker's informants were divided on the sword issue. Two Moons told him that Custer had a sword (Tablet A). Charles Clifford agreed (Tablet 10), but his opinion was based on what other Indians told him. F. E. Server said there was not "a sabre in the command" (Tablet 7). Ricker copied extracts from a letter written by Col. E. S. Godfrey, who said no one had swords. Godfrey was at the Little Bighorn and later wrote about it. He was explicit in his comment, "No one, not even the officer of the day, carried the saber." Edward S. Godfrey, *Custer's Last Battle,* ed. Eugene McAuliffe (Omaha, Nebr., n.p., 1952), 8.

16. Respects Nothing mentioned the attack in his interview (Tablet 29).

17. At the end of Tablet 7 Ricker noted, "Scout Allison's name was Bill Ellis" referring to Edward Allison.

18. Terry's Department of Dakota included both Dakota and Montana territories.

19. William P. Carlin entered the military academy in 1846. At the time of Custer's defeat he was a lieutenant colonel in the Seventeenth Infantry. He retired in 1893. Heitman, *Historical Register,* 282.

20. Ricker must have written to Allison asking him if he meant Frank Grouard, because in the next letter Allison mentions both men in the same paragraph. Frederick F. Gerard was the Arikaras' interpreter at Fort Berthold. John S. Gray, "Arikara Scouts with Custer," *North Dakota History* 35 (1968): 451.

21. Ricker recorded a brief conversation with O. M. Rice in Tablet 3:

> Mr. O. M. Rice, Casper, says Fort Custer was built in 1877. He was there freighting. In 1878 Fort McKinney was built. He was over there also when that was building.
>
> He says further that there used to be graves of soldiers scattered over

the country in various parts, but that the bones have been removed to cemeteries established by the government.

22. Edwin H. Allison, *The Surrender of Sitting Bull, Being a Full and Complete History of the Negotiations Conducted by Scout Allison Which Resulted in the Surrender of Sitting Bull and His Entire Band of Hostile Sioux in 1881* (Dayton, Ohio: Walker Lithograph and Printing, 1891). It was republished as Edwin H. Allison, "Surrender of Sitting Bull," *South Dakota Historical Collections* 6 (1910–12): 231–70.

23. David H. Brotherton served in the army from 1850 until his retirement in 1884. Heitman, *Historical Register,* 250.

24. Second Lt. Henry Moore Harrington was a member of C Company, Seventh Cavalry, and participated in the battle of the Little Bighorn on June 25, 1876. After the engagement, survivors were unable to identify his remains and Harrington was declared MIA and presumed killed. His whereabouts on June 25 have been the subject of continued speculation. Hardorff note, *Death of Crazy* Horse, 46 n. 40.

    Ricker wrote a note in Tablet 22:

    > See Flying Hawk at mouth of W.K. He was in the Custer battle and pursued
    > Lt. Harrington & saw him shoot himself & says it was accidental as he was
    > beating his horse with his revolver.

    Flying Hawk's interview is in Tablet 40.

25. Capt. Miles W. Keogh had been in the army since 1862. Heitman, *Historical Register,* 593.

26. The return address on the envelope is "Comdr., Co. N, Nat. Home D. V. S. Kan."

27. The pamphlet may be Allison's *The Surrender of Sitting Bull.*

28. Born near the forks of the Cheyenne River in 1836, Rain in the Face was one of two Hunkpapa sons born of his father's second marriage. Rain's younger brother was Shave Head, a first sergeant in the Standing Rock Indian Police, who was killed in the line of duty during the arrest of Sitting Bull in 1890. Of Rain's four half brothers, Iron Horn had risen in social standing and was the chief of a minor Hunkpapa band. In 1873 Rain was implicated in the killings of two civilians along the Yellowstone. He was arrested by Capt. Thomas W. Custer late in 1875, and brought to Fort Lincoln, from where he escaped early in 1876, swearing vengeance on the Custers. There are conflicting reports whether Rain actually participated in the Little Bighorn battle; however, the extreme mutilation of Tom Custer's body gave rise to immediate speculation about Rain's involvement. His reputation as Custer's slayer was firmly cemented by the writings of Elizabeth Custer and Longfellow's poem, "The Revenge of Rain in the Face." He died at his home at Standing Rock Agency, North Dakota, on September 14, 1905. Hardorff note, *Lakota Recollections,* 48 n. 26.

29. Sitting Bull had two wives, Four Robes and Seen-by-the-Nation. Four Robes gave birth to twin boys. Robert M. Utley, *The Lance and the Shield: The Life and Times of Sitting Bull* (New York: Henry Holt and Company, 1993), 100, 144.

30. Allison included a hand-drawn map with a note "I make no pretense to accuracy

here but it will help you to understand." The carefully drawn map shows the movements of the various units. It seems likely it was copied from published maps.

31. Louis was the third child of James and Huntkalutawin "Marie" Bordeaux. He was born in 1849, probably at his father's trading post eight miles east of Fort Laramie. Louis's father was a Frenchman from Missouri and his mother was a Brulé. Ricker interviewed him on August 31, 1907. At the time Louis operated a ranch on the Rosebud Reservation. He died in 1917. William J. Bordeaux, *Custer's Conqueror* (Sioux Falls SC: Smith and Co., 1969), 77.

32. Several paintings were commissioned in 1911, including *Custer's Last Stand*. Personal communication from Rich Aarstad, Lewis and Clark Reference Historian, Montana Historical Society, Feb. 28, 2002.

33. Godfrey's article in the *Century Magazine* was published in January 1892. For a more recent republication, see Godfrey, *Custer's Last Battle*.

34. In 1877 Capt. Michael V. Sheridan exhumed the remains of Custer, ten other officers, a surgeon, and two civilians and turned them over to their families. Sheridan's party was accompanied by Company I of the Seventh Cavalry led by Capt. Henry J. Nowlan. Richard G. Hardorff, *The Custer Battle Casualties: Burials, Exhumations and Reinterments* (El Segundo CA: Upton and Sons, Publishers, 1989), 40, 50.

    Captain Nowlan's map is reproduced in W. A. Graham, *The Custer Myth: A Source Book of Custeriana* (Harrisburg PA: Stackpole Co., 1953), 374.

35. Thomas W. Custer, George's brother, joined the army in 1861. Lieutenant Custer was transferred to the Seventh Cavalry in 1866, and was promoted to captain in 1875. Heitman, *Historical Register,* 348.

36. Boston Custer was a civilian employee of the quartermaster. Gray, *Custer's Last Campaign,* 204.

37. George W. Henry Yates joined the army in 1861. Captain Yates was transferred to the Seventh in 1867. William W. Cooke entered the army in 1864, and two years later was assigned to the Seventh. Lieutenant Cooke served as regimental adjutant. Algernon E. Smith joined the army in 1862. Lieutenant Smith was assigned to the Seventh in 1867. William Van W. Reily joined the army in 1875 and was transferred to the Seventh Cavalry a year later. Heitman, *Historical Register,* 1065, 324, 893, and 823.

38. Lt. James E. Porter entered the military academy in 1864, and was assigned to the Seventh Cavalry in 1869. Ibid., 799.

39. Sgt. Francis G. Hughes was transferred from Company K to serve as flag bearer. Gray, *Custer's Last Campaign,* 405.

40. Cassilly Adams painted a diorama of Custer's last battle in 1884. The painting, which measured nine by sixteen feet, attracted little interest. It was destroyed in a fire at Fort Bliss, Texas, in 1946. John M. Carroll, "Anheuser-Busch and Custer's Last Stand," *Greasy Grass* 3 (1987): 26.

41. William B. Franklin attended the military academy, served in the Mexican War,

and the Civil War. General Franklin resigned in 1866. Heitman, *Historical Register,* 434.

42. James W. Forsyth commanded the troops at Wounded Knee. George A. "Sandy" Forsyth fought at Beecher Island. John H. Monnett, *The Battle of Beecher Island and the Indian War of 1867–1869* (Niwot CO: University Press of Colorado, 1992), 117.

43. Edward Ball enlisted in the army in 1844, He received his captaincy in 1865 and transferred to the Seventh Cavalry in 1880. Captain Ball retired four years later. Heitman, *Historical Register,* 187.

44. Two Moons's story was published by Hamlin Garland, "General Custer's Last Fight as Seen by Two Moons," *McClure's* 9 (1898): 443–48.

45. Pvt. David L. Brainard joined the army in 1876, and was assigned to the Second Cavalry. He was honorably discharged in 1899, with the rank of lieutenant colonel. Heitman, *Historical Register,* 240. His account is in Cyrus Townsend Brady, *Indian Fights and Fighters* (Lincoln: University of Nebraska Press, 1971), 335–38. The encounter took place early in May 1877. Lame Deer and Iron Star were killed.

46. The treaty was ratified on July 25, 1868. It provided schools, agricultural equipment, and annuities in addition to defining the boundaries of the reservation. The treaty also awarded $500 to be divided among ten individuals who, in the opinion of the agent, raised the "most valuable crops." Charles J. Kappler, ed., *Indian Affairs, Laws and Treaties* (Washington DC: GPO, 1904), 1008–11.

47. Elizabeth B. Custer, *Boots and Saddles: or, Life in Dakota with General Custer* (New York: Harper and Brothers, 1885).

48. Blackfoot or, more properly, Sits In The Middle Of The Land, led the Crow delegation at the signing of the 1868 treaty. He was about eighty-two years old when he died in 1877. Joseph Medicine Crow, *From the Heart of the Crow Country: The Crow Indians' Own Stories,* ed. Herman J. Viola (New York: Orion Books, 1992), 36.

49. Server must have been thinking about someone else. Bridger died in 1881, on his farm south of Kansas City, Missouri. J. Cecil Alter, *James Bridger: Trapper, Frontiersman, Scout and Guide* (Salt Lake City: Shepard Book Co., 1925), 204, 482.

  Col. Eugene M. Baker's command was sent to punish Mountain Chief's Piegans for killing a miner. Baker attacked a Piegan camp on January 23, 1870, killing 173 men, women, and children. Later he learned it was the wrong Piegan camp. John C. Ewers, *The Blackfeet: Raiders on the Northwestern Plains* (Norman: University of Oklahoma Press, 1958), 249–50.

  John M. Bozeman came to Montana in 1862. Grace Raymond Hebard and E. A. Brininstool, *The Bozeman Trail,* 2 vols. (Glendale CA: Arthur H. Clark Co., 1960).

50. Ricker then listed the names on the Little Bighorn monument. It seemed unnecessary to repeat them here.

51. Dr. Tucker is referring to Godfrey's article in the *Century Magazine,* Godfrey, *Custer's Last Battle.*

52. Henry Mechling was the blacksmith for Company H. He was awarded the Medal of Honor in 1878. David W. Lonich, "Blacksmith Henry Mechling: From Pennsylvania to Little Big Horn," *Greasy Grass* 17 (2001): 31–35. A. N. Grover was the custodian at the battlefield from 1893 to 1906. Hardorff, *The Custer Battle Casualties,* 161.

53. As a result of rank seniority, Capt. Miles W. Keogh commanded Companies I, L, and C in the Little Bighorn battle. On June 27 the remains of Captain Keogh and his immediate command—principally I Company and a few men from L and C— were discovered on the eastern slope of Custer Ridge, near the head of a narrow ravine. Keogh's remains were found in an old buffalo wallow. Across his breast lay the body of his trumpeter, John W. Patton, while near him were found Sgts. James Bustard and Frank E. Varden, both of Company I. Keogh's body did not reveal any signs of mutilation. Contemporary observers concluded that he had been crippled by a gunshot wound that extensively fractured his left knee and leg. Death came later as his trumpeter and noncommissioned staff chose to remain with him to the end. Hardorff note, *Lakota Recollections,* 69 n. 16.

54. Mark Kellogg, a Bismarck, North Dakota, native, was reporting for the *New York Herald.* He wrote his last report on June 21. Stewart, *Custer's Luck,* 240.

4. Beecher Island

1. Monnett, *The Battle of Beecher Island,* 86–87. For other eyewitness accounts of the battle see John Hurst and Sigmund Shlesinger, "The Beecher Island Fight," *Collections of the Kansas State Historical Society* 15 (1919–22): 530–47.

2. Survivors met informally at Beecher Island in 1898. The Beecher Island Battle Memorial Association was incorporated in 1903. Robert Lyman, ed., "The Beecher Island Battle Memorial Association," *The Beecher Island Annual* 4 (1908): 1.

3. Robert Lyman was an organizer of the memorial association, but was not at the battle. J. J. Peate was with the rescue party that came to Beecher Island after the battle. Orvel A. Criqui, *Fifty Fearless Men: The Forsyth Scouts and Beecher Island* (Marceline MO: Walsworth Publishing Co., 1993), 274. Criqui's book includes biographies of the Beecher Island scouts.

4. The names of the fifty-two white participants and a short history of the battle were inscribed on an eighteen-foot-high granite monument. Ibid., 2. A disastrous flood swept the Arikaree valley on May 27, 1935. The deluge washed away most of Beecher Island and toppled the monument. Thomas A. Witty, Jr., "Investigations to Locate Missing Sections of the Beecher Island Monument," MSS, Kansas State Historical Society, Topeka, 1985, 3. The monument has been replaced near the original site.

5. George A. Forsyth and his scouts set out from Fort Hays, Kansas. They arrived at

Fort Wallace on September 5 and learned that two teamsters had been killed by a war party only a few miles from the fort. The scouts went in pursuit. They made camp on Arikaree Creek on September 16 and were attacked the next morning by Cheyenne warriors with their Arapahoe and Brulé allies. Monnett, *The Battle of Beecher Island*, 115–33.

6. Col. Henry C. Bankhead was the commanding officer of the fort. Ibid., 152.

7. S. E. "Comanche Jack" Stilwell was eighteen years old and had been roaming western Kansas for three years. Winfield Freeman, "The Battle of Arickaree," *Transactions of the Kansas State Historical Society* 6 (1900): 347–48. He was accompanied by sixty-year-old Pierre "French Pete" Trudeau. They left Beecher Island about midnight on September 17. Monnett, *The Battle of Beecher Island*, 124, 152.

8. Colonel Bankhead sent Capt. Louis H. Carpenter and seventy men of the Tenth Cavalry to check rumors of depredations west of Fort Wallace. Stilwell and Trudeau arrived at Fort Wallace on the evening of September 22. When Bankhead learned of Forsyth's predicament he sent a courier after the Tenth and they were the first to reach the trapped scouts on September 25. Bankhead arrived the next day with more reinforcements. Ibid., 166–68, 172.

9. Roman Nose led a charge late in the first day of the battle and was wounded by three scouts hiding under the bank of the Arikaree north of the island. He died later that day. Monnett concluded that Roman Nose rode back to the rear after receiving his wound, but points out that there are those who said he fell immediately after being wounded. Monnett, *The Battle of Beecher Island*, 149, 217 n. 56.

Ricker clearly identifies the three scouts who concealed themselves on the riverbank north of the island. Other accounts place Jack Stilwell, Pierre Trudeau, and possibly one more on the riverbank opposite the island and it was this trio who killed Roman Nose. Ibid., 142, 149.

10. Eli S. Ricker, "The Battle of Beecher Island," *The Beecher Island Annual* 4 (1908): 1–22. Ricker's article closely follows the first chapter of George A. Forsyth's *Thrilling Days in Army Life* (New York: Harper and Brothers, 1900).

11. Maj. James Brisbin and two companies of the Second Cavalry were part of the rescue party. Monnett, *The Battle of Beecher Island*, 170.

12. The map is largely unintelligible. It consists of five wavy lines and one in the shape of a Y.

Jack Peate drew a map of the island shortly after being rescued. Robert Lyman, ed., "Map of Beecher Island," *The Beecher Island Annual* 2 (1905): 25.

13. Jim Curry owned a saloon in Hays, Kansas, in the 1870s. There was bad blood between Curry and James Butler "Wild Bill" Hickok but their differences were settled amiably. Hickok gained a notable reputation as a gunfighter. He was murdered in a Deadwood, Dakota, saloon in 1876. Joseph G. Rosa, *They Called Him Wild Bill: The Life and Adventures of James Butler Hickok* (Norman: University of Oklahoma Press, 1964), 100.

14. Ricker put the death toll among the Cheyennes at seventy-five. Colonel Forsyth's

count was thirty-five, but Ricker argued that this low number was only the bodies the colonel saw. Ricker, "The Battle of Beecher Island," 22. Later historians agreed with Forsyth. David Dixon, *Hero of Beecher Island: The Life and Military Career of George A. Forsyth* (Lincoln, University of Nebraska Press, 1994), 87.

15. A doctor with the rescue party amputated Farley's injured leg, but the scout died shortly thereafter. Monnett, *The Battle of Beecher Island,* 172.

5. Lightning Creek Incident

1. Leslie D. Ricker to A. E. Sheldon, June 27, 1926, Ricker Coll. Ricker's articles appeared in the *Chadron Times,* November 5 and 19. The two articles attributed to other papers were on November 12 and December 3. Ricker copied a letter by Clarence Three Stars, which described the incident (Tablet 25). Also see "Sheriffs Battle Indians on Lightning Creek," *The Wyoming Pioneer* 1 (1941): 190–201.

2. William Miller was the sheriff of Weston County, Wyoming. He was killed in the fight. Deputy Sheriff Louis Falkenberg was the other white fatality. Ibid., 191.

6. Biographical Sketches

1. Patrick E. Connor enlisted in the army in 1839. Early in 1865 he took command of the District of the Plains. He was mustered out in April 1866, with the rank of brevet major-general. Fred B. Rogers, *The Soldiers of the Overland: Being Some Account of the Services of General Patrick Edward Connor* (San Francisco: The Grabhorne Press, 1938).

2. On January 29, 1863, Connor and his troops attacked a Shoshone camp on the Bear River near present Preston, Idaho. The battle deteriorated into a massacre in which approximately three hundred Shoshones were killed. Fourteen soldiers lost their lives. Harold Schindler, "The Bear River Massacre: New Historical Evidence," *Utah Historical Quarterly* 67 (1999): 300–308.

3. Elsewhere Ricker used the phonetic spelling "Bisnet." Ricker wrote a brief biographical note in Tablet 17: "The name written in my books as Bisnet should be spelled Bissonette," and later in the tablet he noted, "Herbert Bissonnette lives this winter (1906–7) at the Agency. He is the son of Joseph Bissonnette, Frenchman. His father was an old official interpreter and kept a diary. These papers are in the trunk of Herbert out on W.K. Cr. at the house of his sister Mrs. Red Shirt, 3 miles or over below Manderson."

The elder Bissonette came to Lakota country from St. Louis in 1836. He was a trader, interpreter, and reservation farmer. He died on the Pine Ridge Reservation in 1894. John Dishon McDermott, "Joseph Bissonette," in Vol. 4, *The Mountain Men and the Fur Trade of the Far West,* ed. LeRoy R. Hafen (Glendale CA: Arthur H. Clark Co., 1966), 49–60.

4. After the Lakotas' adamant refusal to sell land in 1888, the government raised the offer of $.50 an acre to $1.25 an acre for land sold during the first three years. It was presumed this would be the best land. A downward sliding scale covered

land sold in later years. Heads of families would receive 320 acres instead of the original offer of 160 acres. There were other concessions as well. There was much opposition to the treaty on the Pine Ridge Reservation, but after American Horse capitulated and signed the agreement a large majority slowly followed suit. The 1889 law was approved on March 2 and published in *Annual Report of the Commissioner*, 1889, 449-58.

5. Charles Allen heard a slightly different story. According to Allen Mr. Miller was a cook for a large ranch run by two white men married to Indian women. They all urged Miller to leave the ranch headquarters for a sanctuary in the Black Hills. He refused because he was convinced the Ghost Dancers were his friends and would not harm him. Allen, *From Fort Laramie to Wounded Knee*, 169-71. Agent Royer identified the body as that of Isaac Miller, an "irregular employee" of the agency. He was killed on January 1, 1891. D. F. Royer to T. J. Morgan, Jan. 2, 1891. *Reports, Campaign of 1890-91*.

6. The granite headstone is about four feet tall. The inscription is, "JOHN Y. SECHLER BORN APR. 10, 1834 DIED AUG. 23, 1898 His memory is blessed."

7. A very light X was penciled across this paragraph. Ricker had reason to mistrust this part of Jones's story. Occasionally Mitch Boyer and Baptiste "Big Bat" Pourier were mistaken for brothers because of the similar-sounding last names. Boyer had at least one half-brother, John or Johnny Boyer. The elder Boyer was killed in the late 1860s. Baptiste Garnier was called Little Bat. Gray, *Custer's Last Campaign*, 8, 21.

8. Geminien P. Beauvais was a trader stationed near Fort Laramie in the 1860s. Charles E. Hanson, Jr., "Geminien P. Beauvais," in Vol. 7, *The Mountain Men and the Fur Trade of the Far West*, ed. LeRoy R. Hafen (Glendale CA: Arthur H. Clark Co., 1969), 35-43.

9. Dr. Valentine T. McGillycuddy began his duties as Pine Ridge Agent on March 10, 1879. McGillycuddy, "Pine Ridge Agency, Dakota," *Annual Report of the Commissioner*, 1879, 40. His wife Fanny died in 1897, and he then married Julia Blanchard, daughter of trader George F. Blanchard. Julia B. McGillycuddy, *McGillycuddy Agent: A Biography of Dr. Valentine T. McGillycuddy* (Stanford CA: Stanford University Press, 1941), 273.

10. In his interview in Tablet 1, William Garnett mentioned in passing that John Hunter was his stepfather.

11. John "Portugee" Phillips carried the news of the defeat. Stewart, *Custer's Luck*, 45.
The so-called Fetterman massacre occurred on December 21, 1866. Capt. William Judd Fetterman and about eighty troops were lured into an ambush by Crazy Horse and annihilated. Robert W. Larson, *Red Cloud: Warrior-Statesman of the Lakota Sioux* (Norman: University of Oklahoma Press, 1997), 100-101.

12. Ricker said Claymore was an Osage Indian (Tablet 9). He may well have had some Osage blood, but from his interview it is apparent he lived primarily in the white world.

13. Troops began construction of a fort near the Platte River bridge in 1864. On July 26, 1865, Lt. Caspar W. Collins and twenty Kansas volunteers went to escort a wagon train into the stockade. They were attacked and Collins and four others were killed. Robert M. Utley, *Frontiersmen in Blue: The United States Army and the Indian, 1848–65* (New York: Macmillan Co., 1967), 319–20. The outpost was named Fort Casper the following September.

14. James Baker entered the fur trade in 1839 and settled near Denver in 1859. He died at Savery, Wyoming, in 1898. Nolie Mumey, "James Baker," in Vol. 3, *The Mountain Men and the Fur Trade of the Far West,* ed. LeRoy R. Hafen (Glendale CA: Arthur H. Clark Co., 1966), 39–47.

15. In Tablet 22 Ricker wrote a note about the tribe: "Daylight's son, Richard Daylight was at 'Bat's' and he speaks good English. He says the Wind River Indians are Snakes or Shoshones. The Indians call them Snakes and the Whites call them Shoshones. He says these are a different tribe from the Crows."

16. Bridger left in the summer of 1868. Alter, *James Bridger,* 469.

17. Bridger claimed the Mormons burned his trading post and stole his merchandise and stock worth $100,000. Ibid., 514.

18. James P. Beckwourth came west with William Henry Ashley's trappers in 1824. For more than forty years he roamed the West. He died in 1866 in the camp of his Crow Indian friends. Delmont R. Oswald, "James P. Beckwourth," in Vol. 6, *The Mountain Men and the Fur Trade of the Far West,* ed. LeRoy R. Hafen (Glendale CA: Arthur H. Clark Co., 1968), 37–60. Oswald pointed out that his biography published in 1856 "did succeed in gaining him the ignominious title, 'Gaudy Liar'." Ibid., 37.

Ricker added the following in Tablet 22:

Richard Daylight, P.O. Crow Agency, Montana, gives information of Jim Beckworth. Richard lives at old Fort Custer.

Mrs. Daylight mother of Richard is the daughter of John Richard and the last wife of Jim Beckworth, viz., Medicine Lands who is now living. Medicine Lands was Beckworth's last wife. ~~About~~ In 1868, Pourier says, she was six months gone with child by her husband John Richard. Daylight says Beckworth had three wives (this is his information) and this Medicine Lands was the third. Daylight saw Beckworth when he was married to his wife's mother. Pourier has seen Beckworth. Daylight says that Beckworth was on a spree and died on a steamboat on the Missouri at or near Fort Benton. Bat thinks he died in 1866. Richard Daylight will find out from his grandmother what he can and write me.

19. Ricker seems to have accepted, without question, one of the myths about democracy and the U.S. Constitution. See Francis Paul Prucha, "The Challenge of Indian History," in "The Western Forum," *Journal of the West* 34 (1995): 3–4.

20. William Garnett told Ricker about American Horse killing Sioux Jim in Tablet 2.

21. Crow Dog killed Spotted Tail on August 5, 1881. Hyde, *Spotted Tail's Folk,* 299. He was tried in Deadwood and condemned to hang. The verdict was appealed to

the U. S. Supreme Court and the tribunal declared that Deadwood did not have jurisdiction in reservation matters and ordered Crow Dog's release. V. T. McGillycuddy, "Pine Ridge Agency, Dakota," *Annual Report of the Commissioner, 1884,* 41. For a recent analysis of the incident see Sidney L. Harring, *Crow Dog's Case: American Indian Sovereignty, Tribal Law, and United States Law in the Ninteenth Century* (Cambridge: Cambridge University Press, 1994), 100–141.

22. William F. Drannan is listed as the author of *Thirty-One Years on the Plains and in the Mountains* (Chicago: Rhodes and McClure Publishing Co., 1900). The frontispiece is a studio photograph of the buckskin-clad Drannan. It is likely the book was ghost-written by his second wife, Belle, because Drannan was illiterate. Dan Thrapp, *Encyclopedia of Western Biography,* 3 vols. (Lincoln: University of Nebraska Press, 1991), 1:423.

23. Vasquez and Bridger were partners at Fort Bridger, a trading post and way station for Oregon Trail travelers from 1843 to about 1853. Alter, *James Bridger,* 176, 246.

24. Virginia and Felix Bridger attended a school in St. Charles, Missouri, and both lived to adulthood. Daughter Josephine probably lived with her Flathead relatives, and daughter Mary probably lived with her Indian relatives. Son William died in 1892 and daughter Mary Ann died in 1841. Ibid., 209-10.

25. Bridger's third wife died in 1858, and was buried near Westport, Missouri. His first two wives died in Indian country. Ibid., 210, 522.

26. Bridger died in 1881, and was buried on the Stubbins Watts farm south of Westport. His body was moved to Mount Washington Cemetery in Kansas City and the monument was unveiled in 1904. Ibid., 497, 512.

7. The Old West

1. Honoré Picotte was hired by the American Fur Company in 1830. Janet Lecompte, "Pierre Chouteau, Junior," in Vol. 9, *The Mountain Men and the Fur Trade of the Far West,* ed. LeRoy R. Hafen (Glendale CA: Arthur H. Clark Co., 1972), 105. A law prohibiting the importation of ardent spirits into Indian country was enacted on July 9, 1832. To circumvent the law a distillery was set up at Fort Union.

2. Little Thunder and his band of about four hundred Brulés were camped along Blue Water Creek opposite Ash Hollow. On September 3, 1855, they were attacked by Bvt. Brig. Gen. William S. Harney in command of nearly seven hundred troops. Donald F. Danker, "A High Price to Pay for a Lame Cow," *Kansas History* 10 (1987): 117. The army believed this show of strength would prevent further attacks on whites traveling on the trail to the West Coast. Many undoubtedly saw it as revenge for killing Lt. John Grattan and his men in 1854.

3. Eugene Ware met the father and son in 1864. He described Col. William Collins as "a very fine old gentleman, rather old for military service, but finely preserved, energetic and soldierly." Ware thought the younger Collins was "full of life and energy" but "exceeedingly reckless." Eugene F. Ware, *The Indian War of 1864* (Lincoln: University of Nebraska Press, 1960), 120, 217.

4. General Harney, in command of about seven hundred troops, arrived at Fort Laramie on September 15, 1855. He left for Fort Pierre on the twenty-ninth with a force of about 425 men. Midway through the march Harney sent three companies back to Fort Laramie. George Rollie Adams, *General William S. Harney: Prince of Dragoons* (Lincoln: University of Nebraska Press, 2001), 134–35.

5. Later, Ricker realized the name was not Laramie but Larimer. Even then he sometimes wrote Laramie.

6. In 1864 Josiah S. Kelly, his wife Fanny, their adopted daughter Mary, and Gardner Wakefield left Kansas hoping for a brighter future in Idaho. Later William and Sarah Larimer, their young son Frank, and a few others joined them. On July 12 their wagon train was attacked by an Oglala Sioux war party east of present Casper, Wyoming. Mr. Kelly and Mr. Larimer survived, but three other men were killed. The two women and their children were taken captive. Mary was killed the next day. Sarah and Frank escaped during the second night of their captivity. Fanny was ransomed five months later and freed at Fort Sully. Fanny Kelly, *Narrative of My Captivity Among the Sioux Indians,* ed. Clark and Mary Lee Spence (Chicago: Donnelley, Gossette & Loyd, 1880; reprint, Chicago: R. R. Donnelley and Sons Co., 1990); Sarah L. Larimer, *The Capture and Escape: or Life Among the Sioux* (Philadelphia: Claxton, Remsen and Haffelfinger, 1870). The two books undoubtedly came from a single manuscript. Sentences and occasionally whole paragraphs are identical.

The decoy girl was Mary Kelly. After the raid the Oglalas fled with their captives. Mrs. Kelly and her daughter rode a horse together and after dark Mrs. Kelly let the young girl slip unnoticed from the horse. Mary was recaptured and later her mother learned that she had been used as a decoy and then killed. Her body was found on July 14. Kelly, *Narrative of My Captivity,* 48, 256.

7. Sarah Larimer and her son escaped from the Oglalas and returned to Deer Creek Station on July 17. She wrote that she crossed the river in a wagon. Larimer, *The Capture and Escape,* 116.

Capt. Levi M. Rinehart, Eleventh Ohio Volunteer Cavalry, enlisted in 1863. He was killed by the Sioux late in 1864. Kelly, *Narrative of My Captivity,* 32. Sarah Larimer wrote that he was accidentally shot and killed by one of his own men while at an Indian village. Larimer, *The Capture and Escape,* 121.

8. Kelly implied that Two Face, his brother, and possibly others were executed for the kidnapping of Lucinda Eubanks. Kelly, *Narrative of My Captivity,* 264. Ricker's informants were uncertain about the names of the executed men. All accounts agree that Two Face was hung. Black Feet, Black Foot or Blackfoot was also executed. Black Shield and Black Crow were also mentioned.

Ricker added the following note in Tablet 25:

> Thunder Bear who is a judge of the Pine Ridge Indians Court was a nephew of Black Shield who was hung at Laramie. I have been told that his name was Calico, but Thunder Bear denies this. Thunder Bear says the woman (was it

Mrs. Kelly?) was taken captive by the Cheyennes, and by these was sexually outraged, and that some Oglalas bought her and brought her in to the fort with the purpose of effecting peace, and that the two who came were hung.

9. It was Mrs. Eubanks who was released at Fort Laramie. Mrs. Kelly was freed at Fort Sully.

10. Mousseau combined two separate events. Mrs. Kelly's husband offered a reward for her return. Before anyone tried to collect the money she was freed at Fort Sully. Two Face learned of the reward, purchased Mrs. Eubanks, and brought her to Fort Laramie expecting to collect the prize.

11. In 1869 Bridger wrote to the war department requesting $6,000, the agreed upon rent when the army took over his post in 1857. It took twenty years before the secretary of war recommended payment, not for rent but for improvements at Fort Bridger. Alter, *James Bridger*, 475, 492.

12. Thomas Moonlight enlisted in the army in 1837. By 1864 he was a colonel. He retired the following year. Heitman, *Historical Register*, 721. The 1865 expedition was to the Wind River valley. Little was acomplished. Alter, *James Bridger*, 409.

13. There are dozens of hearsay stories about Scott but the only points of similarity are his tragic death and his involvement in the fur trade in some manner. Merrill J. Mattes, *The Great Platte River Road* (Lincoln: Nebraska State Historical Society, 1969), 426–27.

14. Baptiste "Little Bat" Garnier lived with E. W. Whitcomb until about 1869. Brininstool, *Fighting Indian Warriors*, 271.

15. Lt. Col. Edward Hatch was the commanding officer for most of 1886 through 1889. Buecker, *Fort Robinson and the American West*, 199.

16. Bartender James Haguewood shot Garnier on December 15, 1900, and he died early the next day. Haguewood's trial was in late March 1901. Betty Loudon, ed., "Pioneer Pharmacist J. Walter Moyer's Notes on Crawford and Fort Robinson in the 1890's," *Nebraska History* 58 (1977): 115.

17. Mousseau's La Bonte might be Lewis B. Myers, who roamed the Plains in the late 1840s. However, Myers died in California in 1893. Ann Woodbury Hafen, "Lewis B. Myers 'La Bonte'," in Vol. 7, *The Mountain Men and the Fur Trade of the Far West*, ed. LeRoy R. Hafen (Glendale CA: Arthur H. Clark Co., 1969), 227–36.

18. William Garnett and George W. Colhoff also told Ricker that Alfred Palladay and John Richard Sr. were killed on the Niobrara River (Tablets 1 and 17).

19. William Garnett witnessed the killing and told Ricker about it in more detail (Tablet 1). This section of the Garnett interview appears in Donald F. Danker, "The Violent Deaths of Yellow Bear and John Richard Jr.," *Nebraska History* 63 (1982): 137–51.

20. John Richard Sr. was a trader in the Fort Laramie area. He married Mary Gardiner, a mixed-blood Oglala, in 1844. They had four sons, Louis, Charles, Peter, and John Jr. John Dishon McDermott, "John Baptiste Richard," in Vol. 2, *The Moun-*

tain Men and the Fur Trade of the Far West, ed. LeRoy R. Hafen (Glendale CA: Arthur H. Clark Co., 1965), 293.

21. Chadron Creek was named for Louis B. Chartran. He had a trading post near present Chadron, Nebraska, in the early 1840s. Charles E. Hanson, Jr., "The Chadron Creek Trading Post," *The Museum of the Fur Trade Quarterly* 12 (1976): 6, 18.

22. James Bordeaux may have entered the fur trade as early as 1826. Later he supervised operations at Fort John/Laramie until it was sold to the army in 1849. He had a store near the Whetstone Agency, which was in the general vicinity of the Bijou Hills. John Dishon McDermott, "James Bordeaux," in Vol. 5, *The Mountain Men and the Fur Trade of the Far West,* ed. LeRoy R. Hafen (Glendale CA: Arthur H. Clark Co., 1968), 65-80.

Joseph Bissonet, uncle of Bordeaux's partner Joseph Bissonette, was in the fur trade for many years as early as 1812. He was from St. Louis. He frequently used the name Bijou, his stepfather's surname. LeRoy R. Hafen, "Joseph Bissonet, dit Bijou," in Vol. 9, *The Mountain Men and the Fur Trade of the Far West,* ed. LeRoy R. Hafen (Glendale CA: Arthur H. Clark Co., 1972), 27.

23. Bordeaux's first wife was an Arikara. She left him in the early 1840s. His second wife was a Brulé. They had ten children. Louis, born in 1849, was the third. McDermott, "James Bordeaux," 68.

24. About 1872 Francis C. Boucher took over James Bordeaux's post on Bordeaux Creek. He was selling guns and ammunition illegally to the Brulés and the army put him out of business in the fall of 1876. Charles E. Hanson, Jr. and Veronica Sue Walters, "The Early Fur Trade in Northwestern Nebraska," *Nebraska History* 57 (1976): 311.

25. Brothers Frank and Luther North became acquainted with the Pawnees in the late 1850s and by 1861 Frank was working as a clerk and interpreter for a trader on the reservation in present Nance County, Nebraska. Troops of Pawnee scouts were organized on seven separate occasions for periods of up to a few months. If other tribes were represented they were a very small minority. In addition to scouting they fought beside the soldiers against the Lakotas, Cheyennes, and other old enemies. Frank commanded the scouts on all their sorties except the first, when he was second in command. Donald F. Danker, "The North Brothers and the Pawnee Scouts," *Nebraska History* 42 (1961): 161-79.

26. There are other accounts of James Beckwith's death. In one he was poisoned by the Crows so his spirit would always remain with them. Another account has him dying of an illness. Oswald, "James P. Beckworth," 59-60. Richard Daylight [Tablet 22] told Ricker that Beckwourth "was on a spree and died on a steamboat on the Missouri River."

27. Christopher Carson and his long-time friend Lucien Maxwell began operations in 1849 on an enormous ranch in New Mexico. Tom Dunlay, *Kit Carson and the Indians* (Lincoln: University of Nebraska Press, 2000), 134.

28. Thomas Fitzpatrick began his career in the West as a fur trapper in 1823. He was

a guide for the army, but was never a soldier. In the summer of 1846 Fitzpatrick received his appointment as agent for the tribes in the Upper Platte and Arkansas river area. He served in that capacity until his death in 1854. LeRoy R. Hafen and W. J. Ghent, *Broken Hand: The Life Story of Thomas Fitzpatrick, Chief of the Mountain Men* (Denver: Old West Publishing Co., 1931), 131.

Tribes east of the Rocky Mountains and north of Texas and New Mexico were invited to attend the 1851 peace treaty negotiations at Fort Laramie. It was attended by the Sioux, Cheyennes, Arapahoes, Crows, Assiniboines, Gros Ventres, Mandans, and Arickaras. Other Plains tribes did not attend fearing an attack by their enemies.

29. Other accounts also based on hearsay tell of Indians killing J. LaRamee in the early 1820s on the Laramie River. John Dishon McDermott, "J. LaRamee," in Vol. 6, *The Mountain Men and the Fur Trade of the Far West,* ed. LeRoy R. Hafen (Glendale CA: Arthur H. Clark Co., 1968), 223–25.

30. Honoré Picotte was hired by the American Fur Company in 1830 at a salary of $1,000 a year. Later he was placed in charge of the Sioux Outfit, which included the Missouri River posts. Lecompte, "Pierre Chouteau, Junior," 91–123.

31. The firm was Berthold, Chouteau, and Pratte commonly called the French Company. In a reorganization it became Bernard Pratte and Company before being absorbed by the American Fur Company. Ibid., 102.

32. Hiram Martin Chittenden, *The American Fur Trade of the Far West,* 2 vols. (New York: Francis P. Harper, 1902).

33. Allen, *From Fort Laramie to Wounded Knee,* 12.

34. This was probably William M. Dye, who served in the Twentieth Iowa Infantry during the Civil War. Heitman, *Historical Register,* 392.

35. Col. Henry E. Maynadier was stationed at Fort Laramie in 1866. A commission headed by Edward B. Taylor met with Lakota leaders in June to discuss safe passage on the Bozeman Trail. Gray, *Custer's Last Campaign,* 36–37.

36. Colhoff's account summarizes a detailed report by Col. Henry E. Maynadier, commanding officer at Fort Laramie. Maynadier called Spotted Tail "Pegaleshka, head chief of the Brule Sioux." Maynadier, "No. 86. Headquarters West Sub-Division of Nebraska," *Annual Report of the Commissioner,* 1866, 207–8.

37. The Sod Agency consisted of ten rooms along two sides of a sod rectangle 100 by 120 feet. Nearby were three large warehouses, also enclosed by a sod wall. One of the warehouses and a stable were of log. "Description of Buildings and Enclosure," Red Cloud Agency letters, roll 715.

38. Lt. John W. Wham was honorably discharged from the army at his request on January 1, 1871. He returned to the army as paymaster from March 1877 until his retirement in 1901. Heitman, *Historical Register,* 1022. His appointment as agent was approved on February 16, 1871. J. Delano to Commissioner of Indian Affairs, Feb. 16, 1871, Red Cloud Agency letters, roll 715. In October he was replaced by Col. John E. Smith. Delano to Commissioner, Nov. 1, 1871, Ibid.

39. Ricker wrote the following note in Tablet 22:

> The Loafer band was a waiting body of Indians which lived around Fort
> Laramie, noted for its friendly disposition toward white people. When the
> Indians started down and the fight came off at Horse Creek, these Loafers
> also went along, but they returned the next year. Big Mouth was the chief
> at fort Laramie. He was the father of Mrs. John Farnham. The Loafer band
> was one band till 1868. Not many Indians besides the Loafers moved down
> to Whetstone; on their way back they split, a part adhering to Red Cloud
> and part to Spotted Tail. The Whetstone movement contemplated but one
> Agency for all. When abt. five yrs. afterwards the two Agencies of Red Cloud
> & Spotted Tail were made, one band of Loafers adhered to one Agency &
> the other band to the other Agency.

40. In 1867 a seven-member commission of army officers and civilians met with small
groups of friendly Indians in Nebraska, Kansas, and Wyoming, but failed to accomplish anything. Olson, *Red Cloud and the Sioux Problem,* 59, 66–69.

   In addition to Harney and Sanborn, the 1868 commission included Maj. Gen.
Alfred H. Terry, Sen. J. B. Henderson, S. S. Tappan, and Commissioner of Indian
Affairs N. G. Taylor. General Sherman had been called back to Washington dur-
ing the 1867 meetings, but was in attendance in 1868. Ibid., 59, 74.

41. Red Cloud did not attend the primary meeting, but came to Fort Laramie and
touched the pen on November 5. Ibid., 81. Charles E. Geren was the interpreter.
Ibid., 75.

42. The west boundary was 104° west longitude. The north and south boundaries
were 46° and 43° north latitude, respectively. Kappler, *Indian Affairs,* 998. The
latitudes are near the Niobrara and Cannonball rivers and because the Indians did
not understand latitude, these landmarks were used instead. It would cause many
problems in the future. See the Sanborn letter, Tablet 36.

43. The delegation arrived in Washington on June 1, 1870. Olson, *Red Cloud and the
Sioux Problem,* 99.

44. Richard shot and killed Corp. Francis Conrad on September 9, 1869. Bryan Jones,
"John Richard, Jr., and the Killing at Fetterman," *Annals of Wyoming* 43 (1971):
242.

45. In November 1875 John Richard Sr. was murdered with Alfred Palladay along the
upper Niobrara River. McDermott, "John Baptiste Richard," 303.

46. Pine Ridge Agency opened in October 1878. It continues today at Pine Ridge,
South Dakota. Olson, *Red Cloud and the Sioux Problem,* 263.

47. In the spring of 1876 the Indians living near the agency burned the slaughter house
and ran off cattle and horses. They attacked one of Yates's supply trains and killed
the draft animals. The agent ordered Yates to send his wife to Fort Robinson,
where she would be safe. Buecker, *Fort Robinson and the American West,* 80.

48. Fort John/Laramie was Sublette and Campbell's trading post, which passed
through several owners until Pierre Chouteau Jr. & Company sold it to the U.S.
government on June 26, 1849. Construction of log and timber buildings adjacent

to the old structures began the following year. Fort Laramie was named for a mountain man killed in the vicinity in the 1820s. Remi Nadeau, *Fort Laramie and the
Sioux Indians* (Englewood Cliffs NJ: Prentice-Hall, Inc., 1967), 64-65.

49. The reference is to Helen "Nellie" Laravie. Born along the South Platte about
1860, she was one of four daughters of Joseph Laravie, a French trader, and a
Southern Cheyenne woman. Among her mother's people, Helen Laravie was
known as Chi-Chi. In 1878 she settled among Lip's *Wajaje* band near Eagle Nest
Butte on Pine Ridge and was known among the Lakotas as *Ista Gli Win,* "Brown
Eyes Woman." Hardorff note, *Death of Crazy Horse,* 26 n. 1.

50. Capt. James M. Bell took over from McGillycuddy on May 18, 1886, and served
briefly. Bell, "Pine Ridge Agency, Dakota," *Annual Report of the Commissioner,*
1886, 76.

51. Three troops of the Ninth Cavalry arrived on December 20 from Fort Robinson.
Jensen, Paul, and Carter, *Eyewitness at Wounded Knee,* 28.

52. Clarence Three Stars's interview is in Tablet 17. He was a teacher at a school north
of the agency.

53. During the Ghost Dance era Father John Jutz, S.J., made at least two trips to the
Stronghold to persuade Ghost Dancers to return to the agency. Jutz was in charge
of the Drexel or Holy Rosary Catholic Mission. He was assigned to the Rosebud
Reservation in 1886, and then to Pine Ridge three years later. Sister Mary Clem-
ent Fitzgerald, "Bishop Marty and His Sioux Missions," *South Dakota Historical
Collections* 20 (1940): 540, 548.

54. Dr. John J. Saville began his duties as agent to the Oglalas in August 1873. He was
replaced by James S. Hastings on December 10, 1875. Saville, "Red Cloud Agency,
Dakota," *Annual Report of the Commissioner,* 1874, 251-52; Hastings, "Red Cloud
Agency, Nebraska," *Annual Report of the Commissioner,* 1876, 33. Edward Rosewater was the editor of the *Omaha Bee.*

55. John G. Bourke alluded to corruption on the reservations in his book, *On the Border with Crook.*

56. Rev. John Robinson first met with the Oglalas at the agency on the Missouri River
and then followed them to Pine Ridge. James Irwin, "Red Cloud Agency, Dakota,"
Annual Report of the Commissioner, 1878, 38.

    Rev. Charles Smith Cook was a Yankton Sioux educated at Trinity College and
Seabury Divinity School. Eastman, *From Deep Woods to Civilization,* 85. Cook
came to Pine Ridge in the summer of 1885. Cook, "Pine Ridge Agency, Dak.," *Annual Report of the Commissioner,* 1888, 52.

57. Maj. Eugene A. Carr, Fifth Cavalry, commanded the so-called Republican River
Expedition in the summer of 1869. The command included the Pawnee Scouts
under Maj. Frank J. North. William F. Cody was chief of scouts for the cavalry. On
July 11 they routed the Cheyennes under Tall Bull near Summit Springs in northeastern Colorado. King, *War Eagle,* 101, 113. Colhoff has reversed the order of the

1873 Massacre Canyon attack by the Sioux on the Pawnees, and Carr's 1869 Republican River campaign against the Cheyenne Dog Soldiers.

58. Col. Anson Mills led the charge on the Lakota village at Slim Buttes on September 9, 1876. Greene, *Slim Buttes,* 59-60.

59. Maj. Guy V. Henry, Ninth Cavalry, entered the miliary academy in 1856, and was a brigadier general when he retired in 1898. He died a year later. Heitman, *Historical Register,* 523. The Ninth Cavalry departed on March 24, 1891. Jensen, Paul, and Carter, *Eyewitness at Wounded Knee,* 176.

60. Heitman, *Historical Register,* 574; Thomas R. Buecker, *Fort Robinson and the American Century, 1900-1948* (Lincoln: Nebraska State Historical Society, 2002), 21.

61. Lt. George F. Chase, Third Cavalry, entered West Point in 1867. Heitman, *Historical Register,* 297. Lt. Col. Luther P. Bradley commanded Fort C. F. Smith in 1867. He was transferred to Fort Laramie and then to Fort Robinson in 1877. Buecker, *Fort Robinson and the American West,* 97. Crazy Horse was killed at Fort Robinson on September 5, 1877.

62. On September 9, 1878, approximately three hundred Northern Cheyennes under Dull Knife and Little Wolf fled their Indian Territory reservation, where they had lived for fifteen months. Orlan J. Svingen, *The Northern Cheyenne Indian Reservation, 1877-1900* (Niwot: University Press of Colorado, 1993), 19.

63. On November 25, 1876, Col. Ranald Mackenzie led ten cavalry troops in the attack on Dull Knife's Cheyennes. Robert M. Utley, *Frontier Regulars: The United States Army and the Indian, 1866-1891* (Lincoln: University of Nebraska Press, 1984), 275-76. They were camped on Red Fork of Powder River.

64. Lt. John A. McKinney was in the Fourth Cavalry when he was killed. Heitman, *Historical Register,* 673.

65. Thomas T. Thornburgh joined the army in 1862, and a year later began attending the military academy. Major Thornburgh was assigned to the Fourth Infantry in 1878. He was killed September 29, 1879. Ibid., 958-59.

66. Estimates of the number killed vary, but eight hundred is much too high.

67. The author consistently wrote Major Ivans, which Ricker changed to Evans. Maj. Andrew W. Evans, Third Cavalry, arrived at the station from Fort Laramie on January 19 and took command. Wessells's men were reinforced by two troops of the Third Cavalry under Capt. John B. Johnson. Buecker, *Fort Robinson and the American West,* 144.

68. Ricker wrote the following note in Tablet 39 in 1906:
   Allen. [S.Dak.] See Louis Mousseau, Capt. Johnson's Stat. [statement] shows that Mousseau was with with Capt. Wessels in pursuit of the Cheyennes when "Woman's Dress" was shot through the arm. He says it was the Mousseau who was at the World's Fair with Buffalo Bill.

69. Ricker consistently misspelled Adolf Cuny's name. In July 1877 Cuny was killed at Six Mile Ranch by Billy Webster, alias Clark Pelton. Susan Bordeaux Bettelyoun

and Josephine Waggoner, *With My Own Eyes: A Lakota Woman Tells Her People's History*, ed. Emily Levine, (Lincoln: University of Nebraska Press, 1999), 150. In Tablet 22 Ricker correctly mentioned that, "Adolph Cooney was a sheriff over on the Laramie and was killed by outlaws."

70. For discussion of a medal presented "For Gallant Services Rendered to the Whites" at the death of Crazy Horse, but whose recipient has not been identified conclusively, see Paul L. Hedren, "The Crazy Horse Medal: An Enigma From the Great Sioux War," *Nebraska History* 75 (Summer 1994): 195-99.

71. Apache Kid killed Rip, the man who killed his father. Kid was a sergeant in the Indian scouts. He was temporarily in command of the scouts when Rip was murdered in late May 1887. Earle R. Forrest and Edwin R. Hill, *Lone War Trail of Apache Kid* (Pasadena CA: Trail's End Publishing Co., 1947), 39-40. The San Carlos Indian agency was on the Gila River south of present San Carlos, Arizona.

72. Al Sieber served in the Civil War with the Minnesota volunteers. He came to Arizona Territory in 1868, and three years later began a twenty-year career as a scout for the army. Ibid., 91-98.

73. William Diehl and William Grace were killed. Ibid., 42.

74. Tom Horn came west in 1874 when he was fourteen years old. He was a scout for the army in the mid-1880s during the search for Geronimo. He was convicted of murder and hung in Cheyenne, Wyoming, in 1903. Jay Monaghan, *Tom Horn: Last of the Bad Men* (Lincoln: University of Nebraska Press, 1997).

75. James B. Hughes entered the military academy in 1880, and was assigned to the Tenth Cavalry after his graduation. Heitman, *Historical Register*, 552.

76. This was probably James W. Watson, who was assigned to the Tenth Cavalry after his graduation from West Point. Ibid., 1009.

77. Theodore J. Wint enlisted in the army in 1861. He was promoted to captain in the Fourth Cavalry in 1872. Ibid., 1050.

78. John Bigelow, Jr. was a captain in the Tenth Cavalry. Ibid., 217.

79. Since the Kid was an army scout he was tried and convicted of desertion in a military court. When this sentence was commuted, civil authorities stepped in. The Kid and eight companions were tried for murder and found guilty on October 18, 1899. They were sentenced to seven years in the state penitentiary at Yuma. Forrest and Hill, *Lone War Trail of Apache Kid*, 43-44.

80. Sheriff Glenn Reynolds and Deputy William H. Holmes were taking Kid, seven of his companions, and a Mexican horse thief to the Yuma prison. Eugene Middleton was the stage driver. Ibid., 45-46.

81. Josh and Nosy were scouts. They killed a man in a drunken brawl and were promised a pardon if they would infiltrate Kid's gang. Josh and Nosy located Kid and killed five of his friends and wounded one called Say-es. Ibid., 54-55.

82. Hilda Gilbert, George Harris, and Bonnie Pourier Harris, *Big Bat Pourier* (Sheridan WY: Mills Publishing Company, 1968).

　　Major portions of this interview have been published. See Donald F. Danker,

"Big Bat Pourier's Version of the Sibley Scout," *Nebraska History* 66 (1985): 129–43; Baptiste Pourier, "Sibley's Ordeal in the Big Horns, July 6–9, 1876," in *Battles and Skirmishes of the Great Sioux War, 1876–1877,* ed. Jerome A. Greene (Norman: University of Oklahoma Press, 1993), 63–78. For other eyewitness accounts of the scouting expedition see John F. Finerty, *War-Path and Bivouac: or the Conquest of the Sioux* (Norman: University of Oklahoma Press, 1961) and Grouard's account in DeBarthe, *Life and Adventures of Frank Grouard.*

83. John Richard and his partners built a bridge across the North Platte River near Deer Creek in 1851, which was destroyed by a flood. It was replaced by a stronger structure. McDermott, "James Bordeaux," 72.

84. James Bridger went west of the Bighorn Mountains and down Clarks Fork of the Yellowstone River. It was not a very direct route. John M. Bozeman began a search for a shorter route to the gold fields in the fall of 1862. The trail he pioneered left the North Platte River near present Douglas, Wyoming, and turned to the northwest past the east and north sides of the Bighorn Mountains and then west to Virginia City. By 1864 the Bozeman Trail was the preferred route. Hebard and Brininstool, *The Bozeman Trail,* 214–20; Susan Badger Doyle, ed., *Journeys to the Land of Gold: Emigrant Diaries from the Bozeman Trail, 1863–1866,* 2 vols. (Helena: Montana Historical Society Press, 2000).

85. Washington Irving, *Astoria, or Anecdotes of an Enterprise beyond the Rocky Mountains* (New York: C. P. Putnam's Sons, 1897).

86. They arrived in early July. Gray, *Custer's Last Campaign,* 28.

87. Pourier's account seems to include elements from two fights. On August 1, 1867, a war party of nearly five hundred Cheyennes and Arapahos attacked a haying party and its military escort near Fort C. F. Smith. Three soldiers were killed before a relief party from the fort drove the attackers away. The next day near Fort Phil Kearny Red Cloud and his warriors attacked some soldiers and woodcutters, who fought from behind an improvised wagon box fortress. Olson, *Red Cloud and the Sioux Problem,* 63–64.

88. Hiram B. Kelly came to Fort Laramie in 1858, and in the 1870s had a ranch near present Chugwater, Wyoming. Virginia Cole Trenholm, *Footprints on the Frontier* (Douglas wy: Douglas Enterprise Co., 1945) 219, 247.

89. While Richard was hauling hay his father went to the fort to report vandalism by Indians at the Richard's home. Jones, "John Richard, Jr., and the Killing at Fetterman," 242.

90. William G. Bullock was hired as the store manager about 1857 by owner Seth E. Ward. Jerome A. Greene, "Sutlers, Post Traders, and the Fort Laramie Experience, 1850s–1860s," *Journal of the West* 41 (2002): 20.

Col. John Smith had been the commanding officer at Fort Laramie. He returned to the fort in the spring of 1870 to escort the delegates to Washington. Catherine Price, *The Oglala People, 1841–1879: A Political History* (Lincoln: University of Nebraska Press, 1996), 90.

91. This was probably Verling K. Hart, who was a captain in the Third Infantry in 1870. He transferred to the Fifth Cavalry in 1875. Heitman, *Historical Register,* 506.

92. James McCloskey was murdered at Six-Mile Ranch On October 27, 1870. John Boyer was hung for the crime on April 21, 1871. Gray, *Custer's Last Campaign,* 9.

93. Pourier was hired as General Crook's Crow interpreter during the campaign. J. W. Vaughn, *With Crook at the Rosebud* (Harrisburg PA: Stackpole Company, 1956), 17.

94. Captain Henry's wound was nearly fatal. A bullet passed through his face and blinded him in one eye. Ibid., 62. Henry continued to serve in the army until his retirement in 1898. He died a year later. Heitman, *Historical Register,* 523.

95. Maj. Thaddeus H. Stanton was the paymaster. When he retired in 1899, he was paymaster general of the army. Ibid., 916.

   Five reporters accompanied the battalion. One of the more prolific writers was John F. Finerty, who wrote *Warpath and Bivouac* in which he detailed his experiences.

96. Charles "Buffalo Chips" White was a scout. Greene, *Slim Buttes,* 75. Bourke's account of the incident varies only in details. Bourke, *On the Border with Crook,* 372.

97. Pourier is mistaken. Crazy Horse died at 11:40 P.M., Wednesday, September 5, 1877. Hardorff note, *Death of Crazy Horse,* 92 n. 1.

98. The third Indian scout was Little Big Man. No Neck was a respected Oglala band leader. After enlisting as a U.S. Indian scout he resided on No Neck Creek, Pine Ridge, where he died in 1887. The escort consisted of Company E, Third Cavalry, commanded by 2d Lt. Henry R. Lemley. Lemley had received orders from General Bradley to escort Crazy Horse to Fort Laramie by ambulance and from there to Cheyenne, where a train was to be boarded for Fort Marion, St. Augustine, Florida, where Crazy Horse was to be imprisoned. Hardorff note, *Death of Crazy Horse,* 93 n. 2.

99. Crazy Horse married Black Shawl in the summer of 1871. He married Nellie Laravie in the spring of 1877, after his surrender at Fort Robinson. Richard G. Hardorff, *The Oglala Lakota Crazy Horse: A Preliminary Genealogical Study and an Annotated Listing of Primary Sources* (Mattituck NJ and Bryan TX: J. M. Carroll and Co., 1985), 34, 35.

   In Tablet 17 Ricker mentioned, "The wife of old Crazy Horse is now the wife of Crazy Horse who lives in third house above Baptiste Pourier's on Wounded Knee Creek." Ricker was referring to Nellie Laravie. Later she married Greasing Hand, a Brulé, who assumed the name Crazy Horse. They lived on the Pine Ridge Reservation. Ibid., 35.

100. One of these councils took place at Camp Robinson on May 25, 1877, during which session, in a very rare display of public speaking, Crazy Horse briefly addressed Gen. Crook on the issue of a Northern Oglala agency. Hardorff note, *Death of Crazy Horse,* 94 n. 4.

101. After the Custer defeat Gen. George Crook sent a scouting party to locate their

Crow Indian allies. The party was led by Lt. Frederick W. Sibley. Danker, "Big Bat Pourier's Version of the Sibley Scout," 129-30.

102. Finerty, *War-Path and Bivouac;* Bourke, *On the Border with Crook.*

103. Grouard wrote that the Indians recognized him and said "they would get me by sundown." DeBarthe, *Life and Adventures of Frank Grouard,* 140.

104. *Publisher's Auxiliary,* Jan. 17, 1942.

105. Duncan "Tom" Blackburn, Bill Bivens, Robert McKemie, and probably others were partners in the late 1870s. They specialized in robbing stagecoaches leaving Deadwood. Little is known about the men. There was a rumor that Blackburn fathered a child by Calamity Jane. Later in life Blackburn supposedly became a prominent Baltimore businessman. Jay Robert Nash, *Encyclopedia of Western Lawmen and Outlaws* (New York: DaCapo Press, 1994), 47, 222.

106. Col. Wesley Merritt assumed command of the Fifth Cavalry on July 1, 1876. Heitman, *Historical Register,* 706. Lt. Col. Eugene A. Carr was also in the Fifth Cavalry. Ibid., 285. The battalion left Fort Laramie on a scouting expedition and confronted a Cheyenne war party on the upper reaches of Warbonnet Creek. Cody was riding ahead of the command and supposedly killed and scalped Yellow Hand, who was leading his party. Ricker interviewed Donald Brown, who said he saw Cody kill Yellow Hand (Tablet 13), but there were others who also claimed to have killed the Cheyenne chief. Historian Don Russell examined these claims and dispelled all of them. Don Russell, *The Lives and Legends of Buffalo Bill* (Norman: University of Oklahoma Press, 1960) 226. The chief's name should be translated Yellow Hair. Paul L. Hedren, *First Scalp for Custer: The Skirmish at Warbonnet Creek, Nebraska, July 17, 1876* (Glendale CA: Arthur H. Clark Co., 1980), 17.

107. Lt. John G. Bourke, Third Cavalry, wrote about the fight in *On the Border with Crook,* 369-75. Bourke was with the reinforcements who arrived after most of the fighting had ended.

108. American Horse, also known as Iron Plume, was a Miniconjou. He was killed in the fight. Greene, *Slim Buttes,* 49, 80.

109. Pvt. Edward Kennedy, Fifth Cavalry, also died of his wound and was buried with Charles White (Buffalo Chips). Ibid., 92.

110. General Crook sent Col. Ranald Mackenzie to disarm the Red Cloud and Red Leaf camps. Mackenzie had eight companies of cavalry and forty-two Pawnee scouts. Guns, ammunition, and 722 horses were taken without resistance on October 23, 1876. Jerome A. Greene, "The Surrounding of Red Cloud and Red Leaf, 1876: A Preemptive Maneuver of the Great Sioux War," *Nebraska History* 82 (2001): 69-75; Olson, *Red Cloud and the Sioux Problem,* 233.

111. Doc Middleton (James M. Riley, 1851-1913) took advantage of the general chaos during the Ghost Dance troubles and stole about thirty-five horses from the Indians and a few belonging to nearby whites. A posse recovered the animals, but Middleton was never charged with the crime. Hutton, *The Luckiest Outlaw,* 167.

112. In September 1878 three hundred Cheyennes under Dull Knife and Little Wolf fled

from virtual incarceration on a reservation in Indian Territory in a daring attempt to return to their homeland in Montana. Dull Knife's group of about 150 was captured by the army and imprisoned in a soldiers' barracks at Fort Robinson, while the government tried to decide what to do with them. On January 9, 1879, they made a desperate dash for freedom. Buecker, *Fort Robinson and the American West*, 127–41.

113. On November 27, 1868, Lt. Col. George A. Custer attacked a Cheyenne village under Black Kettle. More than one hundred men, women, and children were killed. Stan Hoig, *The Battle of the Washita: The Sheridan-Custer Indian Campaign of 1867–69* (Lincoln: University of Nebraska Press, 1976).

114. Colonel Custer was placed under arrest in 1867 for deserting his post at Fort Wallace. At his trial other charges were added and on October 11 he was found guilty and suspended from his command and salary for a year. Robert M. Utley, *Cavalier in Buckskin: George Armstrong Custer and the Western Military Frontier* (Norman: University of Oklahoma Press, 1988), 53.

115. Maj. Gen. John B. Sanborn commanded the Upper Arkansas District until leaving the army in 1866. Brig. Gen. Philip H. Sheridan commanded the Department of the Missouri. Hoig, *The Battle of the Washita*, 3, 23, 40.

116. Mrs. Clara Blinn and her two-year-old son Willie were abducted by the Cheyennes on October 9 near Fort Lyon. On December 11 a reconnaissance party discovered the bodies. Ibid., 96, 154, 160. They were probably killed by the Seventh Cavalry during the attack on Black Kettle's village. Joe D. Haines, Jr., "'For Our Sake Do All You Can': The Indian Captivity and Death of Clara and Willie Blinn," *The Chronicles of Oklahoma* 77 (1999): 181.

117. Construction of the second Red Cloud Agency, in present Dawes County, Nebraska, began in August 1873. J. J. Saville, "Red Cloud Agency, Nebraska," *Annual Report of the Commissioner*, 1875, 250.

The third Red Cloud Agency was established late in 1877, on the Missouri River near the mouth of Medicine Creek. The Lakotas opposed the move and after one year left the Missouri for the Pine Ridge country. Ibid., 254.

118. Dr. James Irwin was agent for the Oglalas from July 1, 1877, through December 1878. Red Cloud, Spotted Tail, and other chiefs were in Washington in September 1877. Olson, *Red Cloud and the Sioux Problem*, 240, 247, 264.

119. Big Mouth, a Loafer band chief, lived with his followers near the Whetstone Agency. He was jealous of Spotted Tail's growing influence in the tribe and hoped to rise above him in the Lakota hierarchy. Agent D. C. Poole confirmed that alcohol was involved and that Spotted Tail had been warned of Big Mouth's intentions. The killing occurred in the early morning hours of October 27, 1869. Poole, *Among the Sioux of Dakota: Eighteen Months' Experience as an Indian Agent, 1869–70* (St. Paul: Minnesota Historical Society Press, 1988), 82–83, 93. Hyde described Big Mouth as "jovial and fat." He became a chief after Smoke died in 1864. Hyde, *Spotted Tail's Folk*, 100.

120. Heitman, *Historical Register*, 338.

121. Little Chief surrendered to Col. Nelson A. Miles in the spring of 1877, and settled near Fort Keogh. That fall Colonel Miles attacked the Nez Perces in the Bear Paw Mountains of northern Montana. Wooster, *Nelson A. Miles and the Twilight of the Frontier Army,* Chapt. 6.

122. Edward G. Mathey joined the army in 1861. In 1867 he was assigned to the Seventh Cavalry and promoted to captain in 1877. Heitman, *Historical Register,* 696.

   William H. Lewis entered the military academy in 1845. Lieutenant Colonel Lewis was transferred to the Nineteenth Infantry in 1873. He was wounded on September 27, 1878, in action with the Cheyennes on Punished Woman's Fork. He died the next day. Ibid., 631. The stream is near present Scott City, Kansas, nearly two hundred miles south of Ogallala, Nebraska.

123. When the Cheyennes reached the North Platte River, Little Wolf's group of 114 people separated from the main body and eluded capture. Dull Knife's band decided to surrender at Fort Robinson, hoping for permission to join the Oglalas. On October 23 they encountered a scouting party of the Third Cavalry under Capt. John B. Johnson. They surrendered without incident and were taken to Fort Robinson. Svingen, *The Northern Cheyenne Indian Reservation,* 19.

124. Edwin Mauck joined the army in 1861. He was promoted from captain to major in 1879. He was made a brevet major for his service in the Atlanta campaign in the Civil War. Heitman, *Historical Register,* 697.

125. John Pope entered the military academy in 1838. He was breveted for his service in both the Mexican and the Civil War. When he retired in 1886, he was a major general. Ibid., 798.

126. Ben Clarke served as an army scout in Kansas and south into Texas. J. W. Vaughn, *The Reynolds Campaign on Powder River* (Norman: University of Oklahoma Press, 1961), 40.

   William Rowland was the Cheyenne interpreter. He married a Cheyenne woman in 1850, and remained with the tribe. George Bird Grinnell, *The Fighting Cheyennes* (Norman: University of Oklahoma Press, 1956), 360.

   Ricker wrote the following in Tablet 22:

   > William Young Rowland was a native of Kentucky. Left home when 12 years old. Got in with the American Fur Company. It is said he went to Salt Lake in 1847 with an expedition. Mrs. Nellie Rowland, relict of Ben Rowland, Kyle, S.D. has photos of William Rowland's father and mother. I have seen them. The above is from Willis Rowland, son of Ben Rowland. James Rowland of Kirby, Montana, can give history of his father William Rowland.

127. Mackenzie's column attacked Dull Knife's Cheyennes. Charles M. Robinson III, *Bad Hand: A Biography of General Ranald S. Mackenzie* (Austin TX: State House Press, 1991), 217. William Garnett's interview in Tablet 1 covers this campaign in detail.

128. David Y. Mears, "Campaigning Against Crazy Horse," *Proceedings and Collections of the Nebraska State Historical Society* 10 (1907): 68–77.

129. E. S. "Zeke" Newman began ranching in 1878 to supply beef at Pine Ridge and Rosebud reservations. The ranch headquarters was about twelve miles south of Gordon, Nebraska. Robert H. Burns, "The Newman Ranches: Pioneer Cattle Ranches of the West," *Nebraska History* 34 (1953): 21–31.

130. Samuel P. Ferris began attending the military academy in 1857. Captain Ferris was assigned to the Fourth Infantry in 1869. Heitman, *Historical Register*, 417.

131. Ibid., 175; Buecker, *Fort Robinson and the American Century*, 3, 159.

132. Letters by a soldier in the Eleventh Ohio Cavalry have been published in William E. Unrau's, *Tending the Talking Wire: A Buck Soldier's View of Indian Country, 1863–1866* (Salt Lake City: University of Utah Press, 1979).

133. Mud Springs Pony Express station was built in 1859 or early in 1860. It also served as a stagecoach and telegraph station. It was approximately ten miles southeast of Courthouse Rock. There were two buildings. One was eighteen by thirty-eight feet with two rooms and the other was twenty by forty feet with three rooms. Both of these were sod. There may have been a third that served as a stable. On February 4, 1865, Indians attacked Mud Springs. The telegraph operator wired for help and soldiers from Camp Mitchell, located forty-five miles to the northwest, arrived the next morning. Col. William Collins arrived from Fort Laramie with 120 cavalrymen later in the day and the Indians were finally driven off. On February 8–10 Collins's command skirmished with the Indians near Rush Creek, before the Indians withdrew north of the Platte. Three soldiers were killed and sixteen wounded in the two fights. Indian fatalities were estimated at forty. Paul Henderson, "The Story of Mud Springs," *Nebraska History* 32 (1951): 108–19; John D. McDermott, "'We Had a Terribly Hard Time Letting Them Go': The Battles of Mud Springs and Rush Creek, February 1865," *Nebraska History* 77 (1996): 78–88.

134. James McClosky served as interpreter when a Lakota delegation went to Washington, D.C. in 1870. Olson, *Red Cloud and the Sioux Problem*, 97.

   On the reverse of the page Ricker noted, "Calico, White Face, and One Side were the three Indian prisoners mounted. The one prisoner in the wagon was kept there as he could not run away."

135. The sun dancer has also been identified as Black Wolf. Nadeau, *Fort Laramie and the Sioux*, 181.

136. William Garnett told Ricker a story he heard from Woman's Dress (Tablet 2). Supposedly "Crazy Horse planned to meet General Crook in an apparently friendly manner and intention, to shake hands, and then treacherously to take his life, while his adherents would kill his attendants." Charles Eastman told Ricker, "Woman's Dress was a liar and was serving the interests of the jealous chiefs who were conspiring against Crazy Horse. It was false that Crazy Horse was planning to compass the death of Gen. Crook" (Tablet 11).

   The entry in Clark's book only describes the sign language for the name Crazy Horse. Clark explained, "It should not be *Crazy Horse*, but *His-Horse-is-Crazy*."

William P. Clark, *The Indian Sign Language* (Philadelphia: L. R. Hamersly Co., 1885), 422.

137. This account is similar to an event described by George Hyde in *Spotted Tail's Folk* and Sidney Harring in *Crow Dog's Case*. It was Spotted Tail's son who stole one of White Thunder's wives. White Thunder retaliated by taking young Spotted Tail's horses. Young Spotted Tail and some of his friends then ambushed White Thunder, killing him. Long Pumpkin was severely wounded. Hyde and determined that the incident occurred on May 29, 1884. Hyde, *Spotted Tail's Folk,* 306–7; Harring, *Crow Dog's Case,* 133.

138. Ricker's notes on his interview with Eastman (Tablet 11) do not mention Custer or the Little Bighorn.

139. Eli Paul was kind enough to let me copy his biography of Sam Deon. R. Eli Paul, ed., *Autobiography of Red Cloud: War Leader of the Oglalas* (Helena: Montana Historical Society Press, 1997), 13–14.

In Tablet 44 Ricker described Deon as a "Pine Ridge old timer; oldest on the Reservation next to McClosky."

140. The American Fur Company held a virtual monopoly on the fur trade in the West. By 1847 buffalo robes were the primary trade item.

John B. Sarpy and Pierre Didier Papin were undoubtedly the men Deon refers to. They arrived in St. Louis from a trip to the upper Missouri on July 8, 1847. Papin set out for the upper river again in September. Charles G. Clarke, "Pierre Didier Papin," in Vol. 9, *The Mountain Men and the Fur Trade of the Far West,* ed. LeRoy R. Hafen (Glendale: Arthur H. Clark Co., 1972), 316–17.

141. Deon seems to be describing true keelboats, not the distinctly different mackinaws.

142. The cholera epidemic was at its worst in April and May 1849. Louise Barry, *The Beginning of the West: Annals of the Kansas Gateway to the American West, 1540–1854* (Topeka: Kansas State Historical Society, 1972), 829–31, 845–47.

143. Joseph Marie La Barge had three sons. Son Joseph was the captain of the steamboat *Martha* that went up the Missouri in 1847. Sons Charles S. and John B. were also riverboat men. Deon failed to mention the attempted highjacking of the boat by the Yanktons. One crewman was killed in the meleé. Hiram Martin Chittenden, *History of Early Steamboat Navigation on the Missouri River* (Minneapolis: Ross and Haines Inc., 1962), 13, 178–83.

144. This may have been Pierre Champaign, who was also a trader about this time. Charles E. Hanson, Jr., "J. B. Moncravie," in Vol. 9, *The Mountain Men and the Fur Trade of the Far West,* ed. LeRoy R. Hafen (Glendale: Arthur H. Clark Co., 1972), 289–98.

145. The tablet continues in Ricker's handwriting in spite of the use of the first person. The steamboat *St. Ange* left St. Louis on June 7. Hiram Martin Chittenden and Alfred Talbot Richardson, *Life, Letters and Travels of Father Pierre-Jean DeSmet, S.J.* (New York: Francis P. Harper, 1905), 638.

146. The 1851 treaty was signed on September 17 near Fort Laramie. It was an attempt

to establish territorial boundaries for the tribes north of the Platte River and to allow emigrant roads through these territories. Kappler, *Indian Affairs*, 594–96. Deon is now on board a steamboat and it would have been going upriver in the early spring. Fur company officials and the Indians went overland from Fort Union to Fort Laramie.

147. Father DeSmet did not mention Champaign or Deon in his writings. Chittenden, *Life of DeSmet*.

148. The American Fur Company was supportive of DeSmet's endeavors, but he was not an employee.

149. Father DeSmet called Four Bears "the most civil and affable Indian I met on the Missouri." Chittenden, *Life of DeSmet*, 651.

150. In addition to the sixty-odd company employees in the boats there was also De-Smet's party of thirty-two that went by land. The latter group included Assiniboines, Minnetarees, Crows, and a few others. The land party had two four-wheeled wagons and two carts. Ibid., 653–54.

151. Alexander Culbertson entered the fur trade in 1830 when he was twenty-one years old. Ten years later was in charge of Fort Union. By the time Deon met him, Culbertson was a very wealthy man. He would make some bad investments and died in near poverty at Orleans, Nebraska in 1879. Ray H. Mattison, "Alexander Culbertson," in Vol. 1, *The Mountain Men and the Fur Trade of the Far West*, ed. LeRoy R. Hafen (Glendale: Arthur H. Clark Co., 1965), 252–56. With his long experience in the West, Deon certainly knew that Culbertson was not "the headman of the Blackfeet." This must be Ricker's error.

152. This was the 1851 treaty. Kappler, *Indian Affairs*, 440–42.

153. Blackfoot was hung on May 26, 1865, at Fort Laramie for kidnapping a white woman and her child. His name is rendered Blackfoot in Nadeau, *Fort Laramie and the Sioux Indians*, 178.

154. For Red Cloud's "Life" see Paul, *Autobiography of Red Cloud*.

155. Jules Ecoffey began trading with the Lakotas about 1854. George E. Hyde, *Red Cloud's Folk, A History of the Oglala Sioux Indians* (Norman: University of Oklahoma Press, 1937), 196. He and his partner, Adolph Cuny, operated a large cattle ranch and a road ranche near Fort Laramie. Paul L. Hedren, *Fort Laramie in 1876: Chronicle of a Frontier Post at War* (Lincoln: University of Nebraska Press, 1988), 45–46.

156. The Cheyennes attacked a wagon train near Plum Creek Station on August 7, 1864. Several members of the train were killed and a woman was taken prisoner. Leroy W. Hagerty, "Indian Raids Along the Platte and Little Blue Rivers, 1864–1865," *Nebraska History* 28 (1947): 240.

Two Face and Blackfoot abducted Lucinda Eubanks and Laura Roper. The women were captured near present Oak, Nebraska, not at Plum Creek.

157. On August 8, 1864, a mule train led by Thomas F. Morton passed Plum Creek, Nebraska, heading west. The train was attacked and eleven whites were killed. Mor-

ton's wife Nancy was taken prisoner. In December Joseph Bissonette, Jr. and Jules Ecoffey made an unsuccessful attempt to ransom her from her Cheyenne captors. A second attempt in January met with success. Old Crow or Black Crow, a Sioux, was hung for his part in the abduction of Mrs. Morton. Russ Czaplewski, *Captive of the Cheyenne: The Story of Nancy Jane Morton and the Plum Creek Massacre* (Lexington NE: Dawson County Historical Society, 1993). Moses Sydenham, in a 1905 letter to the *Nebraska State Journal* (Tablet 34), said the train carrying goods for Denver merchants was attacked by 150 Cheyennes.

158. Bridger's daughter Virginia lived on the Bridger farm near Kansas City. She married a Mr. Wachsman and after his death (?) she married Mr. Hahn. Daughter Mary lived in Indian Territory and she was married, but her husband's name was not given. Alter, *James Bridger*, 212, 518–19.

159. John Shangrau's description of General Crook's expedition to the Powder River in March 1876 is in Tablet 27. Frank Grouard was also a scout on the expedition and his recollection of it is in DeBarthe, *Life and Adventures of Frank Grouard*. Major Bourke wrote about an attack on the camp that occurred the evening of March 5. One soldier was wounded. The herder was wounded on the night of March 1–2. Bourke, *On the Border with Crook*, 256–58.

160. Respects Nothing's interview is in Tablet 29.

161. Col. Ranald S. Mackenzie commanded the District of the Black Hills. On August 13, 1876, he established his headquarters at Fort Robinson. Capt. William H. Jordan, Ninth Infantry, was the commanding officer at the post. Buecker, *Fort Robinson and the American West*, 85, 198.

162. Nathan C. Meeker was in charge of the White River Ute agency in western Colorado. An argument with the chiefs over a plot of land escalated until Meeker panicked and called in the army. The Utes fought off the soldiers, burned the agency, and killed several civilians, including Meeker, on September 29, 1879. Robert Emmitt, *The Last War Trail: The Utes and the Settlement of Colorado* (Norman: University of Oklahoma Press, 1954.

163. On November 11 Agent Daniel Royer ordered the arrest of Little for killing agency cattle. Little's friends prevented his incarceration. Jensen, Paul, and Carter, *Eyewitness at Wounded Knee*, 27.

164. Forty-five Pine Ridge Indians returned from their European tour with William F. Cody's Wild West show. Troops began arriving at Pine Ridge on November 20. Ibid., 29, 78.

165. John M. Burke served as Cody's press agent and general manager of the Wild West shows. His title was honorary. Russell, *The Lives and Legends of Buffalo Bill*, 202.

166. Capt. Augustus W. Corliss and more than two hundred soldiers from the Ninth Cavalry and Eighth Infantry left Fort Robinson on November 19 for the Pine Ridge Agency. The troops guarded the agency, went on scouting missions, and were involved in the Drexel Mission fight. Buecker, *Fort Robinson and the American West*, 174–75.

William R. Shafter joined the army in 1861 and retired forty years later with the rank of major general. Heitman, *Historical Register,* 876. Frank Wheaton joined the army in 1855. Major General Wheaton retired in 1897. Ibid., 1022.

167. Capt. Allyn Capron, First Artillery, was in charge of two Hotchkiss guns at Wounded Knee. Lt. Harry L. Hawthorne commanded the other two. Utley, *The Last Days of the Sioux Nation,* 201–2.

168. In July 1873 Col. David S. Stanley placed Custer under arrest for two days while on a march from Fort Rice to the Yellowstone River. Utley, *Cavalier in Buckskin,* 119.

169. The fight was on August 11 against followers of Sitting Bull near the mouth of the Bighorn River. The arrival of Colonel Stanley's infantry tipped the scales in favor of the army and the Lakotas fled. Ibid., 122.

170. John E. Smith enlisted in the army in 1861, and served until his retirement in 1881. Heitman, *Historical Register,* 900. Smith commanded the troops sent to protect the Red Cloud and Spotted Tail agencies. Col. Smith, Fourteenth Infantry, was at Red Cloud from March 5 to March 9, 1874. Four companies of infantry and one of cavalry were stationed there under Capt. James Van Horn. Smith and the rest of the troops moved on to the Spotted Tail Agency. Buecker, *Fort Robinson and the American West,* 14–16.

171. Crow Dog fired the shot that killed Spotted Tail. Black Crow was implicated in the 1881 assassination, but the case against him was dropped. Hyde, *Spotted Tail's Folk,* 302–3.

172. Either Whalen's memory or Ricker's notes were faulty. Col. Nelson Cole's unit left Omaha on July 1. Troops under Gen. Patrick E. Connor built Fort Connor. Terrain and bad weather delayed Cole's planned rendezvous with Connor. Hunkpapa warriors tried to capture the the soldiers' horses and mules. Six soldiers were killed. By this time starvation was a greater threat than the Indians. On September 20 Cole's bedraggled troops arrived at Fort Connor. Utley, *Frontiersmen in Blue,* 323–30.

173. On September 5 there was a fierce fight with Sioux, Cheyenne, and Arapahoe warriors. Three days later there was another fight near a Sioux village. Ibid., 329.

174. Most of the troops stationed at Fort Casper were in the Eleventh Kansas Cavalry. Ibid., 319–20.

175. Maj. Alexander Chambers was at the Whetstone Agency when the Indians arrived late in 1868. He was replaced by Capt. A. E. Woodson, and then S. L. Nidelt served briefly. Hyde, *Spotted Tail's Folk,* 132. DeWitt Clinton Poole arrived on July 14, 1869, to begin duties as agent. Poole, "Whetstone Agency, D.T.," *Annual Report of the Commissioner,* 1870, 315. J. M. Washburn took charge on November 18, 1870. Washburn, "Whetstone Agency," *Annual Report of the Commissioner,* 1872, 527. Raymond may have been a clerk who managed the affairs of the agency in the absence of the agent.

176. Although it was against the law, there were many whiskey peddlers in Indian country. One of the most cunning was a man who ran a still and liquor store directly across the Missouri from Whetstone Agency, where his operation was legal. Wil-

liam Welch, chairman of the Board of Indian Commissioners, purchased the establishment in the hopes it would end the sale of liquor to the Lakotas. The peddler moved a short distance downstream, where he reopened his business, which he graciously offered to sell to the agent. Poole, *Among the Sioux of Dakota,* 210–12.

177. The commissioners who visited the Lakotas in 1874 included Episcopal Bishop William H. Hare, Rev. S. D. Hinman, C. C. Cox, and R. B. Lines. Hare and Cox became ill after the meeting was concluded. Olson, *Red Cloud and the Sioux Problem,* 167–68.

178. The delegation met with the President on September 27, 1877. Ibid., 248.

179. Commissioner of Indian Affairs Ezra Hayt met with the Lakotas in July 1878 at the agencies on the Missouri River to discuss a permanent agency site. Ibid., 260.

180. Congress appropriated $25,000 in 1875. Ibid., 182.

181. Pro-Indian whites frequently mentioned starvation as a cause for the Lakotas' discontent and the spread of the Ghost Dance. It had the advantage of being an easily understood and logical reason, especially when the recent reduction in the government-supplied rations was mentioned. In spite of the reduction, more than a pound of usable meat and a variety of other foodstuffs were provided per person per day. Richard E. Jensen, "Notes on the Lakota Ghost Dance," paper read before the Thirty-third Annual Missouri Valley History Conference, Omaha, March 8, 1990.

182. The legend about the skinned man may have first appeared in the Lacon *Illinois Gazette* on February 2, 1850. It was repeated on numerous occasions and it was said to have happened a variety of locations from Rawhide Creek in Nebraska to Rawhide Butte in Wyoming. Not one of the people who reported on the alleged incident claimed to have been an eyewitness. It seems likely that such an atrocity would be reported to the military, but it is not mentioned in any of the reports filed at Fort Kearny, the closest army post.

183. In 1850 the Pawnee village was on the south side of the Platte River in northeastern Saunders County, Nebraska. Roger T. Grange, Jr., *Pawnee and Lower Loup Pottery* (Lincoln: Nebraska State Historical Society, 1968), 24–25.

184. This crude map shows the Elkhorn River with a large bend where a road crosses on a ferry. This "old road" goes southwest past "grave" and crosses Rawhide Creek. The old road and grave are southeast of "Government Bridge" across Rawhide Creek. A note reads, "P.S. where the ferry was is now a little place called Bridgeport. The place was called 'Elkhorn Ferry' at the time the bridge was built. Capt. Fifield kept a little store at the ferry. This map was made by Mr. Irion." The map is on the back of a scrap of a legal document about a creditors' meeting in the bankruptcy of Joseph M. Robinson in Chadron, Nebraska.

185. The treaty establishing the Pawnee reservation, which was roughly present-day Nance County, Nebraska, was signed on September 24, 1857. Kappler, *Indian Affairs,* 772. The Pawnees went to Oklahoma in the late 1870s. The Omaha reservation established in 1854 is in present Thurston County, Nebraska. Ibid., 610. The

Oto reservation, formerly in present Gage County, was also established in 1854, but the Otos, too, went to Oklahoma. Ibid., 608. The reservation for the Poncas was in eastern Boyd County, Nebraska, approximately 100 miles northwest of the Omahas. The Poncas also were removed to Oklahoma. Ibid., 772.

186. Perhaps Adam Smith was a descendent of John Simpson Smith, who was present at the Sand Creek massacre as an interpreter. Stan Hoig, *The Sand Creek Massacre* (Norman: University of Oklahoma Press, 1961), 153.

187. Oddly Ricker did not correct this confusion. Fort Laramie was at the mouth of the Laramie River, while Fort Bridger was on a tributary of Ham's Fork, but not far from it. Bridger was a part owner of Fort Laramie in the 1830s, but not in 1849, when it was sold to the government. Alter, *James Bridger*, 150, 177.

188. In early September 1857 a party of about 140 California-bound emigrants camped at Mountain Meadows in the southwest corner of Utah. The anti-Mormon attitude of the travelers was equaled by enmity the Mormons felt for the Gentiles. Paiute Indians, led by John D. Lee, attacked the party. After the emigrants fought off the attack, they were approached by whites who offered to lead them to safety at Cedar City, but only if they would disarm themselves and go on foot to allay the fears of the Paiutes. After the emigrants were disarmed the attack was renewed and approximately 120 men, women, and children were murdered. Lee was executed in 1877 for his part in the Mountain Meadows massacre. Will Bagley, *Blood of the Prophets: Brigham Young and the Massacre at Mountain Meadows* (Norman: University of Oklahoma Press, 2002).

189. An army of two thousand men under Col. Albert Sidney Johnston was ordered to Utah because of concerns about a possible Mormon rebellion. The troops reached Fort Bridger on November 17, 1857, where a blizzard prevented any further advance. Charles P. Roland, *Albert Sidney Johnston: Soldier of Three Republics* (Austin: University of Texas Press, 1987), 196–201.

190. Johnston and his army arrived at Salt Lake City on June 25. In February 1858 he received orders relieving him of the Utah command. He was granted a leave of absence while waiting for a new assignment. Johnston was killed in battle at Shiloh, Tennessee, on April 6, 1862, while in command of the Confederate Army. Ibid., 213, 236, 338.

191. On March 17, 1876, Col. Joseph J. Reynolds's command attacked a Northern Cheyenne village on the Powder River. The Indians were forced into a retreat, the village was burned, and the horse herd captured. Reynolds lost the initiative and the Cheyennes recaptured the horses. Crook brought charges against Reynolds for failure to guard the captured horses, which the Indians recaptured, and for destroying the foodstuffs in the village rather than keeping them for the troops. Reynolds was found guilty, but the sentence was remanded by President Grant. Reynolds retired shortly after the trial. Vaughn, *The Reynolds Campaign*.

192. Four men were killed and six were wounded. Ibid., 93.

193. Capt. James Egan, Second Cavalry, joined the army in 1856. He retired in 1879.

Heitman, *Historical Register,* 399. Custer was not with this unit. Capt. Henry Noyes was reprimanded for this action. Stewart, *Custer's Luck,* 94.

194. Joseph R. Brown played a major role in the development of Minnesota. Musician Brown served at Fort Snelling in 1820. Later he became active in territorial and state politics. He also edited a newspaper and was agent to the Santees. William Watts Folwell, *A History of Minnesota,* 4 vols. (St. Paul: Minnesota Historical Society, 1921) 3:347–50.

195. This is a garbled version of an event near Fort Laramie in 1854. Conquering Bear tried to pay for the Mormon's cow but was refused. Lt. John L. Grattan in command of twenty-nine soldiers was sent to arrest High Forehead who had killed the cow. High Forehead refused to be arrested, tempers flared, and shots were fired, which escalated into a pitched battle. Grattan and his entire command were killed. The interpreter, Lucien Auguste, and Conquering Bear were also killed. Lloyd E. McCann, "The Grattan Massacre," *Nebraska History* 37 (1956): 1–25.

196. Pliley followed his own rules for punctuation and capitalization, which made the letter nearly incomprehensible on first reading. Ricker's edited and typed copy is offered here.

197. It was named for Brig. Gen. John A. Rawlins, who inspected the area with Union Pacific Railroad officials in 1867. Grenville M. Dodge, *How We Built the Union Pacific Railway* (Denver: Sage Books, 1965), 24.

198. Civil War veteran Grenville M. Dodge was the chief construction engineer for the Union Pacific Railroad. He was in the Rawlins vicinity during most of 1868. Ibid., 28.

199. Thomas L. Rosser was at the head of the surveyors and engineers of the Northern Pacific Railroad. Custer wrote about the campaign but failed to make any mention of his altercation with General Stanley. G. A. Custer, "Battling with the Sioux on the Yellowstone," in *The Custer Reader,* ed. Paul Andrew Hutton (Lincoln: University of Nebraska Press, 1992), 203.

200. Allen, *From Fort Laramie to Wounded Knee,* 71.

201. James H. Cook, *Fifty Years on the Old Frontier* (New Haven: Yale University Press, 1923).

202. This section was published. See James H. Cook, "The Texas Trail," *Nebraska History Magazine* 16 (1935): 229–40.

203. Early in his career, Cook worked for Ben Slaughter as a ranch hand in southwestern New Mexico. Cook, *Fifty Years on the Old Frontier,* 8.

204. Col. William H. Emory served in the Fifth U.S. Cavalry from 1865 until his retirement on July 1, 1876. Heitman, *Historical Register,* 405. Col. Wesley Merritt then assumed command of the Fifth. Ibid., 706.

205. Lt. Col. George A. Custer ordered the execution of four deserters. Three were wounded and one died. In September 1867 Custer was court-martialed and found guilty. He was suspended from rank and command for a year, and forfeited his pay for the same period. Custer spent the winter at Fort Leavenworth as a guest

of Gen. William T. Sherman. During the summer Custer relaxed on the shores of Lake Erie, returning to Fort Hays in September 1869. Lawrence A. Frost, *The Court-Martial of General George Armstrong Custer* (Norman: University of Oklahoma Press, 1968).

206. After the Rosebud battle, Gen. George Crook's army found an Indian trail that seemed to be heading for the Black Hills. Crook followed, fearing the Indians would attack the gold miners. The soldiers were on half rations by the end of August. On September 5, near the headwaters of the Heart River, Crook found it necessary to kill horses for food. Charles M. Robinson III, *General Crook and the Western Frontier* (Norman: University of Oklahoma Press, 2001), 193.

207. Col. George A. H. Blake served from 1830 to 1870. He earned commendations in both the Mexican and Civil wars. Heitman, *Historical Register,* 223. Maj. Albert G. Brackett served from 1847 to 1891, winning commendations in the Civil War. Ibid., 237.

208. The letter was two typewritten pages. Box 19, Ricker Coll.

209. James C. Hunt joined the army in 1861. In 1867 he was promoted to lieutenant colonel for gallantry in an engagement with Indians at Steen's Mountain in southeastern Oregon. Heitman, *Historical Register,* 556.

210. Moses Harris began his military career in 1863 as a private. He was awarded the Medal of Honor for bravery in the Civil War. Major Harris resigned in 1893. Ibid., 503-4.

211. The Cheyennes, angered by what they saw as the government's refusal to abide by the Medicine Lodge Creek treaty, raided frontier settlements in western Kansas. On September 14, 1868, Gov. Samuel J. Crawford authorized the formation of the Nineteenth Kansas Volunteer Cavalry. These raw recruits were to punish the Indians and restore peace. Later they would join with the Seventh U.S. Cavalry.

The Kansas Volunteers threatened to mutiny the following February because they had not been paid and they were near starvation. Crawford resigned and went to Washington, hoping to correct the problems. Lt. Col. Horace L. Moore assumed command. Hoig, *The Battle of the Washita,* 98-99, 171.

212. Allison J. Pliley was a survivor of Beecher Island. He commanded Company A of the Nineteenth Kansas Volunteers. Ibid., 102.

213. Maj. Joel Elliott, second in command, with sixteen troopers chased some Cheyennes fleeing from the village. Elliott's men were ambushed by Cheyenne and Arapahoe warriors from camps a few miles away, and all were killed. In all, twenty-two soldiers died in the fight. Ibid., 141, 210. Mrs. Clara Blinn and her two-year-old son, Willie, were killed, probably by the cavalry. Haines, "'For Our Sake Do All You Can': The Indian Captivity and Death of Clara and Willie Blinn," 181.

214. Eighteen-year-old Sarah White was abducted and her father killed on their farm near Concordia, Kansas. The attack was in mid-August. Mrs. Morgan was taken from her farm about twenty miles to the south in October. Hoig, *The Battle of the Washita,* 67.

215. Four minor chiefs were captured. One was released. Custer threatened to hang the remaining three if the white women were not released. Ibid., 177–78.

216. Mrs. Morgan's brother was Daniel Brewster. He accompanied Custer's troops in the hope of finding his sister. Lieutenant Colonel Moore and two other officers met the Cheyennes who surrendered the women. Brewster was detained in the army camp. Ibid., 169, 179. The interpreter's name was Romero, "whom the soldiers facetiously dubbed Romeo, because he was so ugly." Brady, *Indian Fights and Fighters,* 155.

217. It would seem that Bingaman is referring to the Kiowa chief Satanta. If so, this part of his story is questionable.

218. There were talks between the chiefs and army officers rather than a formal treaty.

219. Inkapaduta and his renegade Sioux followers were soundly defeated by troops led by Gen. Alfred Sully. The battle began on September 3, 1863. Clair Jacobson, *Whitestone Hill: The Indians and the Battle* (LaCrosse WI: Pine Tree Publishing, 1991).

220. Benjamin F. Gue, *History of Iowa,* 4 vols. (New York: Century History Co., 1903). Leclere has confused the 1863 and 1864 Sully campaigns, conflating the battles at Whitestone Hill in 1863 and the Badlands Campaign of 1864. See Robert Huhn Jones, *The Civil War in the Northwest: Nebraska, Wisconsin, Iowa, Minnesota, and the Dakotas* (Norman: University of Oklahoma Press, 1960).

221. Maj. Alfred B. Brackett led the charge on July 28, 1864, against the Miniconjous and other northern Lakota bands allied with some Santees. Utley, *Frontiersmen in Blue,* 278; Hyde, *Red Cloud's Folk,* 115–22.

222. Unfortunately, Ricker never received the remainder of the story or it has been lost.

Bibliography

Adams, George Rollie. *General William S. Harney: Prince of Dragoons.* Lincoln: University of Nebraska Press, 2001.

Agonito, Joseph G. "Young Man Afraid of His Horses: The Reservation Years." *Nebraska History* 79 (1998): 116–32.

Allen, Charles W. *From Fort Laramie to Wounded Knee: In the West that Was.* Ed. Richard E. Jensen. Lincoln: University of Nebraska Press, 1997.

Allison, Edwin H. *The Surrender of Sitting Bull, Being a Full and Complete History of the Negotiations Conducted by Scout Allison Which Resulted in the Surrender of Sitting Bull and His Entire Band of Hostile Sioux in 1881.* Dayton OH: Walker Lithograph and Printing, 1891.

———. "Surrender of Sitting Bull." *South Dakota Historical Collections* 6 (1910–12): 231–70.

Alter, J. Cecil. *James Bridger: Trapper, Frontiersman, Scout and Guide.* Salt Lake City: Shepard Book Co., 1925.

Andrews. Ralph W. *Indians as the Westerners Saw Them.* Seattle: Superior Publishing Co., 1963.

Anon. "The Messiah Craze." *Annual Report of the Commissioner of Indian Affairs.* Washington DC: GPO, 1891.

Bagley, Will. *Blood of the Prophets: Brigham Young and the Massacre at Mountain Meadows.* Norman: University of Oklahoma Press, 2002.

Baldwin, Frank D. "Report of Kiowa Agency." *Annual Report of the Commissioner of Indian Affairs.* Washington DC: GPO, 1897.

Barry, Louise. *The Beginning of the West: Annals of the Kansas Gateway to the American West, 1540–1854.* Topeka: Kansas State Historical Society, 1972.

Beach, Rex E. "Wounded Knee." *Appleton's Booklovers Magazine* 7 (1906): 732–36.

Bell, James M. "Pine Ridge Agency, Dakota." *Annual Report of the Commissioner of Indian Affairs.* Washington DC: GPO, 1886.

Bettelyoun, Susan Bordeaux and Josephine Waggoner. *With My Own Eyes: A Lakota Woman Tells Her People's History.* Ed. Emily Levine. Lincoln: University of Nebraska Press, 1999.

Bland, Thomas A. *A Brief History of the Late Military Invasion of the Home of the Sioux.* Washington DC: National Indian Defense Association, 1891.

Bordeaux, William J. *Custer's Conqueror.* Sioux Falls SD: Smith and Co., 1969.

Borst, John C. "Dakota Resources: The John R. Brennan Family Papers at the South Dakota Historical Resource Center." *South Dakota History* 14 (1984): 67–72.

Bourke, John G. *On the Border with Crook.* Lincoln: University of Nebraska Press, 1971.

Brady, Cyrus Townsend. *Indian Fights and Fighters.* Lincoln: University of Nebraska Press, 1971.

Brennan, J. R. "Report of Agent for Pine Ridge Agency." *Annual Report of the Commissioner of Indian Affairs.* Washington DC: GPO, 1902.

Brininstool, E. A. *Fighting Indian Warriors.* Harrisburg PA: Stackpole Co., 1953.

Brown, George LeRoy. "Report of Pine Ridge Agency." *Annual Report of the Commissioner of Indian Affairs.* Washington DC: GPO, 1892.

Buecker, Thomas R. *Fort Robinson and the American West, 1874–1899.* Lincoln: Nebraska State Historical Society, 1999.

———. *Fort Robinson and the American Century, 1900–1948.* Lincoln: Nebraska State Historical Society, 2002.

Burns, Robert H. "The Newman Ranches: Pioneer Cattle Ranches of the West." *Nebraska History* 34 (1953): 21–31.

Carroll, John M., ed. *Custer's Chief of Scouts: The Reminiscences of Charles A. Varnum.* Lincoln: University of Nebraska Press, 1987.

———. "Anheuser-Busch and Custer's Last Stand." *Greasy Grass* 3 (1987): 25–28.

Chittenden, Hiram Martin. *The American Fur Trade of the Far West.* 2 vols. New York: Francis P. Harper, 1902.

———. *History of Early Steamboat Navigation on the Missouri River.* Minneapolis: Ross and Haines Inc., 1962.

Chittenden, Hiram Martin and Alfred Talbot Richardson. *Life, Letters and Travels of Father Pierre-Jean DeSmet, S.J.* New York: Francis P. Harper, 1905.

Clapp, W. H. "Report of Pine Ridge Agency." *Annual Report of the Commissioner of Indian Affairs.* Washington DC: GPO, 1896.

Clark, William P. *The Indian Sign Language.* Philadelphia: L. R. Hamersly Co., 1885.

Clarke, Charles G. "Pierre Didier Papin." *The Mountain Men and the Fur Trade of the Far West.* Vol. 9. Ed. LeRoy R. Hafen. Glendale CA: Arthur H. Clark Co. 1972.

Clary, David A. and Joseph W. A. Whitehorne. *The Inspectors General of the United States Army 1777–1903.* Washington DC: GPO, 1987.

Colby, L. W. "Wanagi Olowan Kin: The Ghost Songs of the Dakotas." *Proceedings and Collections of the Nebraska State Historical Society* 1 (1895): 131–150.

———. "The Sioux Indian War of 1890–91." *Transactions and Reports of the Nebraska State Historical Society* 3 (1891): 144–200.

Cook, Charles Smith. "Pine Ridge Agency, Dak." *Annual Report of the Commissioner of Indian Affairs.* Washington DC: GPO, 1888.

Cook, James H. *Fifty Years on the Old Frontier.* New Haven: Yale University Press, 1923.

————. "The Texas Trail." *Nebraska History Magazine* 16 (1935): 229–40.

Cook, Joseph W. "Greenwood, Dak." *Annual Report of the Commissioner of Indian Affairs.* Washington DC: GPO, 1887.

Cox, W. H. "Report of Superintendent of Fort Sill School." *Annual Report of the Commissioner of Indian Affairs.* Washington DC: GPO, 1897.

Criqui, Orvel A. *Fifty Fearless Men: The Forsyth Scouts and Beecher Island.* Marceline MO: Walsworth Publishing Co., 1993.

Custer, Elizabeth B. *Boots and Saddles: or, Life in Dakota with General Custer.* New York: Harper and Brothers, 1885.

Custer, G. A. "Battling with the Sioux on the Yellowstone." *The Custer Reader.* Ed. Paul Andrew Hutton. Lincoln: University of Nebraska Press, 1992.

Czaplewski, Russ. *Captive of the Cheyenne: The Story of Nancy Jane Morton and the Plum Creek Massacre.* Lexington NE: Dawson County Historical Society, 1993.

Daniels, J. W. "Red Cloud Agency, Washington Territory." *Annual Report of the Commissioner of Indian Affairs.* Washington DC: GPO, 1874.

Danker, Donald F. "The North Brothers and the Pawnee Scouts." *Nebraska History* 42 (1961): 161–79.

————. "The Violent Deaths of Yellow Bear and John Richard Jr." *Nebraska History* 63 (1982): 137–51.

————. "Big Bat Pourier's Version of the Sibley Scout." *Nebraska History* 66 (1985): 129–43.

————. "A High Price to Pay for a Lame Cow." *Kansas History* 10 (1987): 111–17.

Deahl, William E., Jr. "The Chadron-Chicago 1,000 Mile Cowboy Race." *Nebraska History* 52 (1973): 167–93.

DeBarthe, Joe. *Life and Adventures of Frank Grouard.* Ed. Edgar I. Stewart. Norman: University of Oklahoma Press, 1958.

Dixon, David. *Hero of Beecher Island: The Life and Military Career of George A. Forsyth.* Lincoln: University of Nebraska Press, 1994.

Dodge, Grenville M. *How We Built the Union Pacific Railway.* Denver: Sage Books, 1965.

Doyle, Susan Badger, ed. *Journeys to the Land of Gold: Emigrant Diaries from the Bozeman Trail, 1863–1866.* 2 vols. Helena: Montana Historical Society Press, 2000.

Drannan, William F. *Thirty-One Years on the Plains and in the Mountains.* Chicago: Rhodes and McClure Publishing Co., 1900.

Dunlay, Tom. *Kit Carson and the Indians.* Lincoln: University of Nebraska Press, 2000.

Eastman, Charles A. *From Deep Woods to Civilization: Chapters in the Autobiography of an Indian.* Lincoln: University of Nebraska Press, 1977.

Emmitt, Robert. *The Last War Trail: The Utes and the Settlement of Colorado.* Norman: University of Oklahoma Press, 1954.

Ewers, John C. *The Blackfeet: Raiders on the Northwestern Plains.* Norman: University of Oklahoma Press, 1958.

Executive Documents of the Senate of the United States, 51st Cong., 2d sess., 1891–92. Doc. 9. Washington DC: GPO, 1892.

Fanebust, Wayne. *Echoes of November: The Life and Times of Senator R. F. Pettigrew.* Freeman SD: Pine Hill Press, 1997.

Faulk, Odie B. *The Geronimo Campaign.* New York: Oxford University Press, 1969.

Faust, Patricia L., ed. *Historical Times Illustrated Encyclopedia of the Civil War.* New York: Harper Perennial, 1986.

Finerty, John F. *War-Path and Bivouac: or the Conquest of the Sioux.* Norman: University of Oklahoma Press, 1961.

Fitzgerald, Sister Mary Clement. "Bishop Marty and His Sioux Missions." *South Dakota Historical Collections* 20 (1940): 522–88.

Foley, Thomas W. *Father Francis M. Craft: Missionary to the Sioux.* Lincoln: University of Nebraska Press, 2002.

Folwell, William Watts. *A History of Minnesota.* 4 vols. St. Paul: Minnesota Historical Society, 1921.

Forrest, Earle R. and Edwin R. Hill. *Lone War Trail of Apache Kid.* Pasadena CA: Trail's End Publishing Co., 1947.

Forsyth, George A. *Thrilling Days in Army Life.* New York: Harper and Brothers, 1900.

Freeman, Winfield. "The Battle of Arickaree." *Transactions of the Kansas State Historical Society* 6 (1900): 347–48.

Friswold, Carroll, and Robert A. Clark, eds. *The Killing of Chief Crazy Horse.* Glendale CA: Arthur H. Clark Co., 1976.

Frost, Lawrence A. *The Court-Martial of General George Armstrong Custer.* Norman: University of Oklahoma Press, 1968.

Gallagher, Hugh D. "Pine Ridge Agency, Dakota." *Annual Report of the Commissioner of Indian Affairs.* Washington DC: GPO, 1887.

Garland, Hamlin. "General Custer's Last Fight as Seen by Two Moons." *McClure's* 9 (1898): 443–48.

Gilbert, Hilda, George Harris, and Bonnie Pourier Harris. *Big Bat Pourier.* Sheridan WY: Mills Publishing Company, 1968.

Godfrey, Edward S. *Custer's Last Battle.* Ed. Eugene McAuliffe. Omaha: n.p., 1952.

Graham, W. A. *The Custer Myth: A Source Book of Custeriana.* Harrisburg PA: Stackpole Co., 1953.

Grange, Roger T. Jr. *Pawnee and Lower Loup Pottery.* Lincoln: Nebraska State Historical Society, 1968.

Gray, John S. "Arikara Scouts with Custer." *North Dakota History* 35 (1968): 443–78.

———. *Custer's Last Campaign: Mitch Boyer and the Little Big Horn Reconstructed.* Lincoln: University of Nebraska Press, 1991.

Greene, Jerome A. *Slim Buttes, 1876: An Episode of the Great Sioux War.* Norman: University of Oklahoma Press, 1982.

———. "The Surrounding of Red Cloud and Red Leaf, 1876: A Preemptive Maneuver of the Great Sioux War." *Nebraska History* 82 (2001): 69–75.

———. "Sutlers, Post Traders, and the Fort Laramie Experience, 1850s-1860s." *Journal of the West* 41 (2002): 17–25.

Grinnell, George Bird. *The Fighting Cheyennes*. Norman: University of Oklahoma Press, 1956.

Gue, Benjamin F. *History of Iowa*. 4 vols. New York: Century History Co., 1903.

Hafen, Ann Woodbury. "Lewis B. Myers 'La Bonte'." *The Mountain Men and the Fur Trade of the Far West*. Vol. 7. Ed. LeRoy R. Hafen. Glendale CA: Arthur H. Clark Co. 1969.

Hafen, LeRoy R. "Joseph Bissonet, dit Bijou," *The Mountain Men and the Fur Trade of the Far West*. Vol. 9. Ed. LeRoy R. Hafen. Glendale CA: Arthur H. Clark Co. 1972.

Hafen, LeRoy R., and W. J. Ghent. *Broken Hand: The Life Story of Thomas Fitzpatrick, Chief of the Mountain Men*. Denver: Old West Publishing Co., 1931.

Hagan, William T. *The Indian Rights Association: The Herbert Welsh Years, 1882–1904*. Tucson: University of Arizona Press, 1985.

Hagerty, Leroy W. "Indian Raids Along the Platte and Little Blue Rivers, 1864-1865." *Nebraska History* 28 (1947): 239–60.

Haines, Joe D., Jr. "'For Our Sake Do All You Can': The Indian Captivity and Death of Clara and Willie Blinn." *The Chronicles of Oklahoma* 77 (1999): 170–83.

Hammer, Kenneth, ed. *Custer in '76: Walter Camp's Notes on the Custer Fight*. Provo UT: Brigham Young University Press, 1976.

Hanson, Charles E., Jr. "Geminien P. Beauvais." *The Mountain Men and the Fur Trade of the Far West*. Vol. 7. Ed. LeRoy R. Hafen. Glendale CA: Arthur H. Clark Co., 1969.

———. "J. B. Moncravie." *The Mountain Men and the Fur Trade of the Far West*. Vol. 9. Ed. LeRoy R. Hafen. Glendale CA: Arthur H. Clark Co., 1972.

———. "The Chadron Creek Trading Post." *The Museum of the Fur Trade Quarterly* 12 (1976): 1–20.

Hanson, Charles E., Jr., and Veronica Sue Walters. "The Early Fur Trade in Northwestern Nebraska." *Nebraska History* 57 (1976): 291–314.

Hanson, Joseph Mills. *The Conquest of the Missouri*. New York: Murray Hill Books, 1909.

Hardorff, Richard, G. *Lakota Recollections of the Custer Fight: New Sources of Indian-Military History*. Lincoln: University of Nebraska Press, 1997.

———. *The Surrender and Death of Crazy Horse*. Spokane: Arthur H. Clark Co., 1998.

———. *The Oglala Lakota Crazy Horse: A Preliminary Genealogical Study: An Annotated Listing of Primary Sources*. Mattituck NY and Bryan TX: J. M. Carroll and Co., 1985.

———. *The Custer Battle Casualties: Burials, Exhumations and Reinterments*. El Segundo CA: Upton and Sons, Publishers, 1989.

Harring, Sidney L. *Crow Dog's Case: American Indian Sovereignty, Tribal Law, and United States Law in the Nineteenth Century*. Cambridge: Cambridge University Press, 1994.

Hart, Joseph C. "Report of Eastern Cherokee Agency." *Annual Report of the Commissioner of Indian Affairs*. Washington DC: GPO, 1898.

Hastings, James S. "Red Cloud Agency, Nebraska." *Annual Report of the Commissioner of Indian Affairs*. Washington DC: GPO, 1876.

Hebard, Grace Raymond and E. A. Brininstool. *The Bozeman Trail*. 2 vols. Glendale CA: Arthur H. Clark Co., 1960.

Hedren, Paul L. *First Scalp for Custer: The Skirmish at Warbonnet Creek, Nebraska, July 17, 1876*. Glendale CA: Arthur H. Clark Co., 1980.

———. *Fort Laramie in 1876: Chronicle of a Frontier Post at War*. Lincoln: University of Nebraska Press, 1988.

———. "The Crazy Horse Medal: An Enigma From the Great Sioux War." *Nebraska History* 75 (Summer 1994): 195–99.

Heitman, Francis B. *Historical Register and Dictionary of the United States Army*. Washington DC: GPO, 1903.

Henderson, Paul. "The Story of Mud Springs." *Nebraska History* 32 (1951): 108–19.

Hoig, Stan. *The Sand Creek Massacre*. Norman: University of Oklahoma Press, 1961.

———. *The Battle of the Washita: The Sheridan-Custer Indian Campaign of 1867–69*. Lincoln: University of Nebraska Press, 1976.

Howard, E. A. "Spotted Tail Agency, Nebraska." *Annual Report of the Commissioner of Indian Affairs*. Washington DC: GPO, 1876.

Howe, M. A. DeWolfe. *The Life and Labors of Bishop Hare: Apostle to the Sioux*. New York: Sturgis and Walton Co., 1913.

Hurst, John and Sigmund Shlesinger. "The Beecher Island Fight." *Collections of the Kansas State Historical Society* 15 (1919–22): 530–47.

Hutton, Harold. *The Luckiest Outlaw: The Life and Legends of Doc Middleton*. Lincoln: University of Nebraska Press, 1992.

Hyde, George E. *Red Cloud's Folk, A History of the Oglala Sioux Indians*. Norman: University of Oklahoma Press, 1937.

———. *Spotted Tail's Folk: A History of the Brulé Sioux*. Norman: University of Oklahoma Press, 1961.

Irving, Washington. *Astoria, or Anecdotes of an Enterprise beyond the Rocky Mountains*. New York: C. P. Putnam's Sons, 1897.

Irwin, James. "Red Cloud Agency, Nebraska." *Annual Report of the Commissioner of Indian Affairs*. Washington DC: GPO, 1877.

———. "Red Cloud Agency, Dakota." *Annual Report of the Commissioner of Indian Affairs*. Washington DC: GPO, 1878.

Jacobson, Clair. *Whitestone Hill: The Indians and the Battle*. LaCrosse WI: Pine Tree Publishing, 1991.

Jensen, Richard E. "Big Foot's Followers at Wounded Knee." *Nebraska History* 71 (1990): 194–212.

Jensen, Richard E., R. Eli Paul, and John E. Carter. *Eyewitness at Wounded Knee*. Lincoln: University of Nebraska Press, 1991.

Jones, Bryan. "John Richard, Jr., and the Killing at Fetterman." *Annals of Wyoming* 43 (1971): 237–57.

Jones, Robert Huhn. *The Civil War in the Northwest: Nebraska, Wisconsin, Iowa, Minnesota, and the Dakotas.* Norman: University of Oklahoma Press, 1960.

Kappler, Charles J., ed. *Indian Affairs, Laws and Treaties.* Washington DC: GPO, 1904.

Kelley, William Fitch. *Pine Ridge 1890.* Ed. Alexander Kelley and Pierre Bovis. San Francisco: Pierre Bovis, 1971.

Kelly, Fanny. *Narrative of My Captivity Among the Sioux Indians.* Ed. Clark and Mary Lee Spence. Chicago: Donnelley, Gossette, & Loyd, 1880. Reprint, Chicago: R. R. Donnelley and Sons Co., 1990.

King, James T. *War Eagle: A Life of General Eugene A. Carr.* Lincoln: University of Nebraska Press, 1963.

Kolbenschlag, George R. *A Whirlwind Passes: News Correspondents and the Sioux Disturbances of 1890–1891.* Vermillion: University of South Dakota Press, 1990.

Larimer, Sarah L. *The Capture and Escape: or Life Among the Sioux.* Philadelphia: Claxton, Remsen and Haffelfinger, 1870.

Larson, Robert W. *Red Cloud: Warrior-Statesman of the Lakota Sioux.* Norman: University of Oklahoma Press, 1997.

Lecompte, Janet. "Pierre Chouteau, Junior." *The Mountain Men and the Fur Trade of the Far West.* Vol. 9. Ed. LeRoy R. Hafen. Glendale CA: Arthur H. Clark Co. 1972.

Lee, Jesse M. "Spotted Tail Agency, Nebraska." *Annual Report of the Commissioner of Indian Affairs.* Washington DC: GPO, 1877.

Lonich, David W. "Blacksmith Henry Mechling: From Pennsylvania to Little Big Horn." *Greasy Grass* 17 (2001): 31–35.

Loudon, Betty, ed. "Pioneer Pharmacist J. Walter Moyer's Notes on Crawford and Fort Robinson in the 1890s." *Nebraska History* 58 (1977): 89–117.

Lyman, Robert, ed. "Map of Beecher Island." *The Beecher Island Annual* 2 (1905): 25.

———. "The Beecher Island Battle Memorial Association." *The Beecher Island Annual* 4 (1908): 1–2.

Mackintosh, John. "Lakota Bullet Ends Wallace's Life — 14 Years after Little Bighorn." *Greasy Grass* 16 (2000): 21–30.

Mattison, Ray H. "Alexander Culbertson." *The Mountain Men and the Fur Trade of the Far West.* Vol. 1. Ed. LeRoy R. Hafen. Glendale CA: Arthur H. Clark Co. 1965.

Mattes, Merrill J. *The Great Platte River Road.* Lincoln: Nebraska State Historical Society, 1969.

Maynadier, Col. Henry A. "No. 86. Headquarters West Sub-Division of Nebraska." *Annual Report of the Commissioner of Indian Affairs.* Washington DC: GPO, 1866.

McCann, Lloyd E. "The Grattan Massacre." *Nebraska History* 37 (1956): 1–26.

McDermott, John Dishon. "John Baptiste Richard." *The Mountain Men and the Fur Trade of the Far West.* Vol. 2. Ed. LeRoy R. Hafen. Glendale CA: Arthur H. Clark Co. 1965.

————. "Joseph Bissonette." *The Mountain Men and the Fur Trade of the Far West.* Vol. 4. Ed. LeRoy R. Hafen. Glendale CA: Arthur H. Clark Co. 1966.

————. "James Bordeaux." *The Mountain Men and the Fur Trade of the Far West.* Vol. 5. Ed. LeRoy R. Hafen. Glendale CA: Arthur H. Clark Co. 1968.

————. "J. LaRamee," *The Mountain Men and the Fur Trade of the Far West.* Vol. 6. Ed. LeRoy R. Hafen. Glendale CA: Arthur H. Clark Co. 1968.

————. "'We Had a Terribly Hard Time Letting Them Go': The Battles of Mud Springs and Rush Creek, February 1865," *Nebraska History* 77 (1996): 78–88.

McGillycuddy, Julia B. *McGillycuddy Agent: A Biography of Dr. Valentine T. McGillycuddy.* Stanford CA: Stanford University Press, 1941.

McGillycuddy, V. T. "Pine Ridge Agency, Dakota." *Annual Report of the Commissioner of Indian Affairs.* Washington DC: GPO, 1879.

————. "Pine Ridge Agency, Dakota." *Annual Report of the Commissioner of Indian Affairs.* Washington DC: GPO, 1884.

McLemore, Clyde. "Fort Pease: The First Attempted Settlement in the Yellowstone Valley." *Montana Magazine of History* 2 (1952): 17–31.

Mears, David Y. "Campaigning Against Crazy Horse." *Proceedings and Collections of the Nebraska State Historical Society* 10 (1907): 68–77.

Medicine Crow, Joseph. *From the Heart of the Crow Country: The Crow Indians' Own Stories.* Ed. Herman J. Viola. New York: Orion Books, 1992.

Meyer, Roy W. "The Establishment of the Santee Reservation, 1866–1869. *Nebraska History* 45 (1964): 59–97.

Miles, Nelson A. *Personal Recollections and Observations of General Nelson A. Miles.* Lincoln: University of Nebraska Press, 1992.

Miller, George L. "Bishop Clarkson." *Transactions and Reports of the Nebraska State Historical Society* 1 (1885): 106–11.

Milner, Joe. E. and Earle R. Forrest. *California Joe: Noted Scout and Indian Fighter.* Lincoln: University of Nebraska Press, 1987.

Molin, Paulette Fairbanks. "'Training the Hand, the Head, and the Heart': Indian Education at Hampton Institute." *Minnesota History* 51 (1988): 82–98.

Monaghan, Jay. *Tom Horn: Last of the Bad Men.* Lincoln: University of Nebraska Press, 1997.

Monnett, John H. *The Battle of Beecher Island and the Indian War of 1867–1869.* Niwot: University Press of Colorado, 1992.

Mooney, James. "The Ghost-Dance Religion and the Sioux Outbreak of 1890." *Fourteenth Annual Report of the Bureau of American Ethnology, Smithsonian Institution.* Washington DC: GPO, 1896.

Moorehead, Warren K. *Tonda: A Story of the Sioux.* Cincinnati: Robert Clarke Co., 1904.

Mumey, Nolie. "James Baker." *The Mountain Men and the Fur Trade of the Far West.* Vol. 3. Ed. LeRoy R. Hafen. Glendale CA: Arthur H. Clark Co. 1966.

Nadeau, Remi. *Fort Laramie and the Sioux Indians.* Englewood Cliffs NJ: Prentice-Hall Inc., 1967.

Nash, Jay Robert. *Encyclopedia of Western Lawmen and Outlaws*. New York: DaCapo Press, 1994.

Nelson, Peter B. *Fifty Years on the Prairie*. Chadron NE: E. E. Nelson, 1941.

Nelson, John Young. *Fifty Years on the Trail: A True Story of Western Life*. As told to Harrington O'Reilly. Norman: University of Oklahoma Press, 1963.

Olsen, Jon. "Cultural History," *Chadron, Nebraska, Centennial History, 1885–1895*. Chadron NE: Chadron Narrative History Project Comm., 1985.

Olson, James C. *Red Cloud and the Sioux Problem*. Lincoln: University of Nebraska Press, 1975.

Oswald, Delmont R. "James P. Beckwourth." *The Mountain Men and the Fur Trade of the Far West*. Vol. 6. Ed. LeRoy R. Hafen. Glendale CA: Arthur H. Clark Co. 1968.

Paine, Bayard H. "An Indian Depredation Claim that Proved A Boomerang." *Nebraska History Magazine* 15 (1934): 45–55.

Paul, R. Eli, ed. *Autobiography of Red Cloud: War Leader of the Oglalas*. Helena: Montana Historical Society Press, 1997.

Penny, Charles G. "Report of Pine Ridge Agency." *Annual Report of the Commissioner of Indian Affairs*. Washington DC: GPO, 1891.

Peterson, J. B. *The Battle of Wounded Knee*. Gordon NE: News Publishing Co., 1941.

Poole, DeWitt C. "Whetstone Agency, D.T." *Annual Report of the Commissioner of Indian Affairs*. Washington DC: GPO, 1870.

———. *Among the Sioux of Dakota: Eighteen Months' Experience as an Indian Agent, 1869–70*. St. Paul: Minnesota Historical Society Press, 1988.

Pourier, Baptiste. "Sibley's Ordeal in the Big Horns, July 6–9, 1876." *Battles and Skirmishes of the Great Sioux War, 1876–1877*. Ed. Jerome A. Greene. Norman: University of Oklahoma Press, 1993.

Price, Catherine. *The Oglala People, 1841–1879: A Political History*. Lincoln: University of Nebraska Press, 1996.

Prucha, Francis Paul. *A Guide to the Military Posts of the United States*. Madison: State Historical Society of Wisconsin, 1964.

———. "Thomas Jefferson Morgan." *The Commissioners of Indian Affairs, 1824–1977*. Ed. Robert M. Kvasnicka and Herman Viola. Lincoln: University of Nebraska Press, 1979.

———. "The Challenge of Indian History." *Journal of the West* 34 (1995): 3–4.

Ricker, Eli S. "The Battle of Beecher Island." *The Beecher Island Annual* 4 (1908): 1–22.

Robinson, Charles M., III. *Bad Hand: A Biography of General Ranald S. Mackenzie*. Austin TX: State House Press, 1993.

———. *General Crook and the Western Frontier*. Norman: University of Oklahoma Press, 2001.

Rogers, Fred B. *The Soldiers of the Overland: Being Some Account of the Services of General Patrick Edward Connor*. San Francisco: The Grabhorne Press, 1938.

Roland, Charles P. *Albert Sidney Johnston: Soldier of Three Republics*. Austin: University of Texas Press, 1987.

Rosa, Joseph G. *They Called Him Wild Bill: The Life and Adventures of James Butler Hickok.* Norman: University of Oklahoma Press, 1964.

Ross, Ralph H. *Pine Ridge Reservation: A Pictorial Description.* Kendall Park NJ: Lakota Books, 1996.

Russell, Don. *The Lives and Legends of Buffalo Bill.* Norman: University of Oklahoma Press, 1960.

Saville, J. J. "Red Cloud Agency, Dakota." *Annual Report of the Commissioner of Indian Affairs.* Washington DC: GPO, 1874.

———. "Red Cloud Agency, Nebraska." *Annual Report of the Commissioner of Indian Affairs.* Washington DC: GPO, 1875.

Schindler, Harold. "The Bear River Massacre: New Historical Evidence." *Utah Historical Quarterly* 67 (1999): 300–308.

Schmitt, Martin F. *General George Crook: His Autobiography.* Norman: University of Oklahoma Press, 1946.

Sheldon, Addison E. *Nebraska the Land and the People.* 2 vols. Chicago: Lewis Publishing Co., 1931.

"Sheriffs Battle Indians on Lightning Creek," *The Wyoming Pioneer* 1 (1941): 190–201.

Shumway, Grant L. *History of Western Nebraska and Its People.* 2 vols. Lincoln NE: Western Publishing Co., 1921.

Sterling, C. G. "Report of the Missionary, Pine Ridge Agency." *Annual Report of the Commissioner of Indian Affairs.* Washington DC: GPO, 1888.

Stewart, Edgar I. *Custer's Luck.* Norman: University of Oklahoma Press, 1955.

Sutton, Royal, ed. *The Face of Courage: The Indian Photographs of Frank A. Rinehart.* Fort Collins CO: Old Army Press, 1972.

Svingen, Orlan J. *The Northern Cheyenne Indian Reservation, 1877–1900.* Niwot: University Press of Colorado. 1993.

Thrapp, Dan. *Encyclopedia of Western Biography.* 3 vols. Lincoln: University of Nebraska Press, 1991.

Trenholm, Virginia Cole. *Footprints on the Frontier.* Douglas WY: Douglas Enterprise Co., 1945.

Unrau, William E. *Tending the Talking Wire: A Buck Soldier's View of Indian Country, 1863–1866.* Salt Lake City: University of Utah Press, 1979.

Utley, Robert M. *The Last Days of the Sioux Nation.* New Haven: Yale University Press, 1963.

———. *Frontiersmen in Blue: The United States Army and the Indian, 1848–65.* New York: Macmillan Co., 1967.

———. *Frontier Regulars: The United States Army and the Indian, 1866–1891.* Lincoln: University of Nebraska Press, 1984.

———. *Cavalier in Buckskin: George Armstrong Custer and the Western Military Frontier.* Norman: University of Oklahoma Press, 1988.

———. *The Lance and the Shield: The Life and Times of Sitting Bull.* New York: Henry Holt and Co. 1993.

Vaughn, J. W. *With Crook at the Rosebud*. Harrisburg PA: Stackpole Co., 1956.

———. *The Reynolds Campaign on Powder River*. Norman: University of Oklahoma Press, 1961.

Walker, James R. *Lakota Belief and Ritual*. Ed. Raymond J. DeMallie and Elaine A. Jahner. Lincoln: University of Nebraska Press, 1980.

Ware, Eugene F. *The Indian War of 1864*. Lincoln: University of Nebraska Press, 1960.

Washburn, J. M. "Whetstone Agency." *Annual Report of the Commissioner of Indian Affairs*. Washington DC: GPO, 1872.

Watkins, Albert. "Fort Mitchell Cemetery." *Nebraska History and Record of Pioneer Days* (December 1918): 2–3.

Weist, Katherine M. "Ned Casey and His Cheyenne Scouts: A Noble Experiment in an Atmosphere of Tension." *Montana, the Magazine of Western History* 27 (1977): 26–39.

Wells, Phillip H. "Ninety-six Years Among the Indians of the Northwest — Adventures and Reminiscences of an Indian Scout and Interpreter in the Dakotas." *North Dakota History* 15 (1948): 85–133, 169–215, 265–312.

Williamson, John P. "Yankton Agency, Dakota." *Annual Report of the Commissioner of Indian Affairs*. Washington DC: GPO, 1887.

Wissler, Clark. "Societies and Ceremonial Associations in the Oglala Division of the Teton-Dakota." *Anthropological Papers 11*. American Museum of Natural History. Washington DC: GPO, 1912.

Wooster, Robert. *Nelson A. Miles and the Twilight of the Frontier Army*. Lincoln: University of Nebraska Press, 1993.

Young, Gertrude S. *William Joshua Cleveland*. n.p.: n.d.

Manuscripts and Government Records

Aarstad, Rich, Lewis and Clark Reference Historian, Montana Historical Society, Feb. 28, 2002. Personal communication.

Jensen, Richard E. "Notes on the Lakota Ghost Dance." Paper read before the Thirty-third Annual Missouri Valley History Conference, Omaha, March 8, 1990.

National Archives and Records Administration. *Reports and Correspondence Relating to the Army Investigation of the Battle of Wounded Knee and to the Sioux Campaign of 1890–91*. Microcopy 983, roll 148. Records of the Office of the Adjutant General. Record Group 94.

———. Letters Sent to the Office of Indian Affairs from the Pine Ridge Agency. Microcopy 1282, rolls 20, 21. Records of the Bureau of Indian Affairs. Record Group 75.

———. Letters Received by the Office of Indian Affairs from the Red Cloud Agency. Microcopy 234, rolls 715,716,726. Records of the Bureau of Indian Affairs. Record Group 75.

Ricker, Eli S. Papers. Nebraska State Historical Society, Lincoln.

Witty, Thomas A., Jr. "Investigations to Locate Missing Sections of the Beecher Island Monument." MSS. Kansas State Historical Society, Topeka, 1985.

Newspapers and Magazines

Century Magazine

Chadron (NE) Advocate

Chadron (NE) Citizen

Chadron (NE) Democrat

Chadron (NE) Journal

Chadron (NE) Times

Chicago Inter-Ocean

Cincinnati Times-Star

Denver Post

Hay Springs (NE) News

Lincoln Nebraska State Journal

New York Herald

Omaha Bee

Omaha World-Herald

Publisher's Auxiliary

Rushville (NE) Standard

St. Louis Post-Dispatch

Valentine (NE) Democrat

Washington (DC) Evening Star

Index

CPSIA information can be obtained
at www.ICGtesting.com
Printed in the USA
LVHW050209121219
640181LV00003B/254/P